PLAYFAIR CRICKET ANNUAL 2024

77th edition

EDITED BY IAN MARSHALL

All statistics by the Editor unless otherwise stated

FOREWORD

England did not emulate Alastair Cook's side of 2012-13 by winning a Test series in India. It's become the hardest task in cricket. However, it was still a compelling contest and, while England's batters did not score at the rate they did when they visited Pakistan, there were plenty of signs that Bazball is alive and well. The selection of Rehan Ahmed, Shoaib Bashir and Tom Hartley to accompany Jack Leach as England's spin attack was a triumph of instinct over playing it safe. Last summer, Liam Dawson took 49 first-class wickets at an average of exactly 20, while the inexperienced triumvirate picked up a combined 37 wickets at over 55. Yet, the rookie trio took 50 wickets between them, having bowled with control and guile, vindicating their selection and standing comparison with their much more experienced Indian counterparts.

But Brendon McCullum pointed to an obvious concern for the summer ahead. Bashir plays in the same Somerset side as Leach, while Hartley's Lancashire welcome Nathan Lyon as their overseas signing. Will either of them get much of an opportunity to play? With so much early-summer Championship cricket, you fear the worst. Could it make sense for them to be loaned out for a spell? At least England now have a genuine selection dilemma for the spinner's role in the series with West Indies and Sri Lanka. As has been said many times before, we need to amend the calendar to enable our spinners to have a chance to bowl lots of overs when the wickets are at their most suitable, rather than confining them to the edges of the summer when they cannot be as effective.

Our cover star this year is Yorkshire and England's Harry Brook, who has scored 1181 runs in 12 Tests at an average of 62.15 – no other batter has burst upon the scene so successfully since Kevin Pietersen. His technique is simple and effective, and he looks as though he is hugely enjoying himself with bat in hand. Longstanding readers of the Annual will remember the so-called 'Curse of *Playfair*', where cover stars immediately broke mirrors, lost form or picked up a serious injury. So they won't have been surprised when Brook had to withdraw from the India tour for personal reasons – the first of several from both teams to do so.

We do not know the circumstances behid any of these absences, but I do wonder if in some instances we may be seeing a response to the relentless international schedule, supplemented by the franchise tournaments. Since the beginning of 2020, Steve Smith has played just one Sheffield Shield game for New South Wales; Virat Kohli last played a Ranji Trophy match for Delhi in November 2012 – when Rehan Ahmed was just eight years old. It's never going to happen, but I feel sure that our greatest cricketers would benefit from a regular opportunity to play some cricket away from the brightest spotlight – it may be one factor as to why the County Championship draws in so many top names, with Lyon the latest to come to these shores.

And that's just one reason why the Championship remains such an exciting and valuable – but hugely undervalued – competition. The tweak to the point-scoring system last year, with 450 runs now needed (rather than 400) for maximum batting points, seems to have encouraged more positive batting. While compiling the averages this year, I noticed how many bowlers who usually bowl more than a hundred maidens in a season were having to make do with 75 instead. Beyond the action itself, there is a compelling blend of long-serving county pros, international greats and young players hoping to catch the eye of the selectors. Because, with this England set-up, you know they will be given an early opportunity. So why not head to your local ground, *Playfair* in your pocket, and see if you can spot the next star in the making before the selectors do?

Ian Marshall
Eastbourne, 11 March 2024

ACKNOWLEDGEMENTS AND THANKS

This book could not have been compiled without the assistance of many people giving so generously of their time and expertise, so I must thank the following for all they have done to help ensure this edition of *Playfair Cricket Annual* could be written:

At the counties, I would like to thank the following for their help over the last year: Derbyshire – Stephen Martin and Jane Hough; Durham – Sam Blacklock and William Dobson; Essex – Luca Morelli and Tony Choat (for the last time); Glamorgan – Andrew Hignell; Gloucestershire – Cameron Hastie and Adrian Bull; Hampshire – Tim Tremlett and Fiona Newnham; Kent – Becca Smith and Lorne Hart; Lancashire – Diana Lloyd; Leicestershire – Dan Nice and Paul Rogers; Middlesex – Steven Fletcher and Don Shelley; Northamptonshire – Alex Berry and Terry Owen; Nottinghamshire – Matt Freeman and Roger Marshall; Somerset – Spencer Bishop and Polly Rhodes; Surrey – Steve Howes and Debbie Beesley; Sussex – Colin Bowley and Graham Irwin; Warwickshire – Keith Cook and Mel Smith; Worcestershire – Carrie Lloyd and Sue Drinkwater; Yorkshire – Katie Day and John Potter.

Thanks to Andy Smith for the Principal and Second XI Fixtures, and to Richard Logan for the National County Fixtures. Yet again, Philip Bailey has provided the first-class, List A and T20 career records, and I am hugely grateful to him for this.

At Headline, many thanks go to Jonathan Taylor for his encouragement and enthusiasm; Louise Rothwell ensures the swiftest printing of the Annual, so it is as up-to-date as possible; Ana Carter ran the *Playfair* website with supreme efficiency last summer, do visit it during the summer for match reports and information on all the newcomers. Helen Trotter once again handled the proofreading with an eagle eye. At typesetters Letterpart, Chris Leggett and Caroline Leggett coped brilliantly with all that was thrown at them to get everything ready to go to press on time.

Thanks to my daughters, Kiri and Sophia, one of whom even moved up to Durham University so as not to interrupt me; and most of all to my wife, Sugra, for her support, patience and understanding. Thank you all.

GUIDE TO USING PLAYFAIR

The layout of *Playfair* remains the same for this edition. The Annual is divided into five sections, as follows: Test match cricket, county cricket, international limited-overs cricket (including IT20), other cricket (IPL, The Hundred, Ireland and women's international cricket), and fixtures for the coming season. Each section, where applicable, begins with a preview of forthcoming events, followed by events during the previous year, then come the player records, and finally the records sections.

Within the players' register, there has been some debate with the county scorers over those who are defined as 'Released/Retired', pointing out that some players are drafted in for a game or two, and may re-appear in the current season, despite not having a contract as the book goes to press. What I try to do is to ensure that everyone who appeared in last season's games is included somewhere – this way, at least, if they do play in 2024 their details are available to readers. This issue has become more problematic because of the overlap between The Hundred and the 50-over competition. Players' Second XI Championship debuts and their England Under-19 Test appearances are given for those under the age of 25. Players' appearances in The Hundred are listed in the county register, along with appearances in the IPL and Big Bash.

In the county limited-overs records in the Register, those records denoted by '50ov' cover any limited-overs game of 50 or more overs – in the early days, each team could have as many as 65 overs per innings. The '40ov' section refers to games of 40 or 45 overs per innings.

For both men's and women's IT20 records sections, I have taken the decision to limit the records listed to those games that feature at least one side that has appeared in an official LOI. While I welcome the ICC's efforts to broaden the game's profile, there have been some horrible mismatches.

TOURING TEAMS REGISTER 2024

Neither West Indies nor Sri Lanka had selected their 2024 touring teams at the time of going to press. The following players, who had represented those teams in Test matches since 30 November 2022, were still available for selection:

WEST INDIES

Full Names	*Birthdate*	*Birthplace*	*Team*	*Type*	*F-C Debut*
ATHANAZE, Alick Steven	12.07.98	Dominica	Windward Is	LHB/OB	2018-19
BLACKWOOD, Jermaine	20.11.91	St Elizabeth	Jamaica	RHB/OB	2011-12
BONNER, Nkruma Eljego	23.01.89	St Catherine	Jamaica	RHB/LB	2009-10
BRATHWAITE, Kraigg Clairmonte	01.12.92	St Michael	Barbados	RHB/OB	2008-09
BROOKS, Shamarh Shaqad Joshua	01.10.98	St Michael	Combined C&C	RHB/LB	2006-07
CHANDERPAUL, Tagenarine	17.05.96	Georgetown	Guyana	LHB/LB	2012-13
CHASE, Roston Lamar	22.03.92	Christ Church	Barbados	RHB/OB	2010-11
CORNWALL, Rahkeem Rashawn Shane	01.02.93	Antigua	Leeward Is	RHB/OB	2014-15
DA SILVA, Joshua Michael	19.06.98	Trinidad	Trinidad & T	RHB/WK	2018-19
GABRIEL, Shannon Terry	28.04.88	Trinidad	Trinidad & T	RHB/RF	2009-10
GREAVES, Justin Pierre	26.04.94	Barbados	Leeward Is	RHB/RM	2013-14
HODGE, Kaveem Ajoel Rakem	21.02.93	Dominica	Windward Is	RHB/SLA	2011-12
HOLDER, Jason Omar	05.11.91	St George	Barbados	RHB/RMF	2008-09
JOSEPH, Alzarri Shaheim	20.11.96	Antigua	Leeward Is	RHB/RFM	2014-15
JOSEPH, Shamar	31.08.99	Berbice	Guyana	LHB/RF	2022-23
McKENZIE, Kirk Sanjay Alexander	09.11.00	Jamaica	Jamaica	LHB/OB	2022
MAYERS, Kyle Rico	08.09.92	Barbados	Barbados	LHB/RM	2015-16
MINDLEY, Marquino Junior	29.12.94	Jamaica	Jamaica	RHB/RFM	2014-15
MOTIE, Gudakesh	29.03.95	Georgetown	Guyana	LHB/SLA	2015-16
PHILLIP, Anderson	22.08.96	Trinidad	Trinidad & T	RHB/RFM	2016-17
REIFER, Raymon Anton	11.05.91	St Lucy	Barbados	LHB/LM	2010-11
ROACH, Kemar Andre Jamal	30.06.88	St Lucy	Barbados	RHB/RFM	2007-08
SEALES, Jayden Nigel Tristan	10.09.01	Trinidad & T	Trinidad & T	LHB/RM	2020-21
SINCLAIR, Kevin	23.11.99	Guyana	Guyana	RHB/OB	2019-20
THOMAS, Devon Cuthbert	12.11.89	Antigua	Leeward Is	RHB/RM	2007-08
WARRICAN, Jomel Andrel	20.05.92	Richmond Hill	Barbados	RHB/SLA	2011-12

SRI LANKA

Full Names	*Birthdate*	*Birthplace*	*Team*	*Type*	*F-C Debut*
CHANDIMAL, Lokuge Dinesh	18.11.89	Balapitiya	Sri Lanka Army	RHB/OB	2009
De SILVA, Dhananjaya Maduranga	06.09.91	Colombo	Tamil Union	RHB/OB	2010-11
DICKWELLA, D.P.D.Niroshan	23.06.93	Kandy	Nondescripts	LHB/WK	2012-13
FERNANDO, Asitha Madusanka	31.07.97	Katuneriya	Colombo	RHB/RMF	2016
FERNANDO, B.Oshada Piumal	15.04.92	Colombo	Galle	RHB/LB	2011-12
FERNANDO, K.Nishan Madushka	10.09.99	Moratuwa	Ragama	RHB/WK	2018-19
FERNANDO, M.Vishwa Thilina	18.09.91	Colombo	Colombo	RHB/LMF	2011-12
GUNASEKARA, Chamika D.	25.11.99	Colombo	Nondescripts	RHB/RMF	2019-20
JAYASURIYA, N.G.R.Prabath	05.11.91	Matale	Sinhalese	RHB/SLA	2011-12
KARUNARATNE, F.Dimuth M.	28.04.88	Colombo	Sinhalese	LHB/RM	2008-09
KUMARA, C.B.R.Lahiru S.	13.02.97	Kandy	Nondescripts	LHB/RFM	2016-17
MADUSHANKA, L.M.Dilshan	18.09.00	Hambantota	Colts	RHB/LMF	2019-20
MATHEWS, Angelo Davis	02.06.87	Colombo	Colts	RHB/RMF	2006-07
MENDIS, B.Kusal Gimhan	02.02.95	Moratuwa	Sinhalese	RHB/LB	2014-15
RAJITHA, C.A.Kasun	01.06.93	Matara	Sinhalese	RHB/RMF	2014-15
SAMARAWICKRAMA, W.Sadeera R.	30.08.95	Colombo	Tamil Union	RHB/WK	2014-15
WANIGAMUNI, Ramesh T.Mendis	07.07.95	Ambalangoda	Moors	RHB/OB	2014-15

ENGLAND v WEST INDIES

SERIES RECORDS
1928 to 2021-22

HIGHEST INNINGS TOTALS

England	in England	619-6d	Nottingham	1957
	in West Indies	849	Kingston	1929-30
West Indies	in England	692-8d	The Oval	1995
	in West Indies	751-5d	St John's	2003-04

LOWEST INNINGS TOTALS

England	in England	71	Manchester	1976
	in West Indies	46	Port of Spain	1993-94
West Indies	in England	54	Lord's	2000
	in West Indies	47	Kingston	2003-04
HIGHEST MATCH AGGREGATE		1815 for 34 wickets	Kingston	1929-30
LOWEST MATCH AGGREGATE		309 for 29 wickets	Bridgetown	1934-35

HIGHEST INDIVIDUAL INNINGS

England	in England	285*	P.B.H.May	Birmingham	1957
	in West Indies	325	A.Sandham	Kingston	1929-30
West Indies	in England	291	I.V.A.Richards	The Oval	1976
	in West Indies	400*	B.C.Lara	St John's	2003-04

HIGHEST AGGREGATE OF RUNS IN A SERIES

England	in England	506	(av 42.16)	G.P.Thorpe (*6 Tests*)	1995
	in West Indies	693	(av 115.50)	E.H.Hendren	1929-30
West Indies	in England	829	(av 118.42)	I.V.A.Richards	1976
	in West Indies	798	(av 99.75)	B.C.Lara	1993-94

RECORD WICKET PARTNERSHIPS – ENGLAND

1st	229	A.J.Strauss (142)/A.N.Cook (94)	Bridgetown	2008-09
2nd	291	A.J.Strauss (137)/R.W.T.Key (221)	Lord's	2004
3rd	303	M.A.Atherton (135)/R.A.Smith (175)	St John's	1993-94
4th	411	P.B.H.May (285*)/M.C.Cowdrey (154)	Birmingham	1957
5th	218	P.D.Collingwood (161)/M.J.Prior (131*)	Port of Spain	2008-09
6th	205	M.R.Ramprakash (154)/G.P.Thorpe (103)	Bridgetown	1997-98
7th	197	M.J.K.Smith (96)/J.M.Parks (101*)	Port of Spain	1959-60
8th	217	T.W.Graveney (165)/J.T.Murray (112)	The Oval	1966
9th	109	G.A.R.Lock (89)/P.I.Pocock (13)	Georgetown	1967-68
10th	128	K.Higgs (63)/J.A.Snow (59*)	The Oval	1966

RECORD WICKET PARTNERSHIPS – WEST INDIES

1st	298	C.G.Greenidge (149)/D.L.Haynes (167)	St John's	1989-90
2nd	287*	C.G.Greenidge (214*)/H.A.Gomes (92*)	Lord's	1984
3rd	338	E.de C.Weekes (206)/F.M.M.Worrell (167)	Port of Spain	1953-54
4th	399	G.St A.Sobers (226)/F.M.M.Worrell (197*)	Bridgetown	1959-60
5th	265	S.M.Nurse (137)/G.St A.Sobers (174)	Leeds	1966
6th	282*	B.C.Lara (400*)/R.D.Jacobs (107*)	St John's	2003-04
7th	295*	S.O.Dowrich (116*)/J.O.Holder (202*)	Bridgetown	2018-19
8th	99	C.A.McWatt (54)/J.K.C.Holt (48*)	Georgetown	1953-54
9th	150	E.A.E.Baptiste (87*)/M.A.Holding (69)	Birmingham	1984
10th	143	D.Ramdin (107*)/T.L.Best (95)	Birmingham	2012

BEST INNINGS BOWLING ANALYSIS

England	in England	8-103	I.T.Botham	Lord's	1984
	in West Indies	8- 53	A.R.C.Fraser	Port of Spain	1997-98
West Indies	in England	8- 92	M.A.Holding	The Oval	1976
	in West Indies	8- 45	C.E.L.Ambrose	Bridgetown	1989-90

BEST MATCH BOWLING ANALYSIS

England	in England	12-119	F.S.Trueman	Birmingham	1963
	in West Indies	13-156	A.W.Greig	Port of Spain	1973-74
West Indies	in England	14-149	M.A.Holding	The Oval	1976
	in West Indies	11- 84	C.E.L.Ambrose	Port of Spain	1993-94

HIGHEST AGGREGATE OF WICKETS IN A SERIES

England	in England	34	(av 17.47)	F.S.Trueman	1963
	in West Indies	27	(av 18.66)	J.A.Snow	1967-68
		27	(av 18.22)	A.R.C.Fraser	1997-98
West Indies	in England	35	(av 12.65)	M.D.Marshall	1988
	in West Indies	30	(av 14.26)	C.E.L.Ambrose	1997-98

RESULTS SUMMARY

ENGLAND v WEST INDIES – IN ENGLAND

		Series			Lord's			Manchester			The Oval			Nottingham			B'ham			Leeds			Chester-le-S			So'ton		
	Tests	*E*	*WI*	*D*	*E*	*WI*	*D*	*E*	*WI*	*D*	*E*	*WI*	*D*	*E*	*WI*	*D*	*E*	*WI*	*D*	*E*	*WI*	*D*	*E*	*WI*	*D*	*E*	*WI*	*D*
1928	3	3	–	–	1	–	–	1	–	–	1	–	–	–	–	–	–	–	–	–	–	–	–	–	–	–	–	–
1933	3	2	–	1	1	–	–	–	–	1	1	–	–	–	–	–	–	–	–	–	–	–	–	–	–	–	–	–
1939	3	1	–	2	1	–	–	–	–	1	–	–	1	–	–	–	–	–	–	–	–	–	–	–	–	–	–	–
1950	4	1	3	–	–	1	–	1	–	–	–	1	–	–	1	–	–	–	–	–	–	–	–	–	–	–	–	–
1957	5	3	–	2	1	–	–	–	–	–	1	–	–	–	–	1	–	–	1	1	–	–	–	–	–	–	–	–
1963	5	1	3	1	–	–	1	–	1	–	–	1	–	–	–	–	1	–	–	–	1	–	–	–	–	–	–	–
1966	5	1	3	1	–	–	1	–	1	–	1	–	–	–	1	–	–	–	–	–	1	–	–	–	–	–	–	–
1969	3	2	–	1	–	–	1	1	–	–	–	–	–	–	–	–	–	–	–	1	–	–	–	–	–	–	–	–
1973	3	–	2	1	–	1	–	–	–	–	–	1	–	–	–	–	–	–	1	–	–	–	–	–	–	–	–	–
1976	5	–	3	2	–	–	1	–	1	–	–	1	–	–	–	1	–	–	–	–	1	–	–	–	–	–	–	–
1980	5	–	1	4	–	–	1	–	–	1	–	–	1	–	1	–	–	–	–	–	–	1	–	–	–	–	–	–
1984	5	–	5	–	–	1	–	–	1	–	–	1	–	–	–	–	–	1	–	–	1	–	–	–	–	–	–	–
1988	5	–	4	1	–	1	–	–	1	–	–	1	–	–	–	1	–	–	–	–	1	–	–	–	–	–	–	–
1991	5	2	2	1	–	–	1	–	–	–	1	–	–	–	1	–	–	1	–	1	–	–	–	–	–	–	–	–
1995	6	2	2	2	1	–	–	1	–	–	–	–	1	–	–	1	–	1	–	–	1	–	–	–	–	–	–	–
2000	5	3	1	1	1	–	–	–	–	1	1	–	–	–	–	–	–	1	–	1	–	–	–	–	–	–	–	–
2004	4	4	–	–	1	–	–	1	–	–	1	–	–	–	–	–	1	–	–	–	–	–	–	–	–	–	–	–
2007	4	3	–	1	–	–	1	1	–	–	–	–	–	–	–	–	–	–	–	1	–	–	1	–	–	–	–	–
2009	2	2	–	–	1	–	–	–	–	–	–	–	–	–	–	–	–	–	–	–	–	–	1	–	–	–	–	–
2012	3	2	–	1	1	–	–	–	–	–	–	–	–	1	–	–	–	–	1	–	–	–	–	–	–	–	–	–
2017	3	2	1	–	1	–	–	–	–	–	–	–	–	–	–	–	1	–	–	–	1	–	–	–	–	–	–	–
2020	3	2	1	–	–	–	–	2	–	–	–	–	–	–	–	–	–	–	–	–	–	–	–	–	–	–	1	–
	89	36	31	22	10	4	7	8	5	4	7	6	3	1	4	4	3	4	3	5	7	1	2	–	–	–	1	–

ENGLAND v WEST INDIES – IN WEST INDIES

		Series			Bridgetown			P of Spain			Georgetown			Kingston			Antigua*			St George			Gros Islet		
	Tests	*E*	*WI*	*D*	*E*	*WI*	*D*	*E*	*WI*	*D*	*E*	*WI*	*D*	*E*	*WI*	*D*	*E*	*WI*	*D*	*E*	*WI*	*D*	*E*	*WI*	*D*
1929-30	4	1	1	2	–	–	1	1	–	–	–	1	–	–	–	1	–	–	–	–	–	–	–	–	–
1934-35	4	1	2	1	1	–	–	–	1	–	–	–	1	–	1	–	–	–	–	–	–	–	–	–	–
1947-48	4	–	2	2	–	–	1	–	–	1	–	1	–	–	1	–	–	–	–	–	–	–	–	–	–
1953-54	5	2	2	1	–	1	–	–	–	1	1	–	–	1	1	–	–	–	–	–	–	–	–	–	–
1959-60	5	1	–	4	–	–	1	1	–	1	–	–	1	–	–	1	–	–	–	–	–	–	–	–	–
1967-68	5	1	–	4	–	–	1	1	–	1	–	–	1	–	–	1	–	–	–	–	–	–	–	–	–
1973-74	5	1	1	3	–	–	1	1	1	–	–	–	1	–	–	1	–	–	–	–	–	–	–	–	–
1980-81	4	–	2	2	–	1	–	–	1	–	–	–	–	–	–	1	–	–	1	–	–	–	–	–	–
1985-86	5	–	5	–	–	1	–	–	2	–	–	–	–	–	1	–	–	1	–	–	–	–	–	–	–
1989-90	4	1	2	1	–	1	–	–	–	1	–	–	–	1	–	–	–	1	–	–	–	–	–	–	–
1993-94	5	1	3	1	1	–	–	–	1	–	–	1	–	–	1	–	–	–	1	–	–	–	–	–	–
1997-98	6	1	3	2	–	–	1	1	1	–	–	1	–	–	–	1	–	1	–	–	–	–	–	–	–
2003-04	4	3	–	1	1	–	–	1	–	–	–	–	–	1	–	–	–	–	1	–	–	–	–	–	–
2008-09	5	–	1	4	–	–	1	–	–	1	–	–	–	–	1	–	–	–	2	–	–	–	–	–	–
2015	3	1	1	1	–	1	–	–	–	–	–	–	–	–	–	–	–	–	1	1	–	–	–	–	–
2018-19	3	1	2	–	–	1	–	–	–	–	–	–	–	–	–	–	–	1	–	–	–	–	1	–	–
2021-22	3	–	1	2	–	–	1	–	–	–	–	–	–	–	–	–	–	–	1	–	1	–	–	–	–
	74	15	28	31	3	6	8	6	7	6	1	4	4	3	6	6	–	4	7	1	1	–	1	–	–
Totals	163	51	59	53																					

ENGLAND v SRI LANKA

SERIES RECORDS
1981-82 to 2020-21

HIGHEST INNINGS TOTALS

England	in England	575-9d	Lord's	2014
	in Sri Lanka	460	Colombo (PSS)	2011-12
Sri Lanka	in England	591	The Oval	1998
	in Sri Lanka	628-8d	Colombo (SSC)	2003-04

LOWEST INNINGS TOTALS

England	in England	181	The Oval	1998
	in Sri Lanka	81	Galle	2007-08
Sri Lanka	in England	82	Cardiff	2011
	in Sri Lanka	81	Colombo (SSC)	2000-01
HIGHEST MATCH AGGREGATE		1496 for 36 wickets	Lord's	2014
LOWEST MATCH AGGREGATE		508 for 30 wickets	Leeds	2016

HIGHEST INDIVIDUAL INNINGS

England	in England	203	I.J.L.Trott	Cardiff	2011
	in Sri Lanka	228	J.E.Root	Galle	2020-21
Sri Lanka	in England	213	S.T.Jayasuriya	The Oval	1998
	in Sri Lanka	213*	D.P.M.D.Jayawardena	Galle	2007-08

HIGHEST AGGREGATE OF RUNS IN A SERIES

England	in England	390	(av 97.50)	A.N.Cook	2011
	in Sri Lanka	426	(av 106.50)	J.E.Root	2020-21
Sri Lanka	in England	342	(av 85.50)	K.C.Sangakkara	2014
	in Sri Lanka	474	(av 158.00)	D.P.M.D.Jayawardena	2007-08

RECORD WICKET PARTNERSHIPS – ENGLAND

1st	168	M.E.Trescothick (76)/M.P.Vaughan (115)	Lord's	2002
2nd	202	M.E.Trescothick (161)/M.A.Butcher (94)	Birmingham	2002
3rd	251	A.N.Cook (133)/I.J.L.Trott (203)	Cardiff	2011
4th	173	J.E.Root (228)/D.W.Lawrence (73)	Galle	2020-21
5th	173	K.P.Pietersen (158)/P.D.Collingwood (57)	Lord's	2006
6th	171	J.E.Root (200*)/M.J.Prior (86)	Lord's	2014
7th	144	J.M.Bairstow (167*)/C.R.Woakes (66)	Lord's	2016
8th	102	A.J.Stewart (123)/A.F.Giles (45)	Manchester	2002
9th	81	J.E.Root (200*)/L.E.Plunkett (39)	Lord's	2014
10th	91	G.P.Thorpe (123)/M.J.Hoggard (17*)	Birmingham	2002

RECORD WICKET PARTNERSHIPS – SRI LANKA

1st	207	N.T.Paranavitana (65)/T.M.Dilshan (193)	Lord's	2011
2nd	142	F.D.M.Karunaratne (83)/D.M.de Silva (73)	Colombo (SSC)	2018-19
3rd	262	T.T.Samaraweera (142)/ D.P.M.D.Jayawardena (134)	Colombo (SSC)	2003-04
4th	153	D.P.M.D.Jayawardena (52)/T.M.Dilshan (100)	Kandy	2003-04
5th	150	S.Wettimuny (190)/L.R.D.Mendis (111)	Lord's	1984
6th	138	S.A.R.Silva (102*)/L.R.D.Mendis (94)	Lord's	1984
7th	183	D.P.M.D.Jayawardena (213*)/W.P.J.U.C.Vaas (90)	Galle	2007-08
8th	149	A.D.Mathews (160)/H.M.R.K.B.Herath (48)	Leeds	2014
9th	105	W.P.J.U.C.Vaas (50*)/K.D.M.N.Kulasekara (64)	Lord's	2006
10th	64	J.R.Ratnayeke (59*)/G.F.Labrooy (42)	Lord's	1988

BEST INNINGS BOWLING ANALYSIS

England	in England	7-70	P.A.J.DeFreitas	Lord's	1991
	in Sri Lanka	6-33	J.E.Emburey	Colombo (PSS)	1981-82
Sri Lanka	in England	9-65	M.Muralitharan	The Oval	1998
	in Sri Lanka	7-46	M.Muralitharan	Galle	2003-04

BEST MATCH BOWLING ANALYSIS

England	in England	10- 45	J.M.Anderson	Leeds	2016
	in Sri Lanka	10-181	G.P.Swann	Colombo (PSS)	2011-12
Sri Lanka	in England	16-220	M.Muralitharan	The Oval	1998
	in Sri Lanka	12-171	H.M.R.K.B.Herath	Galle	2011-12

HIGHEST WICKET AGGREGATE IN A SERIES

England	in England	21	(av 10.80)	J.M.Anderson	2016
	in Sri Lanka	18	(av 29.94)	A.F.Giles	2003-04
		18	(av 21.38)	M.J.Leach	2018-19
		18	(av 24.50)	M.M.Ali	2018-19
Sri Lanka	in England	24	(av 16.87)	M.Muralitharan	2006
	in Sri Lanka	26	(av 12.30)	M.Muralitharan	2003-04

RESULTS SUMMARY
ENGLAND v SRI LANKA – IN ENGLAND

		Series			Lord's			The Oval			Birmingham			Manchester			Nottingham			Cardiff			Southampton			Leeds			Chester-le-St		
	Tests	*E*	*SL*	*D*	*E*	*SL*	*D*	*E*	*SL*	*D*	*E*	*SL*	*D*	*E*	*SL*	*D*	*E*	*SL*	*D*	*E*	*SL*	*D*	*E*	*SL*	*D*	*E*	*SL*	*D*	*E*	*SL*	*D*
1984	1	–	–	1	–	–	1	–	–	–	–	–	–	–	–	–	–	–	–	–	–	–	–	–	–	–	–	–	–	–	–
1988	1	1	–	–	1	–	–	–	–	–	–	–	–	–	–	–	–	–	–	–	–	–	–	–	–	–	–	–	–	–	–
1991	1	1	–	–	1	–	–	–	–	–	–	–	–	–	–	–	–	–	–	–	–	–	–	–	–	–	–	–	–	–	–
1998	1	–	1	–	–	–	–	–	1	–	–	–	–	–	–	–	–	–	–	–	–	–	–	–	–	–	–	–	–	–	–
2002	3	2	–	1	–	–	1	–	–	–	1	–	–	1	–	–	–	–	–	–	–	–	–	–	–	–	–	–	–	–	–
2006	3	1	1	1	–	–	1	–	–	–	1	–	–	–	–	–	–	1	–	–	–	–	–	–	–	–	–	–	–	–	–
2011	3	1	–	2	–	–	1	–	–	–	–	–	–	–	–	–	–	–	–	1	–	–	–	–	1	–	–	–	–	–	–
2014	2	–	1	1	–	–	1	–	–	–	–	–	–	–	–	–	–	–	–	–	–	–	–	–	–	–	1	–	–	–	–
2016	3	2	–	1	–	–	1	–	–	–	–	–	–	–	–	–	–	–	–	–	–	–	–	–	–	1	–	–	1	–	–
	18	8	3	7	2	–	6	–	1	–	2	–	–	1	–	–	–	1	–	1	–	–	–	–	1	1	1	–	1	–	–

ENGLAND v SRI LANKA – IN SRI LANKA

		Series			Colombo (PSS)			Colombo (SSC)			Galle			Kandy			Pallekele		
	Tests	*E*	*SL*	*D*	*E*	*SL*	*D*	*E*	*SL*	*D*	*E*	*SL*	*D*	*E*	*SL*	*D*	*E*	*SL*	*D*
1981-82	1	1	–	–	1	–	–	–	–	–	–	–	–	–	–	–	–	–	–
1992-93	1	–	1	–	–	–	–	–	1	–	–	–	–	–	–	–	–	–	–
2000-01	3	2	1	–	–	–	–	1	–	–	–	1	–	1	–	–	–	–	–
2003-04	3	–	1	2	–	–	–	–	1	–	–	–	1	–	–	1	–	–	–
2007-08	3	–	1	2	–	–	–	–	–	1	–	–	1	–	1	–	–	–	–
2011-12	2	1	1	–	1	–	–	–	–	–	–	1	–	–	–	–	–	–	–
2018-19	3	3	–	–	–	–	–	1	–	–	1	–	–	–	–	–	1	–	–
2020-21	2	2	–	–	–	–	–	–	–	–	2	–	–	–	–	–	–	–	–
	18	9	5	4	2	–	–	2	2	1	3	2	2	1	1	1	1	–	–
Totals	36	17	8	11															

STATISTICAL HIGHLIGHTS IN 2023 TESTS

Including Tests from No. 2485 (Australia v South Africa, 3rd Test) and No. 2487 (Pakistan v New Zealand, 2nd Test) to No. 2518 (Australia v Pakistan, 2nd Test) and No. 2520 (South Africa v India, 1st Test).
† = National record

TEAM HIGHLIGHTS

HIGHEST INNINGS TOTALS

704-3d	Sri Lanka v Ireland (*2nd Test*)	Galle
592	England v Australia	Manchester
591-6d	Sri Lanka v Ireland	Galle

HIGHEST FOURTH INNINGS TOTAL

334	Australia (set 384) v England	The Oval

LOWEST INNINGS TOTALS

89	Pakistan v Australia	Perth
91	Australia v India	Nagpur

HIGHEST MATCH AGGREGATE

1438-34	New Zealand (449 & 277-5d) v Pakistan (408 & 304-9)	Karachi

BATSMEN'S MATCH (Qualification: 1200 runs, average 60 per wicket)

60.78 (1398-23)	Sri Lanka (704-3d) v Ireland (492 & 202)	Galle

LOWEST MATCH AGGREGATE

547-31	India (109 & 163) v Australia (197 & 78-1)	Indore

LARGE MARGINS OF VICTORY

Inns & 280 runs	Sri Lanka (591-6d) beat Ireland (143 & 168) (*1st Test*)	Galle
Inns & 222 runs	Pakistan (576-5d) beat Sri Lanka (166 & 188)	Colombo (SSC)
546 runs	Bangladesh (382 & 425-4d) beat Afghanistan (146 & 115)	Mirpur

The third highest winning margin (by runs) in Test history.

360 runs	Australia (487 & 233-5d) beat Pakistan (271 & 89)	Perth

NARROW MARGINS OF VICTORY

1 run	New Zealand (209 & 483) beat England (435-8d & 256)	Wellington

Only the second victory in Test match history by 1 run.

2 wkts	New Zealand (373 & 285-8) beat Sri Lanka (355 & 302)	Christchurch
2 wkts	Australia (386 & 282-8) beat England (393-8d & 273)	Birmingham

VICTORY AFTER BEING ASKED TO FOLLOW ON

New Zealand (209 & 483) beat England (435-8d & 256) by 1 run — Wellington

Only the fourth occasion this has happened in Test match history.

FOUR HUNDREDS IN AN INNINGS

Sri Lanka (591-6d) v Ireland (*1st Test*)	Galle
Sri Lanka (704-3d) v Ireland (*2nd Test*)	Galle

SIX FIFTIES IN AN INNINGS

England (592) v Australia — Manchester

MOST EXTRAS IN AN INNINGS

	B	*LB*	*W*	*NB*		
52	20	15	15	2	Australia (318) v Pakistan	Melbourne

UNUSUAL DISMISSAL – OUT OBSTRUCTING THE FIELD

Mushfiqur Rahim	Bangladesh v New Zealand	Mirpur

BATTING HIGHLIGHTS

DOUBLE HUNDREDS

T.Chanderpaul	207*	West Indies v Zimbabwe (*1st Test*)	Bulawayo
K.N.M.Fernando	205	Sri Lanka v Ireland (*2nd Test*)	Galle
B.K.G.Mendis	245	Sri Lanka v Ireland (*2nd Test*)	Galle
H.M.Nicholls	200*	New Zealand v Sri Lanka	Wellington
O.J.D.Pope	205	England v Ireland	Lord's
Saud Shakil	208*	Pakistan v Sri Lanka	Galle
K.S.Williamson	215	New Zealand v Sri Lanka	Wellington

HUNDREDS IN THREE CONSECUTIVE INNINGS

K.S.Williamson	121*	New Zealand v Sri Lanka	Christchurch
	215	New Zealand v Sri Lanka	Wellington
	104	New Zealand v Bangladesh	Sylhet

HUNDRED IN EACH INNINGS OF A MATCH

Nazmul Hossain	146	124	Bangladesh v Afghanistan	Mirpur

MOST SIXES IN AN INNINGS

11 B.K.G.Mendis (245) Sri Lanka v Ireland (*2nd Test*) Galle

The second-equal most sixes in a Test innings.

9 B.A.Stokes (155) England v Australia Lord's

MOST RUNS FROM BOUNDARIES IN AN INNINGS

Runs	*6s*	*4s*			
138	11	18	B.K.G.Mendis	Sri Lanka v Ireland	Galle

HUNDRED ON DEBUT

Y.B.Jaiswal	171	India v West Indies	Roseau
L.J.Tucker	108	Ireland v Bangladesh	Mirpur

LONG INNINGS (Qualification: 600 mins and/or 400 balls)

Min	*Balls*			
596	467	T.Chanderpaul (207*)	West Indies v Zimbabwe (*1st Test*)	Bulawayo
585	422	U.T.Khawaja (180)	Australia v India	Ahmedabad

NOTABLE PARTNERSHIPS

Qualifications: 1st-4th wkts: 225 runs; 5th-6th: 200; 7th: 175; 8th: 150; 9th: 125; 10th: 100.

First Wicket

336	K.C.Brathwaite/T.Chanderpaul	West Indies v Zimbabwe (*1st Test*)	Bulawayo
229	Y.B.Jaiswal/R.G.Sharma	India v West Indies	Roseau
228	K.N.M.Fernando/F.D.M.Karunaratne	Sri Lanka v Ireland (*2nd Test*)	Galle

Second Wicket

281	F.D.M.Karunaratne/B.K.G.Mendis	Sri Lanka v Ireland (*1st Test*)	Galle
268	K.N.M.Fernando/B.K.G.Mendis	Sri Lanka v Ireland (*2nd Test*)	Galle
252	B.M.Duckett/O.J.D.Pope	England v Ireland	Lord's

Third Wicket

363	K.S.Williamson/H.M.Nicholls	New Zealand v Sri Lanka	Wellington

Fourth Wicket

302	J.E.Root/H.C.Brook	England v New Zealand	Wellington
285	S.P.D.Smith/T.M.Head	Australia v India	The Oval

Fifth Wicket

208	U.T.Khawaja/C.D.Green	Australia v India	Ahmedabad

Seventh Wicket

183*	L.D.Chandimal/W.S.R.Samarawickrama	Sri Lanka v Ireland (*1st Test*)	Galle

Tenth Wicket

104	M.J.Henry/A.Y.Patel	New Zealand v Pakistan	Karachi

BOWLING HIGHLIGHTS

EIGHT WICKETS IN AN INNINGS

N.M.Lyon	8-64	Australia v India	Indore

TEN WICKETS IN A MATCH

R.Ashwin	12-131	India v West Indies	Roseau
P.J.Cummins	10- 97	Australia v Pakistan	Melbourne
R.A.Jadeja	10-110	India v Australia	Delhi
N.G.R.P.Jayasuriya	10-108	Sri Lanka v Ireland (*1st Test*)	Galle
N.M.Lyon	11- 99	Australia v India	Indore
G.Motie	13- 99	West Indies v Zimbabwe (*2nd Test*)	Bulawayo
Taijul Islam	10-184	Bangladesh v New Zealand	Sylhet

FIVE WICKETS IN AN INNINGS ON DEBUT

Aamer Jamal	6-111	Pakistan v Australia	Perth
T.R.Murphy	7-124	Australia v India	Nagpur
Nijat Masood	5- 79	Afghanistan v Bangladesh	Mirpur
J.C.Tongue	5- 66	England v Ireland	Lord's

60 OVERS IN AN INNINGS

M.J.Leach	61.3-12-157-5	England v New Zealand	Wellington
N.M.Lyon	65-9-151-3	Australia v India	Ahmedabad

200 RUNS CONCEDED IN AN INNINGS

B.C.White	34-1-203-0	Sri Lanka v Ireland (*2nd Test*)	Galle

WICKET-KEEPING HIGHLIGHTS

SIX OR MORE WICKET-KEEPING DISMISSALS IN AN INNINGS

J.Da Silva	7ct	West Indies v South Africa	Centurion

NINE WICKET-KEEPING DISMISSALS IN A MATCH

A.T.Carey	6ct,3st	Australia v England	Birmingham

FIELDING HIGHLIGHTS

FOUR OR MORE CATCHES IN AN INNINGS IN THE FIELD

S.P.D.Smith	5ct	Australia v England	Leeds

FIVE CATCHES IN A MATCH IN THE FIELD

Agha Salman	5ct	Pakistan v Australia	Melbourne
S.P.D.Smith	5ct	Australia v England	Leeds

LEADING TEST AGGREGATES IN 2023

1000 RUNS IN 2023

	M	*I*	*NO*	*HS*	*Runs*	*Avge*	*100*	*50*
U.T.Khawaja (A)	13	24	1	195*	**1210**	52.60	3	6

RECORD CALENDAR YEAR RUNS AGGREGATE

	M	*I*	*NO*	*HS*	*Runs*	*Avge*	*100*	*50*
M.Yousuf (P) (2006)	11	19	1	202	**1788**	99.33	9	3

RECORD CALENDAR YEAR RUNS AVERAGE

	M	*I*	*NO*	*HS*	*Runs*	*Avge*	*100*	*50*
G.St A.Sobers (WI) (1958)	7	12	3	365*	1193	**132.55**	5	3

1000 RUNS IN DEBUT CALENDAR YEAR

	M	*I*	*NO*	*HS*	*Runs*	*Avge*	*100*	*50*
M.A.Taylor (A) (1989)	11	20	1	219	**1219**	64.15	4	5
A.C.Voges (A) (2015)	12	18	6	269*	**1028**	85.66	4	3
A.N.Cook (E) (2006)	13	24	2	127	**1013**	46.04	4	3

40 WICKETS IN 2023

	M	*O*	*R*	*W*	*Avge*	*Best*	*5wI*	*10wM*
N.M.Lyon (A)	10	400.1	1173	**47**	24.95	8-64	2	1
P.J.Cummins (A)	11	320.1	1155	**42**	27.50	6-91	3	1
R.Ashwin (I)	7	275.3	698	**41**	17.02	7-71	4	1

RECORD CALENDAR YEAR WICKETS AGGREGATE

	M	*O*	*R*	*W*	*Avge*	*Best*	*5wI*	*10wM*
M.Muralitharan (SL) (2006)	11	588.4	1521	**90**	16.90	8-70	9	5
S.K.Warne (A) (2005)	14	691.4	2043	**90**	22.70	6-46	6	2

40 WICKET-KEEPING DISMISSALS IN 2023

	M	*Dis*	*Ct*	*St*
A.T.Carey (A)	13	**54**	44	10

RECORD CALENDAR YEAR DISMISSALS AGGREGATE

	M	*Dis*	*Ct*	*St*
J.M.Bairstow (E) (2016)	17	**70**	66	4

20 CATCHES BY FIELDERS IN 2023

	M	*Ct*
S.P.D.Smith (A)	13	**20**

RECORD CALENDAR YEAR FIELDER'S AGGREGATE

	M	*Ct*
G.C.Smith (SA) (2008)	15	**30**

TEST MATCH SCORES
INDIA v AUSTRALIA (1st Test)

At Vidarbha CA Stadium, Nagpur, on 9, 10, 11 February 2023.
Toss: Australia. Result: **INDIA** won by an innings and 132 runs.
Debuts: India – K.Srikar Bharat, S.A.Yadav; Australia – T.R.Murphy.

AUSTRALIA

D.A.Warner	b Shami	1	(2)	lbw b Ashwin	10
U.T.Khawaja	lbw b Siraj	1	(1)	c Kohli b Ashwin	5
M.Labuschagne	st Srikar Bharat b Jadeja	49		lbw b Jadeja	17
S.P.D.Smith	b Jadeja	37		not out	25
M.T.Renshaw	lbw b Jadeja	0		lbw b Ashwin	2
P.S.P.Handscomb	lbw b Jadeja	31		lbw b Ashwin	6
†A.T.Carey	b Ashwin	36		lbw b Ashwin	10
*P.J.Cummins	c Kohli b Ashwin	6		c Srikar Bharat b Jadeja	1
T.R.Murphy	lbw b Jadeja	0		c Sharma b Patel	2
N.M.Lyon	not out	0		b Shami	8
S.M.Boland	b Ashwin	1		lbw b Shami	0
Extras	(B 7, LB 5, NB 3)	15		(LB 1, NB 4)	5
Total	**(63.5 overs)**	**177**		**(32.3 overs)**	**91**

INDIA

*R.G.Sharma	b Cummins	120
K.L.Rahul	c and b Murphy	20
R.Ashwin	lbw b Murphy	23
C.A.Pujara	c Boland b Murphy	7
V.Kohli	c Carey b Murphy	12
S.A.Yadav	b Lyon	8
R.A.Jadeja	b Murphy	70
†K.Srikar Bharat	lbw b Murphy	8
A.R.Patel	b Cummins	84
Mohammed Shami	c Carey b Murphy	37
M.Siraj	not out	1
Extras	(B 5, LB 2, NB 3)	10
Total	**(139.3 overs)**	**400**

INDIA	*O*	*M*	*R*	*W*		*O*	*M*	*R*	*W*
Mohammed Shami	9	4	18	1		4.3	1	13	2
Siraj	7	3	30	1	(3)	1	1	0	0
Jadeja	22	8	47	5	(4)	12	3	34	2
Patel	10	3	28	0	(5)	3	0	6	1
Ashwin	15.5	2	42	3	(2)	12	3	37	5
AUSTRALIA									
Cummins	20.3	3	78	2					
Boland	17	4	34	0					
Lyon	49	13	126	1					
Murphy	47	12	124	7					
Labuschagne	5	0	24	0					
Renshaw	1	0	7	0					

FALL OF WICKETS

	A	I	A
Wkt	*1st*	*1st*	*2nd*
1st	2	76	7
2nd	2	118	26
3rd	84	135	34
4th	84	151	42
5th	109	168	52
6th	162	229	64
7th	172	240	67
8th	173	328	75
9th	176	380	88
10th	177	400	91

Umpires: R.K.Illingworth (*England*) (62) and N.N.Menon (*India*) (15).
Referee: A.J.Pycroft (*Zimbabwe*) (90). **Test No. 2490/103 (I566/A850)**

INDIA v AUSTRALIA (2nd Test)

At Feroz Shah Kotla, Delhi, on 17, 18, 19 February 2023.
Toss: Australia. Result: **INDIA** won by six wickets.
Debut: Australia – M.P.Kuhnemann.

AUSTRALIA

D.A.Warner	c Srikar Bharat b Shami	15		absent hurt	
U.T.Khawaja	c Rahul b Jadeja	81	(1)	c Iyer b Jadeja	6
M.Labuschagne	lbw b Ashwin	18		b Jadeja	35
S.P.D.Smith	c Srikar Bharat b Ashwin	0		lbw b Ashwin	9
T.M.Head	c Rahul b Shami	12	(2)	c Srikar Bharat b Ashwin	43
P.S.P.Handscomb	not out	72		c Kohli b Jadeja	0
†A.T.Carey	c Kohli b Ashwin	0		b Jadeja	7
*P.J.Cummins	lbw b Jadeja	33		b Jadeja	0
T.R.Murphy	b Jadeja	0	(10)	not out	3
N.M.Lyon	b Shami	10	(9)	b Jadeja	8
M.P.Kuhnemann	b Shami	6		b Jadeja	0
M.T.Renshaw			(5)	lbw b Ashwin	2
Extras	(B 13, LB 1, NB 2)	16			–
Total	**(78.4 overs)**	**263**		**(31.1 overs)**	**113**

INDIA

*R.G.Sharma	b Lyon	32		run out	31
K.L.Rahul	lbw b Lyon	17		c Carey b Lyon	1
C.A.Pujara	lbw b Lyon	0		not out	31
V.Kohli	lbw b Kuhnemann	44		st Carey b Murphy	20
S.S.Iyer	c Handscomb b Lyon	4		c Murphy b Lyon	12
R.A.Jadeja	lbw b Murphy	26			
†K.Srikar Bharat	c Smith b Lyon	6	(6)	not out	23
A.R.Patel	c Cummins b Murphy	74			
R.Ashwin	c Renshaw b Cummins	37			
Mohammed Shami	b Kuhnemann	2			
M.Siraj	not out	1			
Extras	(B 8, LB 11)	19			–
Total	**(83.3 overs)**	**262**		**(4 wkts; 26.4 overs)**	**118**

INDIA	*O*	*M*	*R*	*W*		*O*	*M*	*R*	*W*	FALL OF WICKETS	A	I	A	I
										Wkt	*1st*	*1st*	*2nd*	*2nd*
Mohammed Shami	14.4	4	60	4	(2)	2	0	10	0	1st	50	46	23	6
Siraj	10	2	30	0						2nd	91	53	65	39
Ashwin	21	4	57	3	(1)	16	3	59	3	3rd	91	54	85	69
Jadeja	21	2	68	3	(3)	12.1	1	42	7	4th	108	66	95	88
Patel	12	2	34	0	(4)	1	0	2	0	5th	167	125	95	–
AUSTRALIA										6th	168	135	95	–
Cummins	13	2	41	1						7th	227	139	95	–
Kuhnemann	21.3	4	72	2	(1)	7	0	38	0	8th	227	253	110	–
Lyon	29	5	67	5	(2)	12	3	49	2	9th	246	259	113	–
Murphy	18	2	53	2	(3)	6.4	2	22	1	10th	263	262	113	–
Head	2	0	10	0	(4)	1	0	9	0					

Umpires: M.A.Gough (*England*) (29) and N.N.Menon (*India*) (16).
Referee: A.J.Pycroft (*Zimbabwe*) (91). **Test No. 2491/104 (I567/A851)**
M.T.Renshaw concussion replacement for D.A.Warner (India 1st inns, 8.6 overs).

INDIA v AUSTRALIA (3rd Test)

At Holkar Stadium, Indore, on 1, 2, 3 March 2023.
Toss: India. Result: **AUSTRALIA** won by nine wickets.
Debuts: None.

INDIA

*R.G.Sharma	st Carey b Kuhnemann	12		lbw b Lyon	12
S.Gill	c Smith b Kuhnemann	21		b Lyon	5
C.A.Pujara	b Lyon	1		c Smith b Lyon	59
V.Kohli	lbw b Murphy	22		lbw b Kuhnemann	13
R.A.Jadeja	c Kuhnemann b Lyon	4		lbw b Lyon	7
S.S.Iyer	b Kuhnemann	0		c Khawaja b Starc	26
†K.Srikar Bharat	lbw b Lyon	17		b Lyon	3
A.R.Patel	not out	12	(9)	not out	15
R.Ashwin	c Carey b Kuhnemann	3	(8)	lbw b Lyon	16
U.T.Yadav	lbw b Kuhnemann	17		c Green b Lyon	0
M.Siraj	run out	0		b Lyon	0
Extras		–		(B 3, LB 4)	7
Total	**(33.2 overs)**	**109**		**(60.3 overs)**	**163**

AUSTRALIA

T.M.Head	lbw b Jadeja	9	(2)	not out	49
U.T.Khawaja	c Gill b Jadeja	60	(1)	c Srikar Bharat b Ashwin	0
M.Labuschagne	b Jadeja	31		not out	28
*S.P.D.Smith	c Srikar Bharat b Jadeja	26			
P.S.P.Handscomb	c Iyer b Ashwin	19			
C.D.Green	lbw b Yadav	21			
†A.T.Carey	lbw b Ashwin	3			
M.A.Starc	b Yadav	1			
N.M.Lyon	b Ashwin	5			
T.R.Murphy	b Yadav	0			
M.P.Kuhnemann	not out	0			
Extras	(B 9, LB 8, NB 5)	22		(LB 1)	1
Total	**(76.3 overs)**	**197**		**(1 wkt; 18.5 overs)**	**78**

AUSTRALIA	*O*	*M*	*R*	*W*		*O*	*M*	*R*	*W*
Starc	5	0	21	0		7	1	14	1
Green	2	0	14	0					
Kuhnemann	9	2	16	5	(2)	16	2	60	1
Lyon	11.2	2	35	3	(3)	23.3	1	64	8
Murphy	6	1	23	1	(4)	14	6	18	0
INDIA									
Ashwin	20.3	4	44	3		9.5	3	44	1
Jadeja	32	8	78	4		7	1	23	0
Patel	13	1	33	0					
Yadav	5	0	12	3	(3)	2	0	10	0
Siraj	6	1	13	0					

FALL OF WICKETS

	I	A	I	A
Wkt	*1st*	*1st*	*2nd*	*2nd*
1st	27	12	15	0
2nd	34	108	32	–
3rd	36	125	54	–
4th	44	146	78	–
5th	45	186	113	–
6th	70	188	118	–
7th	82	192	140	–
8th	88	196	155	–
9th	108	197	155	–
10th	109	197	163	–

Umpires: N.N.Menon (*India*) (17) and J.S.Wilson (*West Indies*) (34).
Referee: B.C.Broad (*England*) (118). **Test No. 2492/105 (I568/A852)**

INDIA v AUSTRALIA (4th Test)

At Narendra Modi Stadium, Ahmedabad, on 9, 10, 11, 12, 13 March 2023.
Toss: Australia. Result: **MATCH DRAWN**.
Debuts: None.

AUSTRALIA

T.M.Head	c Jadeja b Ashwin	32	(2)	b Patel	90
U.T.Khawaja	lbw b Patel	180			
M.Labuschagne	b Shami	3		not out	63
*S.P.D.Smith	b Jadeja	38		not out	10
P.S.P.Handscomb	b Shami	17			
C.D.Green	c Srikar Bharat b Ashwin	114			
†A.T.Carey	c Patel b Ashwin	0			
M.A.Starc	c Iyer b Ashwin	6			
N.M.Lyon	c Kohli b Ashwin	34			
T.R.Murphy	lbw b Ashwin	41			
M.P.Kuhnemann	not out	0	(1)	lbw b Ashwin	6
Extras	(B 9, LB 3, NB 2, W 1)	15		(B 4, LB 1, NB 1)	6
Total	**(167.2 overs)**	**480**		**(2 wkts dec; 78.1 overs)**	**175**

INDIA

*R.G.Sharma	c Labuschagne b Kuhnemann	35
S.Gill	lbw b Lyon	128
C.A.Pujara	lbw b Murphy	42
V.Kohli	c Labuschagne b Murphy	186
R.A.Jadeja	c Khawaja b Murphy	28
†K.Srikar Bharat	c Handscomb b Lyon	44
A.R.Patel	b Starc	79
R.Ashwin	c Kuhnemann b Lyon	7
U.T.Yadav	run out	0
Mohammed Shami	not out	0
S.S.Iyer	absent hurt	
Extras	(B 14, LB 4, NB 4)	22
Total	**(178.5 overs)**	**571**

INDIA	*O*	*M*	*R*	*W*		*O*	*M*	*R*	*W*
Mohammed Shami	31	3	134	2	(3)	8	1	19	0
Yadav	25	2	105	0	(5)	5	0	21	0
Ashwin	47.2	15	91	6	(1)	24	9	58	1
Jadeja	35	5	89	1	(2)	20	7	34	0
Patel	28	8	47	1	(4)	19	8	36	1
Iyer	1	0	2	0					
Gill					(6)	1.1	0	1	0
Pujara					(7)	1	0	1	0
AUSTRALIA									
Starc	22	3	97	1					
Green	18	1	90	0					
Lyon	65	9	151	3					
Kuhnemann	25	3	94	1					
Murphy	45.5	10	113	3					
Head	3	0	8	0					

FALL OF WICKETS

	A	I	A
Wkt	*1st*	*1st*	*2nd*
1st	61	74	14
2nd	72	187	153
3rd	151	245	–
4th	170	309	–
5th	378	393	–
6th	378	555	–
7th	387	568	–
8th	409	569	–
9th	479	571	–
10th	480	–	–

Umpires: R.A.Kettleborough (*England*) (78) and N.N.Menon (*India*) (18).
Referee: B.C.Broad (*England*) (119). **Test No. 2493/106 (I569/A853)**

SOUTH AFRICA v WEST INDIES (1st Test)

At SuperSport Park, Centurion, on 28 February, 1, 2 March 2023.
Toss: South Africa. Result: **SOUTH AFRICA** won by 87 runs.
Debuts: South Africa – G.W.Coetzee, T.de Zorzi.

SOUTH AFRICA

D.Elgar	c Blackwood b Joseph	71	(2)	c Reifer b Joseph	1
A.K.Markram	b Joseph	115	(1)	c Da Silva b Roach	47
T.de Zorzi	run out	28		c Da Silva b Roach	0
*T.Bavuma	lbw b Joseph	0		c Da Silva b Joseph	0
K.D.Petersen	lbw b Mayers	14		lbw b Holder	7
†H.Klaasen	c Joseph b Gabriel	20		c Da Silva b Holder	5
S.Muthusamy	lbw b Roach	3		c Da Silva b Gabriel	4
M.Jansen	not out	23		b Roach	6
K.Rabada	c Blackwood b Holder	8		not out	10
G.W.Coetzee	c Holder b Joseph	17		c Da Silva b Roach	20
A.A.Nortje	c Chanderpaul b Joseph	14		c Da Silva b Roach	4
Extras	(B 8, LB 9, NB 10, W 2)	29		(B 4, LB 2, NB 6)	12
Total	**(86.3 overs)**	**342**		**(28 overs)**	**116**

WEST INDIES

*K.C.Brathwaite	b Rabada	11	c Klaasen b Rabada	0
T.Chanderpaul	c Muthusamy b Coetzee	22	c Nortje b Jansen	10
R.A.Reifer	c Klaasen b Jansen	62	c Klaasen b Rabada	8
J.Blackwood	c Klaasen b Nortje	37	c Markram b Rabada	79
R.L.Chase	c Elgar b Rabada	22	b Jansen	0
K.R.Mayers	c Jansen b Nortje	18	c Elgar b Coetzee	0
†J.M.Da Silva	c Jansen b Nortje	4	c Petersen b Rabada	17
J.O.Holder	c Markram b Nortje	0	c Klaasen b Rabada	18
A.S.Joseph	c Jansen b Nortje	4	c Rabada b Nortje	4
K.A.J.Roach	not out	4	lbw b Rabada	12
S.T.Gabriel	lbw b Coetzee	7	not out	1
Extras	(B 5, LB 8, NB 3, W 5)	21	(B 4, LB 4, NB 1, W 1)	10
Total	**(69 overs)**	**212**	**(41 overs)**	**159**

WEST INDIES	*O*	*M*	*R*	*W*		*O*	*M*	*R*	*W*
Roach	17	1	71	1		10	0	47	5
Joseph	18.3	0	81	5		8	0	30	2
Mayers	10	2	23	1					
Gabriel	12	1	49	1		3	0	26	1
Holder	14	1	64	1	(3)	7	2	7	2
Chase	14	0	33	0					
Blackwood	1	0	4	0					
SOUTH AFRICA									
Rabada	16	4	44	2		15	3	50	6
Jansen	17	3	64	1	(3)	7	2	33	2
Nortje	16	5	36	5	(2)	13	0	48	1
Coetzee	12	0	45	2		6	1	20	1
Muthusamy	8	2	10	0					

FALL OF WICKETS

	SA	WI	SA	WI
Wkt	*1st*	*1st*	*2nd*	*2nd*
1st	141	22	31	0
2nd	221	58	33	12
3rd	221	122	34	20
4th	236	169	49	20
5th	262	169	57	33
6th	271	179	69	91
7th	290	179	76	128
8th	300	190	80	139
9th	326	201	109	157
10th	342	212	116	159

Umpires: H.D.P.K.Dharmasena (*Sri Lanka*) (77) and M.Erasmus (*South Africa*) (76).
Referee: R.S.Madugalle (*Sri Lanka*) (210). **Test No. 2496/31 (SA459/WI570)**

SOUTH AFRICA v WEST INDIES (2nd Test)

At Wanderers Stadium, Johannesburg, on 8, 9, 10, 11 March 2023.
Toss: South Africa. Result: **SOUTH AFRICA** won by 284 runs.
Debuts: None.

SOUTH AFRICA

D.Elgar	c Chase b Motie	42	(2)	c Chase b Mayers	5
A.K.Markram	c Blackwood b Motie	96	(1)	c Da Silva b Roach	18
T.de Zorzi	b Motie	85		b Mayers	1
*T.Bavuma	lbw b Holder	28		c Roach b Holder	172
R.D.Rickelton	c Da Silva b Joseph	22		c Da Silva b Reifer	10
†H.Klaasen	c Da Silva b Mayers	17		c Da Silva b Joseph	14
P.W.A.Mulder	b Mayers	12		c Chanderpaul b Joseph	42
S.R.Harmer	c Da Silva b Mayers	1		lbw b Holder	19
K.A.Maharaj	c Motie b Joseph	1		c Motie b Mayers	10
G.W.Coetzee	c Da Silva b Joseph	1		not out	9
K.Rabada	not out	6		c and b Holder	16
Extras	(LB 5, NB 3, W 1)	9		(NB 4, W 1)	5
Total	**(92.2 overs)**	**320**		**(100.4 overs)**	**321**

WEST INDIES

*K.C.Brathwaite	c Elgar b Rabada	17		lbw b Rabada	18
T.Chanderpaul	run out	1		c Elgar b Harmer	2
R.A.Reifer	c de Zorzi b Coetzee	15		c Klaasen b Rabada	0
J.Blackwood	c Klaasen b Coetzee	6		c Bavuma b Harmer	4
R.L.Chase	b Mulder	28		b Maharaj	0
K.R.Mayers	c Elgar b Rabada	29		lbw b Maharaj	7
†J.M.Da Silva	b Harmer	26		b Coetzee	34
J.O.Holder	not out	81		b Coetzee	19
A.S.Joseph	c de Zorzi b Maharaj	4	(10)	st Klaasen b Harmer	18
K.A.J.Roach	c Elgar b Coetzee	13	(9)	c sub (K.D.Petersen) b Coetzee	2
G.Motie	c Bavuma b Harmer	17		not out	0
Extras	(B 4, LB 7, NB 3)	14		(B 1, NB 1)	2
Total	**(79.3 overs)**	**251**		**(35.1 overs)**	**106**

WEST INDIES	*O*	*M*	*R*	*W*		*O*	*M*	*R*	*W*
Roach	16	3	55	0		14	2	54	1
Joseph	18.2	3	60	3		14	1	49	2
Mayers	9	0	32	3	(4)	17	5	46	3
Holder	16	5	39	1	(3)	19.4	2	48	3
Motie	19	3	75	3	(6)	10	1	40	0
Chase	14	2	54	0	(7)	14	1	45	0
Reifer					(5)	11	0	36	1
Blackwood						1	0	3	0
SOUTH AFRICA									
Rabada	12	5	19	2		7	1	19	2
Mulder	15	4	40	1					
Coetzee	14	4	41	3	(5)	8	1	37	3
Harmer	17.3	2	63	2	(2)	17.1	8	45	3
Maharaj	21	4	77	1	(3)	2.5	1	4	2
Markram					(4)	0.1	0	0	0

FALL OF WICKETS

	SA	WI	SA	WI
Wkt	*1st*	*1st*	*2nd*	*2nd*
1st	76	1	6	21
2nd	192	22	8	21
3rd	248	28	32	25
4th	278	51	69	26
5th	286	103	103	26
6th	309	116	206	34
7th	311	157	277	82
8th	312	162	293	87
9th	312	193	297	106
10th	320	251	321	106

Umpires: M.Erasmus (*South Africa*) (77) and P.R.Reiffel (*Australia*) (60).
Referee: R.S.Madugalle (*Sri Lanka*) (211). **Test No. 2497/32 (SA460/WI571)**

NEW ZEALAND v SRI LANKA (1st Test)

At Hagley Oval, Christchurch, on 9, 10, 11, 12, 13 March 2023.
Toss: New Zealand. Result: **NEW ZEALAND** won by two wickets.
Debuts: None. ‡ (C.Karunaratne)

SRI LANKA

B.O.P.Fernando	c Blundell b Southee	13		c Blundell b Tickner	28
*F.D.M.Karunaratne	c Latham b Henry	50		c Nicholls b Tickner	17
B.K.G.Mendis	lbw b Southee	87		c Bracewell b Tickner	14
A.D.Mathews	c Mitchell b Henry	47		c Blundell b Henry	115
L.D.Chandimal	c Latham b Southee	39	(6)	b Southee	42
D.M.de Silva	c Blundell b Southee	46	(7)	not out	47
†D.P.D.N.Dickwella	lbw b Bracewell	7	(8)	c Blundell b Henry	0
C.A.K.Rajitha	c Williamson b Henry	22	(9)	lbw b Henry	14
N.G.R.P.Jayasuriya	c Blundell b Henry	13	(5)	c Blundell b Tickner	6
C.B.R.L.S.Kumara	not out	13		run out	8
A.M.Fernando	lbw b Southee	10		c Williamson b Southee	0
Extras	(LB 6, W 2)	8		(B 4, LB 3, W 4)	11
Total	**(92.4 overs)**	**355**		**(105.3 overs)**	**302**

NEW ZEALAND

T.W.M.Latham	b A.M.Fernando	67	b Jayasuriya	24
D.P.Conway	lbw b A.M.Fernando	30	c and b Rajitha	5
K.S.Williamson	c Karunaratne b Kumara	1	not out	121
H.M.Nicholls	c Rajitha b Kumara	2	c Mendis b Jayasuriya	20
D.J.Mitchell	c Dickwella b Kumara	102	b A.M.Fernando	81
†T.A.Blundell	c Dickwella b Rajitha	7	b A.M.Fernando	3
M.G.Bracewell	c Dickwella b Jayasuriya	25	c sub‡ b A.M.Fernando	10
*T.G.Southee	c Kumara b Rajitha	25	c de Silva b Kumara	1
M.J.Henry	b A.M.Fernando	72	run out	4
N.Wagner	c de Silva b A.M.Fernando	27	not out	0
B.M.Tickner	not out	2		
Extras	(B 4, LB 6, W 3)	13	(B 5, B 4, NB 1, W 6)	16
Total	**(107.3 overs)**	**373**	**(8 wkts; 70 overs)**	**285**

NEW ZEALAND	*O*	*M*	*R*	*W*		*O*	*M*	*R*	*W*
Southee	26.4	10	64	5		26.3	9	57	2
Henry	26	8	80	4		28	5	71	3
Tickner	20	2	103	0		28	1	100	4
Wagner	10	1	68	0		3	0	9	0
Mitchell	7	3	17	0		12	2	31	0
Bracewell	3	0	17	1		8	1	27	0
SRI LANKA									
Rajitha	31	10	104	2		17	5	60	1
A.M.Fernando	29.3	5	85	4		19	4	63	3
Kumara	25	5	76	3	(4)	15	3	61	1
De Silva	9	2	34	0					
Mathews	3	0	18	0					
Jayasuriya	10	1	46	1	(3)	19	1	92	2

FALL OF WICKETS

	SL	NZ	SL	NZ
Wkt	*1st*	*1st*	*2nd*	*2nd*
1st	14	67	28	9
2nd	151	70	47	50
3rd	151	76	81	90
4th	233	134	95	232
5th	260	151	200	238
6th	268	188	260	266
7th	316	235	266	273
8th	331	291	288	280
9th	336	360	298	–
10th	355	373	302	–

Umpires: C.B.Gaffaney (*New Zealand*) (47) and M.A.Gough (*England*) 30.
Referee: Sir R.B.Richardson (*West Indies*) (44). **Test No. 2498/37 (NZ463/SL308)**

NEW ZEALAND v SRI LANKA (2nd Test)

At Basin Reserve, Wellington, on 17, 18, 19, 20 March 2023.
Toss: Sri Lanka. Result: **NEW ZEALAND** won by an innings and 58 runs.
Debut: Sri Lanka – K.N.M.Fernando. ‡ (R.T.M.Wanigamuni) § (W.A.Young)

NEW ZEALAND

T.W.M.Latham	c Jayasuriya b Rajitha	21
D.P.Conway	c and b de Silva	78
K.S.Williamson	c sub‡ b Jayasuriya	215
H.M.Nicholls	not out	200
D.J.Mitchell	c and b Rajitha	17
†T.A.Blundell	not out	17
M.G.Bracewell		
*T.G.Southee		
M.J.Henry		
D.A.J.Bracewell		
B.M.Tickner		
Extras	(B 2, LB 17, NB 8, W 5)	32
Total	**(4 wkts dec; 123 overs)**	**580**

SRI LANKA

B.O.P.Fernando	c Blundell b Henry	6		c sub§ b D.A.J.Bracewell	5
*F.D.M.Karunaratne	c Latham b M.G.Bracewell	89		c Conway b Southee	51
B.K.G.Mendis	c Conway b D.A.J.Bracewell	0		c Williamson b Henry	50
N.G.R.P.Jayasuriya	c Mitchell b Southee	4	(9)	c Tickner b M.G.Bracewell	2
A.D.Mathews	c Blundell b Henry	1	(4)	c M.G.Bracewell b Tickner	2
L.D.Chandimal	st Blundell b M.G.Bracewell	37	(5)	c D.A.J.Bracewell b Tickner	62
D.M.de Silva	c Southee b M.G.Bracewell	0	(6)	c Nicholls b M.G.Bracewell	98
†K.N.M.Fernando	c M.G.Bracewell b Henry	19	(7)	c Henry b Tickner	39
C.A.K.Rajitha	run out	0	(8)	c Williamson b Southee	20
C.B.R.L.S.Kumara	not out	1		c M.G.Bracewell b Southee	7
A.M.Fernando	c Williamson b Tickner	0		not out	0
Extras	(B 4, LB 1, NB 1, W 1)	7		(LB 6, NB 2, W 14)	22
Total	**(66.5 overs)**	**164**		**(142 overs)**	**358**

SRI LANKA	*O*	*M*	*R*	*W*		*O*	*M*	*R*	*W*
Rajitha	32	6	126	2					
A.M.Fernando	26	6	110	0					
Kumara	25	1	164	0					
De Silva	19	3	75	1					
Jayasuriya	21	1	86	1					
NEW ZEALAND									
Southee	15	6	22	1		27	13	51	3
Henry	20	6	44	3		29	8	59	1
D.A.J.Bracewell	12	7	19	1	(4)	18	3	58	1
M.G.Bracewell	12	1	50	3	(3)	42	14	100	2
Tickner	6.5	1	21	1		26	6	84	3
Mitchell	1	0	3	0					

FALL OF WICKETS	NZ	SL	SL
Wkt	*1st*	*1st*	*2nd*
1st	87	13	26
2nd	118	18	97
3rd	481	27	113
4th	530	34	116
5th	–	114	242
6th	–	116	318
7th	–	156	318
8th	–	163	338
9th	–	163	354
10th	–	164	358

Umpires: C.B.Gaffaney (*New Zealand*) (48) and R.K.Illingworth (*England*) 63.
Referee: Sir R.B.Richardson (*West Indies*) (45). **Test No. 2499/38 (NZ464/SL309)**

BANGLADESH v IRELAND (Only Test)

At Shere Bangla National Stadium, Mirpur, on 4, 5, 6, 7 April 2023.
Toss: Ireland. Result: **BANGLADESH** won by seven wickets.
Debuts: Ireland – C.Campher, M.Commins, G.I.Hume, H.T.Tector, L.J.Tucker, B.C.White.

IRELAND

J.A.McCollum	c Nazmul b Ebadat	15	(2)	lbw b Shakib	0
M.Commins	lbw b Shoriful	5	(1)	lbw b Taijul	1
*A.Balbirnie	lbw b Taijul	16		b Taijul	3
H.T.Tector	b Mehedi	50		lbw b Taijul	56
C.Campher	lbw b Taijul	34		c Liton b Shakib	1
P.J.Moor	c Tamim b Taijul	1		c Liton b Shoriful	16
†L.J.Tucker	st Liton b Taijul	37		c Shoriful b Ebadat	108
A.R.McBrine	c Mominul b Ebadat	19		b Ebadat	72
M.R.Adair	lbw b Taijul	32		c Liton b Taijul	13
G.I.Hume	b Mehedi	2		c Liton b Ebadat	14
B.C.White	not out	0		not out	0
Extras	(NB 3)	3		(B 4, LB 2, NB 2)	8
Total	**(77.2 overs)**	**214**		**(116 overs)**	**292**

BANGLADESH

Tamim Iqbal	c Adair b McBrine	21		c Commins b White	31
Nazmul Hossain	b Adair	0	(3)	c Balbirnie b McBrine	4
Mominul Haque	b Adair	17	(5)	not out	20
Mushfiqur Rahim	c Commins b McBrine	126		not out	51
*Shakib Al Hasan	c Tucker b McBrine	87			
†Liton Das	c Tector b White	43	(2)	b Adair	23
Mehedi Hasan	st Tucker b White	55			
Taijul Islam	b McBrine	4			
Shoriful Islam	lbw b McBrine	4			
Ebadat Hossain	c Tucker b McBrine	0			
Khaled Ahmed	not out	4			
Extras	(LB 4, NB 2, W 2)	8		(B 4, LB 4, W 1)	9
Total	**(80.3 overs)**	**369**		**(3 wkts; 27.1 overs)**	**138**

BANGLADESH	*O*	*M*	*R*	*W*		*O*	*M*	*R*	*W*
Shoriful Islam	8	1	22	1	(5)	8	1	35	1
Khaled Ahmed	9	1	29	0	(6)	7	2	38	0
Ebadat Hossain	12	0	54	2	(4)	15	3	37	3
Taijul Islam	28	10	58	5	(2)	42	16	90	4
Mehedi Hasan	17.2	4	43	2	(3)	30	8	58	0
Shakib Al Hasan	3	1	8	0	(1)	13	4	26	2
Mominul Haque						1	0	2	0
IRELAND									
Adair	17	2	64	2		6	0	30	1
Hume	11	2	37	0					
McBrine	28	2	118	6	(2)	13.1	0	52	1
Campher	8	1	54	0					
White	13.3	0	71	2	(3)	7	0	43	1
Tector	3	0	21	0	(4)	1	0	5	0

FALL OF WICKETS	Ire	B	Ire	B
Wkt	*1st*	*1st*	*2nd*	*2nd*
1st	11	2	1	32
2nd	27	34	7	43
3rd	48	40	8	105
4th	122	199	13	–
5th	123	286	51	–
6th	124	331	123	–
7th	159	337	234	–
8th	199	347	265	–
9th	214	354	289	–
10th	214	369	292	–

Umpires: Alim Dar (*Pakistan*) (145) and Sharfuddoula (*Bangladesh*) (9).
Referee: D.C.Boon (*Australia*) (71). **Test No. 2500/1 (B137/Ire4)**

SRI LANKA v IRELAND (1st Test)

At Galle International Stadium, on 16, 17, 18 April 2023.
Toss: Sri Lanka. Result: **SRI LANKA** won by an innings and 280 runs.
Debuts: None.

SRI LANKA

K.N.M.Fernando	c Tucker b Campher	29
*F.D.M.Karunaratne	c Tucker b Adair	179
B.K.G.Mendis	lbw b Dockrell	140
A.D.Mathews	c Tucker b White	0
L.D.Chandimal	not out	102
N.G.R.P.Jayasuriya	lbw b Campher	16
D.M.de Silva	lbw b McBrine	12
†W.S.R.Samarawickrama	not out	104
R.T.M.Wanigamuni		
A.M.Fernando		
M.V.T.Fernando		
Extras	(B 4, LB 3, NB 1, W 1)	9
Total	**(6 wkts dec; 131 overs)**	**591**

IRELAND

J.A.McCollum	b Jayasuriya	35		c de Silva b Jayasuriya	8
M.Commins	b M.V.T.Fernando	0		c Wanigamuni b M.V.T.Fernando	0
*A.Balbirnie	c K.N.M.Fernando b M.V.T.Fernando	4		c de Silva b M.V.T.Fernando	6
H.T.Tector	c de Silva b Jayasuriya	34		run out	42
C.Campher	c Wanigamuni b Jayasuriya	0	(7)	c K.N.M.Fernando b Wanigamuni	30
P.J.Moor	c Samarawickrama b Jayasuriya	14		c K.N.M.Fernando b Wanigamuni	0
†L.J.Tucker	lbw b Jayasuriya	45	(5)	lbw b Jayasuriya	6
G.H.Dockrell	lbw b Jayasuriya	2		lbw b Wanigamuni	32
A.R.McBrine	lbw b Wanigamuni	7		c Mendis b Wanigamuni	10
M.R.Adair	st Samarawickrama b Jayasuriya	0		not out	23
B.C.White	not out	0		lbw b Jayasuriya	1
Extras	(NB 2)	2		(B 4, LB 4, NB 1, W 1)	10
Total	**(52.3 overs)**	**143**		**(54.1 overs)**	**168**

IRELAND	*O*	*M*	*R*	*W*		*O*	*M*	*R*	*W*
Adair	24.3	3	95	1					
Campher	21	2	84	2					
McBrine	40	2	162	1					
White	22	0	119	1					
Dockrell	21.3	0	112	1					
Tector	2	0	12	0					
SRI LANKA									
A.M.Fernando	5	2	9	0	(4)	3	0	15	0
M.V.T.Fernando	9	2	38	2		4	2	3	2
Jayasuriya	23	10	52	7	(1)	24.1	6	56	3
Wanigamuni	14.3	3	40	1	(3)	20	1	76	4
De Silva	1	0	4	0		3	0	10	0

FALL OF WICKETS

Wkt	SL *1st*	Ire *1st*	Ire *2nd*
1st	64	0	0
2nd	345	4	8
3rd	348	74	24
4th	373	74	32
5th	390	85	40
6th	408	92	100
7th	–	108	108
8th	–	143	131
9th	–	143	167
10th	–	143	168

Umpires: H.D.P.K.Dharmasena (*Sri Lanka*) (78) and A.T.Holdstock (*South Africa*) (6).
Referee: J.Srinath (*India*) (64). **Test No. 2501/1 (SL310/Ire5)**

SRI LANKA v IRELAND (2nd Test)

At Galle International Stadium, on 24, 25, 26, 27, 28 April 2023.
Toss: Ireland. Result: **SRI LANKA** won by an innings and 10 runs.
Debut: Ireland – M.J.Humphreys. ‡ (M.A.D.I.Hemantha)

IRELAND

J.A.McCollum	c Samarawickrama b Jayasuriya	10	b Wanigamuni	10
P.J.Moor	lbw b A.M.Fernando	5	c Mathews b Jayasuriya	19
*A.Balbirnie	c de Silva b Wanigamuni	95	c Mathews b Wanigamuni	46
H.T.Tector	c Chandimal b Jayasuriya	18	b A.M.Fernando	85
P.R.Stirling	c de Silva b A.M.Fernando	103	c Mendis b Jayasuriya	1
†L.J.Tucker	b M.V.T.Fernando	80	b A.M.Fernando	13
C.Campher	c de Silva b Jayasuriya	111	c Mendis b Wanigamuni	12
A.R.McBrine	c sub‡ b M.V.T.Fernando	35	c de Silva b Wanigamuni	10
G.I.Hume	lbw b Jayasuriya	6	c Samarawickrama b Wanigamuni	0
M.J.Humphreys	c Wanigamuni b Jayasuriya	7	not out	4
B.C.White	not out	0	b A.M.Fernando	0
Extras	(B 9, LB 11, NB 1, W 1)	22	(LB 2)	2
Total	**(145.3 overs)**	**492**	**(77.3 overs)**	**202**

SRI LANKA

K.N.M.Fernando	lbw b McBrine	205
*F.D.M.Karunaratne	c Humphreys b Campher	115
B.K.G.Mendis	c Humphreys b Hume	245
A.D.Mathews	not out	100
L.D.Chandimal	retired hurt	13
D.M.de Silva	not out	12
†W.S.R.Samarawickrama		
R.T.M.Wanigamuni		
N.G.R.P.Jayasuriya		
A.M.Fernando		
M.V.T.Fernando		
Extras	(B 2, LB 8, NB 2, W 2)	14
Total	**(3 wkts dec; 151 overs)**	**704**

SRI LANKA	*O*	*M*	*R*	*W*		*O*	*M*	*R*	*W*
M.V.T.Fernando	24	1	92	2		6	1	15	0
A.M.Fernando	22	4	78	2	(4)	11.3	3	30	3
Jayasuriya	58.3	13	174	5	(2)	32	9	88	2
Wanigamuni	27	4	108	1	(3)	27	6	64	5
De Silva	14	5	20	0		1	0	3	0
IRELAND									
Hume	22	3	87	1					
McBrine	57	8	191	1					
Campher	20	1	101	1					
Humphreys	10	0	67	0					
White	34	1	203	0					
Tector	8	0	45	0					

FALL OF WICKETS

	Ire	SL	Ire
Wkt	*1st*	*1st*	*2nd*
1st	12	228	10
2nd	43	496	38
3rd	89	629	61
4th	232	–	78
5th	321	–	103
6th	385	–	143
7th	474	–	159
8th	476	–	161
9th	483	–	202
10th	492	–	202

Umpires: H.D.P.K.Dharmasena (*Sri Lanka*) (79) and P.R.Reiffel (*Australia*) (61).
Referee: J.Srinath (*India*) (65). **Test No. 2502/2 (SL311/Ire6)**
L.D.Chandimal retired hurt at 651-3.

ENGLAND v IRELAND (Only Test)

At Lord's, London, on 1, 2, 3, June 2023.
Toss: England. Result: **ENGLAND** won by ten wickets.
Debuts: England – J.C.Tongue; Ireland – F.P.Hand.

IRELAND

J.A.McCollum	c Root b Broad	36	(2)	retired hurt	12
P.J.Moor	lbw b Broad	10	(1)	lbw b Tongue	11
*A.Balbirnie	c Crawley b Broad	0		c Bairstow b Tongue	2
H.T.Tector	c Potts b Broad	0		c Brook b Tongue	51
P.R.Stirling	c Bairstow b Leach	30		c Bairstow b Tongue	15
†L.J.Tucker	lbw b Leach	18		b Leach	44
C.Campher	b Leach	33		c Stokes b Root	19
A.R.McBrine	c Bairstow b Potts	19		not out	86
M.R.Adair	b Broad	14		c Bairstow b Potts	88
F.P.Hand	c Bairstow b Potts	1		c Crawley b Tongue	7
G.I.Hume	not out	0		b Broad	14
Extras	(B 1, LB 9, NB 1)	11		(LB 8, NB 5)	13
Total	**(56.2 overs)**	**172**		**(86.2 overs)**	**362**

ENGLAND

Z.Crawley	c and b Hand	56	not out	12
B.M.Duckett	b Hume	182	not out	0
O.J.D.Pope	st Tucker b McBrine	205		
J.E.Root	b McBrine	56		
H.C.Brook	not out	9		
*B.A.Stokes				
†J.M.Bairstow				
S.C.J.Broad				
M.J.Potts				
J.C.Tongue				
M.J.Leach				
Extras	(B 7, LB 5, NB 1, W 3)	16		–
Total	**(4 wkts dec; 82.4 overs)**	**524**	**(0 wkts; 0.4 overs)**	**12**

ENGLAND	*O*	*M*	*R*	*W*	*O*	*M*	*R*	*W*
Broad	17	5	51	5	14.2	2	62	1
Potts	12.2	4	36	2	21	3	77	1
Tongue	13	4	40	0	21	2	66	5
Leach	14	2	35	3	20	4	90	1
Root					10	0	59	1
IRELAND								
Adair	20	2	127	0	0.4	0	12	0
Hume	17	0	85	1				
Hand	19	2	113	1				
Campher	13	0	88	0				
McBrine	13.4	0	99	2				

FALL OF WICKETS

	Ire	E	Ire	E
Wkt	*1st*	*1st*	*2nd*	*2nd*
1st	15	109	16	–
2nd	19	361	18	–
3rd	19	507	63	–
4th	64	524	126	–
5th	98	–	162	–
6th	104	–	162	–
7th	142	–	325	–
8th	169	–	340	–
9th	172	–	362	–
10th	172	–	–	–

Umpires: A.T.Holdstock (*South Africa*) (7) and P.Wilson (*Australia*) (8).
Referee: Sir R.B.Richardson (*West Indies*) (46). **Test No. 2503/2 (E1061/Ire7)**
J.A.McCollum retired hurt at 25-2.

INDIA v AUSTRALIA (Only Test – ICC Final)

At The Oval, London, on 7, 8, 9, 10, 11 June 2023.
Toss: India. Result: **AUSTRALIA** won by 209 runs.
Debuts: None.

AUSTRALIA

D.A.Warner	c Srikar Bharat b Thakur	43	(2) c Srikar Bharat b Siraj	1
U.T.Khawaja	c Srikar Bharat b Siraj	0	(1) c Srikar Bharat b Yadav	13
M.Labuschagne	b Shami	26	c Pujara b Yadav	41
S.P.D.Smith	b Thakur	121	c Thakur b Jadeja	34
T.M.Head	c Srikar Bharat b Siraj	163	c and b Jadeja	18
C.D.Green	c Gill b Shami	6	b Jadeja	25
†A.T.Carey	lbw b Jadeja	48	not out	66
M.A.Starc	run out	5	c Kohli b Shami	41
*P.J.Cummins	c Rahane b Siraj	9	c sub (A.R.Patel) b Shami	5
N.M.Lyon	b Siraj	9		
S.M.Boland	not out	1		
Extras	(B 13, LB 10, NB 7, W 8)	38	(B 9, LB 9, NB 2, W 6)	26
Total	**(121.3 overs)**	**469**	**(8 wkts dec; 84.3 overs)**	**270**

INDIA

*R.G.Sharma	lbw b Cummins	15	lbw b Lyon	43
S.Gill	b Boland	13	c Green b Boland	18
C.A.Pujara	b Green	14	c Carey b Cummins	27
V.Kohli	c Smith b Starc	14	c Smith b Boland	49
A.M.Rahane	c Green b Cummins	89	c Carey b Starc	46
R.A.Jadeja	c Smith b Lyon	48	c Carey b Boland	0
†K.Srikar Bharat	b Boland	5	c and b Lyon	23
S.N.Thakur	c Carey b Green	51	lbw b Lyon	0
U.T.Yadav	b Cummins	5	c Carey b Starc	1
Mohammed Shami	c Carey b Starc	13	not out	13
M.Siraj	not out	0	c Boland b Lyon	1
Extras	(B 10, LB 10, NB 8, W 1)	29	(LB 2, NB 5, W 6)	13
Total	**(69.4 overs)**	**296**	**(63.3 overs)**	**234**

INDIA	*O*	*M*	*R*	*W*		*O*	*M*	*R*	*W*
Mohammed Shami	29	4	122	2		16.3	6	39	2
Siraj	28.3	4	108	4		20	2	80	1
Yadav	23	5	77	0	(4)	17	1	54	2
Thakur	23	4	83	2	(3)	8	1	21	0
Jadeja	18	2	56	1		23	4	58	3
AUSTRALIA									
Starc	13.4	0	71	2	(3)	14	1	77	2
Cummins	20	2	83	3	(1)	13	1	55	1
Boland	20	6	59	2	(2)	16	2	46	3
Green	12	1	44	2		5	0	13	0
Lyon	4	0	19	1		15.3	2	41	4

FALL OF WICKETS

	A	I	A	I
Wkt	*1st*	*1st*	*2nd*	*2nd*
1st	2	30	2	41
2nd	71	30	24	92
3rd	76	50	86	93
4th	361	71	111	179
5th	376	142	124	179
6th	387	152	167	212
7th	402	261	260	213
8th	453	271	270	220
9th	468	294	–	224
10th	469	296	–	234

Umpires: C.B.Gaffaney (*New Zealand*) (49) and R.K.Illingworth (*England*) (64).
Referee: Sir R.B.Richardson (*West Indies*) (47). **Test No. 2504/177 (I570/A854)**

BANGLADESH v AFGHANISTAN (Only Test)

At Shere Bangla National Stadium, Mirpur, on 14, 15, 16, 17 June 2023.
Toss: Afghanistan. Result: **BANGLADESH** won by 546 runs.
Debuts: Afghanistan – Bahir Shah, Karim Janat, Nijat Masood.

BANGLADESH

Mahmudul Hasan	c Zadran b Rahmat	76		c Zadran b Hotak	17
Zakir Hasan	c Zazai b Masood	1		run out	71
Nazmul Hossain	c Nasir b Hotak	146		c Malik b Khan	124
Mominul Haque	c Zazai b Masood	15		not out	121
Mushfiqur Rahim	c Nasir b Masood	47		c Zadran b Khan	8
*†Liton Das	c Zadran b Khan	9		not out	66
Mehedi Hasan	c Hotak b Yamin	48			
Taskin Ahmed	lbw b Yamin	2			
Taijul Islam	c Malik b Masood	0			
Shoriful Islam	b Masood	6			
Ebadat Hosain	not out	0			
Extras	(B 8, LB 1, NB 16, W 7)	32		(B 2, LB 2, NB 8, W 6)	18
Total	**(86 overs)**	**382**		**(4 wkts dec; 80 overs)**	**425**

AFGHANISTAN

Ibrahim Zadran	c Liton b Shoriful	6		lbw b Shoriful	0
Abdul Malik	c Zakir b Ebadat	17		c Liton b Taskin	5
Rahmat Shah	c Taskin b Ebadat	9		c Liton b Taskin	30
*Hashmatullah Shahidi	c Mehedi b Shoriful	9		retired hurt	13
Nasir Ahmadzai	lbw b Mehedi	35		c Liton b Ebadat	6
†Afsar Zazai	c Shoriful b Ebadat	36		c Mehedi b Shoriful	6
Karim Janat	st Liton b Mehedi	23	(8)	b Taskin	18
Hamza Hotak	c Mominul b Ebadat	6	(9)	c Mominul b Mehedi	5
Yamin Ahmadzai	c Liton b Taijul	0	(10)	c Mushfiqur b Taskin	1
Nijat Masood	c Zakir b Taijul	0	(11)	not out	4
Zahir Khan	not out	0	(12)	retired hurt	4
Bahir Shah			(7)	c Taijul b Shoriful	7
Extras	(LB 1, NB 4)	5		(B 4, NB 6, W 6)	16
Total	**(39 overs)**	**146**		**(33 overs)**	**115**

AFGHANISTAN	*O*	*M*	*R*	*W*		*O*	*M*	*R*	*W*
Yamin Ahmadzai	10	1	39	2		13	1	61	0
Nijat Masood	16	2	79	5		12.5	1	83	0
Karim Janat	11	3	33	0	(4)	8	0	48	0
Zahir Khan	16	0	98	1	(5)	23	0	112	2
Hamza Hotak	24	1	85	1	(3)	16.1	0	90	1
Hashmatullah Shahidi	3	0	9	0		3	0	19	0
Rahmat Shah	6	1	30	1	(8)	2	0	4	0
Nasir Ahmadzai					(7)	2	0	4	0
BANGLADESH									
Taskin Ahmed	7	0	48	0	(2)	9	2	37	4
Shoriful Islam	8	2	28	2	(1)	10	1	28	3
Ebadat Hossain	10	1	47	4	(5)	7	2	22	1
Taijul Islam	5	0	7	2	(3)	5	1	19	0
Mehedi Hasan	9	1	15	2	(4)	2	0	5	1

FALL OF WICKETS

	B	Afg	B	Afg
Wkt	*1st*	*1st*	*2nd*	*2nd*
1st	6	18	18	0
2nd	218	24	191	7
3rd	256	35	274	48
4th	271	51	282	65
5th	290	116	–	78
6th	373	116	–	91
7th	375	128	–	98
8th	375	140	–	106
9th	377	146	–	110
10th	382	146	–	–

Umpires: C.M.Brown (*New Zealand*) (7) and P.R.Reiffel (*Australia*) (62).
Referee: B.C.Broad (*England*) (120). **Test No. 2505/2 (B138/Afg7)**
Bahir Shah replaced Hashmatullah Shahidi, who retired hurt (concussion) at 45-2.

ENGLAND v AUSTRALIA (1st Test)

At Edgbaston, Birmingham, on 16, 17, 18, 19, 20 June 2023.
Toss: England. Result: **AUSTRALIA** won by two wickets.
Debuts: None.

ENGLAND

Z.Crawley	c Carey b Boland	61		c Carey b Boland	7
B.M.Duckett	c Carey b Hazlewood	12		c Green b Cummins	19
O.J.D.Pope	lbw b Lyon	31		b Cummins	14
J.E.Root	not out	118		st Carey b Lyon	46
H.C.Brook	b Lyon	32		c Labuschagne b Lyon	46
*B.A.Stokes	c Carey b Hazlewood	1		lbw b Cummins	43
†J.M.Bairstow	st Carey b Lyon	78		lbw b Lyon	20
M.M.Ali	st Carey b Lyon	18		c Carey b Hazlewood	19
S.C.J.Broad	b Green	16	(10)	not out	10
O.E.Robinson	not out	17	(9)	c Green b Lyon	27
J.M.Anderson				c Carey b Cummins	12
Extras	(LB 6, NB 3)	9		(LB 9, NB 1)	10
Total	**(8 wkts dec; 78 overs)**	**393**		**(66.2 overs)**	**273**

AUSTRALIA

D.A.Warner	b Broad	9	(2)	c Bairstow b Robinson	36
U.T.Khawaja	b Robinson	141	(1)	b Stokes	65
M.Labuschagne	c Bairstow b Broad	0		c Bairstow b Broad	13
S.P.D.Smith	lbw b Stokes	16		c Bairstow b Broad	6
T.M.Head	c Crawley b Ali	50	(6)	c Root b Ali	16
C.D.Green	b Ali	38	(7)	b Robinson	28
†A.T.Carey	b Anderson	66	(8)	c and b Root	20
*P.J.Cummins	c Stokes b Robinson	38	(9)	not out	44
N.M.Lyon	c Duckett b Robinson	1	(10)	not out	16
S.M.Boland	c Pope b Broad	0	(5)	c Bairstow b Broad	20
J.R.Hazlewood	not out	1			
Extras	(B 4, LB 6, NB 15, W 1)	26		(LB 10, NB 8)	18
Total	**(116.1 overs)**	**386**		**(8 wkts; 92.3 overs)**	**282**

AUSTRALIA	*O*	*M*	*R*	*W*		*O*	*M*	*R*	*W*
Cummins	14	0	59	0		18.2	1	63	4
Hazlewood	15	1	61	2		10	1	48	1
Boland	14	0	86	1	(4)	12	2	61	1
Lyon	29	1	149	4	(3)	24	2	80	4
Green	6	0	32	1		2	0	12	0
ENGLAND									
Broad	23	4	68	3	(2)	21	3	64	3
Robinson	22.1	5	55	3	(3)	18.3	7	43	2
Anderson	21	5	53	1	(1)	17	1	56	0
Brook	3	1	5	0					
Ali	33	4	147	2	(4)	14	2	57	1
Stokes	7	0	33	1		7	2	9	1
Root	7	3	15	0	(5)	15	2	43	1

FALL OF WICKETS

	E	A	E	A
Wkt	*1st*	*1st*	*2nd*	*2nd*
1st	22	29	27	61
2nd	92	29	27	78
3rd	124	67	77	89
4th	175	148	129	121
5th	176	220	150	143
6th	297	338	196	192
7th	323	372	210	209
8th	350	377	229	227
9th	–	378	256	–
10th	–	386	273	–

Umpires: Ahsan Raza (*Pakistan*) (8) and M.Erasmus (*South Africa*) (78).
Referee: A.J.Pycroft (*Zimbabwe*) (92). **Test No. 2506/357 (E1062/A855)**

ENGLAND v AUSTRALIA (2nd Test)

At Lord's, London, on 28, 29, 30 June, 1, 2 July 2023.
Toss: England. Result: **AUSTRALIA** won by 43 runs.
Debuts: None.

AUSTRALIA

D.A.Warner	b Tongue	66	(2)	lbw b Tongue	25
U.T.Khawaja	b Tongue	17	(1)	c sub (M.J.Potts) b Broad	77
M.Labuschagne	c Bairstow b Robinson	47		c Brook b Anderson	30
S.P.D.Smith	c Duckett b Tongue	110		c Crawley b Tongue	34
T.M.Head	st Bairstow b Root	77		c Root b Broad	7
C.D.Green	c Anderson b Root	0		c Duckett b Robinson	18
†A.T.Carey	lbw b Broad	22		c Root b Robinson	21
M.A.Starc	c Bairstow b Anderson	6		not out	15
*P.J.Cummins	not out	22		c Duckett b Broad	11
N.M.Lyon	c Tongue b Robinson	7	(11)	c Stokes b Broad	4
J.R.Hazlewood	c Root b Robinson	4	(10)	c Root b Stokes	1
Extras	(B 12, LB 14, NB 12)	38		(B 14, LB 9, NB 6, W 7)	36
Total	**(100.4 overs)**	**416**		**(101.5 overs)**	**279**

ENGLAND

Z.Crawley	st Carey b Lyon	48	c Carey b Starc	3
B.M.Duckett	c Warner b Hazlewood	98	c Carey b Hazlewood	83
O.J.D.Pope	c Smith b Green	42	b Starc	3
J.E.Root	c Smith b Starc	10	c Warner b Cummins	18
H.C.Brook	c Cummins b Starc	50	b Cummins	4
*B.A.Stokes	c Green b Starc	17	c Carey b Hazlewood	155
†J.M.Bairstow	c Cummins b Hazlewood	16	st Carey b Green	10
S.C.J.Broad	lbw b Head	12	c Green b Hazlewood	11
O.E.Robinson	c Carey b Head	9	c Smith b Cummins	1
J.C.Tongue	c sub (M.T.Renshaw) b Cummins	1	b Starc	19
J.M.Anderson	not out	0	not out	3
Extras	(B 9, LB 4, NB 7, W 2)	22	(LB 3, NB 4, W 10)	17
Total	**(76.2 overs)**	**325**	**(81.3 overs)**	**327**

ENGLAND	*O*	*M*	*R*	*W*		*O*	*M*	*R*	*W*
Anderson	20	5	53	1		19	4	64	1
Broad	23	4	99	1		24.5	8	65	4
Robinson	24.4	3	100	3	(4)	26	11	48	2
Tongue	22	3	98	3	(3)	20	4	53	2
Stokes	3	1	21	0		12	1	26	1
Root	8	1	19	2					
AUSTRALIA									
Starc	17	0	88	3		21.3	2	79	3
Cummins	16.2	2	46	1		25	2	69	3
Hazlewood	13	1	71	2		18	0	80	3
Lyon	13	1	35	1					
Green	9	0	54	1		13	3	73	1
Head	7	1	17	2	(4)	4	0	23	0
Smith	1	0	1	0					

FALL OF WICKETS

	A	E	A	E
Wkt	*1st*	*1st*	*2nd*	*2nd*
1st	73	91	63	9
2nd	96	188	123	13
3rd	198	208	187	41
4th	316	222	190	45
5th	316	279	197	177
6th	351	293	239	193
7th	358	311	242	301
8th	393	324	261	302
9th	408	325	264	302
10th	416	325	279	327

Umpires: Ahsan Raza (*Pakistan*) (9) and C.B.Gaffaney (*New Zealand*) (50).
Referee: A.J.Pycroft (*Zimbabwe*) (93). **Test No. 2507/358 (E1063/A856)**

ENGLAND v AUSTRALIA (3rd Test)

At Headingley, Leeds, on 6, 7, 8, 9 July 2023.
Toss: England. Result: **ENGLAND** won by three wickets.
Debuts: None.

AUSTRALIA

D.A.Warner	c Crawley b Broad	4	(2) c Crawley b Broad	1
U.T.Khawaja	b Wood	13	(1) c Bairstow b Woakes	43
M.Labuschagne	c Root b Woakes	21	c Brook b Ali	33
S.P.D.Smith	c Bairstow b Broad	22	c Duckett b Ali	2
T.M.Head	c Root b Woakes	39	c Duckett b Broad	77
M.R.Marsh	c Crawley b Woakes	118	c Bairstow b Woakes	28
†A.T.Carey	c Woakes b Wood	8	b Woakes	5
M.A.Starc	b Wood	2	c Brook b Wood	16
*P.J.Cummins	lbw b Wood	0	c Bairstow b Wood	1
T.R.Murphy	b Wood	13	lbw b Broad	11
S.M.Boland	not out	0	not out	0
Extras	(B 10, LB 10, NB 3)	23	(B 5, LB 2)	7
Total	**(60.4 overs)**	**263**	**(67.1 overs)**	**224**

ENGLAND

Z.Crawley	c Warner b Marsh	33	c Carey b Marsh	44
B.M.Duckett	c Carey b Cummins	2	lbw b Starc	23
H.C.Brook	c Smith b Cummins	3	(5) c Cummins b Starc	75
J.E.Root	c Warner b Cummins	19	c Carey b Cummins	21
†J.M.Bairstow	c Smith b Starc	12	(7) b Starc	5
*B.A.Stokes	c Smith b Murphy	80	c Carey b Starc	13
M.M.Ali	c Smith b Cummins	21	(3) b Starc	5
C.R.Woakes	c Carey b Starc	10	not out	32
M.A.Wood	c Marsh b Cummins	24	not out	16
S.C.J.Broad	c Smith b Cummins	7		
O.E.Robinson	not out	5		
Extras	(B 4, LB 3, NB 9, W 5)	21	(B 7, LB 7, NB 5, W 1)	20
Total	**(52.3 overs)**	**237**	**(7 wkts; 50 overs)**	**254**

ENGLAND	*O*	*M*	*R*	*W*		*O*	*M*	*R*	*W*
Broad	11.4	0	58	2		14.1	3	45	3
Robinson	11.2	2	38	0					
Wood	11.4	4	34	5		17	2	66	2
Woakes	17	1	73	3	(2)	18	0	68	3
Ali	9	1	40	0		17	3	34	2
Root					(4)	1	0	4	0
AUSTRALIA									
Starc	14	3	59	2	(2)	16	0	78	5
Cummins	18	1	91	6	(1)	15	0	77	1
Boland	10	0	35	0		11	1	49	0
Marsh	3	1	9	1		6	0	23	1
Murphy	7.3	0	36	1		2	0	13	0

FALL OF WICKETS

	A	E	A	E
Wkt	*1st*	*1st*	*2nd*	*2nd*
1st	4	18	11	42
2nd	42	22	68	60
3rd	61	65	72	93
4th	85	68	90	131
5th	240	87	131	161
6th	245	131	139	171
7th	249	142	168	230
8th	249	167	170	–
9th	254	199	211	–
10th	263	237	224	–

Umpires: H.D.P.K.Dharmasena (*Sri Lanka*) (80) and N.N.Menon (*India*) (19).
Referee: R.S.Madugalle (*Sri Lanka*) (212). **Test No. 2508/359 (E1064/A857)**

ENGLAND v AUSTRALIA (4th Test)

At Old Trafford, Manchester, on 19, 20, 21, 22, 23 (*no play*) July 2023.
Toss: England. Result: **MATCH DRAWN.**
Debuts: None.

AUSTRALIA

D.A.Warner	c Bairstow b Woakes	32	(2)	b Woakes	28
U.T.Khawaja	lbw b Broad	3	(1)	c Bairstow b Wood	18
M.Labuschagne	lbw b Ali	51		c Bairstow b Root	111
S.P.D.Smith	lbw b Wood	41		c Bairstow b Wood	17
T.M.Head	c Root b Broad	48		c Duckett b Wood	1
M.R.Marsh	c Bairstow b Woakes	51		not out	31
C.D.Green	lbw b Woakes	16		not out	3
†A.T.Carey	c Bairstow b Woakes	20			
M.A.Starc	not out	36			
*P.J.Cummins	c Stokes b Anderson	1			
J.R.Hazlewood	c Duckett b Woakes	4			
Extras	(B 8, LB 3, NB 3)	14		(B 1, LB 2, NB 1, W 1)	5
Total	**(90.2 overs)**	**317**		**(5 wkts; 71 overs)**	**214**

ENGLAND

Z.Crawley	b Green	189
B.M.Duckett	c Carey b Starc	1
M.M.Ali	c Khawaja b Starc	54
J.E.Root	b Hazlewood	84
H.C.Brook	c Starc b Hazlewood	61
*B.A.Stokes	b Cummins	51
†J.M.Bairstow	not out	99
C.R.Woakes	c Carey b Hazlewood	0
M.A.Wood	b Hazlewood	6
S.C.J.Broad	c and b Hazlewood	7
J.M.Anderson	lbw b Green	5
Extras	(B 15, LB 9, NB 11)	35
Total	**(107.4 overs)**	**592**

ENGLAND	*O*	*M*	*R*	*W*		*O*	*M*	*R*	*W*
Broad	14	0	68	2	(2)	12	2	47	0
Anderson	20	4	51	1	(1)	17	5	30	0
Woakes	22.2	4	62	5	(5)	12	5	31	1
Wood	17	5	60	1		11	0	27	3
Ali	17	1	65	1	(3)	13	2	44	0
Root						6	1	32	1
AUSTRALIA									
Starc	25	0	137	2					
Hazlewood	27	2	126	5					
Cummins	23	0	129	1					
Green	15.4	1	64	2					
Head	7	0	52	0					
Marsh	9	0	57	0					
Labuschagne	1	0	3	0					

FALL OF WICKETS

	A	E	A
Wkt	*1st*	*1st*	*2nd*
1st	15	9	32
2nd	61	130	54
3rd	120	336	97
4th	183	351	108
5th	189	437	211
6th	254	474	–
7th	255	486	–
8th	294	506	–
9th	299	526	–
10th	317	592	–

Umpires: N.N.Menon (*India*) (20) and J.S.Wilson (*West Indies*) (35).
Referee: R.S.Madugalle (*Sri Lanka*) (213). **Test No. 2509/360 (E1065/A858)**

ENGLAND v AUSTRALIA (5th Test)

At The Oval, London, on 27, 28, 29, 30, 31 July 2023.
Toss: Australia. Result: **ENGLAND** won by 49 runs.
Debuts: None.

ENGLAND

Z.Crawley	c Smith b Cummins	22		c Smith b Cummins	73
B.M.Duckett	c Carey b Marsh	41		c Carey b Starc	42
M.M.Ali	b Murphy	34	(7)	c Hazlewood b Starc	29
J.E.Root	b Hazlewood	5		b Murphy	91
H.C.Brook	c Smith b Starc	85		c Carey b Hazlewood	7
*B.A.Stokes	b Starc	3	(3)	c Cummins b Murphy	42
†J.M.Bairstow	b Hazlewood	4	(6)	c Carey b Starc	78
C.R.Woakes	c Head b Starc	36		c Khawaja b Starc	1
M.A.Wood	b Murphy	28		c Marsh b Murphy	9
S.C.J.Broad	c Head b Starc	7		not out	8
J.M.Anderson	not out	0		lbw b Murphy	8
Extras	(B 9, LB 7, NB 2)	18		(LB 4, NB 3)	7
Total	**(54.4 overs)**	**283**		**(81.5 overs)**	**395**

AUSTRALIA

U.T.Khawaja	lbw b Broad	47	(2)	lbw b Woakes	72
D.A.Warner	c Crawley b Woakes	24	(1)	c Bairstow b Woakes	60
M.Labuschagne	c Root b Wood	9		c Crawley b Wood	13
S.P.D.Smith	c Bairstow b Woakes	71		c Crawley b Woakes	54
T.M.Head	c Bairstow b Broad	4		c Root b Ali	43
M.R.Marsh	b Anderson	16		c Bairstow b Ali	6
†A.T.Carey	c Stokes b Root	10		c Bairstow b Broad	28
M.A.Starc	c Duckett b Wood	7		c Crawley b Woakes	0
*P.J.Cummins	c Stokes b Root	36		c Stokes b Ali	9
T.R.Murphy	lbw b Woakes	34		c Bairstow b Broad	18
J.R.Hazlewood	not out	6		not out	4
Extras	(B 17, LB 12, NB 1, W 1)	31		(B 10, LB 10, NB 2, W 5)	27
Total	**(103.1 overs)**	**295**		**(94.4 overs)**	**334**

AUSTRALIA	*O*	*M*	*R*	*W*		*O*	*M*	*R*	*W*
Starc	14.4	1	82	4		20	2	100	4
Hazlewood	13	0	54	2		15	0	67	1
Cummins	13	2	66	1		16	0	79	1
Marsh	8	0	43	1		8	0	35	0
Murphy	6	0	22	2		22.5	0	110	4
ENGLAND									
Broad	20	5	49	2		20.4	4	62	2
Anderson	26	9	67	1		14	4	53	0
Wood	22	4	62	2	(6)	9	0	34	1
Woakes	25	8	61	3	(3)	19	4	50	4
Root	7.1	1	20	2		9	0	39	0
Brook	3	1	7	0					
Ali					(4)	23	2	76	3

FALL OF WICKETS	E	A	E	A
Wkt	*1st*	*1st*	*2nd*	*2nd*
1st	62	49	79	140
2nd	66	91	140	141
3rd	73	115	213	169
4th	184	127	222	264
5th	193	151	332	274
6th	208	170	360	274
7th	212	185	364	275
8th	261	239	375	294
9th	270	288	379	329
10th	283	295	395	334

Umpires: H.D.P.K.Dharmasena (*Sri Lanka*) (81) and J.S.Wilson (*West Indies*) (36).
Referee: R.S.Madugalle (*Sri Lanka*) (214). **Test No. 2510/361 (E1066/A859)**

WEST INDIES v INDIA (1st Test)

At Windsor Park, Roseau, on 12, 13, 14 July 2023.
Toss: West Indies. Result: **INDIA** won by an innings and 141 runs.
Debuts: West Indies – A.S.Athenaze; India – Y.B.Jaiswal, I.P.Kishan.

WEST INDIES

*K.C.Brathwaite	c Sharma b Ashwin	20	c Rahane b Ashwin	7
T.Chanderpaul	b Ashwin	12	lbw b Jadeja	7
R.A.Reifer	c Kishan b Thakur	2	lbw b Jadeja	11
J.Blackwood	c Siraj b Jadeja	14	lbw b Ashwin	5
A.S.Athenaze	c Thakur b Ashwin	47	c Jaiswal b Ashwin	28
†J.M.Da Silva	c Kishan b Jadeja	2	lbw b Siraj	13
J.O.Holder	c Thakur b Siraj	18	not out	20
A.S.Joseph	c Unadkat b Ashwin	4	c Gill b Ashwin	13
R.R.S.Cornwall	not out	19	c Gill b Ashwin	4
K.A.J.Roach	lbw b Jadeja	1	b Ashwin	0
J.A.Warrican	c Gill b Ashwin	1	lbw b Ashwin	18
Extras	(B 2, LB 5, NB 2, W 1)	10	(B 2, LB 2)	4
Total	**(64.3 overs)**	**150**	**(50.3 overs)**	**130**

INDIA

Y.B.Jaiswal	c Da Silva b Joseph	171
*R.G.Sharma	c Da Silva b Athanaze	103
S.Gill	c Athanaze b Warrican	6
V.Kohli	c Athanaze b Cornwall	76
A.M.Rahane	c Blackwood b Roach	3
R.A.Jadeja	not out	37
†I.P.Kishan	not out	1
R.Ashwin		
S.N.Thakur		
J.D.Unadkat		
M.Siraj		
Extras	(B 8, LB 11, W 5)	24
Total	**(5 wkts dec; 152.2 overs)**	**421**

INDIA	*O*	*M*	*R*	*W*		*O*	*M*	*R*	*W*
Siraj	12	2	25	1		6	1	16	1
Unadkat	7	2	17	0		2	1	1	0
Ashwin	24.3	6	60	5		21.3	7	71	7
Thakur	7	3	15	1					
Jadeja	14	7	26	3	(4)	21	5	38	2
WEST INDIES									
Roach	24	6	50	1					
Joseph	18.2	2	80	1					
Cornwall	16	5	32	1					
Warrican	45	4	106	1					
Holder	18	5	40	0					
Brathwaite	9	0	21	0					
Athanaze	16	2	53	1					
Reifer	4	0	16	0					
Blackwood	2	0	4	0					

FALL OF WICKETS

	WI	I	WI
Wkt	*1st*	*1st*	*2nd*
1st	31	229	8
2nd	38	240	22
3rd	47	350	32
4th	68	356	32
5th	76	405	58
6th	117	–	78
7th	124	–	100
8th	129	–	108
9th	147	–	108
10th	149	–	130

Umpires: M.A.Gough (*England*) (31) and R.A.Kettleborough (*England*) (79).
Referee: J.J.Crowe (*New Zealand*) (114). **Test No. 2511/99 (WI572/I571)**

WEST INDIES v INDIA (2nd Test)

At Queen's Park Oval, Port of Spain, on 20, 21, 22, 23, 24 (*no play*) July 2023.
Toss: West Indies. Result: **MATCH DRAWN**.
Debuts: West Indies – K.S.A.McKenzie; India – Mukesh Kumar.

INDIA

Y.B.Jaiswal	c McKenzie b Holder	57		c Da Silva b Warrican	38
*R.G.Sharma	b Warrican	80		c Joseph b Gabriel	57
S.Gill	c Da Silva b Roach	10		not out	29
V.Kohli	run out	121			
A.M.Rahane	b Gabriel	8			
R.A.Jadeja	c Da Silva b Roach	61			
†I.P.Kishan	c Da Silva b Holder	25	(4)	not out	52
R.Ashwin	b Roach	56			
J.D.Unadkat	st Da Silva b Warrican	7			
M.Siraj	lbw b Warrican	0			
Mukesh Kumar	not out	0			
Extras	(B 4, NB 8, W 1)	13		(B 1, LB 2, NB 1, W 1)	5
Total	**(128 overs)**	**438**		**(2 wkts dec; 24 overs)**	**181**

WEST INDIES

*K.C.Brathwaite	b Ashwin	75	c Unadkat b Ashwin	28
T.Chanderpaul	c Ashwin b Jadeja	33	not out	24
K.S.A.McKenzie	c Kishan b Mukesh Kumar	32	lbw b Ashwin	0
J.Blackwood	c Rahane b Jadeja	20	not out	20
A.S.Athenaze	lbw b Mukesh Kumar	37		
†J.M.Da Silva	b Siraj	10		
J.O.Holder	c Kishan b Siraj	15		
A.S.Joseph	lbw b Siraj	4		
K.A.J.Roach	c Kishan b Siraj	4		
J.A.Warrican	not out	7		
S.T.Gabriel	lbw b Siraj	0		
Extras	(B 4, LB 1, NB 8, W 5)	18	(B 2, LB 1, NB 1)	4
Total	**(115.4 overs)**	**255**	**(2 wkts; 32 overs)**	**76**

WEST INDIES	*O*	*M*	*R*	*W*		*O*	*M*	*R*	*W*
Roach	22	2	104	3		4	0	46	0
Joseph	22	0	97	0		4	0	37	0
Gabriel	18	0	74	1	(4)	6	0	33	1
Warrican	39	7	89	3	(5)	6	0	36	1
Holder	21	3	57	2	(3)	4	0	26	0
Athanaze	4	0	12	0					
Brathwaite	2	1	1	0					
INDIA									
Siraj	23.4	6	60	5		8	2	24	0
Unadkat	16	3	44	0	(3)	3	2	1	0
Ashwin	33	10	61	1	(4)	11	2	33	2
Mukesh Kumar	18	6	48	2	(2)	5	4	5	0
Jadeja	25	10	37	2		5	1	10	0

FALL OF WICKETS

	I	WI	I	WI
Wkt	*1st*	*1st*	*2nd*	*2nd*
1st	139	71	98	38
2nd	153	117	102	44
3rd	155	157	–	–
4th	182	178	–	–
5th	341	208	–	–
6th	360	229	–	–
7th	393	233	–	–
8th	416	244	–	–
9th	426	255	–	–
10th	438	255	–	–

Umpires: M.Erasmus (*South Africa*) (79) and R.A.Kettleborough (*England*) (80).
Referee: J.J.Crowe (*New Zealand*) (115). **Test No. 2512/100 (WI573/I572)**

SRI LANKA v PAKISTAN (1st Test)

At Galle International Stadium, on 16, 17, 18, 19, 20 July 2023.
Toss: Sri Lanka. Result: **PAKISTAN** won by four wickets.
Debuts: None. ‡ (P.H.K.D.Mendis)

SRI LANKA

K.N.M.Fernando	c Sarfraz b Afridi	4		c Sarfraz b Ali	52
*F.D.M.Karunaratne	c Sarfraz b Afridi	29		c Salman b Abrar	20
B.K.G.Mendis	c Salman b Afridi	12		lbw b Ali	18
A.D.Mathews	c Sarfraz b Abrar	64		c Azam b Ali	7
L.D.Chandimal	c Azam b Shah	1		c Imam b Salman	28
D.M.de Silva	c Masood b Shah	122		c Sarfraz b Afridi	82
†W.S.R.Samarawickrama	c Imam b Salman	36		c Shafiq b Salman	11
R.T.M.Wanigamuni	c Azam b Abrar	5		lbw b Abrar	42
N.G.R.P.Jayasuriya	c Sarfraz b Shah	4		c Masood b Afridi	10
C.A.K.Rajitha	c Shafiq b Abrar	8	(11)	c Masood b Abrar	5
M.V.T.Fernando	not out	21	(10)	not out	0
Extras	(B 4, LB 1, NB 1)	6		(LB 1, NB 1, W 2)	4
Total	**(95.2 overs)**	**312**		**(83.1 overs)**	**279**

PAKISTAN

Abdullah Shafiq	c de Silva b Jayasuriya	19		c Samarawickrama b Jayasuriya	8
Imam-ul-Haq	c sub‡ b Rajitha	1		not out	50
Shan Masood	lbw b Wanigamuni	39		c K.N.M.Fernando b Jayasuriya	7
*Babar Azam	c Samarawickrama b Jayasuriya	13	(5)	lbw b Jayasuriya	24
Saud Shakil	not out	208	(6)	c Samarawickrama b Wanigamuni	30
†Sarfraz Ahmed	lbw b Jayasuriya	17	(7)	c Mendis b Jayasuriya	1
Agha Salman	st Samarawickrama b Wanigamuni	83	(8)	not out	6
Nauman Ali	lbw b Wanigamuni	25	(4)	run out	0
Shaheen Shah Afridi	lbw b M.V.T.Fernando	9			
Naseem Shah	b Wanigamuni	6			
Abrar Ahmed	c Mathews b Wanigamuni	10			
Extras	(B 9, LB 8, NB 6, W 8)	31		(B 4, LB 3)	7
Total	**(121.2 overs)**	**461**		**(6 wkts; 32.5 overs)**	**133**

PAKISTAN	*O*	*M*	*R*	*W*		*O*	*M*	*R*	*W*
Shaheen Shah Afridi	24	3	86	3		13	0	64	2
Naseem Shah	22	2	90	3		12	2	32	0
Abrar Ahmed	31.2	9	68	3	(4)	24.1	5	68	3
Agha Salman	5	1	18	1	(3)	9	0	39	2
Nauman Ali	13	2	45	0		25	5	75	3
SRI LANKA									
M.V.T.Fernando	18	1	69	1		2	1	6	0
Rajitha	19	1	77	1					
Jayasuriya	35	3	145	3		14.5	0	56	4
Wanigamuni	42.2	2	136	5	(2)	14	1	62	1
De Silva	7	1	17	0	(4)	2	1	2	0

FALL OF WICKETS

	SL	P	SL	P
Wkt	*1st*	*1st*	*2nd*	*2nd*
1st	6	3	42	16
2nd	22	47	79	36
3rd	53	67	91	38
4th	54	73	99	79
5th	185	101	159	122
6th	242	278	175	127
7th	257	330	251	–
8th	282	346	269	–
9th	283	440	274	–
10th	312	461	279	–

Umpires: R.J.Tucker (*Australia*) (82) and A.G.Wharf (*England*) (5).
Referee: D.C.Boon (*Australia*) (72). **Test No. 2513/58 (SL312/P452)**

SRI LANKA v PAKISTAN (2nd Test)

At Sinhalese Sports Club, Colombo, on 24, 25, 26, 27 July 2023.
Toss: Sri Lanka. Result: **PAKISTAN** won by an innings and 222 runs.
Debut: Sri Lanka – L.M.D.Madushanka. ‡ (Mohammad Rizwan)

SRI LANKA

K.N.M.Fernando	run out	4	b Ali	33
*F.D.M.Karunaratne	b Shah	17	c Imam b Ali	41
B.K.G.Mendis	c sub‡ b Afridi	6	c Shakil b Ali	14
A.D.Mathews	c Sarfraz b Shah	9	not out	63
L.D.Chandimal	c Imam b Shah	34	c Imam b Ali	1
D.M.de Silva	c Shakil b Abrar	57	c Abrar b Ali	10
†W.S.R.Samarawickrama	c Shafiq b Abrar	0	st Rizwan b Ali	5
R.T.M.Wanigamuni	c Shakil b Abrar	27	lbw b Abrar	16
N.G.R.P.Jayasuriya	run out	1	b Shah	0
A.M.Fernando	b Abrar	8	b Shah	0
L.M.D.Madushanka	not out	0	b Shah	0
Extras	(B 2, NB 1)	3	(LB 4, W 1)	5
Total	**(48.4 overs)**	**166**	**(67.4 overs)**	**188**

PAKISTAN

Abdullah Shafiq	c Madushanka b Jayasuriya	201
Imam-ul-Haq	c K.N.M.Fernando b A.M.Fernando	6
Shan Masood	c Mendis b A.M.Fernando	51
*Babar Azam	lbw b Jayasuriya	39
Saud Shakil	lbw b A.M.Fernando	57
†Sarfraz Ahmed	retired hurt	14
Agha Salman	not out	132
†Mohammad Rizwan	not out	50
Nauman Ali		
Shaheen Shah Afridi		
Naseem Shah		
Abrar Ahmed		
Extras	(B 4, LB 16, NB 3, W 3)	26
Total	**(5 wkts dec; 134 overs)**	**576**

PAKISTAN	*O*	*M*	*R*	*W*	*O*	*M*	*R*	*W*
Shaheen Shah Afridi	11	1	44	1	12	5	30	0
Naseem Shah	14	3	41	3	17.4	5	44	3
Abrar Ahmed	20.4	3	69	4	10	1	34	0
Nauman Ali	3	1	10	0	23	8	70	7
Agha Salman					5	1	6	0
SRI LANKA								
A.M.Fernando	25	1	133	3				
Madushanka	17	3	77	0				
Wanigamuni	36	2	139	0				
Jayasuriya	53	11	194	2				
De Silva	3	1	13	0				

FALL OF WICKETS

	SL	P	SL
Wkt	*1st*	*1st*	*2nd*
1st	9	13	69
2nd	23	121	86
3rd	35	210	99
4th	36	319	109
5th	121	468	131
6th	122	–	141
7th	133	–	177
8th	136	–	184
9th	163	–	188
10th	166	–	188

Umpires: C.B.Gaffaney (*New Zealand*) (51) and A.G.Wharf (*England*) (6).
Referee: D.C.Boon (*Australia*) (73). **Test No. 2514/59 (SL313/P453)**
Sarfraz Ahmed retired hurt at 344-4 (P1) and was replaced by Mohammad Rizwan.

BANGLADESH v NEW ZEALAND (1st Test)

At Sylhet Stadium, on 28, 29, 30 November, 1, 2 December 2023.
Toss: Bangladesh. Result: **BANGLADESH** won by 150 runs.
Debut: Bangladesh – Shahadat Hossain.

BANGLADESH

Mahmudul Hasan	c Mitchell b Sodhi	86	run out	8
Zakir Hasan	b Patel	12	lbw b Patel	17
*Nazmul Hossain	c Williamson b Phillips	37	c Blundell b Southee	105
Mominul Haque	c Blundell b Phillips	37	run out	40
Mushfiqur Rahim	c Williamson b Patel	12	lbw b Patel	67
Shahadat Hossain	c Nicholls b Phillips	24	lbw b Sodhi	18
Mehedi Hasan	c Mitchell b Jamieson	20	not out	50
†Nurul Hasan	c Blundell b Phillips	29	c and b Phillips	10
Nayeem Hasan	c Latham b Jamieson	16	c Latham b Sodhi	4
Taijul Islam	not out	8	c Nicholls b Patel	0
Shoriful Islam	lbw b Southee	13	st Blundell b Patel	10
Extras	(B 12, LB 3, W 1)	16	(B 2, LB 7)	9
Total	**(85.1 overs)**	**310**	**(100.4 overs)**	**338**

NEW ZEALAND

T.W.M.Latham	c Nayeem b Taijul	21	c Nurul b Shoriful	0
D.P.Conway	c Shahadat b Mehedi	12	c Shahadat b Taijul	22
K.S.Williamson	b Taijul	104	lbw b Taijul	11
H.M.Nicholls	c Nurul b Shoriful	19	c Nayeem b Mehedi	2
D.J.Mitchell	st Nurul b Taijul	41	c Taijul b Nayeem	58
†T.A.Blundell	c Nurul b Nayeem	6	c Nurul b Taijul	6
G.D.Phillips	c Nazmul b Mominul	42	lbw b Nayeem	12
K.A.Jamieson	lbw b Mominul	23	lbw b Taijul	9
I.S.Sodhi	c Shahadat b Taijul	0	c Zakir b Taijul	22
*T.G.Southee	b Mominul	35	c Zakir b Taijul	34
A.Y.Patel	not out	1	not out	0
Extras	(B 8, LB 5)	13	(B 4, NB 1)	5
Total	**(101.5 overs)**	**317**	**(71.1 overs)**	**181**

NEW ZEALAND	*O*	*M*	*R*	*W*		*O*	*M*	*R*	*W*
Southee	14.1	2	43	1		15	3	33	1
Jamieson	17	5	52	2		13	3	25	0
Patel	24	1	76	2		36.4	1	148	4
Sodhi	14	1	71	1	(5)	19	2	74	2
Phillips	16	1	53	4	(4)	16	4	47	1
Mitchell						1	0	2	0
BANGLADESH									
Shoriful Islam	13	2	54	1		6	2	13	1
Mehedi Hasan	22	3	64	1		15	4	44	1
Taijul Islam	39	9	109	4		31.1	8	75	6
Nayeem Hasan	24	3	73	1		17	3	40	2
Mominul Haque	3.5	1	4	3		2	0	5	0

FALL OF WICKETS

	B	NZ	B	NZ
Wkt	*1st*	*1st*	*2nd*	*2nd*
1st	39	36	23	0
2nd	92	44	26	19
3rd	180	98	116	30
4th	184	164	214	46
5th	210	175	248	60
6th	233	253	278	81
7th	261	262	291	102
8th	276	264	311	132
9th	290	316	312	178
10th	310	317	338	181

Umpires: Ahsan Raza (*Pakistan*) (10) and P.R.Reiffel (*Australia*) (63).
Referee: D.C.Boon (*Australia*) (74). **Test No. 2515/18 (B139/NZ465)**

BANGLADESH v NEW ZEALAND (2nd Test)

At Shere Bangla National Stadium, Mirpur, on 6, 7 (*no play*), 8, 9 December 2023.
Toss: Bangladesh. Result: **NEW ZEALAND** won by four wickets.
Debuts: None.

BANGLADESH

Mahmudul Hasan	c Latham b Patel	14	(2)	c Mitchell b Patel	2
Zakir Hasan	c Williamson b Santner	8	(1)	c Mitchell b Patel	59
*Nazmul Hossain	lbw b Santner	9		c Williamson b Southee	15
Mominul Haque	c Blundell b Patel	5		lbw b Patel	10
Mushfiqur Rahim	obstructing the field	35		c Mitchell b Santner	9
Shahadat Hossain	c Blundell b Phillips	31		lbw b Santner	4
Mehedi Hasan	c Mitchell b Santner	20		c Santner b Patel	3
†Nurul Hasan	c Santner b Phillips	7		lbw b Patel	0
Nayeem Hasan	not out	13		c Southee b Santner	9
Taijul Islam	lbw b Phillips	6		not out	14
Shoriful Islam	c Blundell b Southee	10		st Blundell b Patel	8
Extras	(B 9, LB 5)	14		(B 10, LB 1)	11
Total	**(66.2 overs)**	**172**		**(35 overs)**	**144**

NEW ZEALAND

T.W.M.Latham	c Nurul b Taijul	4	c Nazmul b Mehedi	26
D.P.Conway	b Mehedi	11	lbw b Shoriful	2
K.S.Williamson	c Shahadat b Mehedi	13	st Nurul b Taijul	11
H.M.Nicholls	c Shoriful b Taijul	1	lbw b Mehedi	3
D.J.Mitchell	c Mehedi b Nayeem	18	c Nazmul b Mehedi	19
†T.A.Blundell	lbw b Mehedi	0	c Nurul b Taijul	2
G.D.Phillips	c Nurul b Shoriful	87	not out	40
M.J.Santner	c Nazmul b Nayeem	1	not out	35
K.A.Jamieson	c Shahadat b Shoriful	20		
*T.G.Southee	c Mehedi b Taijul	14		
A.Y.Patel	not out	0		
Extras	(B 5, LB 5, W 1)	11	(B 1)	1
Total	**(37.1 overs)**	**180**	**(6 wkts; 39.4 overs)**	**139**

NEW ZEALAND	*O*	*M*	*R*	*W*		*O*	*M*	*R*	*W*
Southee	5.2	5	0	1	(3)	6	1	25	1
Jamieson	4	2	8	0					
Patel	17	6	54	2	(1)	18	1	57	6
Santner	28	7	65	3	(2)	11	0	51	3
Phillips	12	1	31	3					
BANGLADESH									
Shoriful Islam	4	1	15	2		5	2	9	1
Mehedi Hasan	11	1	53	3		16.4	2	52	3
Taijul Islam	16.1	0	64	3		14	2	58	2
Nayeem Hasan	4	0	21	2		3	0	15	0
Mominul Haque	2	0	17	0		1	0	4	0

FALL OF WICKETS

	B	NZ	B	NZ
Wkt	*1st*	*1st*	*2nd*	*2nd*
1st	29	20	3	5
2nd	29	22	38	24
3rd	41	30	71	33
4th	47	46	82	48
5th	104	46	88	51
6th	123	95	97	69
7th	135	97	97	–
8th	145	152	112	–
9th	154	180	128	–
10th	172	180	144	–

Umpires: P.R.Reiffel (*Australia*) (64) and R.J.Tucker (*Australia*) (83).
Referee: D.C.Boon (*Australia*) (75). **Test No. 2516/19 (B140/NZ466)**

AUSTRALIA v PAKISTAN (1st Test)

At Perth Stadium, on 14, 15, 16, 17 December 2023.
Toss: Australia. Result: **AUSTRALIA** won by 360 runs.
Debuts: Pakistan – Aamer Jamal, Khurram Shehzad.

AUSTRALIA

D.A.Warner	c Imam b Jamal	164	(2)	c Imam b Shehzad	0
U.T.Khawaja	c Sarfraz b Afridi	41	(1)	c Azam b Afridi	90
M.Labuschagne	lbw b Ashraf	16		c Sarfraz b Shehzad	2
S.P.D.Smith	c Sarfraz b Shehzad	31		lbw b Shehzad	45
T.M.Head	c Salman b Jamal	40		c Imam b Jamal	14
M.R.Marsh	b Shehzad	90		not out	63
†A.T.Carey	b Jamal	34			
M.A.Starc	b Jamal	12			
*P.J.Cummins	c Salman b Jamal	9			
N.M.Lyon	c Salman b Jamal	5			
J.R.Hazlewood	not out	4			
Extras	(B 1, LB 17, NB 9, W 14)	41		(LB 11, NB 7, W 1)	19
Total	**(113.2 overs)**	**487**		**(5 wkts dec; 63.2 overs)**	**233**

PAKISTAN

Abdullah Shafiq	c Warner b Lyon	42		c Carey b Starc	2
Imam-ul-Haq	st Carey b Lyon	62		lbw b Starc	10
*Shan Masood	c Carey b Starc	30		c Carey b Hazlewood	2
Khurram Shehzad	b Cummins	7	(11)	c Warner b Hazlewood	0
Babar Azam	c Carey b Marsh	21	(4)	c Carey b Cummins	14
Saud Shakil	c Warner b Hazlewood	28	(5)	lbw b Hazlewood	24
†Sarfraz Ahmed	b Starc	3	(6)	c Marsh b Starc	4
Agha Salman	not out	28	(7)	run out	5
Faheem Ashraf	c Khawaja b Cummins	9	(8)	lbw b Lyon	5
Aamer Jamal	st Carey b Lyon	10	(9)	b Lyon	4
Shaheen Shah Afridi	c Khawaja b Head	4	(10)	not out	3
Extras	(B 8, LB 7, W 12)	27		(B 6, LB 10)	16
Total	**(101.5 overs)**	**271**		**(30.2 overs)**	**89**

PAKISTAN	*O*	*M*	*R*	*W*	*O*	*M*	*R*	*W*
Shaheen Shah Afridi	27	7	96	1	18.2	4	76	1
Khurram Shehzad	22	5	83	2	16	4	45	3
Aamer Jamal	20.2	1	111	6	9	0	28	1
Faheem Ashraf	17	1	93	1	7	0	37	0
Agha Salman	27	3	86	0	13	1	36	0
AUSTRALIA								
Starc	25	5	68	2	9	2	31	3
Hazlewood	22	7	49	1	7.2	2	13	3
Cummins	20	7	35	2	6	1	11	1
Lyon	24	3	66	3	8	1	18	2
Marsh	9	0	34	1				
Head	1.5	0	4	1				

FALL OF WICKETS

	A	P	A	P
Wkt	*1st*	*1st*	*2nd*	*2nd*
1st	126	74	0	2
2nd	159	123	5	17
3rd	238	133	87	19
4th	304	181	107	48
5th	321	192	233	56
6th	411	195	–	63
7th	449	230	–	79
8th	476	241	–	83
9th	481	258	–	89
10th	487	271	–	89

Umpires: R.K.Illingworth (*England*) (65) and J.S.Wilson (*West Indies*) (37).
Referee: J.Srinath (*India*) (66). **Test No. 2517/70 (A860/P454)**

AUSTRALIA v PAKISTAN (2nd Test)

At Melbourne Cricket Ground, on 26, 27, 28, 29 December 2023.
Toss: Pakistan. Result: **AUSTRALIA** won by 79 runs.
Debuts: None.

AUSTRALIA

D.A.Warner	c Azam b Salman	38	(2) b Hamza	6
U.T.Khawaja	c Salman b Ali	42	(1) c Rizwan b Afridi	0
M.Labuschagne	c Shafiq b Jamal	63	c Rizwan b Afridi	4
S.P.D.Smith	c Rizwan b Jamal	26	c Salman b Afridi	50
T.M.Head	c Salman b Afridi	17	b Hamza	0
M.R.Marsh	c Jamal b Hamza	41	c Salman b Hamza	96
†A.T.Carey	c Rizwan b Afridi	4	lbw b Hamza	53
M.A.Starc	c Salman b Hamza	9	c Azam b Afridi	9
*P.J.Cummins	c Hamza b Jamal	13	c Rizwan b Jamal	16
N.M.Lyon	c Hamza b Ali	8	b Jamal	11
J.R.Hazlewood	not out	5	not out	1
Extras	(B 20, LB 15, NB 2, W 15)	52	(B 1, LB 10, W 5)	16
Total	**(96.5 overs)**	**318**	**(84.1 overs)**	**262**

PAKISTAN

Abdullah Shafiq	c and b Cummins	62	c Khawaja b Starc	4
Imam-ul-Haq	c Labuschagne b Lyon	10	lbw b Cummins	12
*Shan Masood	c Marsh b Lyon	54	c Smith b Cummins	60
Babar Azam	b Cummins	1	b Hazlewood	41
Saud Shakil	b Hazlewood	9	c Carey b Starc	24
†Mohammad Rizwan	c Warner b Cummins	42	c Carey b Cummins	35
Agha Salman	c Carey b Cummins	5	c Marsh b Starc	50
Aamer Jamal	not out	33	c and b Cummins	0
Shaheen Shah Afridi	lbw b Lyon	21	c Labuschagne b Cummins	0
Hassan Ali	b Cummins	2	not out	0
Mir Hamza	st Carey b Lyon	2	c Smith b Starc	0
Extras	(B 4, LB 11, NB 3, W 5)	23	(B 1, LB 6, NB 1, W 3)	11
Total	**(73.5 overs)**	**264**	**(67.2 overs)**	**237**

PAKISTAN	*O*	*M*	*R*	*W*		*O*	*M*	*R*	*W*
Shaheen Shah Afridi	27	5	85	2		27	4	76	4
Mir Hamza	22	5	51	2		18.1	6	32	4
Hassan Ali	23.5	7	61	2		17	2	53	0
Aamer Jamal	19	1	64	3		16	2	74	2
Agha Salman	5	0	22	1		6	1	16	0
AUSTRALIA									
Starc	16	3	69	0		13.2	1	55	4
Hazlewood	16	5	43	1		15	7	34	1
Cummins	20	1	48	5	(4)	18	2	49	5
Lyon	18.5	2	73	4	(3)	19	1	84	0
Marsh	3	0	16	0		2	0	8	0

FALL OF WICKETS

	A	P	A	P
Wkt	*1st*	*1st*	*2nd*	*2nd*
1st	90	34	0	8
2nd	108	124	6	49
3rd	154	131	16	110
4th	204	147	16	146
5th	250	151	169	162
6th	260	170	187	219
7th	275	215	209	219
8th	286	240	237	237
9th	308	255	249	237
10th	318	264	262	237

Umpires: M.A.Gough (*England*) (32) and J.S.Wilson (*West Indies*) (38).
Referee: J.Srinath (*India*) (67). **Test No. 2518/71 (A861/P455)**

AUSTRALIA v PAKISTAN (3rd Test)

At Sydney Cricket Ground, on 3, 4, 5, 6 January 2024.
Toss: Pakistan. Result: **AUSTRALIA** won by eight wickets.
Debut: Pakistan – Saim Ayub.

PAKISTAN

Abdullah Shafiq	c Smith b Starc	0		b Starc	0
Saim Ayub	c Carey b Hazlewood	0		lbw b Lyon	33
*Shan Masood	c Smith b Marsh	35		c Carey b Hazlewood	0
Babar Azam	lbw b Cummins	26		c Carey b Head	23
Saud Shakil	c Carey b Cummins	5		c Smith b Hazlewood	2
†Mohammad Rizwan	c Hazlewood b Cummins	88		c Warner b Lyon	28
Agha Salman	c Head b Starc	53	(8)	c Warner b Hazlewood	0
Sajid Khan	c Lyon b Cummins	15	(7)	b Hazlewood	0
Aamer Jamal	c Starc b Lyon	82		c Head b Cummins	18
Hassan Ali	c Starc b Cummins	0		b Lyon	5
Mir Hamza	not out	7		not out	1
Extras	(LB 1, NB 1)	2		(B 2, LB 3)	5
Total	**(77.1 overs)**	**313**		**(43.1 overs)**	**115**

AUSTRALIA

D.A.Warner	c Azam b Salman	34	(2)	lbw b Khan	57
U.T.Khawaja	c Rizwan b Jamal	47	(1)	lbw b Khan	0
M.Labuschagne	b Salman	60		not out	62
S.P.D.Smith	c Azam b Hamza	38		not out	4
T.M.Head	lbw b Jamal	10			
M.R.Marsh	c Masood b Jamal	54			
†A.T.Carey	b Khan	38			
M.A.Starc	not out	1			
*P.J.Cummins	lbw b Jamal	0			
N.M.Lyon	c Shakil b Jamal	5			
J.R.Hazlewood	c Salman b Jamal	0			
Extras	(B 1, LB 7, NB 2, W 2)	12		(B 5, LB 2)	7
Total	**(109.4 overs)**	**299**		**(2 wkts; 25.5 overs)**	**130**

AUSTRALIA	*O*	*M*	*R*	*W*		*O*	*M*	*R*	*W*
Starc	16	2	75	2		4	1	15	1
Hazlewood	15	2	65	1		9	2	16	4
Cummins	18	1	61	5		7	0	24	1
Lyon	17.1	0	74	1		17.1	2	36	3
Marsh	7	1	27	1					
Labuschagne	3	1	9	0					
Head	1	0	1	0	(5)	6	1	19	1
PAKISTAN									
Sajid Khan	26	5	73	1		11	1	49	2
Mir Hamza	21	9	53	1		2	0	9	0
Hassan Ali	21	6	53	0		4	0	15	0
Aamer Jamal	21.4	2	69	6	(5)	3.5	0	22	0
Agha Salman	20	3	43	2	(4)	5	0	28	0

FALL OF WICKETS

	P	A	P	A
Wkt	*1st*	*1st*	*2nd*	*2nd*
1st	0	70	0	0
2nd	4	108	1	119
3rd	39	187	58	–
4th	47	187	60	–
5th	96	205	67	–
6th	190	289	67	–
7th	220	293	67	–
8th	226	293	109	–
9th	227	299	109	–
10th	313	299	115	–

Umpires: M.A.Gough (*England*) (33) and R.K.Illingworth (*England*) (66).
Referee: J.Srinath (*India*) (68). **Test No. 2519/72 (A862/P456)**

SOUTH AFRICA v INDIA (1st Test)

At SuperSport Park, Centurion, on 26, 27, 28 December 2023.
Toss: South Africa. Result: **SOUTH AFRICA** won by an innings and 32 runs.
Debuts: South Africa – D.G.Bedingham, N.Burger; India – P.M.Krishna.

INDIA

Y.B.Jaiswal	c Verreynne b Burger	17	c Verreynne b Burger	5
*R.G.Sharma	c Burger b Rabada	5	b Rabada	0
S.Gill	c Verreynne b Burger	2	b Jansen	26
V.Kohli	c Verreynne b Rabada	38	c Rabada b Jansen	76
S.S.Iyer	b Rabada	31	b Jansen	6
†K.L.Rahul	b Burger	101	c Markram b Burger	4
R.Ashwin	c sub (P.W.A.Mulder) b Rabada	8	c Bedingham b Burger	0
S.N.Thakur	c Elgar b Rabada	24	c Bedingham b Rabada	2
J.J.Bumrah	b Jansen	1	run out	0
M.Siraj	c Verreynne b Coetzee	5	c Verreynne b Burger	4
P.M.Krishna	not out	0	not out	0
Extras	(B 2, LB 8, NB 1, W 2)	13	(LB 2, W 6)	8
Total	**(67.4 overs)**	**245**	**(34.1 overs)**	**131**

SOUTH AFRICA

A.K.Markram	c Rahul b Siraj	5
D.Elgar	c Rahul b Thakur	185
T.de Zorzi	c Jaiswal b Bumrah	28
K.D.Petersen	b Bumrah	2
D.G.Bedingham	b Siraj	56
†K.Verreynne	c Rahul b Krishna	4
M.Jansen	not out	84
G.W.Coetzee	c Siraj b Ashwin	19
K.Rabada	b Bumrah	1
N.Burger	b Bumrah	0
*T.Bavuma	absent hurt	
Extras	(LB 13, NB 9, W 2)	24
Total	**(108.4 overs)**	**408**

SOUTH AFRICA	*O*	*M*	*R*	*W*		*O*	*M*	*R*	*W*
Rabada	20	4	59	5		12	3	32	2
Jansen	16	2	52	1	(3)	7.1	1	36	3
Burger	15.4	4	50	3	(2)	10	3	33	4
Coetzee	16	1	74	1		5	0	28	0
INDIA									
Bumrah	26.4	5	69	4					
Siraj	24	1	91	2					
Thakur	19	2	101	1					
Krishna	20	2	93	1					
Ashwin	19	6	41	1					

FALL OF WICKETS

	I	SA	I
Wkt	*1st*	*1st*	*2nd*
1st	13	11	5
2nd	23	104	13
3rd	24	113	52
4th	92	244	72
5th	107	249	96
6th	121	360	96
7th	164	391	105
8th	191	392	113
9th	238	408	121
10th	245	–	131

Umpires: P.R.Reiffel (*Australia*) (65) and L.Rusere (*Zimbabwe*) (6).
Referee: B.C.Broad (*England*) (121). **Test No. 2520/43 (SA461/I573)**

SOUTH AFRICA v INDIA (2nd Test)

At Newlands, Cape Town, on 3, 4, January 2024.
Toss: South Africa. Result: **INDIA** won by seven wickets.
Debut: South Africa – T.Stubbs.

SOUTH AFRICA

A.K.Markram	c Jaiswal b Siraj	2	c Sharma b Siraj	106
*D.Elgar	b Siraj	4	c Kohli b Mukesh Kumar	12
T.de Zorzi	c Rahul b Siraj	2	c Rahul b Mukesh Kumar	1
T.Stubbs	c Sharma b Bumrah	3	c Rahul b Bumrah	1
D.G.Bedingham	c Jaiswal b Siraj	12	c Rahul b Bumrah	11
†K.Verreynne	c Gill b Siraj	15	c Siraj b Bumrah	9
M.Jansen	c Rahul b Siraj	0	c and b Bumrah	11
K.A.Maharaj	c Bumrah b Mukesh Kumar	3	c Iyer b Bumrah	3
K.Rabada	c Iyer b Mukesh Kumar	5	c Sharma b Krishna	2
N.Burger	c Jaiswal b Bumrah	4	not out	6
L.T.Ngidi	not out	0	c Jaiswal b Bumrah	8
Extras	(B 4, LB 1)	5	(LB 1, NB 5)	6
Total	**(23.2 overs)**	**55**	**(36.5 overs)**	**176**

INDIA

Y.B.Jaiswal	b Rabada	0	c Stubbs b Burger	28
*R.G.Sharma	c Jansen b Burger	39	not out	16
S.Gill	c Jansen b Burger	36	b Rabada	10
V.Kohli	c Markram b Rabada	46	c Verreynne b Jansen	12
S.S.Iyer	c Verreynne b Burger	0	not out	4
†K.L.Rahul	c Verreynne b Ngidi	8		
R.A.Jadeja	c Jansen b Ngidi	0		
J.J.Bumrah	c Jansen b Ngidi	0		
M.Siraj	run out	0		
P.M.Krishna	c Markram b Rabada	0		
Mukesh Kumar	not out	0		
Extras	(B 4, LB 10, NB 5, W 5)	24	(B 1, LB 2, NB 1, W 6)	10
Total	**(34.5 overs)**	**153**	**(3 wkts; 12 overs)**	**80**

INDIA	*O*	*M*	*R*	*W*		*O*	*M*	*R*	*W*
Bumrah	8	1	25	2		13.5	0	61	6
Siraj	9	3	15	6		9	3	31	1
Krishna	4	1	10	0	(4)	4	1	27	1
Mukesh Kumar	2.2	2	0	2	(3)	10	2	56	2
SOUTH AFRICA									
Rabada	11.5	2	38	3		6	0	33	1
Ngidi	6	1	30	3					
Burger	8	2	42	3	(2)	4	0	29	1
Jansen	9	2	29	0	(3)	2	0	15	1

FALL OF WICKETS

	SA	I	SA	I
Wkt	*1st*	*1st*	*2nd*	*2nd*
1st	5	17	37	44
2nd	8	72	41	57
3rd	11	105	45	75
4th	15	110	66	–
5th	34	153	85	–
6th	34	153	103	–
7th	45	153	111	–
8th	46	153	162	–
9th	55	153	162	–
10th	55	153	176	–

Umpires: Ahsan Raza (*Pakistan*) (11) and L.Rusere (*Zimbabwe*) (7).
Referee: B.C.Broad (*England*) (122). **Test No. 2521/44 (SA462/I574)**

AUSTRALIA v WEST INDIES (1st Test)

At Adelaide Oval, on 17, 18, 19 January 2024.
Toss: Australia. Result: **AUSTRALIA** won by ten wickets.
Debuts: West Indies – J.P.Greaves, K.A.R.Hodge, S.Joseph.

WEST INDIES

*K.C.Brathwaite	b Cummins	13	c Head b Hazlewood	1
T.Chanderpaul	c Green b Cummins	6	c Carey b Hazlewood	0
K.S.A.McKenzie	c Carey b Hazlewood	50	c Labuschagne b Green	26
A.S.Athanaze	b Hazlewood	13	c Carey b Hazlewood	0
K.A.R.Hodge	c Green b Hazlewood	12	c Smith b Hazlewood	3
J.P.Greaves	c Labuschagne b Hazlewood	5	lbw b Lyon	24
†J.M.Da Silva	c Head b Cummins	6	c Hazlewood b Starc	18
A.S.Joseph	c Smith b Cummins	14	c Carey b Starc	16
G.Motie	c Lyon b Starc	1	b Hazlewood	3
K.A.J.Roach	not out	17	not out	11
S.Joseph	lbw b Lyon	36	st Carey b Lyon	15
Extras	(B 12, LB 1, W 2)	15	(LB 1, NB 2)	3
Total	**(62.1 overs)**	**188**	**(35.2 overs)**	**120**

AUSTRALIA

S.P.D.Smith	c Greaves b S.Joseph	12	not out	11
U.T.Khawaja	c Athanaze b Greaves	45	retired hurt	9
M.Labuschagne	c Motie b S.Joseph	10	not out	1
C.D.Green	c Da Silva b S.Joseph	14		
T.M.Head	c Hodge b A.S.Joseph	119		
M.R.Marsh	c Greaves b Roach	5		
†A.T.Carey	c Da Silva b Greaves	15		
M.A.Starc	c Chanderpaul b S.Joseph	10		
*P.J.Cummins	b Roach	12		
N.M.Lyon	b S.Joseph	24		
J.R.Hazlewood	not out	0		
Extras	(LB 8, NB 9)	17	(LB 1, NB 4)	5
Total	**(81.1 overs)**	**283**	**(0 wkts; 6.4 overs)**	**26**

AUSTRALIA	*O*	*M*	*R*	*W*		*O*	*M*	*R*	*W*
Starc	12	5	37	1		10	2	46	2
Hazlewood	15	6	44	4		14	6	35	5
Cummins	17	5	41	4		5	1	25	0
Lyon	12.1	2	36	1	(5)	3.2	0	4	2
Marsh	2	1	5	0					
Green	4	1	12	0	(4)	3	0	9	1
WEST INDIES									
Roach	16.1	5	48	2		2	0	6	0
A.S.Joseph	18	2	55	1		3	0	12	0
S.Joseph	20	2	94	5		1.4	0	7	0
Motie	12	1	42	0					
Greaves	15	3	36	2					

FALL OF WICKETS

	WI	A	WI	A
Wkt	*1st*	*1st*	*2nd*	*2nd*
1st	14	25	0	–
2nd	27	45	1	–
3rd	52	67	7	–
4th	98	113	19	–
5th	107	129	40	–
6th	108	168	73	–
7th	132	222	84	–
8th	133	255	94	–
9th	133	283	94	–
10th	188	283	120	–

Umpires: A.T.Holdstock (*South Africa*) (8) and N.N.Menon (*India*) (21).
Referee: A.J.Pycroft (*Zimbabwe*) (94). **Test No. 2522/119 (A863/WI574)**
U.T.Khawaja retired hurt at 25-0.

AUSTRALIA v WEST INDIES (2nd Test)

At Woolloongabba, Brisbane, on 25, 26, 27, 28 January 2024 (day/night).
Toss: West Indies. Result: **WEST INDIES** won by 8 runs.
Debut: West Indies – K.Sinclair.

WEST INDIES

*K.C.Brathwaite	c Carey b Hazlewood	4	c Labuschagne b Green	16
T.Chanderpaul	c Smith b Starc	21	c Carey b Hazlewood	4
K.S.A.McKenzie	c Khawaja b Cummins	21	lbw b Lyon	41
A.S.Athanaze	c Carey b Starc	8	c Smith b Lyon	35
K.A.R.Hodge	c Smith b Starc	71	run out	29
J.P.Greaves	c Khawaja b Starc	6	c Carey b Hazlewood	33
†J.M.Da Silva	lbw b Lyon	79	c Green b Starc	7
K.Sinclair	st Carey b Lyon	50	not out	14
A.S.Joseph	c Smith b Hazlewood	32	c Smith b Hazlewood	0
K.A.J.Roach	run out	8	lbw b Lyon	1
S.Joseph	not out	3	retired hurt	3
Extras	(B 4, NB 2, W 2)	8	(B 4, LB 3, NB 3)	10
Total	**(108 overs)**	**311**	**(72.3 overs)**	**193**

AUSTRALIA

S.P.D.Smith	lbw b Roach	6	not out	91
U.T.Khawaja	c Athanaze b Sinclair	75	c Da Silva A.S.Joseph	10
M.Labuschagne	c Sinclair b A.S.Joseph	3	c Sinclair b Greaves	5
C.D.Green	c Brathwaite b Roach	8	b S.Joseph	42
T.M.Head	c Da Silva b Roach	0	b S.Joseph	0
M.R.Marsh	c Roach b A.S.Joseph	21	c Greaves b S.Joseph	10
†A.T.Carey	c Chanderpaul b S.Joseph	65	b S.Joseph	2
M.A.Starc	c Da Silva A.S.Joseph	2	c Sinclair b S.Joseph	21
*P.J.Cummins	not out	64	c Da Silva S.Joseph	2
N.M.Lyon	c Da Silva A.S.Joseph	19	c Da Silva A.S.Joseph	9
J.R.Hazlewood			b S.Joseph	0
Extras	(B 9, LB 9, NB 6, W 2)	26	(LB 3, NB 9, W 3)	15
Total	**(9 wkts dec; 53 overs)**	**289**	**(50.5 overs)**	**207**

AUSTRALIA	*O*	*M*	*R*	*W*		*O*	*M*	*R*	*W*
Starc	24	3	82	4		14.3	3	45	1
Hazlewood	20	6	38	2		14	5	23	3
Cummins	23	1	76	1		12	1	39	0
Lyon	28	3	81	2	(5)	22	6	42	3
Marsh	2	0	3	0					
Green	7	2	12	0	(4)	10	2	37	1
Labuschagne	1	0	1	0					
Head	3	0	14	0					
WEST INDIES									
Roach	11	0	47	3		10	1	28	0
A.S.Joseph	14	0	84	4		17	1	62	2
S.Joseph	11	1	56	1	(4)	11.5	0	68	7
Greaves	9	3	31	0	(3)	12	0	46	1
Sinclair	8	1	53	1					

FALL OF WICKETS

	WI	A	WI	A
Wkt	*1st*	*1st*	*2nd*	*2nd*
1st	9	6	13	24
2nd	42	11	63	42
3rd	54	24	86	113
4th	57	24	123	113
5th	64	54	148	132
6th	213	150	157	136
7th	225	161	184	171
8th	266	242	184	175
9th	297	289	185	191
10th	311	–	–	207

Umpires: N.N.Menon (*India*) (22) and Sharfuddoula (*Bangladesh*) (10).
Referee: A.J.Pycroft (*Zimbabwe*) (95). **Test No. 2523/120 (A864/WI575)**

SRI LANKA v AFGHANISTAN (Only Test)

At Sinhalese Sports Club, Colombo, on 2, 3, 4, 5 February 2024.
Toss: Sri Lanka. Result: **SRI LANKA** won by ten wickets.
Debuts: Afghanistan – Mohammad Saleem, Naveed Zadran, Noor Ali Zadran, Zia-ur-Rehman; Sri Lanka – C.D.Gunasekara.

AFGHANISTAN

Batter	1st innings	Runs		2nd innings	Runs
Ibrahim Zadran	lbw b A.M.Fernando	0		b Jayasuriya	114
Noor Ali Zadran	c and b M.V.T.Fernando	31		lbw b A.M.Fernando	47
Rahmat Shah	c Samarawickrama b Jayasuriya	91		c Samarawickrama b Rajitha	54
*Hashmatullah Shahidi	c Samarawickrama b M.V.T.Fernando	17		c Samarawickrama b Jayasuriya	18
Nasir Ahmadzai	b Jayasuriya	0		not out	41
†Ikram Alikhil	c K.N.M.Fernando b M.V.T.Fernando	21		c Mendis b A.M.Fernando	1
Qais Ahmad	lbw b Jayasuriya	21		c de Silva b Jayasuriya	1
Zia-ur-Rehman	lbw b M.V.T.Fernando	4		b Jayasuriya	0
Nijat Masood	c and b A.M.Fernando	12	(10)	c Samarawickrama b Rajitha	0
Naveed Zadran	not out	0	(9)	b Jayasuriya	4
Mohammad Saleem	b A.M.Fernando	0		c de Silva b A.M.Fernando	2
Extras	(W 1)	1		(B 1, LB 6, NB 1, W 6)	14
Total	**(62.4 overs)**	**198**		**(112.3 overs)**	**296**

SRI LANKA

Batter	1st innings	Runs		2nd innings	Runs
K.N.M.Fernando	c Noor Ali b Naveed	37	(2)	not out	22
F.D.M.Karunaratne	c Ibrahim b Ahmad	77	(1)	not out	32
B.K.G.Mendis	c Zia b Masood	10			
A.D.Mathews	hit wkt b Ahmad	141			
L.D.Chandimal	c Alikhil b Zadran	107			
*D.M.de Silva	run out	0			
†W.S.R.Samarawickrama	c Shah b Zadran	27			
C.D.Gunasekara	retired hurt	16			
N.G.R.P.Jayasuriya	b Zadran	2			
M.V.T.Fernando	not out	0			
A.M.Fernando	b Masood	0			
C.A.K.Rajitha					
Extras	(B 5, LB 9, NB 3, W 5)	22		(LB 1, NB 1)	2
Total	**(109.2 overs)**	**439**		**(0 wkts; 7.2 overs)**	**56**

SRI LANKA	*O*	*M*	*R*	*W*		*O*	*M*	*R*	*W*
A.M.Fernando	14.4	1	24	3	(2)	21.3	2	63	3
M.V.T.Fernando	12	1	51	4	(1)	14	3	37	0
Gunasekara	9	1	50	0					
Jayasuriya	25	7	67	3		47	10	107	5
De Silva	2	0	6	0		10	1	23	0
Rajitha					(3)	20	5	59	2
AFGHANISTAN									
Nijat Masood	19.2	3	76	2	(3)	1	0	5	0
Mohammad Saleem	12.1	0	57	0					
Naveed Zadran	22.5	4	83	4	(2)	3	0	30	0
Zia-ur-Rehman	28	2	90	0	(1)	3	0	12	0
Qais Ahmad	22	2	98	2	(4)	0.2	0	8	0
Rahmat Shah	3	0	10	0					
Hashmatullah Shahidi	2	0	11	0					

FALL OF WICKETS

Wkt	Afg *1st*	SL *1st*	Afg *2nd*	SL *2nd*
1st	0	93	106	–
2nd	57	115	214	–
3rd	109	148	237	–
4th	110	380	246	–
5th	155	380	247	–
6th	169	410	248	–
7th	182	427	250	–
8th	190	435	271	–
9th	198	439	284	–
10th	198	–	296	–

Umpires: C.M.Brown (*New Zealand*) (8) and M.A.Gough (*England*) (34).
Referee: B.C.Broad (*England*) (123). **Test No. 2529/1 (SL314/Afg8)**
C.D.Gunasekara retired hurt at 439-8; C.A.K.Rajitha concussion replacement from 4.1 overs (Afg2).

NEW ZEALAND v SOUTH AFRICA (1st Test)

At Bay Oval, Mount Maunganui, on 4, 5, 6, 7 February 2024.
Toss: South Africa. Result: **NEW ZEALAND** won by 281 runs.
Debuts: South Africa – N.Brand, R.de Swardt, C.Fortuin, E.M.Moore, T.L.Moreki, R.van Tonder.

NEW ZEALAND

T.W.M.Latham	c Fortuin b Paterson	20	lbw b Paterson	3
D.P.Conway	lbw b Moreki	1	c Moore b Brand	29
K.S.Williamson	c Moreki b de Swardt	118	st Fortuin b Brand	109
R.Ravindra	b Brand	240	c Brand b de Swardt	12
D.J.Mitchell	c and b Brand	34	not out	11
†T.A.Blundell	c Hamza b de Swardt	11	not out	5
G.D.Phillips	c de Swardt b Brand	39		
M.J.Santner	b Brand	2		
K.A.Jamieson	not out	8		
M.J.Henry	c de Swardt b Brand	27		
*T.G.Southee	b Brand	0		
Extras	(B 2, LB 2, NB 4, W 3)	11	(LB 6, NB 2, W 2)	10
Total	**(144 overs)**	**511**	**(4 wkts dec; 43 overs)**	**179**

SOUTH AFRICA

E.M.Moore	c Conway b Henry	23	c Conway b Henry	0
*N.Brand	c Blundell b Jamieson	4	b Southee	3
R.van Tonder	lbw b Jamieson	0	c Latham b Jamieson	31
M.Z.Hamza	b Santner	22	c Southee b Jamieson	36
D.G.Bedingham	c Santner b Henry	32	c Santner b Jamieson	87
K.D.Petersen	c Williamson b Ravindra	45	c Ravindra b Jamieson	16
R.de Swardt	lbw b Henry	0	not out	35
†C.Fortuin	c Southee b Santner	9	c Blundell b Phillips	11
D.Olivier	not out	15	c Mitchell b Santner	1
T.L.Moreki	b Santner	5	lbw b Santner	6
D.Paterson	b Ravindra	1	c Williamson b Santner	15
Extras	(B 2, LB 3, NB 1)	6	(B 1, LB 1, NB 2, W 2)	6
Total	**(72.5 overs)**	**162**	**(80 overs)**	**247**

SOUTH AFRICA	*O*	*M*	*R*	*W*		*O*	*M*	*R*	*W*
Olivier	30	3	119	0	(4)	4	0	19	0
Moreki	27	2	110	1		8	1	16	0
Paterson	32	5	98	1	(1)	10	1	38	1
De Swardt	29	7	61	2	(3)	8	0	48	1
Brand	26	1	119	6		13	1	52	2
NEW ZEALAND									
Southee	13	3	41	0		10	3	46	1
Henry	14	6	31	3		11	3	33	1
Jamieson	15	6	35	2		17	3	59	4
Santner	21	8	34	3		26	9	59	3
Ravindra	9.5	5	16	2	(6)	7	2	18	0
Phillips					(5)	9	1	30	1

FALL OF WICKETS

	NZ	SA	NZ	SA
Wkt	*1st*	*1st*	*2nd*	*2nd*
1st	2	26	10	3
2nd	39	26	102	5
3rd	271	30	143	68
4th	374	74	173	73
5th	391	83	–	178
6th	473	83	–	181
7th	474	120	–	199
8th	479	152	–	208
9th	511	161	–	223
10th	511	162	–	247

Umpires: Ahsan Raza (*Pakistan*) (12) and R.A.Kettleborough (*England*) (81).
Referee: J.Srinath (*India*) (69). **Test No. 2530/48 (NZ467/SA463)**

NEW ZEALAND v SOUTH AFRICA (2nd Test)

At Seddon Park, Hamilton, on 13, 14, 15, 16 February 2024.
Toss: South Africa. Result: **NEW ZEALAND** won by seven wickets.
Debuts: New Zealand – W.P.O'Rourke; South Africa – S.von Berg. ‡ (M.J.Santner)

SOUTH AFRICA

*N.Brand	lbw b O'Rourke	25		c Blundell b O'Rourke	34
†C.Fortuin	c Phillips b Henry	0		lbw b Ravindra	3
R.van Tonder	c Latham b Wagner	32		c Wagner b O'Rourke	1
M.Z.Hamza	c sub‡ b Ravindra	20		c Young b Wagner	17
D.G.Bedingham	c Young b Ravindra	39		c Phillips b O'Rourke	110
K.D.Petersen	c Southee b Ravindra	2		c Phillips b Henry	43
R.de Swardt	b O'Rourke	64		b Phillips	1
S.von Berg	b O'Rourke	38		c Wagner b O'Rourke	2
D.L.Piedt	c Blundell b Southee	4		c Southee b Phillips	2
T.L.Moreki	not out	4	(11)	not out	0
D.Paterson	c Latham b O'Rourke	0	(10)	c Blundell b O'Rourke	7
Extras	(B 9, LB 2, W 3)	14		(B 10, LB 1, NB 2, W 2)	15
Total	**(97.2 overs)**	**242**		**(69.5 overs)**	**235**

NEW ZEALAND

T.W.M.Latham	b Piedt	40	c Hamza b Piedt	30
D.P.Conway	c Fortuin b Paterson	0	lbw b Piedt	17
K.S.Williamson	c van Tonder b Piedt	43	not out	133
R.Ravindra	b Moreki	29	c Brand b Piedt	20
W.A.Young	c de Swardt b Piedt	36	not out	60
†T.A.Blundell	b Paterson	4		
G.D.Phillips	c Fortuin b Piedt	4		
M.J.Henry	run out	10		
*T.G.Southee	c van Tonder b Paterson	5		
N.Wagner	st Fortuin b Piedt	33		
W.P.O'Rourke	not out	0		
Extras	(B 1, LB 5, W 1)	7	(B 4, LB 3, NB 1, W 1)	9
Total	**(77.3 overs)**	**211**	**(3 wkts; 94.2 overs)**	**269**

NEW ZEALAND	*O*	*M*	*R*	*W*		*O*	*M*	*R*	*W*
Southee	25	8	63	1		9	2	33	0
Henry	17	5	44	1		11	5	15	1
O'Rourke	18.2	4	59	4	(4)	13.5	4	34	5
Wagner	16	6	32	1	(6)	8	1	42	1
Ravindra	21	8	33	3	(3)	13	1	50	1
Phillips					(5)	15	3	50	2
SOUTH AFRICA									
Paterson	17	6	39	3		22	5	58	0
Moreki	13	4	32	1		18.2	4	44	0
Piedt	32.3	5	89	5		32	4	93	3
Von Berg	13	3	40	0		16	0	60	0
De Swardt	2	0	5	0		6	3	7	0

FALL OF WICKETS

	SA	NZ	SA	NZ
Wkt	*1st*	*1st*	*2nd*	*2nd*
1st	4	1	23	40
2nd	40	75	28	53
3rd	63	86	39	117
4th	99	145	104	–
5th	101	157	202	–
6th	150	162	213	–
7th	227	163	219	–
8th	234	170	226	–
9th	242	183	234	–
10th	242	211	235	–

Umpires: Ahsan Raza (*Pakistan*) (13) and R.K.Illingworth (*England*) (67).
Referee: J.Srinath (*India*) (70). **Test No. 2531/49 (NZ468/SA464)**

AFGHANISTAN v IRELAND (Only Test)

At Sheikh Zayed Stadium, Abu Dhabi, on 28, 29 February, 1 March 2024.
Toss: Afghanistan. Result: **IRELAND** won by six wickets.
Debuts: Afghanistan – Rahmanullah Gurbaz; Ireland – B.J.McCarthy, T.F.van Woerkom, C.A.Young.

AFGHANISTAN

Ibrahim Zadran	c Tucker b Young	53		c Moor b Adair	12
Noor Ali Zadran	c Balbirnie b Adair	7		c Adair b McCarthy	32
Rahmat Shah	b Adair	0		c Tucker b Adair	9
*Hashmatullah Shahidi	c Tucker b McCarthy	20		lbw b Adair	55
†Rahmanullah Gurbaz	c Tucker b Adair	5		b Young	46
Nasir Ahmadzai	b Young	0		b McCarthy	2
Karim Janat	not out	41		c Balbirnie b Young	13
Zia-ur-Rehman	c Balbirnie b Adair	6		c Balbirnie b van Woerkom	13
Naveed Zadran	c McBrine b Campher	12		b Young	25
Nijat Masood	c Tucker b Campher	0		b McCarthy	0
Zahir Khan	b Adair	0		not out	4
Extras	(B 4, LB 6, NB 1)	11		(B 7)	7
Total	**(54.5 overs)**	**155**		**(75.4 overs)**	**218**

IRELAND

P.J.Moor	b Naveed	12		b Naveed	0
*A.Balbirnie	lbw b Naveed	2		not out	58
C.Campher	c Gurbaz b Rehman	49		b Naveed	0
H.T.Tector	lbw b Naveed	32		c Gurbaz b Masood	2
T.F.van Woerkom	b Rehman	1			
P.R.Stirling	b Khan	52	(5)	c Shah b Rehman	14
†L.J.Tucker	c Shah b Rehman	46	(6)	not out	27
A.R.McBrine	c Naveed b Masood	38			
M.R.Adair	lbw b Rehman	15			
B.J.McCarthy	lbw b Rehman	5			
C.A.Young	not out	1			
Extras	(B 4, LB 3, NB 3)	10		(LB 7, NB 3)	10
Total	**(83.4 overs)**	**263**		**(4 wkts; 31.3 overs)**	**111**

IRELAND	*O*	*M*	*R*	*W*		*O*	*M*	*R*	*W*
Adair	16.5	5	39	5		16	3	56	3
McCarthy	11	1	28	1		18	5	48	3
Young	11	5	31	2	(5)	10.4	2	24	3
McBrine	7	1	22	0		17	3	38	0
Van Woerkom	5	1	12	0	(3)	13	3	43	1
Campher	4	1	13	2					
Tector					(6)	1	0	2	0
AFGHANISTAN									
Nijat Masood	12.4	2	38	1		8	1	27	1
Naveed Zadran	18	4	59	3		9.3	0	31	2
Karim Janat	6	0	24	0					
Zia-ur-Rehman	30	7	64	5	(3)	11	0	33	1
Zahir Khan	14	0	67	1	(4)	3	0	13	0
Hashmatullah Shahidi	3	0	4	0					

FALL OF WICKETS

Wkt	Afg *1st*	Ire *1st*	Afg *2nd*	Ire *2nd*
1st	11	6	24	8
2nd	11	32	38	8
3rd	66	92	93	13
4th	86	94	140	39
5th	89	106	143	–
6th	90	186	173	–
7th	111	216	174	–
8th	138	242	206	–
9th	138	256	207	–
10th	155	263	218	–

Umpires: A.T.Holdstock (*South Africa*) (9) and R.A.Kettleborough (*England*) (82).
Referee: D.C.Boon (*Australia*) (76). **Test No. 2532/2 (Afg8/Ire8)**

INDIA v ENGLAND (1st Test)

At Rajiv Gandhi International Stadium, Hyderabad, on 25, 26, 27, 28 January 2024.
Toss: England. Result: **ENGLAND** won by 28 runs.
Debut: England – T.W.Hartley.

ENGLAND

Z.Crawley	c Siraj b Ashwin	20	c Sharma b Ashwin	31
B.M.Duckett	lbw b Ashwin	35	b Bumrah	47
O.J.D.Pope	c Sharma b Jadeja	1	b Bumrah	196
J.E.Root	c Bumrah b Jadeja	29	lbw b Bumrah	2
J.M.Bairstow	b Patel	37	b Jadeja	10
*B.A.Stokes	b Bumrah	70	b Ashwin	6
†B.T.Foakes	c Srikar Bharat b Patel	4	b Patel	34
R.Ahmed	c Srikar Bharat b Bumrah	13	c Srikar Bharat b Bumrah	28
T.W.Hartley	b Jadeja	23	b Ashwin	34
M.A.Wood	b Ashwin	11	c Srikar Bharat b Jadeja	0
M.J.Leach	not out	0	not out	0
Extras	(LB 1, NB 2)	3	(B 20, LB 6, NB 6)	32
Total	**(64.3 overs)**	**246**	**(102.1 overs)**	**420**

INDIA

Y.B.Jaiswal	c and b Root	80	(2) c Pope b Hartley	15
*R.G.Sharma	c Stokes b Leach	24	(1) lbw b Hartley	39
S.Gill	c Duckett b Hartley	23	c Pope b Hartley	0
K.L.Rahul	c Ahmed b Hartley	86	lbw b Root	22
S.S.Iyer	c Hartley b Ahmed	35	(6) c Root b Leach	13
R.A.Jadeja	lbw b Root	87	(7) run out	2
†K.Srikar Bharat	lbw b Root	41	(8) b Hartley	28
R.Ashwin	run out	1	(9) st Foakes b Hartley	28
A.R.Patel	b Ahmed	44	(5) c and b Hartley	17
J.J.Bumrah	b Root	0	not out	6
M.Siraj	not out	0	st Foakes b Hartley	12
Extras	(B 5, LB 6, NB 2, W 2)	15	(B 4, LB 14, NB 1, W 1)	20
Total	**(121 overs)**	**436**	**(69.2 overs)**	**202**

INDIA	*O*	*M*	*R*	*W*		*O*	*M*	*R*	*W*
Bumrah	8.3	1	28	2		16.1	4	41	4
Siraj	4	0	28	0	(5)	7	1	22	0
Jadeja	18	4	88	3	(4)	34	1	131	2
Ashwin	21	1	68	3	(2)	29	4	126	3
Patel	13	1	33	2	(3)	16	2	74	1
ENGLAND									
Wood	17	1	47	0	(2)	8	1	15	0
Hartley	25	0	131	2	(3)	26.2	5	62	7
Leach	26	6	63	1	(4)	10	1	33	1
Ahmed	24	4	105	2	(5)	6	0	33	0
Root	29	5	79	4	(1)	19	3	41	1

FALL OF WICKETS

	E	I	E	I
Wkt	*1st*	*1st*	*2nd*	*2nd*
1st	55	80	45	42
2nd	58	123	113	42
3rd	60	159	117	63
4th	121	223	140	95
5th	125	288	163	107
6th	137	356	275	119
7th	155	358	339	119
8th	193	436	419	176
9th	234	436	420	177
10th	246	436	420	202

Umpires: C.B.Gaffaney (*New Zealand*) (52) and P.R.Reiffel (*Australia*) (66).
Referee: Sir R.B.Richardson (*West Indies*) (48). **Test No. 2524/132 (I575/E1067)**

INDIA v ENGLAND (2nd Test)

At Dr Y.S.Rajasekhara Reddy ACA-VDCA Stadium, Visakhapatnam, on 2, 3, 4, 5 February 2024.
Toss: India. Result: **INDIA** won by 106 runs.
Debuts: India – R.M.Patidar; England – S.Bashir.

INDIA

Y.B.Jaiswal	c Bairstow b Anderson	209		c Root b Anderson	17
*R.G.Sharma	c Pope b Bashir	14		b Anderson	13
S.Gill	c Foakes b Anderson	34		c Foakes b Bashir	104
S.S.Iyer	c Foakes b Hartley	27		c Stokes b Hartley	29
R.M.Patidar	b Ahmed	32		c Foakes b Ahmed	9
A.R.Patel	c Ahmed b Bashir	27		lbw b Hartley	45
†K.Srikar Bharat	c Bashir b Ahmed	17		c Stokes b Ahmed	6
R.Ashwin	c Foakes b Anderson	20		c Foakes b Ahmed	29
K.Yadav	not out	8		c Duckett b Hartley	0
J.J.Bumrah	c Root b Ahmed	6		c Bairstow b Hartley	0
Mukesh Kumar	c Root b Bashir	0		not out	0
Extras	(LB 1, NB 1)	2		(LB 2, NB 1)	3
Total	**(112 overs)**	**396**		**(78.3 overs)**	**255**

ENGLAND

Z.Crawley	c Iyer b Patel	76		lbw b Yadav	73
B.M.Duckett	c Patidar b Yadav	21		c Srikar Bharat b Ashwin	28
O.J.D.Pope	b Bumrah	23	(4)	c Sharma b Ashwin	23
J.E.Root	c Gill b Bumrah	5	(5)	c Patel b Ashwin	16
J.M.Bairstow	c Gill b Bumrah	25	(6)	lbw b Bumrah	26
*B.A.Stokes	b Bumrah	47	(7)	run out	11
†B.T.Foakes	b Yadav	6	(8)	c and b Bumrah	36
R.Ahmed	c Gill b Yadav	6	(3)	lbw b Patel	23
T.W.Hartley	c Gill b Bumrah	21		b Bumrah	36
J.M.Anderson	lbw b Bumrah	6	(11)	not out	5
S.Bashir	not out	8	(10)	c Srikar Bharat b Mukesh Kumar	0
Extras	(B 7, LB 1, NB 1)	9		(B 8, LB 5, NB 2)	15
Total	**(55.5 overs)**	**253**		**(69.2 overs)**	**292**

ENGLAND	*O*	*M*	*R*	*W*		*O*	*M*	*R*	*W*
Anderson	25	4	47	3		10	1	29	2
Root	14	0	71	0	(4)	2	1	1	0
Hartley	18	2	74	1	(5)	27	3	77	4
Bashir	38	1	138	3	(2)	15	0	58	1
Ahmed	17	2	65	3	(3)	24.3	5	88	3
INDIA									
Bumrah	15.5	5	45	6		17.2	4	46	3
Mukesh Kumar	7	1	44	0		5	1	26	1
Yadav	17	1	71	3		15	0	60	1
Ashwin	12	0	61	0		18	2	72	3
Patel	4	0	24	1		14	1	75	1

FALL OF WICKETS

	I	E	I	E
Wkt	*1st*	*1st*	*2nd*	*2nd*
1st	40	59	29	50
2nd	89	114	30	95
3rd	179	123	111	132
4th	249	136	122	154
5th	301	159	211	194
6th	330	172	220	194
7th	364	182	228	220
8th	383	229	229	275
9th	395	234	255	281
10th	396	253	255	292

Umpires: M.Erasmus (*South Africa*) (80) and C.B.Gaffaney (*New Zealand*) (53).
Referee: Sir R.B.Richardson (*West Indies*) (49). **Test No. 2525/133 (I576/E1068)**

INDIA v ENGLAND (3rd Test)

At Saurashtra CA Stadium, Rajkot, on 15, 16, 17, 18 February 2024.
Toss: India. Result: **INDIA** won by 434 runs.
Debuts: India – D.C.Jurel, S.N.Khan.

INDIA

Y.B.Jaiswal	c Root b Wood	10		not out	214
*R.G.Sharma	c Stokes b Wood	131		lbw b Root	19
S.Gill	c Foakes b Wood	0		run out	91
R.M.Patidar	c Duckett b Hartley	5		c Ahmed b Hartley	0
R.A.Jadeja	c and b Root	112			
S.N.Khan	run out	62		not out	68
K.Yadav	c Foakes b Anderson	4	(5)	c Root b Ahmed	27
†D.C.Jurel	c Foakes b Ahmed	46			
R.Ashwin	c Anderson b Ahmed	37			
J.J.Bumrah	lbw b Wood	26			
M.Siraj	not out	3			
Extras	(B 2, LB 4, NB 2, W 1)	9		(LB 9, W 2)	11
Total	**(130.5 overs)**	**445**		**(4 wkts dec; 98 overs)**	**430**

ENGLAND

Z.Crawley	c Patidar b Ashwin	15	lbw b Bumrah	11
B.M.Duckett	c Gill b Yadav	153	run out	4
O.J.D.Pope	lbw b Siraj	39	c Sharma b Jadeja	3
J.E.Root	c Jaiswal b Bumrah	18	lbw b Jadeja	7
J.M.Bairstow	lbw b Yadav	0	lbw b Jadeja	4
*B.A.Stokes	c Bumrah b Jadeja	41	lbw b Yadav	15
†B.T.Foakes	c Sharma b Siraj	13	c Jurel b Jadeja	16
R.Ahmed	b Siraj	6	c Siraj b Yadav	0
T.W.Hartley	st Jurel b Jadeja	9	b Ashwin	16
M.A.Wood	not out	4	c Jaiswal b Jadeja	33
J.M.Anderson	b Siraj	1	not out	1
Extras	(B 6, LB 5, NB 4, Pen 5)	20	(B 5, LB 4, NB 3)	12
Total	**(71.1 overs)**	**319**	**(39.4 overs)**	**122**

ENGLAND	*O*	*M*	*R*	*W*		*O*	*M*	*R*	*W*
Anderson	25	7	61	1		13	1	78	0
Wood	27.5	2	114	4	(4)	10	0	46	0
Hartley	40	7	109	1		23	2	78	1
Root	16	3	70	1	(2)	27	3	111	1
Ahmed	22	2	85	2		25	1	108	1
INDIA									
Bumrah	15	1	54	1		8	1	18	1
Siraj	21.1	2	84	4		5	2	16	0
Yadav	18	2	77	2	(4)	8	2	19	2
Ashwin	7	0	37	1	(5)	6	3	19	1
Jadeja	10	0	51	2	(3)	12.4	4	41	5

FALL OF WICKETS

	I	E	I	E
Wkt	*1st*	*1st*	*2nd*	*2nd*
1st	22	89	30	15
2nd	24	182	191	18
3rd	33	224	246	20
4th	237	225	258	28
5th	314	260	–	50
6th	331	299	–	50
7th	331	299	–	50
8th	408	314	–	82
9th	415	314	–	91
10th	445	319	–	122

Umpires: H.D.P.K.Dharmasena (*Sri Lanka*) (82) and J.S.Wilson (*West Indies*) (39).
Referee: J.J.Crowe (*New Zealand*) (116). **Test No. 2526/134 (I577/E1069)**
Y.B.Jaiswal (2) retired hurt from 185-1 to 246-3.

INDIA v ENGLAND (4th Test)

At JSCA International Stadium, Ranchi, on 23, 24, 25, 26 February 2024.
Toss: England. Result: **INDIA** won by five wickets.
Debut: India – A.Deep.

ENGLAND

Z.Crawley	b Deep	42	b Yadav	60
B.M.Duckett	c Jurel b Deep	11	c Khan b Ashwin	15
O.J.D.Pope	lbw b Deep	0	lbw b Ashwin	0
J.E.Root	not out	122	lbw b Ashwin	11
J.M.Bairstow	lbw b Ashwin	38	c Patidar b Jadeja	30
*B.A.Stokes	lbw b Jadeja	3	b Yadav	4
†B.T.Foakes	c Jadeja b Siraj	47	c and b Ashwin	17
T.W.Hartley	b Siraj	13	c Khan b Yadav	7
O.E.Robinson	c Jurel b Jadeja	58	lbw b Yadav	0
S.Bashir	c Patidar b Jadeja	0	not out	1
J.M.Anderson	lbw b Jadeja	0	c Jurel b Ashwin	0
Extras	(B 6, LB 8, NB 5)	19		–
Total	**(104.5 overs)**	**353**	**(53.5 overs)**	**145**

INDIA

Y.B.Jaiswal	b Bashir	73	(2)	c Anderson b Root	37
*R.G.Sharma	c Foakes b Anderson	2	(1)	c Foakes b Hartley	55
S.Gill	lbw b Bashir	38		not out	52
R.M.Patidar	lbw b Bashir	17		c Pope b Bashir	0
R.A.Jadeja	c Pope b Bashir	12		c Bairstow b Bashir	4
S.N.Khan	c Root b Hartley	14		c Pope b Bashir	0
†D.C.Jurel	b Hartley	90		not out	39
R.Ashwin	lbw b Hartley	1			
K.Yadav	b Anderson	28			
A.Deep	lbw b Bashir	9			
M.Siraj	not out	0			
Extras	(B 12, LB 5, NB 6)	23		(B 4, LB 1)	5
Total	**(103.2 overs)**	**307**		**(5 wkts; 61 overs)**	**192**

INDIA	*O*	*M*	*R*	*W*		*O*	*M*	*R*	*W*
Siraj	18	3	78	2	(3)	3	0	16	0
Deep	19	0	83	3					
Jadeja	32.5	7	67	4	(2)	20	5	56	1
Ashwin	22	1	83	1	(1)	15.5	0	51	5
Yadav	12	4	22	0	(4)	15	2	22	4
Jaiswal	1	0	6	0					
ENGLAND									
Anderson	18	4	48	2	(4)	3	1	12	0
Robinson	13	0	54	0					
Bashir	44	8	119	5		26	4	79	3
Hartley	27.2	6	68	3	(2)	25	2	70	1
Root	1	0	1	0	(1)	7	0	26	1

FALL OF WICKETS

	E	I	E	I
Wkt	*1st*	*1st*	*2nd*	*2nd*
1st	47	4	19	84
2nd	47	86	19	99
3rd	57	112	65	100
4th	109	130	110	120
5th	112	161	120	120
6th	225	171	120	–
7th	245	177	133	–
8th	347	253	133	–
9th	349	293	145	–
10th	353	307	145	–

Umpires: H.D.P.K.Dharmasena (*Sri Lanka*) (83) and R.J.Tucker (*Australia*) (84).
Referee: J.J.Crowe (*New Zealand*) (117). **Test No. 2527/135 (I578/E1070)**

INDIA v ENGLAND (5th Test)

At Himachal Pradesh CA Stadium, Dharamsala, on 7, 8, 9 March 2024.
Toss: England. Result: **INDIA** won by an innings and 64 runs.
Debut: India – D.B.Padikkal.

ENGLAND

Z.Crawley	b Yadav	79	c Khan b Ashwin	0
B.M.Duckett	c Gill b Yadav	27	b Ashwin	2
O.J.D.Pope	st Jurel b Yadav	11	c Jaiswal b Ashwin	19
J.E.Root	lbw b Jadeja	26	c Bumrah b Yadav	84
J.M.Bairstow	c Jurel b Yadav	29	lbw b Yadav	39
*B.A.Stokes	lbw b Yadav	0	b Ashwin	2
†B.T.Foakes	b Ashwin	24	b Ashwin	8
T.W.Hartley	c Padikkal b Ashwin	6	lbw b Bumrah	20
M.A.Wood	c Sharma b Ashwin	0	lbw b Bumrah	0
S.Bashir	not out	11	b Jadeja	13
J.M.Anderson	c Padikkal b Ashwin	0	not out	0
Extras	(B 2, LB 1, NB 2)	5	(B 6, LB 1, NB 1)	8
Total	**(57.4 overs)**	**218**	**(48.1 overs)**	**195**

INDIA

Y.B.Jaiswal	st Foakes b Bashir	57
*R.G.Sharma	b Stokes	103
S.Gill	b Anderson	110
D.B.Padikkal	b Bashir	65
S.N.Khan	c Root b Bashir	56
R.A.Jadeja	lbw b Hartley	15
†D.C.Jurel	c Duckett b Bashir	15
R.Ashwin	b Hartley	0
K.Yadav	c Foakes b Anderson	30
J.J.Bumrah	st Foakes b Bashir	20
M.Siraj	not out	0
Extras	(LB 4, NB 2)	6
Total	**(124.1 overs)**	**477**

INDIA	*O*	*M*	*R*	*W*		*O*	*M*	*R*	*W*
Bumrah	13	2	51	0		10	2	38	2
Siraj	8	1	24	0	(5)	1	0	8	0
Ashwin	11.4	1	51	4	(2)	14	0	77	5
Yadav	15	1	72	5		14.1	0	40	2
Jadeja	10	2	17	1	(3)	9	1	25	1
ENGLAND									
Anderson	16	2	60	2					
Wood	15	1	89	0					
Hartley	39	3	126	2					
Bashir	46.1	5	173	5					
Stokes	5	1	17	1					
Root	3	0	8	0					

FALL OF WICKETS

	E	I	E
Wkt	*1st*	*1st*	*2nd*
1st	64	104	2
2nd	100	275	21
3rd	137	279	36
4th	175	376	92
5th	175	403	103
6th	175	427	113
7th	183	427	141
8th	183	428	141
9th	218	477	189
10th	218	477	195

Umpires: R.J.Tucker (*Australia*) (85) and J.S.Wilson (*West Indies*) (40).
Referee: J.J.Crowe (*New Zealand*) (118). **Test No. 2528/136 (I579/E1071)**

INTERNATIONAL UMPIRES AND REFEREES 2024

ELITE PANEL OF UMPIRES 2024

The Elite Panel of ICC Umpires and Referees was introduced in April 2002 to raise standards and guarantee impartial adjudication. Two umpires from this panel stand in Test matches while one officiates with a home umpire from the Supplementary International Panel in limited-overs internationals.

Full Names	*Birthdate*	*Birthplace*	*Tests*	*Debut*	*LOI*	*Debut*
AHSAN RAZA	29.05.74	Lahore, Pakistan	13	2020-21	53	2009-10
DHARMASENA, H.D.P.Kumar	24.04.71	Colombo, Sri Lanka	83	2010-11	127	2008-09
ERASMUS, Marais	27.02.64	George, South Africa	81	2009-10	124	2007-08
GAFFANEY, Christopher Blair	30.11.75	Dunedin, New Zealand	53	2014	86	2010
GOUGH, Michael Andrew	18.12.79	Hartlepool, England	35	2016	86	2013
HOLDSTOCK, Adrian Thomas	27.04.70	Cape Town, South Africa	9	2020-21	58	2012-13
ILLINGWORTH, Richard Keith	23.08.63	Bradford, England	67	2012-13	90	2010
KETTLEBOROUGH, Richard Allan	15.03.73	Sheffield, England	82	2010-11	106	2009
MENON, Nitin Narendra	02.11.83	Indore, India	22	2019-20	58	2016-17
REIFFEL, Paul Ronald	19.04.66	Box Hill, Australia	66	2012	88	2008-09
TUCKER, Rodney James	28.08.64	Sydney, Australia	84	2009-10	102	2008-09
WILSON, Joel Sheldon	30.12.66	Trinidad, West Indies	39	2015	92	2011

ELITE PANEL OF REFEREES 2024

Full Names	*Birthdate*	*Birthplace*	*Tests*	*Debut*	*LOI*	*Debut*
BOON, David Clarence	29.12.60	Launceston, Australia	76	2011	174	2011
BROAD, Brian Christopher	29.09.57	Bristol, England	123	2003-04	361	2003-04
CROWE, Jeffrey John	14.09.58	Auckland, New Zealand	117	2004-05	329	2003-04
MADUGALLE, Ranjan Senerath	22.04.59	Kandy, Sri Lanka	215	1993-94	397	1993-94
PYCROFT, Andrew John	06.06.56	Harare, Zimbabwe	95	2009	225	2009
RICHARDSON, Sir Richard Benjamin	12.01.62	Five Islands, Antigua	49	2016	96	2016
SRINATH, Javagal	31.08.69	Mysore, India	70	2006	269	2006-07

INTERNATIONAL UMPIRES PANEL 2024

Nominated by their respective cricket boards, members from this panel officiate in home LOIs and supplement the Elite panel for Test matches. The number of Test matches/LOI in which they have stood is shown in brackets.

Afghanistan	Ahmed Shah Pakteen (2/37)	Ahmed Shah Durrani (-/8)	Bismillah Jan Shinwari (-/16) Izatullah Safi (-/5)
Australia	D.M.Koch (-/5)	P.Wilson (8/44)	S.J.Nogajski (-/17) P.J.Gillespie (-/-)
Bangladesh	Tanvir Ahmed (-/7)	Sharfuddoula (10/61)	Masudur Rahman (-/20) Gazi Sohel (-/8)
England	A.G.Wharf (6/26) M.J.Saggers (-/9)	R.J.Warren (-/-)	M.Burns (-/7)
India	J.Madanagopal (-/13)	R.Pandit (-/-)	V.K.Sharma (4/6) K.N.Ananthapadmanabhan (-/7)
Ireland	M.Hawthorne (-/33)	R.E.Black (-/26)	J.Kennedy (-/-) A.Seaver (-/-)
New Zealand	W.R.Knights (4/24)	C.M.Brown (8/31)	S.B.Haig (-/9)
Pakistan	Faisal Afridi (-/1)	Alim Dar (145/231)	Asif Yaqoob (-/17) Rashid Riaz (-/15)
South Africa	L.B.Gcuma (-/-) A.Paleker (2/16)	S.D.Harris (-/-)	B.P.Jele (-/29)
Sri Lanka	R.M.P.J.Rambukwella (-/4)	R.S.A.Palliyaguruge (9/94)	R.R.Wimalasiri (-/38) L.E.Hannibal (-/21)
West Indies	G.O.Brathwaite (8/57)	L.S.Reifer (-/25)	P.A.Gustard (-/-) N.Duguid (1/15)
Zimbabwe	L.Rusere (3/34)	I.Chabi (1/13)	C.Phiri (-/6) F.Mutizwa (-/4)

Test Match and LOI statistics to 4 March 2024.

TEST MATCH CAREER RECORDS

These records, complete to 6 March 2024 (except for England, which are updated to 4 April 2024), contain all players registered for county cricket in 2024 at the time of going to press, plus those who have played Test cricket since 30 November 2022 (Test No. 2476 and 2478). Some players who may return to Test action have also been listed, even if their most recent game was earlier than this date.

ENGLAND – BATTING AND FIELDING

	M	*I*	*NO*	*HS*	*Runs*	*Avge*	*100*	*50*	*Ct/St*
R.Ahmed	4	8	–	28	87	10.87	–	–	3
M.M.Ali	68	118	8	155*	3094	28.12	5	15	40
J.M.Anderson	187	264	113	81	1353	8.96	–	1	107
J.C.Archer	13	20	–	30	155	7.75	–	–	2
J.M.Bairstow	100	178	12	167*	6042	36.39	12	26	242/14
J.T.Ball	4	8	–	31	67	8.37	–	–	1
S.Bashir	3	6	3	13	33	11.00	–	–	1
D.M.Bess	14	19	5	57	319	22.78	–	1	3
S.W.Billings	3	3	–	36	66	22.00	–	–	8
S.G.Borthwick	1	2	–	4	5	2.50	–	–	2
J.R.Bracey	2	3	–	8	8	2.66	–	–	6
S.C.J.Broad	167	244	41	169	3662	18.03	1	13	55
H.C.Brook	12	20	1	186	1181	62.15	4	7	9
R.J.Burns	32	59	–	133	1789	30.32	3	11	24
J.C.Buttler	57	100	9	152	2907	31.94	2	18	153/1
M.S.Crane	1	2	–	4	6	3.00	–	–	–
Z.Crawley	44	82	2	267	2611	32.63	4	14	50
S.M.Curran	24	38	5	78	815	24.69	–	3	5
T.K.Curran	2	3	1	39	66	33.00	–	–	–
L.A.Dawson	3	6	2	66*	84	21.00	–	1	2
J.L.Denly	15	28	–	94	827	29.53	–	6	7
B.M.Duckett	20	38	2	182	1464	40.66	3	7	17
M.D.Fisher	1	1	1	0*	0	–	–	–	1
B.T.Foakes	25	46	7	113*	1139	29.20	2	4	69/10
A.D.Hales	11	21	–	94	573	27.28	–	5	8
H.Hameed	10	19	1	82	439	24.38	–	4	7
T.W.Hartley	5	10	–	36	185	18.50	–	–	2
W.G.Jacks	2	4	–	31	89	22.25	–	–	–
K.K.Jennings	17	32	1	146*	781	25.19	2	1	17
C.J.Jordan	8	11	1	35	180	18.00	–	–	14
D.W.Lawrence	11	21	2	91	551	29.00	–	4	3
M.J.Leach	36	55	21	92	446	13.11	–	1	16
A.Z.Lees	10	19	–	67	453	23.84	–	2	6
L.S.Livingstone	1	2	1	9	16	16.00	–	–	–
A.Lyth	7	13	–	107	265	20.38	1	–	8
S.Mahmood	2	2	1	49	52	52.00	–	–	1
D.J.Malan	22	39	–	140	1074	27.53	1	9	13
C.Overton	8	14	2	41*	182	15.16	–	–	7
J.Overton	1	1	–	97	97	97.00	–	1	–
M.W.Parkinson	1	1	–	8	8	8.00	–	–	–
S.R.Patel	6	9	–	42	151	16.77	–	–	3
O.J.D.Pope	43	77	5	205	2451	34.04	5	11	54/1
M.J.Potts	6	6	2	19	30	7.50	–	–	5
A.U.Rashid	19	33	5	61	540	19.28	–	2	4
O.E.Robinson	20	33	5	58	410	14.64	–	1	8
S.D.Robson	7	11	–	127	336	30.54	1	1	5
T.S.Roland-Jones	4	6	2	25	82	20.50	–	–	–
J.E.Root	140	257	21	254	11736	49.72	31	61	193
J.J.Roy	5	10	–	72	187	18.70	–	1	1
D.P.Sibley	22	39	3	133*	1042	28.94	2	5	12

ENGLAND – BATTING AND FIELDING (continued)

	M	I	NO	HS	Runs	Avge	100	50	Ct/St
B.A.Stokes	102	185	7	258	6316	35.48	13	31	106
O.P.Stone	3	6	–	20	55	9.16	–	–	1
M.D.Stoneman	11	20	1	60	526	27.68	–	5	1
J.C.Tongue	2	2	–	19	20	10.00	–	–	1
J.M.Vince	13	22	–	83	548	24.90	–	3	8
T.Westley	5	9	1	59	193	24.12	–	1	1
C.R.Woakes	48	79	15	137*	1754	27.40	1	6	20
M.A.Wood	34	58	10	52	772	16.08	–	1	8

ENGLAND – BOWLING

	O	M	R	W	Avge	Best	5wI	10wM
R.Ahmed	155.2	17	621	18	34.50	5- 48	1	–
M.M.Ali	2101.4	293	7612	204	37.31	6- 53	5	1
J.M.Anderson	6646.1	1720	18569	700	26.52	7- 42	32	3
J.C.Archer	434.5	95	1304	42	31.04	6- 45	3	–
J.T.Ball	102	23	343	3	114.33	1- 47	–	–
S.Bashir	169.1	18	567	17	33.35	5-119	1	–
D.M.Bess	417	82	1223	36	33.97	5- 30	2	–
S.G.Borthwick	13	0	82	4	20.50	3- 33	–	–
S.C.J.Broad	5616.2	1304	16719	604	27.68	8- 15	20	3
H.C.Brook	14	2	37	1	37.00	1- 25	–	–
M.S.Crane	48	3	193	1	193.00	1-193	–	–
S.M.Curran	515.1	96	1669	47	35.51	4- 58	–	–
T.K.Curran	66	14	200	2	100.00	1- 65	–	–
L.A.Dawson	87.4	12	298	7	42.57	4-101	–	–
J.L.Denly	65	11	219	2	109.50	2- 42	–	–
M.D.Fisher	27	6	71	1	71.00	1- 67	–	–
A.D.Hales	3	1	2	0	–	–	–	–
T.W.Hartley	250.4	30	795	22	36.13	7- 62	1	–
W.G.Jacks	54.3	5	232	6	38.66	6-161	1	–
K.K.Jennings	12.1	1	55	0	–	–	–	–
C.J.Jordan	255	74	752	21	35.80	4- 18	–	–
D.W.Lawrence	35	11	97	3	32.33	1- 0	–	–
M.J.Leach	1431.4	295	4335	126	34.40	5- 66	5	1
A.Lyth	1	1	0	0	–	–	–	–
S.Mahmood	61	17	137	6	22.83	2- 21	–	–
D.J.Malan	37	4	131	2	65.50	2- 33	–	–
C.Overton	245.2	43	760	21	36.19	3- 14	–	–
J.Overton	37	4	146	2	73.00	1- 61	–	–
M.W.Parkinson	15.3	0	47	1	47.00	1- 47	–	–
S.R.Patel	143	23	421	7	60.14	2- 27	–	–
M.J.Potts	216.1	48	673	23	29.26	4- 13	–	–
A.U.Rashid	636	50	2390	60	39.83	5- 49	2	–
O.E.Robinson	632.4	159	1742	76	22.92	5- 49	3	–
T.S.Roland-Jones	89.2	23	334	17	19.64	5- 57	1	–
J.E.Root	934.3	156	3068	68	45.11	5- 8	1	–
D.P.Sibley	1	0	7	0	–	–	–	–
B.A.Stokes	1916.5	344	6335	198	31.99	6- 22	4	–
O.P.Stone	59.4	14	194	10	19.40	3- 29	–	–
J.C.Tongue	76	13	257	10	25.70	5- 66	1	–
J.M.Vince	4	1	13	0	–	–	–	–
T.Westley	4	0	12	0	–	–	–	–
C.R.Woakes	1428.1	322	4341	149	29.13	6- 17	5	1
M.A.Wood	1014.2	186	3374	108	31.4	6- 37	4	–

AUSTRALIA – BATTING AND FIELDING

	M	I	NO	HS	Runs	Avge	100	50	Ct/St
A.C.Agar	5	7	1	98	195	32.50	–	1	–
C.T.Bancroft	10	18	1	82*	446	26.23	–	3	16
S.M.Boland	10	11	4	20	47	6.71	–	–	6
A.T.Carey	31	44	4	111	1227	29.92	1	7	111/12
P.J.Cummins	61	87	12	64*	1240	16.53	–	3	31
C.D.Green	27	41	5	174*	1347	37.41	2	6	30
P.S.P.Handscomb	20	35	6	110	1079	37.20	2	5	30
J.R.Hazlewood	69	84	41	39	498	11.58	–	–	26
T.M.Head	48	79	5	175	3134	42.35	7	16	25
U.T.Khawaja	72	129	12	195*	5424	46.35	15	26	52
M.P.Kuhnemann	3	5	2	6	12	4.00	–	–	2
M.Labuschagne	49	88	7	215	4018	49.60	11	19	35
N.M.Lyon	128	162	44	47	1501	12.72	–	–	61
M.R.Marsh	41	71	7	181	1930	30.15	3	8	21
T.R.Murphy	6	10	1	41	122	13.55	–	–	2
M.G.Neser	2	3	–	35	56	18.66	–	–	–
W.J.Pucovski	1	2	–	62	72	36.00	–	1	–
M.T.Renshaw	14	24	2	184	645	29.31	1	3	9
S.P.D.Smith	108	193	25	239	9665	57.52	32	41	183
M.A.Starc	88	127	27	99	2065	20.65	–	10	39
D.A.Warner	112	205	8	335*	8786	44.59	26	37	91

AUSTRALIA – BOWLING

	O	M	R	W	Avge	Best	5wI	10wM
A.C.Agar	167.4	36	468	9	52.00	3- 46	–	–
S.M.Boland	255.1	63	712	35	20.34	6- 7	1	–
P.J.Cummins	2067.2	457	5966	264	22.59	6- 23	12	2
C.D.Green	350	61	1167	33	35.36	5- 27	1	–
J.R.Hazlewood	2390.1	608	6677	267	25.00	6- 67	11	–
T.M.Head	106.4	11	382	12	31.83	4- 10	–	–
U.T.Khawaja	3	0	8	0	–	–	–	–
M.P.Kuhnemann	78.3	11	280	9	31.11	5- 16	1	–
M.Labuschagne	202.5	19	748	13	57.53	3- 45	–	–
N.M.Lyon	5441.5	1043	15997	527	30.35	8- 50	24	5
M.R.Marsh	538.3	86	1893	48	39.43	5- 46	1	–
T.R.Murphy	175.5	33	534	21	25.42	7-124	1	–
M.G.Neser	46.5	11	117	7	16.71	3- 22	–	–
M.T.Renshaw	5	0	20	0	–	–	–	–
S.P.D.Smith	245	28	1008	19	53.05	3- 18	–	–
M.A.Starc	2868.5	555	9779	354	27.62	6- 50	14	2
D.A.Warner	57	1	269	4	67.25	2- 45	–	–

SOUTH AFRICA – BATTING AND FIELDING

	M	I	NO	HS	Runs	Avge	100	50	Ct/St
K.J.Abbott	11	14	–	17	95	6.78	–	–	4
T.Bavuma	57	97	12	172	2997	35.25	2	20	28
D.G.Bedingham	4	7	–	110	347	49.57	1	2	2
N.Brand	2	4	–	34	66	16.50	–	–	3
N.Burger	2	3	1	6*	10	5.00	–	–	1
G.W.Coetzee	3	5	1	20	66	16.50	–	–	–
T.B.de Bruyn	13	25	1	101	468	19.50	1	–	12
M.de Lange	2	2	–	9	9	4.50	–	–	1
R.de Swardt	2	4	1	64	99	33.00	–	1	3
T.de Zorzi	4	7	–	85	145	20.71	–	1	2
M.de Lange	2	2	–	9	9	4.50	–	–	1
D.Elgar	86	152	11	199	5347	37.92	14	23	92
S.J.Erwee	10	19	1	108	479	26.61	1	1	8

SOUTH AFRICA – BATTING AND FIELDING (continued)

	M	I	NO	HS	Runs	Avge	100	50	Ct/St
C.Fortuin	2	4	–	11	23	5.75	–	–	3/2
M.Z.Hamza	8	16	–	62	307	19.18	–	1	7
S.R.Harmer	10	14	2	47	221	18.41	–	–	4
M.Jansen	13	21	4	84*	401	23.58	–	2	13
H.Klaasen	4	8	–	35	104	13.00	–	–	10/2
K.A.Maharaj	50	80	6	84	1135	15.33	–	5	16
A.K.Markram	37	67	1	152	2398	36.33	7	10	37
E.M.Moore	1	2	–	23	23	11.50	–	–	1
T.L.Moreki	2	4	2	6	15	7.50	–	–	1
P.W.A.Mulder	12	21	–	42	326	15.52	–	–	17
S.Muthusamy	3	6	2	49*	105	26.25	–	–	3
L.T.Ngidi	18	29	10	19	97	5.10	–	–	7
A.A.Nortje	19	33	9	40	187	7.79	–	–	6
D.Olivier	16	21	10	15*	66	6.00	–	–	3
D.Paterson	4	8	3	39*	66	13.20	–	–	1
K.D.Petersen	14	25	–	82	704	28.16	–	4	18
D.L.Piedt	10	14	1	56	137	10.53	–	1	5
K.Rabada	62	96	17	47	905	11.45	–	–	30
R.D.Rickelton	4	8	1	42	165	23.57	–	–	1
T.Stubbs	1	2	–	3	4	2.00	–	–	1
H.E.van der Dussen	18	32	2	98	905	30.16	–	6	23
R.van Tonder	2	4	–	32	64	16.00	–	–	2
K.Verreynne	16	26	3	136*	600	26.08	1	2	48/3
S.von Berg	1	2	–	38	40	20.00	–	–	–
K.Zondo	5	7	1	39	120	20.00	–	–	2

SOUTH AFRICA – BOWLING

	O	M	R	W	Avge	Best	5wI	10wM
K.J.Abbott	346.5	95	886	39	22.71	7- 29	3	–
T.Bavuma	16	1	61	1	61.00	1- 29	–	–
N.Brand	39	2	171	8	21.37	6-119	1	–
N.Burger	37.4	9	154	11	14.00	4- 33	–	–
G.W.Coetzee	61	7	245	10	24.50	3- 37	–	–
T.B.de Bruyn	17	1	74	0	–	–	–	–
M.de Lange	74.4	10	277	9	30.77	7- 81	1	–
R.de Swardt	45	10	121	3	40.33	2- 61	–	–
D.Elgar	172.4	12	673	15	44.86	4- 22	–	–
S.R.Harmer	350.5	68	1075	39	27.56	4- 61	–	–
M.Jansen	330	59	1117	49	22.79	5- 35	1	–
K.A.Maharaj	1595.5	299	5055	158	31.99	9-129	9	1
A.K.Markram	41.3	5	130	2	65.00	2- 27	–	–
T.L.Moreki	66.2	11	202	2	101.00	1- 32	–	–
P.W.A.Mulder	175	49	515	19	27.10	3- 1	–	–
S.Muthusamy	45.3	4	190	2	95.00	1- 63	–	–
L.T.Ngidi	391.5	94	1222	54	22.62	6- 39	3	–
A.A.Nortje	509.3	81	1870	70	26.71	6- 56	4	–
D.Olivier	382	64	1432	59	24.27	6- 37	3	1
D.Paterson	138.5	28	399	9	44.33	3- 39	–	–
D.L.Piedt	368.3	55	1357	34	39.91	5- 89	2	–
K.Rabada	1902.4	378	6419	291	22.05	7-112	14	4
S.von Berg	29	3	100	0	–	–	–	–

WEST INDIES – BATTING AND FIELDING

	M	I	NO	HS	Runs	Avge	100	50	Ct/St
A.S.Athanaze	4	7	–	47	168	24.00	–	–	4
J.Blackwood	56	102	6	112*	2898	30.18	3	18	45
N.E.Bonner	15	25	4	123	803	38.23	2	3	14
K.C.Brathwaite	89	171	10	212	5513	34.24	12	29	41
S.S.J.Brooks	13	24	–	111	553	23.04	1	3	12
T.Chanderpaul	10	19	2	207*	560	32.94	1	1	6
R.L.Chase	49	90	4	137*	2265	26.33	5	11	23
R.R.S.Cornwall	10	17	3	73	261	18.64	–	2	15
J.M.Da Silva	26	45	7	100*	992	26.10	1	4	100/6
S.T.Gabriel	59	88	34	20*	229	4.24	–	–	16
J.P.Greaves	2	4	–	33	68	17.00	–	–	3
K.A.R.Hodge	2	4	–	71	115	28.75	–	1	1
J.O.Holder	64	113	18	202*	2797	29.44	3	12	62
A.S.Joseph	32	49	–	86	616	12.57	–	2	13
S.Joseph	2	4	2	36	57	28.50	–	–	–
K.S.A.McKenzie	3	6	–	50	170	28.33	–	1	1
K.R.Mayers	18	32	3	210*	949	32.72	2	2	10
M.J.Mindley	1	2	1	11*	11	11.00	–	–	–
G.Motie	5	6	2	23*	56	14.00	–	–	3
A.Phillip	2	3	1	43	53	26.50	–	–	–
R.A.Reifer	8	14	1	62	298	22.92	–	3	5
K.A.J.Roach	81	129	27	41	1174	11.50	–	–	22
J.N.T.Seales	10	15	8	13	41	5.85	–	–	3
K.Sinclair	1	2	1	50	64	64.00	–	1	3
D.C.Thomas	1	2	–	19	31	15.50	–	–	1
J.A.Warrican	15	26	10	41	189	11.81	–	–	5

WEST INDIES – BOWLING

	O	M	R	W	Avge	Best	5wI	10wM
A.S.Athanaze	20	2	65	1	65.00	1-53	–	–
J.Blackwood	75.4	12	264	4	66.00	2-14	–	–
N.E.Bonner	19	2	82	1	82.00	1-16	–	–
K.C.Brathwaite	456	35	1520	29	52.41	6-29	1	–
R.L.Chase	1132.1	129	3910	85	46.00	8-60	4	–
R.R.S.Cornwall	460.1	84	1316	35	37.60	7-75	2	1
S.T.Gabriel	1563.1	269	5348	166	32.21	8-62	6	1
J.P.Greaves	36	6	113	3	37.66	2-36	–	–
J.O.Holder	1782.1	466	4587	157	29.21	6-42	8	1
A.S.Joseph	907.2	144	3224	92	35.04	5-81	1	–
S.Joseph	44.3	3	225	13	17.30	7-68	2	–
K.R.Mayers	254	77	622	34	18.29	5-18	1	–
M.J.Mindley	2	0	11	0	–	–	–	–
G.Motie	146.2	28	459	22	20.86	7-37	2	1
A.Phillip	46	4	212	3	70.66	2-30	–	–
R.A.Reifer	56	11	170	3	56.66	1-36	–	–
K.A.J.Roach	2410.4	526	7491	270	27.74	6-48	11	1
J.N.T.Seales	265	53	897	37	24.24	5-55	1	–
K.Sinclair	8	1	53	1	53.00	1-53	–	–
D.C.Thomas	16	1	66	2	33.00	2-53	–	–
J.A.Warrican	539.3	75	1675	46	36.41	4-50	–	–

NEW ZEALAND – BATTING AND FIELDING

	M	I	NO	HS	Runs	Avge	100	50	Ct/St
T.A.Blundell	31	52	6	138	1735	37.50	4	10	84/13
D.A.J.Bracewell	28	45	4	47	568	13.85	–	–	11
M.G.Bracewell	8	14	1	74*	259	19.92	–	1	12

NEW ZEALAND – BATTING AND FIELDING (continued)

	M	I	NO	HS	Runs	Avge	100	50	Ct/St
D.P.Conway	20	37	1	200	1497	41.58	4	8	8
M.J.Henry	24	31	6	72	555	22.20	–	4	8
K.A.Jamieson	19	26	4	51*	432	19.63	–	1	5
S.C.Kuggeleijn	2	4	–	26	28	12.00	–	–	1
T.W.M.Latham	79	140	6	264*	5307	39.60	13	27	94
D.J.Mitchell	22	35	5	190	1546	51.53	5	9	32
H.M.Nicholls	56	87	7	200*	2973	37.16	9	12	36
W.P.O'Rourke	2	3	3	0*	0	–	–	–	–
A.Y.Patel	16	22	11	35	127	11.54	–	–	7
G.D.Phillips	6	10	1	87	348	38.66	–	3	5
R.Ravindra	6	12	1	240	433	39.36	1	1	4
M.J.Santner	26	35	2	126	804	24.36	1	2	20
I.S.Sodhi	20	29	4	65	546	21.84	–	4	11
T.G.Southee	99	141	11	77*	2072	15.93	–	6	79
B.M.Tickner	3	3	2	8	13	13.00	–	–	1
N.Wagner	64	84	24	66*	875	14.58	–	1	19
K.S.Williamson	99	174	17	251	8675	55.25	32	33	89
W.A.Young	15	26	1	89	702	28.08	–	7	11

NEW ZEALAND – BOWLING

	O	M	R	W	Avge	Best	5wI	10wM
T.A.Blundell	3	0	13	0	–	–	–	–
D.A.J.Bracewell	860.4	157	2873	74	38.82	6- 40	2	–
M.G.Bracewell	258.3	24	1003	24	41.79	4- 75	–	–
M.J.Henry	948.3	205	2918	86	33.93	7- 23	2	–
K.A.Jamieson	593	187	1579	80	19.73	6- 48	5	1
S.C.Kuggeleijn	50	2	254	6	42.33	2- 75	–	–
D.J.Mitchell	114.1	27	350	3	116.66	1- 7	–	–
W.P.O'Rourke	67	22	191	11	17.36	5- 34	1	–
A.Y.Patel	595.3	109	1845	62	29.75	10-119	4	1
G.D.Phillips	84	14	256	16	16.00	5- 45	1	–
R.Ravindra	119.5	28	331	10	33.10	3- 33	–	–
M.J.Santner	758.5	164	2080	53	39.24	3- 34	–	–
I.S.Sodhi	666.5	91	2464	57	43.22	6- 86	1	–
T.G.Southee	3737	865	11148	378	29.49	7- 64	15	1
B.M.Tickner	105.5	10	435	12	36.25	4-100	–	–
N.Wagner	2287.3	473	7169	260	27.57	7- 39	9	–
K.S.Williamson	358.3	48	1207	30	40.23	4- 44	–	–

INDIA – BATTING AND FIELDING

	M	I	NO	HS	Runs	Avge	100	50	Ct/St
R.Ashwin	99	140	15	124	3309	26.47	5	14	33
J.J.Bumrah	35	54	18	34*	251	6.97	–	–	13
A.Deep	1	1	–	9	9	9.00	–	–	–
S.Gill	24	45	4	128	1382	33.70	3	6	20
S.S.Iyer	14	24	2	105	811	36.86	1	5	15
R.A.Jadeja	71	104	21	175*	3021	36.39	4	20	42
Y.B.Jaiswal	8	15	1	214*	971	69.35	3	3	8
D.C.Jurel	2	3	1	90	175	87.50	–	1	4/1
S.N.Khan	2	4	1	68*	144	48.00	–	2	2
I.P.Kishan	2	3	2	52*	78	78.00	–	1	5
V.Kohli	113	191	11	254*	8848	49.15	29	30	111
P.M.Krishna	2	3	2	0*	0	0.00	–	–	–
Kuldeep Yadav	11	14	1	40	161	12.38	–	–	3
Mohammed Shami	64	89	27	56*	750	12.09	–	2	16
Mukesh Kumar	3	4	3	0*	0	0.00	–	–	–

INDIA – BATTING AND FIELDING (continued)

	M	I	NO	HS	Runs	Avge	100	50	Ct/St
K.K.Nair	6	7	1	303*	374	62.33	1	–	6
R.R.Pant	33	56	4	159*	2271	43.67	5	11	119/14
A.R.Patel	14	22	4	84	646	35.88	–	4	4
R.M.Patidar	3	6	–	32	63	10.50	–	–	4
C.A.Pujara	103	176	11	206*	7195	43.60	19	35	66
A.M.Rahane	85	144	12	188	5077	38.46	12	26	102
K.L.Rahul	50	86	2	199	2863	34.08	8	14	62
R.G.Sharma	58	100	10	212	4034	44.82	11	17	59
P.P.Shaw	5	9	1	134	339	42.37	1	2	2
M.Siraj	26	35	14	16*	104	4.95	–	–	14
K.Srikar Bharat	7	12	1	44	221	20.09	–	–	18/1
S.N.Thakur	11	18	1	67	331	19.47	–	4	5
J.D.Unadkat	4	5	2	14*	36	12.00	–	–	3
S.A.Yadav	1	1	–	8	8	8.00	–	–	–
U.T.Yadav	57	68	27	31	460	11.21	–	–	19

INDIA – BOWLING

	O	M	R	W	Avge	Best	5wI	10wM
R.Ashwin	4335.2	888	12127	507	23.91	7-59	35	8
J.J.Bumrah	1174	276	3202	157	20.39	6-27	10	–
A.Deep	19	0	83	3	27.66	3-83	–	–
S.Gill	1.1	0	1	0	–	–	–	–
S.S.Iyer	1	0	2	0	–	–	–	–
R.A.Jadeja	2853.1	703	7054	292	24.15	7-42	13	2
Y.B.Jaiswal	1	0	6	0	–	–	–	–
V.Kohli	29.1	2	84	0	–	–	–	–
P.M.Krishna	28	4	130	2	65.00	1-27	–	–
Kuldeep Yadav	298.1	44	1004	46	21.82	5-40	3	–
Mohammed Shami	1919.1	364	6346	229	27.71	6-56	6	–
Mukesh Kumar	47.2	16	179	7	25.57	2- 0	–	–
K.K.Nair	2	0	11	0	–	–	–	–
A.R.Patel	423.2	96	1064	55	19.34	6-38	5	1
C.A.Pujara	2	0	3	0	–	–	–	–
R.G.Sharma	63.5	5	224	2	112.00	1-26	–	–
M.Siraj	646	121	2165	74	29.25	6-15	3	–
S.N.Thakur	241.3	36	880	31	28.38	7-61	1	–
J.D.Unadkat	79	17	231	3	77.00	2-50	–	–
U.T.Yadav	1496.3	245	5263	170	30.95	6-88	3	1

PAKISTAN – BATTING AND FIELDING

	M	I	NO	HS	Runs	Avge	100	50	Ct/St
Aamer Jamal	3	6	1	82	143	28.60	–	1	1
Abdullah Shafiq	17	32	2	201	1330	44.33	4	5	13
Abrar Ahmed	6	8	4	17	52	13.00	–	–	2
Agha Salman	12	23	4	132*	809	42.57	2	6	16
Azhar Ali	97	180	11	302*	7142	42.26	19	35	66
Babar Azam	52	94	9	196	3898	45.85	9	26	41
Faheem Ashraf	17	27	1	91	687	26.42	–	4	5
Haris Rauf	1	2	–	12	12	6.00	–	–	–
Hassan Ali	24	38	6	30	382	11.93	–	–	6
Imam-ul-Haq	24	46	4	157	1568	37.33	3	9	21
Khurram Shehzad	1	2	–	7	7	3.50	–	–	–
Mir Hamza	5	10	5	7*	18	3.60	–	–	2
Mohammad Abbas	25	36	16	29	110	5.50	–	–	7
Mohammad Ali	2	4	2	0*	0	0.00	–	–	1
Mohammad Amir	36	67	11	48	751	13.41	–	–	5

PAKISTAN – BATTING AND FIELDING (continued)

	M	I	NO	HS	Runs	Avge	100	50	Ct/St
Mohammad Nawaz	6	10	1	45	144	16.00	–	–	4
Mohammad Rizwan	30	48	8	115*	1616	40.40	2	9	76/3
Mohammad Wasim	2	4	1	43	55	18.33	–	–	1
Naseem Shah	17	22	8	18	102	7.28	–	–	5
Nauman Ali	15	19	4	97	275	18.33	–	1	1
Saim Ayub	1	2	–	33	33	16.50	–	–	–
Sajid Khan	8	9	–	21	88	9.77	–	–	4
Sarfraz Ahmed	54	95	14	118	3031	37.41	4	21	160/22
Saud Shakil	10	19	3	208*	967	60.43	2	6	9
Shaheen Shah Afridi	29	37	9	21	182	6.50	–	–	2
Shan Masood	33	62	–	156	1778	28.67	4	9	22
Zafar Gohar	1	2	–	37	71	35.50	–	–	–
Zahid Mahmood	2	4	–	17	18	4.50	–	–	–

PAKISTAN – BOWLING

	O	M	R	W	Avge	Best	5wI	10wM
Aamer Jamal	89.5	6	368	18	20.44	6- 69	2	–
Abrar Ahmed	324.4	46	1181	38	31.07	7-114	2	1
Agha Salman	183	19	639	12	53.25	3- 75	–	–
Azhar Ali	144.3	8	621	8	77.62	2- 35	–	–
Babar Azam	15	2	42	2	21.00	1- 1	–	–
Faheem Ashraf	318	79	991	25	39.64	3- 42	–	–
Haris Rauf	13	1	78	1	78.00	1- 78	–	–
Hassan Ali	715.5	164	2185	80	27.31	5- 27	6	1
Imam-ul-Haq	2	0	9	0	–	–	–	–
Khurram Shehzad	38	9	128	5	25.60	3- 45	–	–
Mir Hamza	137.1	30	409	9	45.44	4- 32	–	–
Mohammad Abbas	855.4	261	2072	90	23.02	5- 33	4	1
Mohammad Ali	49	2	261	4	65.25	2- 64	–	–
Mohammad Amir	1269.5	292	3627	119	30.47	6- 44	4	–
Mohammad Nawaz	159.5	23	496	16	31.00	5- 88	1	–
Mohammad Wasim	59.4	8	231	2	115.50	1- 71	–	–
Naseem Shah	476	77	1725	51	33.82	5- 31	1	–
Nauman Ali	534.4	101	1576	47	33.53	7- 70	4	–
Sajid Khan	314.4	56	954	25	38.16	8- 42	1	1
Saud Shakil	2	0	30	0	–	–	–	–
Shaheen Shah Afridi	969	202	3019	113	26.71	6- 51	4	1
Shan Masood	24	6	92	2	46.00	1- 6	–	–
Zafar Gohar	32	0	159	0	–	–	–	–
Zahid Mahmood	62.3	3	434	12	36.16	4-235	–	–

SRI LANKA – BATTING AND FIELDING

	M	I	NO	HS	Runs	Avge	100	50	Ct/St
L.D.Chandimal	77	138	15	206*	5402	43.91	15	25	83/10
D.M.de Silva	52	92	8	173	3301	39.29	10	13	66
D.P.D.N.Dickwella	54	96	7	96	2757	30.97	–	22	134/27
A.M.Fernando	13	18	7	10	36	3.27	–	–	3
B.O.P.Fernando	21	37	4	102	1091	33.06	1	7	14
K.N.M.Fernando	6	10	1	205	444	49.33	1	1	6
M.V.T.Fernando	21	28	15	38	106	8.15	–	–	4
C.D.Gunasekara	1	1	1	16*	16	–	–	–	–
N.G.R.P.Jayasuriya	10	14	–	16	73	5.21	–	–	1
F.D.M.Karunaratne	89	170	7	244	6740	41.34	16	35	56
C.B.R.L.S.Kumara	26	36	17	13*	85	4.47	–	–	6
L.M.D.Madushanka	1	2	1	0*	0	0.00	–	–	1
A.D.Mathews	107	189	26	200*	7502	46.02	16	40	73

SRI LANKA – BATTING AND FIELDING (continued)

	M	I	NO	HS	Runs	Avge	100	50	Ct/St
B.K.G.Mendis	61	114	4	245	3998	36.34	9	17	86
C.A.K.Rajitha	17	22	3	22	123	6.47	–	–	7
W.S.R.Samarawickrama	9	14	1	104*	308	23.69	1	–	15/2
R.T.M.Wanigamuni	14	20	1	45*	365	19.21	–	–	5

SRI LANKA – BOWLING

	O	M	R	W	Avge	Best	5wI	10wM
D.M.de Silva	599.3	74	1977	34	58.14	3- 25	–	–
A.M.Fernando	328.3	53	1101	41	26.85	6- 51	1	1
B.O.P.Fernando	3	0	19	0	–	–	–	–
M.V.T.Fernando	533	66	1957	54	36.24	5-101	1	–
C.D.Gunasekara	9	1	50	0	–	–	–	–
N.G.R.P.Jayasuriya	578.5	112	1754	67	26.17	7- 52	7	2
F.D.M.Karunaratne	51.2	5	199	2	99.50	1- 12	–	–
C.B.R.L.S.Kumara	775.5	107	2995	74	40.47	6-122	1	–
L.M.D.Madushanka	17	3	77	0	–	–	–	–
A.D.Mathews	658	159	1784	33	54.06	4- 44	–	–
B.K.G.Mendis	22	1	118	1	118.00	1- 10	–	–
C.A.K.Rajitha	469.2	98	1515	47	32.23	5- 64	1	–
R.T.M.Wanigamuni	621	79	1931	63	30.65	6- 70	5	1

R.T.M.Wanigamuni is also known as W.R.T.Mendis.

ZIMBABWE – BATTING AND FIELDING

	M	I	NO	HS	Runs	Avge	100	50	Ct/St
C.J.Chibhabha	5	10	–	60	175	17.50	–	1	–
T.L.Chivanga	1	2	1	6	9	9.00	–	–	–
C.R.Ervine	20	40	2	160	1332	35.05	3	5	17
B.N.Evans	1	2	–	7	7	3.50	–	–	–
I.Kaia	2	4	–	67	172	43.00	–	1	1
T.Makoni	2	4	–	33	43	10.75	–	–	1
W.P.Masakadza	3	6	1	17	44	8.80	–	–	3
B.A.Mavuta	4	7	–	56	82	11.71	–	1	4
P.J.Moor †	8	16	1	83	533	35.53	–	5	9/1
R.Ngarava	4	7	2	19*	50	10.00	–	–	1
V.M.Nyauchi	8	13	4	13	57	6.33	–	–	3
M.Shumba	4	8	–	41	111	13.87	–	–	1
Sikandar Raza	17	33	–	127	1187	35.96	1	8	5
D.T.Tiripano	16	31	7	95	531	22.12	–	2	5
T.E.Tsiga	2	4	1	24*	28	9.33	–	–	5

ZIMBABWE – BOWLING

	O	M	R	W	Avge	Best	5wI	10wM
C.J.Chibhabha	41	4	162	1	162.00	1- 44	–	–
T.L.Chivanga	14	0	59	0	–	–	–	–
B.N.Evans	36	5	115	2	57.50	2- 41	–	–
W.P.Masakadza	87.1	20	268	7	38.28	3- 71	–	–
B.A.Mavuta	127	11	480	12	40.00	5-140	1	–
R.Ngarava	108	18	369	5	73.80	2-104	–	–
V.M.Nyauchi	229.2	41	734	20	36.70	5- 56	1	–
M.Shumba	61.4	8	250	1	250.00	1- 64	–	–
Sikandar Raza	442.5	56	1441	34	42.38	7-113	2	–
D.T.Tiripano	448.5	99	1273	26	48.96	3- 23	–	–

Since the beginning of 2022, Zimbabwe have played just two Tests (v WI, February 2023).

† *See below for P.J.Moor's Ireland Test career.*

BANGLADESH – BATTING AND FIELDING

	M	I	NO	HS	Runs	Avge	100	50	Ct/St
Ebadat Hossain	20	32	16	21*	50	3.12	–	–	1
Khaled Ahmed	12	20	7	4*	13	1.00	–	–	2
Liton Das	39	68	2	141	2394	36.27	3	16	72/8
Mahmudul Hasan	11	20	–	137	566	28.30	1	4	4
Mehedi Hasan	41	75	8	103	1338	19.97	1	5	26
Mominul Haque	59	110	8	181	3883	38.06	12	16	39
Mushfiqur Rahim	88	163	14	219*	5676	38.09	10	27	110/15
Nayeem Hasan	10	15	4	26	160	14.54	–	–	7
Nazmul Hossain	25	48	1	163	1449	30.82	5	3	19
Nurul Hasan	11	21	1	64	440	22.00	–	3	25/9
Shahadat Hossain	2	4	–	31	77	19.25	–	–	5
Shakib Al Hasan	66	121	7	217	4454	39.07	5	31	26
Shoriful Islam	9	14	2	26	89	7.41	–	–	7
Taijul Islam	44	74	11	39*	565	8.96	–	–	22
Tamim Iqbal	70	134	2	206	5134	38.89	10	31	20
Taskin Ahmed	13	22	3	75	221	11.63	–	1	2
Yasir Ali	6	11	1	55	205	20.50	–	1	5
Zakir Hasan	5	10	–	100	354	35.40	1	3	4

BANGLADESH – BOWLING

	O	M	R	W	Avge	Best	5wI	10wM
Ebadat Hossain	552.5	104	1980	42	47.14	6- 46	1	–
Khaled Ahmed	324	52	1152	21	54.85	5-106	1	–
Liton Das	2	0	13	0	–	–	–	–
Mahmudul Hasan	0.1	0	0	0	–	–	–	–
Mehedi Hasan	1683	262	5263	159	33.10	7- 58	9	2
Mominul Haque	137.1	10	512	10	51.20	3- 4	–	–
Nayeem Hasan	321.2	50	989	36	27.47	6-105	3	–
Nazmul Hossain	18.4	1	81	0	–	–	–	–
Shakib Al Hasan	2462.3	470	7238	233	31.06	7- 36	19	2
Shoriful Islam	197	45	612	20	30.60	3- 28	–	–
Taijul Islam	2003.1	360	6000	192	31.25	8- 39	12	2
Tamim Iqbal	5	0	20	0	–	–	–	–
Taskin Ahmed	410.1	67	1545	30	51.50	4- 37	–	–
Yasir Ali	7	0	35	0	–	–	–	–

IRELAND – BATTING AND FIELDING

	M	I	NO	HS	Runs	Avge	100	50	Ct/St
M.R.Adair	5	9	1	88	196	24.50	–	1	3
A.Balbirnie	8	16	1	95	378	25.20	–	4	8
C.Campher	5	10	–	111	289	28.90	1	–	–
M.Commins	2	4	–	5	6	1.50	–	–	2
G.H.Dockrell	2	4	–	39	98	24.50	–	–	–
F.P.Hand	1	2	–	7	8	4.00	–	–	1
G.I.Hume	3	6	1	14	36	7.20	–	–	–
M.J.Humphreys	1	2	1	7	11	11.00	–	–	2
A.R.McBrine	7	13	1	86*	314	26.16	–	2	1
B.J.McCarthy	1	1	–	5	5	5.00	–	–	–
J.A.McCollum	6	12	1	39	199	18.09	–	–	2
P.J.Moor †	5	10	–	19	88	8.80	–	–	1
P.R.Stirling	6	12	–	103	319	26.58	1	1	4
H.T.Tector	5	10	–	85	370	37.00	–	4	1
L.J.Tucker	5	10	1	108	424	47.11	1	1	10/2
T.F.van Woerkom	1	1	–	1	1	1.00	–	–	–
B.C.White	3	6	4	1	1	0.50	–	–	–
C.A.Young	1	1	1	1*	1	–	–	–	–

IRELAND – BOWLING

	O	*M*	*R*	*W*	*Avge*	*Best*	*5wI*	*10wM*
M.R.Adair	128.4	23	521	18	28.94	5- 39	1	–
A.Balbirnie	1	0	8	0	–	–	–	–
C.Campher	66	5	340	5	68.00	2- 13	–	–
G.H.Dockrell	61.3	11	233	3	77.66	2- 63	–	–
F.P.Hand	19	2	113	1	113.00	1-113	–	–
G.I.Hume	50	5	209	2	104.50	1- 85	–	–
M.J.Humphreys	10	0	67	0	–	–	–	–
A.R.McBrine	225.5	26	841	14	60.07	6-118	1	–
B.J.McCarthy	29	6	76	4	19.00	3- 48	–	–
P.R.Stirling	2	0	11	0	–	–	–	–
H.T.Tector	15	0	85	0	–	–	–	–
T.F.van Woerkom	18	4	55	1	55.00	1- 43	–	–
B.C.White	76.3	1	436	4	109.00	3-114	–	–
C.A.Young	21.4	7	55	5	11.00	3- 24	–	–

† *See above for P.J.Moor's Zimbabwe Test career.*

AFGHANISTAN – BATTING AND FIELDING

	M	*I*	*NO*	*HS*	*Runs*	*Avge*	*100*	*50*	*Ct/St*
Abdul Malik	2	4	–	17	22	5.50	–	–	4
Afsar Zazai	6	10	1	48*	214	23.77	–	–	11/1
Bahir Shah	1	1	–	7	7	7.00	–	–	–
Hamza Hotak	4	6	2	34	83	20.75	–	–	2
Hashmatullah Shahidi	8	16	5	200*	485	44.09	1	2	2
Ibrahim Zadran	7	14	–	114	541	38.64	1	4	11
Ikram Alikhil	2	3	–	21	29	9.66	–	–	5/1
Karim Janat	2	4	1	41*	95	31.66	–	–	–
Mohammad Saleem	1	2	–	2	2	1.00	–	–	–
Nasir Ahmadzai	5	10	3	55*	160	22.85	–	1	4
Naveed Zadran	2	4	1	25	41	13.66	–	–	1
Nijat Masood	3	6	1	12	16	3.20	–	–	–
Noor Ali Zadran	2	4	–	47	117	29.25	–	–	1
Qais Ahmad	2	4	–	21	45	11.25	–	–	–
Rahmanullah Gurbaz	1	2	–	46	51	25.50	–	–	2
Rahmat Shah	9	18	–	102	578	32.11	1	5	7
Rashid Khan	5	7	–	51	106	15.14	–	1	–
Yamin Ahmadzai	6	11	–	18	33	3.00	–	–	–
Zahir Khan	5	10	6	4*	8	2.00	–	–	–
Zia-ur-Rehman	2	4	–	13	23	5.75	–	–	1

AFGHANISTAN – BOWLING

	O	*M*	*R*	*W*	*Avge*	*Best*	*5wI*	*10wM*
Hamza Hotak	164	22	517	18	28.72	6- 75	2	–
Hashmatullah Shahidi	11	0	43	0	–	–	–	–
Ibrahim Zadran	2	0	13	1	13.00	1- 13	–	–
Karim Janat	25	3	105	0	–	–	–	–
Mohammad Saleem	12.1	0	57	0	–	–	–	–
Nasir Ahmadzai	2	0	4	0	–	–	–	–
Naveed Zadran	53.2	8	203	9	22.55	4- 83	–	–
Nijat Masood	69.5	9	308	9	34.22	5- 79	1	–
Qais Ahmad	31.2	4	134	3	44.66	2- 98	–	–
Rahmat Shah	14	1	53	1	53.00	1- 30	–	–
Rashid Khan	255.4	48	760	30	22.35	7-137	4	2
Yamin Ahmadzai	111.3	20	364	13	28.00	3- 41	–	–
Zahir Khan	112	3	529	11	48.09	3- 59	–	–
Zia-ur-Rehman	72	9	199	6	33.16	5- 64	1	–

INTERNATIONAL TEST MATCH RESULTS

Complete to 6 March 2024.

	Opponents	*Tests*	*Won by*												*Tied*	*Drawn*
			E	*A*	*SA*	*WI*	*NZ*	*I*	*P*	*SL*	*Z*	*B*	*Ire*	*Afg*		
England	Australia	361	112	152	–	–	–	–	–	–	–	–	–	–	–	97
	South Africa	156	66	–	35	–	–	–	–	–	–	–	–	–	–	55
	West Indies	163	51	–	–	59	–	–	–	–	–	–	–	–	–	53
	New Zealand	112	52	–	–	–	13	–	–	–	–	–	–	–	–	47
	India	135	51	–	–	–	–	34	–	–	–	–	–	–	–	50
	Pakistan	89	29	–	–	–	–	–	21	–	–	–	–	–	–	39
	Sri Lanka	36	17	–	–	–	–	–	–	8	–	–	–	–	–	11
	Zimbabwe	6	3	–	–	–	–	–	–	–	0	–	–	–	–	3
	Bangladesh	10	9	–	–	–	–	–	–	–	–	1	–	–	–	0
	Ireland	2	2	–	–	–	–	–	–	–	–	–	0	–	–	0
Australia	South Africa	101	–	54	26	–	–	–	–	–	–	–	–	–	–	21
	West Indies	120	–	61	–	33	–	–	–	–	–	–	–	–	1	25
	New Zealand	61	–	35	–	–	8	–	–	–	–	–	–	–	–	18
	India	107	–	45	–	–	–	32	–	–	–	–	–	–	1	29
	Pakistan	72	–	37	–	–	–	–	15	–	–	–	–	–	–	20
	Sri Lanka	33	–	20	–	–	–	–	–	5	–	–	–	–	–	8
	Zimbabwe	3	–	3	–	–	–	–	–	–	0	–	–	–	–	0
	Bangladesh	6	–	5	–	–	–	–	–	–	–	1	–	–	–	0
S Africa	West Indies	32	–	–	22	3	–	–	–	–	–	–	–	–	–	7
	New Zealand	49	–	–	26	–	7	–	–	–	–	–	–	–	–	16
	India	44	–	–	18	–	–	16	–	–	–	–	–	–	–	10
	Pakistan	28	–	–	15	–	–	–	6	–	–	–	–	–	–	7
	Sri Lanka	31	–	–	16	–	–	–	–	9	–	–	–	–	–	6
	Zimbabwe	9	–	–	8	–	–	–	–	–	0	–	–	–	–	1
	Bangladesh	14	–	–	12	–	–	–	–	–	–	0	–	–	–	2
W Indies	New Zealand	49	–	–	–	13	17	–	–	–	–	–	–	–	–	19
	India	100	–	–	–	30	–	23	–	–	–	–	–	–	–	47
	Pakistan	54	–	–	–	18	–	–	21	–	–	–	–	–	–	15
	Sri Lanka	24	–	–	–	4	–	–	–	11	–	–	–	–	–	9
	Zimbabwe	12	–	–	–	8	–	–	–	–	0	–	–	–	–	4
	Bangladesh	20	–	–	–	14	–	–	–	–	–	4	–	–	–	2
	Afghanistan	1	–	–	–	1	–	–	–	–	–	–	–	0	–	0
N Zealand	India	62	–	–	–	–	13	22	–	–	–	–	–	–	–	27
	Pakistan	62	–	–	–	–	14	–	25	–	–	–	–	–	–	23
	Sri Lanka	38	–	–	–	–	18	–	–	9	–	–	–	–	–	11
	Zimbabwe	17	–	–	–	–	11	–	–	–	0	–	–	–	–	6
	Bangladesh	19	–	–	–	–	14	–	–	–	–	2	–	–	–	3
India	Pakistan	59	–	–	–	–	–	9	12	–	–	–	–	–	–	38
	Sri Lanka	46	–	–	–	–	–	22	–	7	–	–	–	–	–	17
	Zimbabwe	11	–	–	–	–	–	7	–	–	2	–	–	–	–	2
	Bangladesh	13	–	–	–	–	–	11	–	–	–	0	–	–	–	2
	Afghanistan	1	–	–	–	–	–	1	–	–	–	–	–	0	–	0
Pakistan	Sri Lanka	59	–	–	–	–	–	–	23	17	–	–	–	–	–	19
	Zimbabwe	19	–	–	–	–	–	–	12	–	3	–	–	–	–	4
	Bangladesh	13	–	–	–	–	–	–	12	–	–	0	–	–	–	1
	Ireland	1	–	–	–	–	–	–	1	–	–	–	0	–	–	0
Sri Lanka	Zimbabwe	20	–	–	–	–	–	–	–	14	0	–	–	–	–	6
	Bangladesh	24	–	–	–	–	–	–	–	18	–	1	–	–	–	5
	Ireland	2	–	–	–	–	–	–	–	2	–	–	0	–	–	0
	Afghanistan	1	–	–	–	–	–	–	–	1	–	–	–	0	–	0
Zimbabwe	Bangladesh	18	–	–	–	–	–	–	–	–	7	8	–	–	–	3
	Afghanistan	2	–	–	–	–	–	–	–	–	1	–	–	1	–	0
Bangladesh	Afghanistan	2	–	–	–	–	–	–	–	–	–	1	–	1	–	0
	Ireland	1	–	–	–	–	–	–	–	–	–	1	0	–	–	0
Ireland	Afghanistan	2	–	–	–	–	–	–	–	–	–	–	1	1	–	0
		2532	392	412	178	183	115	177	148	101	13	19	1	3	2	788

	Tests	Won	Lost	Drawn	Tied	Toss Won
England	1070	392	323	355	–	525
Australia	865†	413†	232	218	2	435†
South Africa	464	178	161	125	–	219
West Indies	575	183	210	181	1	302
New Zealand	469	115	184	170	–	232
India	578	177	178	222	1	287
Pakistan	456	148	142	166	–	214
Sri Lanka	314	101	121	92	–	172
Zimbabwe	117	13	75	29	–	65
Bangladesh	140	19	103	18	–	72
Ireland	8	1	7	–	–	4
Afghanistan	9	3	6	–	–	6

† total includes Australia's victory against the ICC World XI.

INTERNATIONAL TEST CRICKET RECORDS

(To 6 March 2024)

TEAM RECORDS – HIGHEST INNINGS TOTALS

952-6d	Sri Lanka v India	Colombo (RPS)	1997-98
903-7d	England v Australia	The Oval	1938
849	England v West Indies	Kingston	1929-30
790-3d	West Indies v Pakistan	Kingston	1957-58
765-6d	Pakistan v Sri Lanka	Karachi	2008-09
760-7d	Sri Lanka v India	Ahmedabad	2009-10
759-7d	India v England	Chennai	2016-17
758-8d	Australia v West Indies	Kingston	1954-55
756-5d	Sri Lanka v South Africa	Colombo (SSC)	2006
751-5d	West Indies v England	St John's	2003-04
749-9d	West Indies v England	Bridgetown	2008-09
747	West Indies v South Africa	St John's	2004-05
735-6d	Australia v Zimbabwe	Perth	2003-04
730-6d	Sri Lanka v Bangladesh	Mirpur	2013-14
729-6d	Australia v England	Lord's	1930
726-9d	India v Sri Lanka	Mumbai (BS)	2009-10
715-6d	New Zealand v Bangladesh	Hamilton	2018-19
713-3d	Sri Lanka v Zimbabwe	Bulawayo	2003-04
713-9d	Sri Lanka v Bangladesh	Chittagong	2017-18
710-7d	England v India	Birmingham	2011
708	Pakistan v England	The Oval	1987
707	India v Sri Lanka	Colombo (SSC)	2010
705-7d	India v Australia	Sydney	2003-04
704-3d	Sri Lanka v Ireland	Galle	2023
701	Australia v England	The Oval	1934
699-5	Pakistan v India	Lahore	1989-90
695	Australia v England	The Oval	1930
692-8d	West Indies v England	The Oval	1995
690	New Zealand v Pakistan	Sharjah	2014-15
687-8d	West Indies v England	The Oval	1976
687-6d	India v Bangladesh	Hyderabad	2016-17
682-6d	South Africa v England	Lord's	2003
681-8d	West Indies v England	Port of Spain	1953-54
680-8d	New Zealand v India	Wellington	2013-14
679-7d	Pakistan v India	Lahore	2005-06
676-7	India v Sri Lanka	Kanpur	1986-87

675-5d	India v Pakistan	Multan	2003-04
674	Australia v India	Adelaide	1947-48
674-6	Pakistan v India	Faisalabad	1984-85
674-6d	Australia v England	Cardiff	2009
671-4	New Zealand v Sri Lanka	Wellington	1990-91
668	Australia v West Indies	Bridgetown	1954-55
664	India v England	The Oval	2007
662-9d	Australia v England	Perth	2017-18
660-5d	West Indies v New Zealand	Wellington	1994-95
659-8d	Australia v England	Sydney	1946-47
659-4d	Australia v India	Sydney	2011-12
659-6d	New Zealand v Pakistan	Christchurch	2020-21
658-8d	England v Australia	Nottingham	1938
658-9d	South Africa v West Indies	Durban	2003-04
657-8d	Pakistan v West Indies	Bridgetown	1957-58
657-7d	India v Australia	Calcutta	2000-01
657	England v Pakistan	Rawalpindi	2022-23
656-8d	Australia v England	Manchester	1964
654-5	England v South Africa	Durban	1938-39
653-4d	England v India	Lord's	1990
653-4d	Australia v England	Leeds	1993
652-8d	West Indies v England	Lord's	1973
652	Pakistan v India	Faisalabad	1982-83
652-7d	England v India	Madras	1984-85
652-7d	Australia v South Africa	Johannesburg	2001-02
651	South Africa v Australia	Cape Town	2008-09
650-6d	Australia v West Indies	Bridgetown	1964-65

The highest for Zimbabwe is 563-9d (v WI, Harare, 2001), for Bangladesh 638 (v SL, Galle, 2012-13), for Ireland 492 (v SL, Galle, 2023) and for Afghanistan 545-4d (v Z, Abu Dhabi, 2020-21).

LOWEST INNINGS TOTALS – † One batsman absent

26	New Zealand v England	Auckland	1954-55
30	South Africa v England	Port Elizabeth	1895-96
30	South Africa v England	Birmingham	1924
35	South Africa v England	Cape Town	1898-99
36	Australia v England	Birmingham	1902
36	South Africa v Australia	Melbourne	1931-32
36	India v Australia	Adelaide	2020-21
38	Ireland v England	Lord's	2019
42	Australia v England	Sydney	1887-88
42	New Zealand v Australia	Wellington	1945-46
42†	India v England	Lord's	1974
43	South Africa v England	Cape Town	1888-89
43	Bangladesh v West Indies	North Sound	2018
44	Australia v England	The Oval	1896
45	England v Australia	Sydney	1886-87
45	South Africa v Australia	Melbourne	1931-32
45	New Zealand v South Africa	Cape Town	2012-13
46	England v West Indies	Port of Spain	1993-94
47	South Africa v England	Cape Town	1888-89
47	New Zealand v England	Lord's	1958
47	West Indies v England	Kingston	2003-04
47	Australia v South Africa	Cape Town	2011-12
49	Pakistan v South Africa	Johannesburg	2012-13

The lowest for Sri Lanka is 71 (v P, Kandy, 1994-95), for Zimbabwe 51 (v NZ, Napier, 2011-12) and for Afghanistan 103 (v I, Bengaluru, 2018).

BATTING RECORDS – 5000 RUNS IN TESTS

Runs			*M*	*I*	*NO*	*HS*	*Avge*	*100*	*50*
15921	S.R.Tendulkar	I	200	329	33	248*	53.78	51	68
13378	R.T.Ponting	A	168	287	29	257	51.85	41	62
13289	J.H.Kallis	SA/ICC	166	280	40	224	55.37	45	58
13288	R.S.Dravid	I/ICC	164	286	32	270	52.31	36	63
12472	A.N.Cook	E	161	291	16	294	45.35	33	57
12400	K.C.Sangakkara	SL	134	233	17	319	57.40	38	52
11953	B.C.Lara	WI/ICC	131	232	6	400*	52.88	34	48
11867	S.Chanderpaul	WI	164	280	49	203*	51.37	30	66
11814	D.P.M.D.Jayawardena	SL	149	252	15	374	49.84	34	50
11626	J.E.Root	E	139	255	21	254	49.68	31	60
11174	A.R.Border	A	156	265	44	205	50.56	27	63
10927	S.R.Waugh	A	168	260	46	200	51.06	32	50
10122	S.M.Gavaskar	I	125	214	16	236*	51.12	34	45
10099	Younus Khan	P	118	213	19	313	52.05	34	33
9665	S.P.D.Smith	A	108	193	25	239	57.52	32	41
9282	H.M.Amla	SA	124	215	16	311*	46.64	28	41
9265	G.C.Smith	SA/ICC	117	205	13	277	48.25	27	38
8900	G.A.Gooch	E	118	215	6	333	42.58	20	46
8848	V.Kohli	I	113	191	11	254*	49.15	29	30
8832	Javed Miandad	P	124	189	21	280*	52.57	23	43
8830	Inzamam-ul-Haq	P/ICC	120	200	22	329	49.60	25	46
8786	D.A.Warner	A	112	205	8	335*	44.59	26	37
8781	V.V.S.Laxman	I	134	225	34	281	45.97	17	56
8765	A.B.de Villiers	SA	114	191	18	278*	50.66	22	46
8675	K.S.Williamson	NZ	99	174	17	251	55.25	32	33
8643	M.J.Clarke	A	115	198	22	329*	49.10	28	27
8625	M.L.Hayden	A	103	184	14	380	50.73	30	29
8586	V.Sehwag	I/ICC	104	180	6	319	49.34	23	32
8540	I.V.A.Richards	WI	121	182	12	291	50.23	24	45
8463	A.J.Stewart	E	133	235	21	190	39.54	15	45
8231	D.I.Gower	E	117	204	18	215	44.25	18	39
8181	K.P.Pietersen	E	104	181	8	227	47.28	23	35
8114	G.Boycott	E	108	193	23	246*	47.72	22	42
8032	G.St A.Sobers	WI	93	160	21	365*	57.78	26	30
8029	M.E.Waugh	A	128	209	17	153*	41.81	20	47
7728	M.A.Atherton	E	115	212	7	185*	37.70	16	46
7727	I.R.Bell	E	118	205	24	235	42.69	22	46
7696	J.L.Langer	A	105	182	12	250	45.27	23	30
7683	L.R.P.L.Taylor	NZ	112	196	24	290	44.66	19	35
7624	M.C.Cowdrey	E	114	188	15	182	44.06	22	38
7558	C.G.Greenidge	WI	108	185	16	226	44.72	19	34
7530	Mohammad Yousuf	P	90	156	12	223	52.29	24	33
7525	M.A.Taylor	A	104	186	13	334*	43.49	19	40
7515	C.H.Lloyd	WI	110	175	14	242*	46.67	19	39
7502	A.D.Mathews	SL	107	189	26	200*	46.02	16	40
7487	D.L.Haynes	WI	116	202	25	184	42.29	18	39
7422	D.C.Boon	A	107	190	20	200	43.65	21	32
7289	G.Kirsten	SA	101	176	15	275	45.27	21	34
7249	W.R.Hammond	E	85	140	16	336*	58.45	22	24
7214	C.H.Gayle	WI	103	182	11	333	42.18	15	37
7212	S.C.Ganguly	I	113	188	17	239	42.17	16	35
7195	C.A.Pujara	I	103	176	11	206*	44.36	19	35
7172	S.P.Fleming	NZ	111	189	10	274*	40.06	9	46
7142	Azhar Ali	P	97	180	11	302*	42.26	19	35

Runs			M	I	NO	HS	Avge	100	50
7110	G.S.Chappell	A	87	151	19	247*	53.86	24	31
7037	A.J.Strauss	E	100	178	6	177	40.91	21	27
6996	D.G.Bradman	A	52	80	10	334	99.94	29	13
6973	S.T.Jayasuriya	SL	110	188	14	340	40.07	14	31
6971	L.Hutton	E	79	138	15	364	56.67	19	33
6868	D.B.Vengsarkar	I	116	185	22	166	42.13	17	35
6806	K.F.Barrington	E	82	131	15	256	58.67	20	35
6744	G.P.Thorpe	E	100	179	28	200*	44.66	16	39
6740	F.D.M.Karunaratne	SL	89	170	7	244	41.34	16	35
6453	B.B.McCullum	NZ	101	176	9	302	38.64	12	31
6361	P.A.de Silva	SL	93	159	11	267	42.97	20	22
6314	B.A.Stokes	E	101	183	7	258	35.87	13	31
6235	M.E.K.Hussey	A	79	137	16	195	51.52	19	29
6227	R.B.Kanhai	WI	79	137	6	256	47.53	15	28
6215	M.Azharuddin	I	99	147	9	199	45.03	22	21
6167	H.H.Gibbs	SA	90	154	7	228	41.95	14	26
6149	R.N.Harvey	A	79	137	10	205	48.41	21	24
6080	G.R.Viswanath	I	91	155	10	222	41.93	14	35
5974	J.M.Bairstow	E	99	176	12	167*	36.42	12	26
5949	R.B.Richardson	WI	86	146	12	194	44.39	16	27
5842	R.R.Sarwan	WI	87	154	8	291	40.01	15	31
5825	M.E.Trescothick	E	76	143	10	219	43.79	14	29
5807	D.C.S.Compton	E	78	131	15	278	50.06	17	28
5768	Salim Malik	P	103	154	22	237	43.69	15	29
5764	N.Hussain	E	96	171	16	207	37.19	14	33
5762	C.L.Hooper	WI	102	173	15	233	36.46	13	27
5719	M.P.Vaughan	E	82	147	9	197	41.44	18	18
5676	Mushfiqur Rahim	B	88	163	14	219*	38.09	10	27
5570	A.C.Gilchrist	A	96	137	20	204*	47.60	17	26
5515	M.V.Boucher	SA/ICC	147	206	24	125	30.30	5	35
5513	K.C.Brathwaite	WI	89	171	10	212	34.24	12	29
5502	M.S.Atapattu	SL	90	156	15	249	39.02	16	17
5492	T.M.Dilshan	SL	87	145	11	193	40.98	16	23
5462	T.T.Samaraweera	SL	81	132	20	231	48.76	14	30
5444	M.D.Crowe	NZ	77	131	11	299	45.36	17	18
5424	U.T.Khawaja	A	72	129	12	195*	46.35	15	26
5410	J.B.Hobbs	E	61	102	7	211	56.94	15	28
5402	L.D.Chandimal	SL	77	138	15	206*	43.91	15	25
5357	K.D.Walters	A	74	125	14	250	48.26	15	33
5347	D.Elgar	SA	86	152	11	199	37.92	14	23
5345	I.M.Chappell	A	75	136	10	196	42.42	14	26
5334	J.G.Wright	NZ	82	148	7	185	37.82	12	23
5312	M.J.Slater	A	74	131	7	219	42.84	14	21
5307	T.W.M.Latham	NZ	79	140	6	264*	39.60	13	27
5248	Kapil Dev	I	131	184	15	163	31.05	8	27
5234	W.M.Lawry	A	67	123	12	210	47.15	13	27
5222	Misbah-ul-Haq	P	75	132	20	161*	46.62	10	39
5200	I.T.Botham	E	102	161	6	208	33.54	14	22
5138	J.H.Edrich	E	77	127	9	310*	43.54	12	24
5134	Tamim Iqbal	B	70	134	2	206	38.89	10	31
5105	A.Ranatunga	SL	93	155	12	135*	35.69	4	38
5077	A.M.Rahan	I	85	144	12	188	38.46	12	26
5062	Zaheer Abbas	P	78	124	11	274	44.79	12	20

The most for Zimbabwe is 4794 by A.Flower (112 innings); for Ireland by L.J.Tucker 424 (10 innings) and for Afghanistan 578 by Rahmat Shah (18 innings).

750 RUNS IN A SERIES

Runs			*Series*	*M*	*I*	*NO*	*HS*	*Avge*	*100*	*50*
974	D.G.Bradman	A v E	1930	5	7	–	334	139.14	4	–
905	W.R.Hammond	E v A	1928-29	5	9	1	251	113.12	4	–
839	M.A.Taylor	A v E	1989	6	11	1	219	83.90	2	5
834	R.N.Harvey	A v SA	1952-53	5	9	–	205	92.66	4	3
829	I.V.A.Richards	WI v E	1976	4	7	–	291	118.42	3	2
827	C.L.Walcott	WI v A	1954-55	5	10	–	155	82.70	5	2
824	G.St A.Sobers	WI v P	1957-58	5	8	2	365*	137.33	3	3
810	D.G.Bradman	A v E	1936-37	5	9	–	270	90.00	3	1
806	D.G.Bradman	A v SA	1931-32	5	5	1	299*	201.50	4	–
798	B.C.Lara	WI v E	1993-94	5	8	–	375	99.75	2	2
779	E.de C.Weekes	WI v I	1948-49	5	7	–	194	111.28	4	2
774	S.M.Gavaskar	I v WI	1970-71	4	8	3	220	154.80	4	3
774	S.P.D.Smith	A v E	2019	4	7	–	211	110.57	3	3
769	S.P.D.Smith	A v I	2014-15	4	8	2	192	128.16	4	2
766	A.N.Cook	E v A	2010-11	5	7	1	235*	127.66	3	2
765	B.C.Lara	WI v E	1995	6	10	1	179	85.00	3	3
761	Mudassar Nazar	P v I	1982-83	6	8	2	231	126.83	4	1
758	D.G.Bradman	A v E	1934	5	8	–	304	94.75	2	1
753	D.C.S.Compton	E v SA	1947	5	8	–	208	94.12	4	2
752	G.A.Gooch	E v I	1990	3	6	–	333	125.33	3	2

HIGHEST INDIVIDUAL INNINGS

400*	B.C.Lara	WI v E	St John's	2003-04
380	M.L.Hayden	A v Z	Perth	2003-04
375	B.C.Lara	WI v E	St John's	1993-94
374	D.P.M.D.Jayawardena	SL v SA	Colombo (SSC)	2006
365*	G.St A.Sobers	WI v P	Kingston	1957-58
364	L.Hutton	E v A	The Oval	1938
340	S.T.Jayasuriya	SL v I	Colombo (RPS)	1997-98
337	Hanif Mohammed	P v WI	Bridgetown	1957-58
336*	W.R.Hammond	E v NZ	Auckland	1932-33
335*	D.A.Warner	A v P	Adelaide	2019-20
334*	M.A.Taylor	A v P	Peshawar	1998-99
334	D.G.Bradman	A v E	Leeds	1930
333	G.A.Gooch	E v I	Lord's	1990
333	C.H.Gayle	WI v SL	Galle	2010-11
329*	M.J.Clarke	A v I	Sydney	2011-12
329	Inzamam-ul-Haq	P v NZ	Lahore	2001-02
325	A.Sandham	E v WI	Kingston	1929-30
319	V.Sehwag	I v SA	Chennai	2007-08
319	K.C.Sangakkara	SL v B	Chittagong	2013-14
317	C.H.Gayle	WI v SA	St John's	2004-05
313	Younus Khan	P v SL	Karachi	2008-09
311*	H.M.Amla	SA v E	The Oval	2012
311	R.B.Simpson	A v E	Manchester	1964
310*	J.H.Edrich	E v NZ	Leeds	1965
309	V.Sehwag	I v P	Multan	2003-04
307	R.M.Cowper	A v E	Melbourne	1965-66
304	D.G.Bradman	A v E	Leeds	1934
303*	K.K.Nair	I v E	Chennai	2016-17
302*	Azhar Ali	P v WI	Dubai (DSC)	2016-17
302	L.G.Rowe	WI v E	Bridgetown	1973-74
302	B.B.McCullum	NZ v I	Wellington	2013-14
299*	D.G.Bradman	A v SA	Adelaide	1931-32

299	M.D.Crowe	NZ v SL	Wellington	1990-91
294	A.N.Cook	E v I	Birmingham	2011
293	V.Sehwag	I v SL	Mumbai (BS)	2009-10
291	I.V.A.Richards	WI v E	The Oval	1976
291	R.R.Sarwan	WI v E	Bridgetown	2008-09
290	L.R.P.L.Taylor	NZ v A	Perth	2015-16
287	R.E.Foster	E v A	Sydney	1903-04
287	K.C.Sangakkara	SL v SA	Colombo (SSC)	2006
285*	P.B.H.May	E v WI	Birmingham	1957
281	V.V.S.Laxman	I v A	Calcutta	2000-01
280*	Javed Miandad	P v I	Hyderabad	1982-83
278*	A.B.de Villiers	SA v P	Abu Dhabi	2010-11
278	D.C.S.Compton	E v P	Nottingham	1954
277	B.C.Lara	WI v A	Sydney	1992-93
277	G.C.Smith	SA v E	Birmingham	2003
275*	D.J.Cullinan	SA v NZ	Auckland	1998-99
275	G.Kirsten	SA v E	Durban	1999-00
275	D.P.M.D.Jayawardena	SL v I	Ahmedabad	2009-10
274*	S.P.Fleming	NZ v SL	Colombo (PSS)	2003
274	R.G.Pollock	SA v A	Durban	1969-70
274	Zaheer Abbas	P v E	Birmingham	1971
271	Javed Miandad	P v NZ	Auckland	1988-89
270*	G.A.Headley	WI v E	Kingston	1934-35
270	D.G.Bradman	A v E	Melbourne	1936-37
270	R.S.Dravid	I v P	Rawalpindi	2003-04
270	K.C.Sangakkara	SL v Z	Bulawayo	2004
269*	A.C.Voges	A v WI	Hobart	2015-16
268	G.N.Yallop	A v P	Melbourne	1983-84
267*	B.A.Young	NZ v SL	Dunedin	1996-97
267	P.A.de Silva	SL v NZ	Wellington	1990-91
267	Younus Khan	P v I	Bangalore	2004-05
267	Z.Crawley	E v P	Southampton	2020
266	W.H.Ponsford	A v E	The Oval	1934
266	D.L.Houghton	Z v SL	Bulawayo	1994-95
264*	T.W.M.Latham	NZ v SL	Wellington	2018-19
263	A.N.Cook	E v P	Abu Dhabi	2015-16
262*	D.L.Amiss	E v WI	Kingston	1973-74
262	S.P.Fleming	NZ v SA	Cape Town	2005-06
261*	R.R.Sarwan	WI v B	Kingston	2004
261	F.M.M.Worrell	WI v E	Nottingham	1950
260	C.C.Hunte	WI v P	Kingston	1957-58
260	Javed Miandad	P v E	The Oval	1987
260	M.N.Samuels	WI v B	Khulna	2012-13
259*	M.J.Clarke	A v SA	Brisbane	2012-13
259	G.M.Turner	NZ v WI	Georgetown	1971-72
259	G.C.Smith	SA v E	Lord's	2003
258	T.W.Graveney	E v WI	Nottingham	1957
258	S.M.Nurse	WI v NZ	Christchurch	1968-69
258	B.A.Stokes	E v SA	Cape Town	2015-16
257*	Wasim Akram	P v Z	Sheikhupura	1996-97
257	R.T.Ponting	A v I	Melbourne	2003-04
256	R.B.Kanhai	WI v I	Calcutta	1958-59
256	K.F.Barrington	E v A	Manchester	1964
255*	D.J.McGlew	SA v NZ	Wellington	1952-53
254*	V.Kohli	I v SA	Pune	2019-20
254	D.G.Bradman	A v E	Lord's	1930
254	V.Sehwag	I v P	Lahore	2005-06

254	J.E.Root	E v P	Manchester	2016
253*	H.M.Amla	SA v I	Nagpur	2009-10
253	S.T.Jayasuriya	SL v P	Faisalabad	2004-05
253	D.A.Warner	A v NZ	Perth	2015-16
252	T.W.M.Latham	NZ v B	Christchurch	2021-22
251	W.R.Hammond	E v A	Sydney	1928-29
251	K.S.Williamson	NZ v WI	Hamilton	2020-21
250	K.D.Walters	A v NZ	Christchurch	1976-77
250	S.F.A.F.Bacchus	WI v I	Kanpur	1978-79
250	J.L.Langer	A v E	Melbourne	2002-03

The highest for Bangladesh is 219* by Mushfiqur Rahim (v Z, Mirpur, 2018-19), for Ireland 118 by K.J.O'Brien (v P, Dublin, 2018) and for Afghanistan 200* by Hashmatullah Shahidi (v Z, Abu Dhabi, 2020-21).

20 HUNDREDS

					Opponents										
			200	*Inn*	*E*	*A*	*SA*	*WI*	*NZ*	*I*	*P*	*SL*	*Z*	*B*
51	S.R.Tendulkar	I	6	329	7	11	7	3	4	–	2	9	3	5
45	J.H.Kallis	SA	2	280	8	5	–	8	6	7	6	1	3	1
41	R.T.Ponting	A	6	287	8	–	8	7	2	8	5	1	1	1
38	K.C.Sangakkara	SL	11	233	3	1	3	3	4	5	10	–	2	7
36	R.S.Dravid	I	5	286	7	2	2	5	6	–	5	3	3	3
34	Younus Khan	P	6	213	4	4	4	3	2	5	–	8	1	3
34	S.M.Gavaskar	I	4	214	4	8	–	13	2	–	5	2	–	–
34	B.C.Lara	WI	9	232	7	9	4	–	1	2	4	5	1	1
34	D.P.M.D.Jayawardena	SL	7	252	8	2	6	1	3	6	2	–	1	5
33	A.N.Cook	E	5	291	–	5	2	6	3	7	5	3	–	2
32	K.S.Williamson	NZ	6	174	4	2	6	3	–	2	5	5	1	4
32	S.P.D.Smith	A	4	193	12	–	2	3	2	9	2	2	–	–
32	S.R.Waugh	A	1	260	10	–	2	7	2	2	3	3	1	2
31	J.E.Root	E	5	255	–	4	2	5	5	10	1	4	–	–
30	M.L.Hayden †	A	2	184	5	–	6	5	1	6	1	3	2	–
30	S.Chanderpaul	WI	2	280	5	5	5	–	2	7	1	–	1	4
29	D.G.Bradman	A	12	80	19	–	4	2	–	4	–	–	–	–
29	V.Kohli	I	7	191	5	8	3	3	3	–	–	5	–	2
28	M.J.Clarke	A	4	198	7	–	5	1	4	7	1	3	–	–
28	H.M.Amla	SA	4	215	6	5	–	1	4	5	2	2	–	3
27	G.C.Smith	SA	5	205	7	3	–	7	2	–	4	–	1	3
27	A.R.Border	A	2	265	8	–	–	3	5	4	6	1	–	–
26	G.St A.Sobers	WI	2	160	10	4	–	–	1	8	3	–	–	–
26	D.A.Warner	A	3	205	3	–	5	1	5	4	6	–	–	2
25	Inzamam-ul-Haq	P	2	200	5	1	–	4	3	3	–	5	2	2
24	G.S.Chappell	A	4	151	9	–	–	5	3	1	6	–	–	–
24	Mohammad Yousuf	P	4	156	6	1	–	7	1	4	–	1	2	2
24	I.V.A.Richards	WI	3	182	8	5	–	–	1	8	2	–	–	–
23	V.Sehwag	I	6	180	2	3	5	2	2	–	4	5	–	–
23	K.P.Pietersen	E	3	181	–	4	3	3	2	6	2	3	–	–
23	J.L.Langer	A	3	182	5	–	2	3	4	3	4	2	–	–
23	Javed Miandad	P	6	189	2	6	–	2	7	5	–	1	–	–
22	W.R.Hammond	E	7	140	–	9	6	1	4	2	–	–	–	–
22	M.Azharuddin	I	–	147	6	2	4	–	2	–	3	5	–	–
22	M.C.Cowdrey	E	–	188	–	5	3	6	2	3	3	–	–	–
22	A.B.de Villiers	SA	2	191	2	6	–	6	–	3	4	1	–	–
22	G.Boycott	E	1	193	–	7	1	5	2	4	3	–	–	–
22	I.R.Bell	E	1	205	–	4	2	2	1	4	4	2	–	3
21	R.N.Harvey	A	2	137	6	–	8	3	–	4	–	–	–	–
21	G.Kirsten	SA	3	176	5	2	–	3	2	3	2	1	1	2

					Opponents									
			200	*Inn*	*E*	*A*	*SA*	*WI*	*NZ*	*I*	*P*	*SL*	*Z*	*B*
21	A.J.Strauss	E	–	178	–	4	3	6	3	3	2	–	–	–
21	D.C.Boon	A	1	190	7	–	–	3	3	6	1	1	–	–
20	K.F.Barrington	E	1	131	–	5	2	3	3	3	4	–	–	–
20	P.A.de Silva	SL	2	159	2	1	–	–	2	5	8	–	1	1
20	M.E.Waugh	A	–	209	6	–	4	4	1	1	3	1	–	–
20	G.A.Gooch	E	2	215	–	4	–	5	4	5	1	1	–	–

† Includes century scored for Australia v ICC in 2005-06.

The most for Zimbabwe 12 by A.Flower (112), and for Bangladesh 11 by Mominul Haque (102). The most double hundreds by batsmen not included above are 6 by M.S.Atapattu (16 hundreds for Sri Lanka), 4 by L.Hutton (19 for England), 4 by C.G.Greenidge (19 for West Indies), 4 by Zaheer Abbas (12 for Pakistan), and 4 by B.B.McCullum (12 for New Zealand).

HIGHEST PARTNERSHIP FOR EACH WICKET

1st	415	N.D.McKenzie/G.C.Smith	SA v B	Chittagong	2007-08
2nd	576	S.T.Jayasuriya/R.S.Mahanama	SL v I	Colombo (RPS)	1997-98
3rd	624	K.C.Sangakkara/D.P.M.D.Jayawardena	SL v SA	Colombo (SSC)	2006
4th	449	A.C.Voges/S.E.Marsh	A v WI	Hobart	2015-16
5th	405	S.G.Barnes/D.G.Bradman	A v E	Sydney	1946-47
6th	399	B.A.Stokes/J.M.Bairstow	E v SA	Cape Town	2015-16
7th	347	D.St E.Atkinson/C.C.Depeiza	WI v A	Bridgetown	1954-55
8th	332	I.J.L.Trott/S.C.J.Broad	E v P	Lord's	2010
9th	195	M.V.Boucher/P.L.Symcox	SA v P	Johannesburg	1997-98
10th	198	J.E.Root/J.M.Anderson	E v I	Nottingham	2014

BOWLING RECORDS – 200 WICKETS IN TESTS

Wkts			*M*	*Balls*	*Runs*	*Avge*	*5wI*	*10wM*
800	M.Muralitharan	SL/ICC	133	44039	18180	22.72	67	22
708	S.K.Warne	A	145	40705	17995	25.41	37	10
698	J.M.Anderson	E	186	39781	18509	26.51	32	3
619	A.Kumble	I	132	40850	18355	29.65	35	8
604	S.C.J.Broad	E	167	33698	16719	27.68	20	3
563	G.D.McGrath	A	124	29248	12186	21.64	29	3
527	N.M.Lyon	A	128	32651	15997	30.35	24	5
519	C.A.Walsh	WI	132	30019	12688	24.44	22	3
507	R.Ashwin	I	99	26012	12127	23.91	35	8
439	D.W.Steyn	SA	93	18608	10077	22.95	26	5
434	Kapil Dev	I	131	27740	12867	29.64	23	2
433	H.M.R.K.B.Herath	SL	93	25993	12157	28.07	34	9
431	R.J.Hadlee	NZ	86	21918	9612	22.30	36	9
421	S.M.Pollock	SA	108	24453	9733	23.11	16	1
417	Harbhajan Singh	I	103	28580	13537	32.46	25	5
414	Wasim Akram	P	104	22627	9779	23.62	25	5
405	C.E.L.Ambrose	WI	98	22104	8500	20.98	22	3
390	M.Ntini	SA	101	20834	11242	28.82	18	4
383	I.T.Botham	E	102	21815	10878	28.40	27	4
378	T.G.Southee	NZ	99	22422	11148	29.49	15	1
376	M.D.Marshall	WI	81	17584	7876	20.94	22	4
373	Waqar Younis	P	87	16224	8788	23.56	22	5
362	Imran Khan	P	88	19458	8258	22.81	23	6
362	D.L.Vettori	NZ/ICC	113	28814	12441	34.36	20	3
355	D.K.Lillee	A	70	18467	8493	23.92	23	7
355	W.P.J.U.C.Vaas	SL	111	23438	10501	29.58	12	2
354	M.A.Starc	A	88	17213	9779	27.62	14	2
330	A.A.Donald	SA	72	15519	7344	22.25	20	3

Wkts			M	Balls	Runs	Avge	5wI	10wM
325	R.G.D.Willis	E	90	17357	8190	25.20	16	–
317	T.A.Boult	NZ	78	17417	8717	27.49	10	1
313	M.G.Johnson	A	73	16001	8891	28.40	12	3
311	I.Sharma	I	105	19160	10078	32.40	11	1
311	Z.Khan	I	92	18785	10247	32.94	11	1
310	B.Lee	A	76	16531	9554	30.81	10	–
309	M.Morkel	SA	86	16498	8550	27.66	8	–
309	L.R.Gibbs	WI	79	27115	8989	29.09	18	2
307	F.S.Trueman	E	67	15178	6625	21.57	17	3
297	D.L.Underwood	E	86	21862	7674	25.83	17	6
292	R.A.Jadeja	I	71	17119	7054	24.15	13	2
292	J.H.Kallis	SA/ICC	166	20232	9535	32.65	5	–
291	K.Rabada	SA	62	11416	6419	22.05	14	4
291	C.J.McDermott	A	71	16586	8332	28.63	14	2
270	K.A.J.Roach	WI	81	14464	7491	27.74	11	1
267	J.R.Hazlewood	A	69	14341	6677	25.00	11	–
266	B.S.Bedi	I	67	21364	7637	28.71	14	1
264	P.J.Cummins	A	61	12404	5966	22.59	12	2
261	Danish Kaneria	P	61	17697	9082	34.79	15	2
260	N.Wagner	NZ	64	13725	7169	27.57	9	–
259	J.Garner	WI	58	13169	5433	20.97	7	–
259	J.N.Gillespie	A	71	14234	6770	26.13	8	–
255	G.P.Swann	E	60	15349	7642	29.96	17	3
252	J.B.Statham	E	70	16056	6261	24.84	9	1
249	M.A.Holding	WI	60	12680	5898	23.68	13	2
248	R.Benaud	A	63	19108	6704	27.03	16	1
248	M.J.Hoggard	E	67	13909	7564	30.50	7	1
246	G.D.McKenzie	A	60	17681	7328	29.78	16	3
244	Yasir Shah	P	48	14255	7657	31.38	16	3
242	B.S.Chandrasekhar	I	58	15963	7199	29.74	16	2
236	A.V.Bedser	E	51	15918	5876	24.89	15	5
236	J.Srinath	I	67	15104	7196	30.49	10	1
236	Abdul Qadir	P	67	17126	7742	32.80	15	5
235	G.St A.Sobers	WI	93	21599	7999	34.03	6	–
234	A.R.Caddick	E	62	13558	6999	29.91	13	1
233	Shakib Al Hasan	B	66	14775	7238	31.06	19	2
233	C.S.Martin	NZ	71	14026	7878	33.81	10	1
229	Mohammed Shami	I	64	11515	6346	27.71	6	–
229	D.Gough	E	58	11821	6503	28.39	9	–
228	R.R.Lindwall	A	61	13650	5251	23.03	12	–
226	S.J.Harmison	E/ICC	63	13375	7192	31.82	8	1
226	A.Flintoff	E/ICC	79	14951	7410	32.78	3	–
224	V.D.Philander	SA	64	11391	5000	22.32	13	2
221	P.M.Siddle	A	67	13907	6777	30.66	8	–
218	C.L.Cairns	NZ	62	11698	6410	29.40	13	1
216	C.V.Grimmett	A	37	14513	5231	24.21	21	7
216	H.H.Streak	Z	65	13559	6079	28.14	7	–
212	M.G.Hughes	A	53	12285	6017	28.38	7	1
208	S.C.G.MacGill	A	44	11237	6038	29.02	12	2
208	Saqlain Mushtaq	P	49	14070	6206	29.83	13	3
204	M.M.Ali	E	68	12610	7612	37.31	5	1
202	A.M.E.Roberts	WI	47	11136	5174	25.61	11	2
202	J.A.Snow	E	49	12021	5387	26.66	8	1
200	J.R.Thomson	A	51	10535	5601	28.00	8	–

The most wickets for Ireland is 18 by M.R.Adair (9 innings) and for Afghanistan 34 by Rashid Khan (9 innings).

35 OR MORE WICKETS IN A SERIES

Wkts			Series	M	Balls	Runs	Avge	5wI	10wM
49	S.F.Barnes	E v SA	1913-14	4	1356	536	10.93	7	3
46	J.C.Laker	E v A	1956	5	1703	442	9.60	4	2
44	C.V.Grimmett	A v SA	1935-36	5	2077	642	14.59	5	3
42	T.M.Alderman	A v E	1981	6	1950	893	21.26	4	–
41	R.M.Hogg	A v E	1978-79	6	1740	527	12.85	5	2
41	T.M.Alderman	A v E	1989	6	1616	712	17.36	6	1
40	Imran Khan	P v I	1982-83	6	1339	558	13.95	4	2
40	S.K.Warne	A v E	2005	5	1517	797	19.92	3	2
39	A.V.Bedser	E v A	1953	5	1591	682	17.48	5	1
39	D.K.Lillee	A v E	1981	6	1870	870	22.30	2	1
38	M.W.Tate	E v A	1924-25	5	2528	881	23.18	5	1
37	W.J.Whitty	A v SA	1910-11	5	1395	632	17.08	2	–
37	H.J.Tayfield	SA v E	1956-57	5	2280	636	17.18	4	1
37	M.G.Johnson	A v E	2013-14	5	1132	517	13.97	3	–
36	A.E.E.Vogler	SA v E	1909-10	5	1349	783	21.75	4	1
36	A.A.Mailey	A v E	1920-21	5	1465	946	26.27	4	2
36	G.D.McGrath	A v E	1997	6	1499	701	19.47	2	–
35	G.A.Lohmann	E v SA	1895-96	3	520	203	5.80	4	2
35	B.S.Chandrasekhar	I v E	1972-73	5	1747	662	18.91	4	–
35	M.D.Marshall	WI v E	1988	5	1219	443	12.65	3	1

The most for New Zealand is 33 by R.J.Hadlee (3 Tests v A, 1985-86), for Sri Lanka 30 by M.Muralitharan (3 Tests v Z, 2001-02), for Zimbabwe 22 by H.H.Streak (3 Tests v P, 1994-95), and for Bangladesh 19 by Mehedi Hasan (2 Tests v E, 2016-17).

15 OR MORE WICKETS IN A TEST († On debut)

19- 90	J.C.Laker	E v A	Manchester	1956
17-159	S.F.Barnes	E v SA	Johannesburg	1913-14
16-136†	N.D.Hirwani	I v WI	Madras	1987-88
16-137†	R.A.L.Massie	A v E	Lord's	1972
16-220	M.Muralitharan	SL v E	The Oval	1998
15- 28	J.Briggs	E v SA	Cape Town	1888-89
15- 45	G.A.Lohmann	E v SA	Port Elizabeth	1895-96
15- 99	C.Blythe	E v SA	Leeds	1907
15-104	H.Verity	E v A	Lord's	1934
15-123	R.J.Hadlee	NZ v A	Brisbane	1985-86
15-124	W.Rhodes	E v A	Melbourne	1903-04
15-217	Harbhajan Singh	I v A	Madras	2000-01

The best analysis for South Africa is 13-132 by M.Ntini (v WI, Port of Spain, 2004-05), for West Indies 14-149 by M.A.Holding (v E, The Oval, 1976), for Pakistan 14-116 by Imran Khan (v SL, Lahore, 1981-82), for Zimbabwe 11-257 by A.G.Huckle (v NZ, Bulawayo, 1997-98), for Bangladesh 12-117 by Mehedi Hasan (v WI, Dhaka, 2018-19), for Ireland 8-95 by M.R.Adair (v Afg, Abu Dhabi, 2023-24) and for Afghanistan 11-104 by Rashid Khan (v B, Chittagong, 2019).

NINE OR MORE WICKETS IN AN INNINGS

10- 53	J.C.Laker	E v A	Manchester	1956
10- 74	A.Kumble	I v P	Delhi	1998-99
10-119	A.Y.Patel	NZ v I	Mumbai	2021-22
9- 28	G.A.Lohmann	E v SA	Johannesburg	1895-96
9- 37	J.C.Laker	E v A	Manchester	1956
9- 51	M.Muralitharan	SL v Z	Kandy	2001-02
9- 52	R.J.Hadlee	NZ v A	Brisbane	1985-86
9- 56	Abdul Qadir	P v E	Lahore	1987-88

9- 57	D.E.Malcolm	E v SA	The Oval	1994
9- 65	M.Muralitharan	SL v E	The Oval	1998
9- 69	J.M.Patel	I v A	Kanpur	1959-60
9- 83	Kapil Dev	I v WI	Ahmedabad	1983-84
9- 86	Sarfraz Nawaz	P v A	Melbourne	1978-79
9- 95	J.M.Noreiga	WI v I	Port of Spain	1970-71
9-102	S.P.Gupte	I v WI	Kanpur	1958-59
9-103	S.F.Barnes	E v SA	Johannesburg	1913-14
9-113	H.J.Tayfield	SA v E	Johannesburg	1956-57
9-121	A.A.Mailey	A v E	Melbourne	1920-21
9-127	H.M.R.K.B.Herath	SL v P	Colombo (SSC)	2014
9-129	K.A.Maharaj	SA v SL	Colombo (SSC)	2018

The best analysis for Zimbabwe is 8-109 by P.A.Strang (v NZ, Bulawayo, 2000-01), for Bangladesh 8-39 by Taijul Islam (v Z, Dhaka, 2014-15), for Ireland 6-118 by A.R.McBrine (v B, Mirpur, 2022-23) and for Afghanistan 7-137 by Rashid Khan (v Z, Abu Dhabi, 2020-21).

HAT-TRICKS

F.R.Spofforth	Australia v England	Melbourne	1878-79
W.Bates	England v Australia	Melbourne	1882-83
J.Briggs[7]	England v Australia	Sydney	1891-92
G.A.Lohmann	England v South Africa	Port Elizabeth	1895-96
J.T.Hearne	England v Australia	Leeds	1899
H.Trumble	Australia v England	Melbourne	1901-02
H.Trumble	Australia v England	Melbourne	1903-04
T.J.Matthews (2)[2]	Australia v South Africa	Manchester	1912
M.J.C.Allom[1]	England v New Zealand	Christchurch	1929-30
T.W.J.Goddard	England v South Africa	Johannesburg	1938-39
P.J.Loader	England v West Indies	Leeds	1957
L.F.Kline	Australia v South Africa	Cape Town	1957-58
W.W.Hall	West Indies v Pakistan	Lahore	1958-59
G.M.Griffin[7]	South Africa v England	Lord's	1960
L.R.Gibbs	West Indies v Australia	Adelaide	1960-61
P.J.Petherick[1/7]	New Zealand v Pakistan	Lahore	1976-77
C.A.Walsh[3]	West Indies v Australia	Brisbane	1988-89
M.G.Hughes[3/7]	Australia v West Indies	Perth	1988-89
D.W.Fleming[1]	Australia v Pakistan	Rawalpindi	1994-95
S.K.Warne	Australia v England	Melbourne	1994-95
D.G.Cork	England v West Indies	Manchester	1995
D.Gough[7]	England v Australia	Sydney	1998-99
Wasim Akram[4]	Pakistan v Sri Lanka	Lahore	1998-99
Wasim Akram[4]	Pakistan v Sri Lanka	Dhaka	1998-99
D.N.T.Zoysa[5]	Sri Lanka v Zimbabwe	Harare	1999-00
Abdul Razzaq	Pakistan v Sri Lanka	Galle	2000-01
G.D.McGrath	Australia v West Indies	Perth	2000-01
Harbhajan Singh	India v Australia	Calcutta	2000-01
Mohammad Sami[7]	Pakistan v Sri Lanka	Lahore	2001-02
J.J.C.Lawson[7]	West Indies v Australia	Bridgetown	2002-03
Alok Kapali[7]	Bangladesh v Pakistan	Peshawar	2003
A.M.Blignaut	Zimbabwe v Bangladesh	Harare	2003-04
M.J.Hoggard	England v West Indies	Bridgetown	2003-04
J.E.C.Franklin	New Zealand v Bangladesh	Dhaka	2004-05
I.K.Pathan[6/7]	India v Pakistan	Karachi	2005-06
R.J.Sidebottom[7]	England v New Zealand	Hamilton	2007-08
P.M.Siddle	Australia v England	Brisbane	2010-11
S.C.J.Broad	England v India	Nottingham	2011
Sohag Gazi	Bangladesh v New Zealand	Chittagong	2013-14

S.C.J.Broad[7]	England v Sri Lanka	Leeds	2014
H.M.R.K.B.Herath	Sri Lanka v Australia	Galle	2016
M.M.Ali	England v South Africa	The Oval	2017
J.J.Bumrah	India v West Indies	Kingston	2019
Naseem Shah	Pakistan v Bangladesh	Rawalpindi	2019-20
K.A.Maharaj	South Africa v West Indies	Gros Islet	2021

[1] On debut. [2] Hat-trick in each innings. [3] Involving both innings. [4] In successive Tests. [5] His first 3 balls (second over of the match). [6] The fourth, fifth and sixth balls of the match. [7] On losing side.

WICKET-KEEPING RECORDS – 150 DISMISSALS IN TESTS†

Total			*Tests*	*Ct*	*St*
555	M.V.Boucher	South Africa/ICC	147	532	23
416	A.C.Gilchrist	Australia	96	379	37
395	I.A.Healy	Australia	119	366	29
355	R.W.Marsh	Australia	96	343	12
294	M.S.Dhoni	India	90	256	38
270	B.J.Haddin	Australia	66	262	8
270†	P.J.L.Dujon	West Indies	79	265	5
269	A.P.E.Knott	England	95	250	19
265	B.J.Watling	New Zealand	67	257	8
256	M.J.Prior	England	79	243	13
241†	A.J.Stewart	England	82	227	14
232	Q.de Kock	South Africa	52	221	11
228	Wasim Bari	Pakistan	81	201	27
223†	J.M.Bairstow	England	55	209	14
219	R.D.Jacobs	West Indies	65	207	12
219	T.G.Evans	England	91	173	46
217	D.Ramdin	West Indies	74	205	12
206	Kamran Akmal	Pakistan	53	184	22
201†	A.C.Parore	New Zealand	67	194	7
198	S.M.H.Kirmani	India	88	160	38
189	D.L.Murray	West Indies	62	181	8
187	A.T.W.Grout	Australia	51	163	24
182	Sarfraz Ahmed	Pakistan	54	160	22
179†	B.B.McCullum	New Zealand	52	168	11
176	I.D.S.Smith	New Zealand	63	168	8
174	R.W.Taylor	England	57	167	7
165	R.C.Russell	England	54	153	12
160	D.P.D.N.Dickwella	Sri Lanka	53	133	27
157	T.D.Paine	Australia	35	150	7
156	H.A.P.W.Jayawardena	Sri Lanka	58	124	32
152	D.J.Richardson	South Africa	42	150	2
151†	K.C.Sangakkara	Sri Lanka	48	131	20
151†	A.Flower	Zimbabwe	55	142	9

The most for Bangladesh is 113 (98 ct, 15 st) by Mushfiqur Rahim in 84 Tests.
† *Excluding catches taken in the field*

25 OR MORE DISMISSALS IN A SERIES

29	B.J.Haddin	Australia v England	2013
28	R.W.Marsh	Australia v England	1982-83
27 (inc 2st)	R.C.Russell	England v South Africa	1995-96
27 (inc 2st)	I.A.Healy	Australia v England (6 Tests)	1997
26 (inc 3st)	J.H.B.Waite	South Africa v New Zealand	1961-62
26	R.W.Marsh	Australia v West Indies (6 Tests)	1975-76
26 (inc 5st)	I.A.Healy	Australia v England (6 Tests)	1993

26 (inc 1st)	M.V.Boucher	South Africa v England	1998
26 (inc 2st)	A.C.Gilchrist	Australia v England	2001
26 (inc 2st)	A.C.Gilchrist	Australia v England	2006-07
26 (inc 1st)	T.D.Paine	Australia v England	2017-18
26 (inc 5st)	A.T.Carey	Australia v England	2023
25 (inc 2st)	I.A.Healy	Australia v England	1994-95
25 (inc 2st)	A.C.Gilchrist	Australia v England	2002-03
25	A.C.Gilchrist	Australia v India	2007-08

TEN OR MORE DISMISSALS IN A TEST

11	R.C.Russell	England v South Africa	Johannesburg	1995-96
11	A.B.de Villiers	South Africa v Pakistan	Johannesburg	2012-13
11	R.R.Pant	India v Australia	Adelaide	2018-19
10	R.W.Taylor	England v India	Bombay	1979-80
10	A.C.Gilchrist	Australia v New Zealand	Hamilton	1999-00
10	W.P.Saha	India v South Africa	Cape Town	2017-18
10	Sarfraz Ahmed	Pakistan v South Africa	Johannesburg	2018-19

SEVEN DISMISSALS IN AN INNINGS

7	Wasim Bari	Pakistan v New Zealand	Auckland	1978-79
7	R.W.Taylor	England v India	Bombay	1979-80
7	I.D.S.Smith	New Zealand v Sri Lanka	Hamilton	1990-91
7	R.D.Jacobs	West Indies v Australia	Melbourne	2000-01
7	J.Da Silva	West Indies v South Africa	Centurion	2022-23

FIVE STUMPINGS IN AN INNINGS

5	K.S.More	India v West Indies	Madras	1987-88

FIELDING RECORDS – 100 CATCHES IN TESTS

Total			*Tests*
210	R.S.Dravid	India/ICC	164
205	D.P.M.D.Jayawardena	Sri Lanka	149
200	J.H.Kallis	South Africa/ICC	166
196	R.T.Ponting	Australia	168
192	J.E.Root	England	139
183	S.P.D.Smith	Australia	108
181	M.E.Waugh	Australia	128
175	A.N.Cook	England	161
171	S.P.Fleming	New Zealand	111
169	G.C.Smith	South Africa/ICC	117
164	B.C.Lara	West Indies/ICC	131
163	L.R.P.L.Taylor	New Zealand	112
157	M.A.Taylor	Australia	104
156	A.R.Border	Australia	156
139	Younus Khan	Pakistan	118
135	V.V.S.Laxman	India	134
134	M.J.Clarke	Australia	115
128	M.L.Hayden	Australia	103
125	S.K.Warne	Australia	145
122	G.S.Chappell	Australia	87
122	I.V.A.Richards	West Indies	121

Total			*Tests*
121†	A.B.de Villiers	South Africa	114
121	A.J.Strauss	England	100
120	I.T.Botham	England	102
120	M.C.Cowdrey	England	114
115	C.L.Hooper	West Indies	102
115	S.R.Tendulkar	India	200
112	S.R.Waugh	Australia	168
111	V.Kohli	India	113
110	R.B.Simpson	Australia	62
110	W.R.Hammond	England	85
109	G.St A.Sobers	West Indies	93
108	H.M.Amla	South Africa	124
108	S.M.Gavaskar	India	125
107	J.M.Anderson	England	186
106	B.A.Stokes	England	101
105	I.M.Chappell	Australia	75
105	M.Azharuddin	India	99
105	G.P.Thorpe	England	100
103	G.A.Gooch	England	118
102	A.M.Rahane	India	85
100	I.R.Bell	England	118

The most for Zimbabwe is 60 by A.D.R.Campbell (60) and for Bangladesh 39 by Mominul Haque (59).

† *Excluding catches taken when wicket-keeping.*

15 CATCHES IN A SERIES

15	J.M.Gregory	Australia v England	1920-21

SEVEN OR MORE CATCHES IN A TEST

8	A.M.Rahane	India v Sri Lanka	Galle	2015
7	G.S.Chappell	Australia v England	Perth	1974-75
7	Yajurvindra Singh	India v England	Bangalore	1976-77
7	H.P.Tillekeratne	Sri Lanka v New Zealand	Colombo (SSC)	1992-93
7	S.P.Fleming	New Zealand v Zimbabwe	Harare	1997-98
7	M.L.Hayden	Australia v Sri Lanka	Galle	2003-04
7	K.L.Rahul	India v England	Nottingham	2018

FIVE CATCHES IN AN INNINGS

5	V.Y.Richardson	Australia v South Africa	Durban	1935-36
5	Yajurvindra Singh	India v England	Bangalore	1976-77
5	M.Azharuddin	India v Pakistan	Karachi	1989-90
5	K.Srikkanth	India v Australia	Perth	1991-92
5	S.P.Fleming	New Zealand v Zimbabwe	Harare	1997-98
5	G.C.Smith	South Africa v Australia	Perth	2012-13
5	D.J.G.Sammy	West Indies v India	Mumbai	2013-14
5	D.M.Bravo	West Indies v Bangladesh	Kingstown	2014
5	A.M.Rahane	India v Sri Lanka	Galle	2015
5	J.Blackwood	West Indies v Sri Lanka	Colombo (PSS)	2015-16
5	S.P.D.Smith	Australia v South Africa	Cape Town	2017-18
5	B.A.Stokes	England v South Africa	Cape Town	2019-20
5	H.D.R.L.Thirimanne	Sri Lanka v England	Galle	2020-21
5	S.P.D.Smith	Australia v England	Leeds	2023

APPEARANCE RECORDS – 100 TEST MATCH APPEARANCES

			Opponents									
			E	*A*	*SA*	*WI*	*NZ*	*I*	*P*	*SL*	*Z*	*B*
200	S.R.Tendulkar	India	32	39	25	21	24	–	18	25	9	7
186	J.M.Anderson	England	–	39	29	22	20	38	20	14	2	2
168†	R.T.Ponting	Australia	35	–	26	24	17	29	15	14	3	4
168	S.R.Waugh	Australia	46	–	16	32	23	18	20	8	3	2
167*	S.C.J.Broad	England	–	40	25	19	23	24	19	12	–	3
166†	J.H.Kallis	South Africa/ICC	31	28	–	24	18	18	19	15	6	6
164	S.Chanderpaul	West Indies	35	20	24	–	21	25	14	7	8	10
164†	R.S.Dravid	India/ICC	21	32	21	23	15	–	15	20	9	7
161	A.N.Cook	England	–	35	19	20	15	30	20	16	–	6
156	A.R.Border	Australia	47	–	6	31	23	20	22	7	–	–
149	D.P.M.D.Jayawardena	Sri Lanka	23	16	18	11	13	18	29	–	8	13
147†	M.V.Boucher	South Africa/ICC	25	20	–	24	17	14	15	17	6	8
145†	S.K.Warne	Australia	36	–	24	19	20	14	15	13	1	2
139*	J.E.Root	England	–	34	15	14	18	29	15	10	–	2
134	V.V.S.Laxman	India	17	29	19	22	10	–	15	13	6	3
134	K.C.Sangakkara	Sri Lanka	22	11	17	12	12	17	23	–	5	15
133†	M.Muralitharan	Sri Lanka/ICC	16	12	15	12	14	22	16	–	14	11
133	A.J.Stewart	England	–	33	23	24	16	9	13	9	6	–
132	A.Kumble	India	19	20	21	17	11	–	15	18	7	4
132	C.A.Walsh	West Indies	36	38	10	–	10	15	18	3	2	–
131	Kapil Dev	India	27	20	4	25	10	–	29	14	2	–
131†	B.C.Lara	West Indies/ICC	30	30	18	–	11	17	12	8	2	2
128	N.M.Lyon	Australia	30	–	18	12	11	27	15	13	–	2
128	M.E.Waugh	Australia	29	–	18	28	14	14	15	9	1	–
125	S.M.Gavaskar	India	38	20	–	27	9	–	24	7	–	–

			Opponents									
			E	*A*	*SA*	*WI*	*NZ*	*I*	*P*	*SL*	*Z*	*B*
124	H.M.Amla	South Africa	21	21	–	9	14	21	14	14	2	8
124	Javed Miandad	Pakistan	22	24	–	17	18	28	–	12	3	–
124†	G.D.McGrath	Australia	30	–	17	23	14	11	17	8	1	2
121	I.V.A.Richards	West Indies	36	34	–	–	7	28	16	–	–	–
120†	Inzamam-ul-Haq	Pakistan/ICC	19	13	13	15	12	10	–	20	11	6
119	I.A.Healy	Australia	33	–	12	28	11	9	14	11	1	–
118	I.R.Bell	England	–	33	11	12	13	20	13	10	–	6
118	G.A.Gooch	England	–	42	3	26	15	19	10	3	–	–
118	Younus Khan	Pakistan	17	11	14	15	11	9	–	29	5	7
117	D.I.Gower	England	–	42	–	19	13	24	17	2	–	–
117†	G.C.Smith	South Africa/ICC	21	21	–	14	13	15	16	7	2	8
116	D.L.Haynes	West Indies	36	33	1	–	10	19	16	1	–	–
116	D.B.Vengsarkar	India	26	24	–	25	11	–	22	8	–	–
115	M.A.Atherton	England	–	33	18	27	11	7	11	4	4	–
115†	M.J.Clarke	Australia	35	–	14	12	11	22	10	8	–	2
114	M.C.Cowdrey	England	–	43	14	21	18	8	10	–	–	–
114	A.B.de Villiers	South Africa	20	24	–	13	10	20	12	7	4	4
113	S.C.Ganguly	India	12	24	17	12	8	–	12	14	9	5
113	V.Kohli	India	28	25	16	16	11	–	–	11	–	6
113†	D.L.Vettori	New Zealand/ICC	17	18	14	10	–	15	9	11	9	9
112	L.R.P.L.Taylor	New Zealand	19	12	8	14	–	17	15	12	4	11
112	D.A.Warner	Australia	33	–	15	10	10	21	13	8	–	2
111	S.P.Fleming	New Zealand	19	14	15	11	–	13	9	13	11	6
111	W.P.J.U.C.Vaas	Sri Lanka	15	12	11	9	10	14	18	–	15	7
110	S.T.Jayasuriya	Sri Lanka	14	13	15	10	13	10	17	–	13	5
110	C.H.Lloyd	West Indies	34	29	–	–	8	28	11	–	–	–
108	G.Boycott	England	–	38	7	29	15	13	6	–	–	–
108	C.G.Greenidge	West Indies	29	32	–	–	10	23	14	–	–	–
108	S.M.Pollock	South Africa	23	13	–	16	11	12	12	13	5	3
108	S.P.D.Smith	Australia	37	–	12	9	9	19	15	5	–	2
107	D.C.Boon	Australia	31	–	6	22	17	11	11	9	–	–
107*‡	A.D.Mathews	Sri Lanka	11	11	10	8	13	17	23	–	3	8
105†	J.L.Langer	Australia	21	–	11	18	14	14	13	8	3	2
105‡	I.Sharma	India	23	25	15	12	9	–	1	12	–	7
104	K.P.Pietersen	England	–	27	10	14	8	16	14	11	–	4
104†	V.Sehwag	India/ICC	17	23	15	10	12	–	9	11	3	4
104	M.A.Taylor	Australia	33	–	11	20	11	9	12	8	–	–
104	Wasim Akram	Pakistan	18	13	4	17	9	12	–	19	10	2
103	C.H.Gayle	West Indies	20	8	16	–	12	14	8	10	8	7
103	Harbhajan Singh	India	14	18	11	11	13	–	9	16	7	4
103†	M.L.Hayden	Australia	20	–	19	15	11	18	6	7	2	4
103‡	C.A.Pujara	India	27	25	17	9	12	–	–	7	–	5
103	Salim Malik	Pakistan	19	15	1	7	18	22	–	15	6	–
102	I.T.Botham	England	–	36	–	20	15	14	14	3	–	–
102	C.L.Hooper	West Indies	24	25	10	–	2	19	14	6	2	–
101	G.Kirsten	South Africa	22	18	–	13	13	10	11	9	3	2
101	B.B.McCullum	New Zealand	16	16	13	13	–	10	8	12	4	9
101	M.Ntini	South Africa	18	15	–	15	11	10	9	12	3	8
101§	B.A.Stokes	England	–	24	15	15	11	20	9	4	–	2
100	A.J.Strauss	England	–	20	16	18	9	12	13	8	–	4
100	G.P.Thorpe	England	–	16	16	27	13	5	8	9	2	4

† Includes one appearance in the Australia v ICC 'Test' in 2005-06; * includes two appearances v Ireland; ‡ includes one appearance v Afghanistan; § includes one appearance v Ireland. The most for Zimbabwe is 67 by G.W.Flower, and for Bangladesh 88 by Mushfiqur Rahim.

100 CONSECUTIVE TEST APPEARANCES

159	A.N.Cook	England	May 2006 to September 2018
153	A.R.Border	Australia	March 1979 to March 1994
107	M.E.Waugh	Australia	June 1993 to October 2002
106	S.M.Gavaskar	India	January 1975 to February 1987
101	B.B.McCullum	New Zealand	March 2004 to February 2016
100	N.M.Lyon	Australia	August 2013 to June 2023

50 TESTS AS CAPTAIN

			Won	*Lost*	*Drawn*	*Tied*
109	G.C.Smith	South Africa	53	29	27	–
93	A.R.Border	Australia	32	22	38	1
80	S.P.Fleming	New Zealand	28	27	25	–
77	R.T.Ponting	Australia	48	16	13	–
74	C.H.Lloyd	West Indies	36	12	26	–
68	V.Kohli	India	40	17	11	–
64	J.E.Root	England	27	26	11	–
60	M.S.Dhoni	India	27	18	15	–
59	A.N.Cook	England	24	22	13	–
57	S.R.Waugh	Australia	41	9	7	–
56	Misbah-ul-Haq	Pakistan	26	19	11	–
56	A.Ranatunga	Sri Lanka	12	19	25	–
54	M.A.Atherton	England	13	21	20	–
53	W.J.Cronje	South Africa	27	11	15	–
51	M.P.Vaughan	England	26	11	14	–
50	I.V.A.Richards	West Indies	27	8	15	–
50	M.A.Taylor	Australia	26	13	11	–
50	A.J.Strauss	England	24	11	15	–

The most for Zimbabwe is 21 by A.D.R.Campbell and H.H.Streak, and for Bangladesh 34 by Mushfiqur Rahim.

70 TEST UMPIRING APPEARANCES

145	Alim Dar	(Pakistan)	21.10.2003 to 07.04.2023
128	S.A.Bucknor	(West Indies)	28.04.1989 to 22.03.2009
108	R.E.Koertzen	(South Africa)	26.12.1992 to 24.07.2010
95	D.J.Harper	(Australia)	28.11.1998 to 23.06.2011
92	D.R.Shepherd	(England)	01.08.1985 to 07.06.2005
84	B.F.Bowden	(New Zealand)	11.03.2000 to 03.05.2015
84	R.J.Tucker	(Australia)	15.02.2010 to 26.02.2024
83	H.D.P.K.Dharmasena	(Sri Lanka)	04.11.2010 to 26.02.2024
82	R.A.Kettleborough	(England)	15.11.2010 to 01.03.2024
81	M.Erasmus	(South Africa)	17.01.2010 to 03.03.2024
78	D.B.Hair	(Australia)	25.01.1992 to 08.06.2008
74	I.J.Gould	(England)	19.11.2008 to 23.02.2019
74	S.J.A.Taufel	(Australia)	26.12.2000 to 20.08.2012
73	S.Venkataraghavan	(India)	29.01.1993 to 20.01.2004

THE FIRST-CLASS COUNTIES REGISTER, RECORDS AND 2023 AVERAGES

All statistics are to 10 March 2024.

ABBREVIATIONS – General

*	not out/unbroken partnership
b	born
BB	Best innings bowling analysis
Cap	Awarded 1st XI County Cap
f-c	first-class
HS	Highest Score
IT20	International Twenty20
l-o	limited-overs
LOI	Limited-Overs Internationals
Tests	International Test Matches
F-c Tours	Overseas tours involving first-class appearances

Awards

PCA 2023	Professional Cricketers' Association Player of 2023
Wisden 2022	One of *Wisden Cricketers' Almanack*'s Five Cricketers of 2022
YC 2023	Cricket Writers' Club Young Cricketer of 2023

ECB Competitions

CB40	Clydesdale Bank 40 (2010-12)
CC	County Championship
FPT	Friends Provident Trophy (2007-09)
MBC	Metro Bank One-Day Cup (2023)
P40	NatWest PRO 40 League (2006-09)
RLC	Royal London One-Day Cup (2014-2022)
T20	Twenty20 Competition
Y40	Yorkshire Bank 40 (2013)

Education

Ac	Academy
C	College
CS	Comprehensive School
GS	Grammar School
HS	High School
S	School
SFC	Sixth Form College
SS	Secondary School
U	University

Playing Categories

LBG	Bowls right-arm leg-breaks and googlies
LF	Bowls left-arm fast
LFM	Bowls left-arm fast-medium
LHB	Bats left-handed
LM	Bowls left-arm medium pace
LMF	Bowls left-arm medium fast
OB	Bowls right-arm off-breaks
RF	Bowls right-arm fast
RFM	Bowls right-arm fast-medium
RHB	Bats right-handed
RM	Bowls right-arm medium pace
RMF	Bowls right-arm medium-fast
SLA	Bowls left-arm leg-breaks
SLC	Bowls left-arm 'Chinamen'
WK	Wicket-keeper

Teams (see also p 223)

AS	Adelaide Strikers
BH	Brisbane Heat
CC&C	Combined Campuses & Colleges
CD	Central Districts
CSK	Chennai Super Kings
DC	Deccan Chargers
DCa	Delhi Capitals
DD	Delhi Daredevils
EL	England Lions
EP	Eastern Province
FS	Free State
GL	Gujarat Lions
GT	Gujarat Titans
HEC	Higher Education Commision
HH	Hobart Hurricanes
KKR	Kolkata Knight Riders
KRL	Khan Research Laboratories
KXIP	Kings XI Punjab
KZN	KwaZulu-Natal Inland
LSG	Lucknow Super Giants
ME	Mashonaland Eagles
MI	Mumbai Indians
MR	Melbourne Renegades
MS	Melbourne Stars
MT	Matabeleland Tuskers
MWR	Mid West Rhinos
ND	Northern Districts
NSW	New South Wales
NW	North West
PDSC	Prime Doleshwar Sporting Club
PK	Punjab Kings
PS	Perth Scorchers
PW	Pune Warriors
Q	Queensland
RCB	Royal Challengers Bangalore
RPS	Rising Pune Supergiant
RR	Rajasthan Royals
SA	South Australia
SH	Sunrisers Hyderabad
SJD	Sheikh Jamal Dhanmondi
SNGPL	Sui Northern Gas Pipelines Limited
SR	Southern Rocks
SS	Sydney Sixers
SSGC	Sui Southern Gas Corporation
ST	Sydney Thunder
Tas	Tasmania
T&T	Trinidad & Tobago
TU	Tamil Union
Vic	Victoria
WA	Western Australia
WAPDA	Water & power Developemnt Authority
WP	Western Province

DERBYSHIRE

Formation of Present Club: 4 November 1870
Inaugural First-Class Match: 1871
Colours: Chocolate, Amber and Pale Blue
Badge: Rose and Crown
County Champions: (1) 1936
NatWest Trophy Winners: (1) 1981
Benson and Hedges Cup Winners: (1) 1993
Sunday League Winners: (1) 1990
Twenty20 Cup Winners: (0) best – Semi-Finalist 2019

Chief Executive: Ryan Duckett, Derbyshire County Cricket Club, The Incora County Ground, Nottingham Road, Derby, DE21 6DA • Tel: 01332 388101 • Email: info@derbyshireccc.com • Web: www.derbyshireccc.com • Twitter: @DerbyshireCCC (77,937 followers)

Head of Cricket: Mickey Arthur. **Assistant Coaches**: Ajmal Shahzad (bowling) and Ben Smith (batting). **Captains**: D.L.Lloyd (f-c) and S.R.Patel (l-o). **Overseas Players**: Mohammad Amir and B.M.Tickner. **2024 Testimonial**: None. **Head Groundsman**: Neil Godrich. **Scorer**: Jane Hough. **Blast Team Name**: Derbyshire Falcons. ‡ New registration. NQ Not qualified for England.

AITCHISON, Benjamin William (Merchant Taylors' S; Ormskirk Range HS), b Southport, Lancs 6 Jul 1999. RHB, RFM. Squad No 14. Debut (Derbyshire) 2020. Lancashire 2nd XI 2019. Cheshire 2018-19. HS 50 v Notts (Derby) 2021. BB 6-28 v Durham (Derby) 2021. LO HS 19 v Surrey (Derby) 2021 (RLC). LO BB 4-39 v Hants (Derby) 2022 (RLC). T20 HS 2. T20 BB 2-30.

BROWN, Patrick Rhys (Bourne GS, Lincs), b Peterborough, Cambs 23 Aug 1998. 6'2". RHB, RMF. Squad No 36. Worcestershire 2017-18. Derbyshire debut 2023. Birmingham Phoenix 2021. Oval Invincibles 2022. Lincolnshire 2016. **IT20**: 4 (2019-20); HS 4* v NZ (Wellington) 2019-20; BB 1-29 v NZ (Napier) 2019-20. HS 5* Wo v Sussex (Worcester) 2017. De HS –. BB 2-15 Wo v Leics (Worcester) 2017. De BB 1-15 v Sussex (Derby) 2023. LO HS 3 Wo v Somerset (Worcester) 2019 (RLC). LO BB 4-51 v Worcs (Derby) 2023 (MBC). T20 HS 10*. T20 BB 4-21.

CAME, Harry Robert Charles (Bradfield C), b Basingstoke, Hants 27 Aug 1998. Son of P.R.C.Came (Hampshire 2nd XI 1986-87); grandson of K.C.Came (Free Foresters 1957); great-grandson of R.W.V.Robins (Middlesex, Cambridge U & England 1925-58). 5'9". RHB, OB. Squad No 4. Hampshire 2019-20. Derbyshire debut 2021. HS 141* v Glamorgan (Derby) 2023, sharing De record 1st wkt partnership of 360* with L.M.Reece. BB –. LO HS 94 v Sussex (Derby) 2021 (MBC). T20 HS 56.

CHAPPELL, Zachariah John ('**Zak**') (Stamford S), b Grantham, Lincs 21 Aug 1996. 6'4". RHB, RFM. Squad No 32. Leicestershire 2015-18. Nottinghamshire 2019-21. Gloucestershire 2022 (on loan); cap 2022. Derbyshire debut 2023. Oval Invincibles 2023. HS 96 Le v Derbys (Derby) 2015. De HS 46 and De BB 5-69 v Worcs (Derby) 2023. BB 6-44 Le v Northants (Northampton) 2018. LO HS 59* Le v Durham (Gosforth) 2017 (RLC). LO BB 3-35 Nt v Somerset (Taunton) 2022 (RLC). T20 HS 16. T20 BB 4-33.

CONNERS, Samuel (George Spencer Ac), b Nottingham 13 Feb 1999. 6'0". RHB, RM. Squad No 59. Debut (Derbyshire) 2019; cap 2022. HS 39 v Kent (Derby) 2021. 50 wkts (1): 50 (2022). BB 5-51 v Durham (Leicester) 2022. LO HS 36* v Somerset (Derby) 2023 (MBC). LO BB 5-28 v Yorks (Chesterfield) 2022 (RLC). T20 HS 2*. T20 BB 3-25.

DAL, Anuj Kailash (Durban HS; Nottingham HS), b Newcastle-upon-Tyne, Northumb 8 Jul 1996. 5'9". RHB, RM. Squad No 65. Debut (Derbyshire) 2018; cap 2022. HS 146* v Sussex (Hove) 2022. BB 6-69 v Glos (Bristol) 2023. LO HS 110 v Somerset (Derby) 2023 (MBC). LO BB 1-16 v Worcs (Worcester) 2022 (RLC). T20 HS 35.

DONALD, Aneurin Henry Thomas (Pontarddulais CS), b Swansea, Glamorgan 20 Dec 1996. 6'2". RHB, WK, occ OB. Squad No 12. Glamorgan 2014-18. Hampshire 2019-22. Wales MC 2012. 1000 runs (1): 1088 (2016). HS 234 Gm v Derbys (Colwyn Bay) 2016, in 123 balls, equalling world record for fastest 200, inc 15 sixes, going from 0-127* between lunch and tea, and 127-234 after tea. LO HS 115 H v Worcs (Southampton) 2023 (MBC). T20 HS 76.

GUEST, Brooke David (Kent Street Senior HS, Perth, WA; Murdoch U, Perth), b Whitworth Park, Manchester, Lancs 14 May 1997. 5'11". RHB, WK. Squad No 29. Lancashire 2018-19. Derbyshire debut 2020; cap 2022. HS 197 v Durham (Derby) 2023. LO HS 88 v Essex (Chelmsford) 2022 (RLC). T20 HS 54.

LAMB, Matthew James (North Bromsgrove HS; Bromsgrove S), b Wolverhampton, Staffs 19 July 1996. 6'1". RHB, RM. Squad No 7. Warwickshire 2016-22. Derbyshire debut 2023. HS 173 and BB 2-38 Wa v Worcs (Worcester) 2021. De HS 99 v Durham (Chester-le-St) 2023. De BB –. LO HS 119* Wa v Leics (Birmingham) 2021 (RLC). LO BB 4-35 Wa v Somerset (Birmingham) 2021 (RLC). T20 HS 39.

LLOYD, David Liam (Darland HS; Shrewsbury S), b St Asaph, Denbighs 15 May 1992. 5'9". RHB, RM. Squad No 46. Glamorgan 2012-23; cap 2019; captain 2022-23. Joins Derbyshire in 2024 as captain. Welsh Fire 2021. Wales MC 2010-11. HS 313* Gm v Derbys (Cardiff) 2022. BB 4-11 Gm v Kent (Cardiff) 2021. LO HS 92 Gm v Middx (Cardiff) 2018 (RLC). LO BB 5-53 Gm v Kent (Swansea) 2017 (RLC). T20 HS 97*. T20 BB 2-13.

NQ**MADSEN, Wayne** Lee (Kearsney C, Durban; U of South Africa), b Durban, South Africa 2 Jan 1984. Nephew of M.B.Madsen (Natal 1967-68 to 1978-79), T.R.Madsen (Natal 1976-77 to 1989-90) and H.R.Fotheringham (Natal, Transvaal 1971-72 to 1989-90), cousin of G.S.Fotheringham (KwaZulu-Natal 2008-09 to 2009-10). 5'11". RHB, OB. Squad No 77. KwaZulu-Natal 2003-04 to 2007-08. Dolphins 2006-07 to 2007-08. Derbyshire debut 2009, scoring 170 v Glos (Cheltenham); cap 2011; captain 2012-15; testimonial 2017. Manchester Originals 2022 to date. Qualified for England by residence in February 2015. **IT20** (Italy): 4 (2023); HS 52 v Jersey (Edinburgh) 2023. 1000 runs (6); most – 1292 (2016). HS 231* v Northants (Northampton) 2012. BB 3-45 KZN v EP (Pt Elizabeth) 2007-08. De BB 2-8 v Sussex (Hove) 2021. LO HS 138 v Hants (Derby) 2014 (RLC). LO BB 3-27 v Durham (Derby) 2013 (Y40). T20 HS 109*. T20 BB 2-20.

‡NQ**MOHAMMAD AMIR**, b Gujar Khan, Punjab, Pakistan 13 Apr 1992. LHB, LF. Squad No 5. Federal Areas 2008-09. National Bank 2008-09 to 2009-10. SSGC 2015-16 to 2018-19. Essex 2017-19. Gloucestershire 2022; cap 2022. London Spirit 2021. **Tests** (P): 36 (2009 to 2018-19); HS 48 v A (Brisbane) 2016-17; BB 6-44 v WI (Kingston) 2017. **LOI** (P): 61 (2009 to 2019-20); HS 73* v NZ (Abu Dhabi) 2009-10; BB 5-30 v A (Taunton) 2019. **IT20** (P): 50 (2009 to 2020); HS 21* v A (Birmingham) 2010; BB 4-13 v SL (Lahore) 2017-18. F-c Tours (P): E 2010, 2016, 2018; A 2009-10, 2016-17; SA 2018-19; WI 2017; NZ 2009-10, 2016-17; WI 2017; SL 2009; Ire 2018. HS 66 SSGC v Lahore Blues (Lahore) 2015-16. CC HS 28 Ex v Kent (Canterbury) 2019. 50 wkts (0+1): 56 (2008-09). BB 7-61 (10-97 match) NBP v Lahore Shalimar (Lahore) 2008-09. CC BB 5-18 (10-72 match) Ex v Yorks (Scarborough) 2017. LO HS 73* (*see LOI*). LO BB 5-30 (*see LOI*). T20 HS 21*. T20 BB 6-17.

MOORE, Harry John (Repton S), b Derby 26 Apr 2007. RHB, RFM. Awaiting f-c debut. Derbyshire 2nd XI debut 2023. LO HS 2 v Worcs (Derby) 2023 (MBC). LO BB 1-43 v Northants (Northampton) 2023 (MBC).

‡**PATEL, Samit** Rohit (Worksop C), b Leicester 30 Nov 1984. Elder brother of A.Patel (Derbyshire and Notts 2007-11). 5'8". RHB, SLA. Nottinghamshire 2002-22; cap 2008; testimonial 2017. Glamorgan 2019 (on loan). Joins Derbyshire in 2024 as l-o captain. Big Bash: MR 2019-20. Trent Rockets 2021 to date. MCC 2014, 2016. PCA 2017. **Tests**: 6 (2011-12 to 2015-16); HS 42 v P (Sharjah) 2015-16; BB 2-27 v SL (Galle) 2011-12. **LOI**: 36 (2008 to 2012-13); HS 70* v I (Mohali) 2011-12; BB 5-41 v SA (Oval) 2008. **IT20**: 18 (2011 to 2012-13); HS 67 v SL (Pallekele) 2012-13; BB 2-6 v Afg (Colombo, RPS) 2012-13. F-c Tours: NZ 2008-09 (Eng A); I 2012-13; SL 2011-12; UAE 2015-16 (v P). 1000 runs (2); most – 1125 (2014). HS 257* Nt v Glos (Bristol) 2017. BB 7-68 (11-111 match) Nt v Hants (Southampton) 2011. LO HS 136* Nt v Northants (Northampton) 2019 (RLC). LO BB 6-13 Nt v Ireland (Dublin) 2009 (FPT). T20 HS 90*. T20 BB 4-5.

POTTS, Nicholas James (De Ferrers Ac), b Burton-on-Trent, Staffs 17 Jul 2002. RHB, RFM. Squad No 26. Debut (Derbyshire) 2022. Derbyshire 2nd XI debut 2018. HS 13 v Leics (Derby) 2022. BB 4-50 v Notts (Nottingham) 2022. LO HS 6* and LO BB 2-63 v Worcs (Worcester) 2022 (RLC).

REECE, Luis Michael (St Michael's HS, Chorley; Leeds Met U), b Taunton, Somerset 4 Aug 1990. 6'1". LHB, LM. Squad No 10. Leeds/Bradford MCCU 2012-13. Lancashire 2013-15. Derbyshire debut 2017; cap 2019. MCC 2014. Unicorns 2011-12. London Spirit 2021. 1000 runs (1): 1048 (2023). HS 201* (and 131) v Glamorgan (Derby) 2023, sharing De record 1st wkt partnership of 360* with H.R.C.Came – also scored 139 & 119* v Glamorgan (Cardiff) to become the first batter ever to score four hundreds against the same opposition in a season. 50 wkts (1): 55 (2019). BB 7-20 v Glos (Derby) 2018. LO HS 136 v Worcs (Worcester) 2022 (RLC). LO BB 4-35 Unicorns v Glos (Exmouth) 2011 (CB40). T20 HS 97*. T20 BB 3-33.

THOMSON, Alexander Thomas (Kings S, Macclesfield; Denstone C; Cardiff Met U), b Macclesfield, Cheshire 30 Oct 1993. 6'2". RHB, OB. Squad No 15. Cardiff MCCU 2014-16. Warwickshire 2017-20. Derbyshire debut 2021. Staffordshire 2013-16. F-c Tour (MCC): Nepal 2019-20. HS 54 v Worcs (Derby) 2022. BB 6-138 CfU v Hants (Southampton) 2016. De BB 5-110 v Sussex (Hove) 2023. LO HS 68* Wa v Derbys (Derby) 2019 (RLC). LO BB 3-25 v Lancs (Manchester) 2022 (RLC). T20 HS 28. T20 BB 4-35.

‡NQ**TICKNER, Blair** Marshall, b Napier, New Zealand 13 Oct 1993. RHB, RMF. Central Districts 2014-15 to date. **Tests** (NZ): 3 (2022-23); HS 8 v E (Mt Maunganui) 2022-23; BB 4-100 v SL (Christchurch) 2022-23. **LOI** (NZ): 13 (2021-22 to 2023); HS 6* v SL (Auckland) 2022-23; BB 4-50 v Neth (Mt Maunganui) 2021-22. **IT20** (NZ): 18 (2018-19 to 2023); HS 5* v E (Napier) 2019-20; BB 4-27 v Neth (Hague) 2022. F-c Tour (NZ A): UAE (v P A) 2018-19. HS 42 CD v ND (Mt Maunganui) 2023-24. BB 5-23 CD v Canterbury (Napier) 2017-18. LO HS 24* CD v ND (Lincoln) 2019-20. LO BB 4-37 CD v Auckland (Palmerston N) 2021-22. T20 HS 22. T20 BB 5-19.

WAGSTAFF, Mitchell David (John Port S), b Derby 2 Sep 2003. LHB, LB. Squad No 22. Debut (Derbyshire) 2023. Derbyshire 2nd XI debut 2019. HS 78 v Glamorgan (Cardiff) 2023. BB 2-59 v Yorks (Scarborough) 2023. LO HS 36 v Surrey (Derby) 2021 (RLC).

WHITELEY, Ross Andrew (Repton S), b Sheffield, Yorks 13 Sep 1988. 6'2". LHB, LM. Squad No 44. Debut (Derbyshire) 2008. Worcestershire 2013-21; cap 2013. Hampshire 2022. Southern Brave 2021-22. Oval Invincibles 2023. HS 130* v Kent (Derby) 2011. BB 2-6 v Hants (Derby) 2012. LO HS 131 Wo v Leics (Leicester) 2019 (RLC). LO BB 4-58 Wo v West Indies A (Worcester) 2018. T20 HS 91*. T20 BB 2-2.

RELEASED/RETIRED

(Having made a County 1st XI appearance in 2023, even if not formally contracted. Some may return in 2024.)

DU PLOOY, J.L. – *see MIDDLESEX*.

GODLEMAN, Billy Ashley (Islington Green S), b Islington, London 11 Feb 1989. 6'3". LHB, LB. Middlesex 2005-09. Essex 2010-12. Derbyshire 2013-23; cap 2015; captain 2016-22. F-c Tour (MCC): Nepal 2019-20. 1000 runs (2); most – 1087 (2019). HS 227 v Glamorgan (Swansea) 2016. BB –. LO HS 137 v Warwks (Birmingham) 2018 (RLC). T20 HS 92.

NQ**HAIDER ALI**, b Attock, Punjab, Pakistan 2 Oct 2000. RHB, OB. Northern 2019-20 to 2021-22. Derbyshire 2023. Rawalpindi 2023-24. **LOI** (P): 2 (2020-21); HS 29 v Z (Rawalpindi) 2020-21. **IT20** (P): 35 (2020 to 2023-24); HS 68 v WI (Karachi) 2021-22. HS 206 Northern v Central Punjab (Karachi) 2021-22. De HS 146 v Yorks (Chesterfield) 2023. BB –. LO HS 118 P U23 v Oman (Cox's Bazar) 2019-20. T20 HS 91*.

NQ**LAKMAL**, Ranasinghe Arachchige **Suranga**, b Matara, Sri Lanka 10 Mar 1987. RHB, RMF. Tamil Union 2007-08 to 2020. Derbyshire 2022-23. **Tests** (SL): 70 (2010-11 to 2021-22); HS 42 v B (Colombo, PSS) 2016-17; BB 5-47 v WI (North Sound) 2020-21. **LOI** (SL): 86 (2009-10 to 2020-21); HS 26 v P (Cardiff) 2017; BB 4-13 v I (Dharamsala) 2017-18. **IT20** (SL): 11 (2011 to 2018-19); HS 5* v I (Colombo, RPS) 2017-18; BB 2-26 v E (Bristol) 2011. F-c Tours (SL): E 2011, 2016; A 2011-12, 2018-19; SA 2008-09 (SL A), 2016-17, 2018-19; WI 2013 (SL A), 2018, 2020-21; NZ 2014-15, 2015-16, 2018-19; I 2017-18, 2021-22; Z 2016-17, 2019-20; B 2013-14; UAE (v P) 2011-12, 2013-14, 2017-18. HS 58* TU v SL Navy (Welisara) 2012-13. De HS 12* v Yorks (Chesterfield) 2023. BB 6-68 TU v Nondescripts (Colombo, NCC) 2012-13. De BB 5-82 v Glamorgan (Derby) 2022. LO HS 38* SL A v The Rest (Pallekele) 2013. LO BB 5-31 TU v Nondescripts (Colombo, NCC) 2008-09. T20 HS 33. T20 BB 5-34.

McKIERNAN, Matthew Harry ('**Mattie**') (Lowton HS; St John Rigby C, Wigan), b Billinge, Lancs 14 Jun 1994. 6'0". RHB, LB. Derbyshire 2019-22. Cumberland 2016-17. HS 101 v Leics (Leicester) 2022. BB 2-3 v Notts (Nottingham) 2020. LO HS 72* v Essex (Chelmsford) 2022 (RLC). LO BB 1-14 v Northants (Northampton) 2022 (RLC). T20 HS 26. T20 BB 3-9.

SCRIMSHAW, G.L.S. – *see NORTHAMPTONSHIRE*.

NQ**WATT, Mark** Robert James, b Edinburgh, Scotland 29 Jul 1996. LHB, SLA. Scotland 2016 to 2017-18. Derbyshire 2022-23; l-o debut 2019. Lancashire 2018 (T20 only). **LOI** (Scot): 63 (2016 to 2023-24); HS 47 v Ire (Bulawayo) 2023; BB 5-33 v UAE (Aberdeen) 2022. **IT20** (Scot): 58 (2015 to 2023); HS 31* v Jersey (Edinburgh) 2023; BB 5-27 v Netherlands (Dubai, ICCA) 2015-16. HS 81* Scot v PNG (Port Moresby) 2017-18. De HS 55* v Sussex (Hove) 2022. BB 5-83 v Yorks (Chesterfield) 2023. LO HS 47 (*see LOI*). LO BB 5-33 (*see LOI*). T20 HS 31*. T20 BB 5-27.

WOOD, Thomas Anthony (Heanor Gate Science C), b Derby 11 May 1994. 6'3". RHB, RM. Derbyshire 2016-23. HS 31 v Notts (Derby) 2020. LO HS 109 v Notts (Derby) 2021 (RLC). LO BB 1-13 v Surrey (Derby) 2021 (RLC). T20 HS 110*. T20 BB 1-17.

NQ**ZAMAN KHAN**, b Mirpur, Pakistan 10 Sep 2001. RHB, RF. Awaiting f-c debut. Northern l-o debut 2021-22. Lahore Qalanders debut 2021-22. Derbyshire 2023 (T20 only). Big Bash: ST 2023-24. Manchester Originals 2023. **LOI** (P): 1 (2023); BB –. **IT20** (P): 9 (2022-23 to 2023-24); HS 8* v Afg (Sharjah) 2022-23; BB 1-4 v NZ (Christchurch) 2023-24. LO HS 14* Northern v Sindh (Islamabad) 2021-22. LO BB 2-47 Northern v Sindh (Islamabad) 2021-22 – separate matches. T20 HS 8*. T20 BB 4-16.

A.Harrison left the staff without making a County 1st XI appearance in 2023.

DERBYSHIRE 2023

RESULTS SUMMARY

	Place	Won	Lost	Drew	Tied
LV= Insurance County Champ (Div 2)	6th		4	10	
Metro Bank One-Day Cup (Group B)	8th	2	6		
Vitality Blast (North Group)	5th	6	7		1

LV= INSURANCE COUNTY CHAMPIONSHIP AVERAGES
BATTING AND FIELDING

Cap		*M*	*I*	*NO*	*HS*	*Runs*	*Avge*	*100*	*50*	*Ct/St*
2019	L.M.Reece	11	19	7	201*	1048	87.33	4	5	3
2022	J.L.du Plooy	14	21	6	238*	1236	82.40	4	4	5
2011	W.L.Madsen	12	17	–	143	779	45.82	1	7	31
	H.R.C.Came	11	18	2	141*	695	43.43	2	4	4
2022	B.D.Guest	14	21	–	197	741	35.28	2	2	37
2015	B.A.Godleman	3	5	–	86	166	33.20	–	2	2
	M.D.Wagstaff	3	5	–	78	165	33.00	–	2	2
	Haider Ali	10	16	1	146	481	32.06	1	3	8
2022	A.K.Dal	10	13	1	141*	295	24.58	1	–	9/1
	Z.J.Chappell	10	11	2	46	220	24.44	–	–	1
	A.T.Thomson	10	12	2	44	229	22.90	–	–	4
	M.J.Lamb	9	13	–	99	280	21.53	–	1	5
	G.L.S.Scrimshaw	3	5	4	19*	20	20.00	–	–	3
	R.A.S.Lakmal	4	6	4	12*	30	15.00	–	–	1
	M.R.J.Watt	5	6	1	19	72	14.40	–	–	2
2022	S.Conners	12	13	3	34	139	13.90	–	–	3
	B.W.Aitchison	5	6	–	26	56	9.33	–	–	2

Also played: H.J.H.Brookes (2 matches) 13*, 19* (1 ct); P.R.Brown (3) 0 (1 ct); C.McKerr (1) did not bat; N.J.Potts (2) 2*; T.A.Wood (1) 15.

BOWLING

	O	*M*	*R*	*W*	*Avge*	*Best*	*5wI*	*10wM*
L.M.Reece	161	31	612	20	30.60	3- 47	–	–
A.K.Dal	209.1	37	709	22	32.22	6- 69	3	–
M.R.J.Watt	142.5	28	498	15	33.20	5- 83	1	–
A.T.Thomson	335.3	55	1111	31	35.83	5-110	2	–
Z.J.Chappell	240.2	44	869	24	36.20	5- 69	1	–
S.Conners	318	49	1216	27	45.03	5-115	1	–
Also bowled:								
H.J.H.Brookes	54	10	150	9	16.66	6- 20	1	–
G.L.S.Scrimshaw	59	8	269	9	29.88	5- 49	1	–
R.A.S.Lakmal	113	15	437	8	54.62	3- 77	–	–
B.W.Aitchison	112.5	18	481	8	60.12	3-131	–	–

P.R.Brown 43.3-2-190-3; J.L.du Plooy 30-3-104-0; M.J.Lamb 22-5-83-0; C.McKerr 35.5-8-109-2; N.J.Potts 33-2-182-3; M.D.Wagstaff 31-5-88-2.

Derbyshire played no first-class fixtures outside the County Championship in 2023. The First-Class Averages (pp 223–235) give the records of Derbyshire players in all first-class county matches, with the exceptions of H.J.H.Brookes and C.McKerr, whose first-class figures for Derbyshire are as above.

DERBYSHIRE RECORDS

FIRST-CLASS CRICKET

Highest Total	For 801-8d		v	Somerset	Taunton	2007
	V 677-7d		by	Yorkshire	Leeds	2013
Lowest Total	For 16		v	Notts	Nottingham	1879
	V 23		by	Hampshire	Burton upon T	1958
Highest Innings	For 274	G.A.Davidson	v	Lancashire	Manchester	1896
	V 343*	P.A.Perrin	for	Essex	Chesterfield	1904

Highest Partnership for each Wicket

1st	360*	H.R.C.Came/L.M.Reece	v	Glamorgan	Derby	2023
2nd	417	K.J.Barnett/T.A.Tweats	v	Yorkshire	Derby	1997
3rd	316*	A.S.Rollins/K.J.Barnett	v	Leics	Leicester	1997
4th	328	P.Vaulkhard/D.Smith	v	Notts	Nottingham	1946
5th	302*†	J.E.Morris/D.G.Cork	v	Glos	Cheltenham	1993
6th	258*	J.L.du Plooy/A.K.Dal	v	Worcs	Worcester	2023
7th	258	M.P.Dowman/D.G.Cork	v	Durham	Derby	2000
8th	198	K.M.Krikken/D.G.Cork	v	Lancashire	Manchester	1996
9th	283	A.Warren/J.Chapman	v	Warwicks	Blackwell	1910
10th	132	A.Hill/M.Jean-Jacques	v	Yorkshire	Sheffield	1986

† *346 runs were added for this wicket in two separate partnerships*

Best Bowling	For	10- 40	W.Bestwick	v	Glamorgan	Cardiff	1921
(Innings)	V	10- 45	R.L.Johnson	for	Middlesex	Derby	1994
Best Bowling	For	17-103	W.Mycroft	v	Hampshire	Southampton	1876
(Match)	V	16-101	G.Giffen	for	Australians	Derby	1886

Most Runs – Season	2165	D.B.Carr	(av 48.11)	1959
Most Runs – Career	23854	K.J.Barnett	(av 41.12)	1979-98
Most 100s – Season	8	P.N.Kirsten		1982
Most 100s – Career	53	K.J.Barnett		1979-98
Most Wkts – Season	168	T.B.Mitchell	(av 19.55)	1935
Most Wkts – Career	1670	H.L.Jackson	(av 17.11)	1947-63
Most Career W-K Dismissals	1304	R.W.Taylor	(1157 ct; 147 st)	1961-84
Most Career Catches in the Field	563	D.C.Morgan		1950-69

LIMITED-OVERS CRICKET

Highest Total	**50ov**	366-4		v	Comb Univs	Oxford	1991
	40ov	321-5		v	Essex	Leek	2013
	T20	231-4		v	Leics	Derby	2023
Lowest Total	**50ov**	73		v	Lancashire	Derby	1993
	40ov	60		v	Kent	Canterbury	2008
	T20	72		v	Leics	Derby	2013
Highest Innings	**50ov**	173*	M.J.Di Venuto	v	Derbys CB	Derby	2000
	40ov	141*	C.J.Adams	v	Kent	Chesterfield	1992
	T20	111	W.J.Durston	v	Notts	Nottingham	2010
Best Bowling	**50ov**	8-21	M.A.Holding	v	Sussex	Hove	1988
	40ov	6- 7	M.Hendrick	v	Notts	Nottingham	1972
	T20	5-27	T.Lungley	v	Leics	Leicester	2009

DURHAM

Formation of Present Club: 23 May 1882
Inaugural First-Class Match: 1992
Colours: Navy Blue, Yellow and Maroon
Badge: Coat of Arms of the County of Durham
County Champions: (3) 2008, 2009, 2013
Friends Provident Trophy Winners: (1) 2007
Royal London One-Day Cup Winners: (1) 2014
Twenty20 Cup Winners: (0); best – Finalist 2016

Chief Executive: Tim Bostock, Seat Unique Riverside, Chester-le-Street, Co Durham DH3 3QR • Tel: 0191 387 1717 • Email: reception@durhamcricket.co.uk • Web: www.durhamcricket.co.uk • Twitter: @DurhamCricket (93,015 followers)

Director of Cricket: Marcus North. **Head Coach**: Ryan Campbell. **Bowling Coach**: Graham Onions. **Assistant Coaches**: Alan Walker and Will Gidman. **Captain**: S.G.Borthwick. **Overseas Players**: D.G.Bedingham, S.M.Boland and A.J.Turner. **2024 Testimonial**: None. **Head Groundsman**: Vic Demain. **Scorer**: William Dobson. **Blast Team Name**: Durham Jets. ‡ New registration. [NQ] Not qualified for England.

Durham revised their capping system in 2020 and now award players with their County Caps when they make their first-class debut.

‡[NQ]**ACKERMANN, Colin** Neil (Grey HS, Port Elizabeth; U of SA), b George, South Africa 4 Apr 1991. 6'1". RHB, OB. Squad No 48. Eastern Province 2010-11 to 2015-16. Warriors 2013-14 to 2018-19. Leicestershire 2017-23; cap 2019; captain 2020-22. Durham debut 2023-24. Manchester Originals 2021-22. Southern Brave 2023. **LOI** (Neth): 16 (2021-22 to 2023-24); HS 81 v Afg (Doha) 2021-22; BB 2-39 v P (Hyderabad) 2023-24. **IT20** (Neth): 22 (2019-20 to 2022-23); HS 62 v B (Hobart) 2022-23; BB 1-6 v Bermuda (Dubai, DSC) 2019-20. 1000 runs (0+1): 1200 (2013-14). HS 277* Le v Sussex (Hove) 2022, sharing Le and CC record 5th wkt partnership of 477* with P.W.A.Mulder. Du HS 130 and Du BB 1-5 v Zimbabwe A (Harare) 2023-24. BB 5-69 Le v Sussex (Hove) 2019. LO HS 152* Le v Worcs (Leicester) 2019 (RLC). LO BB 4-48 Warriors v Dolphins (Durban) 2017-18. T20 HS 90*. T20 BB 7-18 v Warwks (Leicester) 2019 – 2nd best T20 figures in world.

[NQ]**BEDINGHAM, David** Guy, b George, Cape Province, South Africa 22 Apr 1994. 5'9". RHB, OB, occ WK. Squad No 5. Western Province 2012-13 to date. Boland 2015-16 to 2018-19. Cape Cobras 2018-19 to 2019-20. Durham debut/cap 2020. Birmingham Phoenix 2021. **Tests** (SA): 4 (2023-24); HS 110 v NZ (Hamilton) 2023-24. F-c Tour (SA): NZ 2023-24. 1000 runs (2); most – 1029 (2021). HS 257 v Derbys (Chester-le-St) 2021. BB –. LO HS 152 v Warwks (Birmingham) 2023. LO BB –. T20 HS 73.

‡[NQ]**BOLAND, Scott** Michael, b Melbourne, Australia 11 Apr 1989. RHB, RFM. Victoria 2011-12 to date. IPL: RPS 2016. Big Bash: MS 2013-14 to date; HH 2019-20 to 2021-22. **Tests** (A): 10 (2021-22 to 2023); HS 20 v E (Birmingham) 2023; BB 6-7 v E (Melbourne) 2021-22. **LOI** (A): 14 (2015-16 to 2016-17); HS 4 v SA (Cape Town) 2016-17; BB 3-67 v SA (Centurion) 2016-17. **IT20** (A): 4 (2015-16 to 2016); HS – ; BB 3-26 v SL (Pallekele) 2016. F-c Tours (A): E 2023; I 2022-23; SL 2022 (Aus A). HS 51 Vic v Tas (Hobart) 2013-14 and 51 Vic v Tas (Hobart) 2015-16. BB 7-31 Vic v WA (Perth) 2015-16. LO HS 19 Vic v SA (Melbourne) 2011-12. LO BB 5-63 Vic v SA (Melbourne) 2012-13. T20 HS 10. T20 BB 4-30.

BORTHWICK, Scott George (Farringdon Community Sports C, Sunderland), b Sunderland 19 Apr 1990. 5'9". LHB, LBG. Squad No 16. Debut (Durham) 2009; cap 2009; captain 2021 to date. Chilaw Marians 2014-15. Wellington 2015-16 to 2016-17. Surrey 2017-20; cap 2018. **Tests**: 1 (2013-14); HS 4 and BB 3-33 v A (Sydney) 2013-14. **LOI**: 2 (2011 to 2011-12); HS 15 v Ire (Dublin) 2011; BB –. **IT20**: 1 (2011); HS 14 and BB 1-15 v WI (Oval) 2011. F-c Tours: A 2013-14; SL 2013-14 (EL). 1000 runs (5); most – 1390 (2015). HS 216 v Middx (Chester-le-St) 2014, sharing Du record 2nd wkt partnership of 274 with M.D.Stoneman. BB 6-70 v Surrey (Oval) 2013. LO HS 88 v Somerset (Taunton) 2022 (RLC). LO BB 5-38 v Leics (Leicester) 2015 (RLC). T20 HS 62. T20 BB 4-18.

BUSHNELL, Jonathan James (Durham S), b Durham 6 Sep 2001. 6'1". RHB, RM. Squad No 20. Debut (Durham) 2022; cap 2022. Durham 2nd XI debut 2019. HS 66 and CC BB 1-15 v Worcs (Chester-le-St) 2022. BB 1-9 v Zimbabwe A (Harare) 2023-24. LO HS 60* v Worcs (Chester-le-St) 2023 (MBC). LO BB 3-56 v Warwks (Birmingham) 2023 (MBC). T20 HS 40*. T20 BB 1-6.

CARSE, Brydon Alexander (Pearson HS, Pt Elizabeth), b Port Elizabeth, South Africa 31 Jul 1995. Son of J.A.Carse (Rhodesia, W Province, E Province, Northants, Border, Griqualand W 1977-78 to 1992-93). 6'1½". RHB, RF. Squad No 99. Debut (Durham) 2016; cap 2016. Northern Superchargers 2021 to date. **ECB Two-Year Central Contract from 2023-24**. **LOI**: 14 (2021 to 2023-24); HS 32 v Ire (Nottingham) 2023; BB 5-61 v P (Birmingham) 2021. **IT20**: 3 (2023); HS 0*; BB 3-23 v NZ (Chester-le-St) 2023. F-c Tour (EL): A 2019-20; I 2023-24. HS 108* v Derbys (Chester-le-St) 2023. BB 6-26 v Middx (Lord's) 2019. LO HS 32 (*see LOI*). LO BB 5-61 (*see LOI*). T20 HS 58. T20 BB 3-23.

CLARK, Graham (St Benedict's Catholic HS, Whitehaven), b Whitehaven, Cumbria 16 Mar 1993. Younger brother of J.Clark (*see SURREY*). 6'1". RHB, LB. Squad No 7. Debut (Durham) 2015; cap 2015. HS 128 v Sussex (Chester-le-St) 2023. BB 1-10 v Sussex (Arundel) 2018. LO HS 141* v Kent (Beckenham) 2021 (RLC). LO BB 3-18 v Leics (Leicester) 2018 (RLC). T20 HS 102*. T20 BB –.

COUGHLIN, Paul (St Robert of Newminster Catholic CS, Washington), b Sunderland 23 Oct 1992. Elder brother of J.Coughlin (Durham 2016-19); nephew of T.Harland (Durham 1974-78). 6'3". RHB, RM. Squad No 23. Debut (Durham) 2012; cap 2012. Nottinghamshire 2019. Northumberland 2011. F-c Tour (EL): WI 2017-18. HS 100* v Worcs (Chester-le-St) 2022. BB 5-49 (10-133 match) v Northants (Chester-le-St) 2017. LO HS 77 v Glos (Chester-le-St) 2022 (RLC). LO BB 3-36 v Worcs (Worcester) 2017 (RLC). T20 HS 53. T20 BB 5-42.

NQ**De LEEDE, Bas**tiaan Franciscus Wilhelmus (St Maartens C), b Nootdorp, Netherlands 15 Nov 1999. Son of T.B.M.de Leede (Netherlands 1995 to 2006-07). 5'9". RHB, RMF. Squad No 27. Netherlands 2017-18. Durham debut/cap 2023. MCC YC 2019. **LOI** (Neth): 43 (2018 to 2023-24); HS 123 and BB 5-52 v Scot (Bulawayo) 2023 only the 4th to score a hundred and take five wkts in an LOI. **IT20** (Neth): 31 (2018 to 2022-23); HS 91* v USA (Bulawayo) 2022; BB 3-19 v UAE (Geelong) 2022-23. HS 103 v Sussex (Chester-le-St) 2023. BB 4-76 v Glamorgan (Chester-le-St) 2023. LO HS 123 (*see LOI*). LO BB 5-52 (*see LOI*). T20 HS 91*. T20 BB 3-19.

DRISSELL, George Samuel (Bedminster Down SS; Filton C), b Bristol, Glos 20 Jan 1999. 6'1½". RHB, OB. Squad No 8. Gloucestershire 2017-19; cap 2017. Durham debut/cap 2022. HS 19 Gs v Warwks (Birmingham) 2018. Du HS 16 v Notts (Nottingham) 2022. BB 4-83 Gs v Glamorgan (Newport) 2019. Du BB 1-47 v Sussex (Chester-le-St) 2023. LO HS 37* v Sussex (Chester-le-St) 2022 (RLC). LO BB 3-46 v Northants (Chester-le-St) 2023 (MBC). T20 HS 70. T20 BB 1-20.

GIBSON, Oliver James (Q Elizabeth GS, Hexham; Derwentside SFC), b Northallerton, Yorks 7 Jul 2000. 5'11". RHB, RFM. Squad No 73. Debut (Durham) 2022; cap 2022. Durham 2nd XI debut 2018. HS 6 and CC BB 2-25 v Leics (Leicester) 2022. BB 4-39 v Zimbabwe A (Harare) 2023-24. CC BB 2-25 v Sussex (Chester-le-St) 2022. LO HS 6 v Surrey (Gosforth) 2022 (RLC). LO BB 3-54 v Somerset (Taunton) 2022 (RLC). T20 HS –. T20 BB 3-12.

NQ**GLOVER, Brandon** Dale (St Stithians C), b Johannesburg, South Africa 3 Apr 1997. 6'2½". RHB, RFM. Squad No 6. Boland 2016-17 to 2018-19. Northamptonshire 2020. Durham debut 2023 (l-o only). **LOI** (Neth): 9 (2019 to 2022-23); HS 18 v Ire (Utrecht) 2021; BB 3-43 v Afg (Doha) 2021-22. **IT20** (Neth): 24 (2019 to 2022-23); HS 1* (twice); BB 4-12 v UAE (Dubai, DSC) 2019-20. HS 12* Boland v Gauteng (Paarl) 2018-19. CC HS 0. BB 4-83 Boland v FS (Bloemfontein) 2017-18. CC BB 2-45 Nh v Somerset (Northampton) 2020. LO HS 27 Boland v Easterns (Benoni) 2017-18. LO BB 3-43 (*see LOI*). T20 HS 15. T20 BB 4-12.

HOGG, Daniel Maxwell (Durham Cathedral S), b Manchester 19 Dec 2004. 6'7". RHB, RMF. Durham 2nd XI debut 2023. Awaiting 1st XI debut.

NQ**JONES, Michael** Alexander (Ormskirk S; Myerscough C), b Ormskirk, Lancs 5 Jan 1998. 6'2". RHB, OB. Squad No 10. Debut (Durham) 2018; cap 2018. **LOI** (Scot): 12 (2017-18 to 2022); HS 87 v Ire (Dubai, ICCA) 2017-18. **IT20** (Scot): 4 (2022 to 2022-23); HS 86 v Ire (Hobart) 2022-23. HS 206 v Middx (Chester-le-St) 2020. LO HS 119 v Middx (Chester-le-St) 2022 (RLC). T20 HS 86.

KILLEEN, Mitchell Jack (St Bede's, Lanchester), b Durham 28 Sep 2004. Son of N.Killeen (Durham 1995 to 2008). 5'9". RHB, RM. Durham 2nd XI debut 2021. Awaiting f-c debut. LO HS 32 v Leics (Leicester) 2022 (RLC). LO BB 1-17 v Notts (Grantham) 2022 (RLC).

LEES, Alexander Zak (Holy Trinity SS, Halifax), b Halifax, Yorks 14 Apr 1993. 6'3". LHB, LB. Squad No 19. Yorkshire 2010-18; cap 2014; captain 2016 (l-o). Durham debut/cap 2018. MCC 2017. YC 2014. **Tests**: 10 (2021-22 to 2022); HS 67 v NZ (Nottingham) 2022. F-c Tours: WI 2021-22; I 2023-24 (EL); SL 2022-23 (EL). 1000 runs (3); most – 1347 (2023). HS 275* Y v Derbys (Chesterfield) 2013. Du HS 195 v Glos (Chester-le-St) 2023. BB 2-51 Y v Middx (Lord's) 2016. Du BB 1-12 v Yorks (Chester-le-St) 2020. LO HS 144 v Sussex (Hove) 2023 (MBC). T20 HS 95*.

McALINDON, Stanley James C. (Trinity S), b Carlisle, Cumberland 28 Apr 2004. 6'3". RHB, RFM. Debut (Durham) 2022; cap 2022. Durham 2nd XI debut 2021. England U19 2022. HS 26* and CC BB 2-63 v Derbys (Chester-le-St) 2022. BB 3-34 v Zimbabwe A (Harare) 2023-24. LO HS 50 and LO BB 4-29 v Leics (Leicester) 2022 (RLC).

McKINNEY, Ben Stewart (Seaham HS), b Sunderland 4 Oct 2004. 6'7". LHB, OB. Squad No 9. Debut (Durham) 2023; cap 2023. Durham 2nd XI debut 2021. England U19 2022 to 2022-23. HS 52 v Zimbabwe A (Harare) 2023-24. CC HS 35 v Sussex (Hove) 2023. LO HS 5 v Worcs (Chester-le-St) 2023 (MBC) and 5 v Sussex (Hove) 2023 (MBC). T20 HS 22.

‡**PARKINSON, Callum** Francis (Bolton S), b Bolton, Lancs 24 Oct 1996. Twin brother of M.W.Parkinson (*see KENT*). 5'8". RHB, SLA. Squad No 17. Derbyshire 2016. Leicestershire 2017-23; cap 2022. Durham debut 2023-24. Northern Superchargers 2021 to date. Staffordshire 2015-16. HS 75 Le v Kent (Canterbury) 2017. BB 8-148 (10-185 match) Le v Worcs (Worcester) 2017. LO HS 52* Le v Notts (Leicester) 2018 (RLC). LO BB 1-34 Le v Derbys (Derby) 2018 (RLC). T20 HS 27*. T20 BB 4-20.

POTTS, Matthew ('**Matty**') James (St Robert of Newminster Catholic S), b Sunderland 29 Oct 1998. 6'0". RHB, RFM. Squad No 35. Debut (Durham) 2017; cap 2017. Northern Superchargers 2021 to date. **ECB Two-Year Central Contract from 2023-24**. **Tests**: 6 (2022 to 2023); HS 19 v I (Birmingham) 2022; BB 4-13 v NZ (Lord's) 2022, taking the wicket of K.S.Williamson with his fifth delivery in Test cricket. **LOI**: 4 (2022 to 2023-24); HS 15* v WI (Bridgetown) 2023-24; BB 2-47 v Ire (Nottingham) 2023. F-c Tour (EL): I 2023-24. HS 81 v Northants (Northampton) 2021. 50 wkts (2); most – 78 (2022). BB 7-40 (11-101 match) v Glamorgan (Chester-le-St) 2022. LO HS 30 v Yorks (Chester-le-St) 2018 (RLC). LO BB 4-62 v Northants (Chester-le-St) 2019 (RLC). T20 HS 40*. T20 BB 3-8.

RAINE, Benjamin Alexander (St Aidan's RC SS, Sunderland) b Sunderland, 14 Sep 1991. 6'0". LHB, RMF. Squad No 44. Debut (Durham) 2011; cap 2011. Leicestershire 2013-18; cap 2018. HS 103* v Worcs (Chester-le-St) 2022, sharing Du record 8th wkt partnership of 213* with P.Coughlin. 50 wkts (3); most – 61 (2015). BB 6-27 v Sussex (Hove) 2019. LO HS 83 Le v Worcs (Worcester) 2018 (RLC). LO BB 3-31 Le v Northants (Northampton) 2018 (RLC). T20 HS 113. T20 BB 4-30.

ROBINSON, Luke Stephen (Park View Ac), b Sunderland 12 Oct 2003. 5'11". LHB, RM. Squad No 12. Awaiting f-c debut. Durham 2nd XI 2022. LO HS 0. LO BB 1-42 v Derbys (Chester-le-St) 2023 (MBC). T20 HS –. T20 BB 2-28.

ROBINSON, Oliver Graham (Hurtsmere S, Greenwich), b Sidcup 1 Dec 1998. 5'8". RHB, WK, occ RM. Squad No 21. Kent 2018-22; cap 2022. Durham debut/cap 2023. HS 167* v Leics (Leicester) 2023. LO HS 206* K v Worcs (Worcester) 2022 (RLC) – K record. T20 HS 69*.

SOWTER, Nathan Adam (Hill Sport HS, NSW), b Penrith, NSW, Australia 12 Oct 1992. 5'10". RHB, LB. Squad No 72. Middlesex 2017-21. Durham debut 2022 (T20 only). Oval Invincibles 2021 to date. HS 57* M v Glamorgan (Cardiff) 2019. BB 3-42 M v Lancs (Manchester) 2017. LO HS 31 M v Surrey (Oval) 2019 (RLC). LO BB 6-62 M v Essex (Chelmsford) 2019 (RLC). T20 HS 37*. T20 BB 5-15.

STOKES, Benjamin Andrew (Cockermouth S), b Christchurch, Canterbury, New Zealand 4 Jun 1991. 6'1". LHB, RFM. Squad No 38. Debut (Durham) 2010; cap 2010. IPL: RPS 2017; RR 2018-21; CSK 2023. Big Bash: MR 2014-15. Northern Superchargers 2021. YC 2013. *Wisden* 2015. PCA 2019. BBC Sports Personality of the Year 2019. OBE 2020. **ECB Central Contract 2023-24. Tests**: 102 (2013-14 to 2023-24, 23 as captain); HS 258 v SA (Cape Town) 2015-16, setting E record fastest double century in 163 balls; BB 6-22 v WI (Lord's) 2017. **LOI**: 114 (2011 to 2023-24, 3 as captain); HS 182 v NZ (Oval) 2023 – E record; BB 5-61 v A (Southampton) 2013. **IT20**: 43 (2011 to 2022-23); HS 52* v PA (Melbourne) 2022-23, in World Cup final; BB 3-26 v NZ (Delhi) 2015-16. F-c Tours (C=Captain): A 2013-14, 2021-22; SA 2015-16, 2019-20; WI 2010-11 (EL), 2014-15, 2018-19, 2021-22; NZ 2017-18, 2019-20, 2022-23C; I 2016-17, 2020-21, 2023-24C; P 2022-23C; SL 2018-19; B 2016-17; UAE 2015-16 (v P). HS 258 (*see Tests*). Du HS 185 v Lancs (Chester-le-St) 2011, sharing Du record 4th wkt partnership of 331 with D.M.Benkenstein. BB 7-67 (10-121 match) v Sussex (Chester-le-St) 2014. LO HS 182 (*see LOI*). LO BB 5-61 (*see LOI*). T20 HS 107*. T20 BB 4-16.

NQ**TURNER, Ashton** James, b Subiaco, Perth, W Australia 25 Jan 1993. RHB, OB. W Australia 2013-14 to date. Durham debut 2022 (T20 only). IPL: RR 2019. Big Bash: PS 2013-14 to date. Manchester Originals 2022 to date. **LOI** (A): 9 (2018-19 to 2021); HS 84* v I (Mohali) 2018-19; BB 1-23 v WI (Bridgetown) 2021. **IT20** (A): 19 (2016-17 to 2023); HS 24 v WI (Gros Islet) 2021; BB 2-12 v SL (Melbourne) 2016-17. HS 128 WA v Vic (Perth) 2022-23. BB 6-111 WA v NSW (Perth) 2016-17. LO HS 100 WA v Tas (Perth) 2021-22. LO BB 2-14 Aus A v New Zealand A (Brisbane, AB) 2023. T20 HS 84*. T20 BB 3-20.

WOOD, Mark Andrew (Ashington HS; Newcastle C), b Ashington 11 Jan 1990. 5'11". RHB, RF. Squad No 33. Debut (Durham) 2011; cap 2011. IPL: CSK 2018; LSG 2023. Northumberland 2008-10. **ECB Three-Year Central Contract from 2023-24. Tests**: 34 (2015 to 2023-24); HS 52 v NZ (Christchurch) 2017-18; BB 6-37 v A (Hobart) 2021-22. **LOI**: 66 (2015 to 2023-24); HS 43* v SA (Mumbai) 2023-24; BB 4-33 v A (Birmingham) 2017. **IT20**: 28 (2015 to 2022-23); HS 5* v A (Hobart) 2017-18 and 5* v NZ (Wellington) 2017-18; BB 3-9 v WI (Basseterre) 2018-19. F-c Tours: A 2021-22; SA 2014-15 (EL), 2019-20; WI 2018-19, 2021-22; NZ 2017-18; I 2023-24; P 2022-23; SL 2013-14 (EL), 2020-21; UAE 2015-16 (v P), 2018-19 (EL v P A). HS 72* v Kent (Chester-le-St) 2017. BB 6-37 (*see Tests*). Du BB 6-46 v Derbys (Derby) 2018. LO HS 43* (*see LOI*). LO BB 4-33 (*see LOI*). T20 HS 27*. T20 BB 5-14.

RELEASED/RETIRED

(Having made a County 1st XI appearance in 2023)

DONEATHY, Luke (Prudhoe HS), b Newcastle upon Tyne 26 Jul 2001. RHB, RM. Durham 2nd XI debut 2019. Awaiting f-c debut. LO HS 69* and LO BB 4-36 v Lancs (Gosforth) 2021 (RLC). T20 HS 12. T20 BB 1-19.

NQ**FERNANDO**, Muthuthanthrige **Vishwa** Thilina, b Colombo, Sri Lanka 18 Sep 1991. RHB, LMF. Bloomfield 2011-12 to 2015-16. Colombo 2017-18 to date. Durham 2023; cap 2023. **Tests** (SL): 21 (2016 to 2023-24); HS 38 v Z (Harare) 2019-20; BB 5-101 v SA (Johannesburg) 2020-21. **LOI** (SL): 8 (2017 to 2018-19); HS 7* v I (Colombo, RPS) 2017 and 7* v P (Sharjah) 2017-18; BB 1-35 v I (Pallekele) 2017. **IT20** (SL): 1 (2017-18); HS 2 v I (Cuttack) 2017-18; BB –. F-c tours (SL): E 2016 (SLA); A 2018-19; SA 2018-19, 2020-21; WI 2020-21; NZ 2015-16 (SLA); I 2019 (SLA), 2021-22; P 2019-20; Z 2019-20; B 2018 (SLA), 2022. HS 41 Colombo v Moors (Colombo CC) 2019-20. Du HS –. BB 5-14 Dambulla v Jaffna (Colombo, SSC) 2022-23. Du BB 4-40 v Leics (Chester-le-St) 2023. LO HS 18* Dambulla v Colombo (Dambulla) 2018-19. LO BB 4-61 Colombo v Kandy (Colombo, RPS) 2017. T20 HS 7. T20 BB 3-22.

NQ**KUHNEMANN, Matt**hew Paul, b Brisbane, Australia 20 Sep 1996. LHB, SLA. Queensland 2020-21 to date. Durham 2023; cap 2023. Big Bash: BH 2018-19 to date. **Tests** (A): 3 (2022-23); HS 6 v I (Delhi) 2022-23 and 6 v I (Ahmedabad) 2022-23; BB 5-16 v I (Indore) 2022-23. **LOI** (A): 4 (2022); HS 15 v SL (Colombo, RPS) 2022; BB 2-26 v SL (Colombo, RPS) 2022 – separate matches. F-c Tours (A): I 2022-23; SL 2022 (Aus A). HS 24* Q v Vic (Melbourne, SK) 2021-22. Du HS 5* v Sussex (Hove) 2023. BB 5-16 (*see Tests*). Du BB 5-53 v Worcs (Chester-le-St) 2023. LO HS 36 Q v SA (Adelaide, KR) 2023-24. LO BB 4-37 Q v SA (Brisbane, AB) 2020-21. T20 HS 9. T20 BB 3-17.

NQ**MACKINTOSH, Tom**as Scott Sabater (Merchiston Castle S), b Madrid, Spain 11 Jan 2003. 5'10". RHB, WK. Durham 2022; cap 2022. **LOI** (Scot): 10 (2022-23 to 2023); HS 38* v Neth (Bulawayo) 2023. IT20 (Scot): 2 (2023); HS 16 v Denmark (Edinburgh) 2023. HS 51 v Derbys (Chester-le-St) 2022. LO HS 53 v Warwks (Birmingham) 2023 (MBC).

NQ**PARNELL, Wayne** Dillon (Grey HS), b Port Elizabeth, South Africa 30 Jul 1989. 6'2". LHB, LFM. E Province 2006-07 to 2010-11. Warriors 2008-09 to 2014-15. Kent 2009-17. Sussex 2011. Cape Cobras 2015-16 to 2016-17. Worcestershire 2018-19. Northamptonshire 2021. W Province 2021-22. Glamorgan 2015 (T20 only). Durham 2023 (T20 only). IPL: PW 2011-13; DD 2014; RCB 2023. Northern Superchargers 2022 to date. **Tests** (SA): 6 (2009-10 to 2017-18); HS 23 and BB 4-51 v SL (Johannesburg) 2016-17. **LOI** (SA): 73 (2008-09 to 2022-23); HS 56 v P (Sharjah) 2013-14; BB 5-48 v E (Cape Town) 2009-10. **IT20** (SA): 56 (2008-09 to 2022-23); HS 29* v A (Johannesburg) 2011-12; BB 5-30 v Ire (Bristol) 2022. F-c Tours (SA A): A 2016; I 2009-10 (SA), 2015; Ire 2012. HS 111* Cobras v Warriors (Paarl) 2015-16. CC HS 90 K v Glamorgan (Canterbury) 2009. BB 7-51 Cobras v Dolphins (Cape Town) 2015-16. CC BB 5-47 Wo v Lancs (Manchester) 2019. LO HS 129 Warriors v Lions (Potchefstroom) 2013-14. LO BB 6-51 Warriors v Knights (Kimberley) 2013-14. T20 HS 99. T20 BB 5-30.

NQ**PATEL, Ajaz** Yunus, b Bombay, India 21 Oct 1988. LHB, SLA. Central Districts 2012-13 to date. Yorkshire 2019. Glamorgan 2022. Durham 2023; cap 2023. **Tests** (NZ): 16 (2018-19 to 2023-24); HS 35 v P (Karachi) 2022-23; BB 10-119 (14-225 match) v I (Mumbai) 2021-22 – third best analysis in all Test cricket. **IT20** (NZ): 7 (2018-19 to 2021); HS 4 v B (Mirpur) 2021; BB 4-16 v B (Mirpur) 2021 – separate matches. F-c Tours (NZ): E 2021, 2022; I 2021-22; P 2022-23; SL 2019; B 2023-24; UAE (v P) 2018-19. HS 52 CD v Wellington (Napier) 2020-21. CC HS 51* Gm v Sussex (Hove) 2022. Du HS 34 v Yorks (Chester-le-St) 2023. BB 10-119 (*see Tests*). CC BB 5-68 v Derbys (Cardiff) 2022. Du BB 5-96 (10-209 match) v Glos (Bristol) 2023. LO HS 45 CD v ND (Hamilton) 2020-21. LO BB 3-31 CD v Auckland (New Plymouth) 2022-23. T20 HS 13. T20 BB 4-16.

NQ**PRETORIUS, Migael**, b Vereeniging, South Africa 24 Mar 1995. RHB, RF. Northerns 2016-17 to 2017-18. Titans 2017-18. Lions 2018-19 to 2019-20. North West 2018-19 to date. Knights 2020-21. Free State 2021-22 to 2022-23. Durham 2023; cap 2023. HS 109* NW v EP (Potchefstroom) 2023-24. Du HS 39 and Du BB 1-37 v Glos (Chester-le-St) 2023. BB 6-38 Northerns v N Cape (Pretoria) 2016-17. LO HS 33 FS v WP (Bloemfontein) 2022-23. LO BB 4-21 FS v KZN Coastal (Bloemfontein) 2021-22. T20 HS 38*. T20 BB 4-32.

RELEASED/RETIRED continued on p 101

DURHAM 2023

RESULTS SUMMARY

	Place	Won	Lost	Drew	Tied	NR
LV= Insurance County Champ (Div 2)	1st	7	1	6		
Metro Bank One-Day Cup (Group B)	5th	3	4			1
Vitality Blast (North Group)	7th	4	7		2	1

LV= INSURANCE COUNTY CHAMPIONSHIP AVERAGES
BATTING AND FIELDING

Cap†		*M*	*I*	*NO*	*HS*	*Runs*	*Avge*	*100*	*50*	*Ct/St*
2023	B.F.W.de Leede	6	5	2	103	279	93.00	1	2	4
2018	A.Z.Lees	14	21	2	195	1347	70.89	5	5	5
2016	B.A.Carse	6	8	2	108*	407	67.83	1	3	3
2015	G.Clark	14	15	1	128	818	58.42	3	3	14
2023	O.G.Robinson	14	18	2	167*	931	58.18	3	5	37/10
2020	D.G.Bedingham	14	19	1	156	1019	56.61	5	1	13
2012	P.Coughlin	6	5	2	59*	163	54.33	–	2	–
2009	S.G.Borthwick	13	19	4	134*	667	44.46	2	4	7
2018	M.A.Jones	14	21	2	121*	631	33.21	1	4	9
2011	B.A.Raine	14	13	4	71	232	25.77	–	2	6
2023	A.Y.Patel	3	4	–	34	87	21.75	–	–	–
2017	M.J.Potts	11	10	1	64	147	16.33	–	1	8
2022	J.J.Bushnell	3	4	–	27	62	15.50	–	–	–
2023	M.W.Parkinson	8	4	3	5*	12	12.00	–	–	4

Also played: G.S.Drissell (1 match – cap 2022) 10*; M.V.T.Fernando (2 – cap 2023) did not bat; M.P.Kuhnemann (3 – cap 2023) 5*, 0 (1 ct); S.J.C.McAlindon (2 – cap 2022) 4; B.S.McKinney (1 – cap 2023) 35, 4 (1 ct); C.N.Miles (1 – cap 2023) 33 (2 ct); M.Pretorius (3 – cap 2023) 39, 36 (2 ct); R.L.Toole (1 – cap 2023) did not bat (1 ct); L.Trevaskis (2 – cap 2017) 79, 28, 7 (3 ct).

BOWLING

	O	*M*	*R*	*W*	*Avge*	*Best*	*5wI*	*10wM*
M.J.Potts	372.3	64	1200	54	22.22	5-65	1	–
M.P.Kuhnemann	97.4	13	271	12	22.58	5-53	1	–
B.A.Raine	485	98	1497	60	24.95	5-51	1	–
M.W.Parkinson	194	29	626	23	27.21	4-58	–	–
B.A.Carse	140.3	17	548	19	28.84	3-38	–	–
B.F.W.de Leede	114	19	494	17	29.05	4-76	–	–
P.Coughlin	109.1	19	388	12	32.33	3-27	–	–
A.Y.Patel	139.4	25	446	10	44.60	5-96	2	1
Also bowled:								
S.G.Borthwick	28.1	1	112	5	22.40	4-25	–	–
M.V.T.Fernando	41	6	157	7	22.42	4-40	–	–
C.N.Miles	42	6	169	5	33.80	4-73	–	–

J.J.Bushnell 29-0-131-2; G.S.Drissell 30-4-88-1; S.J.C.McAlindon 25-1-164-1; M.Pretorius 63-8-227-2; R.L.Toole 25-1-105-0; L.Trevaskis 33-5-101-2.

Durham played no first-class fixtures outside the County Championship in 2023. The First-Class Averages (pp 223–235) give the records of Durham players in all first-class county matches, with the exception of C.N.Miles, M.W.Parkinson and M.J.Potts, whose first-class figures for Durham are as above.

† Durham revised their capping policy in 2020 and now award players with their County Caps when they make their first-class debut.

DURHAM RECORDS

FIRST-CLASS CRICKET

Highest Total	For	648-5d		v	Notts	Chester-le-St[2]	2009
	V	810-4d		by	Warwicks	Birmingham	1994
Lowest Total	For	61		v	Leics	Leicester	2018
	V	18		by	Durham MCCU	Chester-le-St[2]	2012
Highest Innings	For	273	M.L.Love	v	Hampshire	Chester-le-St[2]	2003
	V	501*	B.C.Lara	for	Warwicks	Birmingham	1994

Highest Partnership for each Wicket

1st	334*	S.Hutton/M.A.Roseberry	v	Oxford U	Oxford	1996
2nd	274	M.D.Stoneman/S.G.Borthwick	v	Middlesex	Chester-le-St[2]	2014
3rd	305	A.Z.Lees/D.G.Bedingham	v	Derbyshire	Derby	2023
4th	331	B.A.Stokes/D.M.Benkenstein	v	Lancashire	Chester-le-St[2]	2011
5th	254*	D.G.Bedingham/E.J.H.Eckersley	v	Notts	Nottingham	2021
6th	282	C.T.Bancroft/E.J.H.Eckersley	v	Sussex	Hove	2019
7th	315	D.M.Benkenstein/O.D.Gibson	v	Yorkshire	Leeds	2006
8th	213*	B.A.Raine/P.Coughlin	v	Worcs	Chester-le-St[2]	2022
9th	150	P.Mustard/P.Coughlin	v	Northants	Chester-le-St[2]	2014
10th	103	M.M.Betts/D.M.Cox	v	Sussex	Hove	1996

Best Bowling (Innings)	For	10- 47	O.D.Gibson	v	Hampshire	Chester-le-St[2]	2007
	V	9- 34	J.A.R.Harris	for	Middlesex	Lord's	2015
Best Bowling (Match)	For	15- 95	C.Rushworth	v	Northants	Chester-le-St[2]	2014
	V	13-103	J.A.R.Harris	for	Middlesex	Lord's	2015

Most Runs – Season	1654	M.J.Di Venuto	(av 78.76)	2009
Most Runs – Career	12030	P.D.Collingwood	(av 33.98)	1996-2018
Most 100s – Season	7	K.K.Jennings		2016
Most 100s – Career	25	P.D.Collingwood		1996-2018
Most Wkts – Season	88	C.Rushworth	(av 20.09)	2015
Most Wkts – Career	598	C.Rushworth	(av 22.51)	2010-22
Most Career W-K Dismissals	638	P.Mustard	(619 ct; 19 st)	2002-16
Most Career Catches in the Field	246	P.D.Collingwood		1996-2018

LIMITED-OVERS CRICKET

Highest Total	**50ov**	427-9		v	Sussex	Hove	2023
	40ov	325-9		v	Surrey	The Oval	2011
	T20	225-2		v	Leics	Chester-le-St[2]	2010
Lowest Total	**50ov**	82		v	Worcs	Chester-le-St[1]	1968
	40ov	72		v	Warwicks	Birmingham	2002
	T20	78		v	Lancashire	Chester-le-St[2]	2018
Highest Innings	**50ov**	164	B.A.Stokes	v	Notts	Chester-le-St[2]	2014
	40ov	150*	B.A.Stokes	v	Warwicks	Birmingham	2011
	T20	108*	P.D.Collingwood	v	Worcs	Worcester	2017
Best Bowling	**50ov**	7-32	S.P.Davis	v	Lancashire	Chester-le-St[1]	1983
	40ov	6-31	N.Killeen	v	Derbyshire	Derby	2000
	T20	5- 6	P.D.Collingwood	v	Northants	Chester-le-St[2]	2011

[1] Chester-le-Street CC (Ropery Lane) [2] Emirates Riverside

ESSEX

Formation of Present Club: 14 January 1876
Inaugural First-Class Match: 1894
Colours: Blue, Gold and Red
Badge: Three Seaxes above Scroll bearing 'Essex'
County Champions: (8) 1979, 1983, 1984, 1986, 1991, 1992, 2017, 2019
NatWest/Friends Prov Trophy Winners: (3) 1985, 1997, 2008
Benson and Hedges Cup Winners: (2) 1979, 1998
Pro 40/National League (Div 1) Winners: (2) 2005, 2006
Sunday League Winners: (3) 1981, 1984, 1985
Twenty20 Cup Winners: (1) 2019
Bob Willis Trophy Winners: (1) 2020

Chief Executive: John Stephenson, The Cloud County Ground, New Writtle Street, Chelmsford CM2 0PG • Tel: 01245 252420 • Email: questions@essexcricket.org.uk • Web: www.essexcricket.org.uk • Twitter: @EssexCricket (116,410 followers)

Head Coach: Anthony McGrath. **Bowling Coach**: Mick Lewis. **Batting Coach**: Tom Huggins. **Captains**: T.Westley (f-c and 50 ov) and S.R.Harmer (T20). **Vice-Captain**: S.J.Cook. **Overseas Players**: D.Elgar, S.R.Harmer and D.R.Sams (T20 only). **2024 Testimonial**: None. **Head Groundsman**: Stuart Kerrison. **Scorer**: Paul Parkinson. **Blast Team Name**: Essex Eagles. ‡ New registration. [NQ] Not qualified for England.

ALLISON, Benjamin Michael John (New Hall S; Chelmsford C), b Colchester 18 Dec 1999. Elder brother of C.W.J.Allison (*see BELOW*). 6'5". RHB, RFM. Squad No 65. Gloucestershire 2019; cap 2019. Essex debut 2021. Worcestershire 2023; cap 2023 (on loan). Essex 2nd XI debut 2017. Bedfordshire 2018. Cambridgeshire 2019. HS 75 Wo v Yorks (Leeds) 2023. Ex HS 69* and BB 5-32 v Northants (Northampton) 2022. LO HS 21* v Essex (Southampton) 2022 (RLC). LO BB 2-33 v Kent (Chelmsford) 2021 (RLC). T20 HS 6*. T20 BB 3-33.

ALLISON, Charles William James (Royal Hospital S, Ipswich), b Colchester 2 Mar 2005. Younger brother of B.M.J.Allison (*see ABOVE*). 5'7". RHB, RM. Squad No 56. Awaiting f-c debut. Essex 2nd XI debut 2022. England U19 2023. LO HS 85 v Leics (Kibworth) 2023 (MBC).

BEARD, Aaron Paul (Boswells S, Chelmsford), b Chelmsford 15 Oct 1997. 5'9". LHB, RFM. Squad No 14. Debut (Essex) 2016. Sussex 2022 (on loan). HS 58* v Durham MCCU (Chelmsford) 2017. CC HS 41 v Yorks (Chelmsford) 2019. BB 4-21 v Middx (Chelmsford) 2020. LO HS 22* v Kent (Beckenham) 2019 (RLC). LO BB 4-32 v Notts (Chelmsford) 2023 (MBC). T20 HS 13. T20 BB 4-29.

BENKENSTEIN, Luc Martin (Hilton C; Seaford C), b Durban, South Africa 2 Nov 2004. Son of D.M.Benkenstein (Natal, KZN, Dolphins and Durham 1993-94 to 2013); grandson of M.M.Benkenstein (Rhodesia and Natal B 1970-71 to 1980-81); nephew of B.N.Benkenstein (Natal B and Griqualand W 1994-95 to 1996-97) and B.R.Benkenstein (Natal B 1993-94). 5'8". RHB, LBG. Squad No 99. Sussex 2nd XI 2021. Hampshire 2nd XI 2021. Essex 2nd XI debut 2021. Awaiting f-c debut. LO HS 55 v Worcs (Worcester) 2022 (RLC). LO BB 6-42 v Glamorgan (Chelmsford) 2022 (RLC) – Ex 50 ov record.

BROWNE, Nicholas Lawrence Joseph (Trinity Catholic HS, Woodford Green), b Leytonstone 24 Mar 1991. 6'3½". LHB, LB. Squad No 10. Debut (Essex) 2013; cap 2015. MCC 2016. 1000 runs (3); most – 1262 (2016). HS 255 v Derbys (Chelmsford) 2016. BB –. LO HS 99 v Glamorgan (Chelmsford) 2016 (RLC). T20 HS 38.

COOK, Samuel James (Great Baddow HS & SFC; Loughborough U), b Chelmsford 4 Aug 1997. 6'1". RHB, RFM. Squad No 16. Loughborough MCCU 2016-17. Essex debut 2017; cap 2020. MCC 2019. Trent Rockets 2021 to date. F-c Tour (EL): SL 2022-23. HS 38 v Kent (Canterbury) 2022. 50 wkts (2); most – 58 (2021). BB 7-23 (12-65 match) v Kent (Canterbury) 2019. LO HS 6 v Middx (Chelmsford) 2019 (RLC) and 6 EL v South Africans (Worcester) 2022. LO BB 3-37 v Surrey (Oval) 2019 (RLC). T20 HS 18. T20 BB 4-15.

‡**COX, Jordan** Matthew (Felsted S), b Margate, Kent 21 Oct 2000. 5'8". RHB, WK. Squad No 77. Kent 2019-23. Big Bash: HH 2021-22; MR 2023-24. Oval Invincibles 2022 to date. Kent 2nd XI debut 2017. England U19 2018-19. YC 2022. HS 238* K v Sussex (Canterbury) 2020, sharing K record 2nd wkt partnership of 423 with J.A.Leaning. LO HS 46 EL v Sri Lanka A (Colombo, RPS) 2022-23. T20 HS 94.

CRITCHLEY, Matthew James John (St Michael's HS, Chorley), b Preston, Lancs 13 Aug 1996. 6'2". RHB, LB. Squad No 20. Derbyshire 2015-21; cap 2019. Essex debut 2022; cap 2023. Big Bash: MR 2022-23. Welsh Fire 2021-22. London Spirit 2023. 1000 runs (1): 1000 (2021). HS 137* De v Northants (Derby) 2015. Ex HS 132 and Ex BB 4-114 v Kent (Chelmsford) 2022. BB 6-73 De v Leics (Leicester) 2020. LO HS 64* v Northants (Derby) 2019 (RLC). LO BB 4-48 v Northants (Derby) 2015 (RLC). T20 HS 80*. T20 BB 5-28.

DAS, Robin James (Brentwood S), b Leytonstone 27 Feb 2002. 5'8". RHB. Squad No 47. Debut (Essex) 2023, scoring 132 v Ireland (Chelmsford). Essex 2nd XI debut 2018. HS 132 (*see debut*). CC HS 4 v Kent (Chelmsford) 2023. LO HS 63 v Worcs (Worcester) 2022 (RLC). T20 HS 72.

‡NQ**ELGAR, Dean**, b Welkom, OFS, South Africa 11 Jun 1987. 5'8". LHB, SLA. Squad No 64. Free State 2005-06 to 2010-11. Eagles 2006-07 to 2009-10. Knights 2010-11 to 2013-14. Somerset 2013-17; cap 2017. Titans 2014-15 to 2020-21. Surrey 2015-19. Northerns 2021-22 to date. **Tests** (SA): 86 (2012-13 to 2023-24, 18 as captain); 1000 runs (1): 1128 (2017); HS 199 v B (Potchefstroom) 2017-18; BB 4-22 v I (Mohali) 2015-16. **LOI** (SA): 8 (2012 to 2018-19); HS 42 v E (Oval) 2012; BB 1-11 v E (Southampton) 2012. F-c Tours (SA)(C=Captain): E 2017, 2022C; A 2012-13, 2016 (SA A), 2016-17, 2022-23C; WI 2021C; NZ 2016-17, 2021-22C; I 2015-16, 2019-20; P 2020-21; SL 2010 (SA A), 2014, 2018; Z 2014; B 2010 (SA A), 2015; UAE (v P) 2013-14; Ire 2012 (SA A). 1000 runs (0+2); most – 1193 (2009-10). HS 268 SA A v Australia A (Pretoria) 2013. CC HS 158 Sm v Middx (Lord's) 2017. BB 4-22 (*see Tests*). CC BB 1-4 Sm v Essex (Taunton) 2017. LO HS 137 Titans v Lions (Potchefstroom) 2018-19. LO BB 4-37 Titans v Dolphins (Durban) 2018-19. T20 HS 88*. T20 BB 4-23.

NQ**HARMER, Simon** Ross, b Pretoria, South Africa 10 Feb 1989. 6'2". RHB, OB. Squad No 11. Eastern Province 2009-10 to 2011-12. Warriors 2010-11 to 2018-19. Essex debut 2017; cap 2018; captain 2020 to date (T20 only). Northerns 2021-22 to 2022-23. *Wisden* 2019. **Tests** (SA): 10 (2014-15 to 2022-23); HS 47 v A (Sydney) 2022-23; BB 4-61 v I (Mohali) 2015-16. F-c Tours (SA): E 2022; A 2014 (SA A), 2022-23; I 2015-16; B 2015; Ire 2012 (SA A). HS 102* v Surrey (Oval) 2018. 50 wkts (6+1); most – 86 (2019). BB 9-80 (12-202 match) v Derbys (Chelmsford) 2021. LO HS 68 v Hants (Southampton) 2023 (MBC). LO BB 4-42 Warriors v Lions (Potchefstroom) 2011-12. T20 HS 43. T20 BB 4-18.

KHUSHI, Feroze Isa Nazir (Kelmscott S, Walthamstow; Leyton SFC), b Whipps Cross 23 Jun 1999. 6'1". RHB. OB. Squad No 23. Debut (Essex) 2020. Essex 2nd XI debut 2015. Suffolk 2019-21. HS 164 v Kent (Canterbury) 2022. LO HS 118 v Northants (Northampton) 2022 (RLC). T20 HS 67.

PEPPER, Michael-Kyle Steven (The Perse S), b Harlow 25 Jun 1998. Younger brother of C.A.Pepper (Cambridgeshire 2013-16). 6'2". RHB, WK. Squad No 19. Debut (Essex) 2018. Northern Superchargers 2022. Cambridgeshire 2014-19. HS 92 v Durham (Chester-le-St) 2021. LO HS 63 v Yorks (Chelmsford) 2023 (MBC). T20 HS 86*.

PORTER, James Alexander (Oak Park HS, Newbury Park; Epping Forest C), b Leytonstone 25 May 1993. 5'11½". RHB, RFM. Squad No 44. Debut (Essex) 2014, taking a wkt with his 5th ball; cap 2015. *Wisden* 2017. F-c Tours (EL): WI 2017-18; I 2018-19; UAE 2018-19 (v P A). HS 34 v Glamorgan (Cardiff) 2015. 50 wkts (6); most – 85 (2017). BB 7-41 (11-98 match) v Worcs (Chelmsford) 2018. LO HS 10* v Derbys (Chelmsford) 2012 (RLC). LO BB 4-29 v Glamorgan (Chelmsford) 2018 (RLC). T20 HS 1*. T20 BB 4-20.

RICHARDS, Jamal Adrian (Norlington S; Waltham Forest C), b Edmonton, Middx 3 Mar 2004. 5'10". RHB, RFM. Squad No 87. Debut (Essex) 2023. Essex 2nd XI debut 2021. HS 17 and BB 5-96 v Ireland (Chelmsford) 2023 – only f-c match. LO HS 46 v Derbys (Chelmsford) 2022 (RLC). LO BB 2-37 v Northants (Northampton) 2022 (RLC).

ROSSINGTON, Adam Matthew (Mill Hill S), b Edgware, Middx 5 May 1993. 5'11". RHB, WK, occ RM. Squad No 17. Middlesex 2010-14. Northamptonshire 2014-21; cap 2019; captain 2020-21. Essex debut 2022; cap 2023. London Spirit 2021 to date. HS 138* Nh v Sussex (Arundel) 2016. Ex HS 104 v Hants (Chelmsford) 2023. Won 2013 Walter Lawrence Trophy with 55-ball century M v Cambridge MCCU (Cambridge). LO HS 97 Nh v Notts (Nottingham) 2016 (RLC). T20 HS 95.

NQ**SAMS, Daniel** Richard, b Milperra, NSW, Australia 27 Oct 1992. 6'1". RHB, LFM. Squad No 95. Canterbury 2017-18. New South Wales 2018-19. Essex debut 2022 (T20 only). IPL: DCa 2020-21; RCB 2021; MI 2022. Big Bash: SS 2017-18; ST 2018-19 to date. Trent Rockets 2022 to date. **IT20** (A): 10 (2020-21 to 2022-23); HS 41 v NZ (Dunedin) 2020-21; BB 2-33 v I (Hyderabad) 2022-23. HS 88 Cant v ND (Rangiora) 2017-18. BB 4-55 Cant v Auckland (Auckland) 2017-18. LO HS 62 NSW v WA (Perth) 2018-19. LO BB 5-46 NSW v Vic (Melbourne) 2019-20. T20 HS 98*. T20 BB 5-30.

NQ**SNATER, Shane** (St John's C, Harare), b Harare, Zimbabwe 24 Mar 1996. 5'9". RHB, RM. Squad No 29. Netherlands 2016 to 2017-18. Southern Rocks 2020-21. Essex debut 2021; cap 2022. **LOI** (Neth): 4 (2018 to 2022); HS 17* v E (Amstelveen) 2022; BB 1-41 v Nepal (Amstelveen) 2018. **IT20** (Neth): 13 (2018 to 2019-20); HS 10 and BB 3-42 v Scotland (Dublin) 2019. HS 79* v Northants (Chelmsford) 2022. BB 7-98 v Notts (Nottingham) 2021. LO HS 64 v Hants (Southampton) 2022 (RLC). LO BB 5-29 v Kent (Chelmsford) 2022 (RLC). T20 HS 16*. T20 BB 3-13

THAIN, Noah Robin Mostyn (The Leys S), b Hitchinbrooke, Herts 13 Jan 2005. 5'9". RHB, RM. Squad No 8. Debut (Essex) 2023. Essex 2nd XI debut 2022. England U19 2023. HS 36 and BB 1-44 v Ireland (Chelmsford) 2023 – only f-c appearance. LO HS 75* v Leics (Kibworth) 2023 (MBC). LO BB –.

WALTER, Paul Ian (Billericay S), b Basildon 28 May 1994. 6'7". LHB, LMF. Squad No 22. Debut (Essex) 2016; cap 2023. Big Bash: BH 2023-24. Manchester Originals 2022 to date. HS 141 v Yorks (Chelmsford) 2022. BB 3-20 v Lancs (Blackpool) 2023. LO HS 50 v Glamorgan (Cardiff) 2021 (RLC). LO BB 4-37 v Middx (Chelmsford) 2017 (RLC). T20 HS 78. T20 BB 3-20.

WESTLEY, Thomas (Linton Village C; Hills Road SFC), b Cambridge 13 March 1989. 6'2". RHB, OB. Squad No 21. Debut (Essex) 2007; cap 2013; captain 2020 to date. MCC 2007, 2009, 2016, 2019. Durham MCCU 2009-11. Bloomfield 2014-15. Cambridgeshire 2005. **Tests**: 5 (2017); HS 59 v SA (Oval) 2017. F-c Tours: SL 2016-17 (EL); Nepal 2019-20 (MCC). 1000 runs (2); most – 1435 (2016). HS 254 v Worcs (Chelmsford) 2016. BB 4-55 DU v Durham (Durham) 2010. CC BB 4-75 v Surrey (Colchester) 2015. LO HS 134 v Middx (Radlett) 2018 (RLC). LO BB 4-60 v Northants (Northampton) 2014 (RLC). T20 HS 109*. T20 BB 2-27.

RELEASED/RETIRED

(Having made a County 1st XI appearance in 2023)

NQ**BRACEWELL, Doug**las Andrew John, b Tauranga, New Zealand 28 Sep 1990. Son of B.P.Bracewell (Central Districts, Otago, Northern Districts & NZ 1977-78 to 1989-90); nephew of J.G.Bracewell (Otago, Auckland & NZ 1978-79 to 1989-90), D.W.Bracewell (Canterbury and Central Districts 1974-75 to 1979-80) and M.A.Bracewell (Otago 1977-78); cousin of M.G.Bracewell (Otago, Wellington & NZ 2010-11 to date). RHB, RMF. Central Districts 2008-09 to date. Northamptonshire 2018-19. Essex 2023. IPL: DD 2012. **Tests** (NZ): 28 (2011-12 to 2022-23); HS 47 v SL (Dunedin) 2015-16; BB 6-40 v A (Hobart) 2011-12. **LOI** (NZ): 21 (2011-12 to 2021-22); HS 57 v I (Mt Maunganui) 2018-19; BB 4-55 v WI (Whangarei) 2017-18. **IT20** (NZ): 20 (2011-12 to 2021); HS 44 v SL (Auckland) 2018-19; BB 3-25 v Z (Harare) 2011-12. F-c Tours (NZ): E 2013, 2015; A 2011-12, 2015-16; SA 2012-13, 2016; WI 2012; I 2012, 2013-14 (NZA); SL 2012-13, 2013-14 (NZA); Z 2011-12; B 2013-14. HS 105 CD v Otago (Queenstown) 2014-15. CC HS 81 Nh v Warwks (Birmingham) 2018. Ex HS 61* v Lancs (Blackpool) 2023. BB 7-35 CD v Canterbury (Rangiora) 2012-13. CC BB 4-51 v Warwks (Birmingham) 2023. LO HS 94 CD v Canterbury (Christchurch) 2023-24. LO BB 4-43 CD v Canterbury (Rangiora) 2010-11. T20 HS 93*. T20 BB 3-19.

BUTTLEMAN, William Edward Lewis (Felsted S), b Chelmsford 20 Apr 2000. Younger brother of J.E.L.Buttleman (Durham UCCE 2007-09). RHB, WK, occ OB. Essex 2019-23. HS 65 v Ireland (Chelmsford) 2023. CC HS 43 v Warwks (Chelmsford) 2023. LO HS 50* v Kent (Canterbury) 2023 (MBC). T20 HS 56*.

COOK, Sir Alastair Nathan (Bedford S), b Gloucester 25 Dec 1984. 6'3". LHB, OB. Essex 2003-23; cap 2005; benefit 2014. MCC 2004-07, 2015. YC 2005. *Wisden* 2011. Knighted in 2019 New Year's honours list. **Tests**: 161 (2005-06 to 2018, 59 as captain); 1000 runs (5); most – 1364 (2015); HS 294 v I (Birmingham) 2011. Scored 60 and 104* v I (Nagpur) 2005-06 on debut, and 71 and 147 in final Test v I (Oval) 2018. Second, after M.A.Taylor, to score 1000 runs in the calendar year of his debut. Finished career after appearing in world record 159 consecutive Tests. BB 1-6 v I (Nottingham) 2014. **LOI**: 92 (2006 to 2014-15, 69 as captain); HS 137 v P (Abu Dhabi) 2011-12. **IT20**: 4 (2007 to 2009-10); HS 26 v SA (Centurion) 2009-10. F-c Tours (C=Captain): A 2006-07, 2010-11, 2013-14C, 2017-18; SA 2009-10, 2015-16C; WI 2005-06 (Eng A), 2008-09, 2014-15C; NZ 2007-08, 2012-13C, 2017-18; I 2005-06, 2008-09, 2012-13C, 2016-17C; SL 2004-05 (Eng A), 2007-08, 2011-12; B 2009-10C, 2016-17C; UAE 2011-12 (v P), 2015-16C (v P). 1000 runs (8+1); most – 1466 (2005). HS 294 (*see Tests*). CC HS 195 v Northants (Northampton) 2005. BB 3-13 v Northants (Chelmsford) 2005. LO HS 137 (*see LOI*). LO BB –. T20 HS 100*.

KALLEY, Eshun Singh (Barking Abbey S), b Ilford 23 Nov 2001. RHB, RM. Essex 2023. Hertfordshire 2021. HS 0 v Ireland (Chelmsford) 2023 – only 1st XI appearance. BB –.

LAWRENCE, D.W. – *see SURREY.*

NIJJAR, Aron Stuart Singh (Ilford County HS), b Goodmayes 24 Sep 1994. LHB, SLA. Essex 2015-21. Cardiff MCCU 2017. Kent 2023 (on loan). Suffolk 2014. HS 53 v Northants (Chelmsford) 2015. BB 4-67 K v Notts (Canterbury) 2023. Ex BB 2-28 v Cambridge MCCU (Cambridge) 2019. LO HS 32* v Glos (Bristol) 2021 (RLC). LO BB 3-34 v Leics (Kibworth) 2023 (MBC). T20 HS 27*. T20 BB 3-22.

RYMELL, Joshua Sean (Ipswich S; Colchester SFC), b Ipswich, Suffolk 4 Apr 2001. RHB. Essex 2021-23. Suffolk 2021. HS 21 v Ireland (Chelmsford) 2023. CC HS 14 v Glos (Chelmsford) 2021. LO HS 121 v Yorks (Chelmsford) 2021 (RLC). T20 HS 21.

WEBSTER, B.J. – *see GLOUCESTERSHIRE.*

[NQ]**YADAV, Umesh**kumar Tilak, b Nagpur, India 25 Oct 1987. RHB, RFM. Vidarbha 2008-09 to date. Central Zone 2008-09 to 2013-14. Middlesex 2022. Essex 2023. IPL: DD 2009-10 to 2013; KKR 2014 to date; RCB 2018 to 2020-21. **Tests** (I): 57 (2011-12 to 2023); HS 31 v SA (Ranchi) 2019-20; BB 6-88 v WI (Hyderabad) 2018-19. **LOI** (I): 75 (2010 to 2018-19); HS 18* v NZ (Delhi) 2016-17; BB 4-31 v B (Melbourne) 2014-15. **IT20** (I): 9 (2012 to 2022-23); HS 20* v SA (Indore) 2022-23; BB 2-19 v Ire (Dublin) 2018. F-c Tours (I): E 2018, 2021, 2023 (v A); A 2011-12, 2014-15, 2018-19, 2020-21; SA 2021-22; WI 2016, 2019 (I A); NZ 2019-20; SL 2015, 2017; B 2015, 2022-23. HS 128* Vidarbha v Orissa (Nagpur) 2015-16. CC HS 51 v Hants (Chelmsford) 2023. BB 7-48 (12-79 match) Vidarbha v Kerala (Wayanad) 2018-19. CC BB 3-32 v Middx (Chelmsford) 2023. LO HS 30 C Zone v West Zone (Visakhapatnam) 2013-14. LO BB 5-26 Vidarbha v Rajasthan (Jaipur) 2013-14. T20 HS 26. T20 BB 5-18.

DURHAM RELEASED/RETIRED (continued from p 94)

TOOLE, Raymond Lawrence, b Johannesburg, South Africa 30 Oct 1997. LHB, LM. Central Districts 2019-20 to date. Durham 2023; cap 2023. Essex 2022 (l-o only). HS 17* CD v Canterbury (Nelson) 2019-20. BB 7-57 CD v Auckland (Nelson) 2022-23. Du BB –. LO HS 14 Ex v Glamorgan (Chelmsford) 2022 (RLC). LO BB 5-72 CD v Canterbury (New Plymouth) 2023-24. T20 HS 0*. T20 BB 3-23.

TREVASKIS, L. – *see LEICESTERSHIRE.*

H.M.Crawshaw and R.G.Whitfield left the staff without making a County 1st XI appearance in 2023.

COUNTY CAPS AWARDED IN 2023

Derbyshire	–
Durham	B.F.W.de Leede, M.V.T.Fernando, M.P.Kuhnemann, B.S.McKinney, C.N.Miles, M.W.Parkinson, A.Y.Patel, M.Pretorius, O.G.Robinson, R.L.Toole
Essex	M.J.J.Critchley, A.M.Rossington, P.I.Walter
Glamorgan	–
Gloucestershire	Z.Akhter, L.A.Charlesworth, M.de Lange, D.J.Lamb, E.W.O.Middleton, J.P.Phillips, G.Roelofsen, H.T.Tector, P.A.van Meekeren
Hampshire	B.C.Brown
Kent	–
Lancashire	–
Leicestershire	R.Ahmed, P.W.A.Mulder, R.K.Patel
Middlesex	R.F.Higgins, M.D.E.Holden
Northamptonshire	–
Nottinghamshire	A.M.Fernando, O.P.Stone, W.A.Young
Somerset	M.J.Henry
Surrey	J.Overton, K.A.J.Roach, J.L.Smith, D.J.Worrall
Sussex	T.P.Alsop, R.S.Bopara, F.J.Hudson-Prentice, T.S.Mills, S.P.D.Smith
Warwickshire	A.L.Davies, Hassan Ali, C.Rushworth, R.M.Yates
Worcestershire (colours)	B.M.J.Allison, J.A.Brooks, R.M.Edavalath, A.J.Hose, N.Saini, Usama Mir, L.V.van Beek
Yorkshire	–

Durham and Gloucestershire now award caps on first-class debut. Worcestershire award club colours on Championship debut.

ESSEX 2023

RESULTS SUMMARY

	Place	Won	Lost	Drew	NR
LV= Insurance County Champ (Div 1)	2nd	7	3	4	
All First-Class Matches		7	4	4	
Metro Bank One-Day Cup (Group A)	9th	1	6		1
Vitality Blast (South Group)	Finalist	10	7		

LV= INSURANCE COUNTY CHAMPIONSHIP AVERAGES
BATTING AND FIELDING

Cap		*M*	*I*	*NO*	*HS*	*Runs*	*Avge*	*100*	*50*	*Ct/St*
2013	T.Westley	14	27	2	148	1130	45.20	3	4	7
2023	M.J.J.Critchley	14	26	1	121	990	39.60	2	7	11
2017	D.W.Lawrence	11	21	–	152	801	38.14	3	2	7
	F.I.N.Khushi	2	4	1	56*	106	35.33	–	1	3
2005	A.N.Cook	14	26	1	128	836	33.44	1	6	17
2018	S.R.Harmer	14	23	6	83*	524	30.82	–	3	22
	U.T.Yadav	3	6	2	51	121	30.25	–	1	–
	M.S.Pepper	4	7	2	52*	145	29.00	–	1	10
2023	P.I.Walter	9	16	2	76	389	27.78	–	2	7
2015	N.L.J.Browne	14	24	2	159	543	24.68	1	1	12
2023	A.M.Rossington	8	15	1	104	315	22.50	1	–	17/3
	W.E.L.Buttleman	3	5	1	43	75	18.75	–	–	15/1
	B.M.J.Allison	3	4	2	11*	32	16.00	–	–	2
	D.A.J.Bracewell	8	11	1	61*	151	15.10	–	1	–
2022	S.Snater	7	10	–	31	107	10.70	–	–	1
2020	S.J.Cook	13	18	5	31	139	10.69	–	–	3
2015	J.A.Porter	14	15	9	11	36	6.00	–	–	12

Also batted: R.J.Das (1 match) 4.

BOWLING

	O	*M*	*R*	*W*	*Avge*	*Best*	*5wI*	*10wM*
J.A.Porter	334.5	64	1086	57	19.05	6- 34	4	1
S.J.Cook	352.2	89	941	48	19.60	5- 42	1	–
M.J.J.Critchley	127.2	14	469	23	20.39	3- 33	–	–
D.A.J.Bracewell	165.2	18	658	24	27.41	4- 51	–	–
S.R.Harmer	558.4	131	1766	61	28.95	6-149	5	1
Also bowled:								
P.I.Walter	45.1	5	146	9	16.22	3- 20	–	–
S.Snater	128.4	27	437	8	54.62	3- 71	–	–

B.M.J.Allison 38-9-115-1; D.W.Lawrence 8-2-25-0; U.T.Yadav 54-7-211-4.

The First-Class Averages (pp 223–235) give the records of Essex players in all first-class county matches (Essex's other opponents being Ireland), with the exception of B.M.J.Allison, whose first-class figures for Essex are as above.

ESSEX RECORDS

FIRST-CLASS CRICKET

Highest Total	For 761-6d		v	Leics	Chelmsford	1990
	V 803-4d		by	Kent	Brentwood	1934
Lowest Total	For 20		v	Lancashire	Chelmsford	2013
	V 14		by	Surrey	Chelmsford	1983
Highest Innings	For 343*	P.A.Perrin	v	Derbyshire	Chesterfield	1904
	V 332	W.H.Ashdown	for	Kent	Brentwood	1934

Highest Partnership for each Wicket

1st	373	N.L.J.Browne/A.N.Cook	v	Middlesex	Chelmsford	2017
2nd	403	G.A.Gooch/P.J.Prichard	v	Leics	Chelmsford	1990
3rd	347*	M.E.Waugh/N.Hussain	v	Lancashire	Ilford	1992
4th	314	Salim Malik/N.Hussain	v	Surrey	The Oval	1991
5th	339	J.C.Mickleburgh/J.S.Foster	v	Durham	Chester-le-St[2]	2010
6th	253	A.J.A.Wheater/J.S.Foster	v	Northants	Chelmsford	2011
7th	261	J.W.H.T.Douglas/J.R.Freeman	v	Lancashire	Leyton	1914
8th	263	D.R.Wilcox/R.M.Taylor	v	Warwicks	Southend	1946
9th	251	J.W.H.T.Douglas/S.N.Hare	v	Derbyshire	Leyton	1921
10th	218	F.H.Vigar/T.P.B.Smith	v	Derbyshire	Chesterfield	1947

Best Bowling	For	10- 32	H.Pickett	v	Leics	Leyton	1895
(Innings)	V	10- 40	E.G.Dennett	for	Glos	Bristol	1906
Best Bowling	For	17-119	W.Mead	v	Hampshire	Southampton[1]	1895
(Match)	V	17- 56	C.W.L.Parker	for	Glos	Gloucester	1925

Most Runs – Season	2559	G.A.Gooch	(av 67.34)	1984
Most Runs – Career	30701	G.A.Gooch	(av 51.77)	1973-97
Most 100s – Season	9	J.O'Connor		1929, 1934
	9	D.J.Insole		1955
Most 100s – Career	94	G.A.Gooch		1973-97
Most Wkts – Season	172	T.P.B Smith	(av 27.13)	1947
Most Wkts – Career	1610	T.P.B.Smith	(av 26.68)	1929-51
Most Career W-K Dismissals	1231	B.Taylor	(1040 ct; 191 st)	1949-73
Most Career Catches in the Field	519	K.W.R.Fletcher		1962-88

LIMITED-OVERS CRICKET

Highest Total	**50ov**	391-5		v	Surrey	The Oval	2008
	40ov	368-7		v	Scotland	Chelmsford	2013
	T20	254-5		v	Glamorgan	Chelmsford	2022
Lowest Total	**50ov**	57		v	Lancashire	Lord's	1996
	40ov	69		v	Derbyshire	Chesterfield	1974
	T20	74		v	Middlesex	Chelmsford	2013
Highest Innings	**50ov**	201*	R.S.Bopara	v	Leics	Leicester	2008
	40ov	180	R.N.ten Doeschate	v	Scotland	Chelmsford	2013
	T20	152*	G.R.Napier	v	Sussex	Chelmsford	2008
Best Bowling	**50ov**	6-42	L.M.Benkenstein	v	Glamorgan	Chelmsford	2022
	40ov	8-26	K.D.Boyce	v	Lancashire	Manchester	1971
	T20	6-16	T.G.Southee	v	Glamorgan	Chelmsford	2011

GLAMORGAN

Formation of Present Club: 6 July 1888
Inaugural First-Class Match: 1921
Colours: Blue and Gold
Badge: Gold Daffodil
County Champions: (3) 1948, 1969, 1997
Pro 40/National League (Div 1) Winners: (2) 2002, 2004
Sunday League Winners: (1) 1993
Royal London One-Day Cup Winners: (1) 2021
Twenty20 Cup Winners: (0); best – Semi-Finalist 2004, 2017

Chief Executive: Dan Cherry, Sophia Gardens, Cardiff, CF11 9XR • Tel: 02920 409380 • email: info@glamorgancricket.co.uk • Web: www.glamorgancricket.com • Twitter: @GlamCricket (81,982 followers)

Director of Cricket: Mark Wallace. **Head Coach**: Grant Bradburn. **Asst Coaches**: Adrian Shaw and Steve Watkin. **Captains**: S.A.Northest (f-c) and K.S.Carlson (l-o). **Overseas Players**: C.A.Ingram, M.Labuschagne and Mir Hamza. **2024 Testimonial**: C.B.Cooke. **Head Groundsman**: Robin Saxton. **Scorer**: Andrew K.Hignell. ‡ New registration. NQ Not qualified for England.

BEVAN, Thomas Rhys (Millfield S; Cardiff Met U), b Cardiff 9 Sep 1999. RHB, OB. Squad No 13. Debut (Glamorgan) 2022. Glamorgan 2nd XI debut 2018. Wales NC 2017 to date. HS 48 v Derbys (Cardiff) 2022. LO HS 134 v Hants (Neath) 2022 (RLC). T20 HS 21.

BYROM, Edward James (St John's C, Harare; King's C, Taunton), b Harare, Zimbabwe 17 Jun 1997. 5'11". LHB, OB. Squad No 97. Irish passport. Somerset 2017-21. Rising Stars 2017-18. Glamorgan debut 2021. Mid West Rhinos 2022-23. Southern Rocks 2023-24. HS 176 v Sussex (Cardiff) 2022, sharing Gm record 2nd wkt partnership of 328 with C.A.Ingram. BB 2-64 v Surrey (Oval) 2021. LO HS 108 v Somerset (Taunton) 2023 (MBC). T20 HS 78*.

CARLSON, Kiran Shah (Whitchurch HS; Cardiff U), b Cardiff 16 May 1998. 5'8". RHB, OB. Squad No 5. Debut (Glamorgan) 2016; cap 2021; l-o captain 2022 to date. Cardiff MCCU 2019. Mid West Rhinos 2022-23. Wales MC 2014. 1000 runs (1): 1068 (2023). HS 192 v Sussex (Hove) 2023. BB 5-28 v Northants (Northampton) 2016 – on debut, aged 18y 119d (also scored hundred in same match). LO HS 82 v Durham (Nottingham) 2021 (RLC). LO BB 4-41 v Northants (Northampton) 2022 (RLC). T20 HS 77. T20 BB 2-13.

COOKE, Christopher Barry (Bishops S, Cape Town; U of Cape Town), b Johannesburg, South Africa 30 May 1986. 5'11". RHB, WK, occ RM. Squad No 46. W Province 2009-10. Glamorgan debut 2013; cap 2016; captain 2019-21; testimonial 2024. Birmingham Phoenix 2021. HS 205* v Surrey (Oval) 2021. LO HS 161 v Glos (Bristol) 2019 (RLC). T20 HS 113*.

‡**CRANE, Mason** Sidney (Lancing C), b Shoreham-by-Sea, Sussex 18 Feb 1997. 5'10". RHB, LB. Squad No 3. Hampshire 2015-23; cap 2021. NSW 2016-17. Sussex 2022 (on loan). Joins Glamorgan on season-long loan in 2024. MCC 2017. London Spirit 2021 to date. **Test**: 1 (2017-18); HS 4 and BB 1-193 v A (Sydney) 2017-18. **IT20**: 2 (2017); HS – ; BB 1-38 v SA (Cardiff) 2017. F-c Tours: A 2017-18; WI 2017-18 (EL). HS 29 H v Somerset (Taunton) 2017. BB 5-35 H v Warwks (Southampton) 2015. LO HS 31 H v Notts (Mansfield) 2023 (MBC). LO BB 4-30 H v Middx (Southampton) 2015 (RLC). T20 HS 12*. T20 BB 4-24.

DOUTHWAITE, Daniel Alexander (Reed's S, Cobham; Cardiff Met U), b Kingston-upon-Thames, Surrey 8 Feb 1997. RHB, RMF. Squad No 88. Cardiff MCCU 2019. Glamorgan debut 2019. Warwickshire 2018 (l-o only). Manchester Originals 2021. HS 100* CfU v Sussex (Hove) 2019. Gm HS 96 v Durham (Chester-le-St) 2021. BB 4-48 v Derbys (Derby) 2019. LO HS 52* v Sussex (Hove) 2019 (RLC). LO BB 3-43 Wa v West Indies A (Birmingham) 2018. T20 HS 53. T20 BB 4-23.

GORVIN, Andrew William (Portsmouth HS; Cardiff Met U), b Winchester, Hants 10 May 1997. RHB, RM. Squad No 11. Wales NC 2019 to date. Debut (Glamorgan) 2022. HS 47 v Yorks (Cardiff) 2023. BB 3-88 v Durham (Chester-le-St) 2023. LO HS 12* v Somerset (Taunton) 2021 (RLC). LO BB 2-41 v Hants (Neath) 2022 (RLC). T20 HS 12. T20 BB 1-30.

HARRIS, James Alexander Russell (Pontardulais CS; Gorseinon C), b Morriston, Swansea 16 May 1990. 6'0". RHB, RMF. Squad No 9. Debut (Glamorgan) 2007, aged 16y 351d – youngest Gm player to take a f-c wicket; cap 2010. Middlesex 2013-21; cap 2015. Kent 2017 (on loan). MCC 2016. Wales MC 2005-08. F-c Tours (EL): WI 2010-11; SL 2013-14. HS 87* v Notts (Swansea) 2007. 50 wkts (3); most – 73 (2015). BB 9-34 (13-103 match) M v Durham (Lord's) 2015 – record innings and match analysis v Durham. Gm BB 7-66 (12-118 match) v Glos (Bristol) 2007 – youngest (17y 3d) to take 10 wickets in any CC match. LO HS 117 M v Lancs (Lord's) 2019 (RLC). LO BB 4-38 M v Glamorgan (Lord's) 2015 (RLC). T20 HS 18. T20 BB 4-23.

HORTON, Alex Jack (St Edward's, Oxford), b Newport, Monmouths 7 Jan 2004. RHB, WK. Squad No 37. Glamorgan 2nd XI debut 2019. Wales NC 2022. England U19 2022. Awaiting f-c debut. LO HS 44* v Northants (Cardiff) 2023 (MBC). T20 HS 1*.

HURLE, Henry Ellis (Monmouth S), b Cardiff 11 Nov 2004. RHB, WK. Squad No 6. Glamorgan 2nd XI debut 2021. Awaiting 1st XI debut.

[NQ]**INGRAM, Colin** Alexander, b Port Elizabeth, South Africa 3 Jul 1985. LHB, LB. Squad No 41. Free State 2004-05 to 2005-06. Eastern Province 2005-06 to 2008-09. Warriors 2006-07 to 2016-17. Somerset 2014. Glamorgan debut 2015; cap 2017; captain 2018-19 (T20 only). IPL: DD 2011. Big Bash: AS 2017-18 to 2018-19; HH 2020-21. Oval Invincibles 2021. **LOI** (SA): 31 (2010-11 to 2013-14); HS 124 v Z (Bloemfontein) 2010-11 – on debut; BB –. **IT20** (SA): 9 (2010-11 to 2011-12); HS 78 v I (Johannesburg) 2011-12. HS 190 EP v KZN (Pt Elizabeth) 2008-09. Gm HS 178 v Sussex (Cardiff) 2022, sharing Gm record 2nd wkt partnership of 328 with E.J.Byrom. BB 4-16 EP v Boland (Pt Elizabeth) 2005-06. Gm BB 3-90 v Essex (Chelmsford) 2015. LO HS 155 v Kent (Cardiff) 2022 (RLC). LO BB 4-39 v Middx (Radlett) 2017 (RLC). T20 HS 127*. T20 BB 4-32.

KELLAWAY, Benjamin Ian (Chepstow CS; Clifton C; Cardiff U), b Newport 5 Jan 2004. RHB, OB, occ WK. Squad No 8. Debut (Glamorgan) 2023. Glamorgan 2nd XI debut 2021. Wales MC 2019. HS 0. BB –. LO HS 82 v Worcs (Worcester) 2023 (MBC). LO BB 3-41 v Derbys (Derby) 2023 (MBC). T20 HS 3. T20 BB –.

[NQ]**LABUSCHAGNE, Marnus**, b Klerksdorp, South Africa 22 Jun 1994. RHB, LB. Squad No 33. Queensland 2014-15 to date. Glamorgan debut 2019; cap 2019. Big Bash: BH 2016-17 to date. *Wisden* 2019. **Tests** (A): 49 (2018-19 to 2023-24); 1000 runs (1): 1104 (2019); HS 215 v NZ (Sydney) 2019-20; BB 3-45 v P (Abu Dhabi) 2018-19. **LOI** (A): 52 (2019-20 to 2023-24); HS 124 v SA (Bloemfontein) 2023; BB 2-9 v SL (Pallekelle) 2022. **IT20** (A): 1 (2022-23); HS 2 v P (Lahore) 2022-23. F-c Tours (A): E 2019, 2023; NZ 2023-24; I 2018-19 (Aus A), 2022-23; P 2021-22; SL 2022; UAE 2018-19 (v P). 1000 runs (1+2); most – 1530 (2019). HS 215 (*see Tests*). Gm HS 182 v Sussex (Hove) 2019. BB 4-81 v Durham (Cardiff) 2023 LO HS 135 Q v SA (Brisbane) 2019-20. LO BB 3-46 v Somerset (Cardiff) 2019 (RLC). T20 HS 93*. T20 BB 3-13.

McILROY, Jamie Peter (Builth Wells HS), b Hereford 19 Jun 1994. RHB, LFM. Squad No 35. Debut (Glamorgan) 2021. HS 30* v Yorks (Cardiff) 2023. BB 5-34 v Worcs (Worcester) 2023. LO HS 13 v Worcs (Worcester) 2023 (MBC). LO BB 2-13 v Derbys (Derby) 2022 (RLC). T20 HS 2*. T20 BB 4-36.

‡[NQ]**MIR HAMZA**, b Karachi, Pakistan 10 Sep 1992. LHB, LMF. Squad No 92. Karachi Whites 2012-13 to date. Karachi Dolphins 2014-15. United Bank 2015-16 to 2017-18. National Bank 2018-19. Sussex 2019. Sindh 2019-20 to 2022-23. Warwickshire 2023. SNGPL 2023-24. **Tests** (P): 5 (2018-19 to 2023-24); HS 7* v A (Sydney) 2023-24; BB 4-32 v A (Melbourne) 2023-24. HS 40 SNGPL v HEC (Karachi) 2023-24. CC HS 10* Wa v Lancs (Birmingham) 2023. BB 7-59 UB v SSGC (Sialkot) 2016-17. CC BB 4-51 Sx v Northants (Northampton) 2019. LO HS 49 KD v Rawalpindi Rams (Karachi) 2014-15. LO BB 4-12 Sindh v Khyber Pak (Karachi) 2022-23. T20 HS 19*. T20 BB 4-9.

MORRIS, Benjamin James (King Henry VIII S; Cardiff U), b Abergavenny 4 Nov 2003. RHB, RM. Squad No 18. Glamorgan 2nd XI debut 2021. Wales NC 2021-22. Awaiting f-c XI debut. LO HS 2* v Worcs (Worcester) 2023 (MBC). LO BB –.

NORTHEAST, Sam Alexander (Harrow S), b Ashford, Kent 16 Oct 1989. 5'11". RHB, LB. Squad No 16. Kent 2007-17; cap 2012; captain 2016-17. Hampshire 2018-21; cap 2019. Yorkshire 2021 (on loan). Nottinghamshire 2021 (on loan). Glamorgan debut/cap 2022; captain 2024. MCC 2013, 2018. 1000 runs (5); most – 1402 (2016). HS 410* v Leics (Leicester) 2022 – county record score and the 3rd highest in CC history, sharing Gm record 6th wkt partnership of 461* with C.B.Cooke. BB 1-60 K v Glos (Cheltenham) 2013. LO HS 177* v Worcs (Worcester) 2022 (RLC). T20 HS 114.

PODMORE, Harry William (Twyford HS), b Hammersmith, London 23 Jul 1994. 6'3". RHB, RMF. Squad No 23. Debut (Glamorgan) 2016 (on loan). Middlesex 2016 to 2016-17. Derbyshire 2017 (on loan). Kent 2018-22; cap 2019. HS 66* De v Sussex (Hove) 2017. Gm HS 16* v Kent (Canterbury) 2016. 50 wkts (1): 54 (2019). BB 6-36 K v Middx (Canterbury) 2018. Gm BB 3-59 v Glos (Bristol) 2016. LO HS 40 v Hants (Canterbury) 2019 (RLC). LO BB 4-57 v Notts (Nottingham) 2018 (RLC). T20 HS 9. T20 BB 3-13.

ROOT, William ('**Billy**') Thomas (Worksop C; Leeds Beckett U), b Sheffield, Yorks 5 Aug 1992. Younger brother of J.E.Root (*see YORKSHIRE*). LHB, OB. Squad No 7. Leeds/Bradford MCCU 2015-16. Nottinghamshire 2015-18. Glamorgan debut 2019; cap 2021. Suffolk 2014. HS 229 v Northants (Northampton) 2019. BB 3-29 Nt v Sussex (Hove) 2017. Gm BB 2-63 v Northants (Cardiff) 2019. LO HS 113* v Surrey (Cardiff) 2019 (RLC) and 113* v Worcs (Worcester) 2022 (RLC). LO BB 2-36 v Middx (Lord's) 2019 (RLC). T20 HS 41*. T20 BB –.

SISODIYA, Prem (Whitchurch HS; Clifton C; Cardiff Met U), b Cardiff 21 Sep 1998. RHB, SLA. Squad No 32. Debut (Glamorgan) 2018. Cardiff MCCU 2019. Wales MC 2017-19. HS 38 and CC BB 3-54 v Derbys (Swansea) 2018. BB 4-79 CfU v Somerset (Taunton) 2019. LO HS 7 v Lancs (Neath) 2022 (RLC) and 7 v Glos (Cardiff) 2023 (MBC). LO BB 3-76 v Worcs (Worcester) 2022 (RLC). T20 HS 23. T20 BB 3-26.

SMALE, William Timothy Edward (Rougemont S; King's C, Taunton; Cardiff Met U), b Newport, Monmouths 28 Feb 2001. Elder brother of S.A.E.Smale (Western Storm & England U19 women). RHB, WK. Squad No 28. NW Warriors 2019. Derbyshire 2nd XI 2021. Gloucestershire 2nd XI 2021-22. Somerset 2nd XI 2022. Glamorgan 2nd XI debut 2023. Wales MC 2018. HS 0. LO HS NW 48 v Northern (Eglinton) 2019. T20 HS 27.

[NQ]**SMITH, Ruaidhri** Alexander James (Llandaff Cathedral S; Shrewsbury S; Bristol U), b Glasgow, Scotland 5 Aug 1994. 6'1". RHB, RM. Squad No 20. Glamorgan 2013-21. Scotland 2017. Wales MC 2010-16. **LOI** (Scot): 2 (2016); HS 10 and BB 1-34 v Afg (Edinburgh) 2016. **IT20** (Scot): 2 (2018-19); HS 9* v Netherlands (Al Amerat) 2018-19; BB –. HS 57* v Glos (Bristol) 2014. BB 5-87 v Durham (Cardiff) 2018. LO HS 14 v Hants (Swansea) 2018 (RLC). LO BB 4-7 Scot v Oman (Al Amerat) 2018-19. T20 HS 22*. T20 BB 4-6.

TRIBE, Asa Mark (De La Salle C, Jersey; Cardiff U), b Jersey 29 Mar 2004. RHB, OB. Squad No 55. Glamorgan 2nd XI debut 2023. Awaiting 1st XI debut. **LOI** (Jersey): 5 (2022-23); HS 115* v PNG (Windhoek) 2022-23; BB –. **IT20** (Jersey): 21 (2021-22 to 2023); HS 73* v USA (Bulawayo) 2022. LO HS 115* (*see LOI*). LO BB 1-37 Jersey v Uganda (St Martin) 2022. T20 HS 73*.

NQ**van der GUGTEN, Timm**, b Hornsby, Sydney, Australia 25 Feb 1991. 6'1½". RHB, RFM. Squad No 64. New South Wales 2011-12. Netherlands 2012 to date. Glamorgan debut 2016; cap 2018. Big Bash: HH 2014-15. Trent Rockets 2021. Birmingham Phoenix 2022. **LOI** (Neth): 8 (2011-12 to 2021-22); HS 49 v Ire (Utrecht) 2021; BB 5-24 v Canada (King City, NW) 2013. **IT20** (Neth): 47 (2011-12 to 2023-24); HS 40* v PNG (Dubai, ICCA) 2019-20; BB 3-9 v Singapore (Dubai, ICCA) 2019-20. HS 85* v Yorks (Leeds) 2021. 50 wkts (1): 56 (2016). BB 7-42 v Kent (Cardiff) 2018. LO HS 49 (*see LOI*). LO BB 5-24 (*see LOI*). T20 HS 48. T20 BB 5-21.

ZAIN UL HASSAN (Pedmore Tech C, Stourbridge), b Islamabad, Pakistan 28 Oct 2000. LHB, RM. Squad No 27. Debut (Glamorgan) 2023. Worcestershire 2nd XI 2017-21. Gloucestershire 2nd XI 2021. Surrey 2nd XI 2022. Northamptonshire 2nd XI 2022. Kent 2nd XI 2022. Glamorgan 2nd XI debut 2022. Herefordshire 2021. HS 69 v Derbys (Derby) 2023. BB 2-18 v Worcs (Worcester) 2023. LO HS 26* and LO BB 4-25 v Sussex (Hove) 2023 (MBC). T20 HS 11. T20 BB –.

RELEASED/RETIRED

(Having made a County 1st XI appearance in 2023)

NQ**FLETCHER, Cam**eron Dean, b Auckland, New Zealand 1 Mar 1993. RHB, WK. Northern Districts 2012-13 to 2013-14. Canterbury 2014-15 to 2022-23. Auckland 2023-24. Glamorgan 2023 (T20 only). F-c Tour (NZA): I 2022-23. HS 157 Cant v Otago (Christchurch) 2020-21. LO HS 86* Cant v CD (Christchurch) 2022-23. T20 HS 74*.

NQ**HATZOGLOU, Peter**, b Melbourne, Australia 27 Nov 1998. 6'4". RHB, LBG. S Australia 2020-21 (l-o only). Glamorgan 2023 (T20 only). Big Bash: MR 2020-21; PS 2021-22 to 2022-23; HH 2023-24. Oval Invincibles 2022. LO HS 5* SA v WA (Perth) 2020-21. LO BB –. T20 HS 15. T20 BB 3-14.

LLOYD, D.L. – *see DERBYSHIRE.*

NESER, M.G. – *see HAMPSHIRE.*

SALTER, Andrew Graham (Milford Haven SFC; Cardiff Met U), b Haverfordwest 1 Jun 1993. 5'9". RHB, OB. Cardiff MCCU 2012-14. Glamorgan 2013-23; cap 2022. Wales MC 2010-11. HS 90 v Durham (Chester-le-St) 2021. BB 7-45 v Durham (Cardiff) 2022. LO HS 51 v Pakistan A (Newport) 2016. LO BB 3-37 v Surrey (Cardiff) 2021 (RLC). T20 HS 39*. T20 BB 4-12.

NQ**SWEPSON, Mitchell** Joseph, b Herston, Brisbane, Australia 4 Oct 1993. RHB, LB. Queensland 2015-16 to date. Glamorgan 2023. Big Bash: BH 2015-16 to date. **Tests** (A): 4 (2021-22 to 2022); HS 15* v P (Karachi) 2021-22; BB 3-55 v SL (Galle) 2022. **LOI** (A): 3 (2021-22 to 2022); HS 2 v SL (Pallekele) 2022; BB 2-53 v P (Lahore) 2021-22. **IT20** (A): 8 (2018 to 2022-23); HS 14* v WI (Gros Islet) 2021; BB 3-12 v B (Mirpur) 2021. F-c Tours (A): NZ 2022-23 (Aus A); I 2018-19 (Aus A); P 2021-22; SL 2022. HS 69 v Leics (Cardiff) 2023. BB 5-39 Q v Vic (Mackay) 2023-24. Gm BB 4-89 v Sussex (Cardiff) 2023. LO HS 77 Q v Vic (Townsville) 2018-19. BB 3-40 Aus A v South Africa A (Bengaluru) 2018. T20 HS 14*. T20 BB 3-12.

TAYLOR, Callum Zinzan (The Southport S), b Newport, Monmouths 19 Jun 1998. RHB, OB. Glamorgan 2020-22, scoring 106 v Northants (Northampton) on debut. Wales MC 2017. HS 106 (*see above*). BB 2-16 v Yorks (Leeds) 2020. LO HS 36 v Northants (Northampton) 2021 (RLC). LO BB 1-6 v Somerset (Taunton) 2021 (RLC). T20 HS 23. T20 BB 2-9.

T.D.C.Phillips left the staff without making a County 1st XI appearance in 2023.

GLAMORGAN 2023

RESULTS SUMMARY

	Place	*Won*	*Lost*	*Drew*	*NR*
LV= Insurance County Champ (Div 2)	5th	1	1	12	
Metro Bank One-Day Cup (Group B)	4th	4	3		1
Vitality Blast (South Group)	8th	5	9		

LV= INSURANCE COUNTY CHAMPIONSHIP AVERAGES
BATTING AND FIELDING

Cap		*M*	*I*	*NO*	*HS*	*Runs*	*Avge*	*100*	*50*	*Ct/St*
2021	M.G.Neser	6	7	1	176*	487	81.16	2	2	3
2019	M.Labuschagne	5	8	1	170*	502	71.71	2	2	7
2021	W.T.Root	14	23	6	117*	884	52.00	1	6	2
2021	K.S.Carlson	14	23	–	192	1068	46.43	4	5	7
2016	C.B.Cooke	14	21	5	134*	733	45.81	2	2	38/2
	E.J.Byrom	8	15	2	101	475	36.53	1	4	3
	M.J.Swepson	4	4	1	69	103	34.33	–	1	2
2022	S.A.Northeast	13	20	1	166*	646	34.00	2	2	7
	Zain Ul Hassan	9	16	1	69	453	30.20	–	2	2
2019	D.L.Lloyd	8	13	2	81	332	30.18	–	1	5
2017	C.A.Ingram	7	12	–	136	357	29.75	1	1	7
2018	T.van der Gugten	13	15	5	54	280	28.00	–	2	3
2022	A.G.Salter	4	7	–	48	163	23.28	–	–	3
	A.W.Gorvin	5	6	2	47	86	21.50	–	–	–
	D.A.Douthwaite	4	6	2	37	78	19.50	–	–	–
	J.P.McIlroy	10	11	6	30*	79	15.80	–	–	1
2010	J.A.R.Harris	11	12	1	47	159	14.45	–	–	2

Also batted: T.R.Bevan (1 match) 0, 15 (2 ct); B.I.Kellaway (2) 0, 0; H.W.Podmore (2) 3, 2* (1 ct); P.Sisodiya (1) 4.

BOWLING

	O	*M*	*R*	*W*	*Avge*	*Best*	*5wI*	*10wM*
M.G.Neser	155.3	26	523	20	26.15	7- 32	1	–
T.van der Gugten	385.5	89	1140	39	29.23	6- 88	3	–
J.P.McIlroy	259.5	51	736	24	30.66	5- 34	1	–
J.A.R.Harris	292.4	37	1189	32	37.15	4- 18	–	–
M.J.Swepson	176.3	32	585	14	41.78	4- 89	–	–
K.S.Carlson	206	12	853	14	60.92	3-147	–	–
Also bowled:								
M.Labuschagne	39.3	1	217	5	43.40	4- 81	–	–
A.W.Gorvin	96.4	25	318	7	45.42	3- 88	–	–
D.L.Lloyd	59	5	266	5	53.20	2- 32	–	–
Zain ul Hassan	143	22	477	8	59.62	2- 18	–	–

E.J.Byrom 9-1-49-0; C.B.Cooke 0.3-0-4-0; D.A.Douthwaite 54.5-6-204-4; B.I.Kellaway 17-1-60-0; S.A.Northeast 4-1-15-0; H.W.Podmore 55-13-206-3; W.T.Root 3-0-9-0; A.G.Salter 68-8-253-0; P.Sisodiya 15-0-74-1.

Glamorgan played no first-class fixtures outside the County Championship in 2023. The First-Class Averages (pp 223–235) give the records of Glamorgan players in all first-class county matches, with the exception of M.Labuschagne, whose first-class figures for Glamorgan are as above.

GLAMORGAN RECORDS

FIRST-CLASS CRICKET

Highest Total	For	795-5d		v	Leics	Leicester	2022
	V	750		by	Northants	Cardiff	2019
Lowest Total	For	22		v	Lancashire	Liverpool	1924
	V	33		by	Leics	Ebbw Vale	1965
Highest Innings	For	410*	S.A.Northeast	v	Leics	Leicester	2022
	V	322*	M.B.Loye	for	Northants	Northampton	1998

Highest Partnership for each Wicket

1st	374	M.T.G.Elliott/S.P.James	v	Sussex	Colwyn Bay	2000
2nd	328	E.J.Byrom/C.A.Ingram	v	Sussex	Cardiff	2022
3rd	313	D.E.Davies/W.E.Jones	v	Essex	Brentwood	1948
4th	425*	A.Dale/I.V.A.Richards	v	Middlesex	Cardiff	1993
5th	307*	K.S.Carlson/C.B.Cooke	v	Northants	Cardiff	2021
6th	461*	S.A.Northeast/C.B.Cooke	v	Leics	Leicester	2022
7th	211	P.A.Cottey/O.D.Gibson	v	Leics	Swansea	1996
8th	211	C.B.Cooke/M.G.Neser	v	Leics	Leicester	2023
9th	203*	J.J.Hills/J.C.Clay	v	Worcs	Swansea	1929
10th	143	T.Davies/S.A.B.Daniels	v	Glos	Swansea	1982

Best Bowling	For	10- 51	J.Mercer	v	Worcs	Worcester	1936
(Innings)	V	10- 18	G.Geary	for	Leics	Pontypridd	1929
Best Bowling	For	17-212	J.C.Clay	v	Worcs	Swansea	1937
(Match)	V	16- 96	G.Geary	for	Leics	Pontypridd	1929

Most Runs – Season	2276	H.Morris	(av 55.51)	1990
Most Runs – Career	34056	A.Jones	(av 33.03)	1957-83
Most 100s – Season	10	H.Morris		1990
Most 100s – Career	54	M.P.Maynard		1985-2005
Most Wkts – Season	176	J.C.Clay	(av 17.34)	1937
Most Wkts – Career	2174	D.J.Shepherd	(av 20.95)	1950-72
Most Career W-K Dismissals	933	E.W.Jones	(840 ct; 93 st)	1961-83
Most Career Catches in the Field	656	P.M.Walker		1956-72

LIMITED-OVERS CRICKET

Highest Total	**50ov**	429		v	Surrey	The Oval	2002
	40ov	328-4		v	Lancashire	Colwyn Bay	2011
	T20	240-3		v	Surrey	The Oval	2015
Lowest Total	**50ov**	68		v	Lancashire	Manchester	1973
	40ov	42		v	Derbyshire	Swansea	1979
	T20	44		v	Surrey	The Oval	2019
Highest Innings	**50ov**	177*	S.A.Northeast	v	Worcs	Worcester	2022
	40ov	155*	J.H.Kallis	v	Surrey	Pontypridd	1999
	T20	116*	I.J.Thomas	v	Somerset	Taunton	2004
Best Bowling	**50ov**	6-20	S.D.Thomas	v	Comb Univs	Cardiff	1995
	40ov	7-16	S.D.Thomas	v	Surrey	Swansea	1998
	T20	5-14	G.G.Wagg	v	Worcs	Worcester	2013

GLOUCESTERSHIRE

Formation of Present Club: 1871
Inaugural First-Class Match: 1870
Colours: Blue, Gold, Brown, Silver, Green and Red
Badge: Coat of Arms of the City and County of Bristol
County Champions (since 1890): (0); best – 2nd 1930, 1931, 1947, 1959, 1969, 1986
Gillette/NatWest/C&G Trophy Winners: (5) 1973, 1999, 2000, 2003, 2004
Benson and Hedges Cup Winners: (3) 1977, 1999, 2000
Pro 40/National League (Div 1) Winners: (1) 2000
Royal London One-Day Cup Winners: (1) 2015
Twenty20 Cup Winners: (0); best – Finalist 2007

Chief Executive: Will Brown, Seat Unique Stadium, Nevil Road, Bristol BS7 9EJ • Tel: 0117 910 8000 • Email: reception@glosccc.co.uk • Web: www.gloscricket.co.uk • Twitter: @Gloscricket (80,158 followers)

Head Coach: Mark Alleyne. **Head of Talent Pathway**: Mark Thorburn. **2nd XI/Batting Coach**: Owen Dawkins. **Captain**: G.L.van Buuren (f-c & l-o) and J.M.R.Taylor (T20). **Vice-Captain**: J.R.Bracey. **Overseas Players**: C.T.Bancroft, B.J.Webster and Zafar Gohar. **2024 Testimonial**: C.D.J.Dent. **Head Groundsman**: Sean Williams. **Scorer**: Adrian Bull. ‡ New registration. NQ Not qualified for England.

Gloucestershire revised their capping policy in 2004 and now award players with their County Caps when they make their first-class debut.

AKHTER, Zaman (Perse S; Oxford U), b Cambridge 12 Mar 1999. RHB, RMF. Squad No 17. Oxford MCCU 2019. Gloucestershire debut 2023. Cambridgeshire 2018-19. Hertfordshire 2021. HS 41* v Leics (Leicester) 2023. BB 4-33 v Leics (Bristol) 2023. LO HS 27* v Worcs (Worcester) 2023 (MBC). LO BB 3-56 v Derbys (Cheltenham) 2023 (MBC). T20 HS 11*. T20 BB 2-36.

BAILEY, Archie George (Malvern C), b Northampton 28 Jun 2005. RHB, RMF. Squad No 28. Gloucestershire 2nd XI debut 2022. Awaiting 1st XI debut.

NQ**BANCROFT, Cameron** Timothy (Aquinas C, Perth), b Attadale, Perth, Australia 19 Nov 1992. 6'0". RHB, WK, occ RM. Squad No 4. W Australia 2013-14 to date. Gloucestershire debut/cap 2016. Durham 2019-21; cap 2019; captain 2019-20. Somerset 2023. Big Bash: PS 2014-15 to 2022-23; ST 2023-24. **Tests** (A): 10 (2017-18 to 2019); HS 82* v E (Brisbane) 2017-18. **IT20** (A): 1 (2015-16); HS 0* v I (Sydney) 2015-16. F-c Tours (A): E 2019; SA 2017-18; I 2015 (Aus A). HS 228* WA v SA (Perth) 2017-18. CC HS 206* v Kent (Bristol) 2017. BB 1-10 WA v Q (Brisbane) 2019-20. LO HS 176 WA v SA (Sydney, HO) 2015-16. T20 HS 95*.

BOORMAN, Thomas William (Malvern C), b Cheltenham 12 Apr 2005. RHB, OB. Squad No 71. Gloucestershire 2nd XI debut 2021. Awaiting 1st XI debut.

BRACEY, James Robert (Filton CS), b Bristol 3 May 1997. Younger brother of S.N.Bracey (Cardiff MCCU 2014-15). 6'1". LHB, WK, occ RM. Squad No 25. Debut (Gloucestershire) 2016; cap 2016. Loughborough MCCU 2017-18. **Tests**: 2 (2021); HS 8 v NZ (Birmingham) 2021. F-c Tour (EL): A 2019-20. HS 177 v Yorks (Bristol) 2022. BB –. LO HS 224* v Somerset (Bristol) 2023 (MBC) – Gs l-o record. LO BB 1-23 v Essex (Chelmsford) 2019 (RLC). T20 HS 70.

CHARLESWORTH, Ben Geoffrey (St Edward's S), b Oxford 19 Nov 2000. Elder brother of L.A.Charlesworth (*see below*); son of G.M.Charlesworth (Griqualand W and Cambridge U 1989-90 to 1993). 6'2½". LHB, RM/OB. Squad No 64. Debut (Gloucestershire) 2018; cap 2018. Gloucestershire 2nd XI debut 2016. Oxfordshire 2016. England U19 2018 to 2018-19. HS 87 v Derbys (Derby) 2023. BB 3-25 v Middx (Bristol) 2018. LO HS 99* v Hants (Bristol) 2021 (RLC). LO BB –. T20 HS 56. T20 BB 1-32.

CHARLESWORTH, Luke Alexander (St Edward's S; Exeter U), b Oxford 4 Apr 2003. Younger brother of B.G.Charlesworth (*see above*); son of G.M.Charlesworth (Griqualand W and Cambridge U 1989-90 to 1993). RHB, RM. Debut (Gloucestershire) 2023; cap 2023. Squad No 19. Gloucestershire 2nd XI debut 2019. HS 4 and BB 3-54 v Leics (Leicester) 2023. T20 HS 1. T20 BB 1-32.

DALE, Ajeet Singh (Wellington C), b Slough, Berks 3 Jul 2000. 6'1". RHB, RFM. Squad No 39. Hampshire 2020. Gloucestershire debut/cap 2022. Hampshire 2nd XI 2018-21. Gloucestershire 2nd XI debut 2021. HS 52 v Leics (Bristol) 2023. BB 6-41 v Worcs (Worcester) 2023. LO HS 9 and LO BB 4-58 v Northants (Cheltenham) 2023 (MBC). T20 HS 0. T20 BB 2-36.

De LANGE, Marchant, b Tzaneen, South Africa 13 Oct 1990. RHB, RF. Qualified as a domestic player in 2023. Squad No 90. Easterns 2010-11 to 2015-16. Titans 2010-11 to 2015-16. Knights 2016-17 to 2017-18. Free State 2016-17. Glamorgan 2017-20; cap 2019. Somerset 2021-22. Gloucestershire debut/cap 2023. IPL: KKR 2012; MI 2014-15. Trent Rockets 2021. **Tests** (SA): 2 (2011-12); HS 9 and BB 7-81 v SL (Durban) 2011-12 – on debut. **LOI** (SA): 4 (2011-12 to 2015-16); HS – ; BB 4-46 v NZ (Auckland) 2011-12. **IT20** (SA): 6 (2011-12 to 2015-16); HS – ; BB 2-26 v WI (Durban) 2014-15. F-c Tours (SA): A 2014 (SA A); NZ 2011-12. HS 113 Gm v Northants (Northampton) 2020. Gs HS 22 v Worcs (Worcester) 2023. BB 7-23 Knights v Titans (Centurion) 2016-17. CC BB 5-62 Gm v Glos (Bristol) 2018. Gs BB 3-84 v Glamorgan (Cardiff) 2023. LO HS 58* Gm v Surrey (Cardiff) 2019 (RLC). LO BB 5-49 Gm v Hants (Southampton) 2017 (RLC). T20 HS 28*. T20 BB 5-20.

DENT, Christopher David James (Backwell CS; Alton C), b Bristol 20 Jan 1991. 5'9". LHB, SLA, occ WK. Squad No 15. Debut (Gloucestershire) 2010; cap 2010; captain 2018-21; testimonial 2024. 1000 runs (4); most – 1336 (2016). HS 268 v Glamorgan (Bristol) 2015. BB 2-21 v Sussex (Hove) 2016. LO HS 151* v Glamorgan (Cardiff) 2013 (Y40). LO BB 4-43 v Leics (Bristol) 2012 (CB40). T20 HS 87. T20 BB 1-4.

GOODMAN, Dominic Charles (Dr Challenor's GS), b Ashford, Kent 23 Oct 2000. 6'6". RHB, RMF. Squad No 83. Debut (Gloucestershire) 2021; cap 2021. Gloucestershire 2nd XI debut 2019. HS 18 v Hants (Southampton) 2022. BB 4-73 v Durham (Chester-le-St) 2023. LO BB –.

HAMMOND, Miles Arthur Halhead (St Edward's S, Oxford), b Cheltenham 11 Jan 1996. 5'11". LHB, OB. Squad No 88. Debut (Gloucestershire) 2013; cap 2013. Birmingham Phoenix 2021-22. F-c Tour (MCC): Nepal 2019-20. HS 169 v Hants (Cheltenham) 2022. BB 2-37 v Leics (Leicester) 2021. LO HS 109* v Lancs (Bristol) 2023 (MBC). LO BB 2-18 v Northants (Northampton) 2015 (RLC). T20 HS 63. T20 BB –.

MIDDLETON, Edward William Osborne (King's C, Taunton; Oxford Brookes U), b Exeter, Devon 28 Dec 2000. RHB, LB. Squad No 55. Debut (Gloucestershire) 2023; cap 2023. Gloucestershire 2nd XI debut 2022. Devon 2018-22. HS 39* and BB 1-59 v Derbys (Bristol) 2023.

PAYNE, David Alan (Lytchett Minster S), b Poole, Dorset, 15 Feb 1991. 6'2". RHB, LMF. Squad No 14. Debut (Gloucestershire) 2011; cap 2011. Big Bash: PS 2022-23; AS 2023-24. Welsh Fire 2021 to date. Dorset 2009. **LOI**: 1 (2022); HS – ; BB 1-38 v Neth (Amstelveen) 2022. HS 67* v Glamorgan (Cardiff) 2016. BB 6-26 v Leics (Bristol) 2011. LO HS 40 EL v South Africans (Worcester) 2022. LO BB 7-29 v Essex (Chelmsford) 2010 (CB40), inc 4 wkts in 4 balls and 6 wkts in 9 balls – Gs record. T20 HS 16. T20 BB 5-24.

PHILLIPS, Joseph Peter (Penair S, Truro; Clifton C), b Truro, Cornwall 9 Nov 2003. RHB, OB. Squad No 24. Debut (Gloucestershire) 2023; cap 2023. Gloucestershire 2nd XI debut 2022. Cornwall 2021-22. HS 80 v Worcs (Cheltenham) 2023. LO HS 11 v Northants (Cheltenham) 2023 (MBC).

PRICE, Oliver James (Magdalen Coll S), b Oxford 12 Jun 2001. Younger brother of T.J.Price (*see below*). 6'3". RHB, OB. Squad No 67. Debut (Gloucestershire) 2021; cap 2021. Gloucestershire 2nd XI debut 2018. Oxfordshire 2018-19. F-c Tour (EL): I 2023-24. HS 132 v Derbys (Bristol) 2023. BB 3-40 v Leics (Bristol) 2023. LO HS 116* v Derbys (Cheltenham) 2023 (MBC). LO BB 2-12 v Lancs (Bristol) 2023 (MBC). T20 HS 46. T20 BB 3-21.

PRICE, Thomas James (Magdalen Coll S), b Oxford 2 Jan 2000. Elder brother of O.J.Price (*see above*). 6'1". RHB, RM. Squad No 53. Debut (Gloucestershire) 2020; cap 2020. Gloucestershire 2nd XI debut 2015. Oxfordshire 2018-19. HS 109 v Worcs (Worcester) 2023. BB 8-27 (10-73 match) v Warwks (Bristol) 2022. Hat-tricks (2): v Kent (Canterbury) 2022 and v Worcs (Worcester) 2023, becoming the first in all f-c cricket to score a century and take a hat-trick on the same day. LO HS 45 v Leics (Bristol) 2022 (RLC). LO BB 4-26 v Northants (Cheltenham) 2023 (MBC). T20 HS 25. T20 BB 1-29.

SHAW, Joshua (Crofton HS, Wakefield; Skills Exchange C), b Wakefield, Yorks 3 Jan 1996. Son of C.Shaw (Yorkshire 1984-88). 6'1". RHB, RMF. Squad No 5. Debut (Gloucestershire) 2016 (on loan); cap 2016. Yorkshire 2016-19. HS 44 v Durham (Bristol) 2023. BB 5-79 v Sussex (Bristol) 2016. LO HS 8* v Durham (Chester-le-St) 2022 (RLC). LO BB 4-36 v Lancs (Bristol) 2021 (RLC). T20 HS 14. T20 BB 3-32.

SMITH, Thomas Michael John (Seaford Head Community C; Sussex Downs C), b Eastbourne, Sussex 29 Aug 1987. 5'9". RHB, SLA. Squad No 6. Sussex 2007-09. Surrey 2009 (l-o only). Middlesex 2010-13. Gloucestershire debut/cap 2013. HS 84 v Leics (Cheltenham) 2019. BB 4-35 v Kent (Canterbury) 2014. LO HS 65 Sy v Leics (Leicester) 2009 (P40). LO BB 4-26 v Sussex (Cheltenham) 2016 (RLC). T20 HS 36*. T20 BB 5-16 v Warwks (Birmingham) 2020 – Gs record.

SYED, Ahmed Mujtaba (Clifton C), b Enfield, Middx 26 Sep 2004. RHB, LM. Squad No 20. Gloucestershire 2nd XI debut 2021. Awaiting 1st XI debut.

TAYLOR, Jack Martin Robert (Chipping Norton S), b Banbury, Oxfordshire 12 Nov 1991. Elder brother of M.D.Taylor (*see below*). 5'11". RHB, OB. Squad No 10. Debut (Gloucestershire) 2010; cap 2010; captain 2023 to date (white ball only). Oxfordshire 2009-11. HS 156 v Northants (Cheltenham) 2015. BB 4-16 v Glamorgan (Bristol) 2016. LO HS 121 v Worcs (Worcester) 2023 (MBC). LO BB 4-31 v Somerset (Bristol) 2022 (RLC). T20 HS 80. T20 BB 4-16.

TAYLOR, Matthew David (Chipping Norton S), b Banbury, Oxfordshire 8 Jul 1994. Younger brother of J.M.R.Taylor (*see above*). 6'0". RHB, LMF. Squad No 36. Debut (Gloucestershire) 2013; cap 2013. Oxfordshire 2011-12. HS 57* v Derbys (Derby) 2023. BB 5-15 v Cardiff MCCU (Bristol) 2018. CC BB 5-24 v Sussex (Hove) 2023. LO HS 51* v Lancs (Bristol) 2021 (RLC). LO BB 3-39 v Sussex (Eastbourne) 2019 (RLC). T20 HS 23. T20 BB 3-16.

van BUUREN, Graeme Lourens, b Pretoria, South Africa 22 Aug 1990. 5'6". RHB, SLA. Squad No 12. Northerns 2009-10 to 2015-16. Titans 2012-13 to 2014-15. Gloucestershire debut/cap 2016; captain 2022 to date. Birmingham Phoenix 2022. England resident since May 2019. HS 235 Northerns v EP (Centurion) 2014-15. Gs HS 172* v Worcs (Worcester) 2016. BB 4-12 Northerns v SW Districts (Oudtshoorn) 2012-13. Gs BB 4-18 v Durham MCCU (Bristol) 2017. CC BB 3-15 v Glamorgan (Bristol) 2016. LO HS 119* Northerns v EP (Pt Elizabeth, Grey HS) 2013-14. LO BB 5-35 Northerns v SW Districts (Pretoria) 2011-12. T20 HS 64. T20 BB 5-8.

‡NQ**WEBSTER, Beau** Jacob, b Hobart, Tasmania, Australia 1 Dec 1993. RHB, RMF/OB. Squad No 30. Tasmania 2013-14 to date. Essex 2023 (l-o only). Big Bash: HH 2016-17; MR 2017-18 to 2020-21; MS 2021-22 to date. HS 187 Tas v WA (Hobart) 2019-20. BB 4-32 Tas v SA (Adelaide, KR) 2023-24. LO HS 121 Cricket Aus v SA (Brisbane, AB) 2017-18. LO BB 3-38 Ex v Kent (Canterbury) 2023 (MBC). T20 HS 78. T20 BB 4-29.

WELLS, Ben Joseph James (Monkton Combe S), b Bath, Somerset 30 Jul 2000. RHB, WK. Squad No 72. Debut (Gloucestershire) 2021; cap 2021. Somerset 2nd XI 2018-21. Warwickshire 2nd XI 2021. Gloucestershire 2nd XI debut 2021. Dorset 2018. HS 40 v Glamorgan (Cardiff) 2021. LO HS 108* v Durham (Bristol) 2023 (MBC). T20 HS 43*.

NQ**ZAFAR GOHAR**, b Lahore, Pakistan 1 Feb 1995. 5'11". LHB, SLA. Squad No 77. ZT Bank 2013-14. State Bank 2014-15. SSGC 2015-16 to 2016-17. Lahore Blues 2018-19. Central Punjab 2019-20 to 2022-23. Gloucestershire debut/cap 2021. **Tests** (P): 1 (2020-21); HS 37 v NZ (Christchurch) 2020-21; BB –. **LOI** (P): 1 (2015-16); HS 15 and BB 2-54 v E (Sharjah) 2015-16. F-c Tours (P): NZ 2020-21; SL 2015 (PA). HS 100* C Punjab v Baluchistan (Quetta) 2019-20. Gs HS 81 v Essex (Chelmsford) 2022. BB 7-79 (11-133 match) C Punjab v Northern (Faisalabad) 2019-20. Gs BB 6-43 v Glamorgan (Cardiff) 2021. LO HS 62 v Warwks (Cheltenham) 2022 (RLC). LO BB 5-56 ZT v SNGPL (Islamabad) 2013-14. T20 HS 37*. T20 BB 4-14.

RELEASED/RETIRED

(Having made a County 1st XI appearance in 2023)

NQ**ANWAR ALI**, b Karachi, Pakistan 25 Nov 1987. RHB, RMF. Sind 2006-07 to 2011-12. PIA 2007-08 to 2016-17. Karachi Blues 2012-13. Karachi Whites 2015-16 to 2018-19. Sindh 2019-20 to 2022-23. Gloucestershire 2023 (l-o only). **LOI** (P): 22 (2013-14 to 2015-16); HS 43* v SA (Cape Town) 2013-14; BB 3-66 v NZ (Wellington) 2015-16. **IT20** (P): 16 (2008-09 to 2015-16); HS 46 v SL (Colombo, RPS) 2015; BB 2-27 v SL (Colombo, RPS) 2015 (separate matches) and 2-27 v E (Dubai, DSC) 2015-16. F-c Tour (PA): WI 2010-11. HS 100* PIA v Lahore Shalimar (Lahore) 2007-08. 50 wkts (0+2); most – 54 (2012-13). BB 8-16 (13-85 match) PIA v State Bank (Islamabad) 2011-12. LO HS 89 Sindh v Punjab (Karachi) 2014-15. LO BB 5-49 Karachi W v Islamabad (Karachi) 2016-17. T20 HS 65. T20 BB 4-30.

NQ**HARRIS, Marcus** Sinclair, b Perth, W Australia 21 July 1992. 5'8". LHB, OB. W Australia 2010-11 to 2015-16. Victoria 2016-17 to date. Leicestershire 2021. Gloucestershire 2022-23; cap 2022. Big Bash: PS 2014-15 to date; MR 2016-17 to 2022-23. **Tests** (A): 14 (2018-19 to 2021-22); HS 79 v I (Sydney) 2018-19. HS 250* Vic v NSW (Melbourne) 2018-19. CC HS 185 Le v Middx (Leicester) 2021. Gs HS 159 v Somerset (Taunton) 2022. BB –. LO HS 142* Vic v Tas (Launceston) 2022-23. T20 HS 85.

NQ**ROELOFSEN, Grant** (King Edward VII S, Johannesburg), b Roodepoort, South Africa, 27 Jul 1996. RHB, WK. Gauteng 2016-17. KwaZulu-Natal Inland 2017-18 to 2019-20. Dolphins 2018-19 to 2020-21. KwaZulu-Natal Coastal 2021-22 to date. Gloucestershire 2023; cap 2023. Essex 2022 (l-o only). HS 224* KZN Inland v Namibia (Pietermaritzburg) 2017-18. Gs HS 42 v Durham (Chester-le-St) 2023. LO HS 147* Dolphins v Titans (Centurion) 2019-20. T20 HS 91.

NQ**TECTOR, H.T.** – *see IRELAND*.

NQ**VAN MEEKEREN, Paul** Adriaan, b Amsterdam, Netherlands 15 Jan 1993. 6'4". RHB, RMF. Netherlands 2013 to date. Somerset 2016-18. Gloucestershire 2023; cap 2023. Durham 2021 (l-o only). **LOI** (Neth): 22 (2013 to 2023-24); HS 21* v Z (Harare) 2022-23; BB 4-23 v B (Kolkata) 2023-24. **IT20** (Neth): 58 (2013 to 2022-23); HS 24 v B (Hobart) 2022-23; BB 4-11 v Ire (Dharamsala) 2015-16. HS 34 Neth v PNG (Amstelveen) 2015. BB 5-73 v Worcs (Cheltenham) 2023. LO HS 21* (*see LOI*). LO BB 5-48 v Sussex (Hove) 2022 (RLC). T20 HS 24. T20 BB 4-11.

T.C.Lace, W.L.Naish and J.D.Warner left the staff without making a County 1st XI appearance in 2023.

GLOUCESTERSHIRE 2023

RESULTS SUMMARY

	Place	Won	Lost	Drew	Aband
LV= Insurance County Champ (Div 2)	8th		6	7	1
Metro Bank One-Day Cup (Group B)	SF	7	3		
Vitality Blast (South Group)	7th	5	9		

LV= INSURANCE COUNTY CHAMPIONSHIP AVERAGES
BATTING AND FIELDING

Cap†		*M*	*I*	*NO*	*HS*	*Runs*	*Avge*	*100*	*50*	*Ct/St*
2022	M.S.Harris	5	9	1	148	457	57.12	2	2	4
2016	G.L.van Buuren	8	14	5	110*	461	51.22	1	3	4
2020	T.J.Price	8	11	2	109	410	45.55	1	2	3
2021	O.J.Price	11	20	2	132	763	42.38	3	2	22
2013	M.A.H.Hammond	13	23	1	92	812	36.90	–	8	7
2010	C.D.J.Dent	13	23	–	113	694	30.17	1	4	11
2018	B.G.Charlesworth	9	15	–	87	380	25.33	–	2	8
2013	M.D.Taylor	6	10	3	57*	176	25.14	–	1	2
2016	J.R.Bracey	13	23	1	60*	483	21.95	–	3	29/5
2016	J.Shaw	6	9	1	44	171	21.37	–	–	–
2010	J.M.R.Taylor	5	8	–	98	166	20.75	–	1	2
2023	Z.Akhter	7	13	6	41*	143	20.42	–	–	2
2022	A.S.Dale	6	8	1	52	113	16.14	–	1	–
2021	Zafar Gohar	13	21	1	53	319	15.95	–	1	3
2023	M.de Lange	4	4	–	22	33	8.25	–	–	1
2021	D.C.Goodman	4	5	2	15	23	7.66	–	–	1

Also batted: L.A.Charlesworth (2 matches – cap 2023) 0, 4, 0* (1 ct); D.J.Lamb (1 – cap 2023) 70, 0 (1 ct); E.W.O.Middleton (2 – cap 2023) 9, 39*, 2; J.P.Phillips (2 – cap 2023) 17, 80, 26; G.Roelofsen (2 – cap 2023) 19, 42, 11; H.T.Tector (1 – cap 2023) 18, 24; P.A.van Meekeren (2 – cap 2023) 0, 7 (1 ct).

BOWLING

	O	*M*	*R*	*W*	*Avge*	*Best*	*5wI*	*10wM*
P.A.van Meekeren	53.5	7	258	12	21.50	5- 73	1	–
M.D.Taylor	162.2	38	503	20	25.15	5- 24	1	–
A.S.Dale	135.5	19	475	15	31.66	6- 41	1	–
Z.Akhter	181	16	785	19	41.31	4- 33	–	–
J.Shaw	128	26	487	11	44.27	4- 82	–	–
T.J.Price	209.2	30	824	18	45.77	4- 56	–	–
Zafar Gohar	423.5	56	1566	32	48.93	5-122	1	–
Also bowled:								
D.C.Goodman	70.4	9	319	8	39.87	4- 73	–	–
M.de Lange	80	11	310	6	51.66	3- 84	–	–
O.J.Price	99	3	459	8	57.37	3- 40	–	–

B.G.Charlesworth 23-1-145-3; L.A.Charlesworth 30.5-6-134-4; C.D.J.Dent 6.3-1-11-1; M.S.Harris 1-1-0-0; D.J.Lamb 13.2-3-48-2; E.W.O.Middleton 26-2-92-1; J.M.R.Taylor 9-0-56-0; G.L.van Buuren 38-2-145-1.

Gloucestershire played no first-class fixtures outside the County Championship in 2023. The First-Class Averages (pp 223–235) give the records of Gloucestershire players in all first-class county matches, with the exception of D.J.Lamb and H.T.Tector, whose first-class figures for Gloucestershire are as above.

† Gloucestershire revised their capping policy in 2004 and now award players with their County Caps when they make their first-class debut.

GLOUCESTERSHIRE RECORDS

FIRST-CLASS CRICKET

Highest Total	For 695-9d		v	Middlesex	Gloucester	2004
	V 774-7d		by	Australians	Bristol	1948
Lowest Total	For 17		v	Australians	Cheltenham	1896
	V 12		by	Northants	Gloucester	1907
Highest Innings	For 341	C.M.Spearman	v	Middlesex	Gloucester	2004
	V 319	C.J.L.Rogers	for	Northants	Northampton	2006

Highest Partnership for each Wicket

1st	395	D.M.Young/R.B.Nicholls	v	Oxford U	Oxford	1962
2nd	256	C.T.M.Pugh/T.W.Graveney	v	Derbyshire	Chesterfield	1960
3rd	392	G.H.Roderick/A.P.R.Gidman	v	Leics	Bristol	2014
4th	321	W.R.Hammond/W.L.Neale	v	Leics	Gloucester	1937
5th	261	W.G.Grace/W.O.Moberly	v	Yorkshire	Cheltenham	1876
6th	320	G.L.Jessop/J.H.Board	v	Sussex	Hove	1903
7th	248	W.G.Grace/E.L.Thomas	v	Sussex	Hove	1896
8th	239	W.R.Hammond/A.E.Wilson	v	Lancashire	Bristol	1938
9th	193	W.G.Grace/S.A.P.Kitcat	v	Sussex	Bristol	1896
10th	137	C.N.Miles/L.C.Norwell	v	Worcs	Cheltenham	2014

Best Bowling	For	10-40	E.G.Dennett	v	Essex	Bristol	1906
(Innings)	V	10-66	A.A.Mailey	for	Australians	Cheltenham	1921
		10-66	K.Smales	for	Notts	Stroud	1956
Best Bowling	For	17-56	C.W.L.Parker	v	Essex	Gloucester	1925
(Match)	V	15-87	A.J.Conway	for	Worcs	Moreton-in-M	1914

Most Runs – Season	2860	W.R.Hammond	(av 69.75)	1933
Most Runs – Career	33664	W.R.Hammond	(av 57.05)	1920-51
Most 100s – Season	13	W.R.Hammond		1938
Most 100s – Career	113	W.R.Hammond		1920-51
Most Wkts – Season	222	T.W.J.Goddard	(av 16.80)	1937
	222	T.W.J.Goddard	(av 16.37)	1947
Most Wkts – Career	3170	C.W.L.Parker	(av 19.43)	1903-35
Most Career W-K Dismissals	1054	R.C.Russell	(950 ct; 104 st)	1981-2004
Most Career Catches in the Field	719	C.A.Milton		1948-74

LIMITED-OVERS CRICKET

Highest Total	**50ov**	454-3		v	Somerset	Bristol	2023
	40ov	344-6		v	Northants	Cheltenham	2001
	T20	254-3		v	Middlesex	Uxbridge	2011
Lowest Total	**50ov**	82		v	Notts	Bristol	1987
	40ov	49		v	Middlesex	Bristol	1978
	T20	68		v	Hampshire	Bristol	2010
Highest Innings	**50ov**	224*	J.R.Bracey	v	Somerset	Bristol	2023
	40ov	153	C.M.Spearman	v	Warwicks	Gloucester	2003
	T20	126*	M.Klinger	v	Essex	Bristol	2015
Best Bowling	**50ov**	6-13	M.J.Proctor	v	Hampshire	Southampton[1]	1977
	40ov	7-29	D.A.Payne	v	Essex	Chelmsford	2010
	T20	5-16	T.M.J.Smith	v	Warwicks	Birmingham	2020

HAMPSHIRE

Formation of Present Club: 12 August 1863
Inaugural First-Class Match: 1864
Colours: Blue, Gold and White
Badge: Tudor Rose and Crown
County Champions: (2) 1961, 1973
NatWest/C&G/FP Trophy Winners: (3) 1991, 2005, 2009
Benson and Hedges Cup Winners: (2) 1988, 1992
Sunday League Winners: (3) 1975, 1978, 1986
Clydesdale Bank Winners: (1) 2012
Royal London One-Day Cup: (1) 2018
Twenty20 Cup Winners: (3) 2010, 2012, 2022

CEO: David Mann, The Utilita Bowl, Botley Road, West End, Southampton SO30 3XH • Tel: 023 8047 2002 • Email: enquiries@ageasbowl.com • Web: www.ageasbowl.com • Twitter: @hantscricket (104,272 followers)

Cricket Operations Manager: Tim Tremlett. **Director of Cricket**: Giles White. **1st XI Manager**: Adrian Birrell. **Lead Batting Coach**: Jimmy Adams. **Lead Bowling Coach**: Graeme Welch. **Captains**: J.M.Vince and N.R.T.Gubbins (50 ov). **Overseas Players**: K.J.Abbott, B.R.McDermott, Muhammad Abbas, Naveen-ul-Haq and M.G.Neser. **2024 Testimonial**: C.P.Wood. **Head Groundsman**: Simon Lee. **Scorer**: Fiona Newnham. **Blast Team** Name: Hampshire Hawks. ‡ New registration. NQ Not qualified for England.

NQ**ABBOTT, Kyle** John (Kearnsey C, KZN), b Empangeni, South Africa 18 Jun 1987. 6'3½". RHB, RFM. Squad No 87. KwaZulu-Natal 2008-09 to 2009-10. Dolphins 2008-09 to 2014-15. Hampshire debut 2014; cap 2017. Worcestershire 2016. Boland 2021-22. Middlesex 2015 (T20 only). IPL: KXIP 2016. **Tests** (SA): 11 (2012-13 to 2016-17); HS 17 v A (Adelaide) 2016-17; BB 7-29 v P (Centurion) 2012-13. **LOI** (SA): 28 (2012-13 to 2016-17); HS 23 v Z (Bulawayo) 2014; BB 4-21 v Ire (Canberra) 2014-15. **IT20** (SA): 21 (2012-13 to 2015-16); HS 9* v NZ (Centurion) 2015; BB 3-20 v B (Mirpur) 2015. F-c Tours (SA): A 2016-17; I 2015-16. HS 97* v Lancs (Manchester) 2017. 50 wkts (4+1): 72 (2019). BB 9-40 (17-86 match) v Somerset (Southampton) 2019 – 4th best match figures in CC history. Hat-tricks (2): v Worcs (Worcester) 2018 and v Glos (Cheltenham) 2022. LO HS 56 v Surrey (Oval) 2017 (RLC). LO BB 5-43 v Worcs (Southampton) 2021 (RLC). T20 HS 30. T20 BB 5-14.

ALBERT, Toby Edward (Park House S), b Basingstoke 12 Nov 2001. 6'1". RHB, WK. Squad No 15. Debut (Hampshire) 2022. Kent 2023 (on loan). Hampshire 2nd XI debut 2021. HS 69* v SL Dev (Southampton) 2022. CC HS 39 v Essex (Chelmsford) 2023. LO HS 84* v Derbys (Derby) 2022 (RLC). T20 HS 38.

BARKER, Keith Hubert Douglas (Moorhead HS; Fulwood C, Preston), b Manchester 21 Oct 1986. Son of K.H.Barker (British Guiana 1960-61 to 1963-64). Played football for Blackburn Rovers and Rochdale. 6'3". LHB, LMF. Squad No 13. Warwickshire 2009-18; cap 2013. Hampshire debut 2019; cap 2021. HS 125 Wa v Surrey (Guildford) 2013. H HS 84 v Middx (Lord's) 2021. 50 wkts (4); most – 62 (2016). BB 7-46 v Notts (Southampton) 2021. LO HS 56 Wa v Scotland (Birmingham) 2011 (CB40). LO BB 4-33 Wa v Scotland (Birmingham) 2010 (CB40). T20 HS 46. T20 BB 4-19.

BROWN, Ben Christopher (Ardingly C), b Crawley, Sussex 23 Nov 1988. 5'8". RHB, WK. Squad No 10. Sussex 2007-21; cap 2014; captain 2017-20. Hampshire debut 2022; cap 2023. 1000 runs (2); most – 1031 (2015, 2018). HS 163 Sx v Durham (Hove) 2014. H HS 157 v Kent (Canterbury) 2022, sharing H record 5th wkt partnership of 273 with L.A.Dawson. BB 1-48 Sx v Essex (Colchester) 2016. LO HS 105 Sx v Middx (Hove) 2021 (RLC). T20 HS 68.

DAWSON, Liam Andrew (John Bentley S, Calne), b Swindon, Wilts 1 Mar 1990. 5'8". RHB, SLA. Squad No 8. Debut (Hampshire) 2007; cap 2013. Mountaineers 2011-12. Essex 2015 (on loan). London Spirit 2022. Wiltshire 2006-07. **Tests**: 3 (2016-17 to 2017); HS 66* v I (Chennai) 2016-17; BB 2-34 v SA (Lord's) 2017. **LOI**: 6 (2016 to 2022-23); HS 20 v A (Sydney) 2022-23; BB 2-70 v P (Cardiff) 2016. **IT20**: 11 (2016 to 2022-23); HS 34 v P (Karachi) 2022-23; BB 3-27 v SL (Southampton) 2016. F-c Tour: I 2016-17. HS 171 v Kent (Canterbury) 2022, sharing H record 5th wkt partnership of 273 with B.C.Brown. BB 7-51 Mountaineers v ME (Mutare) 2011-12 (also scored 110* in same match). H BB 7-68 (10-139 match) v Essex (Chelmsford) 2022. LO HS 113* SJD v Kalabagan (Savar) 2014-15. LO BB 7-15 v Warwks (Birmingham) 2023 (MBC) – H record. T20 HS 82. T20 BB 5-17.

ECKLAND, Joseph Robert (Millfield S), b Yeovil, Somerset 22 May 2004. Younger brother of A.J.Eckland (Dorset 2017 to date); nephew of V.J.Marks (Oxford U, Somerset, W Australia & England 1975-89). 6'1". RHB, WK. Squad No 9. Hampshire 2nd XI debut 2021. Dorset 2022. Awaiting f-c debut. LO HS 72 v Yorks (York) 2023 (MBC).

FULLER, James Kerr (Otago U, NZ), b Cape Town, South Africa 24 Jan 1990. UK passport. 6'3". RHB, RFM. Squad No 26. Otago 2009-10 to 2012-13. Gloucestershire 2011-15; cap 2011. Middlesex 2016-18. Hampshire debut 2019; cap 2022. HS 93 M v Somerset (Taunton) 2016. H HS 78* v Kent (Southampton) 2022. BB 6-24 (10-79 match) Otago v Wellington (Dunedin) 2012-13. CC BB 6-37 v Northants (Northampton) 2023. Hat-tricks (2): Gs v Worcs (Cheltenham) 2013; v Surrey (Arundel) 2020. LO HS 55* v Somerset (Lord's) 2019 (RLC). LO BB 6-35 M v Netherlands (Amstelveen) 2012 (CB40). T20 HS 57. T20 BB 6-28 M v Hants (Southampton) 2018 – M record.

GUBBINS, Nicholas Richard Trail (Radley C; Leeds U), b Richmond, Surrey 31 Dec 1993. 6'0½". LHB, LB. Squad No 31. Leeds/Bradford MCCU 2013-15. Middlesex 2014-21; cap 2016. Hampshire debut 2021; cap 2022; captain 2024 (50 ov only). Matabeleland Tuskers 2021-22. Southern Rocks 2022-23. F-c Tours (EL): WI 2017-18; SL 2016-17; UAE 2016-17 (v Afg), 2018-19 (v PA). 1000 runs (1): 1409 (2016). HS 201* M v Lancs (Lord's) 2016. H HS 139* v Somerset (Southampton) 2023. BB 4-41 MT v ME (Harare) 2021-22. H BB 1-12 v Middx (Southampton) 2023. LO HS 141 M v Sussex (Hove) 2015 (RLC). LO BB 4-38 v Sussex (Southampton) 2021 (RLC). T20 HS 57*. T20 BB 3-27.

NQ**HOLLAND, Ian** Gabriel (Ringwood Secondary C, Melbourne), b Stevens Point, Wisconsin, USA 3 Oct 1990. 6'0". RHB, RMF. Squad No 22. England qualified at the start of the 2020 season. Victoria 2015-16. Hampshire debut 2017; cap 2021. **LOI** (USA): 15 (2019-20 to 2022-23); HS 75 v Nepal (Kirtipur) 2019-20; BB 3-11 v UAE (Dubai, ICCA) 2019-20. **IT20** (USA): 6 (2021-22); HS 39* v Bahamas (Coolidge) 2021-22; BB 2-3 v Panama (Coolidge) 2021-22. HS 146* v Middx (Southampton) 2021. BB 4-16 v Somerset (Southampton) 2017. LO HS 75 (*see LOI*). LO BB 5-35 v Surrey (Guildford) 2023 (MBC). T20 HS 65. T20 BB 2-3.

HOWELL, Benny Alexander Cameron (The Oratory S), b Bordeaux, France 5 Oct 1988. Son of J.B.Howell (Warwickshire 2nd XI 1978). 5'11". RHB, RM. Squad No 7. Debut (Hampshire) 2011; rejoined in 2023 with white-ball contract. Gloucestershire 2012-19; cap 2012. Big Bash: MR 2020-21. Birmingham Phoenix 2021 to date. Berkshire 2007. HS 163 Gs v Glamorgan (Cardiff) 2017. H HS 71 v Lancs (Southampton) 2011. BB 5-57 Gs v Leics (Leicester) 2013. LO HS 122 v Surrey (Croydon) 2011 (CB40). LO BB 3-37 Gs v Yorks (Leeds) 2015 (RLC). T20 HS 62*. T20 BB 5-18.

JACK, Edward Vaughan ('**Eddie**')(Canford S), b Barnet, Middx 9 Sep 2005. 6'3". LHB, RFM. Awaiting f-c debut. Hampshire 2nd XI debut 2023. England U19 2022 to 2022-23. LO HS 8 v Leics (Southampton) 2023 (MBC). LO BB 3-31 v Yorks (York) 2023 (MBC).

KELLY, Dominic Christopher (Millfield S), b Winchester 1 Oct 2005. 6'0". LHB, RM. Debut (Hampshire) 2022, aged 16y 224d. Hampshire 2nd XI debut 2022. England U19 2022 to 2022-23. HS –. BB 2-55 v SL Dev (Southampton) 2022. LO HS 17 v Lancs (Southampton) 2022 (RLC). LO BB 2-22 v Yorks (York) 2023 (MBC).

NQ**McDERMOTT, Ben**jamin Reginald, b Caboolture, Queensland, Australia 12 Dec 1994. Son of C.J.McDermott (Queensland and Australia 1983-84 to 1995-96); younger brother of A.C.McDermott (Queensland 2009-10 to 2014-15). 6'0". RHB, WK, occ RM. Squad No 28. Queensland 2014-15 to date. Tasmania 2015-16 to 2022-23. Derbyshire 2021. Hampshire debut 2022 (T20 only). Big Bash: BH 2013-14; MR 2015-16; HH 2016-17 to date. London Spirit 2022. **LOI** (A): 5 (2021 to 2021-22); HS 104 v P (Lahore) 2021-22. **IT20** (A): 25 (2018-19 to 2023-24); HS 54 v I (Bengaluru) 2023-24. HS 146* Q v Tas (Brisbane) 2023-24. CC HS 25 De v Worcs (Worcester) 2021. BB –. LO HS 143 Q v Tas (Hobart) 2023-24. T20 HS 127.

MIDDLETON, Fletcha Scott (Wyvern C), b Winchester 21 Jan 2002. Son of T.C.Middleton (Hampshire 1984-95). 5'8½". RHB, OB. Squad No 19. Debut (Hampshire) 2022. Hampshire 2nd XI debut 2018. HS 77 v Lancs (Southport) 2023. LO HS 100 v Middx (Southampton) 2023 (MBC).

NQ**MUHAMMAD ABBAS**, b Sialkot, Pakistan 10 Mar 1990. 5'11". RHB, RMF. Squad No 38. Sialkot 2008-09 to 2012-13. Pakistan TV 2013-14 to 2014-15. KRL 2015-16 to 2016-17. SNGPL 2017-18 to 2018-19. Leicestershire 2018-19; cap 2018. Southern Punjab 2019-20 to 2022-23. Hampshire debut 2021; cap 2022. State Bank of Pakistan 2023-24. **Tests** (P): 25 (2017 to 2021); HS 29 v A (Adelaide) 2019-20; BB 5-33 v A (Abu Dhabi) 2018-19. **LOI** (P): 3 (2018-19); HS – ; BB 1-44 v A (Sharjah) 2018-19. F-c Tours (P): E 2018, 2020; A 2019-20; SA 2018-19; WI 2017, 2021; NZ 2020-21; Ire 2018. HS 40 and BB 8-46 (14-93 match) KRL v Karachi Whites (Karachi) 2016-17. CC HS 32* Le v Sussex (Hove) 2018. H HS 9 v Warwks (Southampton) 2023. 50 wkts (3+2); most – 71 (2016-17). CC BB 6-11 v Middx (Southampton) 2021, inc hat-trick. LO HS 15* KRL v Habib Bank (Karachi) 2016-17. LO BB 4-31 KRL v SNGPL (Karachi) 2016-17. T20 HS 15*. T20 BB 3-22.

‡NQ**NAVEEN-UL-HAQ** Murid, b Logar, Afghanistan 23 Sep 1999. 6'1". RHB, RMF. Squad No 78. Kabul Region 2017-18 to 2018-19. Leicestershire 2021-23 (T20 only); cap 2022. IPL: LSG 2023. Big Bash: SS 2022-23. **LOI** (Afg): 15 (2016 to 2023-24); HS 10* v Ire (Abu Dhabi) 2020-21; BB 4-42 v Ire (Abu Dhabi) 2020-21 – separate matches. **IT20** (Afg): 34 (2019 to 2023-24); HS 10* v Ire (Belfast) 2022; BB 4-20 v UAE (Sharjah) 2023-24. HS 34 Kabul v Mis Ainak (Asadabad) 2017-18. BB 8-35 Kabul v Mis Ainak (Kabul) 2018-19. LO HS 30 Kabul v Band-e-Amir (Kabul) 2018. LO BB 5-40 Afg A v Bangladesh A (Savar) 2019. T20 HS 25*. T20 BB 5-11.

‡NQ**NESER, Michael** Gertges, b Pretoria, South Africa 29 Mar 1990. 6'0". RHB, RMF. Squad No 20. Queensland 2010-11 to date. Glamorgan 2021-23; cap 2021. IPL: KXIP 2013. Big Bash: BH 2011-12 to date; AS 2012-13 to 2020-21. **Tests** (A): 2 (2021-22 to 2022-23); HS 35 v E (Adelaide); BB 3-22 v WI (Adelaide) 2022-23; took wicket of H.Hameed with 2nd ball in Test cricket. **LOI** (A): 4 (2018 to 2023); HS 6 and BB 2-46 v E (Oval) 2018. F-c Tours (Aus A): E 2019; I 2018-19; UAE (v P) 2018-19. HS 176* Gm v Leics (Cardiff) 2023. BB 7-32 (inc hat-trick) v Yorks (Leeds) 2023. LO HS 122 Q v WA (Sydney, DO) 2017-18. LO BB 5-28 Q v WA (Perth) 2022-23. T20 HS 64*. T20 BB 4-25.

ORGAN, Felix Spencer (Canford S), b Sydney, Australia 2 Jun 1999. 5'9". RHB, OB. Squad No 3. Debut (Hampshire) 2017. Hampshire 2nd XI debut 2015. Dorset 2019. HS 118 v Glos (Cheltenham) 2022. BB 6-67 v Lancs (Southport) 2023. LO HS 79 v Durham (Chester-le-St) 2021 (RLC). LO BB 3-39 v Kent (Beckenham) 2022 (RLC). T20 HS 9. T20 BB 2-21.

‡**ORR, Ali**stair Graham Hamilton (Bede's S, Upper Dicker), b Eastbourne, E Sussex 6 Apr 2001. 6'1". LHB, RM. Squad No 27. Sussex 2021-23. Sussex 2nd XI 2018-23. 1000 runs (1): 1047 (2022). HS 198 Sx v Glamorgan (Hove) 2022. LO HS 206 Sx v Somerset (Taunton) 2022 (RLC) – Sx record. T20 HS 41.

PREST, Thomas James (Canford S), b Wimborne, Dorset 24 Mar 2003. 5'11". RHB, OB. Squad No 24. Debut (Hampshire) 2021. Hampshire 2nd XI debut 2019. Dorset 2019. HS 108 v Essex (Chelmsford) 2023. BB 2-32 v Surrey (Southampton) 2023. LO HS 181 v Kent (Beckenham) 2022 (RLC). LO BB 2-28 v Glos (Bristol) 2021 (RLC). T20 HS 64. T20 BB 1-8.

TURNER, John Andrew (Hilton C, Johannesburg; Exeter U), b Johannesburg, South Africa 10 Apr 2001. Grandson of F.G.Turner (rugby union for South Africa 1933-38). 6'1". RHB, RF. Squad No 6. **England Development Contract 2023-24.** Debut (Hampshire) 2022. Hampshire 2nd XI debut 2021. HS 7 and CC BB 3-23 v Essex (Southampton) 2023. BB 5-31 v SL Dev (Southampton) 2022. LO HS 12 v Glamorgan (Neath) 2022 (RLC). LO BB 5-25 v Lancs (Southampton) 2022 (RLC). T20 HS 1*. T20 BB 3-14.

VINCE, James Michael (Warminster S), b Cuckfield, Sussex 14 Mar 1991. 6'2". RHB, RM. Squad No 14. Debut (Hampshire) 2009; cap 2013; captain 2016 to date. Wiltshire 2007-08. Big Bash: ST 2016-17 to 2017-18; SS 2018-19 to date. Southern Brave 2021 to date. **Tests**: 13 (2016 to 2017-18); HS 83 v A (Brisbane) 2017-18; BB –. **LOI**: 25 (2015 to 2022-23); HS 102 v P (Birmingham) 2021; BB 1-18 v Ire (Southampton) 2020. **IT20**: 17 (2015-16 to 2021-22); HS 59 v NZ (Christchurch) 2019-20. F-c Tours: A 2017-18; SA 2014-15 (EL); NZ 2017-18; SL 2013-14 (EL). 1000 runs (3); most – 1525 (2014). HS 240 v Essex (Southampton) 2014. BB 5-41 v Loughborough MCCU (Southampton) 2013. CC BB 2-2 v Lancs (Southport) 2013. LO HS 190 v Glos (Southampton) 2019 (RLC) – H record. LO BB 1-18 EL v Australia A (Sydney) 2012-13 and (*see LOI*). T20 HS 129* v Somerset (Taunton) 2022 – H record. T20 BB 1-5.

WEATHERLEY, Joe James (King Edward VI S, Southampton), b Winchester 19 Jan 1997. 6'1". RHB, OB. Squad No 5. Debut (Hampshire) 2016; cap 2021. Kent 2017 (on loan). HS 168 v Somerset (Southampton) 2022. BB 1-2 v Notts (Southampton) 2018. LO HS 105* v Kent (Southampton) 2018 (RLC). LO BB 4-25 v T&T (Cave Hill) 2017-18. T20 HS 71. T20 BB –.

NQ**WHEAL, Brad**ley Thomas James (Clifton C), b Durban, South Africa 28 Aug 1996. 5'9". RHB, RMF. Squad No 58. Debut (Hampshire) 2015; cap 2021. Gloucestershire 2022 (on loan); cap 2022. Warwickshire 2022 (on loan). London Spirit 2021-22. **LOI** (Scot): 14 (2015-16 to 2023-24); HS 24 v Canada (Dubai, DSC) 2023-24; BB 3-34 v WI (Harare) 2017-18. **IT20** (Scot): 17 (2015-16 to 2022-23); HS 2* (twice); BB 3-20 v Hong Kong (Mong Kok) 2015-16. HS 46* v Warwks (Birmingham) 2021. BB 6-51 v Notts (Nottingham) 2016. LO HS 24 (*see LOI*). LO BB 5-47 v Lancs (Manchester) 2023 (MBC). T20 HS 16. T20 BB 5-38.

WOOD, Christopher Philip (Alton C), b Basingstoke 27 June 1990. 6'2". RHB, LM. Squad No 25. Debut (Hampshire) 2010; cap 2018; testimonial 2024. London Spirit 2021 to date. HS 105* v Leics (Leicester) 2012. BB 5-39 v Kent (Canterbury) 2014. LO HS 41 v Essex (Southampton) 2013 (Y40). LO BB 5-22 v Glamorgan (Cardiff) 2012 (CB40). T20 HS 31. T20 BB 5-32.

RELEASED/RETIRED

(Having made a County 1st XI appearance in 2023)

CRANE, M.S. – *see GLAMORGAN* (season-long loan).

CURRIE, S.W. – *see LEICESTERSHIRE* (season-long loan).

DONALD, A.H.T. – *see DERBYSHIRE.*

NQ**ELLIS, Nathan** Trevor, b Greenacre, NSW, Australia 22 Sep 1994. 6'0". RHB, RMF. Tasmania 2019-20 to date. Hampshire 2022-23 (T20 only). IPL: PK 2021 to date. Big Bash: HH 2018-19 to date. London Spirit 2022 to date. **LOI** (A): 8 (2021-22 to 2023); HS 18 v SA (Centurion) 2023; BB 2-13 v I (Visakhapatnam) 2022-23. **IT20** (A): 14 (2021 to 2023-24); HS 11* v NZ (Auckland) 2023-24; BB 4-28 v P (Lahore) 2021-22. HS 41 Tas v WA (Adelaide, P25) 2020-21. BB 6-43 Tas v NSW (Hobart) 2019-20. LO HS 31 Tas v NSW (Hobart) 2020-21. LO BB 5-38 Tas v NSW (Sydney, NS) 2019-20. T20 HS 24. T20 BB 4-6.

WHITELEY, R.A. – *see DERBYSHIRE.*

J.O.I.Campbell, C.S.Mumford and H.W.Petrie left the staff without making a County 1st XI appearance in 2023.

HAMPSHIRE 2023

RESULTS SUMMARY

	Place	Won	Lost	Drew
LV= Insurance County Champ (Div 1)	3rd	8	4	2
Metro Bank One-Day Cup (Group A)	Finalist	9	2	
Vitality Blast (South Group)	SF	10	6	

LV= INSURANCE COUNTY CHAMPIONSHIP AVERAGES
BATTING AND FIELDING

Cap		*M*	*I*	*NO*	*HS*	*Runs*	*Avge*	*100*	*50*	*Ct/St*
2013	J.M.Vince	14	24	3	186	1007	47.95	1	7	22
2022	N.R.T.Gubbins	14	24	3	139*	969	46.14	3	4	4
2013	L.A.Dawson	14	22	1	141	840	40.00	3	4	14
2021	I.G.Holland	9	14	3	138*	313	28.45	1	–	1
2022	J.K.Fuller	11	17	2	52*	384	25.60	–	2	–
	F.S.Middleton	14	24	–	77	610	25.41	–	4	10
2021	K.H.D.Barker	10	13	1	58	301	25.08	–	1	1
2023	B.C.Brown	14	22	1	95	501	23.85	–	3	51/5
	T.J.Prest	5	9	1	108	173	21.62	1	–	–
	T.E.Albert	3	6	–	39	117	19.50	–	–	1
2021	J.J.Weatherley	5	7	–	58	121	17.28	–	1	3
2017	K.J.Abbott	13	18	3	89*	246	16.40	–	1	5
	F.S.Organ	10	17	1	97	245	15.31	–	1	4
2022	Mohammad Abbas	14	18	10	9	22	2.75	–	–	1

Also batted: M.S.Crane (2 matches – cap 2021) 4, 18, 22 (1 ct); J.A.Turner (2) 0, 4, 7.

BOWLING

	O	*M*	*R*	*W*	*Avge*	*Best*	*5wI*	*10wM*
L.A.Dawson	315.5	68	980	49	20.00	6-40	4	1
Mohammad Abbas	407.4	108	1063	53	20.05	6-49	2	–
K.J.Abbott	327.3	77	958	44	21.77	4-39	–	–
J.K.Fuller	161.3	17	623	24	25.95	6-37	2	–
I.G.Holland	106	24	312	11	28.36	4-19	–	–
F.S.Organ	71.5	9	336	10	33.60	6-67	1	–
K.H.D.Barker	242.1	50	743	20	37.15	5-32	1	–
Also bowled:								
J.A.Turner	28.3	3	74	5	14.80	3-23	–	–

M.S.Crane 12.3-0-48-1; N.R.T.Gubbins 9-0-28-1; T.J.Prest 23-2-98-3; J.M.Vince 4.1-0-21-1; J.J.Weatherley 7-0-18-0.

Hampshire played no first-class fixtures outside the County Championship in 2023. The First-Class Averages (pp 223–235) give the records of Hampshire players in all first-class county matches, with the exception of T.E.Albert, whose first-class figures for Hampshire are as above.

HAMPSHIRE RECORDS

FIRST-CLASS CRICKET

Highest Total	For 714-5d		v	Notts	Southampton[2]	2005
	V 742		by	Surrey	The Oval	1909
Lowest Total	For 15		v	Warwicks	Birmingham	1922
	V 23		by	Yorkshire	Middlesbrough	1965
Highest Innings	For 316	R.H.Moore	v	Warwicks	Bournemouth	1937
	V 303*	G.A.Hick	for	Worcs	Southampton[1]	1997

Highest Partnership for each Wicket

1st	347	V.P.Terry/C.L.Smith	v	Warwicks	Birmingham	1987
2nd	373	J.H.K.Adams/M.A.Carberry	v	Somerset	Taunton	2011
3rd	523	M.A.Carberry/N.D.McKenzie	v	Yorkshire	Southampton[2]	2011
4th	367	J.H.K.Adams/S.M.Ervine	v	Warwicks	Southampton[2]	2017
5th	273	L.A.Dawson/B.C.Brown	v	Kent	Canterbury	2022
6th	411	R.M.Poore/E.G.Wynyard	v	Somerset	Taunton	1899
7th	325	G.Brown/C.H.Abercrombie	v	Essex	Leyton	1913
8th	257	N.Pothas/A.J.Bichel	v	Glos	Cheltenham	2005
9th	230	D.A.Livingstone/A.T.Castell	v	Surrey	Southampton[1]	1962
10th	192	H.A.W.Bowell/W.H.Livsey	v	Worcs	Bournemouth	1921

Best Bowling	For	9- 25	R.M.H.Cottam	v	Lancashire	Manchester	1965
(Innings)	V	10- 46	W.Hickton	for	Lancashire	Manchester	1870
Best Bowling	For	17- 86	K.J.Abbott	v	Somerset	Southampton[2]	2019
(Match)	V	17-103	W.Mycroft	for	Derbyshire	Southampton	1876

Most Runs – Season	2854	C.P.Mead	(av 79.27)	1928
Most Runs – Career	48892	C.P.Mead	(av 48.84)	1905-36
Most 100s – Season	12	C.P.Mead		1928
Most 100s – Career	138	C.P.Mead		1905-36
Most Wkts – Season	190	A.S.Kennedy	(av 15.61)	1922
Most Wkts – Career	2669	D.Shackleton	(av 18.23)	1948-69
Most Career W-K Dismissals	700	R.J.Parks	(630 ct; 70 st)	1980-92
Most Career Catches in the Field	629	C.P.Mead		1905-36

LIMITED-OVERS CRICKET

Highest Total	**50ov**	396-5		v	Kent	Beckenham	2022
	40ov	353-8		v	Middlesex	Lord's	2005
	T20	249-8		v	Derbyshire	Derby	2017
Lowest Total	**50ov**	50		v	Yorkshire	Leeds	1991
	40ov	43		v	Essex	Basingstoke	1972
	T20	74		v	Somerset	Taunton	2023
Highest Innings	**50ov**	190	J.M.Vince	v	Glos	Southampton[2]	2019
	40ov	172	C.G.Greenidge	v	Surrey	Southampton[1]	1987
	T20	129*	J.M.Vince	v	Somerset	Taunton	2022
Best Bowling	**50ov**	7-15	L.A.Dawson	v	Warwicks	Birmingham	2023
	40ov	6-20	T.E.Jesty	v	Glamorgan	Cardiff	1975
	T20	6-19	Shaheen Shah Afridi	v	Middlesex	Southampton[2]	2020

[1] County Ground (Northlands Road) [2] Ageas Bowl

KENT

Formation of Present Club: 1 March 1859
Substantial Reorganisation: 6 December 1870
Inaugural First-Class Match: 1864
Colours: Maroon and White
Badge: White Horse on a Red Ground
County Champions: (6) 1906, 1909, 1910, 1913, 1970, 1978
Joint Champions: (1) 1977
Gillette Cup Winners: (2) 1967, 1974
Benson and Hedges Cup Winners: (3) 1973, 1976, 1978
Pro 40/National League (Div 1) Winners: (1) 2001
Sunday League Winners: (4) 1972, 1973, 1976, 1995
Royal London One-Day Cup Winners: (1) 2022
Twenty20 Cup Winners: (2) 2007, 2021

Cricket Chief Executive: Simon Storey, The Spitfire Ground, Old Dover Road, Canterbury, CT1 3NZ • Tel: 01227 456886 • Email: feedback@kentcricket.co.uk • Web: www.kentcricket.co.uk • Twitter: @kentcricket (107,357 followers)

Director of Cricket: Simon Cook. **Head Coach**: Matt Walker. **Batting Coach**: Toby Radford. **Bowling Coach**: Robbie Joseph. **Captains**: D.J.Bell-Drummond and S.W.Billings (T20). **Vice-captain**: J.A.Leaning. **Overseas Players**: W.A.Agar and X.C.Bartlett. **2024 Testimonial**: None. **Head Groundsman**: Adrian Llong. **Scorer**: Lorne Hart. **Blast Team Name**: Kent Spitfires. ‡ New registration. NQ Not qualified for England.

NQ**AGAR, Wes**ley Austin, b Malvern, Victoria, Australia 5 Feb 1997. Younger brother of A.C.Agar (W Australia and Australia 2012-13 to date). RHB, RFM. Squad No 8. S Australia 2019-20 to date. Kent debut 2023. Big Bash: AS 2016-17 to date. **LOI** (A): 2 (2021); HS 41 v WI (Bridgetown) 2021; BB –. F-c Tour (Aus A): NZ 2022-23. HS 57 SA v NSW (Wollongong) 2022-23. K HS 51 v Surrey (Canterbury) 2023. BB 6-42 SA v WA (Adelaide) 2023-24. K BB 5-63 v Northants (Northampton) 2023. LO HS 41 (*see LOI*). LO BB 5-40 SA v WA (Adelaide, KR) 2019-20. T20 HS 15. T20 BB 4-6.

ARAFAT Hossain **BHUIYAN** (Rokeby S; Newham SFC; London City U), b Dhaka, Bangladesh 11 Oct 1996. RHB, RFM. Squad No 26. Debut (Kent) 2023. Surrey 2nd XI 2017. MCC YC 2019. Essex 2nd XI 2019. Derbyshire 2nd XI 2021. Kent 2nd XI debut 2022. Worcestershire 2nd XI 2023. HS 15* v Somerset (Taunton) 2023. BB 4-65 v Surrey (Oval) 2023.

‡NQ**BARTLETT, Xavier** Colin, b Adelaide, Australia 17 Dec 1998. RHB, RFM. Squad No 15. Queensland 2019-20 to date. Big Bash: BH 2020-21 to date. **LOI** (A): 2 (2023-24); HS – ; BB 4-17 v WI (Melbourne) 2023-24. **IT20** (A): 1 (2023-24) HS – ; BB 2-37 v WI (Perth) 2023-24. F-c Tour (Aus A): NZ 2022-23. HS 32 Q v NSW (Brisbane) 2022-23. BB 5-64 Q v WA (Perth) 2023-24. LO HS 28 Q v Vic (Townsville) 2018-19. LO BB 4-17 (*see LOI*). T20 HS 42*. T20 BB 4-30.

BELL-DRUMMOND, Daniel James (Millfield S), b Lewisham, London 4 Aug 1993. 5'10". RHB, RMF. Squad No 23. Debut (Kent) 2011; cap 2015; captain 2024. MCC 2014, 2018. Birmingham Phoenix 2021. London Spirit 2022 to date. 1000 runs (1): 1058 (2014). HS 300* v Northants (Northampton) 2023. BB 3-37 v Essex (Canterbury) 2022. LO HS 171* EL v Sri Lanka A (Canterbury) 2016. LO BB 2-22 v Surrey (Oval) 2019 (RLC). T20 HS 112*. T20 BB 2-19.

BILLINGS, Samuel William (Haileybury S; Loughborough U), b Pembury 15 Jun 1991. 5'11". RHB, WK. Squad No 7. Loughborough MCCU 2011, scoring 131 v Northants (Loughborough) on f-c debut. Kent debut 2011; cap 2015; captain 2018-23. MCC 2015. IPL: DD 2016-17; CSK 2018-19; KKR 2022. Big Bash: SS 2016-17 to 2017-18; ST 2020-21 to 2021-22; BH 2022-23 to date. Oval Invincibles 2021 to date. **Tests**: 3 (2021-22 to 2022); HS 36 v I (Birmingham) 2022. **LOI**: 28 (2015 to 2022-23); HS 118 v A (Manchester) 2020. **IT20**: 37, inc 1 for ICC World XI (2015 to 2021-22); HS 87 v WI (Basseterre) 2018-19 – world record IT20 score by a No 6 batsman. F-c Tours (EL): A 2021-22 (E); I 2018-19; UAE 2018-19 (v P). HS 171 v Glos (Bristol) 2016. LO HS 175 EL v Pakistan A (Canterbury) 2016. T20 HS 95*.

‡[NQ]**COHEN, Michael** Alexander Robert (Reddam House C), b Cape Town, South Africa 4 Aug 1998. LHB, LFM. Squad No 45. Western Province 2017-18 to 2018-19. Cape Cobras 2017-18. Derbyshire 2020-21. HS 30* De v Notts (Nottingham) 2020. BB 5-40 WP v SW Districts (Rondebosch) 2017-18. CC BB 5-43 De v Warwks (Derby) 2021. LO HS 16 WP v Northerns (Rondebosch) 2017-18. LO BB 1-17 WP v SW Districts (Rondebosch) 2017-18. T20 HS 7*. T20 BB 2-17.

COMPTON, Benjamin Garnet (Clifton C, Durban), b Durban, S Africa 29 Mar 1994. Son of P.M.D.Compton (Natal 1979-80); grandson of D.S.C.Compton (Middlesex and England 1936-58); cousin of N.R.D.Compton (Middlesex, Somerset, ME, Worcs and England 2004-17). 6'1". LHB, OB. Squad No 2. Nottinghamshire 2019-21. Mountaineers 2021-22 to 2022-23. Kent debut 2022. KwaZulu Natal Inland 2023-24. Norfolk 2021. 1000 runs (1): 1193 (2022). HS 217 Mountaineers v SR (Harare) 2022-23. CC HS 140 v Northants (Northampton) 2022. LO HS 110 Mountaineers v Eagles (Harare) 2021-22.

CRAWLEY, Zak (Tonbridge S), b Bromley 3 Feb 1998. 6'6". RHB, RM. Squad No 16. Debut (Kent) 2017; cap 2019. Big Bash: HH 2022-23; PS 2023-24. London Spirit 2021 to date. YC 2020. *Wisden* 2020. **ECB Two-Year Central Contract from 2023-24. Tests**: 44 (2019-20 to 2023-24); HS 267 v P (Southampton) 2020. **LOI**: 8 (2021 to 2023-24); HS 58* v P (Cardiff) 2021. F-c Tours: A 2021-22; SA 2019-20; WI 2021-22; NZ 2019-20, 2022-23; I 2020-21, 2023-24; P 2022-23; SL 2019-20, 2020-21. 1000 runs (1): 1113 (2023). HS 267 (*see Tests*). K HS 170 v Essex (Canterbury) 2023. LO HS 120 v Middx (Canterbury) 2019 (RLC). T20 HS 108*.

DENLY, Jaydn Kennick (Canterbury Ac), b Margate 5 Jan 2006. Nephew of J.L.Denly (*see KENT*). LHB, SLA. Squad No 42. Kent 2nd XI debut 2022. England U19 2023. Awaiting f-c debut. LO HS 37 v Essex (Canterbury) 2023 (MBC). LO BB 1-20 v Surrey (Oval) 2023 (MBC).

DENLY, Joseph Liam (Chaucer Tech C), b Canterbury 16 Mar 1986. 6'0". RHB, LB. Squad No 6. Kent debut 2004; cap 2008; testimonial 2019. Middlesex 2012-14; cap 2012. MCC 2013. IPL: KKR 2019. Big Bash: SS 2017-18 to 2018-19; BH 2020-21. London Spirit 2021. PCA 2018. **Tests**: 15 (2018-19 to 2020); HS 94 v A (Oval) 2019; BB 2-42 v SA (Cape Town) 2019-20. **LOI**: 16 (2009 to 2019-20); HS 87 v SA (Cape Town) 2019-20; BB 1-24 v Ire (Dublin) 2019. **IT20**: 13 (2009 to 2020); HS 30 v WI (Gros Islet) 2018-19; BB 4-19 v SL (Colombo, RPS) 2018-19. F-c Tours: SA 2019-20; WI 2018-19; NZ 2008-09 (Eng A), 2019-20; I 2007-08 (Eng A); SL 2019-20. 1000 runs (4); most – 1266 (2017). HS 227 v Worcs (Worcester) 2017. BB 4-36 v Derbys (Derby) 2018. LO HS 150* v Glamorgan (Canterbury) 2018 (RLC). LO BB 4-35 v Jamaica (North Sound) 2017-18. T20 HS 127 v Essex (Chelmsford) 2017 – K record. T20 BB 4-19.

EVISON, Joseph David Michael (Stamford S), b Peterborough, Cambs 14 Nov 2001. Son of G.M.Evison (Lincolnshire 1993-97); younger brother of S.H.G.Evison (Lincolnshire 2017-18). 6'2". RHB, RM. Squad No 33. Nottinghamshire 2019-22. Leicestershire 2022 (on loan). Kent debut 2022. Nottinghamshire 2nd XI 2017-22. HS 109* Nt v Sussex (Hove) 2022. K HS 99 v Warwks (Birmingham) 2023. BB 5-21 Nt v Durham (Chester-le-St) 2021. K BB 4-62 v Northants (Canterbury) 2023. LO HS 136 v Yorks (Scarborough) 2023 (MBC). LO BB 3-62 v Essex (Chelmsford) 2022 (RLC). T20 HS 46. T20 BB 3-25.

FINCH, Harry Zachariah (St Richard's Catholic C, Bexhill; Eastbourne C), b Hastings, E.Sussex 10 Feb 1995. 5'8". RHB, RM. Squad No 72. Sussex 2013-20. Kent debut 2021. HS 135* and BB 1-9 Sx v Leeds/Bradford MCCU (Hove) 2016. CC HS 115 v Sussex (Canterbury) 2021. CC BB 1-30 Sx v Northants (Arundel) 2016. LO HS 108 Sx v Hants (Hove) 2018 (RLC). LO BB –. T20 HS 47.

‡**GARRETT, George** Anthony (Shrewsbury S), Harpenden, Herts 4 Mar 2000. 6'3". RHB, RM. Squad No 44. Warwickshire 2019-22. Warwickshire 2nd XI 2019-23. Glamorgan 2nd XI 2023. Kent 2nd XI debut 2023. HS 24 Wa v Essex (Birmingham) 2019. BB 2-53 Wa v Notts (Nottingham) 2019. LO HS 18 Wa v Leics (Leicester) 2022 (RLC). LO BB 3-50 Wa v Leics (Birmingham) 2021 (RLC). T20 BB 1-19.

GILCHRIST, Nathan Nicholas (St Stithian's C; King's C, Taunton), b Harare, Zimbabwe 11 Jun 2000. 6'5". RHB, RFM. Squad No 17. Debut (Kent) 2020. Somerset 2nd XI 2016-19. HS 25 v Surrey (Oval) 2020. BB 6-61 v Somerset (Canterbury) 2022. LO HS 33 v Hants (Beckenham) 2022 (RLC). LO BB 5-45 v Middx (Radlett) 2021 (RLC).

HAMIDULLAH QADRI (Derby Moor S; Chellaston Ac), b Kandahar, Afghanistan 5 Dec 2000. 5'9". RHB, OB. Squad No 75. Derbyshire 2017-19, taking 5-60 v Glamorgan (Cardiff), the youngest to take 5 wkts on CC debut, and the first born this century to play f-c cricket in England. Kent debut 2020. Matabeleland Tuskers 2022-23. England U19 2018-19. HS 87 v Somerset (Canterbury) 2022. BB 6-129 v Lancs (Canterbury) 2022. LO HS 42* v Durham (Beckenham) 2021 (RLC). LO BB 4-36 v Northants (Canterbury) 2022 (RLC). T20 BB 1-34. Youngest to play domestic T20 Blast, aged 16y, 223d.

KLAASSEN, Frederick Jack (Sacred Heart C, Auckland, NZ), b Haywards Heath, Sussex 13 Nov 1992. 6'4". RHB, LMF. Squad No 18. England-qualified thanks to UK passport. Debut (Kent) 2019. Manchester Originals 2021-22. **LOI** (Neth): 19 (2018 to 2022-23); HS 13 v Nepal (Amstelveen) 2018; BB 3-23 v Ire (Utrecht) 2021. **IT20** (Neth): 39 (2018 to 2023-24); HS 13 v Z (Rotterdam) 2019; BB 5-19 v Uganda (Bulawayo) 2022. HS 14* v Loughborough MCCU (Canterbury) 2019. CC HS 13 v Yorks (Canterbury) 2019. BB 4-44 v Middx (Canterbury) 2020. LO HS 13 (*see LOI*). LO BB 3-23 (*see LOI*). T20 HS 13. T20 BB 5-19.

LEANING, Jack Andrew (Archbishop Holgate's S, York; York C), b Bristol, Glos 18 Oct 1993. 5'10". RHB, RMF. Squad No 34. Yorkshire 2013-19; cap 2016. Kent debut 2020; cap 2021. YC 2015. HS 220* v Sussex (Canterbury) 2020, sharing K record 2nd wkt partnership of 423 with J.M.Cox. BB 3-64 v Lancs (Canterbury) 2023. LO HS 137* v Essex (Canterbury) 2023 (MBC). LO BB 5-22 Y v Unicorns (Leeds) 2013 (Y40). T20 HS 81*. T20 BB 3-15.

NQ**MUYEYE, Tawanda** Sean (Eastbourne C), b Harare, Zimbabwe 5 March 2001. 6'0". RHB, OB. Squad No 14. Wisden Schools Cricketer of the Year 2020. Debut (Kent) 2021. Oval Invincibles 2023. HS 179 v Northants (Northampton) 2023. BB 2-70 v Hants (Canterbury) 2022. LO HS 40 v Hants (Beckenham) 2022 (RLC). LO BB 1-17 v Northants (Canterbury) 2022 (RLC). T20 HS 62.

O'RIORDAN, Marcus Kevin (Tonbridge S), b Pembury 25 Jan 1998. 5'10". RHB, OB. Squad No 55. Debut (Kent) 2019. HS 102* v SL Dev (Canterbury) 2022. CC HS 52* v Hants (Canterbury) 2020. BB 3-50 v Sussex (Canterbury) 2020. LO HS 60 v Middx (Radlett) 2021 (RLC). LO BB 1-77 v Durham (Beckenham) 2021 (RLC). T20 HS 13*. T20 BB 2-24.

PARKINSON, Matthew William (Bolton S), b Bolton, Lancs 24 Oct 1996. Twin brother of C.F.Parkinson (*see DURHAM*). 6'0". RHB, LB. Squad No 28. Lancashire 2016-23; cap 2019. Eagles 2022-23. Durham 2023 (on loan). Kent debut 2023 (l-o only) – on loan. Manchester Originals 2021-22. Staffordshire 2014. **Tests**: 1 (2022); HS 8 and BB 1-47 v NZ (Lord's) 2022. **LOI**: 5 (2019-20 to 2021); HS 7* v P (Lord's) 2021; BB 2-28 v P (Cardiff) 2021. **IT20**: 6 (2019-20 to 2022); HS 5 v P (Nottingham) 2021; BB 4-47 v NZ (Napier) 2019-20. HS 30 Eagles v Tuskers (Harare) 2022-23. CC HS 21* La v Northants (Manchester) 2021. BB 7-126 La v Kent (Canterbury) 2021. LO HS 15* EL v West Indies A (Coolidge) 2017-18. LO BB 5-51 La v Worcs (Manchester) 2019 (RLC). T20 HS 18. T20 BB 4-9.

QUINN, Matthew Richard, b Auckland, New Zealand 28 Feb 1993. 6'4". RHB, RMF. Squad No 64. Auckland 2012-13 to 2015-16. Essex 2016-20. Kent debut 2021. UK passport. HS 50 Auckland v Canterbury (Auckland) 2013-14. CC HS 37 v Surrey (Canterbury) 2023. BB 7-76 (11-163 match) Ex v Glos (Cheltenham) 2016. K BB 6-23 v Hants (Southampton) 2022. LO HS 36 Auckland v CD (Auckland) 2013-14. LO BB 4-71 Ex v Sussex (Hove) 2016 (RLC). T20 HS 8*. T20 BB 4-20.

SINGH, Jaskaran (Wilmington Ac), b Denmark Hill, London 19 Sep 2002. 6'5". RHB, RFM. Squad No 19. Debut (Kent) 2021, dismissing A.G.H.Orr with his fifth ball in f-c cricket. Kent 2nd XI debut 2021. HS 14* v SL Dev (Canterbury) 2022. CC HS 7* v Notts (Nottingham) 2023. BB 4-51 v Sussex (Canterbury) 2021. LO HS 19* and LO BB 3-74 v Lancs (Blackpool) 2023 (MBC). T20 BB –.

STEWART, Grant (All Saints C, Maitland; U of Newcastle), b Kalgoorlie, W Australia 19 Feb 1994. 6'2". RHB, RMF. Squad No 9. England qualified due to Italian mother. Debut (Kent) 2017. Sussex 2022 (on loan). **IT20** (Italy): 14 (2021-22 to 2023); HS 76 v Germany (Almeria) 2022-23; BB 3-29 v Jersey (Edinburgh) 2023. HS 103 and BB 6-22 v Middx (Canterbury) 2018. LO HS 57 Italy v Saudi Arabia (Bangi) 2023-24. LO BB 4-42 v Leics (Leicester) 2022 (RLC). T20 HS 76. T20 BB 4-48.

RELEASED/RETIRED

(Having made a County 1st XI appearance in 2023. Some may return in 2024.)

NQ**ARSHDEEP SINGH**, b Guna, Madhya Pradesh, India 5 Feb 1999. LHB, LMF. Punjab 2019-20 to date. Kent 2023. IPL: KXIP 2019 to 2020-21; PK 2021 to date. **LOI** (I): 6 (2022-23 to 2023-24); HS 18 v SA (Gqeberha) 2023-24; BB 5-37 v SA (Johannesburg) 2023-24. **IT20** (I): 44 (2022 to 2023-24); HS 12 v WI (Tarouba) 2023; BB 4-37 v NZ (Napier) 2022-23. HS 36 Punjab v Karnataka (Hubli) 2023-24. K HS 12* v Surrey (Canterbury) 2023. BB 5-33 Punjab v Tripura (Delhi) 2021-22. K BB 3-58 v Essex (Chelmsford) 2023. LO HS 18 (*see LOI*). LO BB 5-37 (*see LOI*). T20 HS 12. T20 BB 5-32.

NQ**BAZLEY, James** Jordan, b Buderim, Queensland, Australia 8 Apr 1995. RHB, RFM. Queensland 2020-21 to date. Kent 2023 (l-o only). Big Bash: BH 2020-21 to 2022-23; AS 2023-24. HS 64* Q v SA (Adelaide) 2022-23. BB 2-9 Q v SA (Adelaide, KR) 2021-22. LO HS 45 Cricket Aus v Tas (Brisbane, AB) 2016-17. LO BB 3-12 Q v Tas (Townsville) 2021-22. T20 HS 49*. T20 BB 4-22.

BLAKE, Alexander James (Hayes SS; Leeds Met U), b Farnborough 25 Jan 1989. 6'1". LHB, RMF. Kent 2008-23; cap 2017. Oval Invincibles 2021. HS 105* v Yorks (Leeds) 2010. BB 2-9 v Pakistanis (Canterbury) 2010. CC BB 1-60 v Hants (Southampton) 2010. LO HS 116 v Somerset (Taunton) 2017 (RLC). LO BB 2-13 v Yorks (Leeds) 2011 (CB40). T20 HS 71*. T20 BB 1-17.

NQ**CHAHAL, Yuzvendra** Singh, b Jind, Haryana, India 23 Jul 1990. RHB, LBG. Haryana 2009-10 to date. Kent 2023. IPL: MI 2011-12 to 2013; RCB 2014-21; RR 2022 to date. **LOI** (I): 72 (2016 to 2022-23); HS 18* v NZ (Hamilton) 2018-19; BB 6-42 v A (Melbourne) 2018-19. **IT20** (I): 80 (2016 to 2023); HS 3* v A (Guwahati) 2017-18; BB 6-25 v E (Bangalore) 2016-17. HS 42 Haryana v Bengal (Lahli) 2015-16. K HS 5* v Lancs (Canterbury) 2023. BB 6-44 Haryana v Hyderabad (Jamshedpur) 2016-17. K BB 3-63 v Notts (Canterbury) 2023. LO HS 24* India A v South Africa A (Pretoria) 2017. LO BB 6-24 Haryana v Jammu & K (Delhi) 2011-12. T20 HS 10. T20 BB 6-25.

COX, J.M. – *see ESSEX*.

HOGAN, Michael Garry, b Newcastle, New South Wales, Australia 31 May 1981. British passport. 6'5". RHB, RFM. W Australia 2009-10 to 2015-16. Glamorgan 2013-22; cap 2013; captain 2018; testimonial 2020-22. Kent 2023. Big Bash: HH 2011-12 to 2012-13. Southern Brave 2022. HS 57 Gm v Lancs (Colwyn Bay) 2015. K HS 43 v Surrey (Oval) 2023. 50 wkts (3); most – 67 (2013). BB 7-92 Gm v Glos (Bristol) 2013. K BB 5-63 v Notts (Canterbury) 2023. LO HS 27 WA v Vic (Melbourne) 2011-12. LO BB 5-44 WA v Vic (Melbourne) 2010-11. T20 HS 17*. T20 BB 5-17.

RELEASED/RETIRED continued on p 132

KENT 2023

RESULTS SUMMARY

	Place	Won	Lost	Drew
LV= Insurance County Champ (Div 1)	8th	2	7	5
Metro Bank One-Day Cup (Group A)	4th	4	4	
Vitality Blast (South Group)	5th	7	7	

LV= INSURANCE COUNTY CHAMPIONSHIP AVERAGES
BATTING AND FIELDING

Cap		*M*	*I*	*NO*	*HS*	*Runs*	*Avge*	*100*	*50*	*Ct/St*
2015	D.J.Bell-Drummond	9	15	2	300*	579	44.53	1	2	6
2019	Z.Crawley	7	13	–	170	565	43.46	2	2	3
	H.Z.Finch	6	10	–	114	390	39.00	1	2	14/2
	T.S.Muyeye	9	16	–	179	571	35.68	1	1	8
	J.D.M.Evison	14	22	3	99	597	31.42	–	4	1
	B.G.Compton	14	25	1	114*	735	30.62	1	4	14
2021	J.A.Leaning	14	25	3	68*	563	25.59	–	4	19
	J.M.Cox	10	17	1	133	385	24.06	1	–	12
2008	J.L.Denly	8	13	–	136	293	22.53	1	1	1
	Hamidullah Qadri	6	9	1	72	169	21.12	–	1	2
	G.Stewart	6	10	–	50	206	20.60	–	1	2
	M.G.Hogan	7	10	5	43	94	18.80	–	–	3
	W.A.Agar	6	8	1	51	112	16.00	–	1	2
	M.R.Quinn	9	15	2	37	156	12.00	–	–	4
	Arshdeep Singh	5	9	4	12*	51	10.20	–	–	3
2015	S.W.Billings	6	10	–	31	92	9.20	–	–	13
	Arafat Bhuiyan	3	5	2	15*	22	7.33	–	–	–

Also batted: T.E.Albert (1 match) 37, 0 (1 ct); A.J.Blake (1) 30, 19 (1 ct); Y.S.Chahal (2) 0, 5*; B.B.A.Geddes (1) 36, 1; N.N.Gilchrist (3) 2, 0 (3 ct); C.McKerr (2) 14, 23, 4* (1 ct); A.S.S.Nijjar (2) 12, 5*, 42; M.K.O'Riordan (1) 35; J.Singh (2) 7*, 0*, 0.

BOWLING

	O	*M*	*R*	*W*	*Avge*	*Best*	*5wI*	*10wM*
W.A.Agar	163.4	32	595	21	28.33	5- 63	1	–
A.S.S.Nijjar	123	29	317	10	31.70	4- 67	–	–
M.R.Quinn	241.3	66	695	21	33.09	4- 25	–	–
Hamidullah Qadri	160.2	21	576	15	38.40	3- 51	–	–
J.A.Leaning	99.4	9	472	12	39.33	3- 64	–	–
M.G.Hogan	179.5	37	563	14	40.21	5- 63	1	–
Arshdeep Singh	161.2	37	543	13	41.76	3- 58	–	–
J.D.M.Evison	249	23	992	19	52.21	4- 62	–	–
Also bowled:								
Y.S.Chahal	101	22	246	9	27.33	3- 63	–	–
J.Singh	49	1	254	7	36.28	4- 87	–	–
Arafat Bhuiyan	62.3	11	265	7	37.85	4- 65	–	–
G.Stewart	112.5	30	371	7	53.00	3- 6	–	–
J.L.Denly	87.1	7	328	6	54.66	4-164	–	–

D.J.Bell-Drummond 35-4-139-3; A.J.Blake 2-0-20-0; B.G.Compton 2-0-2-0; N.N.Gilchrist 96.2-12-401-2; C.McKerr 39.2-3-188-3; T.S.Muyeye 5-0-12-0.

Kent played no first-class fixtures outside the County Championship in 2023. The First-Class Averages (pp 223–235) give the records of Kent players in all first-class county matches, with the exception of T.E.Albert, Z.Crawley and C.McKerr, whose first-class figures for Kent are as above.

KENT RECORDS

FIRST-CLASS CRICKET

Highest Total	For 803-4d		v	Essex	Brentwood	1934
	V 676		by	Australians	Canterbury	1921
Lowest Total	For 18		v	Sussex	Gravesend	1867
	V 16		by	Warwicks	Tonbridge	1913
Highest Innings	For 332	W.H.Ashdown	v	Essex	Brentwood	1934
	V 344	W.G.Grace	for	MCC	Canterbury	1876

Highest Partnership for each Wicket

1st	300	N.R.Taylor/M.R.Benson	v	Derbyshire	Canterbury	1991
2nd	423*	J.M.Cox/J.A.Leaning	v	Sussex	Canterbury	2020
3rd	323	R.W.T.Key/M.van Jaarsveld	v	Surrey	Tunbridge Wells	2005
4th	368	P.A.de Silva/G.R.Cowdrey	v	Derbyshire	Maidstone	1995
5th	277	F.E.Woolley/L.E.G.Ames	v	N Zealanders	Canterbury	1931
6th	346	S.W.Billings/D.I.Stevens	v	Yorkshire	Leeds	2019
7th	248	A.P.Day/E.Humphreys	v	Somerset	Taunton	1908
8th	222	S.A.Northeast/J.C.Tredwell	v	Essex	Chelmsford	2016
9th	171	M.A.Ealham/P.A.Strang	v	Notts	Nottingham	1997
10th	235	F.E.Woolley/A.Fielder	v	Worcs	Stourbridge	1909

Best Bowling	For	10- 30	C.Blythe	v	Northants	Northampton	1907
(Innings)	V	10- 48	C.H.G.Bland	for	Sussex	Tonbridge	1899
Best Bowling	For	17- 48	C.Blythe	v	Northants	Northampton	1907
(Match)	V	17-106	T.W.J.Goddard	for	Glos	Bristol	1939

Most Runs – Season	2894	F.E.Woolley	(av 59.06)	1928
Most Runs – Career	47868	F.E.Woolley	(av 41.77)	1906-38
Most 100s – Season	10	F.E.Woolley		1928, 1934
Most 100s – Career	122	F.E.Woolley		1906-38
Most Wkts – Season	262	A.P.Freeman	(av 14.74)	1933
Most Wkts – Career	3340	A.P.Freeman	(av 17.64)	1914-36
Most Career W-K Dismissals	1253	F.H.Huish	(901 ct; 352 st)	1895-1914
Most Career Catches in the Field	773	F.E.Woolley		1906-38

LIMITED-OVERS CRICKET

Highest Total	**50ov**	384-6		v	Berkshire	Finchampstead	1994
		384-8		v	Surrey	Beckenham	2018
	40ov	337-7		v	Sussex	Canterbury	2013
	T20	236-3		v	Essex	Canterbury	2021
Lowest Total	**50ov**	60		v	Somerset	Taunton	1979
	40ov	83		v	Middlesex	Lord's	1984
	T20	72		v	Hampshire	Southampton[2]	2011
Highest Innings	**50ov**	206*	O.G.Robinson	v	Worcs	Worcester	2022
	40ov	146	A.Symonds	v	Lancashire	Tunbridge Wells	2004
	T20	127	J.L.Denly	v	Essex	Chelmsford	2017
Best Bowling	**50ov**	8-31	D.L.Underwood	v	Scotland	Edinburgh	1987
	40ov	6- 9	R.A.Woolmer	v	Derbyshire	Chesterfield	1979
	T20	5-11	A.F.Milne	v	Somerset	Taunton	2017

LANCASHIRE

Formation of Present Club: 12 January 1864
Inaugural First-Class Match: 1865
Colours: Red, Green and Blue
Badge: Red Rose
County Champions (since 1890): (8) 1897, 1904, 1926, 1927, 1928, 1930, 1934, 2011
Joint Champions: (1) 1950
Gillette/NatWest Trophy Winners: (7) 1970, 1971, 1972, 1975, 1990, 1996, 1998
Benson and Hedges Cup Winners: (4) 1984, 1990, 1995, 1996
Pro 40/National League (Div 1) Winners: (1) 1999.
Sunday League Winners: (4) 1969, 1970, 1989, 1998
Twenty20 Cup Winners: (1) 2015

Chief Executive: Daniel Gidney, Emirates Old Trafford, Talbot Road, Manchester M16 0PX • Tel: 0161 282 4000 • Email: enquiries@lancashirecricket.co.uk • Web: www.lancashirecricket.co.uk • Twitter: @lancscricket (150,789 followers)

Head Coach: Dale Benkenstein. **Director of Cricket Performance**: Mark Chilton. **Lead Batting Coach**: William Porterfield. **Lead Bowling Coach**: Craig White. **Captain**: K.K.Jennings. **Overseas Players**: T.C.Bruce and N.M.Lyon. **2024 Testimonial**: None. **Head Groundsman**: Matthew Merchant. **Scorer**: Chris Rimmer. **Blast Team Name**: Lancashire Lightning. ‡ New registration. [NQ] Not qualified for England.

ANDERSON, James Michael (St Theodore RC HS and SFC, Burnley), b Burnley 30 Jul 1982. 6'2". LHB, RFM. Squad No 9. Debut (Lancashire) 2002; cap 2003; benefit 2012. Auckland 2007-08. YC 2003. *Wisden* 2008. OBE 2015. **ECB Central Contract 2023-24. Tests**: 187 (2003 to 2023-24); HS 81 v I (Nottingham) 2014, sharing a world Test record 10th wkt partnership of 198 with J.E.Root; 50 wkts (3); most – 57 (2010); BB 7-42 v WI (Lord's) 2017. **LOI**: 194 (2002-03 to 2014-15); HS 28 v NZ (Southampton) 2013; BB 5-23 v SA (Port Elizabeth) 2009-10. Hat-trick v P (Oval) 2003. **IT20**: 19 (2006-07 to 2009-10); HS 1* v A (Sydney) 2006-07; BB 3-23 v Netherlands (Lord's) 2009. F-c Tours: A 2006-07, 2010-11, 2013-14, 2017-18, 2021-22; SA 2004-05, 2009-10, 2015-16, 2019-20; WI 2003-04, 2005-06 (Eng A) (*part*), 2008-09, 2014-15, 2018-19; NZ 2007-08, 2012-13, 2017-18, 2022-23; I 2005-06 (*part*), 2008-09, 2012-13, 2016-17, 2020-21, 2023-24; P 2022-23; SL 2003-04, 2007-08, 2011-12, 2018-19, 2020-21; UAE 2011-12 (v P), 2015-16 (v P). HS 81 (*see Tests*). La HS 42 v Surrey (Manchester) 2015. 50 wkts (4); most – 60 (2005, 2017). BB 7-19 v Kent (Manchester) 2021. Hat-trick v Essex (Manchester) 2003. LO HS 28 (*see LOI*). LO BB 5-23 (*see LOI*). T20 HS 16. T20 BB 3-23.

ASPINWALL, Thomas Henry (Sedbergh S), b Lancaster 13 Mar 2004. 5'10". RHB, RM. Squad No 13. Lancashire 2nd XI debut 2021. England U19 2022 to 2022-23. Awaiting f-c debut. LO HS 47 v Glos (Bristol) 2023 (MBC). LO BB 4-52 v Middx (Lord's) 2023 (MBC).

BAILEY, Thomas Ernest (Our Lady's Catholic HS, Preston), b Preston 21 Apr 1991. 6'4". RHB, RMF. Squad No 8. Debut (Lancashire) 2012; cap 2018. F-c Tour (EL): I 2018-19. HS 78 v Kent (Canterbury) 2023. 50 wkts (4); most – 65 (2018). BB 7-37 v Hants (Liverpool) 2021. LO HS 60 v Leics (Manchester) 2023 (MBC). LO BB 3-22 v Glamorgan (Neath) 2022 (RLC). T20 HS 10. T20 BB 5-17.

BALDERSON, George Philip (Cheadle Hulme HS), b Manchester 11 Oct 2000. 5'11". LHB, RM. Squad No 10. Debut (Lancashire) 2020. Lancashire 2nd XI debut 2018. England U19 2018-19. HS 116* v Warwks (Birmingham) 2023. BB 5-14 (inc hat-trick) v Essex (Chelmsford) 2022. LO HS 106* v Kent (Canterbury) 2022 (RLC). LO BB 3-25 v Hants (Southampton) 2021 (RLC).

BELL, George Joseph (Manchester GS), b Manchester 25 Sep 2002. 5'8". RHB, WK, occ OB. Squad No 17. Debut (Lancashire) 2022. Lancashire 2nd XI debut 2021. HS 91 v Middx (Manchester) 2023. BB 1-28 v Hants (Southport) 2023. LO HS 78* v Surrey (Guildford) 2023 (MBC). LO BB 1-20 v Glos (Bristol) 2023 (MBC). T20 HS 31.

BLATHERWICK, Jack Morgan (Holgate Ac, Hucknall; Central C, Nottingham), b Nottingham 4 June 1998. 6'2". RHB, RMF. Squad No 4. Nottinghamshire 2019. Lancashire debut 2021. Northamptonshire 2019 (l-o only). HS 35 v Surrey (Oval) 2023. BB 4-28 v Somerset (Taunton) 2021. LO HS 22* v Hants (Manchester) 2023 (MBC). LO BB 4-52 v Kent (Blackpool) 2023 (MBC). T20 HS 7. T20 BB 2-21.

BOHANNON, Joshua James (Harper Green HS), b Bolton 9 Apr 1997. 5'8". RHB, RM. Squad No 20. Debut (Lancashire) 2018; cap 2021. F-c Tours (EL): I 2023-24; SL 2022-23. 1000 runs (1): 1257 (2023). HS 231 v Glos (Manchester) 2022. BB 3-46 v Hants (Southampton) 2018. LO HS 105 v Kent (Blackpool) 2023 (MBC). LO BB 1-33 v Notts (Nottingham) 2019 (RLC). T20 HS 35.

BOYDEN, Joshua Ashton (Parklands HS, Chorley; Runshaw C), b Chorley 16 Apr 2004. 5'11". LHB, LMF. Squad No 27. Lancashire 2nd XI debut 2021. Awaiting 1st XI debut.

‡NQ**BRUCE, Thomas** Charles, b Te Kuiti, New Zealand 2 Aug 1991. RHB, OB. Squad No 42. Central Districts 2014-15 to date. Sussex 2018 (T20 only). **IT20** (NZ): 17 (2016-17 to 2019-20); HS 59* v B (Mt Maunganui) 2016-17. F-c Tours (NZA): A 2023; I 2017-18, 2022; UAE 2018-19 (v P A). HS 208* CD v ND (Whangarei) 2021-22. BB 2-17 CD v Canterbury (Nelson) 2015-16. LO HS 100 CD v ND (New Plymouth) 2016-17. LO BB 3-4 CD v Wellington (Napier) 2022-23. T20 HS 93*. T20 BB 3-9.

BUTTLER, **Jos**eph Charles (King's C, Taunton), b Taunton, Somerset 8 Sep 1990. 6'0". RHB, WK. Squad No 6. Somerset 2009-13; cap 2013. Lancashire debut 2014; cap 2018. IPL: MI 2016-17; RR 2018 to date. Big Bash: MR 2013-14; ST 2017-18 to 2018-19. Manchester Originals 2021 to date. *Wisden* 2018. MBE 2020. **ECB Two-Year Central Contract from 2023-24. Tests**: 57 (2014 to 2021-22); HS 152 v P (Southampton) 2020. **LOI**: 181 (2011-12 to 2023-24, 39 as captain); HS 162* (in 70 balls) v Neth (Amstelveen) 2022. **IT20**: 114 (2011 to 2023-24, 31 as captain); HS 101* v SL (Sharjah) 2021-22. F-c Tours: A 2021-22; SA 2019-20; WI 2015, 2018-19; NZ 2019-20; I 2016-17, 2020-21; SL 2018-19, 2019-20, 2020-21; UAE 2015-16 (v P). CC HS 144 Sm v Hants (Southampton) 2010. La HS 100* v Durham (Chester-le-St) 2014. BB –. LO HS 162* (*see LOI*). T20 HS 124.

CROFT, Steven John (Highfield HS, Blackpool; Myerscough C), b Blackpool 11 Oct 1984. 5'10". RHB, OB. Squad No 15. Debut (Lancashire) 2005; cap 2010; captain 2017; testimonial 2018. Auckland 2008-09. HS 156 v Northants (Manchester) 2014. BB 6-41 v Worcs (Manchester) 2012. LO HS 127 v Warwks (Birmingham) 2017 (RLC). LO BB 4-24 v Scotland (Manchester) 2008 (FPT). T20 HS 101. T20 BB 3-6.

HARTLEY, Tom William (Merchant Taylors S), b Ormskirk 3 May 1999. 6'3". LHB, SLA. Squad No 2. Debut (Lancashire) 2020. Manchester Originals 2021 to date. **Tests**: 5 (2023-24); HS 36 v I (Visakhapatnam) 2023-24; BB 7-62 v I (Hyderabad) 2023-24 – on debut. **LOI**: 2 (2023); HS 12* v Ire (Nottingham) 2023; BB –. F-c Tour: I 2023-24. HS 73* v Essex (Chelmsford) 2021. BB 7-62 (*see Tests*). La BB 5-52 v Surrey (Manchester) 2022. LO HS 23 v Sri Lanka A (Colombo, RPS) 2022-23. LO BB 1-46 v Sri Lanka A (Colombo, RPS) 2022-23 – separate matches. T20 HS 39. T20 BB 4-16.

HURST, Matthew ('**Matty**') Frederick (Byrchall HS, Wigan; Winstanley C), b Billinge, Cheshire 10 Dec 2003. RHB, WK. Squad No 21. Debut (Lancashire) 2023. Lancashire 2nd XI debut 2021. England U19 2022 to 2022-23. HS 76* v Kent (Canterbury) 2023. LO HS 66 v Middx (Lord's) 2023.

JENNINGS, Keaton Kent (King Edward VII S, Johannesburg), b Johannesburg, South Africa 19 Jun 1992. Son of R.V.Jennings (Transvaal 1973-74 to 1992-93), brother of D.Jennings (Gauteng and Easterns 1999 to 2003-04), nephew of K.E.Jennings (Northern Transvaal 1981-82 to 1982-83). 6'4". LHB, RM. Squad No 1. Gauteng 2011-12. Durham 2012-17; captain 2017 (l-o only). Lancashire debut/cap 2018; captain 2023 to date. **Tests**: 17 (2016-17 to 2018-19); HS 146* v SL (Galle) 2018-19; scored 112 v I (Mumbai) on debut;

BB –. F-c Tours (C=Captain): A 2019-20 (EL)C; WI 2017-18 (EL)C, 2018-19; I 2016-17, 2023-24 (EL); SL 2016-17 (EL), 2018-19. 1000 runs (2); most – 1602 (2016), inc seven hundreds (Du record). HS 318 v Somerset (Southport) 2022. BB 3-37 Du v Sussex (Chester-le-St) 2017. La BB 1-8 v Durham (Sedbergh) 2019. LO HS 139 Du v Warwks (Birmingham) 2017 (RLC). LO BB 2-19 v Worcs (Worcester) 2018 (RLC). T20 HS 108 v Durham (Chester-le-St) 2020 – La record. T20 BB 4-37.

LAVELLE, George Isaac Davies (Merchant Taylors S), b Ormskirk 24 Mar 2000. 5'8". RHB. WK. Squad No 24. Debut (Lancashire) 2020. Lancashire 2nd XI debut 2017. England U19 2018. HS 32 v Notts (Nottingham) 2021. LO HS 72 v Middx (Lord's) 2023 (MBC). T20 HS 12.

LIVINGSTONE, Liam Stephen (Chetwynde S, Barrow-in-Furness), b Barrow-in-Furness, Cumberland 4 Aug 1993. 6'1". RHB, LB. Squad No 23. Debut (Lancashire) 2016; cap 2017; captain 2018. IPL: RR 2019 to 2021; PK 2022 to date. Big Bash: PS 2019-20 to 2020-21. Birmingham Phoenix 2021 to date. **ECB Two-Year Central Contract from 2023-24.** **Tests**: 1 (2022-23); HS 9 v P (Rawalpindi) 2022-23. **LOI**: 25 (2020-21 to 2023-24); HS 95* v NZ (Southampton) 2023; BB 3-16 v NZ (Oval) 2023; took wkt of K.L.Rahul with 2nd delivery in international cricket. **IT20**: 38 (2017 to 2023-24); HS 103 v P (Nottingham) 2021; BB 3-17 v Ire (Melbourne) 2022-23. F-c Tours (EL): WI 2017-18; P 2022-23 (E); SL 2016-17. HS 224 v Warwks (Manchester) 2017. BB 6-52 v Surrey (Manchester) 2017. LO HS 129 EL v South Africa A (Northampton) 2017. LO BB 3-16 (*see LOI*). T20 HS 103. T20 BB 4-17.

‡NQ**LYON, Nathan** Michael, b Young, NSW, Australia 20 Nov 1987. 5'9". RHB, OB. Squad No 67. S Australia 2010-11 to 2012-13. New South Wales 2013-14 to date. Worcestershire 2017. Big Bash: AS 2011-12 to 2012-13; SS 2013-14 to date. **Tests** (A): 128 (2011 to 2023-24); HS 47 v SA (Cape Town) 2017-18; 50 wkts (1): 63 (2017); BB 8-50 v I (Bengaluru) 2016-17. **LOI** (A): 29 (2011-12 to 2019); HS 30 v SA (Providence) 2016; BB 4-44 v Z (Harare) 2014. **IT20** (A): 2 (2015-16 to 2018-19); HS 4* and BB 1-33 v P (Dubai, DSC) 2018-19. F-c Tours (A): E 2012 (Aus A), 2013, 2015, 2019, 2023; SA 2011-12, 2013-14, 2017-18; WI 2011-12, 2015; NZ 2015-16, 2023-24; I 2012-13, 2016-17, 2022-23; P 2021-22; SL 2011, 2016, 2022; B 2017; UAE (v P) 2014-15, 2018-19. HS 75 NSW v Vic (Alice Springs) 2015-16. CC HS 6* Wo v Glamorgan (Worcester) 2017. BB 8-50 (*see Tests*). CC BB Wo 3-94 v Northants (Northampton) 2017. LO HS 37* SA v WA (Adelaide) 2011-12. LO BB 4-10 NSW v Q (Sydney) 2016-17. T20 HS 11. T20 BB 5-23.

MAHMOOD, Saqib (Matthew Moss HS, Rochdale), b Birmingham, Warwks 25 Feb 1997. 6'3". RHB, RFM. Squad No 25. Debut (Lancashire) 2016; cap 2021. Big Bash: ST 2021-22. Oval Invincibles 2021. **ECB Development Contract 2023-24**. **Tests**: 2 (2021-22); HS 49 v WI (St George's) 2021-22; BB 2-21 v WI (Bridgetown) 2021-22. **LOI**: 8 (2019-20 to 2022-23); HS 12 v Ire (Southampton) 2020; BB 4-42 v P (Cardiff) 2021. **IT20**: 12 (2019-20 to 2021-22); HS 7* v WI (Bridgetown) 2021-22; BB 3-33 v P (Leeds) 2021. F-c Tours (EL): A 2021-22; WI 2017-18, 2022-23 (E). HS 49 (*see Tests*). La HS 34 v Middx (Manchester) 2019. BB 5-47 v Yorks (Manchester) 2021. LO HS 45 v Warwks (Birmingham) 2019 (RLC). LO BB 6-37 v Northants (Manchester) 2019 (RLC). T20 HS 11*. T20 BB 4-14.

MORLEY, Jack Peter (Siddal Moor Sports C), b Rochdale 25 Jun 2001. 5'10". LHB, SLA. Squad No 18. Debut (Lancashire) 2020. Lancashire 2nd XI debut 2018. England U19 2018-19. HS 9 v Warwks (Birmingham) 2023. BB 5-69 v Somerset (Southport) 2022. LO HS 6 v Durham (Gosforth) 2021 (RLC). LO BB 3-40 v Hants (Manchester) 2023 (MBC).

SALT, Philip Dean (Reed's S, Cobham), b Bodelwyddan, Denbighs 28 Aug 1996. 5'10". RHB, OB. Squad No 7. Sussex 2013-20. Lancashire debut 2022. IPL: DC 2023. Big Bash: AS 2019-20 to 2020-21. Manchester Originals 2021 to date. **LOI**: 19 (2021 to 2023-24); HS 122 v Neth (Amstelveen) 2022. **IT20**: 21 (2021-22 to 2023-24); HS 119 v WI (Tarouba) 2023-24 – E record. HS 148 Sx v Derbys (Hove) 2018. La HS 105 v Northants (Manchester) 2023. BB 1-32 Sx v Warwks (Hove) 2018. LO HS 137* Sx v Kent (Beckenham) 2019 (RLC). T20 HS 119.

SINGH, Harry (Clitheroe RGS), b Blackburn 16 Jun 2004. Son of R.P.Singh (Uttar Pradesh & India 1982-83 to 1995-96). RHB, OB. Squad No 16. Lancashire 2nd XI debut 2021. England U19 2022 to 2022-23. Awaiting 1st XI debut.

‡**STANLEY, Mitchell** Terry (Idsall S, Shifnal; Shrewsbury SFC), b Telford, Shrops 17 Mar 2001. 6'2". RHB, RFM. Squad No 38. Awaiting f-c debut. Worcestershire 2022-23 (T20 only). Manchester Originals 2022. Worcestershire 2nd XI 2021-23. Shropshire 2021. T20 HS 7. T20 BB 2-24.

WELLS, Luke William Peter (St Bede's S, Upper Dicker), b Eastbourne, E Sussex 29 Dec 1990. Son of A.P.Wells (Border, Kent, Sussex and England 1981-2000); elder brother of D.A.C.Wells (Oxford MCCU 2017); nephew of C.M.Wells (Border, Derbyshire, Sussex and WP 1979-96). 6'4". LHB, LB. Squad No 3. Sussex 2010-19; cap 2016. Colombo CC 2011-12. Lancashire debut 2021; cap 2022. 1000 runs (2); most – 1292 (2017). HS 258 Sx v Durham (Hove) 2017. La HS 175* Warwks (Birmingham) 2022. BB 5-25 v Northants (Northampton) 2023. LO HS 88 v Yorks (York) 2022 (RLC). BB 3-19 Sx v Netherlands (Amstelveen) 2011 (CB40). T20 HS 66. T20 BB 2-19.

NQ**WILLIAMS, Will**iam Salter Austen (Christchurch Boys' HS), b Christchurch, New Zealand 6 Oct 1992. 6'2". RHB, RMF. Squad No 30. UK passport. Canterbury 2012-13 to 2021-22. Lancashire debut 2022. HS 61 v Surrey (Oval) 2023. BB 5-26 Cant v ND (Rangiora) 2020-21. La BB 5-41 v Northants (Northampton) 2022. LO HS 19* Cant v Auckland (Auckland) 2017-18. LO BB 4-20 v Derbys (Manchester) 2022 (RLC). T20 HS 29*. T20 BB 5-12.

WOOD, Luke (Portland CS, Worksop), b Sheffield, Yorks 2 Aug 1995. 5'9". LHB, LFM. Squad No 14. Nottinghamshire 2014-19. Worcestershire 2018 (on loan). Northamptonshire 2019 (on loan). Lancashire debut 2020. Big Bash: MS 2022-23. Trent Rockets 2021 to date. **LOI**: 2 (2022-23 to 2023); HS 10 v A (Adelaide) 2022-23; BB –. **IT20**: 5 (2022-23 to 2023); HS 3 v NZ (Birmingham) 2023; BB 3-24 v P (Karachi) 2022-23. HS 119 v Kent (Canterbury) 2021, sharing La record 8th wkt partnership of 187 with D.J.Lamb. BB 5-40 Nt v Cambridge MCCU (Cambridge) 2016. CC BB 5-67 Nt v Yorks (Scarborough) 2019. La BB 3-31 v Northants (Manchester) 2021. LO HS 52 Nt v Leics (Leicester) 2016 (RLC). LO BB 2-36 Nt v Worcs (Worcester) 2019 (RLC). T20 HS 33*. T20 BB 5-50.

RELEASED/RETIRED

(Having made a County 1st XI appearance in 2023)

NQ**De GRANDHOMME, Colin**, b Harare, Zimbabwe 22 Jul 1986. Son of L.L.de Grandhomme (Rhodesia B and Zimbabwe 1979-80 to 1987-88). RHB, RMF. Zimbabwe A 2005-06. Auckland 2006-07 to 2017-18. N Districts 2018-19 to 2022-23. Hampshire 2021. Surrey 2022. Lancashire 2023. Warwickshire 2017-18 (T20 only). IPL: KKR 2017; RCB 2018-19. Big Bash: AS 2022-23. Southern Brave 2021. **Tests** (NZ): 29 (2016-17 to 2022); HS 120* v SA (Christchurch) 2021-22; BB 6-41 v P (Christchurch) 2016-17 – on debut. **LOI** (NZ): 45 (2011-12 to 2019-20); HS 74* v P (Hamilton) 2017-18; BB 3-26 v I (Hamilton) 2018-19. **IT20** (NZ): 41 (2011-12 to 2021); HS 59 v SL (Pallekele) 2019; BB 2-22 v SA (Auckland) 2016-17. F-c Tours (NZ): E 2014 (NZ A), 2021, 2022; A 2019-20; SA 2005-06 (Z U23); SL 2019; UAE 2018-19 (v P). HS 174* H v Surrey (Southampton) 2021. La HS 67* v Surrey (Manchester) 2023. BB 6-24 Auckland v Wellington (Auckland) 2013-14. CC BB 4-31 H v Glos (Cheltenham) 2021. La BB 2-34 v Essex (Chelmsford) 2023. LO HS 151 NZ A v Northants (Northampton) 2014. LO BB 4-37 Auckland v Wellington (Wellington) 2015-16. T20 HS 86. T20 BB 3-4.

GLEESON, R.J. – *see WARWICKSHIRE.*

JONES, R.P. – *see WORCESTERSHIRE.*

LAMB, D.J. – *see SUSSEX.*

[NQ]**MITCHELL, Daryl** Joseph, b Hamilton, New Zealand 20 May 1991. RHB, RM. N Districts 2011-12 to 2019-20. Canterbury 2020-21. Middlesex 2021. Lancashire 2023. IPL: RR 2022. London Spirit 2023. **Tests** (NZ): 22 (2019-20 to 2023-24); HS 190 v E (Nottingham) 2022; BB 1-7 v WI (Hamilton) 2020-21. **LOI** (NZ): 39 (2020-21 to 2023-24); HS 134 v I (Mumbai) 2023-24; BB 3-25 v I (Christchurch) 2022-23. **IT20** (NZ): 63 (2018-19 to 2023-24); HS 72* v E (Abu Dhabi) 2021-22 and 72* v P (Christchurch) 2023-24; BB 2-27 v I (Hamilton) 2018-19. F-c Tours (NZ): E 2021, 2022; I/SL 2013-14 (NZA); I 2021-22; P 2022-23; B 2023-24. HS 190 (*see Tests*). CC HS 105 and CC BB 3-32 v Somerset (Manchester) 2023. BB 5-44 Cant v Otago (Alexandra) 2020-21. LO HS 134 (*see LOI*). LO BB 3-25 (*see LOI*). T20 HS 88*. T20 BB 4-32.

PARKINSON, M.W. – *see KENT.*

[NQ]**VILAS, Dane** James, b Johannesburg, South Africa 10 Jun 1985. 6'2". RHB, WK. Gauteng 2006-07 to 2009-10. Lions 2008-09 to 2009-10. W Province 2010-11. Cape Cobras 2011-12 to 2016-17. Lancashire 2017-23; cap 2018; captain 2019-22. Dolphins 2017-18 to 2018-19. Northern Superchargers 2021. **Tests** (SA): 6 (2015 to 2015-16); HS 26 v E (Johannesburg) 2015-16. **IT20** (SA): 1 (2011-12); HS –. F-c Tours (SA): A 2016 (SA A), I 2015 (SA A), 2015-16; Z 2016 (SA A), B 2015. 1000 runs (1): 1036 (2019). HS 266 v Glamorgan (Colwyn B) 2019. LO HS 166 v Notts (Nottingham) 2019 (RLC). T20 HS 75*.

KENT RELEASED/RETIRED (continued from p 125)

[NQ]**LINDE, George** Fredrik (Pretoria U), b Cape Town, South Africa 4 Dec 1991. 6'2". LHB, SLA. W Province 2011-12 to date. Cape Cobras 2014-15 to 2020-21. Kent 2022. **Tests** (SA): 3 (2019-20 to 2020-21); HS 37 v I (Ranchi) 2019-20; BB 5-64 v P (Rawalpindi) 2020-21. **LOI** (SA): 2 (2021); HS 18 and BB 2-32 v SL (Colombo, RPS) 2021. **IT20** (SA): 14 (2020-21 to 2021); HS 29 v E (Paarl) 2020-21; BB 3-23 v P (Johannesburg) 2020-21. F-c Tours (SA): I 2019-20; P 2020-21. HS 148* Cobras v Titans (Cape Town) 2019-20. K HS 107 SL Dev (Canterbury) 2022. CC HS 31 v Northants (Northampton) 2022. BB 7-29 Cobras v Knights (Cape Town) 2020-21. K BB 3-43 v Northants (Canterbury) 2022. LO HS 93* WP v Northerns (Rondebosch) 2015-16. LO BB 6-47 Cobras v Warriors (Oudtshoorn) 2017-18. T20 HS 63*. T20 BB 4-19.

[NQ]**RICHARDSON, Kane** William, b Eudunda, S Australia 12 Feb 1991. RHB, RMF. S Australia 2010-11 to 2020-21. Kent 2023 (T20 only). IPL: PW 2013; RR 2014; RCB 2016 to 2021. Big Bash: AS 2011-12 to 2016-17; MR 2017-18 to date. Birmingham Phoenix 2022 to date. **LOI** (A): 25 (2012-13 to 2019-20); HS 24* v I (Rajkot) 2019-20; BB 5-68 v I (Canberra) 2015-16. **IT20** (A): 36 (2014-15 to 2023-24); HS 9 v I (Adelaide) 2015-16; BB 4-30 v SL (Colombo, RPS) 2022. HS 49 SA v Tas (Adelaide) 2013-14. BB 5-69 SA v WA (Adelaide, GS) 2016-17. LO HS 36* Q v NSW (Sydney, NS) 2023-24. LO BB 6-48 SA v Q (Adelaide) 2012-13. T20 HS 45. T20 BB 4-22.

J.E.G.Logan left the staff without making a County 1st XI appearance in 2023.

LANCASHIRE 2023

RESULTS SUMMARY

	Place	Won	Lost	Drew	NR
LV= Insurance County Champ (Div 1)	5th	3	1	10	
Metro Bank One-Day Cup (Group A)	QF	4	3		2
Vitality Blast (North Group)	QF	8	6		1

LV= INSURANCE COUNTY CHAMPIONSHIP AVERAGES
BATTING AND FIELDING

Cap		*M*	*I*	*NO*	*HS*	*Runs*	*Avge*	*100*	*50*	*Ct/St*
2021	J.J.Bohannon	14	22	1	175	1257	59.85	4	5	5
2018	K.K.Jennings	11	17	2	189*	794	52.93	1	5	14
	R.P.Jones	2	4	1	111	154	51.33	1	–	2
	G.P.Balderson	11	16	2	116*	702	50.14	2	4	1
	P.D.Salt	7	11	1	105	433	43.30	2	2	23/3
	D.J.Mitchell	4	7	–	105	291	41.57	1	1	1
	T.W.Hartley	10	13	3	73*	371	37.10	–	2	6
2022	L.W.P.Wells	13	20	–	119	676	33.80	2	3	10
2018	T.E.Bailey	13	18	4	78	467	33.35	–	3	4
	G.J.Bell	12	16	–	91	447	27.93	–	3	25/2
2018	D.J.Vilas	10	16	2	124	363	25.92	1	1	6
2010	S.J.Croft	7	11	1	56*	228	22.80	–	1	3
	J.M.Blatherwick	6	9	4	35	92	18.40	–	–	2
	C.de Grandhomme	5	8	1	67*	128	18.28	–	1	6
	W.S.A.Williams	13	13	3	61	135	13.50	–	1	7
	J.P.Morley	5	4	–	9	14	3.50	–	–	2

Also batted: J.M.Anderson (4 matches – cap 2003) 9*, 8, 5 (2 ct); M.F.Hurst (2) 54*, 76*, 0; D.J.Lamb (1) 0, 4*; S.Mahmood (2 – cap 2021) 1, 1*; M.W.Parkinson (1 – cap 2019) 5; L.Wood (2) 0, 2.

BOWLING

	O	*M*	*R*	*W*	*Avge*	*Best*	*5wI*	*10wM*
J.M.Anderson	128	37	325	16	20.31	5- 76	1	–
T.E.Bailey	407.4	102	1133	50	22.66	6- 59	2	–
W.S.A.Williams	361.3	92	904	39	23.17	4- 23	–	–
L.W.P.Wells	73.1	7	268	10	26.80	5- 25	1	–
G.P.Balderson	235	54	784	23	34.08	4- 69	–	–
T.W.Hartley	286.5	68	852	19	44.84	2- 10	–	–
Also bowled:								
D.J.Mitchell	53.1	16	175	7	25.00	3- 32	–	–
M.W.Parkinson	48	2	223	6	37.16	5-120	1	–
L.Wood	60	7	207	5	41.40	3- 52	–	–
J.P.Morley	108	17	334	8	41.75	3- 87	–	–
C.de Grandhomme	89	11	296	7	42.28	2- 34	–	–
J.M.Blatherwick	87.3	11	393	8	49.12	2- 25	–	–

G.J.Bell 18-0-64-1; S.J.Croft 7-0-35-0; D.J.Lamb 4-0-19-0; S.Mahmood 75-12-231-3; D.J.Vilas 11-2-47-0.

Lancashire played no first-class fixtures outside the County Championship in 2023. The First-Class Averages (pp 223–235) give the records of Lancashire players first-class county matches, with the exception of J.M.Anderson, D.J.Lamb and M.W.Parkinson, whose first-class figures for Lancashire are as above.

LANCASHIRE RECORDS

FIRST-CLASS CRICKET

Highest Total	For 863		v	Surrey	The Oval	1990
	V 707-9d		by	Surrey	The Oval	1990
Lowest Total	For 25		v	Derbyshire	Manchester	1871
	V 20		by	Essex	Chelmsford	2013
Highest Innings	For 424	A.C.MacLaren	v	Somerset	Taunton	1895
	V 315*	T.W.Hayward	for	Surrey	The Oval	1898

Highest Partnership for each Wicket

1st	368	A.C.MacLaren/R.H.Spooner	v	Glos	Liverpool	1903
2nd	371	F.B.Watson/G.E.Tyldesley	v	Surrey	Manchester	1928
3rd	501	A.N.Petersen/A.G.Prince	v	Glamorgan	Colwyn Bay	2015
4th	358	S.P.Titchard/G.D.Lloyd	v	Essex	Chelmsford	1996
5th	360	S.G.Law/C.L.Hooper	v	Warwicks	Birmingham	2003
6th	278	J.Iddon/H.R.W.Butterworth	v	Sussex	Manchester	1932
7th	248	G.D.Lloyd/I.D.Austin	v	Yorkshire	Leeds	1997
8th	187	L.Wood/D.J.Lamb	v	Kent	Canterbury	2021
9th	142	L.O.S.Poidevin/A.Kermode	v	Sussex	Eastbourne	1907
10th	173	J.Briggs/R.Pilling	v	Surrey	Liverpool	1885

Best Bowling	For	10-46	W.Hickton	v	Hampshire	Manchester	1870
(Innings)	V	10-40	G.O.B.Allen	for	Middlesex	Lord's	1929
Best Bowling	For	17-91	H.Dean	v	Yorkshire	Liverpool	1913
(Match)	V	16-65	G.Giffen	for	Australians	Manchester	1886

Most Runs – Season	2633	J.T.Tyldesley	(av 56.02)	1901
Most Runs – Career	34222	G.E.Tyldesley	(av 45.20)	1909-36
Most 100s – Season	11	C.Hallows		1928
Most 100s – Career	90	G.E.Tyldesley		1909-36
Most Wkts – Season	198	E.A.McDonald	(av 18.55)	1925
Most Wkts – Career	1816	J.B.Statham	(av 15.12)	1950-68
Most Career W-K Dismissals	925	G.Duckworth	(635 ct; 290 st)	1923-38
Most Career Catches in the Field	556	K.J.Grieves		1949-64

LIMITED-OVERS CRICKET

Highest Total	**50ov**	406-9		v	Notts	Nottingham	2019
	40ov	324-4		v	Worcs	Worcester	2012
	T20	231-4		v	Yorkshire	Manchester	2015
Lowest Total	**50ov**	59		v	Worcs	Worcester	1963
	40ov	68		v	Yorkshire	Leeds	2000
		68		v	Surrey	The Oval	2002
	T20	83		v	Durham	Manchester	2020
Highest Innings	**50ov**	166	D.J.Vilas	v	Notts	Nottingham	2019
	40ov	143	A.Flintoff	v	Essex	Chelmsford	1999
	T20	108	K.K.Jennings	v	Durham	Chester-le-St[2]	2020
Best Bowling	**50ov**	6-10	C.E.H.Croft	v	Scotland	Manchester	1982
	40ov	6-25	G.Chapple	v	Yorkshire	Leeds	1998
	T20	5-13	S.D.Parry	v	Worcs	Manchester	2016

LEICESTERSHIRE

Formation of Present Club: 25 March 1879
Inaugural First-Class Match: 1894
Colours: Dark Green and Scarlet
Badge: Gold Running Fox on Green Ground
County Champions: (3) 1975, 1996, 1998
Benson and Hedges Cup Winners: (3) 1972, 1975, 1985
Sunday League Champions: (2) 1974, 1977
Metro Bank One-Day Cup: (1) 2023
Twenty20 Cup Winners: (3) 2004, 2006, 2011

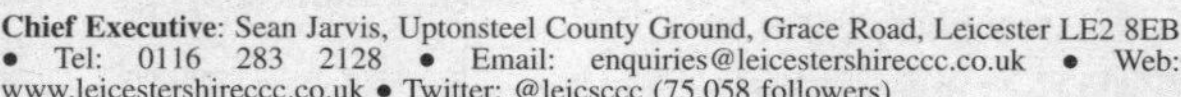
Chief Executive: Sean Jarvis, Uptonsteel County Ground, Grace Road, Leicester LE2 8EB • Tel: 0116 283 2128 • Email: enquiries@leicestershireccc.co.uk • Web: www.leicestershireccc.co.uk • Twitter: @leicsccc (75,058 followers)

Director of Cricket: Claude Henderson. **Head Coach**: Alfonso Thomas. **Assistant Coach**: James Taylor. **Captain**: L.J.Hill. **Overseas Players**: P.S.P.Handscomb, P.W.A.Mulder and W.J.Pucovski. **2024 Testimonial**: None. **Head Groundsman**: Andy Ward. **Scorer**: Paul Rogers. **Blast Team Name**: Leicestershire Foxes. ‡ New registration. [NQ] Not qualified for England.

AHMED, Rehan (Bluecoat Aspley SFC), b Nottingham 13 Aug 2004. 5'8". RHB, LB. Squad No 16. Debut (Leicestershire) 2022; cap 2023. Southern Brave 2022 to date. Leicestershire 2nd XI debut 2021. **ECB Two-Year Central Contract from 2023-24**. **Tests**: 4 (2022-23 to 2023-24); HS 28 v I (Hyderabad) 2023-24; BB 5-48 v P (Karachi) 2022-23 – on debut; youngest Test debutant for England at 18y 126d. **LOI**: 6 (2022-23 to 2023-24); HS 15 v WI (Bridgetown) 2023-24; BB 4-54 v Ire (Nottingham) 2023; youngest LOI debutant for England at 18y 205d. **IT20**: 7 (2022-23 to 2023-24); HS 11 v B (Mirpur) 2022-23 and 11 v NZ (Nottingham) 2023; BB 3-39 v WI (Bridgetown) 2023-24; youngest IT20 debutant for England at 18y 211d. F-c Tours: I 2023-24; P 2022-23. HS 122 and Le BB 5-114 v Derbys (Derby) 2022 – youngest ever to score a century & take five wkts in an innings in f-c career at 18y 57d. BB 5-48 (*see Tests*). LO HS 40* v Northants (Northampton) 2021 (RLC). LO BB 4-54 (*see LOI*). T20 HS 49. T20 BB 4-22.

BUDINGER, Soloman George (Southport S, Queensland), b Colchester, Essex 21 Aug 1999. 6'0". LHB, OB, occ WK. Squad No 1. Debut (Leicestershire) 2022. Nottinghamshire 2021-22 (l-o only). Birmingham Phoenix 2022. Sussex 2nd XI 2016-17. Nottinghamshire 2nd XI 2018-22. HS 72 v Derbys (Leicester) 2023. LO HS 102 v Essex (Kibworth) 2023 (MBC). T20 HS 24. T20 BB 2-21.

COX, Oliver **Ben** (Bromsgrove S), b Wordsley, Stourbridge, Worcs 2 Feb 1992. 5'10". RHB, WK. Squad No 7. Worcestershire 2009-23; testimonial 2023. Leicestershire debut 2023. MCC 2017, 2019. HS 124 Wo v Glos (Cheltenham) 2017. Le HS 58 v Sussex (Hove) 2023. LO HS 122* Wo v Kent (Worcester) 2018 (RLC). T20 HS 61*.

[NQ]**CURRIE, Scott** William (St Edward's RC & C of E S), b Poole, Dorset 2 May 2001. Younger brother of B.J.Currie (*see SUSSEX*). 6'5". RHB, RMF. Squad No 32. Hampshire 2020-21. Leicestershire debut 2023. Joins Leicestershire on season-long loan from Hampshire. Hampshire 2nd XI debut 2018. Dorset 2017-19. **LOI** (Scot): 3 (2023-24); HS 5 (twice) v Canada (Dubai, DSC) 2023-24; BB 2-16 v UAE (Dubai, DSC) 2023-24. HS 38 v Kent (Canterbury) 2020. Le HS 9* v Sussex (Hove) 2023. BB 4-109 v Surrey (Oval) 2021. Le BB 2-32 v Yorks (Leicester) 2023. LO HS 43* v Worcs (Southampton) 2022 (RLC). LO BB 3-25 v Lancs (Southampton) 2022 (RLC). T20 HS 3. T20 BB 4-24.

EVANS, Samuel Thomas (Lancaster S, Leicester; Wyggeston & QE I C; Leicester U), b Leicester 20 Dec 1997. 5'8". RHB, OB. Squad No 21. Loughborough MCCU 2017-18. Leicestershire debut 2017. HS 138 v Surrey (Oval) 2021. BB –. LO HS 60 v Hants (Nottingham) 2023.

^NQ^**HANDSCOMB, Peter** Stephen Patrick (Mt Waverley SC; Deakin U, Melbourne), b Melbourne, Australia 26 Apr 1991. 6'0". RHB, WK. Squad No 54. British passport (English parents). Victoria 2011-12 to date. Gloucestershire 2015; cap 2015. Yorkshire 2017. Durham 2019. Middlesex 2021-22; captain 2021-22. Leicestershire debut 2023. IPL: RPS 2016. Big Bash: MS 2012-13 to date; HH 2020-21 to 2021-22; MR 2022-23. **Tests** (A): 20 (2016-17 to 2022-23); HS 110 v P (Sydney) 2016-17. **LOI** (A): 22 (2016-17 to 2019); HS 117 v I (Mohali) 2018-19. **IT20** (A): 2 (2018-19); HS 20* v I (Bengaluru) 2018-19. F-c Tours (A): SA 2017-18; I 2015 (Aus A), 2016-17, 2018-19, 2022-23; B 2017. HS 281* Vic v WA (Melbourne, SK) 2022-23. CC HS 136* v Durham (Leicester) 2023. LO HS 140 Y v Derbys (Leeds) 2017 (RLC). T20 HS 103*.

HILL, Lewis John (Hastings HS, Hinckley; John Cleveland C), b Leicester 5 Oct 1990. 5'7½". RHB, WK, occ RM. Squad No 23. Debut (Leicestershire) 2015; cap 2021; captain 2023 to date. Unicorns 2012-13. HS 162* v Derbys (Leicester) 2023. LO HS 118 v Worcs (Leicester) 2019 (RLC). T20 HS 59.

HULL, Joshua Owen (Stamford S), b Huntingdon 20 Aug 2004. 6'7". LHB, LFM. Squad No 20. Debut (Leicestershire) 2023. Leicestershire 2nd XI debut 2022. HS 15 and BB 3-68 v Yorks (Leeds) 2023. LO HS 3* and LO BB 4-43 v Notts (Leicester) 2023 (MBC). T20 HS 2*. T20 BB 3-35.

KIMBER, Louis Philip James (William Farr C of E S; Loughborough U), b Lincoln 24 Feb 1997. Elder brother of J.F.Kimber (Lincolnshire 2016-18) and N.J.H.Kimber (*see SURREY*). 6'3". RHB, OB, occ WK. Squad No 17. Loughborough MCCU 2019. Leicestershire debut 2021. Lincolnshire 2015-19. HS 104 v Sussex (Hove) 2022. BB 1-8 v Middx (Leicester) 2022. LO HS 102 v Somerset (Leicester) 2022 (RLC). LO BB 4-61 v Glos (Bristol) 2022 (RLC). T20 HS 59*. T20 BB –.

MIKE, Benjamin Wentworth Munro (Loughborough GS), b Nottingham 24 Aug 1998. Son of G.W.Mike (Nottinghamshire 1989-96). 6'1". RHB, RM. Squad No 8. Debut (Leicestershire) 2018. Warwickshire 2019 (on loan). Yorkshire 2022-23. HS 99* v Middx (Lord's) 2022. BB 5-37 v Sussex (Hove) 2018 – on debut. LO HS 41 v Northants (Leicester) 2019 (RLC). LO BB 4-40 Y v Surrey (York) 2023 (MBC). T20 HS 37. T20 BB 4-22.

^NQ^**MULDER**, Peter Willem Adriaan ('**Wiaan**'), b Johannesburg, South Africa 19 Feb 1998. 6'0". RHB, RMF. Squad No 24. Lions 2016-17 to 2020-21. Gauteng 2017-18 to date. Kent 2019. Leicestershire debut 2022; cap 2023. **Tests** (SA): 12 (2018-19 to 2022); HS 42 v WI (Johannesburg) 2022-23; BB 3-1 v WI (Gros Islet) 2021. **LOI** (SA): 15 (2017-18 to 2023-24); HS 19* v SL (Dambulla) 2018; BB 2-59 v SL (Colombo, RPS) 2018. **IT20** (SA): 5 (2021); HS 36 v Ire (Belfast) 2021; BB 2-10 v Ire (Belfast) 2021 – separate matches. F-c Tours (SA): E 2017 (SA A), 2022; WI 2021; NZ 2021-22; P 2020-21. HS 235* v Sussex (Hove) 2022, sharing Le and CC record 5th wkt partnership of 477* with C.N.Ackermann. BB 7-25 Lions v Dolphins (Potchefstroom) 2016-17. CC BB 5-63 v Sussex (Leicester) 2023. LO HS 116* and LO BB 4-47 v Middx (Radlett) 2022 (RLC). T20 HS 83*. T20 BB 2-10.

PATEL, Rishi Ketan (Brentwood S), b Chigwell, Essex 26 Jul 1998. 6'2". RHB, LB. Squad No 26. Cambridge MCCU 2019. Essex 2019. Leicestershire debut 2020; cap 2023. Hertfordshire 2019. 1000 runs (1): 1075 (2023). HS 179 v Glamorgan (Cardiff) 2023. LO HS 161 v Lancs (Manchester) 2023 (MBC). T20 HS 104.

‡^NQ^**PUCOVSKI, Will**iam Jan, b Malvern, Victoria, Australia 2 Feb 1998. RHB, OB. Squad No 10. Victoria 2016-17 to date. **Tests** (A): 1 (2020-21); HS 62 v I (Sydney) 2020-21. F-c Tour (Aus A): E 2019. HS 255* Vic v SA (Adelaide) 2020-21. LO HS 137 Aus A v Glos (Bristol) 2019.

RAMJI, Uttam (Soar Valley C; Loughborough C), b Udi, Uttar Pradesh, India 26 Nov 2004. RHB, LBG. Squad No 9. Leicestershire 2nd XI debut 2023. Awaiting f-c debut. LO HS –. LO BB 3-58 v Lancs (Manchester) 2023 (MBC).

SALISBURY, Matthew Edward Thomas (Shenfield HS; Anglia Ruskin U), b Chelmsford, Essex 18 Apr 1993. 6'0½". RHB, RMF. Squad No 18. Cambridge MCCU 2012-13. Essex 2014-15. Hampshire 2017. Durham 2018-22; cap 2018. Leicestershire debut 2023. Suffolk 2016. HS 45 Du v Middx (Lord's) 2022. Le HS 4* and Le BB 5-73 v Sussex (Hove) 2023. BB 6-37 Du v Middx (Chester-le-St) 2018. LO HS 5* Ex v Leics (Chelmsford) 2014 (RLC). LO BB 4-55 Ex v Lancs (Chelmsford) 2014 (RLC). T20 HS 1*. T20 BB 2-19.

SCRIVEN, Thomas Antony Rhys (Magdalen Coll S), b Oxford 18 Nov 1998. 6'0½". RHB, RMF. Squad No 88. Hampshire 2020. Leicestershire debut 2022. Berkshire 2022. HS 78 v Sussex (Hove) 2023. BB 4-30 v Glos (Leicester) 2023. LO HS 42 H v Durham (Chester-le-S) 2021 (RLC). LO BB 5-66 v Surrey (Oval) 2023 (MBC). T20 HS 18. T20 BB 4-21.

SWINDELLS, Harry John (Brockington C; Lutterworth C), b Leicester 21 Feb 1999. 5'7". RHB, WK. Squad No 28. Debut (Leicestershire) 2019. HS 171* v Somerset (Taunton) 2021. LO HS 117* v Hants (Nottingham) 2023 (MBC). T20 HS 63.

‡**TREVASKIS, Liam** (Q Elizabeth GS, Penrith), b Carlisle, Cumberland 18 Apr 1999. 5'8". LHB, SLA. Squad No 80. Durham 2017-23; cap 2017. HS 88 Du v Sussex (Hove) 2022. BB 5-78 Du v Glos (Bristol) 2021. LO HS 76* Du v Derbys (Chester-le-St) 2023 (MBC). LO BB 4-50 Du v Worcs (Chester-le-St) 2023 (MBC). T20 HS 31*. T20 BB 4-16.

WALKER, Roman Isaac (Ysgol Bryn Alyn), b Wrexham, Denbighs 6 Aug 2000. 6'4". RHB, RFM. Squad No 49. Debut (Leicestershire) 2022. Glamorgan 2019-21 (l-o only). Glamorgan 2nd XI 2016-21. Wales MC 2018. HS 64 v Glamorgan (Leicester) 2022. BB 3-84 v Derbys (Derby) 2022. LO HS 23 v Sussex (Hove) 2022 (RLC). LO BB 6-43 v Kent (Beckenham) 2023 (MBC). T20 HS 19*. T20 BB 3-15.

WOOD, Samuel Berridge (Charnwood HS; Wyggeston & Q Elizabeth I C), b Leicester 11 Sep 2004. 6'4". LHB, RM. Squad No 19. Leicestershire 2nd XI debut 2021. Awaiting 1st XI debut.

WRIGHT, Christopher Julian Clement (Eggars S, Alton; Anglia Ruskin U), b Chipping Norton, Oxon 14 Jul 1985. 6'3". RHB, RFM. Squad No 31. Cambridge UCCE 2004-05. Middlesex 2004-07. Tamil Union 2005-06. Essex 2008-11. Warwickshire 2011-18; cap 2013. Leicestershire debut 2019; cap 2021. F-c Tour (MCC): Nepal 2019-20. HS 87 v Derbys (Derby) 2021. 50 wkts (2); most – 67 (2012). BB 7-53 v Glos (Bristol) 2021. LO HS 42 Ex v Glos (Cheltenham) 2011 (CB40). LO BB 6-35 v Notts (Leicester) 2022 (RLC). T20 HS 6*. T20 BB 4-24.

RELEASED/RETIRED

(Having made a County 1st XI appearance in 2023)

ACKERMANN, C.N. – *see DURHAM*.

BARNES, Edward (King James S, Knaresborough), b York 26 Nov 1997. 6'0". RHB, RFM. Derbyshire 2020. Leicestershire 2021-23. HS 83* v Somerset (Taunton) 2021. BB 5-101 v Derbys (Leicester) 2022. LO HS 33* v Surrey (Leicester) 2021 (RLC). LO BB 2-32 v Notts (Leicester) 2022 (RLC). T20 HS 7. T20 BB 2-27.

DAVIS, William Samuel (Stafford GS), b Stafford 6 Mar 1996. 6'1". RHB, RFM. Derbyshire 2015-18. Leicestershire 2019-23. HS 58 v Durham (Chester-le-St) 2023. BB 7-146 De v Glamorgan (Colwyn Bay) 2016. Le BB 5-66 v Middx (Northwood) 2021. LO HS 15* v Durham (Chester-le-St) 2019 (RLC) and 15* v Surrey (Leicester) 2021 (RLC). LO BB 2-40 v Northants (Northampton) 2021 (RLC). T20 HS 7*. T20 BB 3-24.

FINAN, Michael George Anthony (Astley Sports C), b Tameside, Lancs 11 Aug 1996. 6'0". RHB, LFM. Leicestershire 2022-23. Cheshire 2019-22. HS 58 v Notts (Nottingham) 2022. BB 5-58 v Middx (Leicester) 2022. LO HS 0* v Notts (Leicester) 2022 (RLC). LO BB –. T20 HS 20. T20 BB 3-39.

LILLEY, Arron Mark (Mossley Hollins HS; Ashton SFC), b Tameside, Lancs 1 Apr 1991. 6'1". RHB, OB. Lancashire 2013-18. Leicestershire 2019-20. HS 63 and BB 5-23 La v Derbys (Southport) 2015. Le HS 13 and Le BB 3-21 v Yorks (Leeds) 2020. LO HS 60 v Durham (Leicester) 2022 (RLC). LO BB 4-30 La v Derbys (Manchester) 2013 (Y40). T20 HS 99*. T20 BB 3-26.

NQ**NASEEM SHAH**, b Lower Dir, NWFP, Pakistan 15 Feb 2003. 5'8". RHB, RF. ZT Bank 2018-19. Central Punjab 2019-20. Southern Punjab 2021-22. Gloucestershire 2022; cap 2022. Leicestershire 2023 (T20 only). **Tests** (P): 17 (2019-20 to 2023); HS 18 v SL (Galle) 2022; BB 5-31 v SL (Karachi) 2019-20. **LOI** (P): 14 (2022 to 2023); HS 18* v Afg (Hambantota) 2023; BB 5-33 v Neth (Rotterdam) 2022. **IT20** (P): 19 (2022 to 2023); HS 14* v Afg (Sharjah) 2022; BB 2-7 v Hong Kong (Sharjah) 2022. F-c Tours (P): E 2020; A 2019-20; NZ 2020-21; SL 2021-22 (PA), 2022, 2023. HS 31 P Shaheens v Sri Lanka A (Pallekele) 2021-22. CC HS 19 and CC BB 1-41 Gs v Northants (Northampton) 2022. BB 6-59 ZT v Pakistan TV (Rawalpindi) 2018-19. LO HS 18* (*see LOI*). LO BB 5-33 (*see LOI*). T20 HS 27. T20 BB 5-20.

NAVEEN-UL-HAQ – *see HAMPSHIRE.*

PARKINSON, C.F. – *see DURHAM.*

NQ**UMAR AMIN**, b Rawalpindi, Pakistan 16 Oct 1989. LHB, RM. Rawalpindi 2007-08 to date. Federal Areas 2008-09 to 2011-12. National Bank 2008-09 to 2011-12. Port Qasim Authority 2012-13 to 2014-15. SSGC 2015-16 to 2018-19. Northern 2019-20 to 2022-23. Leicestershire 2023. State Bank 2023-24. **Tests** (P): 4 (2010); HS 33 v A (Lord's) 2010; BB 1-7 v A (Leeds) 2010. **LOI** (P): 16 (2010 to 2017-18); HS 59 v Z (Harare) 2013; BB –. **IT20** (P): 14 (2013 to 2017-18); HS 47 v WI (Kingstown) 2013. F-c Tours (P A): E 2010 (P); A 2009; WI 2010-11; SL 2009, 2015; Z 2016-17. 1000 runs (0+1): 1321 (2012-13). HS 281 PQA v Habib Bank (Islamabad) 2012-13. Le HS 94 v Sussex (Hove) 2023. BB 3-32 FA v Baluchistan (Lahore) 2010-11. Le BB 1-8 v Glos (Leicester) 2023. LO HS 156 Punjab v Baluchistan (Rawalpindi) 2017. LO BB 3-31 Rawalpindi v Lahore Whites (Rawalpindi) 2017-18. T20 HS 82*. T20 BB 3-14.

WELCH, Nicholas Roy (St John's C, Harare; Loughborough U), b Harare, Zimbabwe 5 Feb 1998. 5'11". RHB, LBG. Mashonaland Eagles 2013-14 to date. Loughborough MCCU 2019. Leicestershire 2022. **IT20** (Z): 7 (2023-24); HS 25 v Namibia (Windhoek) 2023-24. HS 100 ME v MWR (Harare) 2022-23. Le HS 3 v Notts (Leicester) 2022. BB 1-4 ME v Mountaineers (Harare) 2023-24. LO HS 127* v Surrey (Guildford) 2022 (RLC). T20 HS 68.

S.Steel left the staff without making a County 1st XI appearance in 2023.

LEICESTERSHIRE 2023

RESULTS SUMMARY

	Place	Won	Lost	Drew
LV= Insurance County Champ (Div 2)	4th	3	4	7
Metro Bank One-Day Cup (Group A)	**Winner**	9	1	
Vitality Blast (North Group)	9th	2	12	

LV= INSURANCE COUNTY CHAMPIONSHIP AVERAGES
BATTING AND FIELDING

Cap		*M*	*I*	*NO*	*HS*	*Runs*	*Avge*	*100*	*50*	*Ct/St*
2019	C.N.Ackermann	12	22	2	146	987	49.35	3	5	22
	P.S.P.Handscomb	10	18	3	136*	681	45.40	2	4	24/4
2023	R.K.Patel	14	25	1	179	1075	44.79	4	3	6
2021	L.J.Hill	14	24	2	162*	880	40.00	2	5	6
2023	R.Ahmed	9	16	1	90	529	35.26	–	4	2
	O.B.Cox	4	6	2	58	138	34.50	–	1	9/1
	W.S.Davis	4	6	1	58	151	30.20	–	1	–
2023	P.W.A.Mulder	10	16	2	102*	343	24.50	1	1	11
2021	C.J.C.Wright	14	20	6	66*	337	24.07	–	1	4
	T.A.R.Scriven	12	20	4	78	315	19.68	–	2	5
	S.G.Budinger	11	20	–	72	393	19.65	–	2	4
	Umar Amin	4	6	–	94	108	18.00	–	1	1
	L.P.J.Kimber	6	9	–	61	129	14.33	–	1	6
	E.Barnes	3	4	2	5*	17	8.50	–	–	1
2022	C.F.Parkinson	4	5	–	14	31	6.20	–	–	–
	M.G.A.Finan	4	6	1	9	24	4.80	–	–	–
	J.O.Hull	6	8	2	15	23	3.83	–	–	2
	M.E.T.Salisbury	6	7	2	4*	5	1.00	–	–	2

Also batted: S.W.Currie (2 matches) 9*, 2, 0 (1 ct); J.H.Davey (1) 0*, 2; S.T.Evans (2) 15, 22, 10 (2 ct); H.J.Swindells (2) 73, 8, 0.

BOWLING

	O	*M*	*R*	*W*	*Avge*	*Best*	*5wI*	*10wM*
P.W.A.Mulder	168.4	41	467	26	17.96	5- 63	2	–
T.A.R.Scriven	286.3	50	931	39	23.87	4- 30	–	–
C.J.C.Wright	414.1	88	1317	48	27.43	5- 32	2	–
M.E.T.Salisbury	119.3	26	500	14	35.71	5- 73	1	–
C.F.Parkinson	117.3	4	491	11	44.63	4- 63	–	–
Also bowled:								
J.H.Davey	27	3	87	6	14.50	3- 26	–	–
S.W.Currie	46	4	197	5	39.40	2- 32	–	–
M.G.A.Finan	71.4	6	359	8	44.87	3-109	–	–
W.S.Davis	62	10	239	5	47.80	4- 28	–	–
J.O.Hull	116	10	565	9	62.77	3- 68	–	–
R.Ahmed	140	8	529	8	66.12	3- 89	–	–

C.N.Ackermann 99-15-352-4; E.Barnes 53-4-212-2; S.G.Budinger 5-0-27-0; L.P.J.Kimber 8-0-49-0; Umar Amin 19-1-71-1.

Leicestershire played no first-class fixtures outside the County Championship in 2023. The First-Class Averages (pp 223–235) give the records of Leicestershire players in all first-class county matches, with the exception of O.B.Cox and J.H.Davey, whose first-class figures for Leicestershire are as above.

LEICESTERSHIRE RECORDS

FIRST-CLASS CRICKET

Highest Total	For 756-4d		v	Sussex	Hove	2022
	V 795-5d		by	Glamorgan	Leicester	2022
Lowest Total	For 25		v	Kent	Leicester	1912
	V 24		by	Glamorgan	Leicester	1971
	24		by	Oxford U	Oxford	1985
Highest Innings	For 309*	H.D.Ackerman	v	Glamorgan	Cardiff	2006
	V 410*	S.A.Northeast	for	Glamorgan	Leicester	2022

Highest Partnership for each Wicket

1st	390	B.Dudleston/J.F.Steele	v	Derbyshire	Leicester	1979
2nd	320	M.H.Azad/N.J.Dexter	v	Glos	Leicester	2019
3rd	436*	D.L.Maddy/B.J.Hodge	v	L'boro UCCE	Leicester	2003
4th	360*	J.W.A.Taylor/A.B.McDonald	v	Middlesex	Leicester	2010
5th	477*	C.N.Ackermann/P.W.A.Mulder	v	Sussex	Hove	2022
6th	284	P.V.Simmons/P.A.Nixon	v	Durham	Chester-le-St[2]	1996
7th	219*	J.D.R.Benson/P.Whitticase	v	Hampshire	Bournemouth	1991
8th	203*	H.J.Swindells/E.Barnes	v	Somerset	Taunton	2021
9th	160	R.T.Crawford/W.W.Odell	v	Worcs	Leicester	1902
10th	228	R.Illingworth/K.Higgs	v	Northants	Leicester	1977

Best Bowling	For	10- 18	G.Geary	v	Glamorgan	Pontypridd	1929
(Innings)	V	10- 32	H.Pickett	for	Essex	Leyton	1895
Best Bowling	For	16- 96	G.Geary	v	Glamorgan	Pontypridd	1929
(Match)	V	16-102	C.Blythe	for	Kent	Leicester	1909

Most Runs – Season	2446	L.G.Berry	(av 52.04)	1937
Most Runs – Career	30143	L.G.Berry	(av 30.32)	1924-51
Most 100s – Season	7	L.G.Berry		1937
	7	W.Watson		1959
	7	B.F.Davison		1982
Most 100s – Career	45	L.G.Berry		1924-51
Most Wkts – Season	170	J.E.Walsh	(av 18.96)	1948
Most Wkts – Career	2131	W.E.Astill	(av 23.18)	1906-39
Most Career W-K Dismissals	905	R.W.Tolchard	(794 ct; 111 st)	1965-83
Most Career Catches in the Field	426	M.R.Hallam		1950-70

LIMITED-OVERS CRICKET

Highest Total	**50ov**	411-6		v	Lancashire	Manchester	2023
	40ov	344-4		v	Durham	Chester-le-St[2]	1996
	T20	229-5		v	Warwicks	Birmingham	2018
Lowest Total	**50ov**	56		v	Northants	Leicester	1964
		56		v	Minor Cos	Wellington	1982
	40ov	36		v	Sussex	Leicester	1973
	T20	89		v	Derbyshire	Leicester	2022
Highest Innings	**50ov**	201	V.J.Wells	v	Berkshire	Leicester	1996
	40ov	154*	B.J.Hodge	v	Sussex	Horsham	2004
	T20	118*	J.P.Inglis	v	Worcs	Leicester	2021
Best Bowling	**50ov**	6-16	C.M.Willoughby	v	Somerset	Leicester	2005
	40ov	6-17	K.Higgs	v	Glamorgan	Leicester	1973
	T20	7-18	C.N.Ackermann	v	Warwicks	Leicester	2019

MIDDLESEX

Formation of Present Club: 2 February 1864
Inaugural First-Class Match: 1864
Colours: Blue
Badge: Three Seaxes
County Champions (since 1890): (11) 1903, 1920, 1921, 1947, 1976, 1980, 1982, 1985, 1990, 1993, 2016
Joint Champions: (2) 1949, 1977
Gillette/NatWest Trophy Winners: (4) 1977, 1980, 1984, 1988
Benson and Hedges Cup Winners: (2) 1983, 1986
Sunday League Winners: (1) 1992
Twenty20 Cup Winners: (1) 2008

Chief Executive: Andrew Cornish, Lord's Cricket Ground, London NW8 8QN • Tel: 020 7289 1300 • Email: enquiries@middlesexccc.com • Web: www.middlesexccc.com • Twitter: @Middlesex_CCC (98,815 followers)

Head of Men's Cricket: Alan Coleman. **1st Team Coach**: Richard Johnson. **Club Coach**: Rory Coutts. **Coaching Consultants**: Mark Ramprakash and Ian Salisbury. **Captains**: T.S.Roland-Jones (f-c) and S.S.Eskinazi (l-o). **Overseas Players**: None. **2024 Testimonial**: T.S.Roland-Jones. **Head Groundsman**: Karl McDermott. **Scorer**: Don Shelley. ‡ New registration. [NQ] Not qualified for England.

ANDERSSON, Martin Kristoffer (Reading Blue Coat S), b Reading, Berks 6 Sep 1996. 6'1". RHB, RM. Squad No 24. Debut (Leeds/Bradford MCCU) 2017. Derbyshire 2018 (on loan). Middlesex debut 2018. Berkshire 2015-16. HS 92 v Hants (Radlett) 2020. BB 4-25 De v Glamorgan (Derby) 2018. M BB 4-27 v Leics (Leicester) 2021. LO HS 100 v Notts (Radlett) 2023 (MBC). LO BB 3-55 v Lancs (Lord's) 2023 (MBC). T20 HS 25*. T20 BB 3-32.

BAMBER, Ethan Read (Mill Hill S), b Westminster 17 Dec 1998. 5'11". RHB, RMF. Squad No 54. Debut (Middlesex) 2018; cap 2022. Gloucestershire 2019 (on loan). Berkshire 2017. HS 46* v Surrey (Lord's) 2023. 50 wkts (1): 52 (2021). BB 5-20 v Warwks (Birmingham) 2023. LO HS 21 v Kent (Radlett) 2021 (RLC). LO BB 3-27 v Leics (Leicester) 2023 (MBC). T20 HS 3*. T20 BB 3-29.

‡**BROOKES, Henry** James Hamilton (Tudor Grange Ac, Solihull), b Solihull, Warwks 21 Aug 1999. Elder brother of E.A.Brookes (*see WORCESTERSHIRE*). 6'3". RHB, RFM. Squad No 8. Warwickshire 2017-23. Derbyshire 2023 (on loan). Birmingham Phoenix 2022. Warwickshire 2nd XI 2016-23. England U19 2016-17 to 2017. HS 84 Wa v Kent (Birmingham) 2019. BB 6-20 De v Leics (Derby) 2023. LO HS 12* v Derbys (Derby) 2019 (RLC). LO BB 3-44 Wa v Derbys (Birmingham) 2023 (MBC). T20 HS 31*. T20 BB 5-25.

CORNWELL, Noah Bo (Queen's S, Bushey), b Barnet, Herts 10 Sep 2004. 6'1". LHB, LFM. Squad No 10. Middlesex 2nd XI debut 2021. Awaiting 1st XI debut.

CRACKNELL, Joseph Benjamin (London Oratory S), b Enfield 16 Mar 2000. 5'9". RHB, WK. Squad No 48. Debut (Middlesex) 2021. London Spirit 2021. Middlesex 2nd XI debut 2017. Berkshire 2018. HS 33 v Lancs (Manchester) 2023. LO HS 87 v Yorks (Radlett) 2023 (MBC). T20 HS 77.

CULLEN, Blake Carlton (Hampton S), b Hounslow 19 Feb 2002. 6'1". RHB, RMF. Squad No 19. Debut (Middlesex) 2020. London Spirit 2021. Middlesex 2nd XI debut 2017, aged 15y 142d. HS 34 v Sussex (Radlett) 2020. BB 3-30 v Surrey (Oval) 2021. LO HS –. LO BB 2-32 v Yorks (Radlett) 2023 (MBC). T20 HS 20*. T20 BB 4-32.

DAVIES, Jack Leo Benjamin (Wellington C), b Reading, Berks 30 Mar 2000. Son of A.G.Davies (Cambridge U 1982-89). 5'10". LHB, WK. Squad No 17. Debut (Middlesex) 2020. Middlesex 2nd XI debut 2017. Berkshire 2017-19. England U19 2018. HS 65* v Lancs (Manchester) 2023. LO HS 70 v Essex (Chelmsford) 2021 (RLC). T20 HS 47.

De CAIRES, Joshua Michael (St Albans S; Leeds U), b Paddington 25 Apr 2002. Son of M.A.Atherton (Lancashire, Cambridge U & England 1987-2001); great-grandson of F.I.de Caires (British Guiana & West Indies 1928/29-1938). 6'0". RHB, OB. Squad No 25. Middlesex 2nd XI debut 2017. HS 80 v Derbys (Lord's) 2022. BB 8-106 (10-190 match) v Essex (Chelmsford) 2023. LO HS 43 v Kent (Radlett) 2021 (RLC). LO BB 3-52 v Essex (Chelmsford) 2023 (MBC). T20 HS 28. T20 BB 2-34.

‡[NQ]**Du PLOOY,** Jacobus **Leus**, b Pretoria, South Africa 12 Jan 1995. LHB, SLA. Squad No 76. Free State 2014-15 to 2017-18. Knights 2015-16. Northerns 2018-19. Titans 2018-19. Derbyshire 2019-23; cap 2022; captain 2023. SW Districts 2021-22. Welsh Fire 2021-22. Southern Brave 2023. 1000 runs (1): 1236 (2023). HS 238* De v Worcs (Worcester) 2023. BB 3-76 Northerns v WP (Pretoria, TU) 2018-19. CC BB 2-24 De v Glamorgan (Swansea) 2019. LO HS 155 Northerns v WP (Pretoria, TU) 2018-19. LO BB 3-19 Northerns v KZN (Pretoria, TU) 2018-19. T20 HS 92. T20 BB 4-15.

ESKINAZI, Stephen Sean (Christ Church GS, Claremont; U of WA), b Johannesburg, South Africa 28 Mar 1994. 6'2". RHB, WK. Squad No 28. Debut (Middlesex) 2015; cap 2018; captain 2020 and 2023 to date (l-o only). Big Bash: PS 2022-23 to date. Welsh Fire 2023. UK passport. HS 179 v Warwks (Birmingham) 2017. LO HS 182 v Surrey (Radlett) 2022 (RLC) – M record. T20 HS 102*.

FERNANDES, Nathan Shane (St Gregory's Catholic Science C), b Margao, Goa, India 26 Apr 2004. 5'9". LHB, SLA. Squad No 18. Middlesex 2nd XI debut 2021. Awaiting f-c debut. T20 HS 8. T20 BB 1-6.

HELM, Thomas George (Misbourne S, Gt Missenden), b Stoke Mandeville Hospital, Bucks 7 May 1994. 6'4". RHB, RMF. Squad No 7. Debut (Middlesex) 2013; cap 2019. Glamorgan 2014 (on loan). Birmingham Phoenix 2021 to date. Buckinghamshire 2011. F-c Tour (EL): SL 2016-17. HS 52 v Derbys (Derby) 2018. BB 6-110 v Surrey (Lord's) 2023. LO HS 30 v Surrey (Lord's) 2018 (RLC). LO BB 5-33 EL v Sri Lanka A (Colombo, CCC) 2016-17. T20 HS 28*. T20 BB 5-11.

HIGGINS, Ryan Francis (Bradfield C), b Harare, Zimbabwe 6 Jan 1995. 5'10". RHB, RM. Squad No 29. Debut (Middlesex) 2017; cap 2023. Gloucestershire 2018-22; cap 2018. Welsh Fire 2021 to date. HS 199 Gs v Leics (Leicester) 2019. M HS 137 v Notts (Nottingham) 2023. 50 wkts (2); most – 51 (2021). BB 7-42 (11-96 match) Gs v Warwks (Bristol) 2020. M BB 4-59 v Glamorgan (Lord's) 2022. LO HS 88 v Notts (Radlett) 2023 (MBC). LO BB 4-33 v Kent (Beckenham) 2023 (MBC). T20 HS 77*. T20 BB 5-13.

HOLDEN, Max David Edward (Sawston Village C; Hills Road SFC, Cambridge), b Cambridge 18 Dec 1997. 5'11". LHB, OB. Squad No 4. Northamptonshire 2017 (on loan). Middlesex debut 2017; cap 2023. Manchester Originals 2023. F-c Tour (EL): I 2018-19. HS 153 and BB 2-59 Nh v Kent (Beckenham) 2017. M HS 119* v Derbys (Lord's) 2018. M BB 1-15 v Leics (Leicester) 2018. LO HS 166 v Kent (Canterbury) 2019 (RLC). LO BB 1-29 v Australians (Lord's) 2018. T20 HS 121*. T20 BB –.

HOLLMAN, Luke Barnaby Kurt (Acland Burghley S), b Islington 16 Sep 2000. 6'2". LHB, LB. Squad No 56. Debut (Middlesex) 2021. Middlesex 2nd XI debut 2017. Berkshire 2019. England U19 2018 to 2018-19. HS 82 v Sussex (Hove) 2022. BB 5-65 (10-155 match) v Sussex (Hove) 2021. LO HS 35 v Notts (Radlett) 2023 (MBC). LO BB 4-34 v Warwks (Radlett) 2022 (RLC). T20 HS 51. T20 BB 3-18.

KAUSHAL, Ishaan (Dovay Martyrs S; Brunel U), b Hillingdon 9 Feb 2002. 6'1". RHB, RM. Squad No 22. Middlesex 2nd XI debut 2021. Awaiting f-c debut. LO HS 5* v Kent (Beckenham) 2023 (MBC). LO BB 1-38 v Essex (Chelmsford) 2023 (MBC).

ROBSON, Sam David (Marcellin C, Randwick), b Paddington, Sydney, Australia 1 Jul 1989. Elder brother of A.J.Robson (Leicestershire, Sussex and Durham 2013-19). 6'0". RHB, LB. Squad No 12. Qualified for England in April 2013. Debut (Middlesex) 2009; cap 2013. **Tests**: 7 (2014); HS 127 v SL (Leeds) 2014. F-c Tours (EL): SA 2014-15; SL 2013-14. 1000 runs (2); most – 1180 (2013). HS 253 v Sussex (Hove) 2021, sharing M record 1st wkt partnership of 376 with M.D.Stoneman. BB 4-46 v Notts (Nottingham) 2023. LO HS 111 v Warwks (Radlett) 2022 (RLC). LO BB 2-12 v Hants (Southampton) 2023 (MBC). T20 HS 60.

ROLAND-JONES, Tobias Skelton ('**Toby**') (Hampton S; Leeds U), b Ashford 29 Jan 1988. 6'4". RHB, RFM. Squad No 21. Debut (Middlesex) 2010; cap 2012; captain 2023 to date; testimonial 2024. MCC 2011. *Wisden* 2016. Leeds/Bradford UCCE 2009 (not f-c). **Tests**: 4 (2017); HS 25 and BB 5-57 v SA (Oval) 2017. **LOI**: 1 (2017); HS 37* and BB 1-34 v SA (Lord's) 2017. F-c Tours (EL): WI 2017-18; SL 2016-17; UAE 2016-17 (v Afg). HS 103* v Yorks (Lord's) 2015. 50 wkts (3); most – 67 (2022). BB 7-52 (10-79 match) v Glos (Northwood) 2019. Hat-tricks (2): v Derbys (Lord's) 2013, and v Yorks (Lord's) 2016 – at end of match to secure the Championship. LO HS 65 v Glos (Lord's) 2017 (RLC). LO BB 4-10 v Hants (Southampton) 2017 (RLC). T20 HS 40. T20 BB 5-21.

STONEMAN, Mark Daniel (Whickham CS), b Newcastle upon Tyne, Northumb 26 Jun 1987. 5'10". LHB, OB. Squad No 11. Durham 2007-16; captain (l-o only) 2015-16. Surrey 2017-21; cap 2018. Middlesex debut 2021; cap 2022. Yorkshire 2021 (T20 only). **Tests**: 11 (2017 to 2018); HS 60 v NZ (Christchurch) 2017-18. F-c Tour: A 2017-18; NZ 2017-18. 1000 runs (6); most – 1481 (2017). HS 197 Sy v Essex (Guildford) 2017. M HS 174 v Sussex (Hove) 2021, sharing M record 1st wkt partnership of 376 with S.D.Robson. BB 1-34 v Sussex (Hove) 2022. LO HS 144* v Notts (Lord's) 2017 (RLC). LO BB 1-8 Du v Derbys (Derby) 2016 (RLC). T20 HS 89*.

WALALLAWITA, Thilan Nipuna (Oaklands S), b Colombo, Sri Lanka 23 Jun 1998. 5'9". LHB, SLA. Squad No 32. Moved to UK in 2004; granted citizenship in March 2022. Debut (Middlesex) 2020. Pandura 2022-23. HS 20* v Derbys (Lord's) 2021. BB 3-28 v Hants (Radlett) 2020. LO HS 29 v Lancs (Manchester) 2021 (RLC). LO BB 2-54 v Worcs (Worcester) 2021 (RLC). T20 HS 10. T20 BB 3-18.

WHITE, Robert George (Harrow S; Loughborough U), b Ealing 15 Sep 1995. 5'9". RHB, WK, occ RM. Squad No 14. Loughborough MCCU 2015-17. Middlesex debut 2018. Essex 2019 (on loan). HS 120 v Derbys (Lord's) 2021. LO HS 55 v Durham (Radlett) 2021 (RLC). T20 HS 11*.

RELEASED/RETIRED

(Having made a County 1st XI appearance in 2023)

GREATWOOD, Toby Louie (Reading Blue Coats S), b High Wycombe, Bucks 21 Oct 2001. 6'1". RHB, RMF. Middlesex 2nd XI 2019-23. Berkshire 2018-23. Middlesex 2021-23 (l-o only). LO HS 7* and LO BB 2-30 v Kent (Radlett) 2021 (RLC). T20 HS 6. T20 BB 1-35.

HARRIS, Max Benjamin (Alexandra Park S), b Muswell Hill, London 17 Aug 2001. 5'10". RHB, RFM. Middlesex 2nd XI 2019-23. Kent 2nd XI 2023. Middlesex 2022-23 (l-o only). LO HS 12 v Glos (Radlett) 2022 (RLC). LO BB 3-98 v Sussex (Hove) 2022 (RLC). T20 HS 7*. T20 BB 2-26.

NQ**MALAN, Pieter** Jacobus (Waterkloof Hoer S), b Nelspruit, South Africa 13 Aug 1989. Elder brother of J.N.Malan (North West, Cape Cobras, Boland & South Africa 2015-16 to date) and A.J.Malan (Northerns, North West, W Province, Cape Cobras & SW Districts 2010-11 to date). RHB, RMF. Northerns 2006-07 to 2012-13. Titans 2008-09 to 2012-13. W Province 2013-14 to 2019-20. Cape Cobras 2014-15 to 2020-21. Warwickshire 2021. Boland 2021-22 to date. Middlesex 2022-23. **Tests** (SA): 3 (2019-20); HS 84 v E (Cape Town) 2019-20; BB –. F-c Tours (SA A): I 2018, 2019. 1000 runs (0+2); most – 1114 (2017-18). HS 264 Cobras v Knights (Cape Town) 2020-21. CC HS 141 Wa v Worcs (Worcester) 2021. M HS 93 v Worcs (Worcester) 2022. BB 5-35 WP v EP (Pt Elizabeth) 2017-18. LO HS 171 Boland v NW (Potchefstroom) 2023-24. LO BB 1-28 v Leics (Radlett) 2022 (RLC). T20 HS 140*. T20 BB 2-30.

NQ**MURTAGH, Tim**othy James (John Fisher S; St Mary's C), b Lambeth, London 2 Aug 1981. Elder brother of C.P.Murtagh (Loughborough UCCE and Surrey 2005-09), nephew of A.J.Murtagh (Hampshire and EP 1973-77). 6'0". LHB, RMF. British U 2000-03. Surrey 2001-06. Middlesex 2007-23; cap 2008; benefit 2015; captain 2022. Ireland 2012-13 to 2019. MCC 2010. **Tests** (Ire): 3 (2018 to 2019); HS 54* v Afg (Dehradun) 2018-19; BB 5-13 v E (Lord's) 2019. **LOI** (Ire): 58 (2012 to 2019); HS 23* v Scotland (Belfast) 2013; BB 5-21 v Z (Belfast) 2019. **IT20** (Ire): 14 (2012 to 2015-16); HS 12* v UAE (Abu Dhabi) 2015-16; BB 3-23 v PNG (Townsville) 2015-16. HS 74* Sy v Middx (Oval) 2004 and 74* Sy v Warwks (Croydon) 2005. M HS 55 v Leics (Leicester) 2011, sharing M record 9th wkt partnership of 172 with G.K.Berg. 50 wkts (9); most – 85 (2011). BB 7-82 v Derbys (Derby) 2009. LO HS 35* v Surrey (Lord's) 2008 (FPT). LO BB 5-21 (*see LOI*). T20 HS 40*. T20 BB 6-24 Sy v Middx (Lord's) 2005 – Sy record.

SIMPSON, J.A. – *see SUSSEX.*

NQ**YADAV, Jayant**, b Delhi, India 22 Jan 1990. RHB, OB. Haryana 2011-12 to date. Warwickshire 2022. Middlesex 2023. IPL: DD 2015-17; MI 2019-21; GT 2023. **Tests** (I): 6 (2016-17 to 2021-22); HS 104 v E (Mumbai) 2016-17; BB 4-49 v NZ (Mumbai) 2021-22. **LOI** (I): 2 (2016-17 to 2021-22); HS 2 v SA (Cape Town) 2021-22; BB 1-8 v NZ (Visakhapatnam) 2016-17. F-c Tours (IA): E 2018; A 2016. HS 211 Haryana v Karnataka (Hubli) 2012-13. CC HS 56 v Notts (Nottingham) 2023. BB 7-58 Haryana v Jammu & Kashmir (Jammu) 2019-20. CC BB 5-90 Wa v Glos (Bristol) 2022. M BB 5-131 v Lancs (Manchester) 2023. LO HS 71 India EP v Sri Lanka EP (Colombo) 2018-19. LO BB 3-21 Haryana v Kerala (Alur) 2015-16. T20 HS 39. T20 BB 4-22.

D.M.O'Driscoll left the staff without making a County 1st XI appearance in 2023.

MIDDLESEX 2023

RESULTS SUMMARY

	Place	Won	Lost	Drew	NR
LV= Insurance County Champ (Div 1)	9th	3	9	2	
Metro Bank One-Day Cup (Group A)	7th	2	5		1
Vitality Blast (South Group)	9th	3	11		

LV= INSURANCE COUNTY CHAMPIONSHIP AVERAGES
BATTING AND FIELDING

Cap		*M*	*I*	*NO*	*HS*	*Runs*	*Avge*	*100*	*50*	*Ct/St*
2023	R.F.Higgins	14	25	2	137	955	41.52	1	8	9
2013	S.D.Robson	14	28	5	126*	856	37.21	3	2	13
	J.M.De Caires	8	14	3	49	317	28.81	–	–	1
2011	J.A.Simpson	14	25	1	75	564	23.50	–	4	44/8
2022	M.D.Stoneman	14	28	1	76	612	22.66	–	5	3
2023	M.D.E.Holden	13	23	–	55	437	19.00	–	2	5
	J.L.B.Davies	5	10	2	65*	149	18.62	–	1	3
	J.Yadav	3	5	1	56	74	18.50	–	1	1
2018	S.S.Eskinazi	10	18	2	58	283	17.68	–	1	14
2012	T.S.Roland-Jones	11	18	1	39	300	17.64	–	–	3
	L.B.K.Hollman	8	15	1	63*	244	17.42	–	1	3
	J.B.Cracknell	3	6	–	33	90	15.00	–	–	1
	P.J.Malan	8	16	1	66	221	14.73	–	2	3
2022	E.R.Bamber	13	20	9	46*	146	13.27	–	–	5
2019	T.G.Helm	9	14	3	20	113	10.27	–	–	4
2008	T.J.Murtagh	6	11	3	8	27	3.37	–	–	1

Also batted (1 match each): M.K.Andersson 2 (2 ct); R.G.White 0, 3.

BOWLING

	O	*M*	*R*	*W*	*Avge*	*Best*	*5wI*	*10wM*
T.J.Murtagh	182	42	619	30	20.63	6- 42	2	1
J.M.de Caires	213.3	30	691	27	25.59	8-106	2	1
E.R.Bamber	382.2	88	1052	41	25.65	5- 20	1	–
R.F.Higgins	296.5	65	853	31	27.51	4- 74	–	–
T.G.Helm	263.2	47	887	28	31.67	6-110	1	–
T.S.Roland-Jones	304.1	58	953	27	35.29	7- 61	1	–
Also bowled:								
S.D.Robson	35.5	1	173	6	28.83	4- 46	–	–
J.Yadav	105.3	13	387	9	43.00	5-131	1	–
L.B.K.Hollman	103	15	402	5	80.40	2- 37	–	–

M.K.Andersson 21-1-109-1; M.D.Stoneman 0.5-0-11-0.

Middlesex played no first-class fixtures outside the County Championship in 2023. The First-Class Averages (pp 223–235) give the records of Middlesex players in all first-class county matches.

MIDDLESEX RECORDS

FIRST-CLASS CRICKET

Highest Total	For 676-5d		v	Sussex	Hove	2021
	V 850-7d		by	Somerset	Taunton	2007
Lowest Total	For 20		v	MCC	Lord's	1864
	V 31		by	Glos	Bristol	1924
Highest Innings	For 331*	J.D.B.Robertson	v	Worcs	Worcester	1949
	V 341	C.M.Spearman	for	Glos	Gloucester	2004

Highest Partnership for each Wicket

1st	376	S.D.Robson/M.D.Stoneman	v	Sussex	Hove	2021
2nd	380	F.A.Tarrant/J.W.Hearne	v	Lancashire	Lord's	1914
3rd	424*	W.J.Edrich/D.C.S.Compton	v	Somerset	Lord's	1948
4th	325	J.W.Hearne/E.H.Hendren	v	Hampshire	Lord's	1919
5th	338	R.S.Lucas/T.C.O'Brien	v	Sussex	Hove	1895
6th	270	J.D.Carr/P.N.Weekes	v	Glos	Lord's	1994
7th	271*	E.H.Hendren/F.T.Mann	v	Notts	Nottingham	1925
8th	182*	M.H.C.Doll/H.R.Murrell	v	Notts	Lord's	1913
9th	172	G.K.Berg/T.J.Murtagh	v	Leics	Leicester	2011
10th	230	R.W.Nicholls/W.Roche	v	Kent	Lord's	1899

Best Bowling	For	10- 40	G.O.B.Allen	v	Lancashire	Lord's	1929
(Innings)	V	9- 38	R.C.R-Glasgow†	for	Somerset	Lord's	1924
Best Bowling	For	16-114	G.Burton	v	Yorkshire	Sheffield	1888
(Match)		16-114	J.T.Hearne	v	Lancashire	Manchester	1898
	V	16-100	J.E.B.B.P.Q.C.Dwyer	for	Sussex	Hove	1906

Most Runs – Season	2669	E.H.Hendren	(av 83.41)	1923
Most Runs – Career	40302	E.H.Hendren	(av 48.81)	1907-37
Most 100s – Season	13	D.C.S.Compton		1947
Most 100s – Career	119	E.H.Hendren		1907-37
Most Wkts – Season	158	F.J.Titmus	(av 14.63)	1955
Most Wkts – Career	2361	F.J.Titmus	(av 21.27)	1949-82
Most Career W-K Dismissals	1223	J.T.Murray	(1024 ct; 199 st)	1952-75
Most Career Catches in the Field	561	E.H.Hendren		1907-37

LIMITED-OVERS CRICKET

Highest Total	**50ov**	380-5		v	Kent	Canterbury	2019
	40ov	350-6		v	Lancashire	Lord's	2012
	T20	254-3		v	Surrey	The Oval	2023
Lowest Total	**50ov**	41		v	Essex	Westcliff	1972
	40ov	23		v	Yorkshire	Leeds	1974
	T20	80		v	Kent	Lord's	2021
Highest Innings	**50ov**	182	S.S.Eskinazi	v	Surrey	Radlett	2022
	40ov	147*	M.R.Ramprakash	v	Worcs	Lord's	1990
	T20	129	D.T.Christian	v	Kent	Canterbury	2014
Best Bowling	**50ov**	7-12	W.W.Daniel	v	Minor Cos E	Ipswich	1978
	40ov	6- 6	R.W.Hooker	v	Surrey	Lord's	1969
	T20	6-28	J.K.Fuller	v	Hampshire	Southampton[2]	2018

† R.C.Robertson-Glasgow

NORTHAMPTONSHIRE

Formation of Present Club: 31 July 1878
Inaugural First-Class Match: 1905
Colours: Maroon
Badge: Tudor Rose
County Champions: (0); best – 2nd 1912, 1957, 1965, 1976
Gillette/NatWest/C&G/FP Trophy Winners: (2) 1976, 1992
Benson and Hedges Cup Winners: (1) 1980
Twenty20 Cup Winners: (2) 2013, 2016

Chief Executive: Ray Payne, County Ground, Abington Avenue, Northampton, NN1 4PR • Tel: 01604 514455 • Email: info@nccc.co.uk • Web: www.nccc.co.uk • Twitter: @NorthantsCCC (72,193 followers)

Head Coach: John Sadler. **Batting Coach**: Greg Smith. **Captains**: L.A.Procter (f-c) and D.J.Willey (l-o). **Overseas Players**: K.K.Nair, P.P.Shaw, Sikandar Raza and C.P.Tremain. **2024 Testimonial**: R.I.Keogh. **Head Groundsman**: Craig Harvey. **Scorer**: Terry Owen. **Blast Team Name**: Northamptonshire Steelbacks. ‡ New registration. NQ Not qualified for England.

‡**BARTLETT, George** Anthony (Millfield S), b Frimley, Surrey 14 Mar 1998. 6'0". RHB, OB. Squad No 14. Somerset 2017-23. HS 137 Sm v Surrey (Guildford) 2019. BB –. LO HS 108 Sm v Leics (Taunton) 2021 (RLC). T20 HS 82*.

NQ**BROAD, Justin** (Rondesbosch Boys' HS), b Cape Town, South Africa 30 Jun 2000. RHB, RM. Holds German passport. Debut (Northamptonshire) 2023. MCC YC 2019. Surrey 2nd XI 2019-22. Somerset 2nd XI 2022. Northamptonshire 2nd XI debut 2023. **IT20** (Germ): 9 (2021-22 to 2022-23); HS 62 v UAE (Al Amerat) 2021-22; BB 1-9 v Italy (Almeria) 2022-23. HS 56* v Essex (Northampton) 2023. BB 2-39 v Somerset (Northampton) 2023. LO HS 22* v Sussex (Northampton) 2023 (MBC). LO BB –. T20 HS 62. T20 BB 2-11.

GAY, Emilio Nico (Bedford S), b Bedford 14 Apr 2000. 6'2". LHB, RM. Squad No 19. Debut (Northamptonshire) 2019. Northamptonshire 2nd XI debut 2018. HS 145 v Surrey (Northampton) 2022. BB 1-8 v Kent (Northampton) 2021. LO HS 131 v Lancs (Blackpool) 2022 (RLC). LO BB –. T20 HS 53. T20 BB –.

GOWLER, George Edward (Wisbech GS), b Huntingdon 21 Oct 2003. 6'3½". RHB, RM. Squad No 22. Northamptonshire 2nd XI debut 2021. Awaiting 1st XI debut.

HELDREICH, Frederick James (Framlingham C), b Ipswich, Suffolk 12 Sep 2001. 6'3". RHB, SLC. Squad No 80. Northamptonshire 2nd XI debut 2021. Awaiting f-c debut. LO HS 5 and LO BB 2-69 v Glamorgan (Northampton) 2021 (RLC). T20 HS 4. T20 BB 4-27.

KEOGH, Robert Ian (Queensbury S; Dunstable C), b Luton, Beds 21 Oct 1991. 5'11". RHB, OB. Squad No 21. Debut (Northamptonshire) 2012; cap 2019; testimonial 2024. Bedfordshire 2009-10. HS 221 v Hants (Southampton) 2013. BB 9-52 (13-125 match) v Glamorgan (Northampton) 2016. LO HS 134 v Durham (Northampton) 2016 (RLC). LO BB 4-49 v Somerset (Northampton) 2023 (MBC). T20 HS 59*. T20 BB 3-30.

McMANUS, Lewis David (Clayesmore S, Bournemouth; Exeter U), b Poole, Dorset 9 Oct 1994. 5'10". RHB, WK. Squad No 15. Hampshire 2015-21; cap 2021. Northamptonshire debut 2022. Dorset 2011-19. HS 132* H v Surrey (Southampton) 2016. Nh HS 62 v Yorks (Northampton) 2022. LO HS 107 v Derbys (Northampton) 2022 (RLC). T20 HS 60*.

MILLER, Augustus ('**Gus**') Horatio (Bedford S), b Oxford 8 Jan 2002. 6'1". RHB, RFM. Squad No 24. Northamptonshire 2nd XI debut 2021. Awaiting f-c debut. Bedfordshire 2018-21. LO HS 31 v Hants (Newport) 2022 (RLC). T20 HS 5.

NQ**NAIR, Karun** Kaladharan, b Jodhpur, India 6 Dec 1991. 5'6". RHB, OB. Squad No 69. Karnataka 2013-14 to 2022. Northamptonshire debut 2023. Vidarbha 2023-24. IPL: RCB 2013; RR 2014-22; DD 2016-17; KXIP 2018 to 2020-21. **Tests** (I): 6 (2016-17); HS 303* v E (Chennai) 2016-17; BB –. **LOI** (I): 2 (2016); HS 39 v Z (Harare) 2016. F-c Tours (IA): E 2018; A 2014, 2016; SA 2017; NZ 2018-19. HS 328 Karnataka v Tamil Nadu (Mumbai) 2014-15 – the highest score by any No 6 batter in f-c cricket. Nh HS 150 v Surrey (Oval) 2023. BB 2-11 Karnataka v Assam (Guwahati) 2015-16. Nh BB –. LO HS 120 Karnataka v Gujarat (Kolkata) 2013-14. LO BB 2-16 Karnataka v Goa (Secunderabad) 2014-15. T20 HS 111. T20 BB 1-2.

PROCTER, Luke Anthony (Counthill S, Oldham), b Oldham, Lancs 24 June 1988. 5'11". LHB, RM. Squad No 2. Lancashire 2010-17. Northamptonshire debut 2017; cap 2020; captain 2023 to date. Cumberland 2007. HS 144* v Warwks (Northampton) 2022. BB 7-71 La v Surrey (Liverpool) 2012. Nh BB 5-33 v Durham (Chester-le-St) 2017. LO HS 97 La v West Indies A (Manchester) 2010. LO BB 4-34 v Durham (Chester-le-St) 2023 (MBC). T20 HS 25*. T20 BB 3-22.

RUSSELL, Alexander Kian (Chosen Hill S; Hartpury C), b Newport, Monmouths 17 Apr 2002. 5'10". RHB, LB. Squad No 61. Debut (Northamptonshire) 2023. Eagles 2023-24. Gloucestershire 2nd XI 2018-21. Essex 2nd XI 2021. Northamptonshire 2nd XI debut 2022. Herefordshire 2018-21. HS 17* Eagles v Mountaineers (Harare) 2023-24. Nh HS 8* and Nh BB 6-175 v Kent (Northampton) 2023. BB 7-84 (12-122 match) Eagles v Tuskers (Harare) 2023-24. LO HS 3* v Kent (Canterbury) 2022 (RLC). LO BB 3-15 Eagles v Tuskers (Harare) 2023-24. T20 HS 1*. T20 BB 1-27.

SALES, James John Grimwood (Wellingborough S), b Northampton 11 Feb 2003. Son of D.J.G.Sales (Northamptonshire and Wellington 1996-2014). 6'0". RHB, RM. Squad No 5. Debut (Northamptonshire) 2021. Northamptonshire 2nd XI debut 2021. England U19 2022. HS 71 v Glos (Cheltenham) 2022. BB 4-24 v Notts (Northampton) 2023. LO HS 35* v Derbys (Northampton) 2023 (MBC). LO BB 2-31 v Durham (Chester-le-St) 2023 (MBC). T20 HS 12. T20 BB 1-16.

SANDERSON, Ben William (Ecclesfield CS; Sheffield C), b Sheffield, Yorks 3 Jan 1989. 6'0". RHB, RMF. Squad No 26. Yorkshire 2008-10. Northamptonshire debut 2015; cap 2018. Shropshire 2013-15. HS 46 v Kent (Northampton) 2023. 50 wkts (3); most – 61 (2019). BB 8-73 v Glos (Northampton) 2016. Hat-trick v Warwks (Birmingham) 2023. LO HS 31 v Derbys (Derby) 2019 (RLC). LO BB 3-17 v Glamorgan (Northampton) 2022 (RLC). T20 HS 12*. T20 BB 4-21.

‡**SCRIMSHAW, George** Louis Sheridan (John Taylor HS, Burton), b Burton-on-Trent, Staffs 10 Feb 1998. 6'7". RHB, RMF. Squad No 98. Derbyshire 2021-23. Worcestershire 2017 (T20 only). Welsh Fire 2022. **LOI**: 1 (2023); HS – ; BB 3-66 v Ire (Nottingham) 2023. HS 19* and BB 5-49 De v Sussex (Hove) 2023. LO HS 13* De v Surrey (Derby) 2021 (RLC). LO BB 3-66 (*see LOI*). T20 HS 5*. T20 BB 3-16.

NQ**SHAW, Prithvi** Pankaj, b Thane, Maharashtra, India 9 Nov 1999. 5'4". RHB, OB. Squad No 100. Mumbai 2016-17 to date. Northamptonshire debut 2023 (l-o only). IPL: DD 2018; DC 2019 to date. **Tests** (I): 5 (2018-19 to 2020-21); HS 134 v WI (Rajkot) 2018-19 – on debut. **LOI** (I): 6 (2019-20 to 2021); HS 49 v SL (Colombo, RPS) 2021. **IT20** (I): 1 (2021); HS 0. F-c Tours (I): E 2018 (IA); A 2020-21; SA 2021-22 (IA); NZ 2018-19 (IA), 2019-20. HS 379 Mumbai v Assam (Guwahati) 2022-23. BB –. LO HS 244 v Somerset (Northampton) 2023 – Nh record, 6th highest score in all l-o cricket and 2nd highest in UK. T20 HS 134.

‡NQ**SIKANDAR RAZA** Butt (Glasgow Caledonian C), b Sialkot, Pakistan 24 Apr 1986. 5'11". RHB, OB. Squad No 12. Northerns 2006-07 to 2021-22. Southern Rocks 2010-11 to 2021-22. Mashonaland Eagles 2011-12 to 2015-16. Harare Metropolitan Eagles 2016-17. Bulawayo Metropolitan Tuskers 2017-18. Tuskers 2019-20. Southerns 2021-22. **Tests** (Z): 17 (2013 to 2020-21); HS 127 v SL (Colombo, RPS) 2017; BB 7-113 v SL (Harare) 2019-20. **LOI** (Z): 142 (2013 to 2023-24); HS 141 v Afg (Bulawayo) 2014; BB 4-55 v Netherlands (Harare) 2023. **IT20** (Z): 81 (2013 to 2023-24); HS 87 v Singapore (Bulawayo) 2022. F-c Tours (Z): SA 2017-18; SL 2017; B 2014-15, 2018-19, 2019-20; UAE (v Afg) 2020-21. HS 226 SR v Mountaineers (Harare) 2021-22. BB 7-113 (*see Tests*). LO HS 141 (*see LOI*). LO BB 4-33 ME v MT (Harare) 2014-15. T20 HS 95. T20 BB 4-8.

[NQ]**TREMAIN, Chris**topher Peter, b Dubbo, NSW, Australia 10 Aug 1991. 6'4". RHB, RMF. Squad No 20. New South Wales 2011-12 to date. Victoria 2014-15 to 2019-20. Northamptonshire debut 2023. Big Bash: ST 2012-13 to 2020-21; MR 2015-16 to 2018-19. **LOI** (A): 4 (2016-17); HS 23* v SA (Port Elizabeth) 2016-17; BB 3-64 v SA (Cape Town) 2016-17. F-c Tours (A): E 2019; I 2018-19 (Aus A). HS 111 Vic v WA (Alice Springs) 2016-17. Nh HS 16 v Hants (Northampton) 2023. 50 wkts (0+1): 51 (2017-18). BB 7-82 (10-143 match) Vic v WA (Perth) 2017-18. Nh BB 5-44 v Kent (Canterbury) 2023. LO HS 50 Vic v Q (Sydney, NS) 2017-18. LO BB 5-25 Aus A v India A (Townsville) 2016. T20 HS 37*. T20 BB 3-9.

[NQ]**VASCONCELOS, Ricardo** Surrador (St Stithians C), b Johannesburg, South Africa 27 Oct 1997. 5'5". LHB, WK, occ OB. Squad No 27. Boland 2016-17 to 2017-18. Northamptonshire debut 2018; cap 2021. Portuguese passport. HS 185* v Glamorgan (Northampton) 2021. BB –. LO HS 112 v Yorks (Northampton) 2019 (RLC). T20 HS 78*.

WEATHERALL, Raphael Alexander (Dr Challoner's GS), b Kendal, Cumbria 24 Oct 2004. 6'4". RHB, RM. Squad No 84. Northamptonshire 2nd XI debut 2022. England U19 2023. Awaiting 1st XI debut.

WELDON, George Peter le Huray (Eton C), b 17 May 2004. 6'0". RHB, RFM. Squad No 66. Northamptonshire 2nd XI debut 2022. Awaiting 1st XI debut.

WHITE, Curtley-**Jack** (Ullswater Comm C; Queen Elizabeth GS, Penrith), b Kendal, Cumberland 19 Feb 1992. 6'2". LHB, RFM. Squad No 9. Debut (Northamptonshire) 2020. Cumberland 2013. Cheshire 2016-17. HS 59 v Kent (Northampton) 2023. 50 wkts (1): 50 (2023). BB 6-38 v Essex (Northampton) 2022. LO HS 29 v Glos (Cheltenham) 2023 (MBC). LO BB 4-20 v Derbys (Northampton) 2021 (RLC).

WILLEY, David Jonathan (Northampton S), b Northampton 28 Feb 1990. Son of P.Willey (Northants, Leics and England 1966-91). 6'1". LHB, LMF. Squad No 23. Debut (Northamptonshire) 2009; cap 2013; l-o captain 2023 to date. Yorkshire 2016-21; cap 2016; captain 2020 (T20 only). Bedfordshire 2008. IPL: CSK 2018; RCB 2022 to date. Big Bash: PS 2015-16 to 2018-19. Northern Superchargers 2021-22. Welsh Fire 2023. **LOI**: 73 (2015 to 2023-24); HS 51 v Ire (Southampton) 2020; BB 5-30 v Ire (Southampton) 2020 – separate matches. **IT20**: 43 (2015 to 2022-23); HS 33* v I (Birmingham) 2022; BB 4-7 v WI (Basseterre) 2018-19. HS 104* v Glos (Northampton) 2015. BB 5-29 (10-75 match) v Glos (Northampton) 2011. LO HS 167 v Warwks (Birmingham) 2013 (Y40). LO BB 5-30 (*see LOI*). T20 HS 118. T20 BB 4-7.

ZAIB, Saif Ali (RGS High Wycombe), b High Wycombe, Bucks 22 May 1998. 5'7½". LHB, SLA. Squad No 18. Debut (Northamptonshire) 2015. Northern Superchargers 2023. Buckinghamshire 2016. HS 135 v Sussex (Northampton) 2021. BB 6-115 v Loughborough MCCU (Northampton) 2017. CC BB 5-148 v Leics (Northampton) 2016. LO HS 136 v Essex (Northampton) 2022 (RLC). LO BB 4-23 v Glamorgan (Northampton) 2022 (RLC). T20 HS 92. T20 BB 1-17.

RELEASED/RETIRED

(Having made a County 1st XI appearance in 2023)

AZAD, Mohammad **Hasan** (Fernwood S, Nottingham; Bilborough SFC; Loughborough U), b Quetta, Pakistan 7 Jan 1994. Son of Imran Azad (Public Works 1986-87). LHB, OB. Loughborough MCCU 2015-19. Leicestershire 2019-22, scoring 139 v Loughborough MCCU (Leicester) on debut. Northamptonshire 2023. 1000 runs (1): 1189 (2019). HS 152 Le v Sussex (Leicester) 2021. Nh HS 51 v Kent (Canterbury) 2023. BB 1-15 Le v Durham (Leicester) 2020.

BERG, Gareth Kyle (South African College S), b Cape Town, South Africa 18 Jan 1981. 6'0". RHB, RMF. England qualified through residency. Middlesex 2008-14; cap 2010. Hampshire 2015-19; cap 2016. Northamptonshire 2019-23. Italy 2011-12 to date (l-o and T20 only). **IT20** (Italy): 15 (2021-22 to 2023); HS 39* v Finland (Kerava) 2022; BB 4-14 v Denmark (Edinburgh) 2023. HS 130* M v Leics (Leicester) 2011, sharing M record 9th wkt partnership of 172 with T.J.Murtagh. Nh HS 75 v Essex (Chelmsford) 2022. BB 6-56 H v Yorks (Southampton) 2016. Nh BB 5-18 v Sussex (Northampton) 2021. LO HS 75 M v Glamorgan (Lord's) 2013 (Y40). LO BB 5-26 H v Lancs (Southampton) 2019 (RLC). T20 HS 90. T20 BB 4-14.

NQ**BUCKINGHAM, Jordan** Steven Dermott, b Bundoora, Victoria, Australia 17 Mar 2000. RHB, RFM. S Australia 2021-22 to date. Northamptonshire 2023. F-c Tour (Aus A): NZ 2022-23. HS 17 SA v Vic (Melbourne, SK) 2022-23 and 17 v Somerset (Taunton) 2023. BB 7-71 SA v Tas (Adelaide, KR) 2023-24. Nh BB 1-48 v Notts (Northampton) 2023. LO HS 8 SA v Vic (Melbourne) 2023-24. LO BB 6-41 SA v Q (Adelaide) 2023-24.

COBB, J.J. – *see WORCESTERSHIRE.*

GOULDSTONE, Harry Oliver Michael (Bedford S), b Kettering 26 Mar 2001. 5'11". RHB, WK. Northamptonshire 2020-23. Northamptonshire 2nd XI 2019-23. Bedfordshire 2023. HS 67* v Glamorgan (Cardiff) 2021.

KERRIGAN, Simon Christopher (Corpus Christi RC HS, Preston), b Preston, Lancs 10 May 1989. 5'9". RHB, SLA. Lancashire 2010-17; cap 2013. Northamptonshire 2017-23. MCC 2013. **Tests**: 1 (2013); HS 1* and BB – v A (Oval) 2013. F-c Tour (EL): SL 2013-14. HS 62* La v Hants (Southport) 2013. Nh HS 62 v Glamorgan (Cardiff) 2017. 50 wkts (2); most – 58 (2013). BB 9-51 (12-192 match) La v Hants (Liverpool) 2011. Nh BB 5-39 v Yorks (Northampton) 2021. LO HS 10 La v Middx (Lord's) 2012 (CB40). LO BB 4-48 v Somerset (Northampton) 2021 (RLC). T20 HS 4*. T20 BB 3-17.

NQ**LYNN, Chris**topher Austin, b Herston, Brisbane, Australia 10 Apr 1990. 5'11". RHB, SLA. Queensland 2009-10 to 2016-17. Northamptonshire 2022-23 (T20 only). IPL: DC 2012; KKR 2014-19; MI 2021. Big Bash: BH 2011-12 to 2021-22; AS 2022-23 to date. Northern Superchargers 2021. **LOI** (A): 4 (2016-17 to 2018-19); HS 44 v SA (Adelaide) 2018-19. **IT20** (A): 18 (2013-14 to 2018-19); HS 44 v NZ (Sydney) 2017-18. HS 250 Q v Vic (Brisbane) 2014-15. BB –. LO HS 135 Q v NSW (Sydney, DO) 2018-19. LO BB 1-3 Q v WA (Sydney, BO) 2013-14. T20 HS 113* v Worcs (Northampton) 2022 – Nh record. T20 BB 2-15.

TAYLOR, T.A.I. – *see WORCESTERSHIRE.*

NQ**TYE, Andrew** James (Padbury Senior HS, WA), b Perth, Australia 12 Dec 1986. 6'4". RHB, RMF. W Australia 2014-15 to date. Gloucestershire 2016-19 (T20 only). Durham 2022 (T20 only). Northamptonshire 2023 (T20 only). IPL: GL 2017; KXIP 2018-19; RR 2020-21; LSG 2022. Big Bash: ST 2013-14; PS 2014-15 to date. **LOI** (A): 7 (2017-18 to 2018); HS 19 v E (Oval) 2018; BB 5-46 v E (Perth) 2017-18. **IT20** (A): 32 (2015-16 to 2021); HS 20 v E (Birmingham) 2018; BB 4-23 v NZ (Sydney) 2017-18. HS 10 WA v Tas (Hobart) 2014-15. BB 3-47 WA v Q (Brisbane) 2014-15. LO HS 44 WA v Tas (Perth) 2021-22. LO BB 6-46 WA v Q (Sydney, HO) 2018-19. T20 HS 44. T20 BB 5-17.

WHITE, Graeme Geoffrey (Stowe S), b Milton Keynes, Bucks 18 Apr 1987. 5'11". RHB, SLA. Northamptonshire 2006-17; cap 2021. Nottinghamshire 2010-13. Welsh Fire 2021. HS 65 v Glamorgan (Colwyn Bay) 2007. BB 6-44 v Glamorgan (Northampton) 2016. LO HS 41* v Yorks (Leeds) 2018 (RLC). LO BB 6-37 v Lancs (Northampton) 2016 (RLC). T20 HS 37*. T20 BB 5-22 Nt v Lancs (Nottingham) 2013 – Nt record.

NQ**WHITEMAN, Sam** McFarlane, b Doncaster, Yorks 19 Mar 1992. LHB, WK. W Australia 2012-13 to date. Northamptonshire 2023. Big Bash: PS 2013-14 to 2023-24; ST 2021-22 to 2022-23. F-c Tour (Aus A): NZ 2015-16. HS 193 WA v SA (Perth) 2022-23. Nh HS 130* v Somerset (Taunton) 2023. LO HS 137* WA v SA (Perth) 2023-24. T20 HS 68.

O.R.T. Sale left the staff without making a County 1st XI appearance in 2023.

NORTHAMPTONSHIRE 2023

RESULTS SUMMARY

	Place	*Won*	*Lost*	*Drew*
LV= Insurance County Champ (Div 1)	10th	2	8	4
Metro Bank One-Day Cup (Group B)	6th	3	5	
Vitality Blast (North Group)	6th	6	8	

LV= INSURANCE COUNTY CHAMPIONSHIP AVERAGES
BATTING AND FIELDING

Cap		*M*	*I*	*NO*	*HS*	*Runs*	*Avge*	*100*	*50*	*Ct/St*
2019	R.I.Keogh	13	22	2	172	780	39.00	2	3	1
	S.M.Whiteman	11	21	2	130*	719	37.84	2	3	3
	E.N.Gay	10	18	1	144	589	34.64	1	3	11
2020	L.A.Procter	11	19	3	87*	480	30.00	–	4	4
	S.A.Zaib	11	19	1	57*	514	28.55	–	1	5
	G.K.Berg	4	7	1	56	131	21.83	–	1	3
2021	R.S.Vasconcelos	10	20	–	78	389	19.45	–	3	13
	J.Broad	6	10	2	56*	155	19.37	–	1	4
	H.M.Azad	9	16	1	51	290	19.33	–	1	4
	T.A.I.Taylor	10	17	–	66	288	16.94	–	2	1
	J.J.G.Sales	5	10	1	57	132	14.66	–	1	1
2018	J.J.Cobb	3	5	–	44	69	13.80	–	–	2
	L.D.McManus	11	16	1	27	185	12.33	–	–	26/3
	A.K.Russell	3	5	4	8*	11	11.00	–	–	–
2018	B.W.Sanderson	10	16	3	46	125	9.61	–	–	1
	C.P.Tremain	3	6	–	16	56	9.33	–	–	2
	C.J.White	14	22	9	59	112	8.61	–	1	–
	J.S.D.Buckingham	3	6	–	17	34	5.66	–	–	1
	H.O.M.Gouldstone	2	4	–	6	8	2.00	–	–	3

Also batted: S.C.Kerrigan (1 match) 2; D.J.Leech (1) 13; K.K.Nair (3) 78, 150, 21 (5 ct).

BOWLING

	O	*M*	*R*	*W*	*Avge*	*Best*	*5wI*	*10wM*
C.P.Tremain	75.4	16	233	13	17.92	5- 44	1	–
B.W.Sanderson	285.4	66	790	32	24.68	5- 42	1	–
C.J.White	397.5	84	1279	50	25.58	5- 57	3	–
L.A.Procter	132.1	29	462	13	35.53	3- 47	–	–
T.A.I.Taylor	236.4	38	855	19	45.00	4- 59	–	–
R.I.Keogh	178	15	644	14	46.00	3- 52	–	–
Also bowled:								
J.J.G.Sales	37	4	168	6	28.00	4- 24	–	–
G.K.Berg	69	13	253	5	50.60	2- 70	–	–
A.K.Russell	73.5	1	387	6	64.50	6-175	1	–

H.M.Azad 3-1-2-0; J.Broad 27-1-117-2; J.S.D.Buckingham 62-7-256-3; J.J.Cobb 1-0-2-0; S.C.Kerrigan 10-4-13-0; D.J.Leech 19-0-107-0; K.K.Nair 6-1-22-0; S.A.Zaib 46.3-11-165-4.

Northamptonshire played no first-class fixtures outside the County Championship in 2023. The First-Class Averages (pp 223–235) give the records of Northamptonshire players in all first-class county matches, with the exception of D.J.Leech, whose first-class figures for Northamptonshire are as above.

NORTHAMPTONSHIRE RECORDS

FIRST-CLASS CRICKET

Highest Total	For	781-7d		v	Notts	Northampton	1995
	V	701-7d		by	Kent	Beckenham	2017
Lowest Total	For	12		v	Glos	Gloucester	1907.
	V	33		by	Lancashire	Northampton	1977
Highest Innings	For	331*	M.E.K.Hussey	v	Somerset	Taunton	2003
	V	333	K.S.Duleepsinhji	for	Sussex	Hove	1930

Highest Partnership for each Wicket

1st	375	R.A.White/M.J.Powell	v	Glos	Northampton	2002
2nd	344	G.Cook/R.J.Boyd-Moss	v	Lancashire	Northampton	1986
3rd	393	A.Fordham/A.J.Lamb	v	Yorkshire	Leeds	1990
4th	370	R.T.Virgin/P.Willey	v	Somerset	Northampton	1976
5th	401	M.B.Loye/D.Ripley	v	Glamorgan	Northampton	1998
6th	376	R.Subba Row/A.Lightfoot	v	Surrey	The Oval	1958
7th	293	D.J.G.Sales/D.Ripley	v	Essex	Northampton	1999
8th	179	A.J.Hall/J.D.Middlebrook	v	Surrey	The Oval	2011
9th	156	R.Subba Row/S.Starkie	v	Lancashire	Northampton	1955
10th	148	B.W.Bellamy/J.V.Murdin	v	Glamorgan	Northampton	1925

Best Bowling	For	10-127	V.W.C.Jupp	v	Kent	Tunbridge W	1932
(Innings)	V	10- 30	C.Blythe	for	Kent	Northampton	1907
Best Bowling	For	15- 31	G.E.Tribe	v	Yorkshire	Northampton	1958
(Match)	V	17- 48	C.Blythe	for	Kent	Northampton	1907

Most Runs – Season	2198	D.Brookes	(av 51.11)	1952
Most Runs – Career	28980	D.Brookes	(av 36.13)	1934-59
Most 100s – Season	8	R.A.Haywood		1921
Most 100s – Career	67	D.Brookes		1934-59
Most Wkts – Season	175	G.E.Tribe	(av 18.70)	1955
Most Wkts – Career	1102	E.W.Clark	(av 21.26)	1922-47
Most Career W-K Dismissals	810	K.V.Andrew	(653 ct; 157 st)	1953-66
Most Career Catches in the Field	469	D.S.Steele		1963-84

LIMITED-OVERS CRICKET

Highest Total	**50ov**	425		v	Notts	Nottingham	2016
	40ov	324-6		v	Warwicks	Birmingham	2013
	T20	231-5		v	Warwicks	Birmingham	2018
Lowest Total	**50ov**	62		v	Leics	Leicester	1974
	40ov	41		v	Middlesex	Northampton	1972
	T20	47		v	Durham	Chester-le-St[2]	2011
Highest Innings	**50ov**	244	P.P.Shaw	v	Somerset	Northampton	2023
	40ov	172*	W.Larkins	v	Warwicks	Luton	1983
	T20	113*	C.A.Lynn	v	Worcs	Northampton	2022
Best Bowling	**50ov**	7-10	C.Pietersen	v	Denmark	Brondby	2005
	40ov	7-39	A.Hodgson	v	Somerset	Northampton	1976
	T20	6-21	A.J.Hall	v	Worcs	Northampton	2008

NOTTINGHAMSHIRE

Formation of Present Club: March/April 1841
Substantial Reorganisation: 11 December 1866
Inaugural First-Class Match: 1864
Colours: Green and Gold
County Champions (since 1890): (6) 1907, 1929, 1981, 1987, 2005, 2010
NatWest Trophy Winners: (1) 1987
Benson and Hedges Cup Winners: (1) 1989
Sunday League Winners: (1) 1991
Yorkshire Bank 40 Winners: (1) 2013
Royal London Cup Winners: (1) 2017
Twenty20 Cup Winners: (2) 2017, 2020

Chief Executive: Lisa Pursehouse, Trent Bridge, West Bridgford, Nottingham NG2 6AG • Tel: 0115 982 3000 • Email: questions@nottsccc.co.uk • Web: www.trentbridge.co.uk • Twitter: @TrentBridge (99,031 followers)

Director of Cricket: Mick Newell. **Head Coach**: Peter Moores. **Assistant Head Coach**: Paul Franks. **Assistant Coaches**: Ant Botha and Kevin Shine. **Captains**: H.Hameed (f-c), J.M.Clarke (T20). **Overseas Players**: D.Paterson and W.A.Young. **2024 Testimonial**: S.J.Mullaney. **Head Groundsman**: Steve Birks. **Scorer**: Roger Marshall and Anne Cusworth. **Blast Team Name**: Nottinghamshire Outlaws. ‡ New registration. NQ Not qualified for England.

CARTER, Matthew (Branston S), b Lincoln 26 May 1996. Younger brother of A.Carter (Nottinghamshire, Essex, Glamorgan, Derbyshire, Hampshire & Northamptonshire 2009-17). RHB, OB. Squad No 20. Debut (Nottinghamshire) 2015, taking 7-56 v Somerset (Taunton) – the best debut figures for Nt since 1914. Trent Rockets 2021 to date. Lincolnshire 2013-17. HS 33 v Sussex (Hove) 2017. BB 7-56 (10-195 match) (*see above*). LO HS 21* v Warwks (Birmingham) 2019 (RLC). LO BB 4-40 v Warwks (Nottingham) 2018 (RLC). T20 HS 23*. T20 BB 3-14.

CLARKE, Joe Michael (Llanfyllin HS), b Shrewsbury, Shrops 26 May 1996. 5'11". RHB, WK, occ RM. Squad No 33. Worcestershire 2015-18. Nottinghamshire debut 2019; cap 2021; captain (T20 only) 2024. MCC 2017. Big Bash: PS 2020-21; MS 2021-22 to 2022-23; MR 2023-24. Manchester Originals 2021. Welsh Fire 2022 to date. Shropshire 2012-13. F-c Tours (EL): WI 2017-18; UAE 2016-17 (v Afg). 1000 runs (2); most – 1325 (2016). HS 229* v Warwks (Nottingham) 2020. BB –. LO HS 139 v Lancs (Nottingham) 2019 (RLC). T20 HS 136 v Northants (Northampton) 2021 – Nt record.

DUCKETT, Ben Matthew (Stowe S), b Farnborough, Kent 17 Oct 1994. 5'7". LHB, WK, occ OB. Squad No 17. Northamptonshire 2013-18; cap 2016. Nottinghamshire debut 2018; cap 2019. MCC 2017. Big Bash: HH 2018-19; BH 2021-22. Welsh Fire 2021-22. Birmingham Phoenix 2023. PCA 2016. YC 2016. *Wisden* 2016. **ECB Two-Year Central Contract from 2023-24**. **Tests**: 20 (2016-17 to 2023-24); HS 182 v Ire (Lord's) 2023. **LOI**: 11 (2016-17 to 2023-24); HS 107* v Ire (Bristol) 2023. **IT20**: 12 (2019 to 2023-24); HS 70* v P (Karachi) 2022-23. F-c Tours: NZ 2022-23; I 2016-17, 2023-24; P 2022-23; B 2016-17. 1000 runs (3); most – 1338 (2016). HS 282* Nh v Sussex (Northampton) 2016. Nt HS 241 v Derbys (Derby) 2022, sharing in Nt record 2nd wkt partnership of 402 with H.Hameed. BB 1-15 v Middx (Nottingham) 2022. LO HS 220* EL v Sri Lanka A (Canterbury) 2016. T20 HS 96.

FLETCHER, Luke Jack (Henry Mellish S, Nottingham), b Nottingham 18 Sep 1988. 6'6". RHB, RMF. Squad No 19. Debut (Nottinghamshire) 2008; cap 2014; testimonial 2023. Surrey 2015 (on loan). Derbyshire 2016 (on loan). Welsh Fire 2021. Trent Rockets 2022. HS 92 v Hants (Southampton) 2009 and 92 v Durham (Chester-le-St) 2017. 50 wkts (1): 66 (2021). BB 7-37 (10-57 match) v Worcs (Nottingham) 2021. LO HS 53* v Kent (Nottingham) 2018 (RLC). LO BB 5-56 v Derbys (Derby) 2019 (RLC). T20 HS 27. T20 BB 5-32.

HALES, Alexander Daniel (Chesham HS), b Hillingdon, Middx 3 Jan 1989. 6'5". RHB, OB, occ WK. Squad No 10. Debut (Nottinghamshire) 2008; cap 2011. White-ball contract since 2018. Worcestershire 2014 (on loan). Buckinghamshire 2006-07. IPL: SH 2018. Big Bash: MR 2012-13; AS 2013-14; HH 2014-15; ST 2019-20 to date. Trent Rockets 2021 to date. **Tests**: 11 (2015-16 to 2016); HS 94 v SL (Lord's) 2016; BB –. **LOI**: 70 (2014 to 2018-19); HS 171 v P (Nottingham) 2016. **IT20**: 75 (2011 to 2022-23); HS 116* v SL (Chittagong) 2013-14. 1000 runs (3); most – 1127 (2011). HS 236 v Yorks (Nottingham) 2015. BB 2-63 v Yorks (Nottingham) 2009. LO HS 187* v Surrey (Lord's) 2017 (RLC) – Nt record. T20 HS 119*.

HAMEED, Haseeb (Bolton S), b Bolton, Lancs 17 Jan 1997. 6'2". RHB, LB. Squad No 99. Lancashire 2015-19; cap 2016. Nottinghamshire debut/cap 2020; captain 2024. **Tests**: 10 (2016-17 to 2021-22); HS 82 v I (Rajkot) 2016-17 – on debut. F-c Tours: A 2021-22; WI 2017-18 (EL); I 2016-17; SL 2016-17 (EL), 2022-23 (EL). 1000 runs (2): most – 1235 (2022). HS 196 v Derbys (Derby) 2022, sharing in Nt record 2nd wkt partnership of 402 with B.M.Duckett. BB 1-0 v Kent (Nottingham) 2023. LO HS 114 v Middx (Grantham) 2022 (RLC). T20 HS 23.

HARRISON, Calvin Grant (King's C, Taunton; Oxford Brookes U), b Durban, S Africa 29 Apr 1998. 6'4". RHB, LBG. Squad No 31. Oxford MCCU 2019. Nottinghamshire debut 2023. Hampshire 2020 (T20 only). Manchester Originals 2021 to date. HS 39 v Hants (Nottingham) 2023. BB 4-28 v Kent (Nottingham) 2023. LO HS 41 v Middx (Radlett) 2023 (MBC). LO BB 1-0 v Essex (Chelmsford) 2023 (MBC). T20 HS 23. T20 BB 5-11.

HAYES, James Phillip Henry (King's C, Taunton; Richard Huish C), b Haywards Heath, Sussex 27 Jun 2001. RHB, RFM. Squad No 35. Nottinghamshire 2nd XI debut 2021. Awaiting f-c debut. LO HS 1* and LO BB 2-58 v Middx (Grantham) 2022 (RLC).

‡HAYNES, Jack Alexander (Malvern C), b Worcester 30 Jan 2001. Son of G.R.Haynes (Worcestershire 1991-99); younger brother of J.L.Haynes (Worcestershire 2nd XI 2015-16). 6'1". RHB, OB. Squad No 30. Worcestershire 2019-23. Oval Invincibles 2022. England U19 2018. HS 134* Wo v Durham (Chester-le-St) 2023. LO HS 153 Wo v Essex (Chelmsford) 2021 (RLC). T20 HS 63.

HUTTON, Brett Alan (Worksop C), b Doncaster, Yorks 6 Feb 1993. 6'2". RHB, RM. Squad No 16. Debut (Nottinghamshire) 2011. Northamptonshire 2018-20. Surrey 2022 (on loan). HS 84 v Kent (Canterbury) 2023. 50 wkts (1): 62 (2023). BB 8-57 Nh v Glos (Northampton) 2018. Nt BB 6-45 v Somerset (Nottingham) 2023. LO HS 46 v Derbys (Derby) 2021 (RLC). LO BB 7-26 v Leics (Leicester) 2022 (RLC) – Nt record. T20 HS 18*. T20 BB 2-28.

JAMES, Lyndon Wallace (Oakham S), b Worksop 27 Dec 1998. RHB, RMF. Squad No 8. Debut (Nottinghamshire) 2018. HS 164* v Durham (Nottingham) 2022. BB 6-74 v Surrey (Oval) 2023. LO HS 82 v Leics (Leicester) 2023 (MBC). LO BB 5-48 v Warwks (Birmingham) 2021 (RLC). T20 HS 37. T20 BB 1-23.

KING, Samuel Isaac Michael (Nottingham HS; Nottingham U), b Nottingham 12 Jan 2003. RHB, RM. Squad No 1. Nottinghamshire 2nd XI debut 2021. Awaiting f-c debut. LO HS 37 v Lancs (Mansfield) 2023 (MBC).

LOTEN, Thomas William (Pocklington S), b York 8 Jan 1999. 6'5". RHB, RMF. Squad No 24. Yorkshire 2019-22. HS 58 Y v Warwks (Birmingham) 2019. BB 2-31 Y v Warwks (Leeds) 2022. LO HS 44 v Middx (Radlett) 2023 (MBC). LO BB 3-26 v Leics (Leicester) 2023 (MBC).

McCANN, Freddie William (Toothill CS; Trent C), b Nottingham 19 Apr 2005. LHB, OB. Squad No 44. Nottinghamshire 2nd XI debut 2022. Awaiting 1st XI debut.

MARTINDALE, Benjamin John Richardson (Nottingham HS), b Nottingham 12 Dec 2002. Son of D.J.R.Martindale (Nottinghamshire 1985-91). LHB, RMF. Squad No 95. Nottinghamshire 2nd XI debut 2021. Awaiting f-c debut. LO HS 55 v Essex (Chelmsford) 2023 (MBC). LO BB –.

NQ**MONTGOMERY, Matt**hew (Clifton C; Loughborough U), b Johannesburg, South Africa 10 May 2000. RHB, OB. Squad No 14. KwaZulu-Natal 2018-19. Nottinghamshire debut 2022. Nottinghamshire 2nd XI debut 2021. S Africa U19 2018-19. **IT20** (Germany): 1 (2023); HS 13 v Italy (Edinburgh) 2023; BB –. HS 178 v Durham (Nottingham) 2022. BB 1-0 v Kent (Canterbury) 2023. LO HS 104 KZN v WP (Chatsworth) 2018-19 – on debut. LO BB 2-48 v Glos (Bristol) 2022 (RLC). T20 HS 51. T20 BB 1-5.

MOORES, Thomas James (Loughborough GS), b Brighton, Sussex 4 Sep 1996. Son of P.Moores (Worcestershire, Sussex & OFS 1983-98); nephew of S.Moores (Cheshire 1995). LHB, WK, occ RM. Squad No 23. Lancashire 2016 (on loan). Nottinghamshire debut 2016; cap 2021. Trent Rockets 2021-22. HS 106 v Yorks (Nottingham) 2020. LO HS 76 v Leics (Leicester) 2018 (RLC). T20 HS 80*.

MULLANEY, Steven John (St Mary's RC S, Astley), b Warrington, Cheshire 19 Nov 1986. 5'9". RHB, RM. Squad No 5. Lancashire 2006-08. Nottinghamshire debut 2010, scoring 100* v Hants (Southampton); cap 2013; captain 2018-23; testimonial 2024. Trent Rockets 2021. F-c Tour (EL): I 2018-19. 1000 runs (1): 1148 (2016). HS 192 v Sussex (Hove) 2022. BB 5-32 v Glos (Nottingham) 2017. LO HS 124 v Durham (Chester-le-St) 2018 (RLC). LO BB 4-29 v Kent (Nottingham) 2013 (Y40). T20 HS 79. T20 BB 4-19.

NQ**PATERSON, Dane**, b Cape Town, South Africa 4 Apr 1989. RHB, RFM. Squad No 2. Western Province 2009-10 to date. Dolphins 2010-11 to 2012-13. KwaZulu-Natal 2011-12 to 2012-13. Cape Cobras 2013-14 to 2019-20. Nottinghamshire debut/cap 2021. Eastern Province 2021-22. **Tests** (SA): 4 (2019-20 to 2023-24); HS 39* v E (Gqeberha) 2019-20; BB 3-39 v NZ (Hamilton) 2023-24. **LOI** (SA): 4 (2017-18 to 2018-19); HS – ; BB 3-44 v B (East London) 2017-18. **IT20** (SA): 8 (2016-17 to 2018-19); HS 4* v E (Taunton) 2017; BB 4-32 v E (Cardiff) 2017. F-c Tours (SA): E 2017 (SA A); NZ 2023-24. HS 59 KZN v FS (Bloemfontein) 2012-13. Nt HS 22 v Warwks (Nottingham) 2021. 50 wkts (3+2); most – 67 (2013-14). BB 8-52 (10-117 match) v Worcs (Nottingham) 2022. LO HS 29 Cape Cobras v Dolphins (Cape Town) 2017-18. LO BB 5-19 SA A v India A (Bangalore) 2018. T20 HS 24*. T20 BB 4-24.

PATTERSON-WHITE, Liam Anthony (Worksop C), b Sunderland, Co Durham 8 Nov 1998. LHB, SLA. Squad No 22. Debut (Nottinghamshire) 2019, taking 5-73 v Somerset (Taunton). F-c Tour (EL): SL 2022-23. HS 101 v Somerset (Taunton) 2021. BB 5-41 v Hants (Southampton) 2021. LO HS 62* v Sussex (Nottingham) 2022 (RLC). LO BB 5-19 v Northants (Grantham) 2021 (RLC).

‡**PENNINGTON, Dillon** Young (Wrekin C), b Shrewsbury, Shrops 26 Feb 1999. 6'2". RHB, RMF. Squad No 18. Worcestershire 2018-23. Birmingham Phoenix 2021. Shropshire 2017. HS 56 Wo v Essex (Chelmsford) 2021. BB 5-32 Wo v Derbys (Worcester) 2021. LO HS 35 Wo v Derbys (Worcester) 2022 (RLC). LO BB 5-67 Wo v West Indies A (Worcester) 2018. T20 HS 10*. T20 BB 4-9.

PETTMAN, Toby Henry Somerville (Tonbridge S; Jesus C, Oxford), b Kingston-upon-Thames, Surrey 11 May 1998. 6'7". RHB, RFM. Squad No 15. Oxford University 2017-20. Derbyshire 2022 (on loan). Kent 2022 (on loan). Nottinghamshire debut 2023. HS 54* OU v Cambridge U (Oxford) 2018. CC HS 3* K v Surrey (Oval) 2022. Nt HS 1 and Nt BB 1-15 v Hants (Nottingham) 2023. BB 5-19 OU v Cambridge U (Cambridge) 2019. CC BB 3-40 De v Middx (Chesterfield) 2022 and 3-40 De v Durham (Chester-le-St) 2022. LO HS 5* v Leics (Leicester) 2022 (RLC). LO BB 4-44 v Surrey (Mansfield) 2022 (RLC).

[NQ]**SCHADENDORF, Dane** Joshua, b Harare, Zimbabwe 31 Jul 2002. RHB, WK. Squad No 89. Debut (Nottinghamshire) 2021. Mountaineers 2023-24. Zimbabwe U19 2019-20. HS 24 v Derbys (Nottingham) 2021. LO HS 47 Mountaineers v Eagles (Mutare) 2023-24.

SINGH, Fateh Landa (Trent C), b Nottingham 20 Apr 2004. LHB, SLA. Squad No 11. Nottinghamshire 2nd XI debut 2021. Awaiting f-c debut. LO HS 45 v Middx (Grantham) 2022 (RLC). LO BB 2-7 v Leics (Leicester) 2022 (RLC). No 1st XI appearances in 2023.

SLATER, Benjamin Thomas (Netherthorpe S; Leeds Met U), b Chesterfield, Derbys 26 Aug 1991. 5'10". LHB, OB. Squad No 26. Debut (Leeds/Bradford MCCU) 2012. Southern Rocks 2012-13. Derbyshire 2013-18. Nottinghamshire debut 2018; cap 2021. Leicestershire 2020 (on loan). HS 225* v Durham (Chester-le-St) 2022. BB 1-1 v Middx (Nottingham) 2022. LO HS 148* De v Northants (Northampton) 2016 (RLC). T20 HS 57.

STONE, Oliver Peter (Thorpe St Andrew HS), b Norwich, Norfolk 9 Oct 1993. 6'1". RHB, RF. Squad No 9. Northamptonshire 2012-16. Warwickshire 2017-21; cap 2020. Nottinghamshire debut/cap 2023. Big Bash: MS 2023-24. Norfolk 2011. **Tests**: 3 (2019 to 2021); HS 20 v NZ (Birmingham) 2021; BB 3-29 v Ire (Lord's) 2019. **LOI**: 8 (2018-19 to 2022-23); HS 9* v SL (Dambulla) 2018-19; BB 4-85 v A (Melbourne) 2022-23. **IT20**: 1 (2022-23); HS 0; BB –. HS 60 Nh v Kent (Northampton) 2016. Nt HS 22 v Lancs (Nottingham) 2023. BB 8-80 Wa v Sussex (Birmingham) 2018. Nt BB 3-82 v Hants (Southampton) 2023. LO HS 24* Nh v Derbys (Derby) 2015 (RLC). LO BB 4-71 Wa v Worcs (Birmingham) 2018 (RLC). T20 HS 22*. T20 BB 4-14.

‡**TONGUE, Josh**ua Charles (King's S, Worcester; Worcester SFC), b Redditch, Worcs 15 Nov 1997. 6'5". RHB, RFM. Squad No 56. Worcestershire 2016-23. Manchester Originals 2023. **ECB Two-Year Central Contract from 2023-24**. **Tests**: 2 (2023); HS 19 v A (Lord's) 2023; BB 5-66 v Ire (Lord's) 2023. HS 45* Wo v Notts (Worcester) 2022. BB 6-97 Wo v Glamorgan (Worcester) 2017. LO HS 34 Wo v Warwks (Worcester) 2019 (RLC). LO BB 2-35 Wo v Lancs (Manchester) 2019 (RLC). T20 HS 2*. T20 BB 2-32.

[NQ]**YOUNG, Will**iam Alexander, New Plymouth, New Zealand 22 Nov 1992. RHB, OB. Squad No 32. Central Districts 2011-12 to date. Durham 2021; cap 2021. Northamptonshire 2022. Nottinghamshire debut/cap 2023. **Tests** (NZ): 16 (2020-21 to 2023-24); HS 89 v I (Kanpur) 2021-22. **LOI** (NZ): 31 (2020-21 to 2023-24); HS 120 v Neth (Hamilton) 2021-22. **IT20** (NZ): 18 (2020-21 to 2023-24); H6 53 v UAE (Dubai, DSC) 2023. F-c Tours (NZ): E 2021, 2022; I 2017-18 (NZA), 2021-22; UAE 2018-19 (v P A). HS 162 CD v Auckland (Auckland) 2017-18. CC HS 145 v Surrey (Oval) 2023. LO HS 136 NZ A v Pakistan A (Abu Dhabi) 2018-19. T20 HS 101*.

RELEASED/RETIRED

(Having made a County 1st XI appearance in 2023)

BALL, J.T. – *see SOMERSET*.

BROAD, Stuart Christopher John (Oakham S), b Nottingham 24 Jun 1986. Son of B.C.Broad (Glos, Notts, OFS and England 1979-94). 6'6". LHB, RFM. Leicestershire 2005-07; cap 2007. Nottinghamshire 2008-23; cap 2008; testimonial 2019. MCC 2019. Big Bash: HH 2016-17. YC 2006. *Wisden* 2009. **Tests**: 167 (2007-08 to 2023); HS 169 v P (Lord's) 2010, sharing in record Test and UK f-c 8th wkt partnership of 332 with I.J.L.Trott; 50 wkts (2); most – 62 (2013); BB 8-15 v A (Nottingham) 2015. Hat-tricks (2): v I (Nottingham) 2011, and v SL (Leeds) 2014. **LOI**: 121 (2006 to 2015-16, 3 as captain); HS 45* v I (Manchester) 2007; BB 5-23 v SA (Nottingham) 2008. **IT20**: 56 (2006 to 2013-14, 27 as captain); HS 18* v SA (Chester-le-St) 2012 and 18* v A (Melbourne) 2013-14; BB 4-24 v NZ (Auckland) 2012-13. F-c Tours: A 2010-11, 2013-14, 2017-18, 2021-22; SA 2009-10, 2015-16, 2019-20; WI 2005-06 (Eng A), 2008-09, 2014-15, 2018-19; NZ 2007-08, 2012-13, 2017-18, 2019-20, 2022-23; I 2008-09, 2012-13, 2016-17, 2020-21; SL 2007-08, 2011-12, 2018-19, 2020-21; B 2006-07 (Eng A), 2009-10, 2016-17; UAE 2011-12 (v P), 2015-16 (v P). HS 169 (*see Tests*). CC HS 91* Le v Derbys (Leicester) 2007. Nt HS 60 v Worcs (Nottingham) 2009. BB 8-15 (*see Tests*). CC BB 8-52 (11-131 match) v Warwks (Birmingham) 2010. LO HS 45* (*see LOI*). LO BB 5-23 (*see LOI*). T20 HS 18*. T20 BB 4-24.

[NQ]**FERNANDO, Asitha** Madusanka (St Sebastian's C, Katuneriya), b Katuneriya, Sri Lanka 31 July 1997. RHB, RMF. Chilaw Marians 2016-17 to 2020. Nondescripts 2018-19. Colombo 2022-23 to date. Nottinghamshire 2023; cap 2023. **Tests** (SL): 13 (2020-21 to 2023-24); HS 10 v NZ (Christchurch) 2022-23; BB 6-51 v B (Mirpur) 2022. **LOI** (SL): 7 (2017 to 2023-24); HS 1* v E (Oval) 2021; BB 2-23 v Afg (Pallekele) 2023-24. **IT20** (SL): 3 (2022); HS 10* v B (Dubai, DSC) 2022; 1-34 v Afg (Sharjah) 2022. F-c Tours (SL): E 2016 (SLA); SA 2020-21; WI 2017-18 (SLA); NZ 2022-23; B 2022. HS 30 SLA v England Lions (Pallekele) 2016-17. Nt HS 14* and Nt BB 3-40 v Kent (Canterbury) 2023. BB 7-139 Chilaw v Badureliya (Katunayake) 2019-20. LO HS 11 Colombo v Tamil Union (Colombo CC) 2022. LO BB 5-32 Nondescripts v Galle (Colombo) 2018-19. T20 HS 10*. T20 BB 6-8.

[NQ]**IMAD WASIM**, b Swansea, Glamorgan 18 Dec 1988. LHB, SLA. Islamabad 2006-07 to 2017-18. Federal Areas 2008-09 to 2011-12. Islamabad Leopards 2014-15. Northern Areas 2019-20. Nottinghamshire 2019-23 (T20 only). Big Bash: MR 2020-21; MS 2023-24. Trent Rockets 2023. **LOI** (P): 55 (2015 to 2020-21, 2 as captain); HS 63* v E (Lord's) 2016; BB 5-14 v Ire (Dublin) 2016. **IT20** (P): 66 (2015 to 2023); HS 64* v Afg (Sharjah) 2022-23; BB 5-14 v WI (Dubai, DSC) 2016-17. F-c Tour (PA): SL 2015. HS 207 Leopards v Multan Tigers (Multan) 2014-15. BB 8-81 (12-104 match) Islamabad v Multan (Karachi) 2013-14. LO HS 117* P v Kent (Beckenham) 2019. LO BB 5-14 (*see LOI*). T20 HS 92*. T20 BB 5-14.

[NQ]**MUNRO, Colin** (Pakuranga C, Auckland), b Durban, South Africa 11 Mar 1987. LHB, RM. Auckland 2006-07 to 2017-18. Worcestershire 2015. Hampshire 2018 (T20 only). Nottinghamshire 2023 (T20 only). IPL: KKR 2016; DD 2018; DC 2019. Big Bash: SS 2016-17; PS 2020-21 to 2021-22; BH 2022-23 to date. Manchester Originals 2021. Trent Rockets 2022 to date. **Tests** (NZ): 1 (2012-13); HS 15 and BB 2-40 v SA (Pt Elizabeth) 2012-13. **LOI** (NZ): 57 (2012-13 to 2019); HS 87 v B (Christchurch) 2016-17 and 87 v SL (Mt Maunganui) 2018-19; BB 2-10 v P (Dunedin) 2017-18. **IT20** (NZ): 65 (2012-13 to 2019-20); HS 109* v I (Rajkot) 2017-18; BB 1-12 v P (Wellington) 2017-18. F-c Tours (NZ): SA 2012-13; SL 2013-14. HS 281 Auckland v CD (Napier) 2014-15, inc world record 23 sixes. CC HS 34 Wo v Hants (Southampton) 2015. BB 4-36 Auckland v CD (Auckland) 2010-11. LO HS 174* Auckland v Canterbury (Auckland) 2017-18. LO BB 3-45 Auckland v Otago (Oamaru) 2010-11. T20 HS 114*. T20 BB 4-15.

PATEL, S.R. – *see DERBYSHIRE.*

[NQ]**SHAHEEN** Shah **AFRIDI**, b Khyber Agency, Pakistan 6 Apr 2000. 6'4½". LHB, LFM. Khan Research Laboratories 2017-18. Northern Areas 2019-20. Middlesex 2022. Hampshire 2020 (T20 only). Nottinghamshire 2023 (T20 only). Welsh Fire 2023. **Tests** (P): 29 (2018-19 to 2023-24); HS 21 v A (Melbourne) 2023-24; BB 6-51 v WI (Kingston) 2021. **LOI** (P): 53 (2018-19 to 2023-24); HS 25 v E (Kolkata) 2023-24; BB 6-35 v B (Lord's) 2019. **IT20** (P): 57 (2017-18 to 2023-24); HS 22 v NZ (Hamilton) 2023-24; BB 4-22 v B (Adelaide) 2022-23. F-c Tours (P): E 2020; A 2019-20, 2023-24; SA 2018-19; WI 2021; NZ 2020-21; SL 2022, 2023; B 2021-22. HS 29 M v Glamorgan (Cardiff) 2022 and 29 M v Leics (Lord's) 2022. BB 8-39 KRL v Rawalpindi (Rawalpindi) 2017-18 – on f-c debut, aged 17y 174d. LO HS 25 (*see LOI*). LO BB 6-35 (*see LOI*). T20 HS 52. T20 BB 6-19 v Middx (Southampton) 2020 – H record.

NOTTINGHAMSHIRE 2023

RESULTS SUMMARY

	Place	Won	Lost	Drew	NR
LV= Insurance County Champ (Div 1)	6th	4	4	6	
Metro Bank One-Day Cup (Group A)	5th	3	4		1
Vitality Blast (North Group)	5th	8	7		

LV= INSURANCE COUNTY CHAMPIONSHIP AVERAGES
BATTING AND FIELDING

Cap		*M*	*I*	*NO*	*HS*	*Runs*	*Avge*	*100*	*50*	*Ct/St*
2023	W.A.Young	3	6	1	145	299	59.80	1	1	2
2021	J.M.Clarke	14	24	3	229*	1053	50.14	2	7	21
2019	B.M.Duckett	5	9	–	177	401	44.55	1	2	14
2021	B.T.Slater	14	25	–	140	825	33.00	2	3	5
2020	H.Hameed	14	25	1	97	674	28.08	–	4	7
2021	T.J.Moores	10	16	1	94	415	27.66	–	2	28
	M.Montgomery	11	18	1	177	458	26.94	1	1	9
2013	S.J.Mullaney	12	21	2	86	485	25.52	–	1	9
	C.G.Harrison	8	11	2	39	208	23.11	–	–	14
2008	S.C.J.Broad	4	6	3	26	62	20.66	–	–	–
2021	B.A.Hutton	13	18	2	84	282	17.62	–	1	8
	L.W.James	14	24	1	50	405	17.60	–	1	12
2014	L.J.Fletcher	4	6	4	15*	34	17.00	–	–	–
2023	O.P.Stone	2	4	1	22	46	15.33	–	–	–
	L.A.Patterson-White	5	7	–	15	70	10.00	–	–	–
2016	J.T.Ball	4	6	2	11	33	8.25	–	–	2
2021	D.Paterson	13	17	4	16	77	5.92	–	–	1

Also batted: M.Carter (1 match) 8, 15*; A.M.Fernando (2 – cap 2023) 14*, 0; T.H.S.Pettman (1) 1, 0.

BOWLING

	O	*M*	*R*	*W*	*Avge*	*Best*	*5wI*	*10wM*
B.A.Hutton	383.1	62	1327	62	21.40	6-45	6	–
D.Paterson	412.2	62	1390	50	27.80	5-16	3	–
S.C.J.Broad	127	21	426	15	28.40	4-68	–	–
L.W.James	276.4	46	912	28	32.57	6-74	1	–
C.G.Harrison	170	13	612	17	36.00	4-28	–	–
Also bowled:								
L.J.Fletcher	71.5	19	176	9	19.55	3-44	–	–
A.M.Fernando	48.1	11	151	6	25.16	3-40	–	–
O.P.Stone	55	6	225	6	37.50	3-82	–	–
S.J.Mullaney	112.3	17	389	9	43.22	2-32	–	–
J.T.Ball	88	10	386	7	55.14	3-67	–	–

M.Carter 50-9-147-4; H.Hameed 0.3-0-0-1; M.Montgomery 23-3-98-2; T.J.Moores 0.2-0-1-0; L.A.Patterson-White 69-11-228-1; T.H.S.Pettman 25-6-76-2; B.T.Slater 4-1-11-0.

Nottinghamshire played no first-class fixtures outside the County Championship in 2023. The First-Class Averages (pp 223–235) give the records of Nottinghamshire players in all first-class county matches, with the exception of S.C.J.Broad and B.M.Duckett, whose first-class figures for Nottinghamshire are as above.

NOTTINGHAMSHIRE RECORDS

FIRST-CLASS CRICKET

Highest Total	For 791		v	Essex	Chelmsford	2007
	V 781-7d		by	Northants	Northampton	1995
Lowest Total	For 13		v	Yorkshire	Nottingham	1901
	V 16		by	Derbyshire	Nottingham	1879
	16		by	Surrey	The Oval	1880
Highest Innings	For 312*	W.W.Keeton	v	Middlesex	The Oval	1939
	V 345	C.G.Macartney	for	Australians	Nottingham	1921

Highest Partnership for each Wicket

1st	406*	D.J.Bicknell/G.E.Welton	v	Warwicks	Birmingham	2000
2nd	402	H.Hameed/B.M.Duckett	v	Derbyshire	Derby	2022
3rd	367	W.Gunn/J.R.Gunn	v	Leics	Nottingham	1903
4th	361	A.O.Jones/J.R.Gunn	v	Essex	Leyton	1905
5th	359	D.J.Hussey/C.M.W.Read	v	Essex	Nottingham	2007
6th	372*	K.P.Pietersen/J.E.Morris	v	Derbyshire	Derby	2001
7th	301	C.C.Lewis/B.N.French	v	Durham	Chester-le-St[2]	1993
8th	220	G.F.H.Heane/R.Winrow	v	Somerset	Nottingham	1935
9th	170	J.C.Adams/K.P.Evans	v	Somerset	Taunton	1994
10th	152	E.B.Alletson/W.Riley	v	Sussex	Hove	1911
	152	U.Afzaal/A.J.Harris	v	Worcs	Nottingham	2000

Best Bowling	For	10-66	K.Smales	v	Glos	Stroud	1956
(Innings)	V	10-10	H.Verity	for	Yorkshire	Leeds	1932
Best Bowling	For	17-89	F.C.L.Matthews	v	Northants	Nottingham	1923
(Match)	V	17-89	W.G.Grace	for	Glos	Cheltenham	1877

Most Runs – Season	2620	W.W.Whysall	(av 53.46)	1929
Most Runs – Career	31592	G.Gunn	(av 35.69)	1902-32
Most 100s – Season	9	W.W.Whysall		1928
	9	M.J.Harris		1971
	9	B.C.Broad		1990
Most 100s – Career	65	J.Hardstaff jr		1930-55
Most Wkts – Season	181	B.Dooland	(av 14.96)	1954
Most Wkts – Career	1653	T.G.Wass	(av 20.34)	1896-1920
Most Career W-K Dismissals	983	C.M.W.Read	(939 ct; 44 st)	1998-2017
Most Career Catches in the Field	466	A.O.Jones		1892-1914

LIMITED-OVERS CRICKET

Highest Total	**50ov**	445-8		v	Northants	Nottingham	2016
	40ov	296-7		v	Somerset	Taunton	2002
	T20	247-6		v	Derbyshire	Nottingham	2022
Lowest Total	**50ov**	74		v	Leics	Leicester	1987
	40ov	57		v	Glos	Nottingham	2009
	T20	91		v	Lancashire	Manchester	2006
		91		v	Lancashire	Nottingham	2022
Highest Innings	**50ov**	187*	A.D.Hales	v	Surrey	Lord's	2017
	40ov	150*	A.D.Hales	v	Worcs	Nottingham	2009
	T20	136	J.M.Clarke	v	Northants	Northampton	2021
Best Bowling	**50ov**	7-26	B.A.Hutton	v	Leics	Leicester	2022
	40ov	6-12	R.J.Hadlee	v	Lancashire	Nottingham	1980
	T20	5-22	G.G.White	v	Lancashire	Nottingham	2013

SOMERSET

SOMERSET CCC

Formation of Present Club: 18 August 1875
Inaugural First-Class Match: 1882
Colours: Black, White and Maroon
Badge: Somerset Dragon
County Champions: (0); best – 2nd (Div 1) 2001, 2010, 2012, 2016, 2018, 2019
Gillette/NatWest/C&G Trophy Winners: (3) 1979, 1983, 2001
Benson and Hedges Cup Winners: (2) 1981, 1982
Sunday League Winners: (1) 1979
Royal London One-Day Cup Winners: (1) 2019
Twenty20 Cup Winners: (2) 2005, 2023

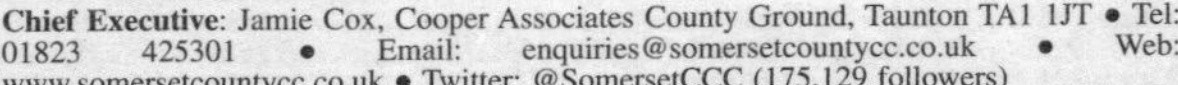

Chief Executive: Jamie Cox, Cooper Associates County Ground, Taunton TA1 1JT • Tel: 01823 425301 • Email: enquiries@somersetcountycc.co.uk • Web: www.somersetcountycc.co.uk • Twitter: @SomersetCCC (175,129 followers)

Director of Cricket: Andy Hurry. **Head Coach**: Jason Kerr. **Batting Coach**: Shane Burger. **Bowling Coach**: Steve Kirby. **Captain**: L.Gregory. **Vice-captain**: C.Overton. **Overseas Players**: M.T.Renshaw and W.J.Sutherland. **2024 Testimonial**: None. **Groundsman**: Nick Pepper. **Scorer**: Polly Rhodes. ‡ New registration. [NQ] Not qualified for England.

ABELL, Thomas Benjamin (Taunton S; Exeter U), b Taunton 5 Mar 1994. 5'10". RHB, RM. Squad No 28. Debut (Somerset) 2014; captain 2017-23; cap 2018. MCC 2019. Big Bash: BH 2021-22. Birmingham Phoenix 2021. Welsh Fire 2023. Wisden Schools Cricketer of the Year 2012. F-c Tours (EL): A 2019-20; SL 2022-23. HS 151 v Lancs (Taunton) 2023. BB 4-39 v Warwks (Birmingham) 2019. Hat-trick v Notts (Nottingham) 2018. LO HS 106 v Sussex (Taunton) 2016 (RLC). LO BB 2-19 v Hants (Lord's) 2019 (RLC). T20 HS 101*. T20 BB 1-11.

ALDRIDGE, Kasey Luke (Millfield S), b Bristol 24 Dec 2000. RHB, RM. Squad No 5. Debut (Somerset) 2021. Somerset 2nd XI debut 2019. Devon 2019. England U19 2018-19. HS 101* v Lancs (Manchester) 2023. BB 6-110 v Kent (Canterbury) 2022. LO HS 12 v Surrey (Oval) 2021 (RLC). LO BB 5-50 v Surrey (Oval) 2022 (RLC). T20 HS 32*. T20 BB –.

BAKER, Sonny (Torquay Boys' GS; King's C, Taunton), b Torbay 13 Mar 2003. Nephew of A.K.Hele (Devon 1998-2001). RHB, RM. Squad No 16. Southern Brave 2022. Somerset 2nd XI debut 2019. Awaiting f-c debut. LO HS 7* v Surrey (Oval) 2021 (RLC). LO BB 6-46 v Durham (Taunton) 2022 (RLC). T20 HS 0. T20 BB 2-28. No 1st XI appearances in 2023.

‡**BALL,** Jacob Timothy ('**Jake**') (Meden CS), b Mansfield, Notts 14 Mar 1991. Nephew of B.N.French (Notts and England 1976-95). 6'0". RHB, RFM. Nottinghamshire 2011-23; cap 2016. MCC 2016. Big Bash: SS 2020-21. Welsh Fire 2021 to date. **Tests**: 4 (2016 to 2017-18); HS 31 and BB 1-47 v I (Mumbai) 2016-17. **LOI**: 18 (2016-17 to 2018); HS 28 v B (Mirpur) 2016-17; BB 5-51 v B (Mirpur) 2016-17 – separate matches. **IT20**: 2 (2018); HS – ; BB 1-39 v I (Bristol) 2018. F-c Tours: A 2017-18; I 2016-17. HS 49* Nt v Warwks (Nottingham) 2015. 50 wkts (1): 54 (2016). BB 6-49 Nt v Sussex (Nottingham) 2015. Hat-trick Nt v Middx (Nottingham) 2016. LO HS 28 (*see LOI*). BB 5-51 (*see LOI*). T20 HS 18*. T20 BB 4-11.

BANTON, Thomas (Bromsgrove S; King's C, Taunton), b Chiltern, Bucks 11 Nov 1998. Son of C.Banton (Nottinghamshire 1995); elder brother of J.Banton (Worcestershire 2021-22 – l-o only). 6'2". RHB, WK, occ OB. Squad No 18. Debut (Somerset) 2018. Big Bash: BH 2019-20. Welsh Fire 2021-22. Northern Superchargers 2023. **LOI**: 6 (2019-20 to 2020); HS 58 v Ire (Southampton) 2020. **IT20**: 14 (2019-20 to 2021-22); HS 73 v WI (Bridgetown) 2021-22. HS 126 v Essex (Chelmsford) 2022. LO HS 112 v Worcs (Worcester) 2019 (RLC). T20 HS 107*.

BASHIR, Shoaib (Fulbrook S; Woking C), b Chertsey, Surrey 13 Oct 2003. RHB, OB. Squad No 13. Debut (Somerset) 2023. Somerset 2nd XI debut 2022. **Tests**: 3 (2023-24); HS 13 v I (Dharamsala) 2023-24; BB 5-119 v I (Ranchi) 2023-24. F-c Tour: I 2023-24. HS 44* and Sm BB 3-67 v Hants (Taunton) 2023. BB 5-119 (*see Tests*). LO HS 7 v Warwks (Taunton) 2023 (MBC). LO BB 1-46 v Northants (Northampton) 2023 (MBC). T20 HS –. T20 BB 3-26.

NQ**DAVEY, Josh**ua Henry (Culford S), b Aberdeen, Scotland 3 Aug 1990. 5'11". RHB, RMF. Squad No 38. Middlesex 2010-12. Scotland 2011-12 to 2016. Somerset debut 2015; cap 2021. Leicestershire 2023 (on loan). Suffolk 2014. **LOI** (Scot): 31 (2010 to 2019-20); HS 64 v Afg (Sharjah) 2012-13; BB 6-28 v Afg (Abu Dhabi) 2014-15 – Scot record. **IT20** (Scot): 31 (2012 to 2022-23); HS 24 v Z (Nagpur) 2015-16; BB 4-18 v PNG (Al Amerat) 2021-22. HS 75* v Leics (Taunton) 2021. BB 5-21 v Yorks (Taunton) 2019. LO HS 91 Scot v Warwks (Birmingham) 2011 (CB40). LO BB 6-28 (*see LOI*). T20 HS 24. T20 BB 4-18.

DICKSON, Sean Robert, b Johannesburg, South Africa 2 Sep 1991. 5'10". RHB, RM. Squad No 58. Northerns 2013-14 to 2014-15. Kent 2015-19. Durham 2020-22; cap 2020. Somerset debut 2023. UK passport holder; England qualified. HS 318 K v Northants (Beckenham) 2017, 2nd highest score in K history. Sm HS 82* v Essex (Chelmsford) 2023. BB 1-15 Northerns v GW (Centurion) 2014-15. CC BB –. LO HS 103* Du v Lancs (Gosforth) 2021 (RLC). T20 HS 53. T20 BB 1-9.

GOLDSWORTHY, Lewis Peter (Cambourne Science & Int Ac), b Truro, Cornwall 8 Jan 2001. RHB, SLA. Squad No 44. Debut (Somerset) 2021. Somerset 2nd XI debut 2017. Cornwall 2017-19. England U19 2018-19. HS 130 v Lancs (Southport) 2022. BB –. LO HS 111 v Warwks (Birmingham) 2022 (RLC). LO BB 2-30 v Worcs (Taunton) 2023 (MBC). T20 HS 48. T20 BB 3-14.

GREEN, Benjamin George Frederick (Exeter S), b Exeter, Devon 28 Sep 1997. 6'2". RHB, RFM. Squad No 54. Debut (Somerset) 2018. Welsh Fire 2023. Devon 2014-18. HS 54 v Glamorgan (Taunton) 2020. BB 3-31 v Hants (Southampton) 2022. LO HS 157 (in 84 balls) v Durham (Taunton) 2022 (RLC). LO BB 3-64 v Derbys (Taunton) 2021 (RLC). T20 HS 43*. T20 BB 5-29.

GREGORY, Lewis (Hele's S, Plympton), b Plymouth, Devon 24 May 1992. 6'0". RHB, RMF. Squad No 24. Debut (Somerset) 2011; cap 2015; T20 captain 2018-21; captain 2024. MCC 2017. Devon 2008. Big Bash: BH 2020-21. Trent Rockets 2021 to date. **LOI**: 3 (2021); HS 77 v P (Birmingham) 2021; BB 3-44 v P (Lord's) 2021. **IT20**: 9 (2019-20 to 2021); HS 15 and BB 1-10 v NZ (Wellington) 2019-20. HS 137 v Middx (Lord's) 2017. 50 wkts (1): 59 (2019). BB 7-84 (11-148 match) v Notts (Nottingham) 2023. LO HS 105* v Durham (Taunton) 2014 (RLC). LO BB 4-23 v Essex (Chelmsford) 2016 (RLC). T20 HS 76*. T20 BB 5-24.

HILL, Finley James (King's C, Taunton), b Exeter, Devon 21 Jun 2006. RHB, RM. Somerset 2nd XI debut 2022. Devon 2023. Awaiting f-c debut. LO HS 1* v Durham (Gosforth) 2023 (MBC) – only 1st XI appearance.

KOHLER-CADMORE, Tom (Malvern C), b Chatham, Kent 19 Aug 1994. 6'2". RHB, OB. Squad No 32. Worcestershire 2014-17. Yorkshire 2017-22; cap 2019. Somerset debut 2023. Big Bash: ST 2023-24. Northern Superchargers 2021. Trent Rockets 2022 to date. 1000 runs (1): 1004 (2019). HS 176 Y v Leeds/Brad MCCU (Leeds) 2019. CC HS 169 Wo v Glos (Worcester) 2016. Sm HS 130 v Northants (Northampton) 2023. LO HS 164 Y v Durham (Chester-le-St) 2018 (RLC). T20 HS 127 Wo v Durham (Worcester) 2016 – Wo record.

LAMMONBY, Thomas Alexander (Exeter S), b Exeter, Devon 2 Jun 2000. LHB, LM. Squad No 15. Debut (Somerset) 2020. Big Bash: HH 2021-22. Manchester Originals 2021 to date. Somerset 2nd XI debut 2015. Devon 2016-18. England U19 2018-19. HS 116 v Essex (Lord's) 2020. BB 3-35 v Essex (Chelmsford) 2022. LO HS 6 EL v Sri Lanka A (Colombo, RPS) 2022-23. T20 HS 90. T20 BB 2-32.

LANGRIDGE, James Thomas (Queen's C; Malvern C), b Plymouth, Devon 3 Nov 2005. LHB, LFM. Somerset 2nd XI debut 2022. Awaiting f-c debut. LO HS 6 v Glos (Bristol) 2023 (MBC). LO BB 1-17 v Sussex (Taunton) 2023 (MBC).

LEACH, Matthew **Jack** (Bishop Fox's Community S, Taunton; Richard Huish C; UWIC), b Taunton 22 Jun 1991. 6'0". LHB, SLA. Squad No 17. Cardiff MCCU 2012. Somerset debut 2012; cap 2017. MCC 2017. Dorset 2011. **ECB Central Contract 2023-24. Tests**: 36 (2017-18 to 2023-24); HS 92 v Ire (Lord's) 2019; BB 5-66 (10-166 match) v NZ (Leeds) 2022. F-c Tours: A 2021-22; WI 2017-18 (EL), 2021-22; NZ 2017-18, 2019-20, 2022-23; I 2020-21, 2023-24; P 2022-23; SL 2016-17 (EL), 2018-19, 2019-20, 2020-21; UAE 2016-17 (v Afg)(EL). HS 92 (*see Tests*). Sm HS 66 v Lancs (Manchester) 2018. 50 wkts (2); most – 68 (2016). BB 8-85 (10-112 match) v Essex (Taunton) 2018. LO HS 18 v Surrey (Oval) 2014 (RLC). LO BB 3-7 EL v UAE (Dubai, DSC) 2016-17. T20 BB 3-28.

LEONARD, Edward Owen ('**Ned**') (Millfield S), b Hammersmith, Middx 15 Aug 2002. RHB, RMF. Squad No 19. Debut (Somerset) 2021. Somerset 2nd XI debut 2018. HS 8 v Hants (Southampton) 2022. BB 1-68 v Lancs (Taunton) 2021. LO HS 32 v Northants (Northampton) 2023 (MBC). LO BB 3-40 v Derbys (Derby) 2023 (MBC). T20 BB 1-8.

OGBORNE, Alfie Richard James (Ansford Ac; Richard Huish C), b Yeovil 15 Jul 2003. RHB, LFM. Squad No 3. Debut (Somerset) 2023. Somerset 2nd XI debut 2021. HS 2 and BB 2-56 v Hants (Taunton) 2023. LO HS 27* v Sussex (Taunton) 2022 (RLC). LO BB 3-49 v Leics (Leicester) 2022 (RLC).

OVERTON, Craig (West Buckland S), b Barnstaple, Devon 10 Apr 1994. Twin brother of Jamie Overton (*see SURREY*). 6'5". RHB, RMF. Squad No 7. Debut (Somerset) 2012; cap 2016. MCC 2017. Southern Brave 2021 to date. Devon 2010-11. **Tests**: 8 (2017-18 to 2021-22); HS 41* v A (Adelaide) 2017-18; BB 3-14 v I (Leeds) 2021. **LOI**: 7 (2018 to 2022); HS 32 v I (Manchester) 2022; BB 2-23 v P (Cardiff) 2021. F-c Tours: A 2017-18, 2019-20 (EL); WI 2021-22; NZ 2017-18. HS 138 v Hants (Taunton) 2016. BB 7-57 (13-87 match) v Essex (Taunton) 2022. LO HS 66* and LO BB 5-18 v Kent (Taunton) 2019 (RLC). T20 HS 35*. T20 BB 4-25.

NQ**RENSHAW, Matt**hew Thomas, b Middlesbrough, Yorks 28 Mar 1996. 6'0". LHB, OB. Queensland 2014-15 to date. Somerset debut 2018; cap 2022. Kent 2019. Big Bash: BH 2017-18 to date; AS 2020-21 to 2021-22. **Tests** (A): 14 (2016-17 to 2022-23); HS 184 v P (Sydney) 2016-17; BB –. F-c Tours (A): SA 2017-18; I 2016-17, 2018-19 (Aus A), 2022-23; B 2017; UAE 2018-19 (v P). HS 200* Q v NSW (Sydney, DO) 2022-23. Sm HS 146 v Essex (Chelmsford) 2022. BB 3-29 v Lancs (Southport) 2022. LO HS 156* Q v SA (Adelaide) 2021-22. LO BB 2-17 v Surrey (Oval) 2019 (RLC). T20 HS 90*. T20 BB 1-2.

REW, James Edward Kenneth (King's C, Taunton), b Lambeth, London 11 Jan 2004. LHB, WK. Squad No 55. Debut County Select XI 2021. Somerset debut 2022. Somerset 2nd XI debut 2019. YC 2023. F-c Tour (EL): I 2023-24. 1000 runs (1): 1086 (2023). HS 221 v Hants (Taunton) 2023. LO HS 114 v Middx (Taunton) 2022 (RLC). T20 HS 47.

SMEED, William Conrad Francis (King's C, Taunton), b Cambridge 26 Oct 2001. RHB, OB. Squad No 23. Somerset debut 2020 (T20 only). Birmingham Phoenix 2021 to date. Somerset 2nd XI debut 2017. Awaiting f-c debut. LO HS 0 EL v South Africans (Worcester) 2022. T20 HS 101*.

‡NQ**SUTHERLAND, Will**iam James, b East Melbourne, Australia 27 Oct 1999. Son of J.A.Sutherland (Victoria 1990-91 to 1992-93); elder brother of A.J.Sutherland (Australia women 2019-20 to date). RHB, RFM. Victoria 2019-20 to date. Big Bash: MR 2018-19 to date. **LOI** (A): 2 (2023-24); HS 18 and BB 2-28 v WI (Sydney) 2023-24. HS 100 Vic v SA (Adelaide, KR) 2022-23. BB 6-67 Vic v SA (Adelaide) 2019-20. LO HS 66 Vic v Q (Melbourne, St K) 2019-20. LO BB 5-45 Vic v Q (Townsville) 2018-19. T20 HS 51*. T20 BB 3-30.

THOMAS, George William (King's C, Taunton), b Musgrove, Taunton 14 Nov 2003. RHB, RM. Elder brother of J.F.Thomas (*see below*). Squad No 46. Somerset 2nd XI debut 2021. Awaiting f-c debut. LO HS 75 v Leics (Taunton) 2021 (RLC). LO BB 2-42 v Durham (Gosforth) 2023 (MBC).

THOMAS, Joshua Frederick (King's C, Taunton), b Musgrove, Taunton 11 Jan 2005. Younger brother of G.W.Thomas (*see above*). LHB, SLA. Somerset 2nd XI debut 2021. Awaiting f-c debut. LO HS 22 v Glos (Bristol) 2023 (MBC). LO BB 3-40 v Durham (Gosforth) 2023 (MBC).

NQ**UMEED, Andrew** Robert Isaac (High School of Glasgow), b Glasgow 19 Apr 1996. 6'1". RHB, LB. Squad No 1. Scotland 2015. Warwickshire 2016-17, scoring 101 v Durham (Birmingham) on debut. Somerset debut 2022. **LOI** (Scot): 1 (2023-24); HS 8 v Canada (Dubai, DSC) 2023-24. HS 113 Wa v Lancs (Birmingham) 2017. Sm HS 49 v Kent (Taunton) 2023. BB 1-19 Wa v Lancs (Manchester) 2017. LO HS 172* v Derbys (Derby) 2023 (MBC).

NQ**VAN DER MERWE, Roelof** Erasmus (Pretoria HS), b Johannesburg, South Africa 31 Dec 1984. RHB, SLA. Squad No 52. Northerns 2006-07 to 2013-14. Titans 2007-08 to 2014-15. Netherlands 2015 to 2017-18. Somerset debut 2016; cap 2018. IPL: RCB 2009 to 2009-10; DD 2011-13. Big Bash: BH 2011-12. London Spirit 2021. Northern Superchargers 2022. Welsh Fire 2023. **LOI** (SA/Neth): 27 (13 for SA 2008-09 to 2010; 14 for Neth 2019 to 2023-24); HS 57 v Z (Deventer) 2019; BB 3-27 v Z (Centurion) 2009-10. **IT20** (SA/Neth): 57 (13 for SA 2008-09 to 2010; 44 for Neth 2015 to 2023-24); HS 75* v Z (Rotterdam) 2019; BB 4-35 v Z (Rotterdam) 2019 – separate matches. HS 205* Titans v Warriors (Benoni) 2014-15. Sm HS 102* v Hants (Taunton) 2016. BB 5-174 v Lancs (Southport) 2022. LO HS 165* v Surrey (Taunton) 2017 (RLC). LO BB 5-26 Titans v Knights (Centurion) 2012-13. T20 HS 89*. T20 BB 6-20.

RELEASED/RETIRED

(Having made a County 1st XI appearance in 2023)

BANCROFT, C.T. – *see GLOUCESTERSHIRE.*

BARTLETT, G.A. – *see NORTHAMPTONSHIRE.*

BROOKS, Jack Alexander (Wheatley Park S), b Oxford 4 Jun 1984. 6'2". RHB, RFM. Northamptonshire 2009-12; cap 2012. Yorkshire 2013-18; cap 2013. Somerset 2019-23. Sussex 2022 (on loan). Worcestershire 2023 (on loan). Oxfordshire 2004-09. F-c Tour (EL): SA 2014-15. HS 109* Y v Lancs (Manchester) 2017. Sm HS 72 v Glamorgan (Taunton) 2020. 50 wkts (4); most – 71 (2014). BB 6-65 Y v Middx (Lord's) 2016. Sm BB 5-33 v Surrey (Guildford) 2019. LO HS 28 v Sussex (Taunton) 2022 (RLC). LO BB 4-38 v Warwks (Birmingham) 2022 (RLC). T20 HS 33*. T20 BB 5-21.

CAMPHER, C. – *see IRELAND.*

DAVIES, Steven Michael (King Charles I S, Kidderminster), b Bromsgrove, Worcs 17 Jun 1986. 5'10". LHB, WK. Worcestershire 2005-09. Surrey 2010-16; cap 2011. Somerset 2017-23; cap 2017. MCC 2006-07, 2011. **LOI**: 8 (2009-10 to 2010-11); HS 87 v P (Chester-le-St) 2010. **IT20**: 5 (2008-09 to 2010-11); HS 33 v P (Cardiff) 2010. F-c Tours: A 2010-11; B 2006-07 (Eng A); UAE 2011-12 (v P). 1000 runs (6); most – 1147 (2016). HS 200* Sy v Glamorgan (Cardiff) 2015. Sm HS 142 v Surrey (Taunton) 2017. LO HS 127* Sy v Hants (Oval) 2013 (Y40). T20 HS 99*.

NQ**HENRY, Matt**hew James (St Bede's C), b Christchurch, New Zealand 14 Dec 1991. RHB, RFM. Canterbury 2010-11 to date. Worcestershire 2016. Kent 2018-22; cap 2018. Somerset 2023; cap 2023. Derbyshire 2017 (T20 only). IPL: KXIP 2017. Welsh Fire 2023. **Tests** (NZ): 25 (2015 to 2023-24); HS 72 v SL (Christchurch) 2022-23; BB 7-23 v SA (Christchurch) 2021-22. **LOI** (NZ): 82 (2013-14 to 2023-24); HS 48* v P (Wellington) 2015-16; BB 5-30 v P (Abu Dhabi) 2014-15. **IT20** (NZ): 17 (2014-15 to 2023-24); HS 10 v

P (Auckland) 2015-16; BB 3-32 v P (Lahore) 2022-23. F-c Tours (NZ): E 2014 (NZA), 2015, 2021, 2022; A 2015-16, 2019-20; I 2016-17, 2017-18 (NZA); P 2022-23; SL 2013-14 (NZA). HS 81 K v Derbys (Derby) 2018. Sm HS 50* v Lancs (Manchester) 2023. 50 wkts (1): 75 (2018). BB 7-23 (*see Tests*). CC BB 7-42 (11-114 match) K v Northants (Canterbury) 2018. Sm BB 6-59 v Notts (Taunton) 2023. LO HS 48* (*see LOI*). LO BB 6-45 Canterbury v Auckland (Auckland) 2012-13. T20 HS 44. T20 BB 4-24.

NQ**SIDDLE, Peter** Matthew, b Traralgon, Victoria, Australia 25 Nov 1984. 6'1½". RHB, RFM. Victoria 2005-06 to date. Nottinghamshire 2014; cap 2014. Lancashire 2015. Essex 2018-21; cap 2021. Tasmania 2020-21 to 2022-23. Somerset 2022-23; cap 2022. Big Bash: MR 2013-14 to date; AS 2017-18 to 2022-23. **Tests** (A): 67 (2008-09 to 2019); HS 51 v I (Delhi) 2012-13; BB 6-54 v E (Brisbane) 2010-11. **LOI** (A): 20 (2008-09 to 2018-19); HS 10* v I (Melbourne) 2018-19; BB 3-55 v E (Centurion) 2009-10. **IT20** (A): 2 (2008-09 to 2010-11); HS 1* and BB 2-24 v NZ (Sydney) 2008-09. F-c Tours (A): E 2009, 2013, 2015, 2019; SA 2008-09, 2011-12, 2013-14; WI 2011-12; NZ 2015-16; I 2008-09 (Aus A), 2008-09, 2012-13; SL 2011; Z 2011 (Aus A); UAE 2014-15 (v P), 2018-19 (v P). HS 103* Aus A v Scotland (Edinburgh) 2013. CC HS 89 La v Northants (Northampton) 2015. Sm HS 42 v Surrey (Taunton) 2022. 50 wkts (0+1): 54 (2011-12). BB 8-54 Vic v SA (Adelaide) 2014-15. CC BB 6-38 Ex v Warwks (Chelmsford) 2021. Sm BB 6-51 v Surrey (Oval) 2022. LO HS 62 Vic v Q (Sydney, NS) 2017-18. LO BB 4-22 Tas v Vic (Hobart) 2021-22. T20 HS 11*. T20 BB 5-16.

NQ**SODHI**, Inderbir Singh ('**Ish**'), b Ludhiana, Punjab, India 31 Oct 1992. RHB, LBG. Northern Districts 2012-13 to 2021-22. Worcestershire 2021. Canterbury 2022-23 to date. Nottinghamshire 2017-18 (T20 only). Somerset 2023 (T20 only). IPL: RR 2018-19. Big Bash: AS 2016-17. Welsh Fire 2022. Trent Rockets 2023. **Tests** (NZ): 20 (2013-14 to 2023-24); HS 65 and BB 6-86 v P (Karachi) 2022-23. **LOI** (NZ): 51 (2015 to 2023-24); HS 35 and BB 6-39 v B (Mirpur) 2023. **IT20** (NZ): 111 (2014 to 2023-24); HS 19 v Neth (The Hague) 2022; BB 4-28 v A (Christchurch) 2020-21, 4-28 v B (Hamilton) 2020-21 and 4-28 v Scot (Edinburgh) 2022. F-c Tours (NZ): WI 2014; I 2013-14, 2016-17, 2017-18 (NZ A); P 2022-23; SL 2013-14 (NZ A); Z 2016; B 2013-14, 2023-24; UAE 2014-15 (v P), 2018-19 (v P). HS 82* ND v Otago (Dunedin) 2014-15. CC HS 13 and CC BB 6-89 Wo v Warwks (Worcester) 2021. BB 7-30 (12-62 match) ND v Wellington (Wellington) 2017-18. LO HS 48* Cant v ND (Whangarei) 2022-23. LO BB 6-39 (*see LOI*). T20 HS 51. T20 BB 6-11.

NQ**WAGNER, Neil**, b Pretoria, South Africa 13 Mar 1986. LHB, LMF. Northerns 2005-06 to 2007-08. Titans 2006-07 to 2007-08. Otago 2008-09 to 2017-18. Northamptonshire 2014. Lancashire 2016. Essex 2017-18. Northern Districts 2018-19 to date. Somerset 2023. **Tests** (NZ): 64 (2012 to 2023-24); HS 66* v WI (Wellington) 2020-21; BB 7-39 v WI (Wellington) 2017-18. F-c Tours (NZ): E 2013, 2015, 2021, 2022; A 2019-20; SA 2012-13, 2016; WI 2012, 2014; I 2016-17; P 2022-23; Z 2007 (SA Acad), 2016; B 2013-14; UAE 2018-19 (v P). HS 72 and Sm BB 3-67 v Warwks (Birmingham) 2023. 50 wkts (0+2); most – 51 (2010-11, 2012-13). BB 7-39 (*see Tests*). CC BB 6-48 Ex v Somerset (Taunton) 2017. LO HS 45* ND v Wellington (Whangarei) 2022-23. LO BB 5-31 ND v Auckland (Hamilton) 2022-23. T20 HS 36. T20 BB 4-33.

SOMERSET 2023

RESULTS SUMMARY

	Place	*Won*	*Lost*	*Drew*
LV= Insurance County Champ (Div 1)	7th	3	4	7
Metro Bank One-Day Cup (Group B)	7th	3	5	
Vitality Blast (South Group)	**Winners**	15	2	

LV= INSURANCE COUNTY CHAMPIONSHIP AVERAGES
BATTING AND FIELDING

Cap		*M*	*I*	*NO*	*HS*	*Runs*	*Avge*	*100*	*50*	*Ct/St*
	J.E.K.Rew	14	22	3	221	1086	57.15	5	2	40/2
	K.L.Aldridge	8	13	2	101*	451	41.00	1	3	6
	T.Kohler-Cadmore	12	20	1	130	735	38.68	1	4	8
	A.R.I.Umeed	4	6	1	49	160	32.00	–	–	4
2017	M.J.Leach	6	7	3	40*	126	31.50	–	–	3
2015	L.Gregory	9	12	1	65	343	31.18	–	1	3
2018	T.B.Abell	13	21	1	151	622	31.10	1	2	11
	G.A.Bartlett	8	13	–	134	395	30.38	2	1	–
	T.A.Lammonby	14	24	2	109	657	29.86	1	4	14
2021	J.H.Davey	7	9	1	60	218	27.25	–	1	–
	S.R.Dickson	11	20	2	82*	410	22.77	–	3	6
2016	C.Overton	9	14	3	70*	249	22.63	–	1	15
2023	M.J.Henry	6	9	2	50*	149	21.28	–	1	2
	C.T.Bancroft	4	7	–	44	137	19.57	–	–	3
	B.G.F.Green	2	4	1	31*	52	17.33	–	–	–
2022	P.M.Siddle	5	6	2	17	57	14.25	–	–	–
	S.Bashir	6	9	4	44*	71	14.20	–	–	2
	J.A.Brooks	5	5	2	19	37	12.33	–	–	–

Also batted: T.Banton (2 matches) 4 (1 ct); D.M.Bess (1) 54; S.M.Davies (2 – cap 2017) 4, 9, 0 (7 ct); L.P.Goldsworthy (2) 122, 1, 8 (3 ct); A.R.J.Ogborne (1) 2 (1 ct); N.Wagner (3) 13, 4, 72 (1 ct).

BOWLING

	O	*M*	*R*	*W*	*Avge*	*Best*	*5wI*	*10wM*
M.J.Henry	173.1	42	518	32	16.18	6- 59	4	–
L.Gregory	208.1	41	733	34	21.55	7- 84	1	1
P.M.Siddle	139	31	386	16	24.12	3- 34	–	–
J.A.Brooks	106.2	29	331	12	27.58	5- 56	1	–
M.J.Leach	154.1	27	532	18	29.55	4-119	–	–
C.Overton	249.5	55	788	26	30.30	5- 46	1	–
J.H.Davey	127	21	473	15	31.53	4- 17	–	–
K.L.Aldridge	161.1	28	758	16	47.37	4- 36	–	–
S.Bashir	203	50	670	10	67.00	3- 67	–	–
Also bowled:								
N.Wagner	70	18	236	7	33.71	3- 67	–	–

T.B.Abell 32-3-131-4; T.Banton 1-1-0-0; G.A.Bartlett 2-0-13-0; D.M.Bess 42.2-21-76-2; S.R.Dickson 0.3-0-1-0; L.P.Goldsworthy 10-1-34-0; B.G.F.Green 46.2-10-133-4; T.A.Lammonby 4-0-34-0; A.R.J.Ogborne 28-3-89-3; A.R.I.Umeed 10-0-37-0.

Somerset played no first-class fixtures outside the County Championship in 2023. The First-Class Averages (pp 223–235) give the records of Somerset players in all first-class county matches, with the exception of D.M.Bess, J.A.Brooks, J.H.Davey and M.J.Leach, whose first-class figures for Somerset are as above.

SOMERSET RECORDS

FIRST-CLASS CRICKET

Highest Total	For 850-7d		v	Middlesex	Taunton	2007
	V 811		by	Surrey	The Oval	1899
Lowest Total	For 25		v	Glos	Bristol	1947
	V 22		by	Glos	Bristol	1920
Highest Innings	For 342	J.L.Langer	v	Surrey	Guildford	2006
	V 424	A.C.MacLaren	for	Lancashire	Taunton	1895

Highest Partnership for each Wicket

1st	346	L.C.H.Palairet/H.T.Hewett	v	Yorkshire	Taunton	1892
2nd	450	N.R.D.Compton/J.C.Hildreth	v	Cardiff MCCU	Taunton Vale	2012
3rd	319	P.M.Roebuck/M.D.Crowe	v	Leics	Taunton	1984
4th	310	P.W.Denning/I.T.Botham	v	Glos	Taunton	1980
5th	320	J.D.Francis/I.D.Blackwell	v	Durham UCCE	Taunton	2005
6th	265	W.E.Alley/K.E.Palmer	v	Northants	Northampton	1961
7th	279	R.J.Harden/G.D.Rose	v	Sussex	Taunton	1997
8th	236	P.D.Trego/R.C.Davies	v	Lancashire	Manchester	2016
9th	183	C.H.M.Greetham/H.W.Stephenson	v	Leics	Weston-s-Mare	1963
	183	C.J.Tavaré/N.A.Mallender	v	Sussex	Hove	1990
10th	163	I.D.Blackwell/N.A.M.McLean	v	Derbyshire	Taunton	2003

Best Bowling	For	10-49	E.J.Tyler	v	Surrey	Taunton	1895
(Innings)	V	10-35	A.Drake	for	Yorkshire	Weston-s-Mare	1914
Best Bowling	For	16-83	J.C.White	v	Worcs	Bath	1919
(Match)	V	17-86	K.J.Abbott	for	Hampshire	Southampton[2]	2019

Most Runs – Season	2761	W.E.Alley	(av 58.74)	1961
Most Runs – Career	21142	H.Gimblett	(av 36.96)	1935-54
Most 100s – Season	11	S.J.Cook		1991
Most 100s – Career	52	M.E.Trescothick		1993-2019
Most Wkts – Season	169	A.W.Wellard	(av 19.24)	1938
Most Wkts – Career	2165	J.C.White	(av 18.03)	1909-37
Most Career W-K Dismissals	1007	H.W.Stephenson	(698 ct; 309 st)	1948-64
Most Career Catches in the Field	443	M.E.Trescothick		1993-2019

LIMITED-OVERS CRICKET

Highest Total	**50ov**	413-4		v	Devon	Torquay	1990
	40ov	377-9		v	Sussex	Hove	2003
	T20	265-5		v	Derbyshire	Taunton	2022
Lowest Total	**50ov**	58		v	Middlesex	Southgate	2000
	40ov	58		v	Essex	Chelmsford	1977
	T20	82		v	Kent	Taunton	2010
Highest Innings	**50ov**	177	S.J.Cook	v	Sussex	Hove	1990
	40ov	184	M.E.Trescothick	v	Glos	Taunton	2008
	T20	151*	C.H.Gayle	v	Kent	Taunton	2015
Best Bowling	**50ov**	8-66	S.R.G.Francis	v	Derbyshire	Derby	2004
	40ov	6-16	Abdur Rehman	v	Notts	Taunton	2012
	T20	6- 5	A.V.Suppiah	v	Glamorgan	Cardiff	2011

SURREY

Formation of Present Club: 22 August 1845
Inaugural First-Class Match: 1864
Colours: Chocolate
Badge: Prince of Wales' Feathers
County Champions (since 1890): (21) 1890, 1891, 1892, 1894, 1895, 1899, 1914, 1952, 1953, 1954, 1955, 1956, 1957, 1958, 1971, 1999, 2000, 2002, 2018, 2022, 2023
Joint Champions: (1) 1950
NatWest Trophy Winners: (1) 1982
Benson and Hedges Cup Winners: (3) 1974, 1997, 2001
Pro 40/National League (Div 1) Winners: (1) 2003
Sunday League Winners: (1) 1996
Clydesdale Bank 40 Winners: (1) 2011
Twenty20 Cup Winners: (1) 2003

Chief Executive: Steve Elworthy, The Kia Oval, London, SE11 5SS • Tel: 0203 946 0100 • Email: enquiries@surreycricket.com • Web: www.kiaoval.com • Twitter: @surreycricket (120,307 followers)

Director of Cricket: Alec Stewart. **Head Coach**: Gareth Batty. **Assistant Coaches**: Azhar Mahmood, Jade Dernbach and Jim Troughton. **Captains**: R.J.Burns (f-c & L-o) and C.J.Jordan (T20). **Overseas Players**: S.A.Abbott, A.M.Hardie and K.A.J.Roach. **2023 Testimonial**: None. **Head Groundsman**: Lee Fortiss. **Scorer**: Debbie Beesley. ‡ New registration. [NQ] Not qualified for England.

[NQ]**ABBOTT, Sean** Anthony, b Windsor, NSW, Australia 29 Feb 1992. 6'1". RHB, RMF. Squad No 77. New South Wales 2011-12 to date. Surrey debut 2021. IPL: RCB 2015; SH 2022. Big Bash: ST 2011-12 to 2012-13; SS 2013-14 to date. Manchester Originals 2022. **LOI** (A): 21 (2014-15 to 2023-24); HS 69 v WI (Sydney) 2023-24; BB 3-23 v I (Visakhapatnam) 2022-23. **IT20** (A): 15 (2014-15 to 2023-24); HS 12* v I (Canberra) 2020-21; BB 4-31 v SA (Durban) 2023. F-c Tour (Aus A): I 2015. HS 102* NSW v Tas (Adelaide) 2020-21. Sy HS 87* v Lancs (Oval) 2023. BB 7-45 NSW v Tas (Hobart) 2018-19. Sy BB 5-50 v Lancs (Manchester) 2023. LO HS 69 (*see LOI*). LO BB 5-43 NSW v Tas (Sydney, NS) 2018-19. T20 HS 110*. T20 BB 5-16.

ATKINSON, Angus (**'Gus'**) Alexander Patrick (Bradfield C), b Chelsea, Middx 19 Jan 1998. 6'2". RHB, RF. Squad No 37. Debut (Surrey) 2020. Oval Invincibles 2023. **ECB Two-Year Central Contract from 2023-24. LOI**: 9 (2023 to 2023-24): HS 35 v SA (Mumbai) 2023-24; BB 2-28 v WI (North Sound) 2023-24. **IT20**: 3 (2023 to 2023-24); HS 8* v NZ (Birmingham) 2023; BB 4-20 v NZ (Manchester) 2023 – on debut. HS 91 v SL Dev (Guildford) 2022. CC HS 66 v Northants (Oval) 2022. BB 6-68 v Essex (Chelmsford) 2023. LO HS 35 (*see LOI*). LO BB 4-43 v Yorks (Scarborough) 2021 (RLC). T20 HS 14. T20 BB 4-20.

BARNWELL, Nathan André (Caterham S), b Ashford, Kent 3 Feb 2003. 6'0". RHB, RFM. Squad No 29. Debut (Surrey) 2022. Surrey 2nd XI debut 2018. HS 22 and BB 1-68 v SL Dev (Guildford) 2022. LO HS 31 v Middx (Radlett) 2022 (RLC). No 1st XI appearances in 2023.

BLAKE, Joshua William (Trinity S, Croydon), b Carshalton 18 Sep 1998. 6'0". RHB, WK, occ LBG. Squad No 18. Awaiting f-c debut. LO HS 44 v Leics (Guildford) 2022 (RLC).

BURNS, Rory Joseph (City of London Freemen's S), b Epsom 26 Aug 1990. 5'10". LHB, WK, occ RM. Squad No 17. Debut (Surrey) 2011; cap 2014; captain 2018 to date. MCC 2016. MCC Univs 2010. *Wisden* 2018. **Tests**: 32 (2018-19 to 2021-22); HS 133 v A (Birmingham) 2019. F-c Tours: A 2021-22; SA 2019-20; WI 2018-19; NZ 2019-20; I 2020-21; SL 2018-19. 1000 runs (7); most – 1402 (2018). HS 219* v Hants (Oval) 2017. BB 1-18 v Middx (Lord's) 2013. LO HS 95 v Glos (Bristol) 2015 (RLC). T20 HS 56*.

CLARK, Jordan (Sedbergh S), b Whitehaven, Cumbria 14 Oct 1990. Elder brother of G.Clark (*see DURHAM*). 6'4". RHB, RMF, occ WK. Squad No 16. Lancashire 2015-18. Surrey debut 2019; cap 2022. Big Bash: HH 2018-19. Oval Invincibles 2021. HS 140 La v Surrey (Oval) 2017. Sy HS 137 v Glos (Bristol) 2022, sharing Sy record 8th wkt partnership of 244 with J.L.Smith. BB 6-21 v Hants (Oval) 2021. Hat-trick La v Yorks (Manchester) 2018, dismissing J.E.Root, K.S.Williamson and J.M.Bairstow. LO HS 79* and LO BB 4-34 La v Worcs (Manchester) 2017 (RLC). T20 HS 60. T20 BB 4-22.

CURRAN, Samuel Matthew (Wellington C), b Northampton 3 Jun 1998. Son of K.M.Curran (Glos, Natal, Northants, Boland and Zimbabwe 1980-81 to 1999), grandson of K.P.Curran (Rhodesia 1947-48 to 1954-55), younger brother of T.K.Curran (*see below*) and B.J.Curran (Northamptonshire, Southern Rocks and Rhinos 2018 to date). 5'9". LHB, LMF. Squad No 58. Debut (Surrey) 2015, taking 5-101 v Kent (Oval); cap 2018. IPL: KXIP 2019; CSK 2020-21 to 2021; PK 2023. Oval Invincibles 2021 to date. YC 2018. *Wisden* 2018. **ECB Two-Year Central Contract from 2023-24. Tests**: 24 (2018 to 2021); HS 78 v I (Southampton) 2018; BB 4-58 v SA (Centurion) 2019-20. **LOI**: 32 (2018 to 2023-24); HS 95* v I (Pune) 2020-21; BB 5-48 v SL (Oval) 2021. **IT20**: 46 (2019-20 to 2023-24); HS 50 v WI (St George's) 2023-24; BB 5-10 v Afg (Perth) 2022-23 – E record. F-c Tours: SA 2019-20; WI 2018-19; NZ 2019-20; SL 2016-17 (EL), 2018-19, 2019-20, 2020-21; UAE 2016-17 (v Afg)(EL). HS 126 v Kent (Oval) 2022. BB 7-58 v Durham (Chester-le-St) 2016. LO HS 95* (*see LOI*). LO BB 5-48 (*see LOI*). T20 HS 72*. T20 BB 5-10.

CURRAN, Thomas Kevin (Hilton C, Durban), b Cape Town, South Africa 12 Mar 1995. Son of K.M.Curran (Glos, Natal, Northants, Boland and Zimbabwe 1980-81 to 1999), grandson of K.P.Curran (Rhodesia 1947-48 to 1954-55), elder brother of S.M.Curran (*see above*) and B.J.Curran (Northamptonshire, Southern Rocks and Rhinos 2018 to date). 6'0". RHB, RFM. Squad No 59. Debut (Surrey) 2014; cap 2016. IPL: KKR 2018; RR 2020-21; DC 2021. Big Bash: SS 2018-19 to date. Oval Invincibles 2021 to date. **Tests**: 2 (2017-18); HS 39 v A (Sydney) 2017-18; BB 1-65 v A (Melbourne) 2017-18. **LOI**: 28 (2017 to 2021); HS 47* v Ire (Dublin) 2019; BB 5-35 v A (Perth) 2017-18. **IT20**: 30 (2017 to 2021); HS 14* v NZ (Nelson) 2019-20; BB 4-36 v WI (Gros Islet) 2018-19. F-c Tours: A 2017-18; SL 2016-17 (EL); UAE 2016-17 (v Afg)(EL). HS 115 v Northants (Northampton) 2022. 50 wkts (1): 76 (2015). BB 7-20 v Glos (Oval) 2015. LO HS 47* (*see LOI*). LO BB 5-16 EL v UAE (Dubai, DSC) 2016-17. T20 HS 67*. T20 BB 4-22.

DUNN, Matthew Peter (Bearwood C, Wokingham), b Egham 5 May 1992. 6'1". LHB, RFM. Squad No 4. Debut (Surrey) 2010. MCC 2015. HS 31* v Kent (Guildford) 2014. BB 5-43 v Somerset (Guildford) 2019. LO HS 34 v Warwks (Oval) 2022 (RLC). LO BB 2-32 Eng Dev XI v Sri Lanka A (Manchester) 2011. T20 HS 2. BB 3-8.

EALHAM, Tommy Mark (Cranleigh S), b Guildford 26 Mar 2004. Son of M.A.Ealham (Kent, Nottinghamshire & England 1989 to 2009); grandson of A.G.E.Ealham (Kent 1966-82); nephew of S.C.Willis (Kent 1993-99). 5'9". LHB, OB. Squad No 5. Surrey 2nd XI debut 2022. Awaiting f-c debut. LO HS 5 v Essex (Chelmsford) 2023 (MBC).

EVANS, Laurie John (Whitgift S; The John Fisher S; St Mary's C, Durham U), b Lambeth, London 12 Oct 1987. 6'0". RHB, RM. Squad No 10. Durham UCCE 2007. Surrey debut 2009; signed white-ball contract in 2022. Warwickshire 2010-16. Northamptonshire 2016 (on loan). Sussex 2017-19. MCC 2007. Big Bash: PS 2021-22 to date. Oval Invincibles 2021. Manchester Originals 2022 to date. HS 213* and BB 1-29 Wa v Sussex (Birmingham) 2015, sharing Wa 6th wkt record partnership of 327 with T.R.Ambrose. Sy HS 98 and Sy BB 1-30 v Bangladeshis (Oval) 2010. LO HS 134* Sx v Kent (Canterbury) 2017 (RLC). LO BB 1-29 Sx v Middx (Lord's) 2019 (RLC). T20 HS 118*. T20 BB 1-5.

FOAKES, Benjamin Thomas (Tendring TC), b Colchester, Essex 15 Feb 1993. 6'1". RHB, WK. Squad No 7. Essex 2011-14. Surrey debut 2015; cap 2016. MCC 2016. **ECB Central Contract 2023-24. Tests**: 25 (2018-19 to 2023-24); HS 113* v SA (Manchester) 2022; made 107 v SL (Galle) 2018-19 on debut. **LOI**: 1 (2019); HS 61* v Ire (Dublin) 2019. **IT20**: 1 (2019) did not bat. F-c Tours: WI 2017-18 (EL), 2018-19, 2021-22; NZ 2022-23; I 2020-21, 2023-24; P 2022-23; SL 2013-14 (EL), 2016-17 (EL), 2018-19; UAE 2016-17 (v Afg)(EL). HS 141* v Hants (Southampton) 2016. LO HS 106 v Leics (Oval) 2023 (MBC). T20 HS 75*.

GEDDES, Benedict Brodie Albert (St John's S, Leatherhead), b Epsom 31 Jul 2001. 6'1". RHB. Squad No 14. Debut (Surrey) 2021. Kent 2023 (on loan). Surrey 2nd XI debut 2019. HS 124 v Kent (Oval) 2022. LO HS 92 v Yorks (York) 2023 (MBC). T20 HS 28.

NQ**HARDIE, Aaron** Mark, b Bournemouth, Dorset 7 Jan 1999. 6'3". RHB, RM. Squad No 15. W Australia 2018-19 to date. Surrey debut 2022. Big Bash: PS 2018-19 to date. **LOI** (A): 4 (2023 to 2023-24); HS 26 v WI (Sydney) 2023-24; BB 2-62 v SA (Bloemfontein) 2023. **IT20** (A): 7 (2023 to 2023-24); HS 23 v SA (Durban) 2023; BB 1-20 v I (Raipur) 2023-24. F-c Tour (Aus A): NZ 2022-232; SL 2022. HS 174* WA v Vic (Perth) 2021-22. BB 4-24 WA v Vic (Perth) 2021-22 – separate matches. Sy HS 46 and Sy BB 1-19 v Yorks (Scarborough) 2022. LO HS 58 Aus A v Sri Lanka A (Colombo, SSC) 2022. LO BB 3-28 WA v Vic (Melbourne, SK) 2021-22. T20 HS 90*. T20 BB 3-31.

JACKS, William George (St George's C, Weybridge), b Chertsey 21 Nov 1998. 6'1". RHB, OB. Squad No 9. Debut (Surrey) 2018; cap 2022. Big Bash: HH 2020-21. Oval Invincibles 2021 to date. **Tests**: 2 (2022-23); HS 31 v P (Multan) 2022-23; BB 6-161 v P (Rawalpindi) 2022-23. **LOI**: 7 (2022-23 to 2023-24); HS 94 v Ire (Nottingham) 2023; BB 3-22 v WI (Bridgetown) 2023-24. **IT20**: 11 (2022-23 to 2023-24); HS 40 v P (Karachi) 2022-23; BB 1-5 v NZ (Manchester) 2023. F-c Tours: I 2018-19 (EL); P 2022-23. HS 150* v Essex (Oval) 2022. BB 6-161 (*see Tests*). Sy BB 5-87 v Hants (Southampton) 2023. LO HS 121 v Glos (Oval) 2018 (RLC). LO BB 3-22 (*see LOI*). T20 HS 108*. T20 BB 4-15.

JORDAN, Christopher James (Comber Mere S, Barbados; Dulwich C), b Christ Church, Barbados 4 Oct 1988. 6'1". RHB, RFM. Squad No 34. Debut (Surrey) 2007; returned in 2022 as T20 captain. Barbados 2011-12 to 2012-13. Sussex 2013-19; cap 2014. IPL: RCB 2016; SH 2017-18; KXIP 2020-21; PK 2021; CSK 2022; MI 2023. Big Bash: AS 2016-17; ST 2018-19; PS 2019-20; SS 2021-22 to 2022-23; HH 2023-24. Southern Brave 2021 to date. **Tests**: 8 (2014 to 2014-15); HS 35 v SL (Lord's) 2014; BB 4-18 v I (Oval) 2014. **LOI**: 35 (2013 to 2023); HS 38* v SL (Oval) 2014; BB 5-29 v SL (Manchester) 2014. **IT20**: 88 (2013-14 to 2022-23); HS 36 v NZ (Wellington) 2019-20; BB 4-6 v WI (Basseterre) 2018-19. F-c Tour: WI 2014-15. HS 166 Sx v Northants (Northampton) 2019. Sy HS 79* and Sy BB 4-57 v Essex (Chelmsford) 2011. 50 wkts (1): 61 (2013). BB 7-43 Barbados v CC&C (Bridgetown) 2012-13. CC BB 6-48 Sx v Yorks (Leeds) 2013. LO HS 55 Sx v Surrey (Guildford) 2016 (RLC). LO BB 5-28 Sx v Middx (Hove) 2016 (RLC). T20 HS 73. T20 BB 4-6.

LAWES, Thomas Edward (Cranleigh S), b Singapore 25 Dec 2002. 6'0". RHB, RMF. Squad No 30. Debut (Surrey) 2022. Surrey 2nd XI debut 2021. F-c Tour (EL): I 2023-24. HS 55 v Notts (Oval) 2023. BB 5-22 v Kent (Oval) 2023. LO HS 75 v Notts (Mansfield) 2022 (RLC). LO BB 2-20 v Somerset (Oval) 2022 (RLC). T20 HS 6. T20 BB 2-17.

‡**LAWRENCE, Dan**iel William (Trinity Catholic HS, Woodford Green), b Whipps Cross, Essex 12 Jul 1997. 6'2". RHB, LB. Squad No 28. Essex 2015-23; cap 2017. MCC 2019. Big Bash: BH 2020-21; MS 2023-24. London Spirit 2021 to date. **Tests**: 11 (2020-21 to 2021-22); HS 91 v WI (Bridgetown) 2021-22; BB 1-0 v WI (North Sound) 2021-22. F-c Tours: A 2019-20 (EL); WI 2021-22; I 2020-21; SL 2020-21. 1000 runs (1): 1070 (2016). HS 161 Ex v Surrey (Oval) 2015. BB 3-98 Ex v Kent (Chelmsford) 2022. LO HS 115 Ex v Kent (Chelmsford) 2018 (RLC). LO BB 3-35 Ex v Middx (Lord's) 2016 (RLC). T20 HS 93. T20 BB 4-20.

McKERR, Conor (St John's C, Johannesburg), b Johannesburg, South Africa 19 Jan 1998. 6'6". RHB, RFM. Squad No 3. UK passport, qualified for England in March 2020. Derbyshire 2017-23 (on loan), taking wkt of J.D.Libby with 4th ball in f-c cricket. Surrey debut 2017. Kent 2022-23 (on loan). HS 37 v Warwks (Oval) 2022. BB 5-54 (10-141 match) De v Northants (Northampton) 2017. Sy BB 4-26 v Notts (Oval) 2018. LO HS 32 v Yorks (York) 2023 (MBC). LO BB 4-55 v Essex (Chelmsford) 2023 (MBC). T20 HS 7*. T20 BB 2-19.

MAJID, Yousef (Cranleigh S), b Slough, Bucks 8 Sep 2003. 6'2". LHB, SLA. Squad No 68. Surrey 2nd XI debut 2021. England U19 2022. Awaiting f-c debut. LO HS 5* v Warwks (Oval) 2022 (RLC). LO BB 3-74 v Glos (Oval) 2022 (RLC).

OVERTON, Jamie (West Buckland S), b Barnstaple, Devon 10 Apr 1994. Twin brother of Craig Overton (*see SOMERSET*). 6'5". RHB, RFM. Squad No 88. Somerset 2012-20; cap 2019. Northamptonshire 2019 (on loan). Surrey debut 2020; cap 2023. Big Bash: AS 2023-24. Manchester Originals 2023. Devon 2011. **ECB Pace Bowling Development Contract 2022-23. Tests**: 1 (2022); HS 97 and BB 1-61 v NZ (Leeds) 2022. F-c Tour (EL): UAE 2018-19 (v PA). HS 120 Sm v Warwks (Birmingham) 2020. Sy HS 93 v Kent (Beckenham) 2022. BB 6-61 v Yorks (Scarborough) 2022. Hat-trick Sm v Notts (Nottingham) 2018. LO HS 40* Sm v Glos (Taunton) 2016 (RLC). LO BB 4-42 Sm v Durham (Chester-le-St) 2012 (CB40). T20 HS 83*. T20 BB 5-47.

PATEL, Ryan Samir (Whitgift S), b Sutton 26 Oct 1997. 5'10". LHB, RMF. Squad No 26. Debut (Surrey) 2017. HS 126 v SL Dev (Guildford) 2022. CC HS 102 v Somerset (Oval) 2022. BB 6-5 v Somerset (Guildford) 2018. LO HS 131 v Notts (Guildford) 2021 (RLC). LO BB 2-65 v Hants (Oval) 2019 (RLC). T20 HS 5*. T20 BB –.

POPE, Oliver John Douglas (Cranleigh S), b Chelsea, Middx 2 Jan 1998. 5'9". RHB, WK. Squad No 32. Debut (Surrey) 2017; cap 2018. Welsh Fire 2022. **ECB Two-Year Central Contract from 2023-24. Tests**: 43 (2018 to 2023-24); HS 205 v Ire (Lord's) 2023. F-c Tours: A 2021-22; SA 2019-20; NZ 2019-20, 2022-23; I 2018-19 (EL), 2020-21, 2023-24; P 2022-23; SL 2019-20. 1000 runs (3); most – 1156 (2022). HS 274 v Glamorgan (Oval) 2021. LO HS 93* EL v Pakistan A (Abu Dhabi) 2018-19. T20 HS 62.

NQ**ROACH, Kemar** Andre Jamal, b St Lucy, Barbados 30 Jun 1988. 6'1". RHB, RFM. Squad No 66. Barbados 2007-08 to 2019-20. Worcestershire 2011. Surrey debut 2021; cap 2023. IPL: DC 2009-10. Big Bash: BH 2012-13 to 2013-14. **Tests** (WI): 81 (2009 to 2023-24); HS 41 v NZ (Kingston) 2012; BB 6-48 v B (St George's) 2009. **LOI** (WI): 95 (2008 to 2021-22); HS 34 v I (Port of Spain) 2013; BB 6-27 v Netherlands (Delhi) 2010-11. **IT20** (WI): 11 (2008 to 2012-13); HS 3* and BB 2-25 v SA (North Sound) 2010. F-c Tours (WI): E 2012, 2017, 2020; A 2009-10, 2015-16, 2022-23, 2023-24; SA 2014-15, 2022-23; NZ 2008-09, 2017-18, 2020-21; I 2011-12, 2019-20 (v Afg); SL 2010-11, 2015-16, 2021-22; Z 2017-18, 2022-23; B 2011-12, 2018-19, 2020-21. HS 53 Barbados v Leeward Is (Basseterre) 2015-16. Sy HS 29 v Essex (Oval) 2022. BB 8-40 (10-80 match) v Hants (Oval) 2021. LO HS 34 (*see LOI*). LO BB 6-27 (*see LOI*). T20 HS 12. T20 BB 3-18.

ROY, Jason Jonathan (Whitgift S), b Durban, South Africa 21 Jul 1990. 6'0". RHB, RM. Squad No 20. Debut (Surrey) 2010; cap 2014. IPL: GL 2017; DD 2018; SH 2021; KKR 2023. Big Bash: ST 2014-15; SS 2016-17 to 2017-18; PS 2020-21. Oval Invincibles 2021 to date. **Tests**: 5 (2019); HS 72 v Ire (Lord's) 2019. **LOI**: 116 (2015 to 2022-23); HS 180 v A (Melbourne) 2017-18. **IT20**: 64 (2014 to 2022); HS 78 v NZ (Delhi) 2015-16. 1000 runs (1): 1078 (2014). HS 143 v Lancs (Oval) 2015. BB 3-9 v Glos (Bristol) 2014. LO HS 180 (*see LOI*). LO BB –. T20 HS 145*. T20 BB 1-23.

SIBLEY, Dominic Peter (Whitgift S, Croydon), b Epsom 5 Sep 1995. 6'3". RHB, OB. Squad No 45. Debut (Surrey) 2013. Warwickshire 2017-22; cap 2019. MCC 2019. *Wisden* 2020. **Tests**: 22 (2019-20 to 2021); HS 133* v SA (Cape Town) 2019-20. F-c Tours: SA 2019-20; NZ 2019-20; I 2020-21; SL 2019-20, 2020-21. 1000 runs (1): 1428 (2019). HS 244 Wa v Kent (Canterbury) 2019. Sy HS 242 v Yorks (Oval) 2013. BB 2-103 v Hants (Southampton) 2016. LO HS 115 Wa v West Indies A (Birmingham) 2018. LO BB 1-20 v Essex (Chelmsford) 2016 (RLC). T20 HS 74*. T20 BB 2-33.

SMITH, Jamie Luke (Whitgift S), b Epsom 12 Jul 2000. 5'10". RHB, WK. Squad No 11. Debut (Surrey) 2018-19, scoring 127 v MCC (Dubai, ICCA); cap 2023. Birmingham Phoenix 2023. Surrey 2nd XI debut 2018. England U19 2018-19. **LOI**: 2 (2023): HS 9 v Ire (Nottingham) 2023. F-c Tour (EL): SL 2022-23. HS 234* v Glos (Bristol) 2022, sharing Sy record 8th wkt partnership of 244 with J.Clark. LO HS 85 v Durham (Chester-le-St) 2021 (RLC). T20 HS 60.

STEEL, Cameron Tate (Scotch C, Perth, Australia; Millfield S; Durham U), b San Francisco, USA 13 Sep 1995. 5'10". RHB, LB. Squad No 44. Durham MCCU 2014-16. Durham 2017-20. Hampshire 2021 (on loan). Surrey debut 2021. HS 224 Du v Leics (Leicester) 2017. Sy HS 141* v Lancs (Manchester) 2023. BB 4-40 v Hants (Southampton) 2023. LO HS 77 Du v Notts (Nottingham) 2017 (RLC). LO BB 4-33 v Leics (Leicester) 2021 (RLC). T20 HS 37. T20 BB 3-41.

TAYLOR, James Philip Arthur (Trentham HS), b Stoke-on-Trent, Staffs 19 Jan 2001. Younger brother of T.A.I.Taylor (*see WORCESTERSHIRE*). 6'3". RHB, RM. Squad No 25. Derbyshire 2017-19. Surrey debut 2020. Derbyshire 2nd XI 2016-19. HS 31* v Warwks (Birmingham) 2022. BB 3-26 De v Leeds/Brad MCCU (Derby) 2019. Sy BB 3-56 v Hants (Oval) 2022. LO HS 6* and LO BB 2-66 De v Australia A (Derby) 2019. T20 HS 3. T20 BB 1-6. No 1st XI appearances in 2023.

TOPLEY, Reece James William (Royal Hospital S, Ipswich), b Ipswich, Suffolk 21 February 1994. Son of T.D.Topley (Surrey, Essex, GW 1985-94); nephew of P.A.Topley (Kent 1972-75). 6'7". RHB, LFM. Squad No 24. Essex 2011-15; cap 2013. Hampshire 2016-17. Sussex 2019. Surrey debut 2021. IPL: RCB 2023. Big Bash: MR 2021-22. Oval Invincibles 2021-22. Northern Superchargers 2023. **ECB Central Contract 2023-24. LOI**: 29 (2015 to 2023-24); HS 15* v Afg (Delhi) 2023-24; BB 6-24 v I (Lord's) 2022 – E record. **IT20**: 25 (2015 to 2023-24); HS 9 v I (Southampton) 2022; BB 3-22 v I (Nottingham) 2022. F-c Tour (EL): SL 2013-14. HS 16 H v Yorks (Southampton) 2017. Sy HS 10 v Middx (Lord's) 2021. BB 6-29 (11-85 match) Ex v Worcs (Chelmsford) 2013. Sy BB 5-66 v Glos (Bristol) 2021. LO HS 19 Ex v Somerset (Taunton) 2011 (CB40). LO BB 6-24 (*see LOI*). T20 HS 14*. T20 BB 4-20.

VIRDI, Guramar Singh ('**Amar**') (Guru Nanak Sikh Ac, Hayes), b Chiswick, Middx 19 Jul 1998. 5'10". RHB, OB. Squad No 19. Debut (Surrey) 2017. Somerset 2022 (on loan). HS 47 v Northants (Northampton) 2021. BB 8-61 (14-139 match) v Notts (Nottingham) 2019. LO HS 8 v Warwks (Oval) 2022 (RLC) and 8 v Middx (Radlett) 2022 (RLC). LO BB 3-38 v Essex (Chelmsford) 2023 (MBC).

NQ**WORRALL, Daniel** James (Kardina International C; U of Melbourne), b Melbourne, Australia 10 Jul 1991. 6'0". RHB, RFM. Squad No 8. UK passport. S Australia 2012-13 to 2021-22. Gloucestershire 2018-21; cap 2018. Surrey debut 2022; cap 2023. Big Bash: MS 2013-14 to 2019-20; AS 2020-21 to 2021-22. London Spirit 2023. **LOI** (A): 3 (2016-17); HS 6* v SA (Centurion) 2016-17; BB 1-43 v SA (Benoni) 2016-17. HS 51 v Lancs (Oval) 2023. BB 7-64 (10-148 match) SA v WA (Adelaide) 2018-19. CC BB 6-56 (11-122 match) v Essex (Oval) 2022. LO HS 31* SA v WA (Perth) 2021-22. LO BB 5-62 SA v Vic (Hobart) 2017-18. T20 HS 62*. T20 BB 4-23.

RELEASED/RETIRED

(Having made a County 1st XI appearance in 2023, even if not formally contracted. Some may return in 2024.)

GRIFFITHS, Luke Aaron (Charterhouse S), b Frimley 16 Nov 2005. RHB, RFM. Surrey 2023 (l-o only). Surrey 2nd XI 2023. England U19 2023. LO HS 25 v Lancs (Guildford) 2023 (MBC). LO BB 1-24 v Yorks (York) 2023 (MBC).

[NQ]**LATHAM, Thomas** William Maxwell, b Christchurch, New Zealand 2 Apr 1992. Son of R.T.Latham (Canterbury and New Zealand 1980-81 to 1994-95). 5'9". LHB, RM, WK. Canterbury 2010-11 to date. Kent 2016. Durham 2017-18; l-o captain 2018. Surrey 2023. **Tests** (NZ): 80 (2013-14 to 2023-24, 9 as captain); HS 264* v SL (Wellington) 2018-19. **LOI** (NZ): 147 (2011-12 to 2023-24, 44 as captain); HS 145* v I (Auckland) 2022-23. **IT20** (NZ): 26 (2012 to 2023, 13 as captain); HS 65* v B (Mirpur) 2021. F-c Tours (NZ): E 2013, 2014 (NZ A), 2015, 2021, 2022; A 2015-16, 2019-20; SA 2016; WI 2014; I 2013-14 (NZ A), 2016-17, 2021-22; P 2022-23; SL 2013-14 (NZ A), 2019; Z 2016; B 2023-24; UAE 2014-15 (v P), 2018-19 (v P). HS 264* (*see Tests*). CC HS 147 Du v Glos (Cheltenham) 2018. Sy HS 99 v Somerset (Taunton) 2023. BB 1-7 NZ v Cricket Australia (Sydney) 2015-16. LO HS 145* (*see LOI*). T20 HS 110.

MORIARTY, D.T. – *see YORKSHIRE*.

[NQ]**NARINE, Sunil** Philip, b Arima, Trinidad 26 May 1988. 5'10". LHB, OB. Trinidad & Tobago 2008-09 to 2012-13. Surrey 2022-23 (T20 only). IPL: KKR 2012 to date. Big Bash: SS 2012-13; MR 2016-17. Oval Invincibles 2021 to date. **Tests** (WI): 6 (2012 to 2013-14); HS 22* v B (Dhaka) 2012-13; BB 6-91 v NZ (Hamilton) 2013-14. **LOI** (WI): 65 (2011-12 to 2016-17); HS 36 v B (Khulna) 2012-13; BB 6-27 v SA (Providence) 2016. **IT20** (WI): 51 (2011-12 to 2019); HS 30 v P (Dubai, DSC) 2016-17; BB 4-12 v NZ (Lauderhill) 2012. F-c Tours (WI): E 2012; NZ 2013-14; B 2012-13. HS 40* WI A v Bangladesh A (Gros Islet) 2011-12. BB 8-17 (13-39 match) T&T v CC&C (Cave Hill) 2011-12. LO HS 51 T&T v Barbados (Bridgetown) 2017-18. LO BB 6-9 T&T v Guyana (Port of Spain) 2014-15. T20 HS 79. T20 BB 5-19.

PATEL, Krish K. (St Paul's S, Hampton), b Kingston-upon-Thames 2 Dec 2005. RHB, LBG. Surrey 2023 (l-o only). Surrey 2nd XI 2021-23. LO HS 30 v Essex (Chelmsford) 2023 (MBC).

[NQ]**SAI SUDHARSAN**, Bhardwaj, b Chennai, India 15 Oct 2001. LHB, LBG. Tamil Nadu 2022-23 to date. Surrey 2023. IPL: GT 2022 to date. **LOI** (I): 3 (2023-24); HS 62 v SA (Gqeberha) 2023-24; BB –. HS 179 TN v Hyderabad (Hyderabad) 2022-23 – on debut. Sy HS 73 v Hants (Southampton) 2023. BB –. LO HS 154 TN v Arunachal Pradesh (Bengaluru) 2022-23. LO BB 1-0 TN v Punjab (Mumbai) 2023-24. T20 HS 96.

N.J.H.Kimber and N.M.J.Reifer left the staff without making a County 1st XI appearance in 2023.

SURREY 2023

RESULTS SUMMARY

	Place	Won	Lost	Drew	NR
LV= Insurance County Champ (Div 1)	**1st**	8	2	4	
Metro Bank One-Day Cup (Group A)	8th	2	5		1
Vitality Blast (South Group)	QF	9	7		

LV= INSURANCE COUNTY CHAMPIONSHIP AVERAGES
BATTING AND FIELDING

Cap		*M*	*I*	*NO*	*HS*	*Runs*	*Avge*	*100*	*50*	*Ct/St*
2018	O.J.D.Pope	5	8	1	122*	379	54.14	1	1	7
	S.A.Abbott	9	12	2	87*	456	45.60	–	3	5
2023	J.L.Smith	13	19	1	138	736	40.88	2	4	9
	A.A.P.Atkinson	5	5	2	55*	120	40.00	–	1	1
2016	B.T.Foakes	13	19	1	125	716	39.77	3	1	55/1
	T.W.M.Latham	5	9	1	99	318	39.75	–	3	14
	D.P.Sibley	14	25	6	140*	746	39.26	1	5	22
2022	W.G.Jacks	9	15	1	99	484	34.57	–	3	11
	C.T.Steel	7	10	1	141*	291	32.33	1	1	4
2023	J.Overton	6	8	2	51	186	31.00	–	1	14
2014	R.J.Burns	14	27	4	88	631	27.43	–	4	3
2022	J.Clark	14	20	4	107	427	26.68	1	2	2
2023	D.J.Worrall	13	17	3	51	221	15.78	–	1	4
	R.S.Patel	7	9	1	37*	125	15.62	–	–	5
	T.E.Lawes	10	12	1	55	126	11.45	–	1	2
2023	K.A.J.Roach	8	9	5	18	42	10.50	–	–	3

Also batted: S.M.Curran (1 match – cap 2018) 52, 12 (1 ct); D.T.Moriarty (1) 13*; B.Sai Sudharsan (2) 3, 73, 40.

BOWLING

	O	*M*	*R*	*W*	*Avge*	*Best*	*5wI*	*10wM*
T.E.Lawes	205.4	30	771	39	19.76	5-22	3	–
A.A.P.Atkinson	115.1	16	404	20	20.20	6-68	1	–
J.Clark	355	70	1025	48	21.35	5-79	1	–
D.J.Worrall	407.5	92	1162	48	24.20	5-25	3	–
J.Overton	104.4	14	345	14	24.64	3-45	–	–
S.A.Abbott	295.2	64	917	37	24.78	5-50	1	–
K.A.J.Roach	225	43	683	26	26.26	5-34	1	–
W.G.Jacks	89	9	336	10	33.60	5-87	1	–
Also bowled:								
C.T.Steel	72.3	6	254	6	42.33	4-40	–	–

R.J.Burns 2.2-0-2-0; S.M.Curran 37-9-101-3; D.T.Moriarty 17-0-86-1; R.S.Patel 2-0-14-0; O.J.D.Pope 1-0-10-0; D.P.Sibley 1.1-0-15-0.

Surrey played no first-class fixtures outside the County Championship in 2023. The First-Class Averages (pp 223–235) give the records of Surrey players in all first-class county matches, with the exception of D.T.Moriarty and O.J.D.Pope, whose first-class figures for Surrey are as above.

SURREY RECORDS

FIRST-CLASS CRICKET

Highest Total	For 811		v	Somerset	The Oval	1899
	V 863		by	Lancashire	The Oval	1990
Lowest Total	For 14		v	Essex	Chelmsford	1983
	V 16		by	MCC	Lord's	1872
Highest Innings	For 357*	R.Abel	v	Somerset	The Oval	1899
	V 366	N.H.Fairbrother	for	Lancashire	The Oval	1990

Highest Partnership for each Wicket

1st	428	J.B.Hobbs/A.Sandham	v	Oxford U	The Oval	1926
2nd	371	J.B.Hobbs/E.G.Hayes	v	Hampshire	The Oval	1909
3rd	413	D.J.Bicknell/D.M.Ward	v	Kent	Canterbury	1990
4th	448	R.Abel/T.W.Hayward	v	Yorkshire	The Oval	1899
5th	318	M.R.Ramprakash/Azhar Mahmood	v	Middlesex	The Oval	2005
6th	298	A.Sandham/H.S.Harrison	v	Sussex	The Oval	1913
7th	262	C.J.Richards/K.T.Medlycott	v	Kent	The Oval	1987
8th	244	J.L.Smith/J.Clark	v	Glos	Bristol	2022
9th	168	E.R.T.Holmes/E.W.J.Brooks	v	Hampshire	The Oval	1936
10th	173	A.Ducat/A.Sandham	v	Essex	Leyton	1921

Best Bowling	For	10-43	T.Rushby	v	Somerset	Taunton	1921
(Innings)	V	10-28	W.P.Howell	for	Australians	The Oval	1899
Best Bowling	For	16-83	G.A.R.Lock	v	Kent	Blackheath	1956
(Match)	V	15-57	W.P.Howell	for	Australians	The Oval	1899

Most Runs – Season	3246	T.W.Hayward	(av 72.13)	1906
Most Runs – Career	43554	J.B.Hobbs	(av 49.72)	1905-34
Most 100s – Season	13	T.W.Hayward		1906
	13	J.B.Hobbs		1925
Most 100s – Career	144	J.B.Hobbs		1905-34
Most Wkts – Season	252	T.Richardson	(av 13.94)	1895
Most Wkts – Career	1775	T.Richardson	(av 17.87)	1892-1904
Most Career W-K Dismissals	1221	H.Strudwick	(1035 ct; 186 st)	1902-27
Most Career Catches in the Field	605	M.J.Stewart		1954-72

LIMITED-OVERS CRICKET

Highest Total	**50ov**	496-4		v	Glos	The Oval	2007
	40ov	386-3		v	Glamorgan	The Oval	2010
	T20	258-6		v	Sussex	Hove	2023
Lowest Total	**50ov**	74		v	Kent	The Oval	1967
	40ov	64		v	Worcs	Worcester	1978
	T20	88		v	Kent	The Oval	2012
Highest Innings	**50ov**	268	A.D.Brown	v	Glamorgan	The Oval	2002
	40ov	203	A.D.Brown	v	Hampshire	Guildford	1997
	T20	131*	A.J.Finch	v	Sussex	Hove	2018
Best Bowling	**50ov**	7-33	R.D.Jackman	v	Yorkshire	Harrogate	1970
	40ov	7-30	M.P.Bicknell	v	Glamorgan	The Oval	1999
	T20	6-24	T.J.Murtagh	v	Middlesex	Lord's	2005

SUSSEX

Formation of Present Club: 1 March 1839
Substantial Reorganisation: August 1857
Inaugural First-Class Match: 1864
Colours: Dark Blue, Light Blue and Gold
Badge: County Arms of Six Martlets
County Champions: (3) 2003, 2006, 2007
Gillette/NatWest/C&G Trophy Winners: (5) 1963, 1964, 1978, 1986, 2006
Pro 40/National League (Div 1) Winners: (2) 2008, 2009
Sunday League Winners: (1) 1982
Twenty20 Cup Winners: (1) 2009

Chief Executive: Pete Fitzboydon, The 1st Central County Ground, Eaton Road, Hove BN3 3AN • Tel: 01273 827100 • Email: info@sussexcricket.co.uk • Web: www.sussexcricket.co.uk • Twitter: @SussexCCC (134,962 followers)

Head Coach: Paul Farbrace. **Batting Coach**: Grant Flower. **Lead Bowling Coach**: James Kirtley. **Captains**: J.A.Simpson and T.S.Mills (T20). **Vice-Captain**: O.E.Robinson. **Overseas Players**: D.P.Hughes, N.J.McAndrew, C.A.Pujara and J.N.T.Seales. **2024 Testimonial**: None. **Head Groundsman**: Ben Gibson. **Scorer**: Graham Irwin. **Vitality Blast Name**: Sussex Sharks. ‡ New registration. NQ Not qualified for England.

ALSOP, Thomas Philip (Lavington S), b High Wycombe, Bucks 26 Nov 1995. Younger brother of O.J.Alsop (Wiltshire 2010-12). 5'11". LHB, WK, occ SLA. Squad No 45. Hampshire 2014-21; cap 2021. Sussex debut 2022; cap 2023. MCC 2017. F-c Tours (EL): SL 2016-17. UAE 2016-17 (v Afg). HS 182* v Leics (Leicester) 2023. BB 2-59 H v Yorks (Leeds) 2016. Sx BB –. LO HS 189* v Middx (Hove) 2022 (RLC). T20 HS 85.

ARCHER, Jofra Chioke (Christchurch Foundation), b Bridgetown, Barbados 1 Apr 1995. 6'3". RHB, RF. Squad No 22. Debut (Sussex) 2016; cap 2017. IPL: RR 2018 to 2020-21. Big Bash: HH 2017-18 to 2018-19. *Wisden* 2019. Missed entire 2022 season due to injury. **ECB Two-Year Central Contract from 2023-24. Tests**: 13 (2019 to 2020-21); HS 30 v NZ (Mt Maunganui) 2019-20; BB 6-45 v A (Leeds) 2019. **LOI**: 21 (2019 to 2022-23); HS 8* v A (Manchester) 2020; BB 6-40 v SA (Kimberley) 2022-23. **IT20**: 15 (2019 to 2022-23); HS 18* and BB 4-33 v I (Ahmedabad) 2020-21. F-c Tours: SA 2019-20; NZ 2019-20; I 2020-21. HS 81* v Northants (Northampton) 2017. 50 wkts (1): 61 (2017). BB 7-67 v Kent (Hove) 2017. LO HS 45 v Essex (Chelmsford) 2017 (RLC). LO BB 6-40 (*see LOI*). T20 HS 36. T20 BB 4-18.

CARSON, Jack Joshua (Bainbridge Ac; Hurstpierpoint C), b Craigavon, Co Armagh 3 Dec 2000. 6'2". RHB, OB. Squad No 16. Debut (Sussex) 2020. Sussex 2nd XI debut 2018. F-c Tours (EL): I 2023-24; SL 2022-23. HS 87 v Worcs (Worcester) 2021. BB 5-79 v Yorks (Hove) 2023. LO HS 20* v Somerset (Taunton) 2023 (MBC). LO BB 4-83 v Durham (Hove) 2023 (MBC).

CARTER, Oliver James (Eastbourne C), b Eastbourne 2 Nov 2001. 5'8½". RHB, WK. Squad No 11. Debut (Sussex) 2021. Sussex 2nd XI debut 2018. HS 185 v Glamorgan (Cardiff) 2022. LO HS 59 v Glos (Hove) 2021 (RLC). T20 HS 64.

CLARK, Thomas Geoffrey Reeves (Ardingly C), b Haywards Heath 27 Feb 2001. 6'2". LHB, RM. Squad No 27. Debut (Sussex) 2019. Sussex 2nd XI debut 2017. HS 138 v Leics (Leicester) 2022. BB 3-21 v Durham (Hove) 2022. LO HS 104 v Surrey (Hove) 2022 (RLC). T20 HS 47.

COLES, James Matthew (Magdalen Coll S), b Aylesbury, Bucks 2 Apr 2004. 6'0½". RHB, SLA. Squad No 30. Debut (Sussex) 2020, aged 16y 157d – youngest ever player for the county. F-c Tour (EL): I 2023-24. HS 180 v Derbys (Hove) 2023. BB 3-91 v Durham (Chester-le-St) 2022. LO HS 59 v Glamorgan (Hove) 2023 (MBC). LO BB 3-27 v Worcs (Worcester) 2021 (RLC). T20 HS 35. T20 BB 1-15.

CROCOMBE, Henry Thomas (Bede's S, Upper Dicker), b Eastbourne 20 Sep 2001. 6'2". RHB, RMF. Squad No 5. Debut (Sussex) 2020. Sussex 2nd XI debut 2018. HS 46* v Northants (Hove) 2021. BB 4-47 v Durham (Hove) 2023. LO HS 47 v Durham (Hove) 2023 (MBC). LO BB 4-63 v Glos (Hove) 2023 (MBC). T20 HS 12*. T20 BB 3-31.

NQ**CURRIE, Brad**ley James (Poole GS; Millfield S; Bournemouth U), b Poole, Dorset 8 Nov 1998. Elder brother of S.W.Currie (*see HAMPSHIRE*). RHB, LMF. Squad No 12. Debut (Sussex) 2022, taking 6-93 v Middx (Lord's). Dorset 2016-21. **LOI** (Scot): 3 (2023-24); HS 8* v Canada (Dubai, DSC) 2023-24; BB 3-21 v UAE (Dubai, DSC) 2023-24. **IT20** (Scot): 6 (2023); HS – ; BB 5-13 v Ire (Edinburgh) 2023. HS 7 v Worcs (Hove) 2022. BB 6-93 (*see above*). LO HS 18* v Durham (Hove) 2023 (MBC). LO BB 3-21 (*see LOI*). T20 HS 0*. T20 BB 5-13.

FOREMAN, Albert ('**Bertie**') Michael (Hurstpierpoint C), b Worthing 13 May 2004. Grandson of D.J.Foreman (W Province and Sussex 1951-52 to 1967 and football for Brighton & HA). 5'9". LHB, OB. Squad No 13. Sussex 2nd XI debut 2021. England U19 2022 to 2022-23. Awaiting f-c debut. LO HS 35 and LO BB 1-40 v Worcs (Worcester) 2023 (MBC).

HAINES, Thomas Jacob (Tanbridge House S, Horsham; Hurstpierpoint C), b Crawley 28 Oct 1998. 5'10". LHB, RM. Squad No 20. Debut (Sussex) 2016; cap 2021; captain 2022. F-c Tour (EL): SL 2022-23. 1000 runs (1): 1176 (2021). HS 243 v Derbys (Derby) 2022. BB 3-50 v Worcs (Worcester) 2022. LO HS 123 v Middx (Hove) 2021 (RLC). LO BB –. T20 HS 27.

HUDSON-PRENTICE, Fynn Jake (Warden Park S, Cuckfield; Bede's S, Upper Dicker), b Haywards Heath, 12 Jan 1996. 6'0½". RHB, RMF. Squad No 33. Debut (Sussex) 2015; cap 2023. Derbyshire 2019-21. HS 99 De v Middx (Derby) 2019. Sx HS 73 v Glamorgan (Hove) 2023 and 73 v Yorks (Leeds) 2023. BB 5-68 De v Notts (Nottingham) 2021. Sx BB 4-27 v Durham (Hove) 2023. LO HS 93 De v Somerset (Taunton) 2021 (RLC). LO BB 3-37 De v Notts (Derby) 2021 (RLC). T20 HS 49*. T20 BB 3-36.

‡NQ**HUGHES, Daniel** Peter, b Bathurst, NSW, Australia 16 Feb 1989. LHB, RM. Squad No 89. New South Wales 2012-13 to date. Big Bash: SS 2012-13 to date; ST 2013-14 to 2014-15. HS 178 NSW v Tas (Sydney) 2022-23. LO HS 152 NSW v WA (Sydney, DO) 2019-20. T20 HS 96.

HUNT, Sean Frank (Howard of Effingham S), b Guildford, Surrey 7 Dec 2001. 6'5½". RHB, LMF. Squad No 21. Debut (Sussex) 2021. Surrey 2nd XI 2019. HS 22 v Glos (Hove) 2023. BB 3-36 v Glos (Bristol) 2023. LO HS 13 v Worcs (Worcester) 2023 (MBC). LO BB 2-59 v Notts (Nottingham) 2022 (RLC).

IBRAHIM, Danial Kashif (Eastbourne C; Bede's S, Upper Dicker), b Burnley, Lancs 8 Aug 2004. 5'10". RHB, RM. Squad No 40. Debut (Sussex) 2021, aged 16y 298d, scoring 55 v Yorks (Leeds) on 2nd day to become the youngest-ever to score a fifty in the County Championship. Sussex 2nd XI debut 2021. HS 100* v Glamorgan (Hove) 2022. BB 2-9 v Worcs (Worcester) 2021. LO HS 50 and LO BB 2-48 v Warwks (Hove) 2023 (MBC). T20 HS 18.

NQ**KARVELAS, Ari**stides (St Benedict's C, Johannesburg; U of South Africa), b Alberton, South Africa 20 Mar 1994. 6'5". RHB, RMF. Squad No 36. Gauteng 2018-19. Central Gauteng 2019-20 to 2020-21. Sussex debut 2022. **IT20** (Greece): 1 (2022); HS 10 v Italy (Vantaa) 2022. HS 57 v Middx (Lord's) 2022. BB 6-71 Gauteng v NW (Potchefstroom) 2018-19 – on debut. Sx BB 4-14 v Leics (Hove) 2023. LO HS 33 C Gauteng v WP (Cape Town) 2019-20. LO BB 5-16 C Gauteng v Boland (Johannesburg) 2019-20. T20 HS 10. T20 BB 4-20.

‡**LAMB, Daniel** John (St Michael's HS, Chorley; Cardinal Newman C, Preston), b Preston, Lancs 7 Sep 1995. 6'0". RHB, RMF. Squad No 10. Lancashire 2018-23. Gloucestershire 2023 (on loan); cap 2023. HS 125 La v Kent (Canterbury) 2021, sharing La record 8th wkt partnership of 187 with L.Wood. BB 4-55 La v Yorks (Leeds) 2019. LO HS 86* La v Sussex (Sedbergh) 2021 (RLC). LO BB 5-30 La v Glos (Bristol) 2021 (RLC). T20 HS 29*. T20 BB 3-23.

LENHAM, Archie David (Bede's S, Upper Dicker), b Eastbourne 23 Jul 2004. Grandson of L.J.Lenham (Sussex 1956-70); son of N.J.Lenham (Sussex 1984-97); younger brother of S.H.Lenham (Sussex 2nd XI 2018-19). 5'8½". RHB, LBG. Squad No 41. Debut (Sussex) 2021. Sussex 2nd XI debut 2021. HS 48 and BB 4-84 v Leics (Leicester) 2022. LO HS 18* v Notts (Nottingham) 2022 (RLC). LO BB 4-59 v Lancs (Sedbergh) 2021 (RLC) – on debut. T20 HS 7*. T20 BB 4-26. Became second youngest debutant in Blast aged 16y, 323d.

LION-CACHET, Zach Benjamin (Bradfield C), b Oxford 15 Dec 2003. RHB, OB. Squad No 24. Sussex 2nd XI debut 2021. Oxfordshire 2021-23. Awaiting f-c debut. LO HS 34 v Worcs (Worcester) 2023 (MBC) – only 1st XI appearance.

NQ**McANDREW, Nathan** John, b Woollongong, NSW, Australia 14 Jul 1993. RHB, RFM. Squad No 43. Auckland 2015-16. S Australia 2021-22 to date. Warwickshire 2022. Sussex debut 2023. Big Bash: ST 2015-16 to date. F-c Tour (Aus A): SL 2022. HS 92 Aus A v Sri Lanka A (Hambantota) 2022. CC HS 65 v Worcs (Hove) 2023. BB 6-41 SA v Q (Brisbane) 2023-24. CC BB 5-63 v Glos (Bristol) 2023. LO HS 55 SA v Q (Brisbane, AB) 2022-23. LO BB 3-22 SA v Vic (Adelaide) 2022-23. T20 HS 30. T20 BB 4-32.

MILLS, Tymal Solomon (Mildenhall TC), b Dewsbury, Yorks 12 Aug 1992. 6'1". RHB, LF. Squad No 7. Essex 2011-14. Sussex debut 2015; cap 2023; T20 captain 2024; has played T20 only since start of 2016. IPL: RCB 2017; MI 2022. Big Bash: BH 2016-17; HH 2017-18; PS 2021-22. Southern Brave 2021 to date. **IT20**: 16 (inc 1 ICC World XI 2018) (2016 to 2023-24); HS 7 v I (Southampton) 2022; BB 3-27 v B (Abu Dhabi) 2021-22. F-c Tour (EL): SL 2013-14. HS 31* EL v Sri Lanka A (Colombo, RPS) 2013-14. CC HS 30 Ex v Kent (Canterbury) 2014. Sx HS 8 v Worcs (Hove) 2015. BB 4-25 Ex v Glamorgan (Cardiff) 2012. Sx BB 2-28 v Hants (Southampton) 2015. LO HS 3* v Notts (Hove) 2015 (RLC). LO BB 3-23 Ex v Durham (Chelmsford) 2013 (Y40). T20 HS 27. T20 BB 4-13.

NQ**PUJARA, Cheteshwar** Arvindbhai, b Rajkot, India 25 Jan 1988. Son of A.S.Pujara (Saurashtra 1976-77 to 1979-80), nephew of B.S.Pujara (Saurashtra 1983-84 to 1996-97). 5'11". RHB, LB. Squad No 8. Saurashtra 2005-06 to date. Derbyshire 2014. Yorkshire 2015-18. Nottinghamshire 2017; cap 2017. Sussex debut/cap 2022; captain 2023. IPL: KKR 2009-10; RCB 2011-13; KXIP 2014. **Tests** (I): 103 (2010-11 to 2023); 1000 runs (1): 1140 (2017); HS 206* v E (Ahmedabad) 2012-13. **LOI** (I): 5 (2013 to 2014); HS 27 v B (Mirpur) 2014. F-c Tours (I): E 2010 (I A), 2014, 2018, 2021, 2022, 2023 (v A); A 2006 (I A), 2014-15, 2018-19, 2020-21; SA 2010-11, 2013 (I A), 2013-14, 2017-18, 2021-22; WI 2012 (I A), 2016, 2019; NZ 2013-14, 2019-20; SL 2015, 2017; Z/Ken 2007-08 (I A); B 2022-23. 1000 runs (1+3); most – 2064 (2016-17). HS 352 Saur v Karnataka (Rajkot) 2012-13. CC HS 231 v Middx (Lord's) 2022. BB 2-4 Saur v Rajasthan (Jaipur) 2007-08. LO HS 174 v Surrey (Hove) 2022 (RLC). T20 HS 100*.

ROBINSON, Oliver Edward ('**Ollie**') (King's S, Canterbury), b Margate, Kent 1 Dec 1993. 6'5". RHB, RMF. Squad No 25. Debut (Sussex) 2015; cap 2019. Yorkshire 2013 (l-o only). Hampshire 2014 (l-o only). **ECB Central Contract 2023-24. Tests**: 20 (2021 to 2023-24); HS 58 v I (Ranchi) 2023-34; BB 5-49 v SA (Oval) 2022. F-c Tours: A 2019-20 (EL), 2021-22; NZ 2022-23; I 2023-24; P 2022-23. HS 110 v Durham (Chester-le-St) 2015, on debut, sharing Sx record 10th wkt partnership of 164 with M.E.Hobden. 50 wkts (3); most – 81 (2018). BB 9-78 (13-128 match) v Glamorgan (Cardiff) 2021. LO HS 30 v Kent (Canterbury) 2015 (RLC). LO BB 3-31 v Kent (Hove) 2018 (RLC). T20 HS 31. T20 BB 4-15.

ROGERS, Henry Peter (Hurst C), b Guildford, Surrey 1 Apr 2006. RHB, RMF. Squad No 42. Sussex 2nd XI debut 2022. Awaiting 1st XI debut.

‡NQ**SEALES, Jayden** Nigel Tristan, b Trinidad & Tobago 10 Sep 2001. Cousin of J.N.N.Seales (CC & C 2019-20 – l-o only). LHB, RFM. Squad No 14. Debut West Indies A 2020-21. Trinidad & Tobago 2021-22 to date. **Tests** (WI): 10 (2021 to 2022-23); HS 13 v E (St George's) 2021-22; BB 5-55 v P (Kingston) 2021. **LOI** (WI): 10 (2022 to 2023); HS 16* v B (Providence) 2022; BB 1-21 v I (Bridgetown) 2023. F-c Tours (WI): A 2022-23; SA 2023-24 (WIA); NZ 2020-21 (WIA). HS 33 and BB 5-49 T&T v Leeward Is (Diego Martin) 2022. LO HS 16* (*see LOI*). LO BB 3-40 T&T v Guyana (Coolidge) 2020-21. T20 HS 1*. T20 BB 4-13.

‡**SIMPSON, John** Andrew (St Gabriel's RC HS), b Bury, Lancs 13 Jul 1988. 5'10". LHB, WK. Squad No 9. Middlesex 2009-23; cap 2011; testimonial 2023. Joins Sussex as captain in 2024. MCC 2018. Northern Superchargers 2021-22. Cumberland 2007. **LOI**: 3 (2021); HS 17 v P (Lord's) 2021. 1000 runs (1): 1039 (2022). HS 167* M v Lancs (Manchester) 2019. LO HS 82* M v Sussex (Lord's) 2017 (RLC). T20 HS 84*.

NQ**TEAR, Charles** Joseph (Seaford S), b Chichester 12 Jun 2004. 5'8½". RHB, WK. Squad No 28. Debut (Sussex) 2022. Sussex 2nd XI debut 2021. England U19 2022-23. **LOI** (Scot): 2 (2023-24); HS 54* v UAE (Dubai, DSC) 2023-24. HS 56 v Glamorgan (Hove) 2022. LO HS 54* (*see LOI*).

WARD, Harrison David (St Edward's S, Oxford), b Oxford 25 Oct 1999. 6'1½". LHB, OB. Squad No 35. Debut (Sussex) 2021. Sussex 2nd XI debut 2016. Hampshire 2nd XI 2019. Oxfordshire 2015-18. England U19 2018. HS 19 v Derbys (Hove) 2021. LO HS 37 v Glos (Hove) 2022 (RLC). LO BB –. T20 HS 54. T20 BB 1-5.

RELEASED/RETIRED

(Having made a County 1st XI appearance in 2023)

ATKINS, Jamie Ardley (Eastbourne C), b Redhill, Surrey 20 May 2002. 6'6". RHB, RMF. Sussex 2021-22. HS 17 v Worcs (Worcester) 2022. BB 5-51 v Kent (Canterbury) 2021. LO HS 1* v Worcs (Worcester) 2023 (MBC). LO BB –.

BOPARA, Ravinder Singh (Brampton Manor S; Barking Abbey Sports C), b Newham, London 4 May 1985. 5'8". RHB, RM. Essex 2002-19; cap 2005; benefit 2015; captain (l-o only) 2016. Auckland 2009-10. Dolphins 2010-11. Sussex 2020-23 (T20 only); cap 2023. MCC 2006, 2008. IPL: KXIP 2009 to 2009-10; SH 2015. Big Bash: SS 2013-14. London Spirit 2021 to date. YC 2008. **Tests**: 13 (2007-08 to 2012); HS 143 v WI (Lord's) 2009; BB 1-39 v SL (Galle) 2007-08. **LOI**: 120 (2006-07 to 2014-15); HS 101* v Ire (Dublin) 2013; BB 4-38 v B (Birmingham) 2010. **IT20**: 38 (2008 to 2014); HS 65* v A (Hobart) 2013-14; BB 4-10 v WI (Oval) 2011. F-c Tours: WI 2008-09, 2010-11 (EL); SL 2007-08, 2011-12. 1000 runs (1): 1256 (2008). HS 229 Ex v Northants (Chelmsford) 2007. BB 5-49 Ex v Derbys (Chelmsford) 2016. LO HS 201* Ex v Leics (Leicester) 2008 (FPT) – Ex record. LO BB 5-63 Dolphins v Warriors (Pietermaritzburg) 2010-11. T20 HS 105*. T20 BB 6-16.

FINN, Steven Thomas (Parmiter's S, Garston), b Watford, Herts 4 Apr 1989. 6'7½". RHB, RFM. Middlesex 2005-21; cap 2009. Otago 2011-12. Sussex 2022; cap 2022. Manchester Originals 2021. YC 2010. **Tests**: 36 (2009-10 to 2016-17); HS 56 v NZ (Dunedin) 2012-13; BB 6-79 v A (Birmingham) 2015. **LOI**: 69 (2010-11 to 2017); HS 35 v A (Brisbane) 2010-11; BB 5-33 v I (Brisbane) 2014-15. **IT20**: 21 (2011 to 2015); HS 8* v I (Colombo, RPS) 2012-13; BB 3-16 v NZ (Pallekele) 2012-13. F-c Tours: A 2010-11, 2013-14; SA 2015-16; NZ 2012-13; I 2012-13; SL 2011-12; B 2009-10, 2016-17; UAE 2011-12 (v P). HS 56 (*see Tests*) and 56 M v Sussex (Hove) 2019. Sx HS 10* v Middx (Lord's) 2022. 50 wkts (2); most – 64 (2010). BB 9-37 (14-106 match) M v Worcs (Worcester) 2010. Sx BB 3-84 v Notts (Hove) 2022. LO HS 42* M v Glamorgan (Cardiff) 2014 (RLC). LO BB (*see LOI*) and 5-33 M v Derbys (Lord's) 2011 (CB40). T20 HS 11*. T20 BB 5-16.

GARTON, G.H.S. – *see WARWICKSHIRE.*

ORR, A.G.H. – *see HAMPSHIRE.*

[NQ]**SHADAB KHAN**, b Mianwali, Punjab, Pakistan 4 Oct 1998. 5'10". RHB, LBG. Rawalpindi 2016-17. SNGPL 2017-18. Northern 2019-20. Yorkshire 2022 (T20 only). Sussex 2023 (T20 only). Big Bash: BH 2017-18; SS 2021-22; HH 2022-23. Birmingham Phoenix 2023. **Tests** (P): 6 (2017 to 2020); HS 56 v E (Leeds) 2018; BB 3-31 v Ire (Dublin) 2018. **LOI** (P): 70 (2017 to 2023-24); HS 86 v WI (Multan) 2022; BB 4-27 v Nepal (Multan) 2023. **IT20** (P): 92 (2016-17 to 2023); HS 52 v SA (Sydney) 2022-23; BB 4-8 v Hong Kong (Sharjah) 2022. F-c Tours (P): E 2016 (PA), 2018, 2020; SA 2018-19; WI 2017; Z 2016-17 (PA); Ire 2018. HS 132 PA v Zimbabwe A (Bulawayo) 2016-17. BB 6-77 (10-157 match) P v Northants (Northampton) 2018. LO HS 86 (*see LOI*). LO BB 4-27 (*see LOI*). T20 HS 91. T20 BB 5-28.

[NQ]**SHIPLEY, Henry** Burton, b Darfield, Canterbury, New Zealand 10 May 1996. Nephew of M.W.Priest (Canterbury and New Zealand 1984-85 to 1998-99). RHB, RFM. Canterbury 2016-17 to date. Sussex 2023. **LOI** (NZ): 8 (2022-23 to 2023); HS 7 v P (Karachi) 2023; BB 5-31 v SL (Auckland) 2022-23. **IT20** (NZ): 5 (2022-23 to 2023); HS 1* (twice); BB 1-25 v SL (Dunedin) 2022-23. HS 82 Cant v Otago (Christchurch) 2022-23. Sx HS 41 v Worcs (Hove) 2023. BB 5-37 Cant v Wellington (Wellington) 2017-18. Sx BB 4-124 v Derbys (Hove) 2023. LO HS 78 Cant v Otago (Rangiora) 2021-22. LO BB 6-40 Cant v Wellington (Wellington) 2022-23. T20 HS 39*. T20 BB 4-23.

[NQ]**SMITH, Steven** Peter Devereux, b Kogarah, Sydney, NSW, Australia 2 Jun 1989. RHB, LBG. NSW 2007-08 to date. Sussex 2023; cap 2023. Worcestershire 2010 (T20 only). IPL: PW 2012-13; RR 2014 to 2020-21; RPS 2016-17; DC 2021. Big Bash: SS 2011-12 to date. *Wisden* 2015. **Tests** (A): 109 (2010 to 2023-24, 38 as captain); 1000 runs (4); most – 1474 (2015); HS 239 v E (Perth) 2017-18; BB 3-18 v E (Lord's) 2013. **LOI** (A): 158 (2009-10 to 2023-24, 51 as captain); 1000 runs (1): 1154 (2016); HS 164 v NZ (Sydney) 2016-17; BB 3-16 v Z (Harare) 2014. **IT20** (A): 67 (2009-10 to 2023-24, 8 as captain); HS 90 v E (Cardiff) 2015; BB 3-20 v WI (Gros Islet) 2010. F-c Tours (A)(C=Captain): E 2010 (v P), 2013, 2015, 2019, 2023; SA 2013-14; 2017-18C; WI 2015; NZ 2015-16C, 2023-24; I 2010-11, 2012-13, 2016-17C I 2022-23; P 2021-22 SL 2016C, 2022; B 2017C; UAE (v P) 2014-15. HS 239 (*see Tests*). Sx HS 89 and Sx BB 2-55 v Glamorgan (Hove) 2023. BB 7-64 NSW v SA (Sydney) 2009-10. LO HS 164 (*see LOI*). LO BB 3-16 (*see LOI*). T20 HS 125*. T20 BB 4-13.

[NQ]**UNADKAT, Jaydev** Dipakbhai, b Porbandar, Saurashtra, India 18 Oct 1991. RHB, LFM. Saurashtra 2010-11 to date. Sussex 2023. IPL: KKR 2009-10 to 2016; RCB 2013; DD 2014 to 2015; RPS 2017; RR 2018-21; MI 2022; LSG 2023. **Tests** (I): 4 (2010-11 to 2023); HS 14* and BB 2-50 v B (Mirpur) 2022-23. **LOI** (I): 8 (2013 to 2023); HS – ; BB 4-41 v Z (Harare) 2013. **IT20** (I): 10 (2016 to 2017-18); HS – ; BB 3-38 v B (Colombo, RPS) 2017-18. F-c Tours (I): E 2010 (IA); SA 2010-11, 2013 (IA); WI 2023; NZ 2012-13 (IA); B 2022-23. HS 92 Saurashtra v Jammu & K (Jammu) 2015-16. Sx HS 10 v Durham (Chester-le-St) 2023. 50 wkts (0+1): 76 (2019-20). BB 8-39 Saurashtra v Delhi (Rajkot) 2022-23. Sx BB 6-94 v Leics (Hove) 2023. LO HS 57 Saurashtra v Services (Kalyani) 2016-17. LO BB 5-23 Saurashtra v Himachal Pradesh (Delhi) 2022-23. T20 HS 58*. T20 BB 5-25.

D.M.W.Rawlins left the staff without making a County 1st XI appearance in 2023.

SUSSEX 2023

RESULTS SUMMARY

	Place	Won	Lost	Drew
LV= Insurance County Champ (Div 2)	3rd	3	1	10
Metro Bank One-Day Cup (Group B)	9th	1	7	
Vitality Blast (South Group)	6th	6	8	

LV= INSURANCE COUNTY CHAMPIONSHIP AVERAGES
BATTING AND FIELDING

Cap		*M*	*I*	*NO*	*HS*	*Runs*	*Avge*	*100*	*50*	*Ct/St*
	H.B.Shipley	3	6	4	41	116	58.00	–	–	2
2022	C.A.Pujara	8	12	–	151	649	54.08	3	2	5
2023	F.J.Hudson-Prentice	14	22	4	73	879	48.83	–	9	5
	J.M.Coles	12	20	–	180	849	42.45	3	3	11
2023	T.P.Alsop	14	23	2	182*	820	39.04	2	4	16
	O.J.Carter	14	23	3	80	779	38.95	–	7	43/2
2021	T.J.Haines	11	20	–	91	662	33.10	–	6	4
	T.G.R.Clark	12	22	1	96	645	30.71	–	6	18
	J.J.Carson	11	19	4	75	438	29.20	–	3	9
	A.G.H.Orr	8	13	1	67	322	26.83	–	1	6
	N.J.McAndrew	7	11	1	65	265	26.50	–	1	1
	H.T.Crocombe	10	13	6	25*	107	15.28	–	–	6
	S.F.Hunt	5	5	2	22	43	14.33	–	–	–
	D.K.Ibrahim	5	10	1	36	109	12.11	–	–	5
2019	O.E.Robinson	3	4	–	33	48	12.00	–	–	–
	A.Karvelas	8	12	2	23	78	7.80	–	–	2
	J.D.Unadkat	3	4	1	10	18	6.00	–	–	–

Also batted: B.J.Currie (2 matches) 0, 2*; G.H.S.Garton (1) 28; S.P.D.Smith (3 – cap 2023) 30, 3, 89 (6 ct); C.J.Tear (1) 5; H.D.Ward (1) 2.

BOWLING

	O	*M*	*R*	*W*	*Avge*	*Best*	*5wI*	*10wM*
O.E.Robinson	97.4	24	273	20	13.65	7- 58	2	1
A.Karvelas	241.4	53	800	35	22.85	4- 14	–	–
J.D.Unadkat	86	15	266	11	24.18	6- 94	1	–
N.J.McAndrew	208.1	35	750	31	24.19	5- 63	2	–
S.F.Hunt	119	16	493	14	35.21	3- 36	–	–
H.P.Shipley	112.5	15	471	13	36.23	4-124	–	–
H.T.Crocombe	173	23	756	20	37.80	4- 47	–	–
J.J.Carson	314.2	43	1250	31	40.32	5- 79	1	–
F.J.Hudson-Prentice	261	50	953	20	47.65	4- 27	–	–
Also bowled:								
B.J.Currie	62	12	234	9	26.00	3- 27	–	–
T.J.Haines	92.2	19	298	7	42.57	2- 27	–	–
J.M.Coles	144.3	17	530	5	106.00	2- 93	–	–

T.P.Alsop 7-2-10-0; G.H.S.Garton 10-1-64-1; D.K.Ibrahim 10-1-56-1; A.G.H.Orr 3-0-12-0; S.P.D.Smith 14.3-2-68-2.

Sussex played no first-class fixtures outside the County Championship in 2023. The First-Class Averages (pp 223–235) give the records of Sussex players in all first-class county matches, with the exception of C.A.Pujara, O.E.Robinson and S.P.D.Smith, whose first-class figures for Sussex are as above.

SUSSEX RECORDS

FIRST-CLASS CRICKET

Highest Total	For 742-5d		v	Somerset	Taunton	2009
	V 756-4d		by	Leics	Hove	2022
Lowest Total	For 19		v	Surrey	Godalming	1830
	19		v	Notts	Hove	1873
	V 18		by	Kent	Gravesend	1867
Highest Innings	For 344*	M.W.Goodwin	v	Somerset	Taunton	2009
	V 322	E.Paynter	for	Lancashire	Hove	1937

Highest Partnership for each Wicket

1st	490	E.H.Bowley/J.G.Langridge	v	Middlesex	Hove	1933
2nd	385	E.H.Bowley/M.W.Tate	v	Northants	Hove	1921
3rd	385*	M.H.Yardy/M.W.Goodwin	v	Warwicks	Hove	2006
4th	363	M.W.Goodwin/C.D.Hopkinson	v	Somerset	Taunton	2009
5th	297	J.H.Parks/H.W.Parks	v	Hampshire	Portsmouth	1937
6th	335	L.J.Wright/B.C.Brown	v	Durham	Hove	2014
7th	344	K.S.Ranjitsinhji/W.Newham	v	Essex	Leyton	1902
8th	291	R.S.C.Martin-Jenkins/M.J.G.Davis	v	Somerset	Taunton	2002
9th	178	H.W.Parks/A.F.Wensley	v	Derbyshire	Horsham	1930
10th	164	O.E.Robinson/M.E.Hobden	v	Durham	Chester-le-St[2]	2015

Best Bowling	For	10- 48	C.H.G.Bland	v	Kent	Tonbridge	1899
(Innings)	V	9- 11	A.P.Freeman	for	Kent	Hove	1922
Best Bowling	For	17-106	G.R.Cox	v	Warwicks	Horsham	1926
(Match)	V	17- 67	A.P.Freeman	for	Kent	Hove	1922

Most Runs – Season	2850	J.G.Langridge	(av 64.77)	1949
Most Runs – Career	34150	J.G.Langridge	(av 37.69)	1928-55
Most 100s – Season	12	J.G.Langridge		1949
Most 100s – Career	76	J.G.Langridge		1928-55
Most Wkts – Season	198	M.W.Tate	(av 13.47)	1925
Most Wkts – Career	2211	M.W.Tate	(av 17.41)	1912-37
Most Career W-K Dismissals	1176	H.R.Butt	(911 ct; 265 st)	1890-1912
Most Career Catches in the Field	779	J.G.Langridge		1928-55

LIMITED-OVERS CRICKET

Highest Total	**50ov**	400-4		v	Middlesex	Hove	2022
	40ov	399-4		v	Worcs	Horsham	2011
	T20	242-5		v	Glos	Bristol	2016
Lowest Total	**50ov**	49		v	Derbyshire	Chesterfield	1969
	40ov	59		v	Glamorgan	Hove	1996
	T20	67		v	Hampshire	Hove	2004
Highest Innings	**50ov**	206	A.G.H.Orr	v	Somerset	Taunton	2022
	40ov	163	C.J.Adams	v	Middlesex	Arundel	1999
	T20	153*	L.J.Wright	v	Essex	Chelmsford	2014
Best Bowling	**50ov**	6- 9	A.I.C.Dodemaide	v	Ireland	Downpatrick	1990
	40ov	7-41	A.N.Jones	v	Notts	Nottingham	1986
	T20	5-11	Mushtaq Ahmed	v	Essex	Hove	2005

WARWICKSHIRE

Formation of Present Club: 8 April 1882
Substantial Reorganisation: 19 January 1884
Inaugural First-Class Match: 1894
Colours: Dark Blue, Gold and Silver
Badge: Bear and Ragged Staff
County Champions: (8) 1911, 1951, 1972, 1994, 1995, 2004, 2012, 2021
Gillette/NatWest Trophy Winners: (5) 1966, 1968, 1989, 1993, 1995
Benson and Hedges Cup Winners: (2) 1994, 2002
Sunday League Winners: (3) 1980, 1994, 1997
Clydesdale Bank 40 Winners: (1) 2010
Royal London Cup Winners: (1) 2015
Twenty20 Cup Winners: (1) 2014

Chief Executive: Stuart Cain, Edgbaston Stadium, Edgbaston, Birmingham, B5 7QU • Tel: 0121 369 1994 • Email: enquiries@edgbaston.com • Web: www.edgbaston.com • Twitter: @WarwickshireCCC (86,613 followers)

Head Coach: Mark Robinson. **Batting Coach**: Tony Frost. **Bowling Coach**: Stuart Barnes. **Assistant Coach**: Ian Westwood. **Captains**: A.L.Davies (f-c and 50 ov) and M.M.Ali (T20). **Overseas Players**: Hassan Ali. **2024 Testimonial**: O.J.Hannon-Dalby. **Head Groundsman**: Gary Barwell. **Scorer**: Mel Smith. **T20 Blast Name**: Birmingham Bears. ‡ New registration. NQ Not qualified for England.

ALI, Moeen Munir (Moseley S), b Birmingham 18 Jun 1987. Brother of A.K.Ali (Worcs, Glos and Leics 2000-12), cousin of Kabir Ali (Worcs, Rajasthan, Hants and Lancs 1999-2014). 6'0". LHB, OB. Squad No 1. Debut (Warwickshire) 2005; captain 2024 (T20). Worcestershire 2007-19; captain 2020-22 (T20 only). Moors SC 2011-12. MT 2012-13. MCC 2012. IPL: RCB 2018 to 2020-21; CSK 2021 to date. Birmingham Phoenix 2021 to date. PCA 2013. *Wisden* 2014. **ECB Central Contract 2023-24. Tests**: 68 (2014 to 2023); 1000 runs (1): 1078 (2016); HS 155* v SL (Chester-le-St) 2016; BB 6-53 v SA (Lord's) 2017. Hat-trick v SA (Oval) 2017. **LOI**: 138 (2013-14 to 2023-24, 1 as captain); HS 128 v Scotland (Christchurch) 2014-15; BB 4-46 v A (Manchester) 2018. **IT20**: 82 (2013-14 to 2023-24, 11 as captain); HS 72* v A (Cardiff) 2015; BB 3-24 v WI (Bridgetown) 2021-22. F-c Tours: A 2017-18; SA 2015-16; WI 2014-15, 2018-19; NZ 2017-18; I 2016-17, 2020-21; SL 2013-14 (EL), 2018-19; B 2016-17; UAE 2015-16 (v P). 1000 runs (2); most – 1420 (2013). HS 250 Wo v Glamorgan (Worcester) 2013. BB 6-29 (12-96 match) Wo v Lancs (Manchester) 2012. LO HS 158 Wo v Sussex (Horsham) 2011 (CB40). LO BB 4-33 Wo v Notts (Nottingham) 2018 (RLC). T20 HS 121*. T20 BB 5-34.

ALI, Tazeem Chaudry (Moseley S), b Amsterdam, Netherlands 13 June 2006. RHB, LB. Warwickshire 2nd XI debut 2021. Awaiting f-c debut. LO HS –. LO BB 1-49 v Derbys (Birmingham) 2023 (MBC) – only 1st XI appearance.

BARNARD, Edward George (Shrewsbury S), b Shrewsbury, Shrops 20 Nov 1995. Younger brother of M.R.Barnard (Oxford MCCU 2010). 6'1". RHB, RMF. Squad No 30. Worcestershire 2015-22. Warwickshire debut 2023. Shropshire 2012. HS 163* Wo v Notts (Nottingham) 2022. Wa HS 95 v Hants (Southampton) 2023. BB 6-37 (11-89 match) Wo v Somerset (Taunton) 2018. Wa BB 5-66 v Surrey (Oval) 2023. LO HS 161 v Durham (Birmingham) 2023 (MBC). LO BB 3-14 v Worcs (Worcester) 2023 (MBC). T20 HS 43*. T20 BB 3-29.

BENJAMIN, Christopher Gavin (St Andrew's C, Johannesburg; Durham U), b Johannesburg, South Africa 29 Apr 1999. 5'11". RHB, RMF, WK. Squad No 12. Durham MCCU 2019. Warwickshire debut 2021, scoring 127 v Lancs (Manchester); also scored fifties on l-o and T20 debuts. Durham 2022 (on loan); cap 2022. Birmingham Phoenix 2022 to date. HS 127 (*see above*). LO HS 50 v Glamorgan (Cardiff) 2021 (RLC). T20 HS 68*.

BETHELL, Jacob Graham (Rugby S), b Bridgetown, Barbados 23 Oct 2003. 5'10". LHB, SLA. Squad No 2. Debut (Warwickshire) 2021. Gloucestershire 2022 (on loan); cap 2022. Welsh Fire 2022. Birmingham Phoenix 2023. Warwickshire 2nd XI debut 2019. HS 61 Gs v Somerset (Bristol) 2022. Wa HS 37 v Essex (Chelmsford) 2023. BB –. LO HS 66 v Yorks (York) 2021 (RLC). LO BB 4-36 v Glamorgan (Cardiff) 2021 (RLC). T20 HS 32*. T20 BB 1-21.

BOOTH, Michael Gary (Hilton C, KZN; Durham U), b Harare, Zimbabwe 12 Feb 2001. RHB, RF. Squad No 27. Surrey 2nd XI 2019. Hampshire 2nd XI 2021. Warwickshire 2nd XI debut 2021. Awaiting f-c debut. LO HS –. LO BB 1-21 v Worcs (Worcester) 2023 (MBC). T20 HS –. T20 BB 2-24.

BRIGGS, Danny Richard (Isle of Wight C), b Newport, IoW, 30 Apr 1991. 6'2". RHB, SLA. Squad No 14. Hampshire 2009-15; cap 2012. Sussex 2016-19. Warwickshire debut 2021; cap 2021. Big Bash: AS 2020-21. Southern Brave 2021. Oval Invincibles 2022 to date. **LOI**: 1 (2011-12); BB 2-39 v P (Dubai) 2011-12. **IT20**: 7 (2012 to 2013-14); HS 0*; BB 2-25 v A (Chester-le-St) 2013. F-c Tours (EL): WI 2010-11; I 2018-19. HS 120* Sx v South Africa A (Arundel) 2017. CC HS 99 v Middx (Lord's) 2023. BB 6-45 EL v Windward Is (Roseau) 2010-11. CC BB 6-65 H v Notts (Southampton) 2011. Wa BB 4-31 v Essex (Birmingham) 2022. LO HS 37* Sx v Essex (Chelmsford) 2019 (RLC). LO BB 4-32 H v Glamorgan (Cardiff) 2012 (CB40). T20 HS 35*. T20 BB 5-19.

BURGESS, Michael Gregory Kerran (Cranleigh S; Loughborough U), b Epsom, Surrey 8 Jul 1994. 6'1". RHB, WK, occ RM. Squad No 61. Loughborough MCCU 2014-15. Leicestershire 2016. Sussex 2017-19. Warwickshire debut 2019; cap 2021. HS 178 v Surrey (Birmingham) 2022. BB 1-17 v Northants (Northampton) 2022. LO HS 93 v Surrey (Oval) 2022 (RLC). T20 HS 64*.

DAVIES, Alexander Luke (Queen Elizabeth GS, Blackburn), b Darwen, Lancs 23 Aug 1994. 5'7". RHB, WK. Squad No 71. Lancashire 2012-21; cap 2017. Warwickshire debut 2022; cap 2023; captain 2024. Southern Brave 2021-22. F-c Tour (EL): WI 2017-18. 1000 runs (1): 1046 (2017). HS 147 La v Northants (Northampton) 2019. Wa HS 121 v Lancs (Birmingham) 2022. LO HS 147 La v Durham (Manchester) 2018 (RLC). T20 HS 94*.

‡**GARTON, George** Henry Simmons (Hurstpierpoint C), b Brighton, Sussex 15 Apr 1997. 5'10½". LHB, LF. Squad No 7. Sussex 2016-23. IPL: RCB 2021. Big Bash: AS 2021-22. Southern Brave 2021 to date. **IT20**: 1 (2021-22); HS 2 and BB 1-57 v WI (Bridgetown) 2021-22. HS 97 Sx v Glamorgan (Cardiff) 2021. BB 5-26 Sx v Essex (Hove) 2020. LO HS 38 Sx v Essex (Chelmsford) 2019 (RLC). LO BB 4-43 EL v Sri Lanka A (Canterbury) 2016. T20 HS 46. T20 BB 4-16.

‡**GLEESON, Richard** James (Baines HS), b Blackpool, Lancs 2 Dec 1987. 6'3". RHB, RFM. Squad No 33. Northamptonshire 2015-18. Lancashire 2018-20. MCC 2018. T20 only after 2020. Big Bash: MR 2019-20. Manchester Originals 2022 to date. Cumberland 2010-15. **IT20**: 6 (2022 to 2022-23); HS 2 and BB 3-15 v I (Birmingham) 2022. F-c Tour (EL): WI 2017-18. HS 31 Nh v Glos (Bristol) 2016. BB 6-43 La v Leics (Leicester) 2019. Hat-trick MCC v Essex (Bridgetown) 2017-18. LO HS 13 EL v West Indies A (Coolidge) 2017-18. LO BB 5-47 Nh v Worcs (Worcester) 2016 (RLC). T20 HS 8. T20 BB 5-33.

HAIN, Samuel Robert (Southport S, Gold Coast), b Hong Kong 16 July 1995. 5'10". RHB, OB. Squad No 16. Debut (Warwickshire) 2014; cap 2018. MCC 2018. Big Bash: BH 2022-23; HH 2023-24. Manchester Originals 2021. Welsh Fire 2022. Trent Rockets 2023. UK passport (British parents). **LOI**: 2 (2023); HS 89 v Ire (Nottingham) 2023. 1000 runs (1): 1137 (2022). HS 208 v Northants (Birmingham) 2014. BB –. LO HS 161* v Worcs (Worcester) 2019 (RLC). T20 HS 112*.

HANNON-DALBY, Oliver James (Brooksbank S, Leeds Met U), b Halifax, Yorkshire 20 Jun 1989. 6'7". LHB, RMF. Squad No 20. Yorkshire 2008-12. Warwickshire debut 2013; cap 2019; testimonial 2024. F-c Tour (MCC): Nepal 2019-20. HS 40 v Somerset (Taunton) 2014. 50 wkts (2); most – 54 (2023). BB 7-46 v Northants (Birmingham) 2023. LO HS 21* Y v Warwks (Scarborough) 2012 (CB40). LO BB 5-27 v Glamorgan (Birmingham) 2015 (RLC). T20 HS 14*. T20 BB 4-20.

NQ**HASSAN ALI**, b Mandi Bahauddin, Pakistan 7 Feb 1994. 5'8". RHB, RMF. Squad No 32. Sialkot 2013-14. Sialkot Stallions 2014-15. Islamabad 2015-16 to 2016-17. Central Punjab 2019-20 to 2020-21. Lancashire 2022; cap 2022. Southern Punjab 2022-23. Warwickshire debut/cap 2023. **Tests** (P): 24 (2017 to 2023-24); HS 30 v Z (Harare) 2021; BB 5-27 v Z (Harare) 2021 – separate matches. **LOI** (P): 66 (2016 to 2023-24); HS 59 v SA (Durban) 2018-19; BB 5-34 v SL (Abu Dhabi) 2017-18. **IT20** (P): 50 (2016 to 2022); HS 23 v NZ (Wellington) 2017-18; BB 4-18 v Z (Harare) 2021. F-c Tours (P): E 2016 (PA), 2018; A 2023-24; SA 2018-19; WI 2017, 2021; SL 2022; Z 2020-21; B 2021-22. HS 106* C Punjab v Khyber Paktunkhwa (Karachi) 2020-21. CC HS 54 v Notts (Nottingham) 2023. 50 wkts (0+1): 55 (2020-21). BB 8-107 Sialkot S v State Bank (Sialkot) 2014-15. CC BB 6-47 La v Glos (Manchester) 2022. Wa BB 4-48 v Essex (Birmingham) 2023. LO HS 59 (*see LOI*). LO BB 5-34 (*see LOI*). T20 HS 45. T20 BB 5-20.

KHAN, Amir Hamza (Cockshut Hill S), b Solihull 15 Sep 2005. 5'10". LHB, OB/SLA. Squad No 3. Warwickshire 2nd XI debut 2021. Awaiting 1st XI debut.

LINTOTT, Jacob ('**Jake**') Benedict (Queen's C, Taunton), b Taunton, Somerset 22 Apr 1993. 5'11". RHB, SLA. Squad No 23. Debut (Warwickshire) 2021. Hampshire 2017 (T20 only). Gloucestershire 2018 (T20 only). Southern Brave 2021-22. Dorset 2011-15. Wiltshire 2016-19. HS 78 and BB 3-68 v Essex (Chelmsford) 2023. LO HS 28 and LO BB 5-37 Mohammedan SC v Brothers Union (Fatullah) 2022-23. LO HS 28 v Sussex (Hove) 2023 (MBC). T20 HS 41. T20 BB 4-20.

MADDY, George William, b 13 Oct 2005. Son of D.L.Maddy (Leicestershire, Warwickshire and England 1994-2013). 5'10". LHB, WK. Squad No 8. Warwickshire 2nd XI debut 2021. Awaiting f-c debut. LO HS 7 v Somerset (Birmingham) 2022 (RLC). No 1st XI appearances in 2023.

MILES, Craig Neil (Bradon Forest S, Swindon; Filton C, Bristol), b Swindon, Wilts 20 July 1994. Brother of A.J.Miles (Cardiff MCCU 2012). 6'4". RHB, RMF. Squad No 18. Gloucestershire 2011-18; cap 2011. Warwickshire debut 2019. Durham 2023 (on loan). Northern Superchargers 2022. HS 62* Gs v Worcs (Cheltenham) 2014. Wa HS 32 v Surrey (Birmingham) 2022. 50 wkts (3); most – 58 (2018). BB 6-63 Gs v Northants (Northampton) 2015. Wa BB 5-28 v Lancs (Lord's) 2021. Hat-trick Gs v Essex (Cheltenham) 2016. LO HS 31* v Surrey (Oval) 2021 (RLC). LO BB 4-29 Gs v Yorks (Scarborough) 2015 (RLC). T20 HS 11*. T20 BB 4-29.

MOUSLEY, Daniel Richard (Bablake S, Coventry), b Birmingham 8 Jul 2001. 5'11". LHB, OB. Squad No 80. Debut (Warwickshire) 2019. Birmingham Phoenix 2022 to date. Staffordshire 2019. England U19 2018-19. F-c Tour (EL): I 2023-24. HS 94 v Kent (Birmingham) 2023. BB 3-43 EL v India A (Ahmedabad) 2023-24. CC BB –. LO HS 105 Burgher Rec v Nugegoda (Colombo) 2021-22. LO BB 3-32 Burgher Rec v SL Air Force (Colombo) 2021-22. T20 HS 63*. T20 BB 4-28.

NORWELL, Liam Connor (Redruth SS), b Bournemouth, Dorset 27 Dec 1991. 6'3". RHB, RMF. Squad No 24. Gloucestershire 2011-18, taking 6-46 v Derbys (Bristol) on debut; cap 2011. Warwickshire debut 2019. HS 102 Gs v Derbys (Bristol) 2016. Wa HS 64 v Surrey (Birmingham) 2019. 50 wkts (3); most – 68 (2015). BB 9-62 (13-100 match) v Hants (Birmingham) 2022. LO HS 16 Gs v Somerset (Bristol) 2017 (RLC). LO BB 6-52 Gs v Leics (Leicester) 2012 (CB40). T20 HS 2*. T20 BB 3-27. No 1st XI appearances in 2023 due to injury.

RHODES, William Michael Henry (Cottingham HS, Cottingham SFC, Hull), b Nottingham 2 Mar 1995. 6'2". LHB, RMF. Squad No 35. Yorkshire 2014-15 to 2016. Essex 2016 (on loan). Warwickshire debut 2018; cap 2020; captain 2020-23. MCC 2019. F-c Tour (MCC): Nepal 2019-20. HS 207 v Worcs (Worcester) 2020. BB 5-17 v Essex (Chelmsford) 2019. LO HS 113 v Notts (Birmingham) 2022 (RLC). LO BB 3-22 v Northants (Birmingham) 2023 (MBC). T20 HS 79. T20 BB 4-34.

RUSHWORTH, Christopher (Castle View CS, Sunderland), b Sunderland, Co Durham 11 Jul 1986. Cousin of P.Mustard (Durham, Mountaineers, Auckland, Lancashire and Gloucestershire 2002-17). 6'2". RHB, RMF. Squad No 22. Durham 2010-22; cap 2010; testimonial 2019. Warwickshire debut/cap 2023. MCC 2013, 2015. Northumberland 2004-05. PCA 2015. HS 57 Du v Kent (Canterbury) 2017. Wa HS 22 v Surrey (Birmingham) 2023. 50 wkts (7); most – 88 (2015) – Du record. BB 9-52 (15-95 match – Du record) Du v Northants (Chester-le-St) 2014. Wa BB 7-38 (10-76 match) v Hants (Southampton) 2023. Hat-trick Du v Hants (Southampton) 2015. LO HS 38* Du v Derbys (Chester-le-St) 2015 (RLC). LO BB 5-31 Du v Notts (Chester-le-St) 2010 (CB40). T20 HS 5. T20 BB 3-14.

SHAIKH, Hamza (Eden Boys S), b 29 May 2006. 5'11". RHB, LB. Squad No 15. Warwickshire 2nd XI debut 2021. Awaiting f-c debut. LO HS 38 v Somerset (Taunton) 2023 (MBC).

NQ**SIMMONS, Che** Brandon (Sandwell C), b Barbados 18 Dec 2003. 6'1". RHB, RFM. Squad No 99. Warwickshire 2nd XI debut 2021. Awaiting 1st XI debut. Will qualify for England in 2024 thanks to UK passport.

SMITH, Kai (King's S, Canterbury), b Dubai 28 Nov 2004. RHB, WK. Warwickshire 2nd XI debut 2021. Awaiting f-c debut. LO HS 29* v Notts (Birmingham) 2022 (RLC).

WOAKES, Christopher Roger (Barr Beacon Language S, Walsall), b Birmingham 2 March 1989. 6'2". RHB, RFM. Squad No 19. Debut (Warwickshire) 2006; cap 2009. Wellington 2012-13. MCC 2009. IPL: KKR 2017; RCB 2018; DC 2021. Big Bash: ST 2013-14. Herefordshire 2006-07. *Wisden* 2016. PCA 2020. **ECB Two-Year Central Contract from 2023-24. Tests**: 48 (2013 to 2023); HS 137* v I (Lord's) 2018; BB 6-17 v Ire (Lord's) 2019. **LOI**: 122 (2010-11 to 2023-24); HS 95* v SL (Nottingham) 2016; BB 6-45 v A (Brisbane) 2010-11. **IT20**: 33 (2010-11 to 2023-24); HS 37 v P (Sharjah) 2015-16; BB 3-4 v A (Canberra) 2022-23. F-c Tours: A 2017-18, 2021-22; SA 2015-16, 2019-20; WI 2010-11 (EL), 2021-22; NZ 2017-18, 2019-20; I 2016-17; SL 2013-14 (EL), 2019-20; B 2016-17; UAE 2015-16 (v P). HS 152* v Derbys (Derby) 2013. 50 wkts (3); most – 59 (2016). BB 9-36 v Durham (Birmingham) 2016. LO HS 95* (*see LOI*). LO BB 6-45 (*see LOI*). T20 HS 57*. T20 BB 4-21.

YATES, Robert Michael (Warwick S), b Solihull 19 Sep 1999. 6'0". LHB, OB. Squad No 17. Debut (Warwickshire) 2019; cap 2023. Warwickshire 2nd XI debut 2017. Staffordshire 2018. HS 228* and BB 2-45 v Kent (Canterbury) 2023. LO HS 114 v Sussex (Birmingham) 2022 (RLC). LO BB 1-27 v Surrey (Oval) 2021 (RLC). T20 HS 71. T20 BB 1-13.

RELEASED/RETIRED

(Having made a County 1st XI appearance in 2023, even if not formally contracted. Some may return in 2024.)

NQ**BRATHWAITE, Kraigg** Clairmonte (Combermere S), b Belfield, St Michael, Barbados 1 Dec 1992. RHB, OB. Barbados 2008-09 to date. Sagicor HPC 2014. Yorkshire 2017. Nottinghamshire 2018; cap 2018. Glamorgan 2019. Gloucestershire 2021; cap 2021. Warwickshire 2023. **Tests** (WI): 89 (2011 to 2023-24, 30 as captain); HS 212 v B (Kingstown) 2014; BB 6-29 v SL (Colombo, PSS) 2015-16. **LOI** (WI): 10 (2016-17); HS 78 v Z (Bulawayo) 2016-17; BB 1-56 v SL (Bulawayo) 2016-17. F-c Tours (WI)(C=Captain): E 2010 (WI A), 2017, 2020; A 2015-16, 2022-23C, 2023-24C; SA 2014-15, 2022-23C; NZ 2013-14, 2017-18, 2020-21; I 2011-12, 2013-14 (WI A), 2018-19, 2019-20 (v Afg); SL 2014-15 (WI A), 2015-16, 2021-22C; Z 2017-18, 2022-23C; B 2011-12, 2018-19C, 2020-21C; UAE (v P) 2016-17. HS 276 Bar v Jamaica (Bridgetown) 2021-22. CC HS 103* Gm v Leics (Cardiff) 2019. Wa HS 16 v Surrey (Oval) 2023. BB 6-29 (*see Tests*). LO HS 108 Bar v ICC Americas (Lucas Street) 2016-17. LO BB 2-54 WI A v Sri Lanka A (Dambulla) 2014-15.

BROOKES, E.A. – *see WORCESTERSHIRE.*

BROOKES, H.J.H. – *see MIDDLESEX.*

NQ**DRAKES, Dominic** Conneil, b Barbados 2 Jun 1998. Son of V.C.Drakes (Barbados, Sussex, Border, Nottinghamshire, Warwickshire, Leicestershire and West Indies 1991-92 to 2003-04). LHB, LFM. Barbados 2017-18 to date. Yorkshire 2022. Warwickshire 2023 (T20 only). **LOI** (WI): 3 (2023); HS 8 v UAE (Sharjah) 2023; BB 2-29 v UAE (Sharjah) 2023 – separate matches. **IT20** (WI): 10 (2021-22 to 2022); HS 5 v P (Karachi) 2021-22 and 5 v I (Lauderhill) 2022; BB 1-19 v NZ (Kingston) 2022. HS 33 Bar v Jamaica (Bridgetown) 2017-18. CC HS 21 and CC BB 1-37 Y v Hants (Southampton) 2022. BB 3-17 Team Weekes v Team Headley (Coolidge) 2023. LO HS 40* Bar v Jamaica (St Augustine) 2023-24. LO BB 4-44 Bar v USA (Cave Hill) 2018-19. T20 HS 48*. T20 BB 3-26.

GARRETT, G.A. – *see KENT.*

NQ**MAXWELL, Glenn** James, b Kew, Melbourne, Australia 14 Oct 1988. 5'9". RHB, OB. Victoria 2010-11 to date. Hampshire 2014. Yorkshire 2015. Lancashire 2019. Warwickshire 2023. IPL: DD 2012-18; MI 2013 to 2013-13; KXIP 2014 to 2020-21; RCB 2021 to date. Big Bash: MR 2011-12; MS 2012-13 to date. London Spirit 2022. **Tests** (A): 7 (2012-13 to 2017); HS 104 v I (Ranchi) 2016-17; BB 4-127 v I (Hyderabad) 2012-13. **LOI** (A): 138 (2012 to 2023-24); HS 201* v Afg (Mumbai) 2023-24 – A record, while batting at No 6 out of 293-7; BB 4-40 v I (Rajkot) 2023-24. **IT20** (A): 106 (2012 to 2023-24); HS 145* v SL (Pallekele) 2016; BB 3-10 v E (Hobart) 2017-18. F-c Tours (A): I 2012-13, 2016-17; SA/Z 2013 (Aus A); B 2017; UAE 2014-15 (v P). HS 278 Vic v NSW (Sydney, NS) 2017-18. CC HS 140 Y v Durham (Scarborough) 2015. Wa HS 81 and Wa BB 1-45 v Kent (Canterbury) 2023. BB 5-40 La v Middx (Lord's) 2019. LO HS 201* (*see LOI*). LO BB 4-40 (*see LOI*). T20 HS 154*. T20 BB 3-10.

MIR HAMZA – *see GLAMORGAN.*

STIRLING, P.R. – *see IRELAND.*

M.S.Johal left the staff without making a County 1st XI appearance in 2023.

WARWICKSHIRE 2023

RESULTS SUMMARY

	Place	*Won*	*Lost*	*Drew*
LV= Insurance County Champ (Div 1)	4th	6	4	4
Metro Bank One-Day Cup (Group B)	SF	7	2	
Vitality Blast (North Group)	QF	11	4	

LV= INSURANCE COUNTY CHAMPIONSHIP AVERAGES
BATTING AND FIELDING

Cap		*M*	*I*	*NO*	*HS*	*Runs*	*Avge*	*100*	*50*	*Ct/St*
2018	S.R.Hain	11	16	1	165*	706	47.06	3	2	9
	H.J.H.Brookes	3	5	2	52*	103	34.33	–	1	–
2023	R.M.Yates	13	19	2	228*	583	34.29	2	–	26
2020	W.M.H.Rhodes	14	20	–	102	618	30.90	1	2	11
	E.G.Barnard	14	20	4	95	482	30.12	–	2	5
	D.R.Mousley	13	20	1	94	571	30.05	–	6	7
2021	M.G.K.Burgess	14	19	3	88	476	29.75	–	4	45/1
2021	D.R.Briggs	8	10	2	99	238	29.75	–	1	3
2023	A.L.Davies	12	17	–	118	437	25.70	1	2	6
2023	Hassan Ali	6	7	1	54	150	25.00	–	2	2
	J.G.Bethell	4	6	–	37	138	23.00	–	–	1
2023	C.Rushworth	13	12	4	22	95	11.87	–	–	3
2019	O.J.Hannon-Dalby	13	13	7	18	60	10.00	–	–	2
	K.C.Brathwaite	4	6	–	16	45	7.50	–	–	–

Also batted: C.G.Benjamin (1 match) 0, 3 (1 ct); D.M.Bess (1) 7, 63; J.B.Lintott (1) 8, 78; G.J.Maxwell (1) 81 (1 ct); C.N.Miles (3) 1, 29, 5 (2 ct); Mir Hamza (2) 10*, 6, 0; C.R.Woakes (3 – cap 2009) 27, 13, 1.

BOWLING

	O	*M*	*R*	*W*	*Avge*	*Best*	*5wI*	*10wM*
O.J.Hannon-Dalby	384	110	1030	54	19.07	7-46	2	–
C.R.Woakes	76	18	199	10	19.90	3-45	–	–
C.Rushworth	333.3	61	1074	53	20.26	7-38	2	1
Hassan Ali	144.3	22	518	24	21.58	4-48	–	–
E.G.Barnard	269.4	66	845	29	29.13	5-66	1	–
Also bowled:								
Mir Hamza	51.4	9	191	7	27.28	3-49	–	–
C.N.Miles	55	10	187	5	37.40	3-53	–	–
D.R.Briggs	134.5	27	346	9	38.44	2-28	–	–
H.J.H.Brookes	55	6	281	7	40.14	3-55	–	–

D.M.Bess 44-1-191-3; J.G.Bethell 11-3-36-0; M.G.K.Burgess 10-3-24-0; J.B.Lintott 18.1-0-90-3; G.J.Maxwell 24-3-62-1; D.R.Mousley 15.1-2-52-0; W.M.H.Rhodes 62-17-201-2; R.M.Yates 76.3-18-236-2.

Warwickshire played no first-class fixtures outside the County Championship in 2023. The First-Class Averages (pp 223–235) give the records of Warwickshire players in all first-class county matches, with the exception of D.M.Bess, C.N.Miles and C.R.Woakes, whose first-class figures for Warwickshire are as above.

WARWICKSHIRE RECORDS

FIRST-CLASS CRICKET

Highest Total	For 810-4d		v	Durham	Birmingham	1994
	V 887		by	Yorkshire	Birmingham	1896
Lowest Total	For 16		v	Kent	Tonbridge	1913
	V 15		by	Hampshire	Birmingham	1922
Highest Innings	For 501*	B.C.Lara	v	Durham	Birmingham	1994
	V 322	I.V.A.Richards	for	Somerset	Taunton	1985

Highest Partnership for each Wicket

1st	377*	N.F.Horner/K.Ibadulla	v	Surrey	The Oval	1960
2nd	465*	J.A.Jameson/R.B.Kanhai	v	Glos	Birmingham	1974
3rd	327	S.P.Kinneir/W.G.Quaife	v	Lancashire	Birmingham	1901
4th	470	A.I.Kallicharran/G.W.Humpage	v	Lancashire	Southport	1982
5th	335	J.O.Troughton/T.R.Ambrose	v	Hampshire	Birmingham	2009
6th	327	L.J.Evans/T.R.Ambrose	v	Sussex	Birmingham	2015
7th	289*	I.R.Bell/T.Frost	v	Sussex	Horsham	2004
8th	228	A.J.W.Croom/R.E.S.Wyatt	v	Worcs	Dudley	1925
9th	233	I.J.L.Trott/J.S.Patel	v	Yorkshire	Birmingham	2009
10th	214	N.V.Knight/A.Richardson	v	Hampshire	Birmingham	2002

Best Bowling	For	10-41	J.D.Bannister	v	Comb Servs	Birmingham	1959
(Innings)	V	10-36	H.Verity	for	Yorkshire	Leeds	1931
Best Bowling	For	15-76	S.Hargreave	v	Surrey	The Oval	1903
(Match)	V	17-92	A.P.Freeman	for	Kent	Folkestone	1932

Most Runs – Season	2417	M.J.K.Smith	(av 60.42)	1959
Most Runs – Career	35146	D.L.Amiss	(av 41.64)	1960-87
Most 100s – Season	9	A.I.Kallicharran		1984
	9	B.C.Lara		1994
Most 100s – Career	78	D.L.Amiss		1960-87
Most Wkts – Season	180	W.E.Hollies	(av 15.13)	1946
Most Wkts – Career	2201	W.E.Hollies	(av 20.45)	1932-57
Most Career W-K Dismissals	800	E.J.Smith	(662 ct; 138 st)	1904-30
Most Career Catches in the Field	422	M.J.K.Smith		1956-75

LIMITED-OVERS CRICKET

Highest Total	**50ov**	392-5		v	Oxfordshire	Birmingham	1984
	40ov	321-7		v	Leics	Birmingham	2010
	T20	261-2		v	Notts	Nottingham	2022
Lowest Total	**50ov**	93		v	Hampshire	Birmingham	2023
	40ov	59		v	Yorkshire	Leeds	2001
	T20	63		v	Notts	Birmingham	2021
Highest Innings	**50ov**	206	A.I.Kallicharran	v	Oxfordshire	Birmingham	1984
	40ov	137	I.R.Bell	v	Yorkshire	Birmingham	2005
	T20	158*	B.B.McCullum	v	Derbyshire	Birmingham	2015
Best Bowling	**50ov**	7-32	R.G.D.Willis	v	Yorkshire	Birmingham	1981
	40ov	6-15	A.A.Donald	v	Yorkshire	Birmingham	1995
	T20	5-19	N.M.Carter	v	Worcs	Birmingham	2005

WORCESTERSHIRE

Formation of Present Club: 11 March 1865
Inaugural First-Class Match: 1899
Colours: Dark Green and Black
Badge: Shield Argent a Fess between three Pears Sable
County Championships: (5) 1964, 1965, 1974, 1988, 1989
NatWest Trophy Winners: (1) 1994
Benson and Hedges Cup Winners: (1) 1991
Pro 40/National League (Div 1) Winners: (1) 2007
Sunday League Winners: (3) 1971, 1987, 1988
Twenty20 Cup Winners: (1) 2018

Chief Executive: Ashley Giles, County Ground, New Road, Worcester, WR2 4QQ • Tel: 01905 748474 Email: info@wccc.co.uk • Web: www.wccc.co.uk • Twitter: @WorcsCCC (88,654 followers)

Head Coach: Alan Richardson. **Assistant Head Coach**: Kadeer Ali. **Assistant Coach**: Richard Jones. **Captains**: B.L.D'Oliveira (f-c and T20) and J.D.Libby (50 ov). **Vice Captains**: J.D.Libby (f-c) and A.J.Hose (l-o). **Overseas Players**: N.G.Smith and Usama Mir. **2024 Testimonial**: J.Leach. **Head Groundsman**: Stephen Manfield. **Scorer**: Sue Drinkwater. **Vitality Blast Name**: Worcestershire Rapids. ‡ New registration. NQ Not qualified for England.

Worcestershire revised their capping policy in 2002 and now award players with their County Colours when they make their Championship debut.

BAKER, Josh Oliver (Warkwood Middle S; Malvern C), b Redditch 16 May 2003. 6'3". RHB, SLA. Squad No 33. Debut (Worcestershire) 2021. HS 75 v Glos (Cheltenham) 2023. BB 4-51 v Leics (Leicester) 2022. LO HS 25 v Durham (Worcester) 2021 (RLC). LO BB 3-29 v Derbys (Derby) 2023 (MBC). T20 HS 5. T20 BB 2-26.

‡**BROOKES, Ethan** Alexander (Solihull S & SFC), b Solihull, Warwks 23 May 2001. Younger brother of H.J.H.Brookes (*see MIDDLESEX*). 6'1". RHB, RMF. Squad No 77. Warwickshire 2019-21. Warwickshire 2nd XI 2018-23. Staffordshire 2019. HS 15* Wa v Glamorgan (Cardiff) 2020. BB –. LO HS 63 Wa v Leics (Birmingham) 2021 (RLC). LO BB 3-15 v Northants (Birmingham) 2021 (RLC).

‡**COBB, Josh**ua James (Oakham S), b Leicester 17 Aug 1990. Son of R.A.Cobb (Leics and N Transvaal 1980-89). 5'11½". RHB, OB. Squad No 3. Leicestershire 2007-14; l-o captain 2014. Northamptonshire 2015-23; cap 2018; captain 2020-22. Welsh Fire 2021-22. HS 148* Le v Middx (Lord's) 2008. BB 2-11 Le v Glos (Leicester) 2008. LO HS 146* Nh v Pakistanis (Northampton) 2019. LO BB 3-34 Le v Glos (Leicester) 2013 (Y40). T20 HS 103. T20 BB 5-25.

COX, Oliver Hugo (**'Olly'**) (Malvern C; Exeter U), b Peterborough, Canada 21 Nov 2003. 5'8". RHB, OB. Squad No 14. Worcestershire 2nd XI debut 2022. Herefordshire 2022. Awaiting 1st XI debut.

CULLEN, Henry James (St Benedict's HS, Alcester; St Augustine's SFC, Redditch), b Redditch 29 Apr 2003. RHB, WK. Squad No 13. Worcestershire 2nd XI debut 2021. Awaiting f-c debut. Herefordshire 2021-22. LO HS 8 v Derbys (Worcester) 2022 (RLC). No 1st XI appearances in 2023.

DARLEY, Harry Charles, b Shrewsbury, Shrops 21 Nov 2004. RHB, RFM. Squad No 41. Worcestershire 2nd XI debut 2022. Awaiting 1st XI debut.

D'OLIVEIRA, Brett Louis (Worcester SFC), b Worcester 28 Feb 1992. Son of D.B.D'Oliveira (Worcs 1982-95), grandson of B.L.D'Oliveira (Worcs, EP and England 1964-80). 5'9". RHB, LB. Squad No 15. Debut (Worcestershire) 2012; captain 2022 to date. MCC 2018. Birmingham Phoenix 2022. HS 202* v Glamorgan (Cardiff) 2016. BB 7-92 v Glamorgan (Cardiff) 2019. LO HS 123 and LO BB 3-8 v Essex (Chelmsford) 2021 (RLC). T20 HS 71. T20 BB 4-11.

EDAVALATH, Rehaan Mahamood (Newcastle-under-Lyme S; Malvern C; Loughborough U), b Wolverhampton, Staffs 4 Mar 2004. 5'9". RHB, OB. Squad No 11. Debut (Worcestershire) 2023. Worcestershire 2nd XI debut 2021. HS 15 v Derbys (Worcester) 2023 – only 1st XI appearance.

FINCH, Adam William (Kingswinford S; Oldswinford Hospital SFC), b Wordsley, Stourbridge 28 May 2000. 6'4". RHB, RMF. Squad No 61. Debut (Worcestershire) 2019. Surrey 2020 (on loan). Worcestershire 2nd XI debut 2017. England U19 2018 to 2018-19. HS 33* v Glos (Cheltenham) 2023. BB 5-74 v Glamorgan (Cardiff) 2023. LO HS 24 and LO BB 3-54 v Derbys (Worcester) 2022 (RLC). T20 HS 30*. T20 BB 3-38.

GIBBON, Benjamin James, b Chester 9 Jun 2000. 6'3". RHB, LMF. Squad No 21. Debut (Worcestershire) 2022. Lancashire 2nd XI 2019-21. Worcestershire 2nd XI debut 2021. Cheshire 2019-21. HS 41* v Yorks (Worcester) 2023. BB 4-87 v Glamorgan (Cardiff) 2022. LO HS 13* v Durham (Chester-le-St) 2023 (MBC). LO BB 3-58 v Somerset (Taunton) 2023 (MBC).

HOSE, Adam John (Carisbrooke S), b Newport, IoW 25 Oct 1992. 6'2". RHB, RMF. Squad No 54. Somerset 2016-17. Warwickshire 2018-19. Worcestershire debut 2023. Big Bash: AS 2022-23. Northern Superchargers 2022. HS 111 Wa v Notts (Birmingham) 2019. Wo HS 85 v Sussex (Hove) 2023. LO HS 101* Sm v Glos (Bristol) 2017 (RLC). T20 HS 119.

JONES, Robert Peter (Bridgewater HS), b Warrington, Cheshire 3 Nov 1995. 5'10". RHB, LB. Squad No 88. Lancashire 2016-23. Worcestershire debut 2023 (l-o only). Cheshire 2014. HS 122 La v Middx (Lord's) 2019. BB 1-4 La v Northants (Manchester) 2021. LO HS 122 v Northants (Northampton) 2023 (MBC). LO BB 1-3 La v Leics (Manchester) 2019 (RLC). T20 HS 61*.

KASHIF ALI (Dunstable C), b Kashmir, Pakistan 7 Feb 1998. 5'8". RHB, LB. Squad No 27. Debut (Worcestershire) 2022. Ghani Glass 2023-24. Bedfordshire 2021. HS 93 v Yorks (Leeds) 2023. BB 1-51 v Durham (Worcester) 2023. LO HS 114 v Kent (Worcester) 2022 (RLC) – on debut. T20 HS 69. T20 BB –.

LEACH, Joseph (Shrewsbury S; Leeds U), b Stafford 30 Oct 1990. Elder brother of S.G.Leach (Oxford MCCU 2014-16). 6'1". RHB, RMF. Squad No 23. Leeds/Bradford MCCU 2012. Worcestershire debut 2012; captain 2017-21; testimonial 2024. Staffordshire 2008-09. HS 114 v Glos (Cheltenham) 2013. 50 wkts (3); most – 69 (2017). BB 6-44 v Glamorgan (Worcester) 2022. LO HS 88 v Kent (Worcester) 2021 (RLC). LO BB 4-30 v Northants (Worcester) 2015 (RLC). T20 HS 24. T20 BB 5-33.

LIBBY, Jacob ('**Jake**') Daniel (Plymouth C; UWIC), b Plymouth, Devon 3 Jan 1993. 5'9". RHB, OB. Squad No 2. Cardiff MCCU 2014. Nottinghamshire 2014-19, scoring 108 v Sussex (Nottingham) on debut. Northamptonshire 2016 (on loan). Worcestershire debut 2020. Cornwall 2011-14. 1000 runs (2); most – 1153 (2023). HS 215 v Sussex (Hove) 2022. BB 2-10 v Middx (Worcester) 2022. LO HS 126* v Derbys (Worcester) 2022 (RLC). LO BB 2-47 v Lancs (Manchester) 2022 (RLC). T20 HS 78*. T20 BB 1-11.

POLLOCK, Edward John (RGS Worcester; Shrewsbury S; Collingwood C, Durham U), b High Wycombe, Bucks 10 Jul 1995. Son of A.J.Pollock (Cambridge U 1982-84); younger brother of A.W.Pollock (Cambridge MCCU & U 2013-15). 5'10". LHB, OB. Squad No 7. Durham MCCU 2015-17. Worcestershire debut 2022. Warwickshire 2017-21 (white-ball only). Herefordshire 2014-16. HS 113 v Middx (Northwood) 2022. LO HS 103* Wa v Derbys (Derby) 2021 (RLC). T20 HS 77.

RODERICK, Gareth Hugh (Maritzburg C), b Durban, South Africa 29 Aug 1991. 6'0". RHB, WK. Squad No 9. UK passport, qualifying for England in October 2018. KZN 2010-11 to 2011-12. Gloucestershire 2013-20; cap 2013; captain 2016-17. Worcestershire debut 2021. HS 172* v Glamorgan (Cardiff) 2022. LO HS 137 v Glos (Worcester) 2023 (MBC). T20 HS 32.

‡[NQ]**SMITH, Nathan** Gregory, b Dunedin, New Zealand 15 Jul 1998. 6'0". RHB, RMF. Squad No 20. Otago 2015-16 to 2020-21. Wellington 2021-22 to date. HS 114 Otago v ND (Dunedin) 2019-20. BB 6-36 Wellington v Canterbury (Rangiora) 2023-24. LO HS 81 Otago v ND (Dunedin) 2020-21. LO BB 3-21 Otago v ND (Hamilton) 2019-20. T20 HS 38*. T20 BB 5-14.

‡**TAYLOR, Thomas** Alex Ian (Trentham HS, Stoke-on-Trent), b Stoke-on-Trent, Staffs 21 Dec 1994. Elder brother of J.P.A.Taylor (*see SURREY*). 6'2". RHB, RMF. Squad No 12. Derbyshire 2014-17. Leicestershire 2018-20. Northamptonshire debut 2021. HS 80 De v Kent (Derby) 2016. BB 6-47 (10-122 match) Le v Sussex (Hove) 2019. LO HS 112 Nh v Glos (Cheltenham) 2023 (MBC). LO BB 3-24 v Notts (Grantham) 2021 (RLC). T20 HS 50*. T20 BB 5-28.

[NQ]**USAMA MIR**, b Sialkot, Pakistan 23 Dec 1995. 6'3". RHB, LB. Squad No 18. Khan Research Laboratories 2014-15. Sui Southern Gas Corporation 2015-16 to 2018-19. Lankan CC 2018-19. Baluchistan 2020-21. Central Punjab 2022-23. Worcestershire debut 2023. Big Bash: MS 2023-24. Manchester Originals 2023. **LOI** (P): 12 (2022-23 to 2023-24); HS 20 v NZ (Karachi) 2023; BB 4-43 v NZ (Karachi) 2023 – separate matches. **IT20** (P): 3 (2023-24); HS 1* and BB 1-21 v NZ (Christchurch) 2023-24. HS 77* Lankan v Panadura (Panagoda) 2018-19. BB 6-91 C Punjab v Khyber Pak (Faisalabad) 2022-23. Wo HS 1 and Wo BB 1-66 v Sussex (Hove) 2023. LO HS 42 C Punjab v Baluchistan (Karachi) 2022-23. LO BB 7-14 P Emerging v Hong Kong (Cox's Bazar) 2016-17. T20 HS 39. T20 BB 6-40.

WAITE, Matthew James (Brigshaw HS), b Leeds 24 Dec 1995. 6'0". RHB, RFM. Squad No 6. Yorkshire 2017-22. Worcestershire debut 2022. HS 109* v Derbys (Derby) 2023. BB 5-16 Y v Leeds/Brad MCCU (Leeds) 2019. CC BB 4-21 v Leics (Leicester) 2023. LO HS 71 Y v Warwks (Birmingham) 2017 (RLC). LO BB 5-59 Y v Leics (Leicester) 2021 (RLC). T20 HS 35*. T20 BB 3-18.

YADVINDER Singh **CHAHAL**, b Rajasthan, India 18 Jan 1996. 6'0" RHB, RMF. Squad No 8. Worcestershire 2nd XI debut 2019. Northamptonshire 2nd XI 2022. Somerset 2nd XI 2022. Awaiting 1st XI debut.

RELEASED/RETIRED

(Having made a County 1st XI appearance in 2023, even if not formally contracted. Some may return in 2024.)

[NQ]**AZHAR ALI**, b Lahore, Pakistan 19 Feb 1985. 5'9". RHB, LB. Lahore Blues 2001-02. KRL 2002-03 to 2011-12. Lahore 2003-04. Punjab 2008-09 to 2010-11. SNGPL 2012-13 to 2018-19. Somerset 2018-21; cap 2019. Central Punjab 2019-20 to 2022-23. Worcestershire 2022-23. **Tests** (P): 97 (2010 to 2021-22, 9 as captain); 1000 runs (1): 1198 (2016); HS 302* v WI (Dubai, DSC) 2016-17; BB 2-35 v SL (Pallekele) 2015. **LOI** (P): 53 (2011 to 2017-18, 31 as captain); HS 102 v Z (Lahore) 2015; BB 2-26 v E (Dubai, DSC) 2015-16. F-c Tours (P)(C=Captain): E 2010, 2016, 2018, 2020C; A 2009 (PA), 2016-17, 2019-20C; SA 2012-13, 2018-19; WI 2011, 2016-17, 2021; NZ 2010-11, 2016-17, 2020-21; SL 2009 (PA), 2012, 2014, 2015, 2022; Z 2011, 2013, 2021; B 2011-12, 2014-15, 2021-22; Ire 2018. HS 302* (*see Tests*). CC HS 225 v Leics (Worcester) 2022. BB 4-34 KRL v Peshawar (Peshawar) 2002-03. CC BB 1-5 Sm v Essex (Taunton) 2018. Wo BB 1-12 v Leics (Leicester) 2022. LO HS 132* SNGPL v Lahore Blues (Islamabad) 2015-16. LO BB 5-23 Lahore Whites v Peshawar (Karachi) 2001 – on debut. T20 HS 72. T20 BB 3-10.

NQ**BRACEWELL, Michael** Gordon, b Masterton, New Zealand 14 Feb 1991. Son of M.A.Bracewell (Otago 1977-78); nephew of B.P.Bracewell (C Districts, Otago, N Distsricts & New Zealand 1977-78 to 1989-90), D.W.Bracewell (Canterbury & C Districts 1974-75 to 1979-80) and J.G.Bracewell (Otago, Auckland & New Zealand 1978-79 to 1989-90); cousin of D.A.J.Bracewell (C Districts, Northamptonshire & New Zealand 2008-09 to date). LHB, OB. Otago 2010-11 to 2016-17. Wellington 2017-18 to 2021-22. Worcestershire 2023 (T20 only). IPL: RCB 2023. **Tests** (NZ): 8 (2022 to 2022-23); HS 74* and BB 4-75 v P (Karachi) 2022-23. **LOI** (NZ): 19 (2021-22 to 2022-23); HS 140 v I (Hyderabad) 2022-23; BB 3-21 v Neth (Hamilton) 2021-22. **IT20** (NZ): 16 (2022 to 2022-23); HS 61* v Scot (Edinburgh) 2022; BB 3-5 v Ire (Belfast) 2022. F-c Tours (NZ): E 2014 (NZA), 2022; P 2022-23. HS 190 Otago v Wellington (Dunedin) 2012-13. BB 5-43 Wellington v Auckland (Auckland) 2019-20. LO HS 140 (*see LOI*). LO BB 3-21 (*see LOI*). T20 HS 141*. T20 BB 4-28.

BROWN, P.R. – *see DERBYSHIRE.*

CORNALL, Taylor Ryan, b Lytham St Anne's, Lancs 9 Oct 1998. 6'0". LHB, SLA. Leeds/Bradford MCCU 2019. Worcestershire 2022-23. Lancashire 2021 (l-o only). HS 31* v Middx (Northwood) 2022. LO HS 97 v Essex (Worcester) 2022 (RLC). LO BB 2-23 v Derbys (Worcester) 2022 (RLC).

COX, O.B. – *see LEICESTERSHIRE.*

HAYNES, J.A. – *see NOTTINGHAMSHIRE.*

JONES, Cameron William (Wombourne HS; Invictus SFC, Wombourne), b Wolverhampton, Staffs 17 Jan 2005. LHB, RMF. Worcestershire 2nd XI 2022-23. Awaiting f-c debut. LO HS 0 and LO BB 1-28 v Somerset (Taunton) 2023 (MBC).

PENNINGTON, D.Y. – *see NOTTINGHAMSHIRE.*

NQ**SAINI, Navdeep**, b Kamal, Haryana, India 23 Nov 1992. RHB, RFM. Delhi 2013-14 to date. Kent 2022. Worcestershire 2023. IPL: RCB 2019-21; RR 2022 to date. **Tests** (I): 2 (2020-21); HS 5 v A (Brisbane) 2020-21; BB 2-54 v A (Sydney) 2020-21. **LOI** (I): 8 (2019-20 to 2021); HS 45 v NZ (Auckland) 2019-20; BB 2-58 v WI (Cuttack) 2019-20. **IT20** (I): 11 (2019 to 2021); HS 11* v NZ (Wellington) 2019-20; BB 3-17 v WI (Lauderhill) 2019. F-c Tours (IA): E 2018; A 2020-21 (I); SA 2017, 2021-22; NZ 2018-19; B 2022-23. HS 50* IA v Bangladesh A (Sylhet) 2022-23. CC HS 5* and CC BB 5-72 K v Warwks (Birmingham) 2022. Wo HS 0* and Wo BB 1-122 v Derbys (Worcester) 2023. BB 6-32 Delhi v Maharashtra (Delhi) 2015-16. LO HS 45 (*see LOI*). LO BB 5-46 IA v West Indies A (North Sound) 2019. T20 HS 12*. T20 BB 4-17.

NQ**SANTNER, Mitchell** Josef, b Hamilton, New Zealand 5 Feb 1992. LHB, SLA. N Districts 2011-12 to date. Worcestershire 2016. IPL: CSK 2019 to date. Southern Brave 2023. **Tests** (NZ): 26 (2015-16 to 2023-24); HS 126 v E (Mt Maunganui) 2019-20; BB 3-34 v SA (Mt Maunganui) 2023-24. **LOI** (NZ): 104 (2015 to 2023-24); HS 67 v E (Christchurch) 2017-18; BB 5-50 v Ire (Dublin) 2017. **IT20** (NZ): 100 (2015 to 2023-24); HS 77* v Neth (Hague) 2022; BB 4-11 v I (Nagpur) 2015-16. F-c Tours (NZ): E 2015, 2021; A 2015-16, 2019-20; SA 2016; I 2016-17; SL 2019; Z 2016; B 2023-24. HS 136 and BB 5-51 ND v CD (Mt Maunganui) 2022-23. CC HS 23* v Glamorgan (Cardiff) 2016. LO HS 86 ND v CD (New Plymouth) 2014-15. LO BB 5-50 (*see LOI*). T20 HS 92*. T20 BB 4-11.

STANLEY, M.T. – *see LANCASHIRE.*

TONGUE, J.C. – *see NOTTINGHAMSHIRE.*

NQ**VAN BEEK, Logan** Verjus, b Christchurch, New Zealand 7 Sep 1990. Grandson of S.C.Guillen (Trinidad, Canterbury, West Indies and New Zealand 1947-48 to 1960-61). 6'1". RHB, RMF. Canterbury 2009-10 to 2016-17. Netherlands 2017. Wellington 2017-18 to date. Derbyshire 2019. Worcestershire 2023. **LOI** (Neth): 33 (2021 to 2023-24); HS 59 v SL (Lucknow) 2023-24; BB 4-24 v Nepal (Harare) 2023. **IT20** (Neth): 23 (2013-14 to 2022-23); HS 19* v PNG (Bulawayo) 2022; BB 4-27 v Hong Kong (Bulawayo) 2022. F-c Tours (NZA): I 2022-23; UAE 2018-19 (v PA). HS 111* Cant v Otago (Christchurch) 2015-16. CC HS 53 and CC BB 4-42 v Glamorgan (Worcester) 2023. BB 6-46 Well v Auckland (Auckland) 2017-18. LO HS 136 Wellington v CD (Wellington) 2023-24. LO BB 6-18 Neth v UAE (Voorburg) 2017. T20 HS 61*. T20 BB 4-15.

WORCESTERSHIRE 2023

RESULTS SUMMARY

	Place	*Won*	*Lost*	*Drew*	*Tied*
LV= Insurance County Champ (Div 2)	2nd	5	3	6	
Metro Bank One-Day Cup (Group B)	QF	6	3		
Vitality Blast (North Group)	QF	8	6		1

LV= INSURANCE COUNTY CHAMPIONSHIP AVERAGES
BATTING AND FIELDING

Cap†		*M*	*I*	*NO*	*HS*	*Runs*	*Avge*	*100*	*50*	*Ct/St*
2020	J.D.Libby	12	23	3	198	1153	57.65	4	5	11
2012	B.L.D'Oliveira	12	21	3	103	661	36.72	1	4	4
2022	M.J.Waite	11	20	4	109*	565	35.31	1	3	4
2023	B.M.J.Allison	3	4	–	75	134	33.50	–	1	–
2023	A.J.Hose	11	19	1	85	566	31.44	–	3	8
2021	G.H.Roderick	13	24	1	123	696	30.26	1	3	38/2
2019	J.A.Haynes	12	22	3	134*	573	30.15	2	1	15
2019	A.W.Finch	7	11	6	33*	128	25.60	–	–	3
2022	Azhar Ali	14	26	1	103*	612	24.48	2	1	1
2022	B.J.Gibbon	8	9	4	41*	116	23.20	–	–	7
2022	Kashif Ali	4	6	–	93	133	22.16	–	1	–
2021	J.O.Baker	5	7	1	75	130	21.66	–	1	6
2022	E.J.Pollock	8	15	–	56	255	17.00	–	1	6
2012	J.Leach	14	22	4	53	259	14.38	–	1	3
2017	J.C.Tongue	5	7	4	16*	40	13.33	–	–	–
2018	D.Y.Pennington	8	10	1	26	101	11.22	–	–	2

Also batted: J.A.Brooks (1 match – cap 2023) 18; T.R.Cornall (1 – cap 2022) 6, 4 (1 ct); O.B.Cox (1 – cap 2009) 15, 2* (6 ct); R.M.Edavalath (1 – cap 2023) 0, 15; N.Saini (1 – cap 2023) 0*; Usama Mir (1 – cap 2023) 0, 1; L.V.van Beek (2 – cap 2023) 53, 0, 6 (1 ct).

BOWLING

	O	*M*	*R*	*W*	*Avge*	*Best*	*5wI*	*10wM*
A.W.Finch	174.4	23	720	28	25.71	5-74	2	–
D.Y.Pennington	203.5	39	718	26	27.61	4-36	–	–
J.Leach	433.1	87	1414	48	29.45	6-78	2	–
J.C.Tongue	114.5	11	485	16	30.31	5-29	1	–
M.J.Waite	244.5	48	815	26	31.34	4-21	–	–
B.J.Gibbon	200.3	28	861	20	43.05	4-92	–	–
Also bowled:								
L.V.van Beek	40.1	7	162	8	20.25	4-42	–	–
B.M.J.Allison	53	6	217	5	43.40	2-40	–	–

J.O.Baker 110-5-474-4; J.A.Brooks 22-4-83-1; T.R.Cornall 1-0-5-0; B.L.D'Oliveira 61-4-266-3; Kashif Ali 10-0-77-1; J.D.Libby 13-1-68-0; N.Saini 29-4-122-1; Usama Mir 41.1-2-173-2.

Worcestershire played no first-class fixtures outside the County Championship in 2023. The First-Class Averages (pp 223–235) give the records of Worcestershire players in all first-class county matches, with the exception of B.M.J.Allison, J.A.Brooks, O.B.Cox and J.C.Tongue, whose first-class figures for Worcestershire are as above.

† Worcestershire revised their capping policy in 2002 and now award players with their County Colours when they make their Championship debut.

WORCESTERSHIRE RECORDS

FIRST-CLASS CRICKET

Highest Total	For 701-6d		v	Surrey	Worcester	2007
	V 701-4d		by	Leics	Worcester	1906
Lowest Total	For 24		v	Yorkshire	Huddersfield	1903
	V 30		by	Hampshire	Worcester	1903
Highest Innings	For 405*	G.A.Hick	v	Somerset	Taunton	1988
	V 331*	J.D.B.Robertson	for	Middlesex	Worcester	1949

Highest Partnership for each Wicket

1st	309	H.K.Foster/F.L.Bowley	v	Derbyshire	Derby	1901
2nd	316	S.C.Moore/V.S.Solanki	v	Glos	Cheltenham	2008
3rd	438*	G.A.Hick/T.M.Moody	v	Hampshire	Southampton[1]	1997
4th	330	B.F.Smith/G.A.Hick	v	Somerset	Taunton	2006
5th	393	E.G.Arnold/W.B.Burns	v	Warwicks	Birmingham	1909
6th	265	G.A.Hick/S.J.Rhodes	v	Somerset	Taunton	1988
7th	256	D.A.Leatherdale/S.J.Rhodes	v	Notts	Nottingham	2002
8th	184	S.J.Rhodes/S.R.Lampitt	v	Derbyshire	Kidderminster	1991
9th	181	J.A.Cuffe/R.D.Burrows	v	Glos	Worcester	1907
10th	136	A.G.Milton/S.J.Magoffin	v	Somerset	Worcester	2018

Best Bowling	For	9- 23	C.F.Root	v	Lancashire	Worcester	1931
(Innings)	V	10- 51	J.Mercer	for	Glamorgan	Worcester	1936
Best Bowling	For	15- 87	A.J.Conway	v	Glos	Moreton-in-M	1914
(Match)	V	17-212	J.C.Clay	for	Glamorgan	Swansea	1937

Most Runs – Season	2654	H.H.I.H.Gibbons	(av 52.03)	1934
Most Runs – Career	34490	D.Kenyon	(av 34.18)	1946-67
Most 100s – Season	10	G.M.Turner		1970
	10	G.A.Hick		1988
Most 100s – Career	106	G.A.Hick		1984-2008
Most Wkts – Season	207	C.F.Root	(av 17.52)	1925
Most Wkts – Career	2143	R.T.D.Perks	(av 23.73)	1930-55
Most Career W-K Dismissals	1095	S.J.Rhodes	(991 ct; 104 st)	1985-2004
Most Career Catches in the Field	528	G.A.Hick		1984-2008

LIMITED-OVERS CRICKET

Highest Total	**50ov**	404-3		v	Devon	Worcester	1987
	40ov	376-6		v	Surrey	The Oval	2010
	T20	227-6		v	Northants	Kidderminster	2007
Lowest Total	**50ov**	58		v	Ireland	Worcester	2009
	40ov	86		v	Yorkshire	Leeds	1969
	T20	53		v	Lancashire	Manchester	2016
Highest Innings	**50ov**	192	C.J.Ferguson	v	Leics	Worcester	2018
	40ov	160	T.M.Moody	v	Kent	Worcester	1991
	T20	127	T.Kohler-Cadmore	v	Durham	Worcester	2016
Best Bowling	**50ov**	7-19	N.V.Radford	v	Beds	Bedford	1991
	40ov	6-16	Shoaib Akhtar	v	Glos	Worcester	2005
	T20	5-24	A.Hepburn	v	Notts	Worcester	2017

YORKSHIRE

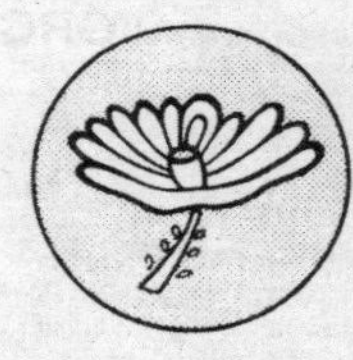

Formation of Present Club: 8 January 1863
Substantial Reorganisation: 10 December 1891
Inaugural First-Class Match: 1864
Colours: Dark Blue, Light Blue and Gold
Badge: White Rose
County Championships (since 1890): (32) 1893, 1896, 1898, 1900, 1901, 1902, 1905, 1908, 1912, 1919, 1922, 1923, 1924, 1925, 1931, 1932, 1933, 1935, 1937, 1938, 1939, 1946, 1959, 1960, 1962, 1963, 1966, 1967, 1968, 2001, 2014, 2015
Joint Champions: (1) 1949
Gillette/C&G Trophy Winners: (3) 1965, 1969, 2002
Benson and Hedges Cup Winners: (1) 1987
Sunday League Winners: (1) 1983
Twenty20 Cup Winners: (0); best – Finalist 2012

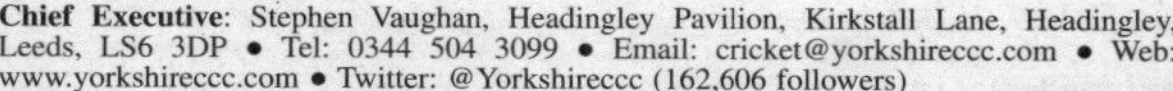

Chief Executive: Stephen Vaughan, Headingley Pavilion, Kirkstall Lane, Headingley, Leeds, LS6 3DP • Tel: 0344 504 3099 • Email: cricket@yorkshireccc.com • Web: www.yorkshireccc.com • Twitter: @Yorkshireccc (162,606 followers)

MD Cricket: Darren Gough. **Head Coach**: Ottis Gibson. **Assistant Coaches**: Kabir Ali and Alastair Maiden. **Captain**: Shan Masood. **Overseas Players**: D.Ferreira and Shan Masood. **2023 Testimonial**: J.M.Bairstow. **Head Groundsman**: Richard Robinson. **Scorers**: John Potter and John Virr. **Vitality Blast Name**: Yorkshire Vikings. ‡ New registration. NQ Not qualified for England.

BAIRSTOW, Jonathan Marc (St Peter's S, York; Leeds Met U), b Bradford 26 Sep 1989. Son of D.L.Bairstow (Yorkshire, GW and England 1970-90); brother of A.D.Bairstow (Derbyshire 1995). 6'0". RHB, WK, occ RM. Squad No 21. Debut (Yorkshire) 2009; cap 2011; testimonial 2023. IPL: SH 2019-21; PK 2022. Welsh Fire 2021 to datse. Inaugural winner of Young Wisden Schools Cricketer of the Year 2008. YC 2011. PCA 2022. **ECB Two-Year Central Contract from 2023-24. Tests**: 100 (2012 to 2023-24); 1000 runs (2); most – 1470 (2016); HS 167* v SL (Lord's) 2016. Took a world record 70 dismissals in 2016, as well as scoring a record number of runs in a calendar year for a keeper. **LOI**: 107 (2011 to 2023-24); 1000 runs (1): 1025 (2018); HS 141* v WI (Southampton) 2017. **IT20**: 70 (2011 to 2023): HS 90 v SA (Bristol) 2022. F-c Tours: A 2013-14, 2017-18, 2021-22; SA 2014-15 (EL), 2015-16, 2019-20; WI 2010-11 (EL), 2018-19, WI 2021-22; NZ 2017-18; I 2012-13, 2016-17, 2020-21, 2023-24; SL 2013-14 (EL), 2018-19, 2020-21; B 2016-17; UAE 2015-16 (v P). 1000 runs (3); most – 1286 (2016). HS 246 v Hants (Leeds) 2016. LO HS 174 v Durham (Leeds) 2017 (RLC). T20 HS 114.

BEAN, Finlay Joseph (Q Ethelburga's C), b Harrogate 16 Apr 2002. LHB, WK. Squad No 33. Debut (Yorkshire) 2022. Yorkshire 2nd XI debut 2019. Warwickshire 2nd XI 2022. HS 135 v Worcs (Worcester) 2023. BB –. LO HS 61 v Kent (Canterbury) 2022 (RLC).

BESS, Dominic Mark (Blundell's S), b Exeter, Devon 22 Jul 1997. Cousin of Z.G.G.Bess (Devon 2015-19), J.J.Bess (Devon 2007-18) and L.F.O.Bess (Devon 2017-19). 5'11". RHB, OB. Squad No 47. Somerset 2016-23. Yorkshire debut 2019 (on loan); cap 2021. Warwickshire 2023 (on loan). Southern Rocks 2023-24. MCC 2018, 2019. Devon 2015-16. **Tests**: 14 (2018 to 2020-21); HS 57 v P (Lord's) 2018; BB 5-30 v SL (Galle) 2020-21. F-c Tours: A 2019-20 (EL), 2021-22 (EL); SA 2019-20; WI 2017-18 (EL); I 2018-19 (EL), 2020-21; SL 2019-20, 2020-21. HS 107 MCC v Essex (Bridgetown) 2018. CC HS 92 Sm v Hants (Taunton) 2018. Y HS 91* v Essex (Leeds) 2019. BB 7-43 v Northants (Northampton) 2021. LO HS 51 v Middx (Radlett) 2023 (MBC). LO BB 5-37 v Essex (Chelmsford) 2023 (MBC). T20 HS 42*. T20 BB 3-15.

BROOK, Harry Cherrington (Sedbergh S), b Keighley 22 Feb 1999. 5'11". RHB, RM. Squad No 88. Debut (Yorkshire) 2016. IPL: SH 2023. Big Bash: HH 2021-22. Northern Superchargers 2021 to date. YC 2021. **ECB Three-Year Central Contract from 2023-24. Tests**: 12 (2022 to 2023); HS 186 and BB 1-25 v NZ (Wellington) 2022-23. **LOI**: 15 (2022-23 to 2023-24); HS 80 v SA (Bloemfontein) 2022-23. **IT20**: 29 (2021-22 to 2023-24); HS 81* v P (Karachi) 2022-23. F-c Tours: A 2021-22 (EL); NZ 2022-23; P 2022-23. HS 194 v Kent (Leeds) 2022. BB 3-15 v Glamorgan (Cardiff) 2021. LO HS 103 v Leics (Leeds) 2019 (RLC). T20 HS 106*. T20 BB 1-13.

CHOHAN, Jafer Ali (Harrow S; Loughborough U), b Camden, Middx 11 Jul 2002. RHB, LB. Squad No 5. Yorkshire 2nd XI debut 2023. Berkshire 2022. Awaiting f-c debut. T20 HS 37. T20 BB 1-13.

CLIFF, Benjamin Michael (Brighouse HS; Huddersfield New C), b Halifax 23 Oct 2002. RHB, RFM. Squad No 26. Debut (Yorkshire) 2023. Yorkshire 2nd XI debut 2021. England U19 2022. HS 1 v Glamorgan (Cardiff) 2023. BB 2-27 v Leics (Leicester) 2023. LO HS 0. LO BB 1-44 v Northants (York) 2022 (RLC).

COAD, Benjamin Oliver (Thirsk S & SFC), b Harrogate 10 Jan 1994. 6'2". RHB, RM. Squad No 10. Debut (Yorkshire) 2016; cap 2018. HS 69 v Essex (Leeds) 2022. 50 wkts (1): 53 (2017). BB 6-25 v Lancs (Leeds) 2017. LO HS 45 v Leics (Leicester) 2023 (MBC). LO BB 4-63 v Derbys (Leeds) 2017 (RLC). T20 HS 7. T20 BB 3-40.

DUKE, Harry George (QEGS, Wakefield; Leeds U), b Wakefield 6 Sep 2001. 5'8". RHB, WK, occ RM. Squad No 22. Debut (Yorkshire) 2021. Yorkshire 2nd XI debut 2019. HS 54 v Sussex (Leeds) 2021. LO HS 125 v Leics (Leicester) 2021 (RLC). T20 HS –.

NQ**EDWARDS, Michael** William (St Augustus C), b Manly, NSW, Australia 23 Dec 1994. 6'7". RHB, RFM. Squad No 90. UK passport through British-born parents. New South Wales 2017-18 to 2022-23. Yorkshire debut 2023. Big Bash: SS 2017-18 to 2021-22. HS 19* v Sussex (Hove) 2023. BB 3-54 v Glamorgan (Leeds) 2023. LO HS 11 NSW v SA (Sydney, HO) 2017-18. LO BB 4-31 NSW v Tas (Perth) 2017-18. T20 HS 0*. T20 BB 1-19.

‡NQ**FERREIRA, Donovan**, b Pretoria, South Africa 21 Jul 1998. RHB, OB, occ WK. Squad No 2. Easterns 2020-21. Northerns 2022-23 to date. **IT20** (SA): 2 (2023 to 2023-24); HS 48 v A (Durban) 2023. HS 127 Easterns v KZN Inland (Bloemfontein) 2020-21. BB 6-38 Northerns v NW (Potchefstroom) 2023-24. LO HS 138* and LO BB 3-53 v KZN Coastal (Durban) 2023-24. T20 HS 82*. T20 BB 2-18.

FISHER, Matthew David (Easingwold SS), b York 9 Nov 1997. 6'1". RHB, RFM. Squad No 7. Debut (Yorkshire) 2015; cap 2022. MCC 2018. Northern Superchargers 2021. Southern Brave 2023. **ECB Development Contract 2023-24**. **Tests**: 1 (2021-22); HS 0* and BB 1-67 v WI (Bridgetown) 2021-22. F-c Tours (EL): A 2021-22; WI 2021-22 (E); I 2023-24; SL 2022-23. HS 53 EL v Sri Lanka A (Galle) 2022-23. Y HS 47* v Kent (Leeds) 2019. BB 5-30 v Derbys (Chesterfield) 2023. LO HS 36* v Worcs (Worcester) 2017 (RLC). LO BB 3-32 v Leics (Leeds) 2015 (RLC). T20 HS 19. T20 BB 5-22.

HILL, George Christopher Hindley (Sedbergh S), b Keighley 24 Jan 2001. 6'2½". RHB, RMF. Squad No 18. Debut (Yorkshire) 2020. Yorkshire 2nd XI debut 2018. England U19 2018-19. HS 151* v Northants (Northampton) 2022. BB 6-26 v Lancs (Manchester) 2022. LO HS 130 v Worcs (Scarborough) 2022 (RLC). LO BB 3-47 v Warwks (York) 2021 (RLC). T20 HS 19*. T20 BB 1-9.

LEECH, Dominic James (Nunthorpe Ac; Q Ethelburga's S, York), b Middlesbrough 10 Jan 2001. 6'2½". RHB, RMF. Squad No 8. Debut (Yorkshire) 2020. Northamptonshire 2023 (on loan). Yorkshire 2nd XI debut 2018. HS 32 and BB 3-78 v Glos (Leeds) 2023. LO HS 23 v Hants (York) 2023 (MBC). LO BB 2-34 v Surrey (York) 2023 (MBC). T20 HS 1*. T20 BB 3-13.

LUXTON, William Andrew (Bradford GS), b Keighley 6 May 2003. RHB, OB. Squad No 68. Debut (Yorkshire) 2022. Yorkshire 2nd XI debut 2021. HS 31 v Surrey (Scarborough) 2022. LO HS 84 v Northants (York) 2022 (RLC). T20 HS 7.

LYTH, Adam (Caedmon S, Whitby; Whitby Community C), b Whitby 25 Sep 1987. 5'8". LHB, RM. Squad No 9. Debut (Yorkshire) 2007; cap 2010; testimonial 2020-21. MCC 2017. Big Bash: PS 2022-23. Northern Superchargers 2021 to date. PCA 2014. *Wisden* 2014. **Tests**: 7 (2015); HS 107 v NZ (Leeds) 2015. F-c Tours (EL): SA 2014-15; WI 2010-11. 1000 runs (4); most – 1619 (2014). HS 251 v Lancs (Manchester) 2014. BB 2-9 v Middx (Scarborough) 2016. LO HS 144 v Lancs (Manchester) 2018 (RLC). LO BB 2-27 v Derbys (Leeds) 2019 (RLC). T20 HS 161 v Northants (Leeds) 2017 – Y & UK record; 6th highest score in all T20 cricket. T20 BB 5-31.

MALAN, Dawid Johannes (Paarl HS), b Roehampton, Surrey 3 Sep 1987. Son of D.J.Malan (WP B and Transvaal B 1978-79 to 1981-82), elder brother of C.C.Malan (Loughborough MCCU 2009-10). 6'0". LHB, LB. Squad No 29. Boland 2005-06. Middlesex 2008-19, scoring 132* v Northants (Uxbridge) on debut; cap 2010; T20 captain 2016-19; captain 2018-19. Yorkshire debut/cap 2020. MCC 2010-11, 2013. IPL: PK 2021. Big Bash: HH 2020-21. Trent Rockets 2021 to date. **ECB Central Contract 2023-24. Tests**: 22 (2017 to 2021-22); HS 140 v A (Perth) 2017-18; BB 2-33 v A (Adelaide) 2021-22. **LOI**: 30 (2019 to 2023-24); HS 140 v B (Dharamsala) 2023-24; BB 1-5 v Neth (Amstelveen) 2022. **IT20**: 62 (2017 to 2023); HS 103* v NZ (Napier) 2019-20; BB 1-27 v NZ (Hamilton) 2017-18. F-c Tours: A 2017-18, 2021-22; NZ 2017-18. 1000 runs (3); most – 1137 runs (2014). HS 219 v Derbys (Leeds) 2020. BB 5-61 M v Lancs (Liverpool) 2012. Y BB 2-24 v Notts (Nottingham) 2020. LO HS 185* EL v Sri Lanka A (Northampton) 2016. LO BB 4-25 PDSC v Partex (Savar) 2014-15. T20 HS 117. T20 BB 2-10.

MILNES, Matthew Edward (West Bridgford CS; Durham U), b Nottingham 29 Jul 1994. 6'1". RHB, RMF. Squad No 4. Durham MCCU 2014. Nottinghamshire 2018. Kent 2019-22; cap 2021. Yorkshire debut 2023. Welsh Fire 2021. Oval Invincibles 2022. HS 78 K v Yorks (Canterbury) 2021. Y HS 75 and Y BB 3-72 v Leics (Leeds) 2023. 50 wkts (1): 58 (2019). BB 6-53 K v Leics (Leicester) 2021. LO HS 26 and LO BB 5-79 K v Hants (Canterbury) 2019 (RLC). T20 HS 14*. T20 BB 5-22.

MORIARTY, Daniel Thornhill (Rondesbosch Boys' HS), b Reigate, Surrey 2 Dec 1999. 6'0". LHB, SLA. Squad No 11. Surrey 2020-23, taking 5-64 v Middx (Oval) on debut. Yorkshire debut 2023. Southern Brave 2022. Surrey 2nd XI 2019-23. Essex 2nd XI 2019. MCC YC 2019. South Africa U19 2016. HS 29 Sy v SL Dev (Guildford) 2022. CC HS 13* Sy v Kent (Canterbury) 2023. Y HS 4* and Y BB 5-139 v Glos (Leeds) 2023. BB 6-60 Sy v Glos (Oval) 2021. LO HS 15 Sy v Lancs (Guildford) 2023 (MBC). LO BB 4-30 Sy v Somerset (Oval) 2021 (RLC). T20 HS 9*. T20 BB 3-25.

RASHID, Adil Usman (Belle Vue S, Bradford), b Bradford 17 Feb 1988. 5'8". RHB, LBG. Squad No 3. Debut (Yorkshire) 2006; cap 2008; testimonial 2018. Signed white ball only contract in 2020. MCC 2007-09. IPL: PK 2021, SH 2023. Big Bash: AS 2015-16. Northern Superchargers 2021 to date. YC 2007. Match double (114, 48, 8-157 and 2-45) for England U19 v India U19 (Taunton) 2006. **ECB Two-Year Central Contract from 2023-24. Tests**: 19 (2015-16 to 2018-19), taking 5-64 v P (Abu Dhabi) on debut; HS 61 v P (Dubai, DSC) 2015-16; BB 5-49 v SL (Colombo, SSC) 2018-19. **LOI**: 135 (2009 to 2023-24); HS 69 v NZ (Birmingham) 2015; BB 5-27 v Ire (Bristol) 2017. **IT20**: 104 (2009 to 2023-24); HS 22 v WI (Bridgetown) 2021-22; BB 4-2 v WI (Dubai, DSC) 2021-22. F-c Tours: WI 2010-11 (EL), 2018-19; I 2007-08 (EL), 2016-17; SL 2018-19; B 2006-07 (Eng A), 2016-17; UAE 2015-16 (v P). HS 180 v Somerset (Leeds) 2013. 50 wkts (2); most – 65 (2008). BB 7-107 v Hants (Southampton) 2008. LO HS 71 v Glos (Leeds) 2014 (RLC). LO BB 5-27 (*see LOI*). T20 HS 36*. T20 BB 4-2.

REVIS, Matthew Liam (Ilkley GS), b Steeton 15 Nov 2001. 6'4½". RHB, RM. Squad No 77. Debut (Yorkshire) 2019. Yorkshire 2nd XI debut 2019. HS 106 v Derbys (Scarborough) 2023. BB 5-50 v Glamorgan (Cardiff) 2023. LO HS 58* v Somerset (Taunton) 2021 (RLC). LO BB 4-54 v Essex (Chelmsford) 2023 (MBC). T20 HS 42. T20 BB 2-18.

ROOT, Joseph Edward (King Ecgbert S, Sheffield; Worksop C), b Sheffield 30 Dec 1990. Elder brother of W.T.Root (*see GLAMORGAN*). 6'0". RHB, OB. Squad No 66. Debut (Yorkshire) 2010; cap 2012. IPL: RR 2023. Big Bash: ST 2018-19. Trent Rockets 2021 to date. YC 2012. *Wisden* 2013. PCA 2021. **ECB Three-Year Central Contract from 2023-24. Tests**: 140 (2012-13 to 2023-24, 64 as captain); 1000 runs (4); most – 1708 (2021); HS 254 v P (Manchester) 2016; BB 5-8 v I (Ahmedabad) 2020-21. **LOI**: 171 (2012-13 to 2023-24); HS 133* v B (Oval) 2017; BB 3-52 v Ire (Lord's) 2017. **IT20**: 32 (2012-13 to 2019); HS 90* v A (Southampton) 2013; BB 2-9 v WI (Kolkata) 2015-16. F-c Tours(C=Captain): A 2013-14, 2017-18C, 2021-22C; SA 2015-16, 2019-20C; WI 2014-15, 2018-19C, 2021-22C; NZ 2012-13, 2017-18C, 2019-20C, 2022-23; I 2012-13, 2016-17, 2020-21C, 2023-24; P 2022-23; SL 2018-19C, 2019-20C, 2020-21C; B 2016-17; UAE 2015-16 (v P). 1000 runs (3); most – 1228 (2013). HS 254 (*see Tests*). CC HS 236 v Derbys (Leeds) 2013. BB 5-8 (*see Tests*). Y BB 4-5 v Lancs (Manchester) 2018. LO HS 133* (*see LOI*). LO BB 3-52 (*see LOI*). T20 HS 92*. T20 BB 2-7.

NQ**SHAN MASOOD**, b Kuwait 14 Oct 1989. LHB, RMF. Squad No 94. Karachi Whites 2007-08 to date. Habib Bank 2009-10 to 2013-14. Durham MCCU 2011. Federal Areas 2011-12. Islamabad 2012-13. United Bank 2015-16 to 2017-18. National Bank 2018-19. Southern Punjab 2019-20 to 2020-21. Baluchistan 2021-22. Derbyshire 2022; cap 2022. Yorkshire debut 2023; captain 2023 to date. **Tests** (P): 33 (2013-14 to 2023-24); HS 156 v E (Manchester) 2020; BB 1-6 v SA (Centurion) 2018-19. **LOI** (P): 9 (2018-19 to 2023); HS 50 v A (Dubai) 2018-19. **IT20** (P): 19 (2022-23); HS 65* v E (Karachi) 2022-23. F-c Tours (P): E 2016, 2020; A 2019-20, 2023-24; SA 2018-19; WI 2010-11 (P A), 2016-17; NZ 2020-21; SL 2015 (P A), 2023. 1000 runs (1+1); most – 1123 (2012-13). HS 239 De v Sussex (Derby) 2022. Y HS 192 v Glamorgan (Cardiff) 2023. BB 2-52 DU v Warwks (Durham) 2011. LO HS 182* Islamabad v Rawalpindi (Rawalpindi) 2017-18. LO BB 2-0 HB v Islamabad Leopards (Islamabad) 2010-11. T20 HS 103*.

TATTERSALL, Jonathan Andrew (King James S, Knaresborough), b Harrogate 15 Dec 1994. 5'8". RHB, WK, occ LB. Squad No 12. Debut (Yorkshire) 2018; cap 2022. Gloucestershire 2021 (on loan). Surrey 2021 (on loan). HS 180* v Surrey (Scarborough) 2022. LO HS 89 v Hants (Southampton) 2018 (RLC). T20 HS 53*.

THOMPSON, Jordan Aaron (Benton Park S), b Leeds 9 Oct 1996. 5'11". LHB, RM. Squad No 44. Debut (Yorkshire) 2019; cap 2022. Big Bash: HH 2021-22. Northern Superchargers 2021. London Spirit 2022 to date. HS 98 v Notts (Nottingham) 2020. BB 5-31 Leics (Leeds) 2020. LO BB –. T20 HS 74. T20 BB 5-21.

VAGADIA, Yash (Teesside HS; Durham U), b Newcastle upon Tyne 7 May 2004. RHB, OB. Squad No 45. Yorkshire 2nd XI debut 2021. Awaiting 1st XI debut.

WHARTON, James Henry (Holmfirth HS; Greenhead C), b Huddersfield 1 Feb 2001. 6'4". RHB, OB. Squad No 23. Debut (Yorkshire) 2022. Yorkshire 2nd XI debut 2018. HS 89 v Worcs (Leeds) 2023. LO HS 54* v Essex (Chelmsford) 2023 (MBC). T20 HS 111*.

RELEASED/RETIRED

(Having made a County 1st XI appearance in 2023)

FRAINE, William Alan Richard (Silcoates S; Bromsgrove SFC; Durham U), b Huddersfield, Yorks 13 Jun 1996. 6'2". RHB, RM. Durham MCCU 2017-18. Nottinghamshire 2018. Yorkshire 2019-22. Herefordshire 2016. HS 106 v Surrey (Scarborough) 2019. LO HS 143 v Northants (York) 2022 (RLC). T20 HS 44*.

NQ**HOPE, Shai** Diego (Queens C; Bede's S, Upper Dicker), b Barbados 10 Nov 1993. Younger brother of K.A.Hope (Barbados, Trinidad & Tobago and West Indies 2009-10 to 2019-20). RHB, WK. Barbados 2012-13 to date. Yorkshire 2023. *Wisden* 2017. **Tests** (WI): 38 (2015 to 2021-22); HS 147 (and 117*) v E (Leeds) 2017. **LOI** (WI): 124 (2016-17 to 2023-24, 20 as captain); HS 170 v Ire (Dublin) 2019. **IT20** (WI): 28 (2017-18 to 2023-24); HS 55 v B (Sylhet) 2018-19. F-c Tours (WI): E 2017, 2020; A 2015-16; NZ 2017-18; I 2018-19, 2019-20; SL 2015-16, 2021-22; Z 2017-18; B 2018-19; UAE (v P) 2016-17. HS 215* Barbados v Guyana (Bridgetown) 2016-17. Y HS 83 v Leics (Leeds) 2023. LO HS 170 (*see LOI*). T20 HS 106.

MIKE, B.W.M. – *see LEICESTERSHIRE.*

NQ**RICKELTON, Ryan** David (St Stithians C), b Johannesburg, South Africa 11 Jul 1996. LHB, WK, occ SLA. Gauteng 2015-16 to date. Lions 2019-20 to 2020-21. Central Gauteng 2019-20. Northamptonshire 2022. Yorkshire 2023. **Tests** (SA): 4 (2021-22 to 2022-23); HS 42 v B (Gqeberha) 2021-22. **LOI** (SA): 2 (2022-23); HS 14 v WI (E London) 2022-23. F-c Tours (SA): E 2022; Z 2021 (SAA). HS 202* C Gauteng v FS (Johannesburg) 2019-20. CC HS 133 Nh v Kent (Canterbury) 2022. Y HS 46 v Sussex (Leeds) 2023. BB –. LO HS 169 SAA v Zimbabwe A (Harare) 2021. LO BB 1-7 Gauteng v FS (Johannesburg) 2017-18. T20 HS 98. T20 BB 1-14.

NQ**SAUD SHAKIL**, b Karachi, Pakistan 5 Sep 1995. LHB, SLA. Karachi Whites 2015-16. Karachi Blues 2016-17. Pakistan TV 2017-18 to 2018-19. Sindh 2019-20 to 2022-23. Yorkshire 2023. SNGPL 2023-24. **Tests** (P): 10 (2022-23 to 2023-24); HS 208* v SL (Galle) 2023; BB –. **LOI** (P): 15 (2021 to 2023-24); HS 68 v Neth (Hyderabad) 2023-24; BB 1-14 v E (Lord's) 2021. F-c Tours (P): E 2016 (PA); A 2023-24; SL 2021-22 (PA), 2023; Z 2016-17 (PA); UAE 2018-19 (PA). 1000 runs (0+1): 1334 (2022-23). HS 208* (*see Tests*). Y HS 35 v Glamorgan (Leeds) 2023. BB 2-7 PT v Rawalpindi (Rawalpindi) 2017-18. LO HS 134* Rawalpindi v FATA (Rawalpindi) 2017-18. LO BB 3-23 PT v Habib Bank (Karachi) 2017-18. T20 HS 74. T20 BB 1-14.

SHUTT, Jack William (Kirk Balk S; Thomas Rotherham C), b Barnsley 24 Jun 1997. 6'0". RHB, OB. Yorkshire 2020-22. HS 7* v Durham (Chester-le-St) 2020. BB 2-14 v Notts (Nottingham) 2020. LO HS 6* v Leics (Leicester) 2023 (MBC). LO BB 4-46 v Glamorgan (Cardiff) 2022 (RLC). T20 HS 0*. T20 BB 5-11.

NQ**STEKETEE, Mark** Thomas, b Warwick, Queensland, Australia 17 Jan 1994. RHB, RFM. Queensland 2014-15 to date. Essex 2022. Yorkshire 2023. Big Bash: BH 2013-14 to 2022-23; MS 2023-24. HS 53 Q v NSW (Sydney) 2016-17. CC HS 26 v Glos (Leeds) 2023. BB 7-44 (10-92 match) Q v SA (Adelaide) 2021-22. CC BB 4-130 Ex v Warwks (Birmingham) 2022. Y BB 3-55 v Worcs (Worcester) 2023. LO HS 35* Q v Tas (Brisbane, AB) 2022-23. LO BB 4-25 Q v Vic (Melbourne, St K) 2019-20. T20 HS 33. T20 BB 4-33.

NQ**WIESE, David** (Witbank HS), b Roodepoort, South Africa 18 May 1985. 6'3". RHB, RMF. Easterns 2005-06 to 2011-12. Titans 2009-10 to 2016-17. Sussex 2016-20; cap 2016. Yorkshire 2023 (T20 only). IPL: RCB 2015-16; KKR 2023. London Spirit 2021. Northern Superchargers 2022 to date. **LOI** (SA/Nam): 15 (6 for SA 2015 to 2015-16; 9 for Nam 2021-22 to 2022); HS 67 Nam v UAE (Dubai) 2021-22; BB 3-50 SA v E (Cape Town) 2015-16. **IT20** (SA/Nam): 45 (20 for SA 2013 to 2015-16; 25 for Nam 2021-22 to 2023-24); HS 66* Nam v Neth (Abu Dhabi) 2021-22; BB 5-23 SA v WI (Durban) 2014-15. F-c Tour (SA A): A 2014. HS 208 Easterns v GW (Benoni) 2008-09. UK HS 139 Sx v Cardiff MCCU (Hove) 2019. CC HS 106 Sx v Warwks (Birmingham) 2018. BB 6-58 Titans v Knights (Centurion) 2014-15. CC BB 5-26 Sx v Middx (Lord's) 2019. LO HS 171 Sx v Hants (Southampton) 2019 (RLC). LO BB 5-25 Easterns v Boland (Benoni) 2010-11. T20 HS 79*. T20 BB 5-19.

YORKSHIRE 2023

RESULTS SUMMARY

	Place	Won	Lost	Drew	Aband	NR
LV= Insurance County Champ (Div 2)	7th	3	2	8	1	
Metro Bank One-Day Cup (Group A)	6th	2	4			2
Vitality Blast (North Group)	8th	6	6			2

LV= INSURANCE COUNTY CHAMPIONSHIP AVERAGES
BATTING AND FIELDING

Cap		*M*	*I*	*NO*	*HS*	*Runs*	*Avge*	*100*	*50*	*Ct/St*
	S.D.Hope	2	4	1	83	187	62.33	–	2	6/1
	Shan Masood	7	13	1	192	720	60.00	2	3	2
2010	A.Lyth	13	22	1	174	1019	48.52	3	5	18
	F.J.Bean	13	21	–	135	983	46.80	3	2	14
	M.L.Revis	10	15	4	106	487	44.27	2	1	4
2020	D.J.Malan	7	13	–	132	542	41.69	2	1	–
	J.H.Wharton	6	10	1	89	349	38.77	–	4	2
	G.C.H.Hill	13	21	2	101	694	36.52	1	7	11
2022	J.A.Tattersall	9	13	1	79	338	28.16	–	1	24/1
2011	J.M.Bairstow	2	4	1	36	83	27.66	–	–	7
2022	J.A.Thompson	11	14	1	64	299	23.00	–	3	4
2021	D.M.Bess	8	13	3	49	216	21.60	–	–	5
2022	M.D.Fisher	9	14	6	37*	140	17.50	–	–	2
	Saud Shakil	3	5	–	35	71	14.20	–	–	1
2018	B.O.Coad	11	12	3	45	119	13.22	–	–	1
	M.W.Edwards	3	5	1	19*	52	13.00	–	–	–

Also batted: B.M.Cliff (2 matches) 1, 0*; D.J.Leech (1) 32 (1 ct); B.W.M.Mike (1) 25; M.E.Milnes (2) 75, 15* (1 ct); D.T.Moriarty (4) 4*, 1*, 2* (1 ct); R.D.Rickelton (3) 6, 46, 13 (2 ct); M.T.Steketee (4) 26, 3, 2.

BOWLING

	O	*M*	*R*	*W*	*Avge*	*Best*	*5wI*	*10wM*
B.O.Coad	279.2	84	728	36	20.22	5- 33	2	–
M.D.Fisher	238.3	52	799	28	28.53	5- 30	1	–
J.A.Thompson	249	47	918	30	30.60	3- 48	–	–
M.L.Revis	124.4	14	528	15	35.20	5- 50	1	–
G.C.H.Hill	206.5	41	681	19	35.84	4- 43	–	–
D.M.Bess	259.3	39	934	22	42.45	5-158	1	–
Also bowled:								
M.E.Milnes	60	8	224	7	32.00	3- 72	–	–
D.T.Moriarty	83.1	23	245	7	35.00	5-139	1	–
M.T.Steketee	70.3	13	272	6	45.33	3- 55	–	–
M.W.Edwards	65	8	254	5	50.80	3- 54	–	–

F.J.Bean 11-0-105-0; B.M.Cliff 26-1-116-3; D.J.Leech 16-2-78-3; A.Lyth 49-8-147-2; D.J.Malan 3-0-8-0; Saud Shakil 5-1-23-0; J.A.Tattersall 4-0-19-0; J.H.Wharton 12.1-1-114-1.

Yorkshire played no first-class fixtures outside the County Championship in 2023. The First-Class Averages (pp 223–235) give the records of Yorkshire players in all first-class county matches, with the exception of J.M.Bairstow, D.M.Bess, D.J.Leech and D.T.Moriarty, whose first-class figures for Yorkshire are as above.

YORKSHIRE RECORDS

FIRST-CLASS CRICKET

Highest Total	For 887		v	Warwicks	Birmingham	1896
	V 681-7d		by	Leics	Bradford	1996
Lowest Total	For 23		v	Hampshire	Middlesbrough	1965
	V 13		by	Notts	Nottingham	1901
Highest Innings	For 341	G.H.Hirst	v	Leics	Leicester	1905
	V 318*	W.G.Grace	for	Glos	Cheltenham	1876

Highest Partnership for each Wicket

1st	555	P.Holmes/H.Sutcliffe	v	Essex	Leyton	1932
2nd	346	W.Barber/M.Leyland	v	Middlesex	Sheffield	1932
3rd	346	J.J.Sayers/A.McGrath	v	Warwicks	Birmingham	2009
4th	372	J.E.Root/J.M.Bairstow	v	Surrey	Leeds	2016
5th	340	E.Wainwright/G.H.Hirst	v	Surrey	The Oval	1899
6th	305	A.Lyth/J.A.Tattersall	v	Surrey	Scarborough	2022
7th	366*	J.M.Bairstow/T.T.Bresnan	v	Durham	Chester-le-St[2]	2015
8th	292	R.Peel/Lord Hawke	v	Warwicks	Birmingham	1896
9th	246	T.T.Bresnan/J.N.Gillespie	v	Surrey	The Oval	2007
10th	149	G.Boycott/G.B.Stevenson	v	Warwicks	Birmingham	1982

Best Bowling	For	10-10	H.Verity	v	Notts	Leeds	1932
(Innings)	V	10-37	C.V.Grimmett	for	Australians	Sheffield	1930
Best Bowling	For	17-91	H.Verity	v	Essex	Leyton	1933
(Match)	V	17-91	H.Dean	for	Lancashire	Liverpool	1913

Most Runs – Season	2883	H.Sutcliffe	(av 80.08)	1932
Most Runs – Career	38558	H.Sutcliffe	(av 50.20)	1919-45
Most 100s – Season	12	H.Sutcliffe		1932
Most 100s – Career	112	H.Sutcliffe		1919-45
Most Wkts – Season	240	W.Rhodes	(av 12.72)	1900
Most Wkts – Career	3597	W.Rhodes	(av 16.02)	1898-1930
Most Career W-K Dismissals	1186	D.Hunter	(863 ct; 323 st)	1888-1909
Most Career Catches in the Field	665	J.Tunnicliffe		1891-1907

LIMITED-OVERS CRICKET

Highest Total	**50ov**	411-6		v	Devon	Exmouth	2004
	40ov	352-6		v	Notts	Scarborough	2001
	T20	260-4		v	Northants	Leeds	2017
Lowest Total	**50ov**	76		v	Surrey	Harrogate	1970
	40ov	54		v	Essex	Leeds	2003
	T20	68		v	Derbyshire	Chesterfield	2023
Highest Innings	**50ov**	175	T.M.Head	v	Leics	Leicester	2016
	40ov	191	D.S.Lehmann	v	Notts	Scarborough	2001
	T20	161	A.Lyth	v	Northants	Leeds	2017
Best Bowling	**50ov**	7-27	D.Gough	v	Ireland	Leeds	1997
	40ov	7-15	R.A.Hutton	v	Worcs	Leeds	1969
	T20	6-19	T.T.Bresnan	v	Lancashire	Leeds	2017

PROFESSIONAL UMPIRES' TEAM 2024

† New appointment. See page 83 for key to abbreviations.

BAILEY, Robert John (Biddulph HS), b Biddulph, Staffs 28 Oct 1963. 6'3". RHB, OB. Northamptonshire 1982-99; cap 1985; benefit 1993; captain 1996-97. Derbyshire 2000-01; cap 2000. Staffordshire 1980. YC 1984. **Tests:** 4 (1988 to 1989-90); HS 43 v WI (Oval) 1988. **LOI**: 4 (1984-85 to 1989-90); HS 43* v SL (Oval) 1988. F-c Tours: SA 1991-92 (Nh); WI 1989-90; Z 1994-95 (Nh). 1000 runs (13); most – 1987 (1990). HS 224* Nh v Glamorgan (Swansea) 1986. BB 5-54 Nh v Notts (Northampton) 1993. F-c career: 374 matches; 21844 runs @ 40.52, 47 hundreds; 121 wickets @ 42.51; 272 ct. Appointed 2006. Umpired 24 LOI (2011 to 2021). **ICC International Panel 2011-19.**

BAINTON, Neil Laurence, b Romford, Essex 2 October 1970. No f-c appearances. Appointed 2006.

BALDWIN, Paul Kerr, b Epsom, Surrey 18 Jul 1973. No f-c appearances. Umpired 18 LOI (2006 to 2009). Reserve List 2010-14. Appointed 2015.

BAMBURY, Grace, b Stafford 28 Jun 2001.

BLACKWELL, Ian David (Brookfield Community S), b Chesterfield, Derbys 10 Jun 1978. 6'2". LHB, SLA. Derbyshire 1997-99. Somerset 2000-08; cap 2001; captain 2006 (*part*). Durham 2009-12. Warwickshire 2012 (on loan). MCC 2012. **Tests**: 1 (2005-06); HS 4 and BB-v I (Nagpur) 2005-06. **LOI**: 34 (2002-03 to 2005-06); HS 82 v I (Colombo) 2002-03; BB 3-26 v A (Adelaide) 2002-03. F-c Tour: I 2005-06. 1000 runs (3); most – 1256 (2005). HS 247* Sm v Derbys (Taunton) 2003 – off 156 balls and including 204 off 98 balls in reduced post-lunch session. BB 7-52 Du v Australia A (Chester-le-St) 2012. CC BB 7-85 Du v Lancs (Manchester) 2009. F-c career: 210 matches; 11595 runs @ 39.57, 27 hundreds; 398 wickets @ 35.91; 66 ct. Reserve List 2015-17. Appointed 2018.

BROWN, Gabi, b Ashton-under-Lyne, Lancs 1 Sep 1989.

BURNS, Michael (Walney CS), b Barrow-in-Furness, Lancs 6 Feb 1969. 6'0". RHB, RM, WK. Warwickshire 1992-96. Somerset 1997-2005; cap 1999; captain 2003-04. 1000 runs (2); most – 1133 (2003). HS 221 Sm v Yorks (Bath) 2001. BB 6-54 Sm v Leics (Taunton) 2001. F-c career: 154 matches; 7648 runs @ 32.68, 8 hundreds; 68 wickets @ 42.42; 142 ct, 7 st. Appointed 2016. Umpired 7 LOI (2020 to 2023). **ICC International Panel 2020 to date.**

CLARK, Amy, b Corbridge, Northumberland 9 Feb 2001.

DEBENHAM, Benjamin John, b Chelmsford, Essex 11 Oct 1967. LHB. No f-c appearances. Reserve List 2012-17. Appointed 2018.

DOVEY, Rose, b Wennappuwa, Sri Lanka 28 Jul 1979.

GOUGH, Michael Andrew (English Martyrs RCS; Hartlepool SFC), b Hartlepool, Co Durham 18 Dec 1979. Son of M.P.Gough (Durham 1974-77). 6'5". RHB, OB. Durham 1998-2003. F-c Tours (Eng A): NZ 1999-00; B 1999-00. HS 123 Du v CU (Cambridge) 1998. CC HS 103 Du v Essex (Colchester) 2002. BB 5-56 Du v Middx (Chester-le-St) 2001. F-c career: 67 matches; 2952 runs @ 25.44, 2 hundreds; 30 wickets @ 45.00; 57 ct. Reserve List 2006-08. Appointed 2009. Umpired 34 Tests (2016 to 2023-24) and 85 LOI (2013 to 2023-24). **ICC Elite Panel 2020 to date.**

HARRIS, Anna Yolanda, b High Wycombe, Bucks 15 Oct 1998.

HARRIS, Anthony Charles, b Durban, South Africa 23 Nov 1973. No f-c appearances. Appointed 2022.

HARTLEY, Peter John (Greenhead GS; Bradford C), b Keighley, Yorks 18 Apr 1960. 6'0". RHB, RMF. Warwickshire 1982. Yorkshire 1985-97; cap 1987; benefit 1996. Hampshire 1998-2000; cap 1998. F-c Tours (Y): SA 1991-92; WI 1986-87; Z 1995-96. HS 127* Y v Lancs (Manchester) 1988. 50 wkts (7); most – 81 (1995). BB 9-41 (inc hat-trick, 4 wkts in 5 balls and 5 in 9; 11-68 match) Y v Derbys (Chesterfield) 1995. Hat-trick 1995. F-c career: 232 matches; 4321 runs @ 19.91, 2 hundreds; 683 wickets @ 30.21; 68 ct. Appointed 2003. Umpired 6 LOI (2007 to 2009). **ICC International Panel 2006-09.**

HASSAN ADNAN (MAO C, Lahore), b Lahore, Pakistan 15 May 1975. 5'9". RHB, OB. Islamabad 1994-95 to 2000-01. WAPDA 1997-98 to 2010-11. Gujranwala 1997-98 to 1998-99. Derbyshire 2003-07; cap 2004. Lahore 2003-04. Pakistan Customs 2009-10. Suffolk 2008-12. 1000 runs (1): 1380 (2004). HS 191 De v Somerset (Taunton) 2005. BB 1-4 De v Glos (Derby) 2006. F-c career: 137 matches; 7609 runs @ 37.11, 10 hundreds; 4 wickets @ 88.00; 76 ct. Reserve list 2020-21. Appointed 2022.

IBBOTSON, Joanne, b Rotherham, Yorks 29 Dec 1971.

ILLINGWORTH, Richard Keith (Salts GS), b Bradford, Yorks 23 Aug 1963. 5'11". RHB, SLA. Worcestershire 1982-2000; cap 1986; benefit 1997. Natal 1988-89. Derbyshire 2001. Wiltshire 2005. **Tests:** 9 (1991 to 1995-96); HS 28 v SA (Pt Elizabeth) 1995-96; BB 4-96 v WI (Nottingham) 1995. Took wicket of P.V.Simmons with his first ball in Tests – v WI (Nottingham) 1991. **LOI:** 25 (1991 to 1995-96); HS 14 v P (Melbourne) 1991-92; BB 3-33 v Z (Albury) 1991-92. F-c Tours: SA 1995-96; NZ 1991-92; P 1990-91 (Eng A); SL 1990-91 (Eng A); Z 1989-90 (Eng A), 1990-91 (Wo), 1993-94 (Wo), 1996-97 (Wo). HS 120* Wo v Warwks (Worcester) 1987 – as night-watchman. Scored 106 for England A v Z (Harare) 1989-90 – also as night-watchman. 50 wkts (5); most – 75 (1990). BB 7-50 Wo v OU (Oxford) 1985. F-c career: 376 matches; 7027 runs @ 22.45, 4 hundreds; 831 wickets @ 31.54; 161 ct. Appointed 2006. Umpired 66 Tests (2012-13 to 2023-24) and 90 LOI (2010 to 2023-24). **ICC Elite Panel 2013 to date**.

JARVIS, Julia, b Haywards Heath, Sussex 2 Jul 1968.

KETTLEBOROUGH, Richard Allan (Worksop C), b Sheffield, Yorks 15 Mar 1973. 6'0". LHB, RM. Yorkshire 1994-97. Middlesex 1998-99. F-c Tour (Y): Z 1995-96. HS 108 Y v Essex (Leeds) 1996. BB 2-26 Y v Notts (Scarborough) 1996. F-c career: 33 matches; 1258 runs @ 25.16, 1 hundred; 3 wickets @ 81.00; 20 ct. Appointed 2006. Umpired 81 Tests (2010-11 to 2023-24) and 106 LOI (2009 to 2023-24). **ICC Elite Panel 2011 to date**.

LLONG, Nigel James (Ashford North S), b Ashford, Kent 11 Feb 1969. 6'0". LHB, OB. Kent 1990-98; cap 1993. F-c Tour (K): Z 1992-93. HS 130 K v Hants (Canterbury) 1996. BB 5-21 K v Middx (Canterbury) 1996. F-c career: 68 matches; 3024 runs @ 31.17, 6 hundreds; 35 wickets @ 35.97; 59 ct. Appointed 2002. Umpired 62 Tests (2007-08 to 2019-20) and 130 LOI (2006 to 2019-20). **ICC Elite Panel 2012-20**.

LLOYD, Graham David (Hollins County HS), b Accrington, Lancs 1 Jul 1969. Son of D.Lloyd (Lancs and England 1965-83). 5'9". RHB, RM. Lancashire 1988-2002; cap 1992; benefit 2001. **LOI:** 6 (1996 to 1998-99); HS 22 v A (Oval) 1997. F-c Tours: A 1992-93 (Eng A); WI 1995-96 (La). 1000 runs (5); most – 1389 (1992). HS 241 La v Essex (Chelmsford) 1996. BB 1-4. F-c career: 203 matches; 11279 runs @ 38.23, 24 hundreds; 2 wickets @ 220.00; 140 ct. Reserve List 2009-13. Appointed 2014.

LUNGLEY, Tom (St John Houghton SS; SE Derbyshire C), b Derby 25 Jul 1979. 6'1". LHB, RM. Derbyshire 2000-10; cap 2007. HS 50 De v Warwks (Derby) 2008. 50 wkts (1): 59 (2007). BB 5-20 De v Leics (Derby) 2007. F-c career: 55 matches; 885 runs @ 14.50; 149 wickets @ 32.10; 25 ct. Reserve list 2015-21. Appointed 2022.

McLELLAND, Isobel **Sophie**, b Bournemouth, Hants 9 May 1989.

MALLENDER, Neil Alan (Beverley GS), b Kirk Sandall, Yorks 13 Aug 1961. 6'0". RHB, RFM. Northamptonshire 1980-86 and 1995-96; cap 1984. Somerset 1987-94; cap 1987; benefit 1994. Otago 1983-84 to 1992-93; captain 1990-91 to 1992-93. **Tests:** 2 (1992); HS 4 v P (Oval) 1992; BB 5-50 v P (Leeds) 1992 – on debut. F-c Tour (Nh): Z 1994-95. HS 100* Otago v CD (Palmerston N) 1991-92. UK HS 87* Sm v Sussex (Hove) 1990. 50 wkts (6); most – 56 (1983). BB 7-27 Otago v Auckland (Auckland) 1984-85. UK BB 7-41 Nh v Derbys (Northampton) 1982. F-c career: 345 matches; 4709 runs @ 17.18, 1 hundred; 937 wickets @ 26.31; 111 ct. Appointed 1999. Umpired 3 Tests (2003-04) and 22 LOI (2001 to 2003-04). **ICC Elite Panel 2004**.

MIDDLEBROOK, James Daniel (Pudsey Crawshaw S), b Leeds, Yorks 13 May 1977. 6'1". RHB, OB. Yorkshire 1998-2015. Essex 2002-09; cap 2003. Northamptonshire 2010-14, cap 2011. MCC 2010, 2013. HS 127 Ex v Middx (Lord's) 2007. 50 wkts (1): 56 (2003). BB 6-78 Nh v Kent (Northampton) 2013. Hat-trick Ex v Kent (Canterbury) 2003. F-c career: 226 matches; 7873 runs @ 27.72, 10 hundreds; 475 wickets @ 38.15; 112 ct. Reserve list 2017-21. Appointed 2022.

MILLNS, David James (Garibaldi CS; N Notts C; Nottingham Trent U), b Clipstone, Notts 27 Feb 1965. 6'3". LHB, RF. Nottinghamshire 1988-89, 2000-01; cap 2000. Leicestershire 1990-99; cap 1991; benefit 1999. Tasmania 1994-95. Boland 1996-97. F-c Tours: A 1992-93 (Eng A); SA 1996-97 (Le). HS 121 Le v Northants (Northampton) 1997. 50 wkts (4); most – 76 (1994). BB 9-37 (12-91 match) Le v Derbys (Derby) 1991. F-c career: 171 matches; 3082 runs @ 22.01, 3 hundreds; 553 wickets @ 27.35; 76 ct. Reserve List 2007-08. Appointed 2009. Umpired 7 LOI (2020 to 2023). **ICC International Panel 2020 to date.**

NAEEM ASHRAF, b Lahore, Pakistan 10 Nov 1972. LHB, LFM. Lahore City 1987-88 to 1998-99. National Bank of Pakistan 1992-93 to 1999-00. Lahore Whites 2000-01. **LOI** (P): 2 (1995); HS 16 v SL (Sharjah) 1995; BB –. HS 139 Lahore City v Gujranwala (Gujranwala) 1997-98. BB 7-41 (10-70 match) NBP v Allied Bank (Lahore) 1997-98. F-c career: 86 matches; 3009 runs @ 26.16, 5 hundreds; 289 wickets @ 24.12; 47 ct. Appointed 2022.

NAEEM, Jasmine, b Ropary, Pakistan 10 Mar 1981. Wife of Naeem Ashraf (*above*).

NEWELL, Mark (Hazelwick SS; City of Westminster C), b Crawley, Sussex 19 Dec 1973. Brother of K.Newell (Sussex, Matabeleland and Glamorgan 1995-2001). 6'1½". RHB, OB. Sussex 1996-98. Derbyshire 1999. Buckinghamshire 2007. HS 135* Sx v Derbys (Horsham) 1998. BB –. 24 matches; 889 runs @ 23.39; 3 hundreds; 17 ct. Reserve list 2017-21. Appointed 2022.

O'SHAUGHNESSY, Steven Joseph (Harper Green SS, Franworth), b Bury, Lancs 9 Sep 1961. 5'10½". RHB, RM. Lancashire 1980-87; cap 1985. Worcestershire 1988-89. Scored 100 in 35 min to equal world record for La v Leics (Manchester) 1983. 1000 runs (1): 1167 (1984). HS 159* La v Somerset (Bath) 1984. BB 4-66 La v Notts (Nottingham) 1982. F-c career: 112 matches; 3720 runs @ 24.31, 5 hundreds; 114 wickets @ 36.03; 57 ct. Reserve List 2009-10. Appointed 2011.

PEVERALL, Benjamin John, b Bristol 23 Jan 1992. No f-c appearances. Appointed 2023.

POLLARD, Paul Raymond (Gedling CS), b Carlton, Nottingham 24 Sep 1968. 5'11". LHB, RM. Nottinghamshire 1987-98; cap 1992. Worcestershire 1999-2001. F-c Tour (Nt): SA 1996-97. 1000 runs (3); most – 1463 (1993). HS 180 Nt v Derbys (Nottingham) 1993. BB 2-79 Nt v Glos (Bristol) 1993. F-c career: 192 matches; 9685 runs @ 31.44, 15 hundreds; 4 wkts @ 68.00; 158 ct. Reserve List 2012-17. Appointed 2018.

PRATT, Neil, b Bishop Auckland, Co Durham 8 Jun 1972. Brother of A.Pratt (Durham 1997-2004) and G.Pratt (Durham 2000-06). RHB, RM. No f-c appearances. Reserve list 2020-21. Appointed 2022.

REDFERN, Suzanne, b Mansfield, Notts 26 Oct 1977. LHB, LM. MBE 2018. **Tests**: 6 (1995-96 to 1999); HS 30 v NZ (Worcester) 1996; BB 2-27 v I (Shenley) 1999. **LOI**: 15 (1995 to 1999); HS 27 v I (Nottingham) 1999; BB 4-21 v SA (Bristol) 1997. Test career: 6 matches; 146 runs @ 29.20; 6 wickets @ 64.50; 5 ct. Became the first woman to stand in a men's f-c game in England when she umpired Derbys v Glamorgan (Cardiff) 2023. Appointed 2022.

RICHARDS, Fiona, b Leeds, Yorks 8 Apr 1971.

SAGGERS, Martin John (Springwood HS, King's Lynn; Huddersfield U), b King's Lynn, Norfolk 23 May 1972. 6'2". RHB, RMF. Durham 1996-98. Kent 1999-2009; cap 2001; benefit 2009. MCC 2004. Essex 2007 (on loan). Norfolk 1995-96. **Tests**: 3 (2003-04 to 2004); HS 1 and BB 2-29 v B (Chittagong) 2003-04 – on debut. F-c Tour: B 2003-04. HS 64 K v Worcs (Canterbury) 2004. 50 wkts (4); most – 83 (2002). BB 7-79 K v Durham (Chester-le-St) 2000. F-c career: 119 matches; 1165 runs @ 11.20; 415 wickets @ 25.33; 27 ct. Reserve List 2010-11. Appointed 2012. Umpired 9 LOI (2020 to 2023). **ICC International Panel 2020 to date.**

SHANMUGAM, Surendiran ('**Suri**')(Sri Krishna C of Engineering & Technology; Manchester U), b Coimbatore, Tamil Nadu, India 2 Jun 1984. No f-c appearances. Appointed 2022.

SHANTRY, Jack David (Priory SS; Shrewsbury SFC; Liverpool U), b Shrewsbury, Shrops 29 Jan 1988. Son of B.K.Shantry (Gloucestershire 1978-79), brother of A.J.Shantry (Northants, Warwicks, Glamorgan 2003-11). 6'4". LHB, LM. Worcestershire 2009-17. Shropshire 2007-09. HS 106 v Glos (Worcester) 2016. 50 wkts (2); most – 67 (2015). BB 7-60 v Oxford MCCU (Oxford) 2013. CC BB 7-69 v Essex (Worcester) 2013. F-c career: 92 matches; 1640 runs @ 19.06, 2 hundreds; 266 wickets @ 29.25; 30 ct. Appointed 2022.

TREDWELL, James Cullum (Southlands Community CS, New Romney), b Ashford 27 Feb 1982. 6'0". LHB, OB. Kent 2001-17; cap 2007; captain 2013; testimonial 2017. Sussex (on loan) 2014. MCC 2004, 2008, 2016. **Tests**: 2 (2009-10 to 2014-15); HS 37 v B (Dhaka) 2009-10; BB 4-47 v WI (North Sound) 2014-15. **LOI**: 45 (2009-10 to 2014-15); HS 30 v I (Nottingham) 2014; BB 4-41 v Scotland (Aberdeen) 2014. **IT20**: 17 (2012-13 to 2014); HS 22 and BB 1-16 v WI (Bridgetown) 2013-14. F-c Tours: WI 2014-15; NZ 2012-13 (*part*); I 2003-04 (Eng A, captain); B 2009-10. HS 124 K v Essex (Chelmsford) 2016, sharing K record 8th wkt partnership of 222 with S.A.Northeast. 50 wkts (1): 69 (2009). BB 8-66 (11-120 match) K v Glamorgan (Canterbury) 2009. F-c career: 177 matches; 4728 runs @ 21.88, 4 hundreds; 426 wickets @ 36.24; 196 ct. Appointed 2023.

WARREN, Russell John (Kingsthorpe Upper S), b Northampton 10 Sep 1971. 6'1". RHB, OB, WK. Northamptonshire 1992-2002; cap 1995. Nottinghamshire 2003-06; cap 2004. 1000 runs (1): 1030 (2001). HS 201* Nh v Glamorgan (Northampton) 2001. F-c career: 146 matches; 7776 runs @ 36.67, 15 hundreds; 128 ct, 5 st. Reserve List: 2015-17. Appointed 2018.

WATTS, Christopher Mark (Stalham HS; Paston C), b Acle, Norfolk 3 Jul 1967. No f-c appearances. Reserve list 2015-21. Appointed 2022.

WHARF, Alexander George (Buttershaw Upper S; Thomas Danby C), b Bradford, Yorks 4 Jun 1975. 6'5". RHB, RMF. Yorkshire 1994-97. Nottinghamshire 1998-99. Glamorgan 2000-08, scoring 100* v OU (Oxford) on debut; cap 2000; benefit 2009. **LOI**: 13 (2004 to 2004-05); HS 9 v India (Lord's) 2004; BB 4-24 v Z (Harare) 2004-05. F-c Tour (Eng A): WI 2005-06. HS 128* Gm v Glos (Bristol) 2007. 50 wkts (1): 52 (2003). BB 6-59 Gm v Glos (Bristol) 2005. F-c career: 121 matches; 3570 runs @ 23.03, 6 hundreds; 293 wickets @ 37.34; 63 ct. Reserve List 2011-13. Appointed 2014. Umpired 6 Tests (2021 to 2023) and 26 LOI (2018 to 2023-24). **ICC International Panel 2018 to date**.

WHITE, Robert Allan (Stowe S; Durham U; Loughborough U), b Chelmsford, Essex 15 Oct 1979. 5'11". RHB, LB. Northamptonshire 2000-12; cap 2008. Loughborough UCCE 2003. British U 2003. 1000 runs (1): 1037 (2008). HS 277 and BB 2-30 v Glos (Northampton) 2002 – highest maiden f-c hundred in UK; included 107 before lunch on first day. F-c career: 112 matches; 5706 runs @ 32.98, 8 hundreds; 18 wickets @ 59.50; 67 ct. Reserve list 2018-21. Appointed 2022.

WIDDUP, Simon, b Doncaster, Yorks 10 Nov 1977. RHB, OB, occ WK. Yorkshire 2000-01. HS 44 and BB 1-22 Y v Somerset (Scarborough) 2000. F-c career: 11 matches; 245 runs @ 14.41; 1 wkt @ 22.00; 11 ct. Appointed 2023.

Test Match and LOI statistics to 11 February 2024.

TOURING TEAMS REGISTER 2023

AUSTRALIA

Full Names	*Birthdate*	*Birthplace*	*Team*	*Type*	*F-C Debut*
BOLAND, Scott Michael	11.04.89	Melbourne	Victoria	RHB/RFM	2011-12
CAREY, Alex Tyson	27.08.91	Loxton	S Australia	LHB/WK	2012-13
CUMMINS, Patrick James	08.05.93	Sydney	NSW	RHB/RF	2010-11
GREEN, Cameron David	03.06.99	Subiaco	W Australia	RHB/RFM	2016-17
HAZLEWOOD, Josh Reginald	08.01.91	Tamworth	NSW	LHB/RFM	2008-09
HEAD, Travis Michael	29.12.93	Adelaide	S Australia	LHB/OB	2011-12
KHAWAJA, Usman Tariq	18.12.86	Islamabad, Pak	Queensland	LHB/RM	2007-08
LABUSCHAGNE, Marnus	22.06.94	Klerksdorp, SA	Queensland	RHB/LB	2014-15
LYON, Nathan Michael	20.11.87	Young	NSW	RHB/OB	2010-11
MARSH, Mitchell Ross	20.10.91	Perth	W Australia	RHB/RMF	2009-10
MURPHY, Todd Raymond	15.11.00	Echuca	Victoria	LHB/OB	2020-21
SMITH, Steven Peter Devereux	02.06.89	Sydney	NSW	RHB/LB	2007-08
STARC, Mitchell Aaron	30.01.90	Sydney	NSW	LHB/LF	2008-09
WARNER, David Andrew	27.10.86	Paddington	NSW	LHB/LB	2008-09

INDIA

Full Names	*Birthdate*	*Birthplace*	*Team*	*Type*	*F-C Debut*
GILL, Shubman	08.09.99	Firozpur	Punjab	RHB/OB	2017-18
JADEJA, Ravindrasinh Anirudsinh	06.12.88	Navagam-Khed	Saurashtra	LHB/SLA	2006-07
KOHLI, Virat	05.11.88	Delhi	Delhi	RHB/RM	2006-07
MOHAMMED SHAMI	03.09.90	Jonagar	Bengal	RHB/RFM	2010-11
PUJARA, Cheteshwar Arvindbhai	25.01.88	Rajkot	Saurashtra	RHB/LB	2005-06
RAHANE, Ajinkya Madhukar	06.06.88	Ashwi Khurd	Mumbai	RHB/RM	2007-08
SIRAJ, Mohammed	13.03.94	Hyderabad	Hyderabad	RHB/RFM	2015-16
SHARMA, Rohit Gurunath	30.04.87	Nagpur	Mumbai	RHB/OB	2006
SRIKAR BHARAT, Kona	03.10.93	Visakhapatnam	Andhra	RHB/WK	2012-13
THAKUR, Shardul Narendra	16.10.91	Palghar	Mumbai	RHB/RFM	2012-13
YADAV, Umeshkumar Tilak	25.10.87	Nagpur	Vidarbha	RHB/RFM	2008-09

For the Ireland register, go to page 321 for further details.

THE 2023 FIRST-CLASS SEASON STATISTICAL HIGHLIGHTS

FIRST TO INDIVIDUAL TARGETS

1000 RUNS	A.Z.Lees	Durham	20 July
2000 RUNS	–	Most – 1347 A.Z.Lees (Durham)	
50 WICKETS	B.A.Hutton	Nottinghamshire	28 July
100 WICKETS	–	Most – 62 B.A.Hutton (Nottinghamshire)	

TEAM HIGHLIGHTS († Team record)
HIGHEST INNINGS TOTALS

737 Glamorgan v Sussex — Hove

The highest second-innings total in all UK f-c cricket, also the greatest variation in a team's totals (scored 123 in 1st innings).

630	Durham v Glamorgan	Chester-le-St
621	Kent v Northamptonshire	Northampton
592	England v Australia	Manchester

HIGHEST FOURTH INNINGS TOTALS

501-5 Surrey (set 501) v Kent — Canterbury

The second highest successful run chase in County Championship history.

483	Leicestershire (set 499) v Sussex	Hove
412-9	Yorkshire (set 492) v Glamorgan	Leeds

LOWEST INNINGS TOTALS

56	Northamptonshire v Hampshire	Southampton
60	Warwickshire v Middlesex	Birmingham
63	Northamptonshire v Hampshire	Northampton
72	Northamptonshire v Nottinghamshire	Northampton

HIGHEST MATCH AGGREGATES

1610-35 Yorkshire (517 & 286-8d) v Leics (415 & 392-7) — Leeds

This was the highest match aggregate for any game featuring Leicestershire.

1586-35	Sussex (348 & 447-7d) v Worcs (410 & 381-8)	Hove
1554-37	Sussex (402 & 384-9d) v Derbyshire (407 & 361-8)	Hove
1541-28	Durham (517-6d & 343-4d) v Leics (422 & 259-8)	Leicester

LOWEST MATCH AGGREGATE

485-30	Northamptonshire (158 & 72) v Nottinghamshire (255)	Northampton

LARGE MARGINS OF VICTORY

399 runs	Somerset (163 & 514-8d) beat Nottinghamshire (186 & 92)	Taunton
339 runs	Sussex (202 & 505-7d) beat Glos (195 & 173)	Hove
321 runs	Nottinghamshire (350 & 372-6d) beat Kent (316 & 85)	Nottingham
Inns & 270 runs	Hampshire (482-8d) beat Northants (149 & 63)	Northampton

NARROW MARGINS OF VICTORY

15 runs	Sussex (262 & 344-9d) beat Leicestershire (108 & 483)	Hove
1 wkt	Durham (227 & 246-9) beat Yorkshire (254 & 218)	Chester-le-St
2 wkts	Australia (386 & 282-8) beat England (393-8d & 273)	Birmingham
2 wkts	Notts (384 & 210-8) beat Middlesex (366 & 224-6d)	Nottingham
2 wkts	Sussex (335 & 232-8) beat Durham (376 & 189)	Hove
2 wkts	Warwickshire (147-4d & 176-8) beat Northants (250 & 72-0d)	Birmingham

SIX FIFTIES IN AN INNINGS

6	England (592) v Australia	Manchester

MOST EXTRAS IN AN INNINGS

	B	*LB*	*W*	*NB*		
64	28	15	9	12	Glamorgan (737) v Sussex	Hove
60	13	19	2	26	Worestershire (473) v Derbyshire	Derby

Under ECB regulations, Test matches excluded, two penalty extras were scored for each no-ball.

UNUSUAL DISMISSAL – OUT OBSTRUCTING THE FIELD

L.P.J.Kimber	Leicestershire v Gloucestershire	Bristol

BATTING HIGHLIGHTS
TREBLE HUNDREDS

D.J.Bell-Drummond	300*	Kent v Northamptonshire	Northampton

DOUBLE HUNDREDS

J.M.Clarke	229*	Nottinghamshire v Warwickshire	Nottingham
J.L.du Plooy	238*	Derbyshire v Worcestershire	Worcester
O.J.D.Pope	205	England v Ireland	Lord's
L.M.Reece	201*	Derbyshire v Glamorgan	Derby
J.E.K.Rew	221	Somerset v Hampshire	Taunton
R.M.Yates	228*	Warwickshire v Kent	Canterbury

HUNDREDS IN THREE CONSECUTIVE INNINGS

A.Z.Lees	101	145	Durham v Leicestershire	Leicester
	195		Durham v Gloucestershire	Chester-le-St

HUNDRED IN EACH INNINGS OF A MATCH

A.Z.Lees	101	145	Durham v Leicestershire	Leicester
L.M.Reece (2)	131	201*	Derbyshire v Glamorgan	Derby
	139	119*	Derbyshire v Glamorgan	Cardiff

The first batter ever to score four centuries in a season against another county.

J.E.K.Rew	105	118*	Somerset v Lancashire	Manchester

FASTEST HUNDRED AGAINST GENUINE BOWLING

J.L.Smith (114)	70 balls	Surrey v Kent	Canterbury

MOST SIXES IN AN INNINGS

9	D.W.Lawrence (135)	Essex v Lancashire	Blackpool
9	B.A.Stokes (155)	England v Australia	Lord's

200 RUNS IN A DAY

D.J.Bell-Drummond (48*-271*)	Kent v Northamptonshire	Northampton

MOST RUNS FROM BOUNDARIES IN AN INNINGS

Runs	*6s*	*4s*			
146	1	35	J.M.Clarke	Nottinghamshire v Warwickshire	Nottingham

HUNDRED ON FIRST-CLASS DEBUT

R.J.Das	132	Essex v Ireland	Chelmsford

HUNDRED ON FIRST-CLASS DEBUT IN BRITAIN

P.J.Moor	118*	Ireland v Essex	Chelmsford

CARRYING BAT THROUGH COMPLETED INNINGS

S.R.Dickson	82*	Somerset (167) v Essex	Chelmsford
M.S.Harris	122*	Gloucestershire (300) v Durham	Bristol
S.D.Robson	107*	Middlesex (251) v Warwickshire	Birmingham

60% OF A COMPLETED INNINGS TOTAL

61.34%	P.I.Walter	Essex (73/119) v Northamptonshire	Northampton

LONG INNINGS (Qualification 600 mins and/or 400 balls)

Mins	*Balls*			
526	439	D.J.Bell-Drummond (300*)	Kent v Northamptonshire	Northampton
578	415	D.P.Sibley (140*)	Surrey v Kent	Canterbury
528	421	R.M.Yates (228*)	Warwickshire v Kent	Canterbury

FIRST-WICKET PARTNERSHIP OF 100 IN EACH INNINGS

165/360*	H.R.C.Came/L.M.Reece	Derbyshire v Glamorgan	Derby

OTHER NOTABLE PARTNERSHIPS

Qualifications: 1st-4th wkts: 250 runs; 5th-6th: 225; 7th: 200; 8th: 175; 9th: 150; 10th: 100; highest partnership for that wicket otherwise. († Team record)

First Wicket

360*†	H.R.C.Came/L.M.Reece	Derbyshire v Glamorgan	Derby

Second Wicket

318	T.S.Muyeye/D.J.Bell-Drummond	Kent v Northamptonshire	Northampton
265	N.L.J.Browne/T.Westley	Essex v Kent	Canterbury
252	B.M.Duckett/O.J.D.Pope	England v Ireland	Lord's

Third Wicket

305†	A.Z.Lees/D.G.Bedingham	Durham v Derbyshire	Derby

Fourth Wicket

288	M.Labsuchagne/K.S.Carlson	Glamorgan v Sussex	Hove
285	S.P.D.Smith/T.M.Head	Australia v India	The Oval
267	W.L.Madsen/J.L.du Plooy	Derbyshire v Worcestershire	Worcester

Fifth Wicket

277	J.L.du Plooy/Haider Ali	Derbyshire v Yorkshire	Chesterfield
244	T.B.Abell/J.E.K.Rew	Somerset v Lancashire	Taunton
236	N.R.T.Gubbins/L.A.Dawson	Hampshire v Middlesex	Southampton
227	O.G.Robinson/G.Clark	Durham v Leicestershire	Leicester

Sixth Wicket

258*†	J.L.du Plooy/A.K.Dal	Derbyshire v Worcestershire	Worcester

Seventh Wicket

163	A.R.McBrine/M.R.Adair	Ireland v England	Lord's

Eighth Wicket

211†	C.B.Cooke/M.G.Neser	Glamorgan v Leicestershire	Leicester

Ninth Wicket

177	F.S.Organ/K.J.Abbott	Hampshire v Somerset	Taunton

Tenth Wicket

130	S.A.Abbott/D.J.Worrall	Surrey v Lancashire	The Oval
108	J.E.K.Rew/S.Bashir	Somerset v Hampshire	Taunton

BOWLING HIGHLIGHTS

EIGHT OR MORE WICKETS IN AN INNINGS

J.M.De Caires	8-106	Middlesex v Essex	Chelmsford

TEN OR MORE WICKETS IN A MATCH

L.A.Dawson	12-130	Hampshire v Middlesex	Southampton
J.M.De Caires	10-190	Middlesex v Essex	Chelmsford
L.Gregory	11-148	Somerset v Nottinghamshire	Nottingham
S.R.Harmer	10-230	Essex v Warwickshire	Chelmsford
T.J.Murtagh	10- 82	Middlesex v Kent	Lord's
A.Y.Patel	10-209	Durham v Gloucestershire	Bristol
J.A.Porter	10- 83	Essex v Hampshire	Southampton
O.E.Robinson	14-117	Sussex v Worcestershire	Worcester
C.Rushworth	10- 76	Warwickshire v Hampshire	Southampton

FIVE WICKETS ON FIRST-CLASS DEBUT

J.A.Richards	5-96	Essex v Ireland	Chelmsford

HAT-TRICK

M.G.Neser	Glamorgan v Yorkshire	Leeds
T.J.Price	Gloucestershire v Worcestershire	Worcester
B.W.Sanderson	Northamptonshire v Warwickshire	Birmingham

MOST RUNS CONCEDED IN AN INNINGS

J.J.Carson	54-8-216-2	Sussex v Glamorgan	Hove

MOST OVERS BOWLED IN AN INNINGS

J.J.Carson	54-8-216-2	Sussex v Glamorgan	Hove

WICKET-KEEPING HIGHLIGHTS
SIX OR MORE WICKET-KEEPING DISMISSALS IN AN INNINGS

B.D.Guest	7ct†	Derbyshire v Sussex	Derby
B.C.Brown	6ct	Hampshire v Nottinghamshire	Nottingham
B.T.Foakes	6ct	Surrey v Middlesex	The Oval
B.D.Guest	6ct	Derbyshire v Yorkshire	Scarborough
T.J.Moores	6ct	Nottinghamshire v Surrey	The Oval
J.E.K.Rew	6ct	Somerset v Lancashire	Taunton

NINE WICKET-KEEPING DISMISSALS IN A MATCH

A.T.Carey	6ct, 3st	Australia v England	Birmingham

NO BYES CONCEDED IN AN INNINGS OF 550

575	B.D.Guest	Derbyshire v Durham	Derby
569-7d	C.B.Cooke	Glamorgan v Gloucestershire	Cardiff

FIELDING HIGHLIGHTS
FOUR OR MORE CATCHES IN THE FIELD IN AN INNINGS

T.W.M.Latham	5ct	Surrey v Nottinghamshire	The Oval
J.A.Leaning	5ct	Kent v Nottinghamshire	Canterbury
S.P.D.Smith	5ct	Australia v England	Leeds
W.L.Madsen	4ct	Derbyshire v Leicestershire	Leicester
J.Overton	4ct	Surrey v Hampshire	Southampton
O.J.Price	4ct	Gloucestershire v Leicestershire	Bristol
R.S.Vasconcelos	4ct	Northamptonshire v Nottinghamshire	Northampton
R.M.Yates	4ct	Warwickshire v Somerset	Taunton

SIX CATCHES IN THE FIELD IN A MATCH

J.A.Leaning	6ct	Kent v Nottinghamshire	Canterbury
J.Overton	6ct	Surrey v Hampshire	Southampton

ALL-ROUND HIGHLIGHTS
HUNDRED AND TEN WICKETS IN A MATCH

L.A.Dawson	141	6-40 6-90	Hampshire v Middlesex	Southampton

HUNDRED AND FIVE WICKETS IN AN INNINGS

A.K.Dal	141*	5-45	Derbyshire v Worcestershire	Worcester
P.W.A.Mulder	102*	5-63	Leicestershire v Sussex	Leicester

HUNDRED AND A HAT-TRICK IN A MATCH

T.J.Price	109	Gloucestershire v Worcestershire	Worcester

First in all f-c cricket to complete the feat on the same day.

HUNDRED AND SIX DISMISSALS IN AN INNINGS

J.E.K.Rew	117	6ct	Somerset v Lancashire	Taunton

LV= INSURANCE COUNTY CHAMPIONSHIP 2023
FINAL TABLES

DIVISION 1

		P	W	L	T	D	Bonus Bat	Points Bowl	Deduct Points	Total Points
1	**SURREY** (1)	14	8	2	–	4	27	41	–	216
2	Essex (4)	14	7	3	–	4	25	39	–	196
3	Hampshire (3)	14	8	4	–	2	18	39	3	192
4	Warwickshire (8)	14	6	4	–	4	22	41	–	179
5	Lancashire (2)	14	3	1	–	10	29	35	1	161
6	Nottinghamshire (-)	14	4	4	–	6	18	39	–	151
7	Somerset (7)	14	3	4	–	7	25	40	–	148
8	Kent (5)	14	2	7	–	5	20	34	–	111
9	Middlesex (-)	14	3	9	–	2	5	39	1	104
10	Northamptonshire (6)	14	2	8	–	4	10	34	–	96

DIVISION 2

		P	W	L	D	Ab	Bonus Bat	Points Bowl	Deduct Points	Total Points
1	Durham (6)	14	7	1	6	–	54	39	2	233
2	Worcestershire (4)	14	5	3	6	–	21	36	–	167
3	Sussex (7)	14	3	1	10	–	29	39	16	150
4	Leicestershire (8)	14	3	4	7	–	25	35	1	142
5	Glamorgan (3)	14	1	1	12	–	29	34	–	139
6	Derbyshire (5)	14	–	4	10	–	25	38	–	113
7	Yorkshire (-)	14	3	2	8	1	31	35	50	109
8	Gloucestershire (-)	14	–	6	7	1	23	35	1	97

SCORING OF CHAMPIONSHIP POINTS 2023

(a) For a win, 16 points, plus any points scored in the first innings.

(b) In a tie, each side to score eight points, plus any points scored in the first innings.

(c) In a drawn match, each side to score five points, plus any points scored in the first innings (see also paragraph (e) below); if the scores are level in a drawn match, the side batting last to score eight points, plus any points scored in the first innings.

(d) **First Innings Points** (awarded only for performances **in the first 110 overs** of each first innings and retained whatever the result of the match).

(i) A maximum of five batting points to be available as under:
250 to 299 runs – 1 point; 300 to 349 runs – 2 points; 350 to 399 runs – 3 points; 400 to 449 runs – 4 points; 450 runs or over – 5 points.

(ii) A maximum of three bowling points to be available as under:
3 to 5 wickets taken – 1 point; 6 to 8 wickets taken – 2 points; 9 to 10 wickets taken – 3 points.

(e) If a match is abandoned without a ball being bowled, each side to score five points.

(f) The bottom two sides from Division 1 were relegated, with the top two sides in Division 2 being promoted. Should any sides in the Championship table be equal on points, the following tie-breakers will be applied in the order stated: most wins, fewest losses, team achieving most points in contests between teams level on points, most wickets taken, most runs scored.

COUNTY CHAMPIONSHIP RESULTS 2023

DIVISION 1

	ESSEX	HANTS	KENT	LANCS	MIDDX	N'HANTS	NOTTS	SOM'T	SURREY	WARKS
ESSEX		C'ford	C'ford	C'ford	C'ford			C'ford	C'ford	C'ford
		H 3w	E 7w	Drawn	E 297			E 196	Drawn	E 9w
HANTS	So'ton				So'ton	So'ton	So'ton	So'ton	So'ton	So'ton
	E 6w				H I/61	H I/135	H 8w	H 185	H 52	Wa I/84
KENT	Cant	Cant		Cant		Cant	Cant		Cant	Cant
	Drawn	Drawn		Drawn		K 7w	Drawn		Sy 5w	Wa I/46
LANCS	B'pool	S'port			Man	Man	Man	Man	Man	
	Ex 46	La 6w			Drawn	Drawn	Drawn	Drawn	Drawn	
MIDDX	Lord's		Lord's			N'wood	Lord's	Lord's	Lord's	Lord's
	E 97		M 9w			Drawn	M 4w	Sm I/13	Sy 8w	Wa 8w
N'HANTS	No'ton	No'ton	No'ton	No'ton	No'ton		No'ton	No'ton		
	Nh I/39	H I/270	K I/15	La I/26	Nh 7w		Nt I/25	Sm 9w		
NOTTS	N'ham	N'ham	N'ham	N'ham	N'ham			N'ham		N'ham
	Drawn	H 116	Nt 321	Drawn	Nt 2w			Nt 165		Drawn
SOM'T		Taunton	Taunton	Taunton		Taunton	Taunton		Taunton	Taunton
		Drawn	Drawn	Drawn		Drawn	Sm 399		Sy 10w	Drawn
SURREY		Oval	Oval	Oval	Oval	Oval	Oval			Oval
		Sy 9w	Sy 10w	La 123	Sy 9w	Drawn	Drawn			Sy I/97
WARKS	Birm		Birm	Birm	Birm	Birm		Birm	Birm	
	Wa 4w		Wa I/14	Drawn	M 8w	Wa 2w		Drawn	Sy 9w	

DIVISION 2

	DERBYS	DURHAM	GLAM	GLOS	LEICS	SUSSEX	WORCS	YORKS
DERBYS		Derby	Derby	Derby	Derby	Derby	Derby	Cfield
		Drawn	Drawn	Drawn	Drawn	Drawn	Wo 8w	Y 3w
DURHAM	C-le-St		C-le-St	C-le-St	C-le-St	C-le-St	C-le-St	C-le-St
	Du I/7		Drawn	Du 9w	Du I/141	Du 7w	Du 121	Du 1w
GLAM	Cardiff	Cardiff		Cardiff	Cardiff	Cardiff	Cardiff	Cardiff
	Drawn	Drawn		Drawn	Drawn	Drawn	Gm 10w	Drawn
GLOS	Bristol	Bristol	Chelt		Bristol	Bristol	Chelt	Bristol
	Drawn	Du 125	Drawn		Le 5w	Drawn	Wo 110	Aband
LEICS	Leics	Leics	Leics	Leics		Leics	Oakham	Leics
	Drawn	Drawn	Drawn	Le 8w		Drawn	Wo 100	Drawn
SUSSEX	Hove	Hove	Hove	Hove	Hove		Hove	Hove
	Drawn	Sx 2w	Drawn	Sx 339	Sx 15		Drawn	Drawn
WORCS	Worcs	Worcs	Worcs	Worcs	Worcs	Worcs		Worcs
	Drawn	Drawn	Wo 80	Drawn	Wo 3w	Drawn		Drawn
YORKS	Scar	Scar	Leeds	Leeds	Leeds	Leeds	Leeds	
	Y 277	Drawn	Drawn	Drawn	Le 3w	Drawn	Y 6w	

COUNTY CHAMPIONS

The English County Championship was not officially constituted until December 1889. Prior to that date there was no generally accepted method of awarding the title; although the 'least matches lost' method existed, it was not consistently applied. Rules governing playing qualifications were agreed in 1873 and the first unofficial points system 15 years later.

Research has produced a list of champions dating back to 1826, but at least seven different versions exist for the period from 1864 to 1889 (see *The Wisden Book of Cricket Records*). Only from 1890 can any authorised list of county champions commence.

That first official Championship was contested between eight counties: Gloucestershire, Kent, Lancashire, Middlesex, Nottinghamshire, Surrey, Sussex and Yorkshire. The remaining counties were admitted in the following seasons: 1891 – Somerset, 1895 – Derbyshire, Essex, Hampshire, Leicestershire and Warwickshire, 1899 – Worcestershire, 1905 – Northamptonshire, 1921 – Glamorgan, and 1992 – Durham.

The Championship pennant was introduced by the 1951 champions, Warwickshire, and the Lord's Taverners' Trophy was first presented in 1973. The first sponsors, Schweppes (1977-83), were succeeded by Britannic Assurance (1984-98), PPP Healthcare (1999-2000), CricInfo (2001), Frizzell (2002-05), Liverpool Victoria (2006-15 and 2021-23) and Specsavers (from 2016-19). Based on their previous season's positions, the 18 counties were separated into two divisions in 2000. From 2000 to 2005 the bottom three Division 1 teams were relegated and the top three Division 2 sides promoted. This was reduced to two teams from the end of the 2006 season.

1890	Surrey
1891	Surrey
1892	Surrey
1893	Yorkshire
1894	Surrey
1895	Surrey
1896	Yorkshire
1897	Lancashire
1898	Yorkshire
1899	Surrey
1900	Yorkshire
1901	Yorkshire
1902	Yorkshire
1903	Middlesex
1904	Lancashire
1905	Yorkshire
1906	Kent
1907	Nottinghamshire
1908	Yorkshire
1909	Kent
1910	Kent
1911	Warwickshire
1912	Yorkshire
1913	Kent
1914	Surrey
1919	Yorkshire
1920	Middlesex
1921	Middlesex
1922	Yorkshire
1923	Yorkshire
1924	Yorkshire
1925	Yorkshire
1926	Lancashire
1927	Lancashire
1928	Lancashire
1929	Nottinghamshire
1930	Lancashire
1931	Yorkshire
1932	Yorkshire
1933	Yorkshire
1934	Lancashire
1935	Yorkshire
1936	Derbyshire
1937	Yorkshire
1938	Yorkshire
1939	Yorkshire
1946	Yorkshire
1947	Middlesex
1948	Glamorgan
1949	Middlesex Yorkshire
1950	Lancashire Surrey
1951	Warwickshire
1952	Surrey
1953	Surrey
1954	Surrey
1955	Surrey
1956	Surrey
1957	Surrey
1958	Surrey
1959	Yorkshire
1960	Yorkshire
1961	Hampshire
1962	Yorkshire
1963	Yorkshire
1964	Worcestershire
1965	Worcestershire
1966	Yorkshire
1967	Yorkshire
1968	Yorkshire
1969	Glamorgan
1970	Kent
1971	Surrey
1972	Warwickshire
1973	Hampshire
1974	Worcestershire
1975	Leicestershire
1976	Middlesex
1977	Kent Middlesex
1978	Kent
1979	Essex
1980	Middlesex
1981	Nottinghamshire
1982	Middlesex
1983	Essex
1984	Essex
1985	Middlesex
1986	Essex
1987	Nottinghamshire
1988	Worcestershire
1989	Worcestershire
1990	Middlesex
1991	Essex
1992	Essex
1993	Middlesex
1994	Warwickshire
1995	Warwickshire
1996	Leicestershire
1997	Glamorgan
1998	Leicestershire
1999	Surrey
2000	Surrey
2001	Yorkshire
2002	Surrey
2003	Sussex
2004	Warwickshire
2005	Nottinghamshire
2006	Sussex
2007	Sussex
2008	Durham
2009	Durham
2010	Nottinghamshire
2011	Lancashire
2012	Warwickshire
2013	Durham
2014	Yorkshire
2015	Yorkshire
2016	Middlesex
2017	Essex
2018	Surrey
2019	Essex
2021	Warwickshire
2022	Surrey
2023	Surrey

COUNTY CHAMPIONSHIP FIXTURES 2024

DIVISION 1

	DURHAM	ESSEX	HANTS	KENT	LANCS	NOTTS	SOM'T	SURREY	WARKS	WORCS
DURHAM		C-le-St	C-le-St	C-le-St	C-le-St	C-le-St	C-le-St			C-le-St
ESSEX	C'ford			C'ford	C'ford	C'ford		C'ford	C'ford	C'ford
HANTS	So'ton	So'ton		So'ton	So'ton			So'ton	So'ton	So'ton
KENT		Cant	Cant		Cant	Cant	Cant	Cant		Cant
LANCS	B'pool		Man	Man		S'port	Man	Man	Man	
NOTTS		N'ham	N'ham		N'ham		N'ham	N'ham	N'ham	N'ham
SOM'T	Taunton	Taunton	Taunton	Taunton		Taunton		Taunton	Taunton	
SURREY	Oval	Oval	Oval		Oval		Oval		Oval	Oval
WARKS	Birm	Birm	Birm	Birm		Birm	Birm			Birm
WORCS	Kidd			Worcs	Worcs	Worcs	Kidd	Worcs	Worcs	

DIVISION 2

	DERBYS	GLAM	GLOS	LEICS	MIDDX	N'HANTS	SUSSEX	YORKS
DERBYS		Derby	Derby	Derby	Derby	Derby	Derby	C'field
GLAM	Cardiff		Cardiff	Cardiff	Cardiff	Cardiff	Cardiff	Cardiff
GLOS	Bristol	Chelt		Bristol	Bristol	Bristol	Bristol	Bristol
LEICS	Leics	Leics	Leics		tba	Leics	Leics	Leics
MIDDX	Lord's	Lord's	Lord's	Lord's		N'wood	Lord's	Lord's
N'HANTS	No'ton	No'ton	No'ton	No'ton	No'ton		No'ton	No'ton
SUSSEX	Hove	Hove	Hove	Hove	Hove	Hove		Hove
YORKS	Leeds	Leeds	Scar	Leeds	Leeds	Leeds	Scar	

METRO BANK ONE-DAY CUP 2023

This latest format of limited-overs competition was launched in 2014, and is now the only List-A tournament played in the UK. The top team from each group went through to the semi-finals, with a home draw; the second team from each group (drawn at home) played off against the third team from the other division to qualify for the semi-finals. The winner was decided in the final at Trent Bridge.

	GROUP A	*P*	*W*	*L*	*T*	*NR*	*Pts*	*Net RR*
1	Leicestershire	8	7	1	–	–	14	+1.30
2	Hampshire	8	7	1	–	–	14	+1.04
3	Lancashire	8	4	2	–	2	10	+0.82
4	Kent	8	4	4	–	–	8	–0.33
5	Nottinghamshire	8	3	4	–	1	7	–0.27
6	Yorkshire	8	2	4	–	2	6	–1.05
7	Middlesex	8	2	5	–	1	5	+0.10
8	Surrey	8	2	5	–	1	5	–1.25
9	Essex	8	1	6	–	1	3	–0.77

	GROUP B	*P*	*W*	*L*	*T*	*NR*	*Pts*	*Net RR*
1	Warwickshire	8	7	1	–	–	14	+1.30
2	Gloucestershire	8	6	2	–	–	12	+0.83
3	Worcestershire	8	6	2	–	–	12	+0.53
4	Glamorgan	8	4	3	–	1	9	–0.06
5	Durham	8	3	4	–	1	7	–0.84
6	Northamptonshire	8	3	5	–	–	6	+0.39
7	Somerset	8	3	5	–	–	6	–0.28
8	Derbyshire	8	2	6	–	–	4	–0.47
9	Sussex	8	1	7	–	–	2	–1.45

Win = 2 points. Tie (T)/No Result (NR) = 1 point.

Positions of counties finishing equal on points are decided by most wins or, if equal, the team that achieved the most points in the matches played between them; if still equal, the team with the higher net run rate (ie deducting from the average runs per over scored by that team in matches where a result was achieved, the average runs per over scored against that team). In the event the teams still cannot be separated, the winner will be decided by drawing lots.

Statistical Highlights in 2023

Highest total	454-3		Gloucestershire v Somerset	Bristol
Biggest win (runs)	264	Leics (380-5) beat Kent (116)		Beckenham
Biggest win (wkts)	10 (167 balls)	Lancs (157-0) beat Surrey (153)		Guildford
Most runs	616 (ave 77.00)	E.G.Barnard (Warwickshire)		
Highest innings	244	P.P.Shaw	Northants v Somerset	Northampton
	224*	J.R.Bracey	Glos v Somerset	Bristol
Most sixes (inns)	11	P.P.Shaw	Northants v Somerset	Northampton
Highest partnership	219	J.D.M.Evison/B.G.Compton	Kent v Yorkshire	Scarborough
Most wickets	24 (ave 13.20)	O.J.Hannon-Dalby (Warwickshire)		
Best bowling	7-15	L.A.Dawson	Hampshire v Warwicks	Birmingham
Most economical	10-3-16-3	B.O.Coad	Yorkshire v Kent	Scarborough
Most expensive	8-0-95-1	J.T.Langridge	Somerset v Glos	Bristol
Most w/k dismissals	23	P.S.P.Handscomb (Leicestershire)		
Most w/k dismissals (inns)	5	P.S.P.Handscomb	Leics v Kent	Beckenham
Most catches (inns)	4	J.A.Leaning	Kent v Lancashire	Blackpool

2023 METRO BANK ONE-DAY CUP FINAL
LEICESTERSHIRE v HAMPSHIRE

At Trent Bridge, Nottingham, on 16 September.

Result: **LEICESTERSHIRE** won by 2 runs.

Toss: Leicestershire. Award: H.J.Swindells.

LEICESTERSHIRE		*Runs*	*Balls*	*4/6*	*Fall*
R.K.Patel	c Brown b Barker	1	2	–	1- 4
S.G.Budinger	c Weatherley b Barker	7	12	1	2- 9
* L.J.Hill	c Brown b Currie	42	57	3	6- 89
C.N.Ackermann	c Middleton b Holland	6	16	1	3- 16
P.W.A.Mulder	lbw b Barker	0	5	–	4- 19
L.P.J.Kimber	c Brown b Currie	18	22	2	5- 56
S.T.Evans	c Weatherley b Currie	60	84	4	7-240
† H.J.Swindells	not out	117	96	8/3	
T.A.R.Scriven	not out	5	6	–	
C.J.C.Wright					
J.O.Hull					
Extras	(LB 1, W 10)	11			
Total	**(7 wkts; 50 overs)**	**267**			

HAMPSHIRE		*Runs*	*Balls*	*4/6*	*Fall*
F.S.Middleton	b Mulder	15	24	1	2- 38
* N.R.T.Gubbins	run out	20	24	3	1- 34
T.J.Prest	c and b Hull	51	62	6/1	5-136
† B.C.Brown	c Ackermann b Wright	33	43	3	3-117
A.H.T.Donald	c Ackermann b Wright	6	8	1	4-123
J.J.Weatherley	c sub (W.S.Davis) b Ackermann	40	52	1/1	6-218
L.A.Dawson	c Wright b Hull	57	64	3/1	8-263
I.G.Holland	c Hull b Mulder	16	13	2	7-243
K.H.D.Barker	not out	12	11	1	
S.W.Currie	not out	1	1	–	
M.S.Crane					
Extras	(LB 1, NB 4, W 9)	14			
Total	**(8 wkts; 50 overs)**	**265**			

HAMPSHIRE	*O*	*M*	*R*	*W*	**LEICESTERSHIRE**	*O*	*M*	*R*	*W*
Barker	10	1	65	3	Mulder	10	0	43	2
Holland	10	1	30	1	Wright	10	0	44	2
Dawson	10	0	47	0	Scriven	10	0	46	0
Currie	10	0	63	3	Hull	10	0	75	2
Crane	9	0	56	0	Ackermann	10	0	56	1
Prest	1	0	5	0					

Umpires: G.D.Lloyd and J.D.Middlebrook

SEMI-FINALS

At Edgbaston, Birmingham, on 29 August. Toss: Hampshire. **HAMPSHIRE** won by nine wickets. Warwickshire 93 (25.5; L.A.Dawson 7-15, K.H.D.Barker 3-28). Hampshire 95-1 (19.1; F.S.Middleton 54*).

At Grace Road, Leicester, 29 August. Toss: Leicestershire. **LEICESTERSHIRE** won by six wickets. Gloucestershire 125 (32.3; T.A.R.Scriven 3-19, P.W.A.Mulder 3-38). Leicestershire 126-4 (28.3; P.W.A.Mulder 55*).

PRINCIPAL LIST A RECORDS 1963-2023

These records cover all the major limited-overs tournaments played by the counties since the inauguration of the Gillette Cup in 1963.

Record	Figure	Player	Match	Venue	Year
Highest Totals	496-4		Surrey v Glos	The Oval	2007
	454-3		Glos v Somerset	Bristol	2023
Highest Total Batting Second	429		Glamorgan v Surrey	The Oval	2002
Lowest Totals	23		Middlesex v Yorks	Leeds	1974
	36		Leics v Sussex	Leicester	1973
Largest Victory (Runs)	346		Somerset beat Devon	Torquay	1990
	304		Sussex beat Ireland	Belfast	1996
Highest Scores	268	A.D.Brown	Surrey v Glamorgan	The Oval	2002
	244	P.P.Shaw	Northants v Somerset	Northampton	2023
	224*	J.R.Bracey	Glos v Somerset	Bristol	2023
	206*	O.G.Robinson	Kent v Worcestershire	Worcester	2022
	206	A.I.Kallicharran	Warwicks v Oxfords	Birmingham	1984
	206	A.G.H.Orr	Sussex v Somerset	Taunton	2022
Fastest Hundred	36 balls	G.D.Rose	Somerset v Devon	Torquay	1990
	43 balls	R.R.Watson	Scotland v Somerset	Edinburgh	2003
	44 balls	M.A.Ealham	Kent v Derbyshire	Maidstone	1995
	44 balls	T.C.Smith	Lancashire v Worcs	Worcester	2012
	44 balls	D.I.Stevens	Kent v Sussex	Canterbury	2013
Most Sixes (Inns)	15	R.N.ten Doeschate	Essex v Scotland	Chelmsford	2013
Highest Partnership for each Wicket					
1st	342	M.J.Lumb/M.H.Wessels	Notts v Northants	Nottingham	2016
2nd	302	M.E.Trescothick/C.Kieswetter	Somerset v Glos	Taunton	2008
3rd	309*	T.S.Curtis/T.M.Moody	Worcs v Surrey	The Oval	1994
4th	245*	S.A.Northeast/W.T.Root	Glamorgan v Worcs	Worcester	2022
5th	221*	R.R.Sarwan/M.A.Hardinges	Glos v Lancashire	Manchester	2005
6th	232	D.Wiese/B.C.Brown	Sussex v Hampshire	Southampton	2019
7th	170	D.R.Brown/A.F.Giles	Warwicks v Essex	Birmingham	2003
8th	174	R.W.T.Key/J.C.Tredwell	Kent v Surrey	The Oval	2007
9th	155	C.M.W.Read/A.J.Harris	Notts v Durham	Nottingham	1984
10th	88	A.K.Dal/S.Conners	Derbyshire v Somerset	Derby	2023
Best Bowling	8-21	M.A.Holding	Derbyshire v Sussex	Hove	1988
	8-26	K.D.Boyce	Essex v Lancashire	Manchester	1971
	8-31	D.L.Underwood	Kent v Scotland	Edinburgh	1987
	8-66	S.R.G.Francis	Somerset v Derbys	Derby	2004
Four Wkts in Four Balls		A.Ward	Derbyshire v Sussex	Derby	1970
		S.M.Pollock	Warwickshire v Leics	Birmingham	1996
		V.C.Drakes	Notts v Derbyshire	Nottingham	1999
		D.A.Payne	Gloucestershire v Essex	Chelmsford	2010
		G.R.Napier	Essex v Surrey	Chelmsford	2013
Most Economical Analyses					
	8-8-0-0	B.A.Langford	Somerset v Essex	Yeovil	1969
	8-7-1-1	D.R.Doshi	Notts v Northants	Northampton	1977
	12-9-3-1	J.Simmons	Lancashire v Suffolk	Bury St Eds	1985
	8-6-2-3	F.J.Titmus	Middlesex v Northants	Northampton	1972
Most Expensive Analyses					
	9-0-110-0	M.K.Andersson	Middlesex v Sussex	Hove	2022
	9-0-108-3	S.D.Thomas	Glamorgan v Surrey	The Oval	2002
	10-0-107-0	J.W.Dernbach	Surrey v Essex	The Oval	2008
	11-0-103-0	G.Welch	Warwicks v Lancs	Birmingham	1995
	10-0-101-1	M.J.J.Critchley	Derbyshire v Worcs	Worcester	2016
Century and Five Wickets in an Innings					
	154*, 5-26	M.J.Procter	Glos v Somerset	Taunton	1972
	206, 6-32	A.I.Kallicharran	Warwicks v Oxfords	Birmingham	1984
	103, 5-41	C.L.Hooper	Kent v Essex	Maidstone	1993
	113, 5-40	A.R.Roberts	Bedfords v Derbyshire CB	Tottenhow	2002
	125, 5-41	I.R.Bell	Warwicks v Essex	Chelmsford	2003
Most Wicket-Keeping Dismissals in an Innings					
	8 (8 ct)	D.J.S.Taylor	Somerset v British Us	Taunton	1982
	8 (8 ct)	D.J.Pipe	Worcs v Herts	Hertford	2001
Most Catches in an Innings by a Fielder					
	5	V.J.Marks	Combined Us v Kent	Oxford	1976
	5	J.M.Rice	Hampshire v Warwicks	Southampton	1978
	5	D.J.G.Sales	Northants v Essex	Northampton	2007

VITALITY BLAST 2023

In 2023, the Twenty20 competition was again sponsored by Vitality. Between 2003 and 2009, three regional leagues competed to qualify for the knockout stages, but this was reduced to two leagues in 2010, before returning to the three-division format in 2012. Since 2014, the competition has reverted to two regional leagues, except for 2020 when, due to Covid constraints, the three-division format applied.

NORTH GROUP

		P	*W*	*L*	*T*	*NR*	*Pts*	*Net RR*
1.	Warwickshire (1)	14	11	3	–	–	22	+0.81
2.	Lancashire (2)	14	8	5	–	1	17	+0.42
3.	Worcestershire (9)	14	8	5	1	–	17	+0.34
4.	Nottinghamshire (5)	14	8	6	–	–	16	–0.22
5.	Derbyshire (3)	14	6	7	1	–	13	+0.39
6.	Northamptonshire (7)	14	6	9	–	–	12	+0.27
7.	Durham (8)	14	4	7	2	1	11	+0.07
8.	Yorkshire (4)	14	6	6	–	2	10	–0.73
9.	Leicestershire (6)	14	2	12	–	–	4	–1.40

Yorkshire were deducted four points after the racism scandal.

SOUTH GROUP

		P	*W*	*L*	*T*	*NR*	*Pts*	*Net RR*
1.	Somerset (2)	14	12	2	–	–	24	+1.46
2.	Hampshire (4)	14	9	5	–	–	18	+0.82
3.	Surrey (1)	14	8	6	–	–	16	+1.19
4.	Essex (3)	14	8	6	–	–	16	+0.08
5.	Kent (9)	14	7	7	–	–	14	+0.28
6.	Sussex (7)	14	6	8	–	–	12	–0.87
7.	Gloucestershire (5)	14	5	9	–	–	10	–0.99
8.	Glamorgan (6)	14	5	9	–	–	10	–1.06
9.	Middlesex (8)	14	3	11	–	–	6	–0.93

2022 positions in brackets.

QUARTER-FINALS: ESSEX beat Warwickshire by two wickets at Birmingham.
SURREY beat Lancashire by 13 runs at Manchester.
SOMERSET beat Nottinghamshire by five wickets at Taunton.
HAMPSHIRE beat Worcestershire by five wickets at Southampton.

SEMI-FINALS: ESSEX beat Hampshire by five wickets at Birmingham.
SOMERSET beat Surrey by 24 runs at Birmingham.

LEADING AGGREGATES AND RECORDS 2023

BATTING (600 runs)	*M*	*I*	*NO*	*HS*	*Runs*	*Avge*	*100*	*50*	*R/100b*	*Sixes*
J.M.Vince (Hants)	16	16	5	103	670	60.90	1	7	154.0	22
D.J.Bell-Drummond (Kent)	13	13	3	111	600	60.00	1	5	148.5	16

BOWLING (30 wkts)	*O*	*M*	*R*	*W*	*Avge*	*BB*	*4w*	*R/Over*
M.J.Henry (Somerset)	52.2	–	411	31	13.25	4-24	2	7.85
B.G.F.Green (Somerset)	54.1	1	500	30	16.66	4-20	2	9.23

Highest total	258-6	Surrey v Sussex		Hove
Biggest win (runs)	144	Derbyshire (212-4) beat Yorkshire (68)		Chesterfield
Biggest win (wkts)	10	Durham (141-0) beat Northants (137)		Northampton
	10	Hampshire (145-0) beat Sussex (144)		Southampton
Highest innings	121*	M.D.E.Holden	Middlesex v Kent	Lord's
Most sixes	31	W.G.Jacks (Surrey)		
Highest partnership	187*	C.A.Ingram/C.B.Cooke	Glamorgan v Middlesex	Northwood
Best bowling	5-15	N.A.Sowter	Durham v Northamptonshire	Northampton
Most economical	4-0-8-3	C.Overton	Somerset v Hampshire	Taunton
Most expensive	4-0-74-1	B.W.M.Mike	Yorkshire v Derbyshire	Chesterfield
Most w/k dismissals	14	B.R.McDermott (Hampshire)		
Most catches	22	C.Overton (Somerset)		

2023 VITALITY BLAST FINAL
SOMERSET v ESSEX

At Edgbaston, Birmingham, on 15 July (floodlit).
Result: **SOMERSET** won by 14 runs.
Toss: Essex. Award: M.J.Henry.

SOMERSET		*Runs*	*Balls*	*4/6*	*Fall*
† T.Banton	c Das b Snater	20	16	1/1	2- 46
W.C.F.Smeed	b Snater	9	9	2	1- 17
T.Kohler-Cadmore	b Critchley	19	19	2/1	3- 54
T.B.Abell	c Beard b Walter	8	14	–	4- 68
S.R.Dickson	c Rossington b Walter	53	35	7	8-133
* L.Gregory	c and b Snater	11	9	1	5-113
B.G.F.Green	c Das b Walter	2	4	–	6-121
C.Overton	run out	4	3	–	7-127
K.L.Aldridge	not out	6	6	–	
M.J.Henry	c Snater b Sams	5	3	1	9-140
I.S.Sodhi	run out	2	2	–	10-145
Extras	(B 4, LB 1, W 1)	6			
Total	**(20 overs)**	**145**			

ESSEX		*Runs*	*Balls*	*4/6*	*Fall*
† A.M.Rossington	c Aldridge b Henry	19	9	4	1- 27
D.W.Lawrence	lbw b Henry	16	8	2/1	3- 38
M.S.Pepper	b Henry	1	4	–	2- 35
R.J.Das	c Henry b Overton	8	7	1	4- 44
P.I.Walter	b Sodhi	26	24	3	6- 80
M.J.J.Critchley	lbw b Gregory	3	10	–	5- 55
D.R.Sams	c Kohler-Cadmore b Henry	45	26	1/3	10-131
* S.R.Harmer	c Banton b Gregory	3	9	–	7-106
S.Snater	b Sodhi	0	3	–	8-107
A.P.Beard	b Sodhi	7	9	–	9-117
S.J.Cook	not out	1	2	–	
Extras	(LB 1, W 1)	2			
Total	**(18.3 overs)**	**131**			

ESSEX	*O*	*M*	*R*	*W*	**SOMERSET**	*O*	*M*	*R*	*W*
Sams	4	0	26	1	Overton	4	0	30	1
Cook	3	0	26	0	Henry	3.3	0	24	4
Snater	4	1	13	3	Gregory	4	0	25	2
Beard	1	0	11	0	Green	1	0	10	0
Critchley	3	0	23	1	Aldridge	2	0	19	0
Walter	4	0	29	3	Sodhi	4	0	22	3
Harmer	1	0	12	0					

Umpires: M.J.Saggers and R.J.Warren

TWENTY20 CUP WINNERS

2003	Surrey	2010	Hampshire	2017	Nottinghamshire
2004	Leicestershire	2011	Leicestershire	2018	Worcestershire
2005	Somerset	2012	Hampshire	2019	Essex
2006	Leicestershire	2013	Northamptonshire	2020	Nottinghamshire
2007	Kent	2014	Warwickshire	2021	Kent
2008	Middlesex	2015	Lancashire	2022	Hampshire
2009	Sussex	2016	Northamptonshire	2023	Somerset

PRINCIPAL TWENTY20 CUP RECORDS 2003-23

Highest Total	265-5		Somerset v Derbyshire	Taunton	2022
Highest Total Batting 2nd	254-3		Middlesex v Surrey	The Oval	2023
Lowest Total	44		Glamorgan v Surrey	The Oval	2019
Largest Victory (Runs)	191		Somerset v Derbyshire	Taunton	2022
Largest Victory (Balls)	82		Nottinghamshire v Worcs	Nottingham	2021
Highest Scores	161	A.Lyth	Yorkshire v Northants	Leeds	2017
	158*	B.B.McCullum	Warwickshire v Derbys	Birmingham	2015
	153*	L.J.Wright	Sussex v Essex	Chelmsford	2014
	152*	G.R.Napier	Essex v Sussex	Chelmsford	2008
	151*	C.H.Gayle	Somerset v Kent	Taunton	2015
Fastest Hundred	34 balls	A.Symonds	Kent v Middlesex	Maidstone	2004
Most Sixes (Innings)	16	G.R.Napier	Essex v Sussex	Chelmsford	2008
Most Runs in Career	5547	J.M.Vince	Hampshire		2010-23
	5080	J.L.Denly	Kent & Middlesex		2004-23
	5026	L.J.Wright	Sussex		2004-22
Most Sixes in Career	184	A.D.Hales	Nottinghamshire		2009-23

Highest Partnership for each Wicket

1st	207	J.L.Denly/D.J.Bell-Drummond	Kent v Essex	Chelmsford	2017
2nd	186	J.L.Langer/C.L.White	Somerset v Glos	Taunton	2006
3rd	174*	S.R.Hain/A.J.Hose	Warwickshire v Notts	Nottingham	2022
4th	187*	C.A.Ingram/C.B.Cooke	Glamorgan v Middlesex	Northwood	2023
5th	171	A.J.Hose/D.R.Mousley	Warwickshire v Northants	Birmingham	2020
6th	141*	H.C.Brook/J.A.Thompson	Yorkshire v Worcestershire	Leeds	2021
7th	88	D.A.Douthwaite/W.J.Weighell	Glamorgan v Middlesex	Radlett	2021
8th	86*	J.A.Simpson/T.G.Southee	Middlesex v Hampshire	Southampton	2017
9th	69	C.J.Anderson/J.H.Davey	Somerset v Surrey	The Oval	2017
10th	59	H.H.Streak/J.E.Anyon	Warwickshire v Worcs	Birmingham	2005

Best Bowling	7-18	C.N.Ackermann	Leics v Warwicks	Leicester	2019
	6- 5	A.V.Suppiah	Somerset v Glamorgan	Cardiff	2011
	6-16	T.G.Southee	Essex v Glamorgan	Chelmsford	2011
	6-19	T.T.Bresnan	Yorkshire v Lancashire	Leeds	2017
	6-19	Shaheen Shah Afridi	Hampshire v Middlesex	Southampton	2020
	6-21	A.J.Hall	Northants v Worcs	Northampton	2008
	6-24	T.J.Murtagh	Surrey v Middlesex	Lord's	2005
	6-28	J.K.Fuller	Middlesex v Hampshire	Southampton	2018
Most Wkts in Career	219	D.R.Briggs	Hampshire, Sussex, Warwickshire		2010-23
	208	S.R.Patel	Nottinghamshire		2003-23

Most Economical Innings Analysis (Qualification: 4 overs)

4-1-4-3	S.R.Patel	Nottinghamshire v Worcs	Nottingham	2021

Most Maiden Overs in an Innings

4-2-9-1	M.Morkel	Kent v Surrey	Beckenham	2007
4-2-5-2	A.C.Thomas	Somerset v Hampshire	Southampton	2010
4-2-14-1	S.M.Curran	Surrey v Sussex	Hove	2018

Most Expensive Innings Analyses

4-0-82-0	M.H.McKiernan	Derbyshire v Somerset	Taunton	2022
4-0-77-0	B.W.Sanderson	Northants v Yorkshire	Leeds	2017

Most Wicket-Keeping Dismissals in Career

114	J.S.Foster	Essex		2003-17
110	P.Mustard	Durham & Gloustershire		2003-17

Five Wicket-Keeping Dismissals in an Innings

This feat has been completed ten times, the most recent being:

5 (4 ct, 1 st)	L.D.McManus	Northants v Leics	Leicester	2023

Most Catches in Career

126	S.J.Croft	Lancashire		2006-23
107	J.M.Vince	Hampshire		2010-23

Most Catches in an Innings by a Fielder

5	M.W.Machan	Sussex v Glamorgan	Hove	2016

Most Appearances in Career

232	S.R.Patel	Nottinghamshire		2003-23
221	S.J.Croft	Lancashire		2006-23
207	R.S.Bopara	Essex & Sussex		2003-23

YOUNG CRICKETER OF THE YEAR

This annual award, made by The Cricket Writers' Club, is currently restricted to players qualified for England, Andrew Symonds meeting that requirement at the time of his award, and under the age of 23 on 1st May. In 1986 their ballot resulted in a dead heat. Up to 4 April 2024 their selections have gained a tally of 3,061 international Test match caps (shown in brackets).

1950	R.Tattersall (16)	1975	A.Kennedy	1999	A.J.Tudor (10)
1951	P.B.H.May (66)	1976	G.Miller (34)	2000	P.J.Franks
1952	F.S.Trueman (67)	1977	I.T.Botham (102)	2001	O.A.Shah (6)
1953	M.C.Cowdrey (114)	1978	D.I.Gower (117)	2002	R.Clarke (2)
1954	P.J.Loader (13)	1979	P.W.G.Parker (1)	2003	J.M.Anderson (187)
1955	K.F.Barrington (82)	1980	G.R.Dilley (41)	2004	I.R.Bell (118)
1956	B.Taylor	1981	M.W.Gatting (79)	2005	A.N.Cook (161)
1957	M.J.Stewart (8)	1982	N.G.Cowans (19)	2006	S.C.J.Broad (167)
1958	A.C.D.Ingleby-Mackenzie	1983	N.A.Foster (29)	2007	A.U.Rashid (19)
1959	G.Pullar (28)	1984	R.J.Bailey (4)	2008	R.S.Bopara (13)
1960	D.A.Allen (39)	1985	D.V.Lawrence (5)	2009	J.W.A.Taylor (7)
1961	P.H.Parfitt (37)	1986	A.A.Metcalfe	2010	S.T.Finn (36)
1962	P.J.Sharpe (12)		J.J.Whitaker (1)	2011	J.M.Bairstow (100)
1963	G.Boycott (108)	1987	R.J.Blakey (2)	2012	J.E.Root (140)
1964	J.M.Brearley (39)	1988	M.P.Maynard (4)	2013	B.A.Stokes (102)
1965	A.P.E.Knott (95)	1989	N.Hussain (96)	2014	A.Z.Lees (10)
1966	D.L.Underwood (86)	1990	M.A.Atherton (115)	2015	J.A.Leaning
1967	A.W.Greig (58)	1991	M.R.Ramprakash (52)	2016	B.M.Duckett (20)
1968	R.M.H.Cottam (4)	1992	I.D.K.Salisbury (15)	2017	D.W.Lawrence (11)
1969	A.Ward (5)	1993	M.N.Lathwell (2)	2018	S.M.Curran (24)
1970	C.M.Old (46)	1994	J.P.Crawley (37)	2019	T.Banton
1971	J.Whitehouse	1995	A.Symonds (26 – Australia)	2020	Z.Crawley (44)
1972	D.R.Owen-Thomas	1996	C.E.W.Silverwood (6)	2021	H.C.Brook (12)
1973	M.Hendrick (30)	1997	B.C.Hollioake (2)	2022	J.M.Cox
1974	P.H.Edmonds (51)	1998	A.Flintoff (79)	2023	J.E.K.Rew

THE PROFESSIONAL CRICKETERS' ASSOCIATION

PLAYER OF THE YEAR

Founded in 1967, the Professional Cricketers' Association introduced this award, decided by their membership, in 1970. The award, now known as the Reg Hayter Cup, is presented at the PCA's Annual Awards Dinner in London.

1970	M.J.Procter	1988	G.A.Hick	2007	O.D.Gibson
	J.D.Bond	1989	S.J.Cook	2008	M.van Jaarsveld
1971	L.R.Gibbs	1990	G.A.Gooch	2009	M.E.Trescothick
1972	A.M.E.Roberts	1991	Waqar Younis	2010	N.M.Carter
1973	P.G.Lee	1992	C.A.Walsh	2011	M.E.Trescothick
1974	B.Stead	1993	S.L.Watkin	2012	N.R.D.Compton
1975	Zaheer Abbas	1994	B.C.Lara	2013	M.M.Ali
1976	P.G.Lee	1995	D.G.Cork	2014	A.Lyth
1977	M.J.Procter	1996	P.V.Simmons	2015	C.Rushworth
1978	J.K.Lever	1997	S.P.James	2016	B.M.Duckett
1979	J.K.Lever	1998	M.B.Loye	2017	S.R.Patel
1980	R.D.Jackman	1999	S.G.Law	2018	J.L.Denly
1981	R.J.Hadlee	2000	M.E.Trescothick	2019	B.A.Stokes
1982	M.D.Marshall	2001	D.P.Fulton	2020	C.R.Woakes
1983	K.S.McEwan	2002	M.P.Vaughan	2021	J.E.Root
1984	R.J.Hadlee	2003	Mushtaq Ahmed	2022	J.M.Bairstow
1985	N.V.Radford	2004	A.Flintoff	2023	H.C.Brook
1986	C.A.Walsh	2005	A.Flintoff		
1987	R.J.Hadlee	2006	M.R.Ramprakash		

2023 FIRST-CLASS AVERAGES

These averages involve the 416 players who appeared in the 133 first-class matches played by 22 teams in England and Wales during the 2023 season.

'Cap' denotes the season in which the player was awarded a 1st XI cap by the county he represented in 2023. If he played for more than one county in 2023, the county(ies) who awarded him his cap is (are) underlined. Durham and Gloucestershire now cap players on first-class debut. Worcestershire now award county colours when players make their Championship debut.

Team abbreviations: A – Australia; De – Derbyshire; Du – Durham; E – England; Ex – Essex; Gm – Glamorgan; Gs – Gloucestershire; H – Hampshire; I – India; Ire – Ireland; K – Kent; La – Lancashire; Le – Leicestershire; M – Middlesex; Nh – Northamptonshire; Nt – Nottinghamshire; Sm – Somerset; Sy – Surrey; Sx – Sussex; Wa – Warwickshire; Wo – Worcestershire; Y – Yorkshire.

† Left-handed batsman. Cap: a dash (–) denotes a non-county player. A blank denotes uncapped by his current county.

BATTING AND FIELDING

		Cap	*M*	*I*	*NO*	*HS*	*Runs*	*Avge*	*100*	*50*	*Ct/St*
	K.J.Abbott (H)	2017	13	18	3	89*	246	16.40	–	1	5
	S.A.Abbott (Sy)		9	12	2	87*	456	45.60	–	3	5
	T.B.Abell (Sm)	2018	13	21	1	151	622	31.10	1	2	13
	C.N.Ackermann (Le)	2019	12	22	2	146	987	49.35	3	5	22
	M.R.Adair (Ire/Ex)		2	4	–	88	249	62.25	–	3	–
	W.A.Agar (K)		6	8	1	51	112	16.00	–	1	2
	R.Ahmed (Le)	2023	9	16	1	90	529	35.26	–	4	2
	B.W.Aitchison (De)		5	6	–	26	56	9.33	–	–	2
	Z.Akhter (Gs)	2023	7	13	6	41*	143	20.42	–	–	2
	T.E.Albert (H/K)		4	8	–	39	154	19.25	–	–	2
	K.L.Aldridge (Sm)		8	13	2	101*	451	41.00	1	3	6
†	M.M.Ali (E)	–	4	7	–	54	180	25.71	–	1	–
	B.M.J.Allison (Ex/Wo)	2023	6	8	2	75	166	27.66	–	1	2
†	T.P.Alsop (Sx)	2024	14	23	2	182*	820	39.04	2	4	18
†	J.M.Anderson (E/La)	2003	8	9	4	12	50	10.00	–	–	3
	M.K.Andersson (M)		1	1	–	2	2	2.00	–	–	2
	Arafat Bhuiyan (K)		3	5	2	15*	22	7.33	–	–	–
†	Arshdeep Singh (K)		5	9	4	12*	51	10.20	–	–	3
	A.A.P.Atkinson (Sy)		5	5	2	55*	120	40.00	–	1	1
†	M.H.Azad (Nh)		9	16	1	51	290	19.33	–	1	4
	Azhar Ali (Wo)	2022	14	26	1	103*	612	24.48	2	1	1
	T.E.Bailey (La)	2018	13	18	4	78	467	33.35	–	3	4
	J.M.Bairstow (E/Y)	2011	8	13	2	99*	405	36.81	–	3	36/1
	J.O.Baker (Wo)	2021	5	7	1	75	130	21.66	–	1	6
	A.Balbirnie (Ire)	–	2	3	–	2	2	0.66	–	–	2
†	G.P.Balderson (La)		11	16	2	116*	702	50.14	2	4	1
	J.T.Ball (Nt)	2016	4	6	2	11	33	8.25	–	–	2
	E.R.Bamber (M)	2022	13	20	9	46*	146	13.27	–	–	5
	C.T.Bancroft (Sm)		4	7	–	44	137	19.57	–	–	3
	T.Banton (Sm)		2	1	–	4	4	4.00	–	–	1
†	K.H.D.Barker (H)	2021	10	13	1	58	301	25.08	–	1	1
	E.G.Barnard (Wa)		14	20	4	95	482	30.12	–	2	5
	E.Barnes (Le)		3	4	2	5*	17	8.50	–	–	1
	G.A.Bartlett (Sm)		8	13	–	134	395	30.38	2	1	–
	S.Bashir (Sm)		6	9	4	44*	71	14.20	–	–	2
†	F.J.Bean (Y)		13	21	–	135	983	46.80	3	2	14
	D.G.Bedingham (Du)	2020	14	19	1	156	1019	56.61	5	1	13
	G.J.Bell (La)		12	16	–	91	447	27.93	–	3	25/2
	D.J.Bell-Drummond (K)	2015	9	15	2	300*	579	44.53	1	2	6

	Cap	M	I	NO	HS	Runs	Avge	100	50	Ct/St
C.G.Benjamin (Wa)		1	2	–	3	3	3.00	–	–	1
G.K.Berg (Nh)		4	7	1	56	131	21.83	–	1	3
D.M.Bess (Sm/Wa/Y)	2021	10	16	3	63	340	26.15	–	2	5
† J.G.Bethell (Wa)		4	6	–	37	138	23.00	–	–	1
T.R.Bevan (Gm)		1	2	–	15	15	7.50	–	–	2
S.W.Billings (K)	2015	6	10	–	31	92	9.20	–	–	13
† A.J.Blake (K)	2017	1	2	–	30	49	24.50	–	–	1
J.M.Blatherwick (La)		6	9	4	35	92	18.40	–	–	2
J.J.Bohannon (La)	2021	14	22	1	175	1257	59.85	4	5	5
S.M.Boland (A)	–	3	5	3	20	21	10.50	–	–	1
S.G.Borthwick (Du)	2009	13	19	4	134*	667	44.46	2	4	7
D.A.J.Bracewell (Ex)		8	11	1	61*	151	15.10	–	1	–
† J.R.Bracey (Gs)	2016	13	23	1	60*	483	21.95	–	3	29/5
K.C.Brathwaite (Wa)		4	6	–	16	45	7.50	–	–	–
D.R.Briggs (Wa)	2021	8	10	2	99	238	29.75	–	1	3
J.Broad (Nh)		6	10	2	56*	155	19.37	–	1	4
† S.C.J.Broad (E/Nt)	2008	10	14	5	26	140	15.55	–	–	–
H.C.Brook (E)		6	10	1	85	372	41.33	–	4	4
H.J.H.Brookes (De/Wa)		5	7	4	52*	135	45.00	–	1	1
J.A.Brooks (Sm/Wo)	2023	6	6	2	19	55	13.75	–	–	–
B.C.Brown (H)	2023	14	22	1	95	501	23.85	–	3	51/5
P.R.Brown (De)		3	1	–	0	0	0.00	–	–	1
† N.L.J.Browne (Ex)	2015	15	26	2	159	575	23.95	1	1	13
J.S.D.Buckingham (Nh)		3	6	–	17	34	5.66	–	–	1
S.G.Budinger (Le)		11	20	–	72	393	19.65	–	2	4
M.G.K.Burgess (Wa)	2021	14	19	3	88	476	29.75	–	4	45/1
† R.J.Burns (Sy)	2014	14	27	4	88	631	27.43	–	4	3
J.J.Bushnell (Du)	2022	3	4	–	27	62	15.50	–	–	–
W.E.L.Buttleman (Ex)		4	7	1	65	141	23.50	–	1	16/1
† E.J.Byrom (Gm)		8	15	2	101	475	36.53	1	4	3
H.R.C.Came (De)		11	18	2	141*	695	43.43	2	4	4
J.O.I.Campbell (H)		1	–	–	–	–	–	–	–	1
C.Campher (Ex/Ire)		2	4	–	33	88	22.00	–	–	1
† A.T.Carey (A)	–	6	11	1	66*	314	31.40	–	2	27/5
K.S.Carlson (Gm)	2021	14	23	–	192	1068	46.43	4	5	7
B.A.Carse (Du)	2016	6	8	2	108*	407	67.83	1	3	3
J.J.Carson (Sx)		11	19	4	75	438	29.20	–	3	9
M.Carter (Nt)		1	2	1	15*	23	23.00	–	–	–
O.J.Carter (Sx)		14	23	3	80	779	38.95	–	7	43/2
Y.S.Chahal (K)		2	2	1	5*	5	5.00	–	–	–
Z.J.Chappell (De)		10	11	2	46	220	24.44	–	–	1
† B.G.Charlesworth (Gs)	2018	9	15	–	87	380	25.33	–	2	8
L.A.Charlesworth (Gs)	2023	2	3	1	4	4	2.00	–	–	1
G.Clark (Du)	2015	14	15	1	128	818	58.42	3	3	14
J.Clark (Sy)	2022	14	20	4	107	427	26.68	1	2	2
† T.G.R.Clark (Sx)		12	22	1	96	645	30.71	–	6	18
J.M.Clarke (Nt)	2021	14	24	3	229*	1053	50.14	2	7	21
B.M.Cliff (Y)		2	2	1	1	1	1.00	–	–	–
B.O.Coad (Y)	2018	11	12	3	45	119	13.22	–	–	1
J.J.Cobb (Nh)	2018	3	5	–	44	69	13.80	–	–	2
J.M.Coles (Sx)		12	20	–	180	849	42.45	3	3	11
B.G.Compton (K)		14	25	1	114*	735	30.62	1	4	14
S.Conners (De)	2022	12	13	3	34	139	13.90	–	–	3
† A.N.Cook (Ex)	2005	14	26	1	128	836	33.44	1	6	17
S.J.Cook (Ex)	2020	13	18	5	31	139	10.69	–	–	3
C.B.Cooke (Gm)	2016	14	21	5	134*	733	45.81	2	2	38/2
† T.R.Cornall (Wo)	2022	1	2	–	6	10	5.00	–	–	1
P.Coughlin (Du)	2012	6	5	2	59*	163	54.33	–	2	–

	Cap	M	I	NO	HS	Runs	Avge	100	50	Ct/St
J.M.Cox (K)		10	17	1	133	385	24.06	1	–	12
O.B.Cox (Le/Wo)	2009	5	8	3	58	155	31.00	–	1	15/1
J.B.Cracknell (M)		3	6	–	33	90	15.00	–	–	1
M.S.Crane (H)	2021	2	3	–	22	44	14.66	–	–	1
Z.Crawley (E/K)	2019	13	24	1	189	1113	48.39	3	5	14
M.J.J.Critchley (Ex)	2023	14	26	1	121	990	39.60	2	7	11
H.T.Crocombe (Sx)		10	13	6	25*	107	15.28	–	–	6
S.J.Croft (La)	2010	7	11	1	56*	228	22.80	–	1	3
P.J.Cummins (A)	–	6	11	2	44*	176	19.55	–	–	4
† S.M.Curran (Sy)	2018	1	2	–	52	64	32.00	–	1	1
B.J.Currie (Sx)		2	2	1	2*	2	2.00	–	–	–
S.W.Currie (Le)		2	3	1	9*	11	5.50	–	–	1
A.K.Dal (De)	2022	10	13	1	141*	295	24.58	1	–	9
A.S.Dale (Gs)	2022	6	8	1	52	113	16.14	–	1	–
R.J.Das (Ex)		2	3	–	132	168	56.00	1	–	1
J.H.Davey (Le/Sm)	2021	8	11	2	60	220	24.44	–	1	–
A.L.Davies (Wa)	2023	12	17	–	118	437	25.70	1	2	6
† J.L.B.Davies (M)		5	10	2	65*	149	18.62	–	1	3
† S.M.Davies (Sm)	2017	2	3	–	9	13	4.33	–	–	7
W.S.Davis (Le)		4	6	1	58	151	30.20	–	1	–
L.A.Dawson (H)	2013	14	22	1	141	840	40.00	3	4	14
J.M.de Caires (M)		8	14	3	49	317	28.81	–	–	1
C.de Grandhomme (La)		5	8	1	67*	128	18.28	–	1	6
M.de Lange (Gs)	2023	4	4	–	22	33	8.25	–	–	1
B.F.W.de Leede (Du)		6	5	2	103	279	93.00	1	2	4
J.L.Denly (K)	2008	8	13	–	136	293	22.53	1	1	1
† C.D.J.Dent (Gs)	2010	13	23	–	113	694	30.17	1	4	11
S.R.Dickson (Sm)		11	20	2	82*	410	22.77	–	3	6
B.L.D'Oliveira (Wo)	2012	12	21	3	103	661	36.72	1	4	4
G.H.Dockrell (Ex)		1	2	–	74	100	50.00	–	1	2
D.A.Douthwaite (Gm)		4	6	2	37	78	19.50	–	–	–
G.S.Drissell (Du)	2022	1	1	1	10*	10	–	–	–	–
† J.L.du Plooy (De)	2022	14	21	6	238*	1236	82.40	4	4	5
† B.M.Duckett (E/Nt)	2020	11	20	1	182	904	47.57	2	4	23
R.M.Edavalath (Wo)	2023	1	2	–	15	15	7.50	–	–	–
M.W.Edwards (Y)		3	5	1	19*	52	13.00	–	–	–
S.S.Eskinazi (M)	2018	10	18	2	58	283	17.68	–	1	14
S.T.Evans (Le)		2	3	–	22	47	15.66	–	–	2
J.D.M.Evison (K)		14	22	3	99	597	31.42	–	4	1
A.M.Fernando (Nt)	2023	2	2	1	14*	14	14.00	–	–	–
M.V.T.Fernando (Du)	2023	2	–	–	–	–	–	–	–	–
M.G.A.Finan (Le)		4	6	1	9	24	4.80	–	–	–
A.W.Finch (Wo)	2019	7	11	6	33*	128	25.60	–	–	3
H.Z.Finch (K)		6	10	–	114	390	39.00	1	2	14/2
M.D.Fisher (Y)	2022	9	14	6	37*	140	17.50	–	–	2
L.J.Fletcher (Nt)	2014	4	6	4	15*	34	17.00	–	–	–
B.T.Foakes (Sy)	2016	13	19	1	125	716	39.77	3	1	55/1
† M.T.Foster (Ex)		1	2	1	1	1	1.00	–	–	–
J.K.Fuller (H)	2022	11	17	2	52*	384	25.60	–	2	–
† G.H.S.Garton (Sx)		1	1	–	28	28	28.00	–	–	–
† E.N.Gay (Nh)		10	18	1	144	589	34.64	1	3	11
B.B.A.Geddes (K)		1	2	–	36	37	18.50	–	–	–
B.J.Gibbon (Wo)	2022	8	9	4	41*	116	23.20	–	–	7
N.N.Gilchrist (K)		3	2	–	2	2	1.00	–	–	3
S.Gill (I)	–	1	2	–	18	31	15.50	–	–	1
† B.A.Godleman (De)	2015	3	5	–	86	166	33.20	–	2	2
L.P.Goldsworthy (Sm)		2	3	–	122	131	43.66	1	–	3
D.C.Goodman (Gs)	2021	4	5	2	14	23	7.66	–	–	1

	Cap	M	I	NO	HS	Runs	Avge	100	50	Ct/St
A.W.Gorvin (Gm)		5	6	2	47	86	21.50	–	–	–
H.O.M.Gouldstone (Nh)		2	4	–	6	8	2.00	–	–	3
B.G.F.Green (Sm)		2	4	1	31*	52	17.33	–	–	–
C.D.Green (A)	–	4	8	1	38	134	19.14	–	–	6
L.Gregory (Sm)	2015	9	12	1	65	343	31.18	–	1	3
† N.R.T.Gubbins (H)	2022	14	24	3	139*	969	46.14	3	4	4
B.D.Guest (De)	2022	14	21	–	197	741	35.28	2	2	37/1
Haider Ali (De)		10	16	1	146	481	32.06	1	3	8
S.R.Hain (Wa)	2018	11	16	1	165*	706	47.06	3	2	9
† T.J.Haines (Sx)	2021	11	20	–	91	662	33.10	–	6	4
H.Hameed (Nt)	2020	14	25	1	97	674	28.08	–	4	7
Hamidullah Qadri (K)		6	9	1	72	169	21.12	–	1	2
M.A.H.Hammond (Gs)	2013	13	23	1	92	812	36.90	–	8	7
F.P.Hand (Ire)	–	2	3	1	48*	56	28.00	–	–	3
P.S.P.Handscomb (Le)		10	18	3	136*	681	45.40	2	4	24/4
† O.J.Hannon-Dalby (Wa)	2019	13	13	7	18	60	10.00	–	–	2
S.R.Harmer (Ex)	2018	14	23	6	83*	524	30.82	–	3	22
J.A.R.Harris (Gm)	2010	11	12	1	47	159	14.45	–	–	2
† M.S.Harris (Gs)	2022	5	9	1	148	457	57.12	2	2	4
C.G.Harrison (Nt)		8	11	2	39	208	23.11	–	–	14
† T.W.Hartley (La)		10	13	3	73*	371	37.10	–	2	6
Hassan Ali (Wa)	2023	6	7	1	54	150	25.00	–	2	2
J.A.Haynes (Wo)	2019	12	22	3	134*	573	30.15	2	1	15
† J.R.Hazlewood (A)	–	4	6	3	6*	20	6.66	–	–	2
† T.M.Head (A)	–	6	12	–	163	543	45.25	1	3	2
T.G.Helm (M)	2019	9	14	3	20	113	10.27	–	–	4
M.J.Henry (Sm)	2023	6	9	2	50*	149	21.28	–	1	2
R.F.Higgins (M)	2023	14	25	2	137	955	41.52	1	8	9
G.C.H.Hill (Y)		13	21	2	101	694	36.52	1	7	11
L.J.Hill (Le)	2021	14	24	2	162*	880	40.00	2	5	6
M.G.Hogan (K)		7	10	5	43	94	18.80	–	–	3
† M.D.E.Holden (M)	2023	13	23	–	55	437	19.00	–	2	5
I.G.Holland (H)	2021	9	14	3	138*	313	28.45	1	–	1
† L.B.K.Hollman (M)		8	15	1	63*	244	17.42	–	1	3
S.D.Hope (Y)		2	4	1	83	187	62.33	–	2	6
A.J.Hose (Wo)	2023	11	19	1	85	566	31.44	–	3	8
F.J.Hudson-Prentice (Sx)	2023	14	22	4	73	879	48.83	–	9	5
† J.O.Hull (Le)		6	8	2	15	23	3.83	–	–	2
† G.I.Hume (Ire)	–	2	3	1	14	23	11.50	–	–	–
S.F.Hunt (Sx)		5	5	2	22	43	14.33	–	–	–
M.F.Hurst (La)		2	3	2	76*	130	130.00	–	2	–
B.A.Hutton (Nt)	2021	13	18	2	84	282	17.62	–	1	8
D.K.Ibrahim (Sx)		5	10	1	36	109	12.11	–	–	5
† C.A.Ingram (Gm)	2017	7	12	–	136	357	29.75	1	1	7
W.G.Jacks (Sy)	2022	9	15	1	99	484	34.57	–	3	11
† R.A.Jadeja (I)	–	1	2	–	48	48	24.00	–	–	1
L.W.James (Nt)		14	24	1	50	405	17.60	–	1	12
† K.K.Jennings (La)	2018	11	17	2	189*	794	52.93	1	5	14
M.A.Jones (Du)	2018	14	21	2	121*	631	33.21	1	4	9
R.P.Jones (La)		2	4	1	111	154	51.33	1	–	2
E.S.Kalley (Ex)		1	1	–	0	0	0.00	–	–	–
A.Karvelas (Sx)		8	12	2	23	78	7.80	–	–	2
Kashif Ali (Wo)	2022	4	6	–	93	133	22.16	–	1	–
B.I.Kellaway (Gm)		2	2	–	0	0	0.00	–	–	–
R.I.Keogh (Nh)	2019	13	22	2	172	780	39.00	2	3	1
S.C.Kerrigan (Nh)		1	1	–	2	2	2.00	–	–	–
† U.T.Khawaja (A)	–	6	12	–	141	509	42.41	1	3	2
F.I.N.Khushi (Ex)		2	4	1	56*	106	35.33	–	1	3

	Cap	M	I	NO	HS	Runs	Avge	100	50	Ct/St
L.P.J.Kimber (Le)		6	9	–	61	129	14.33	–	1	6
T.Kohler-Cadmore (Sm)		12	20	1	130	735	38.68	1	4	8
V.Kohli (I)	–	1	2	–	49	63	31.50	–	–	1
† M.P.Kuhnemann (Du)	2023	3	2	1	5*	5	5.00	–	–	1
M.Labuschagne (A/Gm)	2019	11	20	1	170*	897	47.21	3	3	8
R.A.S.Lakmal (De)		4	6	4	12*	30	15.00	–	–	1
D.J.Lamb (Gs/La)	2023	2	4	1	70	74	24.66	–	1	1
M.J.Lamb (De)		9	13	–	99	280	21.53	–	1	5
† T.A.Lammonby (Sm)		14	24	2	109	657	29.86	1	4	14
† T.W.M.Latham (Sy)		5	9	1	99	318	39.75	–	3	14
T.E.Lawes (Sy)		10	12	1	55	126	11.45	–	1	2
D.W.Lawrence (Ex)	2017	11	21	–	152	801	38.14	3	2	7
J.Leach (Wo)	2012	14	22	4	53	259	14.38	–	1	3
† M.J.Leach (E/Sm)	2017	7	7	3	40*	126	31.50	–	–	3
J.A.Leaning (K)	2021	14	25	3	68*	563	25.59	–	4	19
D.J.Leech (Nh/Y)		2	2	–	32	45	22.50	–	–	1
† A.Z.Lees (Du)	2018	14	21	2	195	1347	70.89	5	5	5
J.D.Libby (Wo)	2020	12	23	3	198	1153	57.65	4	5	11
J.B.Lintott (Wa)		1	2	–	78	86	43.00	–	1	–
D.L.Lloyd (Gm)	2019	8	13	2	81	332	30.18	–	1	5
N.M.Lyon (A)	–	3	5	1	16*	37	9.25	–	–	1
† A.Lyth (Y)	2010	13	22	1	174	1019	48.52	3	5	18
S.J.C.McAlindon (Du)	2022	2	1	–	4	4	4.00	–	–	–
N.J.McAndrew (Sx)		7	11	1	65	265	26.50	–	1	1
† A.R.McBrine (Ire)	–	2	3	1	86*	172	86.00	–	2	–
J.A.McCollum (Ire)	–	2	4	2	100*	154	77.00	1	–	1
J.P.McIlroy (Gm)		10	11	6	30*	79	15.80	–	–	1
C.McKerr (De/K)		3	3	1	23	41	20.50	–	–	1
† B.S.McKinney (Du)	2023	1	2	–	35	39	19.50	–	–	1
L.D.McManus (Nh)		11	16	1	27	185	12.33	–	–	26/3
W.L.Madsen (De)	2011	12	17	–	143	779	45.82	1	7	31
S.Mahmood (La)	2021	2	2	1	1*	2	2.00	–	–	–
† D.J.Malan (Y)	2020	7	13	–	132	542	41.69	2	1	–
P.J.Malan (M)		8	16	1	66	221	14.73	–	2	3
M.R.Marsh (A)	–	3	6	1	118	250	50.00	1	1	2
G.J.Maxwell (Wa)		1	1	–	81	81	81.00	–	1	1
T.Mayes (Ire)	–	1	1	–	17	17	17.00	–	–	–
E.W.O.Middleton (Gs)	2023	2	3	1	39*	50	25.00	–	–	–
F.S.Middleton (H)		14	24	–	77	610	25.41	–	4	10
B.W.M.Mike (Y)		1	1	–	25	25	25.00	–	–	–
C.N.Miles (Du/Wa)	2023	4	4	–	33	68	17.00	–	–	4
M.E.Milnes (Y)		2	2	1	75	90	90.00	–	1	1
† Mir Hamza (Wa)		2	3	1	10*	16	8.00	–	–	–
D.J.Mitchell (La)		4	7	–	105	291	41.57	1	1	1
Mohammad Abbas (H)	2022	14	18	10	9	22	2.75	–	–	1
Mohammed Shami (I)	–	1	2	1	13*	26	26.00	–	–	–
M.Montgomery (Nt)		11	18	1	177	458	26.94	1	1	9
P.J.Moor (Ire)	–	2	4	1	118*	176	58.66	1	–	1
T.J.Moores (Nt)	2021	10	16	1	94	415	27.66	–	2	28
† D.T.Moriarty (Sy/Y)		5	4	4	13*	20	–	–	–	1
† J.P.Morley (La)		5	4	–	9	14	3.50	–	–	2
† D.R.Mousley (Wa)		13	20	1	94	571	30.05	–	6	7
P.W.A.Mulder (Le)	2023	10	16	2	102*	343	24.50	1	1	11
S.J.Mullaney (Nt)	2013	12	21	2	86	485	25.52	–	1	9
† T.R.Murphy (A)	–	2	4	–	34	76	19.00	–	–	–
† T.J.Murtagh (M)	2008	6	11	3	8	27	3.37	–	–	1
T.S.Muyeye (K)		9	16	–	179	571	35.68	1	1	8
K.K.Nair (Nh)		3	3	–	150	249	83.00	1	1	5

	Cap	M	I	NO	HS	Runs	Avge	100	50	Ct/St
M.G.Neser (Gm)	2021	6	7	1	176*	487	81.16	2	2	3
† A.S.S.Nijjar (K)		2	3	1	42	59	29.50	–	–	–
S.A.Northeast (Gm)	2022	13	20	1	166*	646	34.00	2	2	7
A.R.J.Ogborne (Sm)		1	1	–	2	2	2.00	–	–	1
F.S.Organ (H)		10	17	1	97	245	15.31	–	1	4
M.K.O'Riordan (K)		1	1	–	35	35	35.00	–	–	–
A.G.H.Orr (Sx)		8	13	1	67	322	26.83	–	1	6
C.Overton (Sm)	2016	9	14	3	70*	249	22.63	–	1	15
J.Overton (Sy)	2023	6	8	2	51	186	31.00	–	1	14
C.F.Parkinson (Le)	2022	4	5	–	14	31	6.20	–	–	–
M.W.Parkinson (Du/La)	2023/2019	9	5	3	5*	17	8.50	–	–	4
† A.Y.Patel (Du)	2023	3	4	–	34	87	21.75	–	–	–
R.K.Patel (Le)	2023	14	25	1	179	1075	44.79	4	3	6
† R.S.Patel (Sy)		7	9	1	37*	125	15.62	–	–	5
D.Paterson (Nt)	2021	13	17	4	16	77	5.92	–	–	1
† L.A.Patterson-White (Nt)		5	7	–	15	70	10.00	–	–	–
D.Y.Pennington (Wo)	2018	8	10	1	26	101	11.22	–	–	2
M.S.Pepper (Ex)		4	7	2	52*	145	29.00	–	1	10
T.H.S.Pettman (Nt)		1	2	–	1	1	0.50	–	–	–
J.P.Phillips (Gs)	2023	2	3	–	80	123	41.00	–	1	–
H.W.Podmore (Gm)		2	2	1	3	5	5.00	–	–	1
† E.J.Pollock (Wo)	2022	8	15	–	56	255	17.00	–	1	6
O.J.D.Pope (E/Sy)	2018	8	13	1	205	674	56.16	2	1	8
J.A.Porter (Ex)	2015	14	15	9	11	36	6.00	–	–	12
M.J.Potts (Du/E)	2017	12	10	1	64	147	16.33	–	1	9
N.J.Potts (De)		2	1	1	2*	2	–	–	–	–
T.J.Prest (H)		5	9	1	108	173	21.62	1	–	–
M.Pretorius (Du)	2023	3	2	–	39	75	37.50	–	–	2
O.J.Price (Gs)	2021	11	20	2	132	763	42.38	3	2	22
T.J.Price (Gs)	2020	8	11	2	109	410	45.55	1	2	3
† L.A.Procter (Nh)	2020	11	19	3	87*	480	30.00	–	4	4
C.A.Pujara (I/Sx)	2022	9	14	–	151	690	49.28	3	2	6
M.R.Quinn (K)		9	15	2	37	156	12.00	–	–	4
A.M.Rahane (I)	–	1	2	–	89	135	67.50	–	1	1
† B.A.Raine (Du)	2011	14	13	4	71	232	25.77	–	2	6
† L.M.Reece (De)	2019	11	19	7	201*	1048	87.33	4	5	3
M.L.Revis (Y)		10	15	4	106	487	44.27	2	1	4
† J.E.K.Rew (Sm)		14	22	3	221	1086	57.15	5	2	40/2
† W.M.H.Rhodes (Wa)	2020	14	20	–	102	618	30.90	1	2	11
J.A.Richards (Ex)		1	2	2	17*	19	–	–	–	–
† R.D.Rickelton (Y)		3	3	–	46	65	21.66	–	–	2
K.A.J.Roach (Sy)	2023	8	9	5	18	42	10.50	–	–	3
O.E.Robinson (E/Sx)	2019	6	9	2	33	107	15.28	–	–	–
O.G.Robinson (Du)	2023	14	18	2	167*	931	58.18	3	5	37/10
S.D.Robson (M)	2013	14	28	5	126*	856	37.21	3	2	13
G.H.Roderick (Wo)	2021	13	24	1	123	696	30.26	1	3	38/2
G.Roelofsen (Gs)	2023	2	3	–	42	72	24.00	–	–	–
T.S.Roland-Jones (M)	2012	11	18	1	39	300	17.64	–	–	3
J.E.Root (E)	–	6	10	1	118*	468	52.00	1	3	12
† W.T.Root (Gm)	2021	14	23	6	117*	884	52.00	1	6	2
A.M.Rossington (Ex)	2023	8	15	1	104	315	22.50	1	–	17/3
C.Rushworth (Wa)	2023	13	12	4	22	95	11.87	–	–	3
A.K.Russell (Nh)		3	5	4	8*	11	11.00	–	–	–
J.S.Rymell (Ex)		1	2	–	21	26	13.00	–	–	2
N.Saini (Wo)	2023	1	1	1	0*	0	0.00	–	–	–
† B.Sai Sudharsan (Sy)		2	3	–	73	116	38.66	–	1	–
J.J.G.Sales (Nh)		5	10	1	57	132	14.66	–	1	1
M.E.T.Salisbury (Le)		6	7	2	4*	5	1.00	–	–	2

	Cap	M	I	NO	HS	Runs	Avge	100	50	Ct/St
P.D.Salt (La)		7	11	1	105	433	43.30	2	2	23/3
A.G.Salter (Gm)	2022	4	7	–	48	163	23.28	–	–	3
B.W.Sanderson (Nh)	2018	10	16	3	46	125	9.61	–	–	1
† Saud Shakil (Y)		3	5	–	35	71	14.20	–	–	1
G.L.S.Scrimshaw (De)		3	5	4	19*	20	20.00	–	–	3
T.A.R.Scriven (Le)		12	20	4	78	315	19.68	–	2	5
† Shan Masood (Y)		7	13	1	192	720	60.00	2	3	2
R.G.Sharma (I)	–	1	2	–	43	58	29.00	–	–	–
J.Shaw (Gs)	2016	6	9	1	44	171	21.37	–	–	–
H.B.Shipley (Sx)		3	6	4	41	116	58.00	–	–	2
D.P.Sibley (Sy)		14	25	6	140*	746	39.26	1	5	22
P.M.Siddle (Sm)	2022	5	6	2	17	57	14.25	–	–	–
J.A.Simpson (M)	2011	14	25	1	75	564	23.50	–	4	44/8
J.Singh (K)		2	3	2	7*	7	7.00	–	–	–
M.Siraj (I)	–	1	2	1	1	1	1.00	–	–	–
P.Sisodiya (Gm)		1	1	–	4	4	4.00	–	–	–
B.T.Slater (Nt)	2021	14	25	–	140	825	33.00	2	3	5
J.L.Smith (Sy)	2023	13	19	1	138	736	40.88	2	4	9
S.P.D.Smith (A/Sx)	2023	9	15	–	121	650	43.33	2	3	20
S.Snater (Ex)	2022	7	10	–	31	107	10.70	–	–	1
K.Srikar Bharat (I)	–	1	2	–	23	28	14.00	–	–	5
† M.A.Starc (A)	–	5	9	2	41	128	18.28	–	–	1
C.T.Steel (Sy)		7	10	1	141*	291	32.33	1	1	4
M.T.Steketee (Y)		4	3	–	26	31	10.33	–	–	–
G.Stewart (K)		6	10	–	50	206	20.60	–	1	2
P.R.Stirling (Ire)	–	2	3	–	107	152	50.66	1	–	–
† B.A.Stokes (E)	–	6	9	–	155	405	45.00	1	2	7
O.P.Stone (Nt)	2023	2	4	1	22	46	15.33	–	–	–
† M.D.Stoneman (M)	2022	14	28	1	76	612	22.66	–	5	3
M.J.Swepson (Gm)		4	4	1	69	103	34.33	–	1	2
H.J.Swindells (Le)		2	3	–	73	81	27.00	–	1	–
J.A.Tattersall (Y)	2022	9	13	1	79	338	28.16	–	1	24/1
J.M.R.Taylor (Gs)	2010	5	8	–	98	166	20.75	–	1	2
M.D.Taylor (Gs)	2013	6	10	3	57*	176	25.14	–	1	2
T.A.I.Taylor (Nh)		10	17	–	66	288	16.94	–	2	1
C.J.Tear (Sx)		1	1	–	5	5	5.00	–	–	–
H.T.Tector (Gs/Ire)	2023	3	5	–	51	97	19.40	–	1	1
N.R.M.Thain (Ex)		1	2	–	36	39	19.50	–	–	1
S.N.Thakur (I)	–	1	2	–	51	51	25.50	–	1	1
† J.A.Thompson (Y)	2022	11	14	1	64	299	23.00	–	3	4
A.T.Thomson (De)		10	12	2	44	229	22.90	–	–	4
J.C.Tongue (E/Wo)	2017	7	9	4	19	60	12.00	–	–	1
† R.L.Toole (Du)	2023	1	–	–	–	–	–	–	–	1
C.P.Tremain (Nh)		3	6	–	16	56	9.33	–	–	2
† L.Trevaskis (Du)	2017	2	3	–	79	114	38.00	–	1	3
L.J.Tucker (Ire)	–	2	3	–	97	159	53.00	–	1	6/1
J.A.Turner (H)		2	3	–	7	11	3.66	–	–	–
† Umar Amin (Le)		4	6	–	94	108	18.00	–	1	1
A.R.I.Umeed (Sm)		4	6	1	49	160	32.00	–	–	4
J.D.Unadkat (Sx)		3	4	1	10	18	6.00	–	–	–
Usama Mir (Wo)	2023	1	2	–	1	1	0.50	–	–	–
L.V.van Beek (Wo)	2023	2	3	–	53	59	19.66	–	1	1
G.L.van Buuren (Gs)	2016	8	14	5	110*	461	51.22	1	3	4
T.van der Gugten (Gm)	2018	13	15	5	54	280	28.00	–	2	3
P.A.van Meekeren (Gs)	2023	2	2	–	7	7	3.50	–	–	1
† R.S.Vasconcelos (Nh)	2021	10	20	–	78	389	19.45	–	3	13
D.J.Vilas (La)	2018	10	16	2	124	363	25.92	1	1	6
J.M.Vince (H)	2013	14	24	3	186	1007	47.95	1	7	22

	Cap	M	I	NO	HS	Runs	Avge	100	50	Ct/St
† N.Wagner (Sm)		3	3	–	72	89	29.66	–	1	1
† M.D.Wagstaff (De)		3	5	–	78	165	33.00	–	2	2
M.J.Waite (Wo)	2022	11	20	4	109*	565	35.31	1	3	4
† P.I.Walter (Ex)	2023	9	16	2	76	389	27.78	–	2	7
† H.D.Ward (Sx)		1	1	–	2	2	2.00	–	–	–
† D.A.Warner (A)	–	6	12	–	66	329	27.41	–	2	4
† M.R.J.Watt (De)		5	6	1	19	72	14.40	–	–	2
J.J.Weatherley (H)	2021	5	7	–	58	121	17.28	–	1	3
† L.W.P.Wells (La)	2022	13	20	–	119	676	33.80	2	3	10
T.Westley (Ex)	2013	14	27	2	148	1130	45.20	3	4	7
J.H.Wharton (Y)		6	10	1	89	349	38.77	–	4	2
† C.J.White (Nh)		14	22	9	59	112	8.61	–	1	–
R.G.White (M)		1	2	–	3	3	1.50	–	–	–
† S.M.Whiteman (Nh)		11	21	2	130*	719	37.84	2	3	3
W.S.A.Williams (La)		13	13	3	61	135	13.50	–	1	7
C.R.Woakes (E/Wa)	2009	6	8	1	36	120	17.14	–	–	1
† L.Wood (La)		2	2	–	2	2	1.00	–	–	–
M.A.Wood (E)	–	3	5	1	28	83	20.75	–	–	–
T.A.Wood (De)		1	1	–	15	15	15.00	–	–	–
D.J.Worrall (Sy)	2023	13	17	3	51	221	15.78	–	1	4
C.J.C.Wright (Le)	2021	14	20	6	66*	337	24.07	–	1	4
J.Yadav (M)		3	5	1	56	74	18.50	–	1	1
U.T.Yadav (Ex/I)		4	8	2	51	127	21.16	–	1	–
† R.M.Yates (Wa)	2023	13	19	2	228*	583	34.29	2	–	26
C.A.Young (Ire)	–	1	1	–	2	2	2.00	–	–	–
W.A.Young (Nt)	2023	3	6	1	145	299	59.80	1	1	2
† Zafar Gohar (Gs)	2021	13	21	1	53	319	15.95	–	1	3
† S.A.Zaib (Nh)		11	19	1	57*	514	28.55	–	1	5
† Zain Ul Hassan (Gm)		9	16	1	69	453	30.20	–	2	2

BOWLING

See BATTING AND FIELDING section for details of matches and caps

	Cat	O	M	R	W	Avge	Best	5wI	10wM
K.J.Abbott (H)	RFM	327.3	77	958	44	21.77	4- 39	–	–
S.A.Abbott (Sy)	RMF	295.2	64	917	37	24.78	5- 50	1	–
T.B.Abell (Sm)	RM	32	3	131	4	32.75	4- 54	–	–
C.N.Ackermann (Le)	OB	99	15	352	4	88.00	1- 8	–	–
M.R.Adair (Ex/Ire)	RFM	43:4	8	222	2	111.00	2- 64	–	–
W.A.Agar (K)	RFM	163.4	32	595	21	28.33	5- 63	1	–
R.Ahmed (Le)	LB	140	8	529	8	66.12	3- 89	–	–
B.W.Aitchison (De)	RFM	112.5	18	481	8	60.12	3-131	–	–
Z.Akhter (Gs)	RM	181	16	785	19	41.31	4- 33	–	–
K.L.Aldridge (Sm)	RM	161.1	28	758	16	47.37	4- 36	–	–
M.M.Ali (E)	OB	126	15	463	9	51.44	3- 76	–	–
B.M.J.Allison (Ex/Wo)	RFM	91	15	332	6	55.33	2- 40	–	–
T.P.Alsop (Sx)	SLA	7	2	10	0				
J.M.Anderson (E/La)	RFM	282	74	752	21	35.80	5- 76	1	–
M.K.Andersson (M)	RM	21	2	109	1	109.00	1- 86	–	–
Arafat Bhuiyan (K)	RFM	62.3	11	265	7	37.85	4- 65	–	–
Arshdeep Singh (K)	LMF	161.2	37	543	13	41.76	3- 58	–	–
A.A.P.Atkinson (Sy)	RF	115.1	16	404	20	20.20	6- 68	1	–
M.H.Azad (Nh)	OB	3	1	2	0				
T.E.Bailey (La)	RMF	407.4	102	1133	50	22.66	6- 59	2	–
J.O.Baker (Wo)	SLA	110	5	474	4	118.50	3-117	–	–
G.P.Balderson (La)	RM	235	54	784	23	34.08	4- 69	–	–
J.T.Ball (Nt)	RFM	88	10	386	7	55.14	3- 67	–	–
E.R.Bamber (M)	RMF	382.2	88	1052	41	25.65	5- 20	1	–
T.Banton (Sm)	OB	1	1	0	0				

	Cat	O	M	R	W	Avge	Best	5wI	10wM
K.H.D.Barker (H)	LMF	242.1	50	743	20	37.15	5- 32	1	–
E.G.Barnard (Wa)	RMF	269.4	66	845	29	29.13	5- 66	1	–
E.Barnes (Le)	RFM	53	4	212	2	106.00	1- 23	–	–
G.A.Bartlett (Sm)	OB	2	0	13	0				
S.Bashir (Sm)	OB	203	50	670	10	67.00	3- 67	–	–
F.J.Bean (Y)		11	0	105	0				
G.J.Bell (La)	OB	18	0	64	1	64.00	1- 28	–	–
D.J.Bell-Drummond (K)	RMF	35	4	139	3	46.33	2- 42	–	–
G.K.Berg (Nh)	RMF	69	13	253	5	50.60	2- 70	–	–
D.M.Bess (Sm/Wa/Y)	OB	345.5	61	1201	27	44.48	5-158	1	–
J.G.Bethell (Wa)	SLA	11	3	36	0				
A.J.Blake (K)	RM	2	0	20	0				
J.M.Blatherwick (La)	RFM	87.3	11	393	8	49.12	2- 25	–	–
S.M.Boland (A)	RFM	83	11	336	7	48.00	3- 46	–	–
S.G.Borthwick (Du)	LBG	28.1	1	112	5	22.40	4- 25	–	–
D.A.J.Bracewell (Ex)	RMF	165.2	18	658	24	27.41	4- 51	–	–
D.R.Briggs (Wa)	SLA	134.5	27	346	9	38.44	2- 28	–	–
J.Broad (Nh)	RM	27	1	117	2	58.50	2- 39	–	–
S.C.J.Broad (E/Nt)	RFM	342.4	61	1164	43	27.06	5- 51	1	–
H.C.Brook (E)	RM	6	2	12	0				
H.J.H.Brookes (De/Wa)	RFM	109	16	431	16	26.93	6- 20	1	–
J.A.Brooks (Sm/Wo)	RFM	128.2	33	414	13	31.84	5- 56	1	–
P.R.Brown (De)	RMF	43.3	2	190	3	63.33	1- 15	–	–
N.L.J.Browne (Ex)	LB	1.4	0	14	0				
J.S.D.Buckingham (Nh)	RFM	62	7	256	3	85.33	1- 48	–	–
S.G.Budinger (Le)	OB	5	0	27	0				
M.G.K.Burgess (Wa)	RM	10	3	24	0				
R.J.Burns (Sy)	RM	2.2	0	2	0				
J.J.Bushnell (Du)	RM	29	0	131	2	65.50	1- 20	–	–
E.J.Byrom (Gm)	OB	9	1	49	0				
C.Campher (Ex/Ire)	RM	29.5	1	153	1	153.00	1- 45	–	–
K.S.Carlson (Gm)	OB	206	12	853	14	60.92	3-147	–	–
B.A.Carse (Du)	RF	140.3	17	548	19	28.84	3- 38	–	–
J.J.Carson (Sx)	OB	314.2	43	1250	31	40.32	5- 79	1	–
M.Carter (Nt)	OB	50	9	147	4	36.75	3- 43	–	–
Y.S.Chahal (K)	LBG	101	22	246	9	27.33	3- 63	–	–
Z.J.Chappell (De)	RFM	240.2	44	869	24	36.20	5- 69	1	–
B.G.Charlesworth (Gs)	RM/OB	23	1	145	3	48.33	1- 23	–	–
L.A.Charlesworth (Gs)	RM	30.5	6	134	4	33.50	3- 54	–	–
J.Clark (Sy)	RMF	355	69	1025	48	21.35	5- 79	1	–
T.G.R.Clark (Sx)	RM	82	16	232	6	38.66	3- 21	–	–
B.M.Cliff (Y)	RFM	26	1	116	3	38.66	2- 27	–	–
B.O.Coad (Y)	RMF	279.2	84	728	36	20.22	5- 33	2	–
J.J.Cobb (Nh)	OB	1	0	2	0				
J.M.Coles (Sx)	SLA	144.3	17	530	5	106.00	2- 93	–	–
B.G.Compton (K)	OB	2	0	12	0				
S.Conners (De)	RM	318	49	1216	27	45.03	5-115	1	–
S.J.Cook (Ex)	RFM	352.2	89	941	48	19.60	5- 42	1	–
C.B.Cooke (Gm)	RM	0.3	0	4	0				
T.R.Cornall (Wo)	SLA	1	0	5	0				
P.Coughlin (Du)	RM	109.1	19	388	12	32.33	3- 27	–	–
M.S.Crane (H)	LB	12.3	0	48	1	48.00	1- 15	–	–
M.J.J.Critchley (Ex)	LB	127.2	14	469	23	20.39	3- 33	–	–
H.T.Crocombe (Sx)	RMF	173	14	469	23	20.39	3- 33	–	–
S.J.Croft (La)	RMF	7	0	35	0				
P.J.Cummins (A)	RF	191.4	11	817	22	37.13	6- 91	1	–
S.M.Curran (Sy)	LMF	37	9	101	3	33.66	2- 65	–	–
B.J.Currie (Sx)	LMF	62	12	234	9	26.00	3- 27	–	–

	Cat	*O*	*M*	*R*	*W*	*Avge*	*Best*	*5wI*	*10wM*
S.W.Currie (Le)	RMF	46	4	197	5	39.40	2- 32	–	–
A.K.Dal (De)	RM	209.1	37	709	22	32.22	6- 69	3	–
A.S.Dale (Gs)	RFM	135.5	19	475	15	31.66	6- 41	1	–
J.H.Davey (Le/Sm)	RMF	154	24	560	21	26.66	4- 17	–	–
W.S.Davis (Le)	RFM	62	10	239	5	47.80	4- 28	–	–
L.A.Dawson (H)	SLA	315.5	68	980	49	20.00	6- 40	4	1
J.M.de Caires (M)	OB	213.3	30	691	27	25.59	8-106	2	1
C.de Grandhomme (La)	RMF	89	11	296	7	42.28	2- 34	–	–
M.de Lange (Gs)	RF	80	11	310	6	51.66	3- 84	–	–
B.F.W.de Leede (Du)	RM	114	19	494	17	29.05	4- 76	–	–
J.L.Denly (K)	LB	87.1	7	328	6	54.66	4-164	–	–
C.D.J.Dent (Gs)	SLA	6.3	1	11	1	11.00	1- 0	–	–
S.R.Dickson (Sm)	RM	0.3	0	1	0				
G.H.Dockrell (Ex)	SLA	27	1	148	1	148.00	1- 86	–	–
B.L.D'Oliveira (Wo)	LB	61	4	266	3	88.66	2- 37	–	–
D.A.Douthwaite (Gm)	RMF	54.5	6	204	4	51.00	2- 44	–	–
G.S.Drissell (Du)	OB	30	4	88	1	88.00	1- 47	–	–
J.L.du Plooy (De)	SLA	30	3	104	0				
M.W.Edwards (Y)	RFM	65	8	254	5	50.80	3- 54	–	–
J.D.M.Evison (K)	RM	249	23	992	19	52.21	4- 62	–	–
A.M.Fernando (Nt)	RMF	48.1	11	151	6	25.16	3- 40	–	–
M.V.T.Fernando (Du)	LMF	41	6	157	7	22.42	4- 40	–	–
M.G.A.Finan (Le)	LFM	71.4	6	359	8	44.87	3-109	–	–
A.W.Finch (Wo)	RMF	174.4	23	720	28	25.71	5- 74	2	–
M.D.Fisher (Y)	RFM	238.3	52	799	28	28.53	5- 30	1	–
L.J.Fletcher (Nt)	RMF	71.5	19	176	9	19.55	3- 44	–	–
M.T.Foster (Ex)	RFM	11	1	72	0				
J.K.Fuller (H)	RFM	161.3	17	623	24	25.95	6- 37	2	–
G.H.S.Garton (Sx)	LF	10	1	64	1	64.00	1- 64	–	–
B.J.Gibbon (Wo)	LMF	200.3	28	861	20	43.05	4- 92	–	–
N.N.Gilchrist (K)	RFM	96.2	12	401	2	200.50	1- 60	–	–
L.P.Goldsworthy (Sm)	SLA	10	1	34	0				
D.C.Goodman (Gs)	RMF	70.4	9	319	8	39.87	4- 73	–	–
A.W.Gorvin (Gm)	RM	96.4	25	318	7	45.42	3- 88	–	–
B.G.F.Green (Sm)	RFM	46.2	10	133	4	33.25	3- 39	–	–
C.D.Green (A)	RFM	62.4	5	292	7	41.71	2- 44	–	–
L.Gregory (Sm)	RMF	208.1	41	733	34	21.55	7- 84	1	1
N.R.T.Gubbins (H)	LB	9	0	28	1	28.00	1- 12	–	–
T.J.Haines (Sx)	RM	92.2	19	298	7	42.57	2- 27	–	–
H.Hameed (Nt)	LB	0.3	0	0	1	0.00	1- 0	–	–
Hamidullah Qadri (K)	OB	160.2	21	576	15	38.40	3- 51	–	–
F.P.Hand (Ire)	RMF	48	6	260	4	65.00	2- 50	–	–
O.J.Hannon-Dalby (Wa)	RMF	384	110	1030	54	19.07	7- 46	2	–
S.R.Harmer (Ex)	OB	558.4	131	1766	61	28.95	6-149	5	1
J.A.R.Harris (Gm)	RFM	292.4	37	1189	32	37.15	4- 18	–	–
M.S.Harris (Gs)	OB	1	1	0	0				
C.G.Harrison (Nt)	LBG	170	13	612	17	36.00	4- 28	–	–
T.W.Hartley (La)	SLA	286.5	68	852	19	44.84	2- 10	–	–
Hassan Ali (Wa)	RMF	144.3	22	518	24	21.58	4- 48	–	–
J.R.Hazlewood (A)	RFM	111	5	507	16	31.68	5-126	1	–
T.M.Head (A)	OB	18	1	92	2	46.00	2- 17	–	–
T.G.Helm (M)	RMF	263.2	47	887	28	31.67	6-110	1	–
M.J.Henry (Sm)	RFM	173.1	42	518	32	16.18	6- 59	4	–
R.F.Higgins (M)	RM	296.5	65	853	31	27.51	4- 74	–	–
G.C.H.Hill (Y)	RMF	206.5	41	681	19	35.84	4- 43	–	–
M.G.Hogan (K)	RFM	179.5	37	563	14	40.21	5- 63	1	–
I.G.Holland (H)	RMF	106	24	312	11	28.36	4- 19	–	–
L.B.K.Hollman (M)	LB	103	15	402	5	80.40	2- 37	–	–

	Cat	O	M	R	W	Avge	Best	5wI	10wM
F.J.Hudson-Prentice (Sx)	RMF	261	50	953	20	47.65	4- 27	–	–
J.O.Hull (Le)	LFM	116	10	565	9	62.77	3- 68	–	–
G.I.Hume (Ire)	RMF	43	6	179	5	35.80	3- 50	–	–
S.F.Hunt (Sx)	LMF	119	16	493	14	35.21	3- 36	–	–
B.A.Hutton (Nt)	RM	383.1	62	1327	62	21.40	6- 45	6	–
D.K.Ibrahim (Sx)	RM	10	1	56	1	56.00	1- 42	–	–
W.G.Jacks (Sy)	OB	89	9	336	10	33.60	5- 87	1	–
R.A.Jadeja (I)	SLA	41	6	114	4	28.50	3- 58	–	–
L.W.James (Nt)	RMF	276.4	46	912	28	32.57	6- 74	1	–
E.S.Kalley (Ex)	RM	13	1	58	0				
A.Karvelas (Sx)	RMF	241.4	53	800	35	22.85	4- 14	–	–
Kashif Ali (Wo)	LB	10	0	77	1	77.00	1- 51	–	–
B.I.Kellaway (Gm)	OB	17	1	60	0				
R.I.Keogh (Nh)	OB	178	15	644	14	46.00	3- 52	–	–
S.C.Kerrigan (Nh)	SLA	10	4	13	0				
L.P.J.Kimber (Le)	OB	8	0	49	0				
M.P.Kuhnemann (Du)	SLA	97.4	13	271	12	22.58	5- 52	1	–
M.Labuschagne (A/Gm)	LB	40.3	1	220	5	44.00	4- 81	–	–
R.A.S.Lakmal (De)	RMF	113	15	437	8	54.62	3- 77	–	–
D.J.Lamb (Gs/La)	RMF	17.2	3	67	2	33.50	2- 27	–	–
M.J.Lamb (De)	RM	22	5	83	0				
T.A.Lammonby (Sm)	LM	4	0	34	0				
T.E.Lawes (Sy)	RMF	205.4	30	771	39	19.76	5- 22	3	–
D.W.Lawrence (Ex)	LB	8	2	25	0				
J.Leach (Wo)	RMF	433.1	87	1414	48	29.45	6- 78	2	–
M.J.Leach (E/Sm)	SLA	188.1	33	657	22	29.86	4-119	–	–
J.A.Leaning (K)	RMF	99.4	9	472	12	39.33	3- 64	–	–
D.J.Leech (Nh/Y)	RMF	35	2	185	3	61.66	3- 78	–	–
J.D.Libby (Wo)	OB	13	1	68	0				
J.B.Lintott (Wa)	SLA	18.1	0	90	3	30.00	3- 68	–	–
D.L.Lloyd (Gm)	RM	59	5	266	5	53.20	2- 32	–	–
N.M.Lyon (A)	OB	85.3	6	324	14	23.14	4- 41	–	–
A.Lyth (Y)	RM	49	8	147	2	73.50	1- 17	–	–
S.J.C.McAlindon (Du)	RFM	25	1	164	1	164.00	1- 44	–	–
N.J.McAndrew (Sx)	RFM	208.1	35	750	31	24.19	5- 63	2	–
A.R.McBrine (Ire)	OB	34.4	1	247	5	49.40	2- 98	–	–
J.P.McIlroy (Gm)	LFM	259.5	51	736	24	30.66	5- 34	1	–
C.McKerr (De/K)	RFM	75.1	11	297	5	59.40	2- 39	–	–
S.Mahmood (La)	RFM	75	12	231	3	77.00	1- 46	–	–
D.J.Malan (Y)	LB	3	0	8	0				
M.R.Marsh (A)	RMF	34	1	167	3	55.66	1- 9	–	–
G.J.Maxwell (Wa)	OB	24	3	62	1	62.00	1- 45	–	–
T.Mayes (Ire)	RMF	23.5	1	123	7	17.57	4- 68	–	–
E.W.O.Middleton (Gs)	LB	26	2	92	1	92.00	1- 59	–	–
C.N.Miles (Du/Wa)	RMF	97	16	356	10	35.60	4- 73	–	–
M.E.Milnes (Y)	RMF	60	8	224	7	32.00	3- 72	–	–
Mir Hamza (Wa)	LMF	51.4	9	191	7	27.28	3- 49	–	–
D.J.Mitchell (La)	RM	53.1	16	175	7	25.00	3- 32	–	–
Mohammad Abbas (H)	RMF	407.4	108	1063	53	20.05	6- 49	2	–
Mohammed Shami (I)	RFM	45.3	10	161	4	40.25	2- 39	–	–
M.Montgomery (Nt)	OB	23	3	98	2	49.00	1- 0	–	–
T.J.Moores (Nt)	RM	0.2	0	1	0				
D.T.Moriarty (Sy/Y)	SLA	100.1	23	331	8	41.37	5-139	1	–
J.P.Morley (La)	SLA	108	17	334	8	41.75	3- 87	–	–
D.R.Mousley (Wa)	OB	15.1	2	52	0				
P.W.A.Mulder (Le)	RMF	168.4	41	467	26	17.96	5- 63	2	–
S.J.Mullaney (Nt)	RM	112.3	17	389	9	43.22	2- 32	–	–
T.R.Murphy (A)	OB	38.2	0	181	7	25.85	4-110	–	–

	Cat	O	M	R	W	Avge	Best	5wI	10wM
T.J.Murtagh (M)	RMF	182	42	619	30	20.63	6- 42	2	1
T.S.Muyeye (K)	OB	5	0	12	0				
K.K.Nair (Nh)	OB	6	1	22	0				
M.G.Neser (Gm)	RMF	155.3	26	523	20	26.15	7- 32	1	–
A.S.S.Nijjar (K)	SLA	123	29	317	10	31.70	4- 67	–	–
S.A.Northeast (Gm)	LB	4	1	15	0				
A.R.J.Ogborne (Sm)	LFM	28	3	89	3	29.66	2- 56	–	–
F.S.Organ (H)	OB	71.5	9	336	10	33.60	6- 67	1	–
A.G.H.Orr (Sx)	RM	3	0	12	0				
C.Overton (Sm)	RMF	249.5	55	788	26	30.30	5- 46	1	–
J.Overton (Sy)	RFM	104.4	14	345	14	24.64	3- 45	–	–
C.F.Parkinson (Le)	SLA	117.3	4	491	11	44.63	4- 63	–	–
M.W.Parkinson (Du/La)	LB	242	31	849	29	29.27	5-120	1	–
A.Y.Patel (Du)	SLA	139.4	25	446	10	44.60	5- 96	1	–
R.S.Patel (Sy)	RMF	2	0	14	0				
D.Paterson (Nt)	RFM	412.2	62	1390	50	27.80	5- 16	3	–
S.A.Patterson (Y)	RMF	427	132	1020	37	27.56	5- 46	2	–
L.A.Patterson-White (Nt)	SLA	69	11	228	1	228.00	1- 41	–	–
D.Y.Pennington (Wo)	RMF	203.5	39	718	26	27.61	4- 36	–	–
T.H.S.Pettman (Nt)	RFM	25	6	76	2	38.00	1- 15	–	–
H.W.Podmore (Gm)	RMF	55	13	206	3	68.66	2- 95	–	–
O.J.D.Pope (E/Sy)		1	0	10	0				
J.A.Porter (Ex)	RFM	334.5	64	1086	57	19.05	6- 34	4	1
M.J.Potts (Du/E)	RFM	405.5	71	1313	57	23.03	5- 65	1	–
N.J.Potts (De)	RFM	33	2	182	3	60.66	2- 39	–	–
T.J.Prest (H)	OB	23	2	98	3	32.66	2- 32	–	–
M.Pretorius (Du)	RF	63	8	227	2	113.50	1- 37	–	–
O.J.Price (Gs)	OB	99	3	459	8	57.37	3- 40	–	–
T.J.Price (Gs)	RM	209.2	30	824	18	45.77	4- 56	–	–
L.A.Procter (Nh)	RM	132.1	29	462	13	35.53	3- 47	–	–
M.R.Quinn (K)	RMF	241.3	66	695	21	33.09	4- 25	–	–
B.A.Raine (Du)	RMF	485	98	1497	60	24.95	5- 51	1	–
L.M.Reece (De)	LM	161	31	612	20	30.60	3- 47	–	–
M.L.Revis (Y)	RM	124.4	14	528	15	35.20	5- 50	1	–
W.M.H.Rhodes (Wa)	RMF	62	17	201	2	100.50	2- 4	–	–
J.A.Richards (Ex)	RFM	26	6	130	5	26.00	5- 96	1	–
K.A.J.Roach (Sy)	RF	225	43	683	26	26.26	5- 34	1	–
O.E.Robinson (E/Sx)	RMF	200.2	52	557	30	18.56	7- 58	2	1
S.D.Robson (M)	LB	35.5	1	173	6	28.83	4- 46	–	–
T.S.Roland-Jones (M)	RFM	304.1	58	953	27	35.29	7- 61	1	–
J.E.Root (E)	OB	63.1	8	231	7	33.00	2- 19	–	–
W.T.Root (Gm)	OB	3	0	9	0				
C.Rushworth (Wa)	RMF	333.3	61	1074	53	20.26	7- 38	2	1
A.K.Russell (Nh)	LB	73.5	1	387	6	64.50	6-175	1	–
N.Saini (Wo)	RFM	29	4	122	1	122.00	1-122	–	–
J.J.G.Sales (Nh)	RM	37	4	168	6	28.00	4- 24	–	–
M.E.T.Salisbury (Le)	RMF	119.3	26	500	14	35.71	5- 73	1	–
A.G.Salter (Gm)	OB	68	8	253	0				
B.W.Sanderson (Nh)	RMF	285.4	66	790	32	24.68	5- 42	1	–
Saud Shakil (Y)	SLA	5	1	23	0				
G.L.S.Scrimshaw (De)	RMF	59	8	269	9	29.88	5- 49	1	–
T.A.R.Scriven (Le)	RMF	286.3	50	931	39	23.87	4- 30	–	–
J.Shaw (Gs)	RMF	128	26	487	11	44.27	4- 82	–	–
H.B.Shipley (Sx)	RFM	112.5	15	471	13	36.23	4-124	–	–
D.P.Sibley (Sy)	OB	1.1	0	15	0				
P.M.Siddle (Sm)	RFM	139	31	386	16	24.12	3- 34	–	–
J.Singh (K)	RFM	49	1	254	7	36.28	4- 87	–	–
M.Siraj (I)	RFM	48.3	6	188	5	37.60	4-108	–	–

	Cat	O	M	R	W	Avge	Best	5wI	10wM
P.Sisodiya (Gm)	SLA	15	0	74	1	74.00	1- 74	–	–
B.T.Slater (Nt)	OB	4	1	11	0				
S.P.D.Smith (A/Sx)	LB	15.3	2	69	2	34.50	2- 55	–	–
S.Snater (Ex)	RM	128.4	27	437	8	54.62	3- 71	–	–
M.A.Starc (A)	LF	155.5	9	771	27	28.55	5- 78	1	–
C.T.Steel (Sy)	LB	72.3	6	254	6	42.33	4- 40	–	–
M.T.Steketee (Y)	RFM	70.3	13	272	6	45.33	3- 55	–	–
G.Stewart (K)	RMF	112.5	30	371	7	53.00	3- 6	–	–
B.A.Stokes (E)	RFM	29	4	89	3	29.66	1- 9	–	–
O.P.Stone (Nt)	RF	55	6	225	6	37.50	3- 82	–	–
M.D.Stoneman (M)	OB	0.5	0	11	0				
M.J.Swepson (Gm)	LB	176.3	32	585	14	41.78	4- 89	–	–
J.A.Tattersall (Y)	LB	4	0	19	0				
J.M.R.Taylor (Gs)	OB	9	0	56	0				
M.D.Taylor (Gs)	LMF	162.2	38	503	20	25.15	5- 24	1	–
T.A.I.Taylor (Nh)	RMF	236.4	38	855	19	45.00	4- 59	–	–
H.T.Tector (Gs/Ire)	OB	2	0	18	0				
N.R.M.Thain (Ex)	RM	12	0	58	1	58.00	1- 44	–	–
S.N.Thakur (I)	RFM	31	5	104	2	52.00	2- 83	–	–
J.A.Thompson (Y)	RM	249	47	918	30	30.60	3- 48	–	–
A.T.Thomson (De)	OB	335.3	55	1111	31	35.83	5-110	1	–
J.C.Tongue (E/Wo)	RFM	190.5	24	742	26	28.53	5- 29	2	–
R.L.Toole (Du)	LM	25	1	105	0				
C.P.Tremain (Nh)	RMF	75.4	16	233	13	17.92	5- 44	1	–
L.Trevaskis (Du)	SLA	33	5	101	2	50.50	1- 24	–	–
J.A.Turner (H)	RF	28.3	3	74	5	14.80	3- 23	–	–
Umar Amin (Le)	RM	19	1	71	1	71.00	1- 8	–	–
A.R.I.Umeed (Sm)	LB	10	0	37	0				
J.D.Unadkat (Sx)	LFM	86	15	266	11	24.18	6- 94	1	–
Usama Mir (Wo)	LB	41.1	2	173	2	86.50	1- 66	–	–
L.V.van Beek (Wo)	RFM	40.1	7	162	8	20.25	4- 42	–	–
G.L.van Buuren (Gs)	SLA	38	2	145	1	145.00	1- 31	–	–
T.van der Gugten (Gm)	RFM	385.5	89	1140	39	29.23	6- 88	3	–
P.A.van Meekeren (Gs)	RMF	53.5	7	258	12	21.50	5- 73	1	–
D.J.Vilas (La)		11	2	47	0				
J.M.Vince (H)	RM	4.1	0	21	1	21.00	1- 14	–	–
N.Wagner (Sm)	LMF	70	18	236	7	33.71	3- 67	–	–
M.D.Wagstaff (De)	LB	31	5	88	2	44.00	2- 59	–	–
M.J.Waite (Wo)	RFM	244.5	48	815	26	31.34	4- 21	–	–
P.I.Walter (Ex)	LMF	45.1	5	146	9	16.22	3- 20	–	–
M.R.J.Watt (De)	SLA	142.5	28	498	15	33.20	5- 83	1	–
J.J.Weatherley (H)	OB	7	0	18	0				
L.W.P.Wells (La)	LB	73.1	7	268	10	26.80	5- 25	1	–
J.H.Wharton (Y)	OB	12.1	1	114	1	114.00	1- 1	–	–
C.J.White (Nh)	RFM	397.5	84	1279	50	25.58	5- 57	3	–
W.S.A.Williams (La)	RMF	361.3	92	904	39	23.17	4- 23	–	–
C.R.Woakes (E/Wa)	RFM	189.2	40	544	29	18.75	5- 62	1	–
L.Wood (La)	LFM	60	7	207	5	41.40	3- 52	–	–
M.A.Wood (E)	RF	87.4	15	283	14	20.21	5- 34	1	–
D.J.Worrall (Sy)	RFM	407.5	92	1162	48	24.20	5- 25	3	–
C.J.C.Wright (Le)	RFM	414.1	88	1317	48	27.43	5- 32	2	–
J.Yadav (M)	OB	105.3	13	387	9	43.00	5-131	1	–
U.T.Yadav (Ex/I)	RFM	94	13	342	6	57.00	3- 32	–	–
R.M.Yates (Wa)	OB	76.3	18	236	2	118.00	2- 45	–	–
C.A.Young (Ire)	RM	23	3	107	1	107.00	1- 61	–	–
Zafar Gohar (Gs)	SLA	423.5	56	1566	32	48.93	5-122	1	–
S.A.Zaib (Nh)	SLA	46.3	11	165	4	41.25	2- 80	–	–
Zain Ul Hassan (Gm)	RM	143	22	477	8	59.62	2- 18	–	–

FIRST-CLASS CAREER RECORDS

Compiled by Philip Bailey

The following career records are for all players who appeared in first-class, county cricket and The Hundred during the 2023 season, and are complete to the end of that season. Some players who did not appear in 2023 but may do so in 2024 are included.

BATTING AND FIELDING

'1000' denotes instances of scoring 1000 runs in a season. Where these have been achieved outside the British Isles they are shown after a plus sign.

	M	*I*	*NO*	*HS*	*Runs*	*Avge*	*100*	*50*	*1000*	*Ct/St*
Abbott, K.J.	155	210	41	97*	3128	18.50	–	12	–	25
Abbott, S.A.	81	117	11	102*	2606	24.58	1	15	–	46
Abell, T.B.	122	215	19	151	6660	33.97	14	34	1	94
Ackermann, C.N.	164	288	32	277*	10459	40.85	23	62	0+1	176
Adair, M.R.	16	25	3	91	671	30.50	–	4	–	12
Agar, W.A.	30	42	10	57	432	13.50	–	2	–	8
Ahmed, R.	13	24	1	122	735	31.95	1	4	–	4
Aitchison, B.W.	27	37	6	50	383	12.35	–	1	–	20
Akhter, Z.	8	14	7	41*	154	22.00	–	–	–	2
Albert, T.E.	5	9	1	69*	223	27.87	–	1	–	4
Aldridge, K.L.	17	25	4	101*	579	27.57	1	3	–	10
Ali, M.M.	202	346	27	250	11514	36.09	20	70	2	119
Allison, B.M.J.	12	17	4	75	399	30.69	–	4	–	4
Alsop, T.P.	90	152	10	182*	4313	30.37	10	22	–	109
Anderson, J.M.	292	371	156	81	2026	9.42	–	1	–	163
Andersson, M.K.	32	55	4	92	1096	21.49	–	7	–	17
Anwar Ali	108	151	26	100*	2670	21.36	1	11	–	40
Arafat Bhuiyan	3	5	2	15*	22	7.33	–	–	–	0
Archer, J.C.	43	63	10	81*	1201	22.66	–	6	–	21
Arshdeep Singh	12	16	5	26	126	11.45	–	–	–	6
Atkins, J.A.	8	14	7	17	57	8.14	–	–	–	0
Atkinson, A.A.P.	14	18	4	91	394	28.14	–	3	–	2
Azad, M.H.	61	103	9	152	3190	33.93	7	17	1	25
Azhar Ali	262	453	35	302*	16327	39.05	48	69	–	160
Bailey, T.E.	99	130	19	78	2180	19.63	–	11	–	20
Bairstow, J.M.	210	351	39	246	13535	43.38	30	68	3	538/25
Baker, J.O.	20	26	4	75	392	17.81	–	2	–	18
Balbirnie, A.	38	57	3	205*	1525	28.24	2	9	–	34
Balderson, G.P.	33	48	8	116*	1322	33.05	2	8	–	4
Ball, J.T.	72	110	26	49*	1077	12.82	–	–	–	15
Bamber, E.R.	49	76	23	46*	566	10.67	–	–	–	12
Bancroft, C.T.	137	249	21	228*	8800	38.59	23	30	–	188/1
Banton, T.	30	48	1	126	1198	25.48	1	8	–	15
Barker, K.H.D.	163	223	35	125	5293	28.15	6	25	–	39
Barnard, E.G.	106	152	26	163*	4235	33.61	5	22	–	64
Barnes, E.	25	34	8	83*	540	20.76	–	2	–	9
Bartlett, G.A.	55	92	5	137	2562	29.44	8	8	–	12
Bartlett, X.C.	18	23	9	32	225	16.07	–	–	–	10
Bashir, S.	6	9	4	44*	71	14.20	–	–	–	2
Bazley, J.J.	12	17	7	64*	284	28.40	–	3	–	9
Bean, F.J.	16	27	0	135	1121	41.51	3	3	–	15
Beard, A.P.	28	31	14	58*	333	19.58	–	1	–	10
Bedingham, D.G.	81	127	13	257	5716	50.14	18	19	2	72
Bell, G.J.	14	19	0	91	489	25.73	–	3	–	26/2
Bell-Drummond, D.J.	150	258	24	300*	7918	33.83	16	37	1	61
Benjamin, C.G.	13	23	2	127	537	25.57	1	1	–	12

	M	I	NO	HS	Runs	Avge	100	50	1000	Ct/St
Berg, G.K.	152	226	28	130*	5565	28.10	2	31	–	76
Bess, D.M.	89	134	20	107	2753	24.14	1	14	–	37
Bethell, J.G.	9	14	0	61	272	19.42	–	1	–	6
Bevan, T.R.	2	3	0	48	63	21.00	–	–	–	2
Billings, S.W.	88	128	12	171	3628	31.27	6	15	–	219/12
Blake, A.J.	47	74	6	105*	1560	22.94	1	6	–	26
Blatherwick, J.M.	12	16	6	35	115	11.50	–	–	–	3
Bohannon, J.J.	67	96	8	231	4184	47.54	10	20	1	32
Boland, S.M.	98	118	42	51	946	12.44	–	2	–	30
Bopara, R.S.	221	357	40	229	12821	40.44	31	55	1	118
Borthwick, S.G.	209	348	31	216	11193	35.30	22	62	4	261
Bracewell, D.A.J.	129	192	24	105	4349	25.88	3	23	–	57
Bracewell, M.G.	104	185	14	190	5521	32.28	11	23	–	106
Bracey, J.R.	80	142	10	177	4122	31.22	9	20	–	164/9
Brathwaite, K.C.	201	362	25	276	13065	38.76	30	64	–	120
Briggs, D.R.	142	188	45	120*	2717	19.00	1	6	–	48
Broad, J.	6	10	2	56*	155	19.37	–	1	–	4
Broad, S.C.J.	265	372	66	169	5840	19.08	1	25	–	93
Brook, H.C.	68	110	6	194	4248	40.84	11	24	–	53
Brookes, E.A.	3	3	1	15*	21	10.50	–	–	–	0
Brookes, H.J.H.	33	48	8	84	806	20.15	–	5	–	11
Brooks, J.A.	154	193	67	109*	2103	16.69	1	5	–	35
Brown, B.C.	184	292	39	163	9846	38.91	23	51	2	527/27
Brown, P.R.	8	7	4	5*	14	4.66	–	–	–	3
Browne, N.L.J.	138	228	17	255	7569	35.87	19	31	3	102
Bruce, T.C.	70	122	22	208*	4878	48.78	8	31	–	108
Buckingham, J.S.D.	10	15	5	17	59	5.90	–	–	–	4
Budinger, S.G.	14	26	0	72	519	19.96	–	3	–	7
Burgess, M.G.K.	79	114	7	178	3695	34.53	5	20	–	173/8
Burns, R.J.	187	327	21	219*	12264	40.07	24	69	7	140
Bushnell, J.J.	7	11	2	66	278	30.88	–	1	–	0
Buttleman, W.E.L.	5	8	1	65	141	20.14	–	1	–	19/1
Buttler, J.C.	122	199	16	152	5888	32.17	7	33	–	274/3
Byrom, E.J.	55	97	6	176	2901	31.87	6	14	–	28
Came, H.R.C.	24	38	3	141*	1135	32.42	2	7	–	9
Campher, C.	6	12	0	111	337	28.08	1	–	–	1
Carey, A.T.	74	122	12	143	3673	33.39	6	20	–	268/11
Carlson, K.S.	80	137	8	192	4367	33.85	11	20	1	37
Carse, B.A.	41	53	13	108*	1274	31.85	1	5	–	8
Carson, J.J.	35	59	10	87	1003	20.46	–	7	–	16
Carter, M.	18	29	3	33	264	10.15	–	–	–	16
Carter, O.J.	29	50	4	185	1643	35.71	1	13	–	77/2
Chahal, Y.S.	35	52	11	42	345	8.41	–	–	–	12
Chappell, Z.J.	40	58	10	96	930	19.37	–	2	–	7
Charlesworth, B.G.	32	52	2	87	1117	22.34	–	8	–	18
Charlesworth, L.A.	2	3	1	4	4	2.00	–	–	–	1
Clark, G.	51	82	3	128	2444	30.93	4	13	–	39
Clark, J.	89	124	16	140	3008	27.85	3	18	–	13
Clark, T.G.R.	37	68	4	138	1773	27.70	2	12	–	35
Clarke, J.M.	121	206	17	229*	7344	38.85	20	35	2	78
Cliff, B.M.	2	2	1	1	1	1.00	–	–	–	0
Coad, B.O.	64	84	27	69	868	15.22	–	1	–	4
Cobb, J.J.	138	237	23	148*	5552	25.94	4	32	–	59
Cohen, M.A.R.	22	28	15	30*	172	13.23	–	–	–	2
Coles, J.M.	20	34	2	180	1121	35.03	3	5	–	13
Compton, B.G.	42	77	9	217	3219	47.33	11	12	1	35
Conners, S.	43	50	12	39	383	10.07	–	–	–	10
Cook, A.N.	352	619	45	294	26643	46.41	74	125	9+1	386

	M	I	NO	HS	Runs	Avge	100	50	1000	Ct/St
Cook, S.J.	74	88	30	38	586	10.10	–	–	–	14
Cooke, C.B.	130	216	37	205*	7161	40.00	12	40	–	286/14
Cornall, T.R.	8	13	1	31*	142	11.83	–	–	–	5
Coughlin, P.	57	82	12	100*	1891	27.01	1	10	–	29
Cox, J.M.	42	70	4	238*	2276	34.48	4	10	–	43
Cox, O.B.	147	234	34	124	5499	27.49	4	31	–	409/17
Cracknell, J.B.	4	8	0	33	110	13.75	–	–	–	3
Crane, M.S.	53	70	20	29	576	11.52	–	–	–	13
Crawley, Z.	105	188	5	267	5914	32.31	10	33	1	104
Critchley, M.J.J.	94	160	14	137*	4690	32.12	7	26	1	62
Crocombe, H.T.	32	50	13	46*	363	9.81	–	–	–	9
Croft, S.J.	212	320	31	156	9857	34.10	16	56	–	202
Cullen, B.C.	7	9	0	34	105	11.66	–	–	–	2
Cummins, P.J.	69	95	19	82*	1434	18.86	–	5	–	34
Curran, S.M.	80	122	14	126	3250	30.09	1	23	–	26
Curran, T.K.	61	84	11	115	1367	18.72	1	5	–	23
Currie, B.J.	6	9	5	7	17	4.25	–	–	–	1
Currie, S.W.	4	7	1	38	54	9.00	–	–	–	4
Dal, A.K.	50	75	14	146*	2095	34.34	5	9	–	33
Dale, A.S.	16	26	10	52	191	11.93	–	1	–	0
Das, R.J.	2	3	0	132	168	56.00	1	–	–	1
Davey, J.H.	66	99	26	75*	1483	20.31	–	5	–	20
Davies, A.L.	119	184	9	147	5859	33.48	7	38	1	201/19
Davies, J.L.B.	11	19	2	65*	236	13.88	–	1	–	7
Davies, S.M.	254	423	39	200*	14298	37.23	25	68	6	621/34
Davis, W.S.	39	54	18	58	539	14.97	–	1	–	7
Dawson, L.A.	190	307	31	171	9239	33.47	14	49	1	197
de Caires, J.M.	13	24	3	80	446	21.23	–	1	–	3
de Grandhomme, C.	136	220	31	174*	7035	37.22	15	41	–	121
de Lange, M.	102	136	18	113	1933	16.38	1	5	–	42
de Leede, B.F.W.	7	7	3	103	340	85.00	1	3	–	4
Denly, J.L.	237	406	26	227	13537	35.62	31	68	4	92
Dent, C.D.J.	182	328	26	268	11119	36.81	21	66	4	182
Dickson, S.R.	98	167	12	318	5180	33.41	14	20	–	74
Dockrell, G.H.	62	79	22	92	1108	19.43	–	4	–	27
D'Oliveira, B.L.	103	169	14	202*	5069	32.70	12	17	–	44
Donald, A.H.T.	58	101	5	234	3024	31.50	3	18	1	55
Douthwaite, D.A.	31	47	5	100*	1163	27.69	1	6	–	7
Drakes, D.C.	5	7	0	33	115	16.42	–	–	–	3
Drissell, G.S.	11	17	2	19	135	9.00	–	–	–	1
Duckett, B.M.	134	229	12	282*	9269	42.71	25	43	3	119/3
Duke, H.G.	17	25	2	54	436	18.95	–	2	–	50/1
Dunn, M.P.	43	50	22	31*	197	7.03	–	–	–	10
du Plooy, J.L.	102	164	24	238*	6624	47.31	19	33	1	70
Edavalath, R.M.	1	2	0	15	15	7.50	–	–	–	0
Edwards, M.W.	8	15	2	19*	101	7.76	–	–	–	2
Elgar, D.	239	419	30	268	16053	41.26	45	68	0+2	199
Ellis, N.T.	10	14	0	41	205	14.64	–	–	–	3
Eskinazi, S.S.	83	146	10	179	4198	30.86	9	16	–	83
Evans, L.J.	73	125	6	213*	3495	29.36	6	18	–	58
Evans, S.T.	34	57	3	138	1492	27.62	4	6	–	11
Evison, J.D.M.	26	41	4	109*	1060	28.64	1	5	–	5
Fernando, A.M.	63	82	37	30	232	5.15	–	–	–	14
Fernando, M.V.T.	102	121	54	41	651	9.71	–	–	–	29
Ferreira, D.	5	8	1	127	445	63.57	2	1	–	6
Finan, M.G.A.	7	12	3	58	126	14.00	–	1	–	1
Finch, A.W.	24	34	15	33*	337	17.73	–	–	–	4
Finch, H.Z.	61	103	6	135*	2719	28.03	5	15	–	83/2

	M	I	NO	HS	Runs	Avge	100	50	1000	Ct/St
Finn, S.T.	164	202	65	56	1317	9.61	–	2	–	51
Fisher, M.D.	35	50	15	53	588	16.80	–	1	–	13
Fletcher, C.D.	79	124	27	157	3372	34.76	6	17	–	247/14
Fletcher, L.J.	144	206	40	92	2335	14.06	–	7	–	31
Foakes, B.T.	157	245	41	141*	8040	39.41	16	41	–	396/32
Foster, M.T.	4	5	1	6	14	3.50	–	–	–	0
Fraine, W.A.R.	30	50	2	106	1032	21.50	1	3	–	18
Fuller, J.K.	83	116	16	93	2245	22.45	–	10	–	29
Garrett, G.A.	4	6	3	24	42	14.00	–	–	–	1
Garton, G.H.S.	26	36	6	97	650	21.66	–	5	–	14
Gay, E.N.	38	66	2	145	1926	30.09	4	9	–	41
Geddes, B.B.A.	6	9	0	124	336	37.33	2	–	–	3
Gibbon, B.J.	15	15	6	41*	153	17.00	–	–	–	8
Gibson, O.J.	7	7	2	6	7	1.40	–	–	–	1
Gilchrist, N.N.	21	25	1	25	149	6.20	–	–	–	7
Gill, S.	45	77	8	268	3508	50.84	10	16	–	31
Glover, B.D.	10	15	6	12*	38	4.22	–	–	–	1
Godleman, B.A.	188	336	15	227	10193	31.75	23	46	2	110
Goldsworthy, L.P.	22	35	3	130	986	30.81	2	3	–	5
Goodman, D.C.	9	12	5	18	62	8.85	–	–	–	4
Gorvin, A.W.	8	10	2	47	113	14.12	–	–	–	2
Gouldstone, H.O.M.	7	12	2	67*	163	16.30	–	1	–	4
Green, B.G.F.	15	29	2	54	468	17.33	–	1	–	9
Green, C.D.	54	85	13	251	3319	46.09	9	12	0+1	37
Gregory, L.	118	172	19	137	3833	25.05	4	15	–	72
Gubbins, N.R.T.	122	215	10	201*	7272	35.47	16	38	1	46
Guest, B.D.	43	69	1	197	2189	32.19	7	5	–	120/4
Haider Ali	21	34	1	206	1459	44.21	4	7	–	14
Hain, S.R.	118	188	18	208	6767	39.80	17	36	1	111
Haines, T.J.	59	105	3	243	3769	36.95	9	17	1	17
Hales, A.D.	107	182	6	236	6655	37.81	13	38	3	84
Hameed, H.	117	200	17	196	6259	34.20	12	36	2	71
Hamidullah Qadri	29	48	13	87	615	17.57	–	3	–	10
Hammond, M.A.H.	63	113	8	169	3209	30.56	3	23	–	51
Hand, F.P.	3	3	1	48*	56	28.00	–	–	–	3
Handscomb, P.S.P.	160	270	21	281*	9745	39.13	21	55	–	271/8
Hannon-Dalby, O.J.	110	134	54	40	638	7.97	–	–	–	14
Harmer, S.R.	205	301	59	102*	5925	24.48	2	31	–	209
Harris, J.A.R.	175	249	56	87*	4273	22.13	–	18	–	47
Harris, M.S.	148	268	17	250*	10012	39.88	26	42	0+1	80
Harrison, C.G.	10	14	3	39	273	24.81	–	–	–	15
Hartley, T.W.	20	25	7	73*	522	29.00	–	2	–	13
Hassan Ali	78	113	23	106*	1505	16.72	1	7	–	23
Haynes, J.A.	45	73	7	134*	2338	35.42	5	8	–	40
Hazlewood, J.R.	104	121	48	43*	813	11.13	–	–	–	39
Head, T.M.	154	274	17	223	10520	40.93	21	60	0+1	69
Helm, T.G.	50	71	17	52	928	17.18	–	3	–	15
Henry, M.J.	96	128	21	81	2170	20.28	–	9	–	40
Higgins, R.F.	79	128	13	199	3809	33.12	7	19	–	29
Hill, G.C.H.	36	58	4	151*	1719	31.83	3	9	–	18
Hill, L.J.	76	130	12	162*	3786	32.08	7	19	–	106/3
Hogan, M.G.	193	262	104	57	2546	16.11	–	4	–	87
Holden, M.D.E.	80	141	7	153	3542	26.43	3	17	–	30
Holland, I.G.	68	110	11	146*	2584	26.10	4	12	–	35
Hollman, L.B.K.	26	39	2	82	938	25.35	–	5	–	17
Hope, S.D.	69	123	9	215*	4019	35.25	9	15	–	84/2
Hose, A.J.	30	54	2	111	1312	25.23	1	7	–	13
Howell, B.A.C.	86	136	13	163	3378	27.46	2	18	–	52

	M	I	NO	HS	Runs	Avge	100	50	1000	Ct/St
Hudson-Prentice, F.J.	44	73	11	99	1885	30.40	–	14	–	12
Hughes, D.P.	68	128	14	178	4323	37.92	8	24	–	47
Hull, J.O.	6	8	2	15	23	3.83	–	–	–	2
Hume, G.I.	102	134	33	105	1782	17.64	1	4	–	55
Hunt, S.F.	19	27	12	22	98	6.53	–	–	–	1
Hurst, M.F.	2	3	2	76*	130	130.00	–	2	–	0
Hutton, B.A.	86	127	16	84	1940	17.47	–	6	–	54
Ibrahim, D.K.	17	32	3	100*	634	21.86	1	3	–	8
Imad Wasim	77	115	24	207	3702	40.68	6	20	–	35
Ingram, C.A.	124	218	17	190	7628	37.95	18	32	–	86
Jacks, W.G.	52	78	9	150*	2363	34.24	3	15	–	54
Jadeja, R.A.	122	180	29	331	6900	45.69	12	36	–	92
James, L.W.	42	65	5	164*	1930	32.16	3	11	–	23
Jennings, K.K.	170	288	19	318	10105	37.56	26	38	2	147
Jones, M.A.	37	60	4	206	1952	34.85	3	12	–	14
Jones, R.P.	46	67	7	122	1734	28.90	3	8	–	54
Jordan, C.J.	114	159	23	166	3443	25.31	3	15	–	137
Kalley, E.S.	1	1	0	0	0	0.00	–	–	–	0
Karvelas, A.	25	33	5	57	366	13.07	–	1	–	9
Kashif Ali	5	8	0	93	191	23.87	–	2	–	0
Kellaway, B.I.	2	2	0	0	0	0.00	–	–	–	0
Kelly, D.C.	1	–	–	–	–	–	–	–	–	1
Keogh, R.I.	124	206	12	221	6037	31.11	16	19	–	28/1
Kerrigan, S.C.	125	153	50	62*	1425	13.83	–	3	–	45
Khawaja, U.T.	192	329	31	214	13367	44.85	39	66	0+1	146
Khushi, F.I.N.	12	19	1	164	481	26.72	1	2	–	10
Kimber, L.P.J.	23	37	1	104	882	24.50	1	7	–	19
Klaassen, F.J.	5	8	3	14*	45	9.00	–	–	–	3
Kohler-Cadmore, T.	95	157	10	176	4893	33.28	11	22	1	134/1
Kohli, V.	143	235	18	254*	10925	50.34	36	37	0+1	141
Kuhnemann, M.P.	19	20	10	24*	124	12.40	–	–	–	7
Labuschagne, M.	139	243	20	215	10447	46.84	30	49	1+2	120
Lakmal, R.A.S.	139	179	41	58*	1552	11.24	–	1	–	48
Lamb, D.J.	25	34	7	125	727	26.92	1	4	–	10
Lamb, M.J.	50	80	8	173	2123	29.48	3	9	–	19
Lammonby, T.A.	47	82	7	116	2193	29.24	6	8	–	32
Latham, T.W.M.	152	261	18	264*	10703	44.04	26	58	–	206/1
Lavelle, G.I.D.	5	9	0	32	105	11.66	–	–	–	17/1
Lawes, T.E.	17	21	4	55	246	14.47	–	1	–	3
Lawrence, D.W.	118	191	16	161	6360	36.34	15	29	1	83
Leach, J.	128	188	26	114	3821	23.58	2	23	–	31
Leach, M.J.	138	189	53	92	1859	13.66	–	3	–	55
Leaning, J.A.	112	182	21	220*	5319	33.03	8	30	–	107
Leech, D.J.	5	4	1	32	46	15.33	–	–	–	1
Lees, A.Z.	160	274	18	275*	9692	37.85	24	46	3	103
Lenham, A.D.	7	12	2	48	206	20.60	–	–	–	2
Leonard, E.O.	2	4	2	8	18	9.00	–	–	–	1
Libby, J.D.	101	174	15	215	6017	37.84	16	24	2	42
Lilley, A.M.	16	20	5	63	444	29.60	–	2	–	5
Linde, G.F.	73	104	11	148*	2911	31.30	5	14	–	38
Lintott, J.B.	2	3	0	78	101	33.66	–	1	–	1
Livingstone, L.S.	63	96	15	224	3085	38.08	7	15	–	74
Lloyd, D.L.	105	179	17	313*	4998	30.85	6	22	–	55
Loten, T.W.	7	9	0	58	137	15.22	–	1	–	2
Luxton, W.A.	1	2	0	31	45	22.50	–	–	–	0
Lynn, C.A.	41	71	8	250	2743	43.53	6	12	–	26
Lyon, N.M.	201	257	69	75	2358	12.54	–	2	–	89
Lyth, A.	222	372	17	251	13522	38.09	32	69	4	296

	M	I	NO	HS	Runs	Avge	100	50	1000	Ct/St
McAlindon, S.J.C.	4	3	2	26*	48	48.00	–	–	–	0
McAndrew, N.J.	34	50	11	92	1299	33.30	–	7	–	11
McBrine, A.R.	23	36	3	86*	834	25.27	–	6	–	16
McCollum, J.A.	23	38	4	119*	1339	39.38	3	6	–	4
McDermott, B.R.	53	94	10	107*	2641	31.44	2	18	–	35
McIlroy, J.P.	12	12	6	30*	79	13.16	–	–	–	1
McKerr, C.	22	23	5	37	218	12.11	–	–	–	5
McKiernan, M.H.	8	12	0	101	307	25.58	1	2	–	8
McKinney, B.S.	1	2	0	35	39	19.50	–	–	–	1
Mackintosh, T.S.S.	4	4	0	51	90	22.50	–	1	–	21
McManus, L.D.	76	109	11	132*	2471	25.21	1	13	–	175/16
Madsen, W.L.	226	398	27	231*	14904	40.17	36	83	6	271
Mahmood, S.	30	36	16	49	298	14.90	–	–	–	5
Malan, D.J.	212	363	21	219	13201	38.59	30	68	3	205
Malan, P.J.	188	313	24	264	12673	43.85	38	53	0+2	119
Marsh, M.R.	108	187	17	211	5707	33.57	13	23	–	57
Maxwell, G.J.	69	115	10	278	4147	39.49	7	24	–	58
Mayes, T.	1	1	0	17	17	17.00	–	–	–	0
Middleton, E.W.O.	2	3	1	39*	50	25.00	–	–	–	0
Middleton, F.S.	15	25	0	77	674	26.96	–	5	–	11
Mike, B.W.M.	38	60	5	99*	1349	24.52	–	10	–	10
Miles, C.N.	100	137	23	62*	1795	15.74	–	5	–	32
Mills, T.S.	32	38	15	31*	260	11.30	–	–	–	9
Milnes, M.E.	47	71	19	78	990	19.03	–	3	–	18
Mir Hamza	97	117	47	25	545	7.78	–	–	–	19
Mitchell, D.J.	98	158	20	190	5653	40.96	15	31	–	109
Mohammad Abbas	164	226	90	40	820	6.02	–	–	–	41
Mohammad Amir	69	104	16	66	1384	15.72	–	2	–	15
Mohammed Shami	88	122	36	56*	1049	12.19	–	2	–	22
Montgomery, M.	19	32	2	178	1002	33.40	2	3	–	21
Moor, P.J.	75	135	6	157	4234	32.82	6	25	–	76/4
Moores, T.J.	74	118	7	106	2658	23.94	2	8	–	210/5
Moriarty, D.T.	13	13	6	29	65	9.28	–	–	–	3
Morley, J.P.	9	8	3	9	20	4.00	–	–	–	5
Mousley, D.R.	20	32	2	94	833	27.76	–	7	–	14
Mulder, P.W.A.	71	120	18	235*	3401	33.34	9	10	–	54
Mullaney, S.J.	183	305	13	192	9862	33.77	19	50	1	172
Munro, C.	48	74	4	281	3611	51.58	13	15	–	21
Murphy, T.R.	14	20	3	41	231	13.58	–	–	–	6
Murtagh, T.J.	264	357	103	74*	4360	17.16	–	11	–	70
Muyeye, T.S.	19	32	2	179	985	32.83	1	5	–	15
Nair, K.K.	88	139	15	328	6171	49.76	16	28	–	76
Narine, S.P.	13	18	6	40*	213	17.75	–	–	–	10
Naseem Shah	31	38	11	31	206	7.62	–	–	–	6
Naveen-ul-Haq	10	13	1	34	93	7.75	–	–	–	5
Neser, M.G.	97	131	16	176*	3256	28.31	4	15	–	46
Nijjar, A.S.S.	16	19	6	53	298	22.92	–	1	–	3
Northeast, S.A.	209	350	28	410*	12674	39.36	29	63	5	109
Ogborne, A.R.J.	1	1	0	2	2	2.00	–	–	–	1
Organ, F.S.	43	72	3	118	1560	22.60	3	7	–	19
O'Riordan, M.K.	15	20	4	102*	545	34.06	1	1	–	5
Orr, A.G.H.	27	50	2	198	1917	39.93	4	8	1	11
Overton, C.	125	184	23	138	3384	21.01	1	14	–	110
Overton, J.	94	132	27	120	2298	21.88	1	13	–	66
Parkinson, C.F.	58	88	16	75	1316	18.27	–	1	–	8
Parkinson, M.W.	54	58	24	30	309	9.08	–	–	–	12
Parnell, W.D.	84	113	14	111*	2728	27.55	2	17	–	25
Patel, A.Y.	91	128	31	52	1450	14.94	–	2	–	61

	M	I	NO	HS	Runs	Avge	100	50	1000	Ct/St
Patel, R.K.	34	57	1	179	1806	32.25	4	6	1	21
Patel, R.S.	54	85	8	126	2146	27.87	3	7	–	37
Patel, S.R.	231	376	20	257*	12692	35.65	26	64	4	140
Paterson, D.	147	180	54	59	1476	11.71	–	1	–	45
Patterson-White, L.A.	41	57	6	101	1204	23.60	1	6	–	18
Payne, D.A.	115	142	47	67*	1779	18.72	–	6	–	40
Pennington, D.Y.	45	63	12	56	542	10.62	–	1	–	11
Pepper, M.S.	15	24	2	92	423	19.22	–	3	–	25
Pettman, T.H.S.	11	13	3	54*	126	12.60	–	1	–	4
Phillips, J.P.	2	3	0	80	123	41.00	–	1	–	0
Podmore, H.W.	55	78	20	66*	1055	18.18	–	4	–	13
Pollock, E.J.	26	42	1	113	1084	26.43	2	5	–	19
Pope, O.J.D.	90	143	16	274	6403	50.41	18	24	3	114/1
Porter, J.A.	124	143	58	34	505	5.94	–	–	–	40
Potts, M.J.	45	52	9	81	678	15.76	–	3	–	20
Potts, N.J.	7	8	1	13	48	6.85	–	–	–	2
Prest, T.J.	8	11	1	108	226	22.60	1	–	–	2
Pretorius, M.	49	60	9	81*	1228	24.07	–	6	–	12
Price, O.J.	23	42	2	132	1259	31.47	3	7	–	37
Price, T.J.	23	37	8	109	777	26.79	1	3	–	6
Procter, L.A.	135	218	27	144*	6346	33.22	7	35	–	34
Pucovski, W.J.	29	45	4	255*	2008	48.97	6	8	–	12
Pujara, C.A.	256	423	44	352	19533	51.53	60	77	1+3	158/1
Quinn, M.R.	61	81	25	50	606	10.82	–	1	–	13
Rahane, A.M.	180	305	28	265*	13011	46.97	39	55	0+3	189
Raine, B.A.	123	182	26	103*	3495	22.40	1	15	–	27
Reece, L.M.	99	177	17	201*	5704	35.65	12	31	1	42
Revis, M.L.	20	30	7	106	797	34.65	2	3	–	13
Rew, J.E.K.	22	35	6	221	1425	49.13	6	3	1	59/3
Rhodes, W.M.H.	99	160	8	207	5204	34.23	9	23	–	68
Richards, J.A.	1	2	2	17*	19	–	–	–	–	0
Richardson, K.W.	34	52	4	49	664	13.83	–	–	–	10
Rickelton, R.D.	50	84	8	202*	3993	52.53	15	14	–	108/3
Roach, K.A.J.	160	218	48	53	2172	12.77	–	3	–	47
Robinson, O.E.	89	132	22	110	2137	19.42	1	7	–	29
Robinson, O.G.	62	95	7	167*	3136	35.63	7	16	–	180/12
Robson, S.D.	203	363	28	253	12576	37.54	32	46	3	199
Roderick, G.H.	128	207	27	172*	6212	34.51	9	36	–	347/8
Roelofsen, G.	55	82	6	224*	2864	37.68	8	10	–	115/12
Roland-Jones, T.S.	144	205	38	103*	3616	21.65	1	14	–	40
Root, J.E.	203	355	31	254	16029	49.47	42	79	3	228
Root, W.T.	67	111	12	229	3495	35.30	7	15	–	17
Rossington, A.M.	111	178	16	138*	5375	33.17	9	34	–	244/20
Roy, J.J.	87	144	11	143	4850	36.46	9	23	1	75
Rushworth, C.	168	222	74	57	1765	11.92	–	1	–	37
Russell, A.K.	3	5	4	8*	11	11.00	–	–	–	0
Rymell, J.S.	4	5	0	21	49	9.80	–	–	–	4
Saini, N.	62	65	26	50*	405	10.38	–	1	–	17
Sai Sudharsan, B.	10	17	0	179	714	42.00	2	2	–	5
Sales, J.J.G.	12	24	3	71	403	19.19	–	3	–	3
Salisbury, M.E.T.	49	72	13	45	518	8.77	–	–	–	6
Salt, P.D.	52	85	3	148	2749	33.52	6	14	–	75/4
Salter, A.G.	82	122	23	90	2297	23.20	–	9	–	38
Sams, D.R.	5	10	0	88	255	25.50	–	2	–	2
Sanderson, B.W.	98	133	42	46	850	9.34	–	–	–	12
Santner, M.J.	59	91	5	136	2656	30.88	4	14	–	50
Saud Shakil	67	112	17	208*	5152	54.23	17	24	0+1	39
Schadendorf, D.J.	1	1	0	24	24	24.00	–	–	–	4

	M	I	NO	HS	Runs	Avge	100	50	1000	Ct/St
Scrimshaw, G.L.S.	8	13	9	19*	37	9.25	–	–	–	4
Scriven, T.A.R.	17	29	4	78	577	23.08	–	5	–	6
Seales, J.N.T.	15	22	8	33	85	6.07	–	–	–	6
Shadab Khan	17	24	2	132	595	27.04	1	3	–	11
Shaheen Shah Afridi	36	42	8	29	275	8.08	–	–	–	5
Shan Masood	156	268	12	239	9955	38.88	23	45	1+1	95
Sharma, R.G.	113	179	18	309*	8663	53.80	27	36	–	97
Shaw, J.	54	76	14	44	834	13.45	–	–	–	9
Shaw, P.P.	44	78	2	379	3802	50.02	12	16	–	33
Shipley, H.B.	25	40	6	82	909	26.73	–	6	–	13
Shutt, J.W.	5	7	5	7*	12	6.00	–	–	–	3
Sibley, D.P.	128	220	25	244	7580	38.87	19	40	1	100
Siddle, P.M.	218	295	62	103*	3851	16.52	1	6	–	62
Simpson, J.A.	201	320	45	167*	9068	32.97	10	52	1	626/38
Singh, J.	7	7	3	14*	27	6.75	–	–	–	1
Siraj, M.	61	78	19	46	426	7.22	–	–	–	16
Sisodiya, P.	5	8	1	38	87	12.42	–	–	–	2
Slater, B.T.	130	234	13	225*	7394	33.45	12	36	1	51
Smale, W.T.E.	1	1	0	0	0	0.00	–	–	–	5
Smith, J.L.	50	77	7	234*	2756	39.37	8	9	–	56/4
Smith, N.G.	39	63	9	114	1460	27.03	1	8	–	20
Smith, R.A.J.	31	46	6	57*	693	17.32	–	2	–	4
Smith, S.P.D.	164	283	32	239	13942	55.54	48	60	–	260
Smith, T.M.J.	55	77	14	84	1422	22.57	–	4	–	17
Snater, S.	34	45	6	79*	755	19.35	–	5	–	5
Sodhi, I.S.	93	137	19	82*	2587	21.92	–	13	–	38
Sowter, N.A.	13	23	4	57*	292	15.36	–	2	–	12
Srikar Bharat, K.	91	143	12	308	4836	36.91	9	27	–	309/36
Starc, M.A.	133	172	44	99	2852	22.28	–	13	–	62
Steel, C.T.	56	94	3	224	2513	27.61	4	12	–	30
Steketee, M.T.	73	93	17	53	1118	14.71	–	2	–	26
Stewart, G.	40	63	8	103	1327	24.12	1	9	–	6
Stirling, P.R.	73	115	5	146	3188	28.98	8	14	–	40
Stokes, B.A.	177	301	15	258	10194	35.64	22	50	–	144
Stone, O.P.	46	62	13	60	754	15.38	–	1	–	17
Stoneman, M.D.	236	413	12	197	13750	34.28	29	71	6	100
Sutherland, W.J.	31	43	6	100	768	20.75	1	1	–	25
Swepson, M.J.	66	83	17	69	890	13.48	–	1	–	39
Swindells, H.J.	41	64	5	171*	1584	26.84	2	8	–	75/3
Tattersall, J.A.	51	79	9	180*	2358	33.68	2	12	–	125/10
Taylor, C.Z.	11	17	3	106	425	30.35	1	2	–	2
Taylor, J.M.R.	91	141	9	156	3771	28.56	7	12	–	47
Taylor, M.D.	78	105	38	57*	968	14.44	–	2	–	11
Taylor, T.A.I.	64	100	13	80	1646	18.91	–	8	–	21
Tear, C.J.	3	5	0	56	129	25.80	–	1	–	2
Tector, H.T.	16	27	1	146	776	29.84	1	6	–	6
Thain, N.R.M.	1	2	0	36	39	19.50	–	–	–	1
Thakur, S.N.	75	103	7	87	1592	16.58	–	10	–	23
Thompson, J.A.	45	64	5	98	1257	21.30	–	7	–	12
Thomson, A.T.	39	51	4	54	844	17.95	–	2	–	15
Tickner, B.M.	64	70	27	37*	454	10.55	–	–	–	28
Tongue, J.C.	50	64	16	45*	632	13.16	–	–	–	6
Toole, R.L.	26	34	19	17*	109	7.26	–	–	–	6
Tremain, C.P.	82	114	21	111	1251	13.45	1	1	–	20
Trevaskis, L.	27	41	8	88	992	30.06	–	7	–	10
Tucker, L.J.	19	28	3	108	821	32.84	1	4	–	42/6
Turner, A.J.	45	73	6	128	2304	34.38	4	10	–	50
Turner, J.A.	3	4	0	7	11	2.75	–	–	–	0

	M	I	NO	HS	Runs	Avge	100	50	1000	Ct/St
Tye, A.J.	9	10	0	10	52	5.20	–	–	–	1
Umar Amin	167	282	16	281	10810	40.63	28	54	0+1	130
Umeed, A.R.I.	20	33	2	113	664	21.41	2	–	–	17
Unadkat, J.D.	106	136	32	92	1873	18.00	–	8	–	47
Usama Mir	18	27	2	77*	452	18.08	–	2	–	10
van Beek, L.V.	72	100	20	111*	1842	23.02	1	8	–	48
van Buuren, G.L.	116	183	30	235	6272	40.99	13	38	–	64
van der Gugten, T.	80	109	35	85*	1427	19.28	–	7	–	20
van der Merwe, R.E.	80	128	16	205*	3587	32.02	6	22	–	61
van Meekeren, P.A.	10	16	3	34	113	8.69	–	–	–	3
Vasconcelos, R.S.	75	136	7	185*	4089	31.69	8	20	–	120/7
Vilas, D.J.	199	298	32	266	10633	39.97	25	47	1	472/20
Vince, J.M.	203	337	25	240	12354	39.59	28	53	3	191
Virdi, G.S.	41	50	26	47	229	9.54	–	–	–	10
Wagner, N.	202	268	59	72	3515	16.81	–	10	–	64
Wagstaff, M.D.	3	5	0	78	165	33.00	–	2	–	2
Waite, M.J.	27	42	7	109*	957	27.34	1	4	–	8
Walallawita, T.N.	12	17	6	20*	92	8.36	–	–	–	3
Walker, R.I.	3	6	1	64	103	20.60	–	1	–	1
Walter, P.I.	44	62	9	141	1854	34.98	1	9	–	19
Ward, H.D.	4	7	0	19	32	4.57	–	–	–	2
Warner, D.A.	140	252	11	335*	10966	45.50	33	45	–	102
Watt, M.R.J.	12	13	3	81*	257	25.70	–	2	–	4
Weatherley, J.J.	63	101	4	168	2344	24.16	2	11	–	52
Webster, B.J.	71	123	11	187	3657	32.65	8	14	–	98
Welch, N.R.	14	19	1	100	445	24.72	1	2	–	4
Wells, B.J.J.	1	1	0	40	40	40.00	–	–	–	2
Wells, L.W.P.	181	297	21	258	10059	36.44	24	43	2	101
Westley, T.	227	380	28	254	12620	35.85	27	57	2	133
Wharton, J.H.	9	16	1	89	394	26.26	–	4	–	4
Wheal, B.T.J.	46	57	21	46*	402	11.16	–	–	–	15
White, C.J.	31	47	22	59	205	8.20	–	1	–	3
White, G.G.	39	55	5	65	659	13.18	–	2	–	12
White, R.G.	40	65	5	120	1481	24.68	2	8	–	51/2
Whiteley, R.A.	90	146	14	130*	3632	27.51	3	20	–	60
Whiteman, S.M.	96	162	11	193	5555	36.78	12	28	–	188/6
Wiese, D.	124	194	20	208	5814	33.41	11	32	–	70
Willey, D.J.	77	108	16	104*	2515	27.33	2	14	–	18
Williams, W.S.A.	62	81	23	61	781	13.46	–	1	–	27
Woakes, C.R.	167	249	53	152*	6422	32.76	10	25	–	68
Wood, C.P.	43	62	6	105*	1326	23.67	1	6	–	14
Wood, L.	62	90	16	119	1884	25.45	2	7	–	19
Wood, M.A.	72	116	21	72*	1890	19.89	–	5	–	17
Wood, T.A.	12	20	0	31	217	10.85	–	–	–	9
Worrall, D.J.	85	122	40	51	1104	13.46	–	2	–	23
Wright, C.J.C.	203	269	61	87	3904	18.76	–	14	–	40
Yadav, J.	78	121	15	211	2670	25.18	3	13	–	37
Yadav, U.T.	115	139	53	128*	1332	15.48	1	2	–	38
Yates, R.M.	56	91	5	228*	2537	29.50	9	6	–	70
Young, C.A.	18	18	6	23	97	8.08	–	–	–	5
Young, W.A.	115	195	14	162	7262	40.12	15	42	–	70
Zafar Gohar	78	118	13	100*	2290	21.80	1	10	–	32
Zaib, S.A.	51	83	6	135	1921	24.94	2	8	–	17
Zain Ul Hassan	9	16	1	69	453	30.20	–	2	–	2

BOWLING

'50wS' denotes instances of taking 50 or more wickets in a season. Where these have been achieved outside the British Isles they are shown after a plus sign.

	Runs	*Wkts*	*Avge*	*Best*	*5wI*	*10wM*	*50wS*
Abbott, K.J.	12599	597	21.10	9- 40	37	6	4+1
Abbott, S.A.	7355	238	30.90	7- 45	7	–	–
Abell, T.B.	2024	64	31.62	4- 39	–	–	–
Ackermann, C.N.	3836	82	46.78	5- 69	1	–	–
Adair, M.R.	1085	28	38.75	3- 22	–	–	–
Agar, W.A.	3123	99	31.54	5- 53	3	–	–
Ahmed, R.	937	24	39.04	5- 48	2	–	–
Aitchison, B.W.	2083	68	30.63	6- 28	1	–	–
Akhter, Z.	897	19	47.21	4- 33	–	–	–
Aldridge, K.L.	1563	39	40.07	6-110	1	–	–
Ali, M.M.	14953	391	38.24	6- 29	12	2	–
Allison, B.M.J.	726	23	31.56	5- 32	1	–	–
Alsop, T.P.	112	3	37.33	2- 59	–	–	–
Anderson, J.M.	27153	1104	24.59	7- 19	54	6	4
Andersson, M.K.	2074	67	30.95	4- 25	–	–	–
Anwar Ali	9632	349	27.59	8- 16	20	4	0+2
Arafat Bhuiyan	265	7	37.85	4- 65	–	–	–
Archer, J.C.	4510	181	24.91	7- 67	8	1	1
Arshdeep Singh	1139	38	29.97	5- 33	1	–	–
Atkins, J.A.	723	24	30.12	5- 51	2	–	–
Atkinson, A.A.P.	1199	45	26.64	6- 68	1	–	–
Azad, M.H.	25	1	25.00	1- 15	–	–	–
Azhar Ali	2336	50	46.72	4- 34	–	–	–
Bailey, T.E.	8419	359	23.45	7- 37	15	3	4
Bairstow, J.M.	1	0					
Baker, J.O.	1908	39	48.92	4- 51	–	–	–
Balbirnie, A.	262	13	20.15	4- 23	–	–	–
Balderson, G.P.	2244	66	34.00	5- 14	1	–	–
Ball, J.T.	6259	213	29.38	6- 49	6	–	1
Bamber, E.R.	4327	166	26.06	5- 20	3	–	1
Bancroft, C.T.	77	2	38.50	1- 10	–	–	–
Banton, T.	0	0					
Barker, K.H.D.	12986	517	25.11	7- 46	22	1	4
Barnard, E.G.	8608	290	29.68	6- 37	6	1	–
Barnes, E.	1911	42	45.50	5-101	1	–	–
Bartlett, G.A.	40	0					
Bartlett, X.C.	1614	62	26.03	5- 85	1	–	–
Bashir, S.	670	10	67.00	3- 67	–	–	–
Bazley, J.J.	709	19	37.31	2- 9	–	–	–
Bean, F.J.	105	0					
Beard, A.P.	2016	61	33.04	4- 21	–	–	–
Bedingham, D.G.	18	0					
Bell, G.J.	64	1	64.00	1- 28	–	–	–
Bell-Drummond, D.J.	745	25	29.80	3- 37	–	–	–
Berg, G.K.	10136	321	31.57	6- 56	7	–	–
Bess, D.M.	8247	243	33.93	7- 43	14	1	–
Bethell, J.G.	187	0					
Bevan, T.R.	6	0					
Billings, S.W.	4	0					
Blake, A.J.	158	3	52.66	2- 9	–	–	–
Blatherwick, J.M.	821	19	43.21	4- 28	–	–	–
Bohannon, J.J.	562	13	43.23	3- 46	–	–	–
Boland, S.M.	8575	346	24.78	7- 31	8	–	–
Bopara, R.S.	9381	257	36.50	5- 49	3	–	–

	Runs	Wkts	Avge	Best	5wI	10wM	50wS
Borthwick, S.G.	9109	227	40.12	6-70	3	–	–
Bracewell, D.A.J.	12605	398	31.67	7-35	11	–	–
Bracewell, M.G.	2286	51	44.82	5-43	1	–	–
Bracey, J.R.	35	0					
Brathwaite, K.C.	2077	45	46.15	6-29	1	–	–
Briggs, D.R.	11777	343	34.33	6-45	8	–	–
Broad, J.	117	2	58.50	2-39	–	–	–
Broad, S.C.J.	25438	952	26.72	8-15	32	4	–
Brook, H.C.	479	9	53.22	3-15	–	–	–
Brookes, E.A.	76	0					
Brookes, H.J.H.	3396	89	38.15	6-20	1	–	–
Brooks, J.A.	14690	531	27.66	6-65	22	–	4
Brown, B.C.	109	1	109.00	1-48	–	–	–
Brown, P.R.	456	10	45.60	2-15	–	–	–
Browne, N.L.J.	189	0					
Bruce, T.C.	803	23	34.91	2-17	–	–	–
Buckingham, J.S.D.	920	28	32.85	6-58	1	–	–
Budinger, S.G.	27	0					
Burgess, M.G.K.	55	1	55.00	1-17	–	–	–
Burns, R.J.	172	2	86.00	1-18	–	–	–
Bushnell, J.J.	238	3	79.33	1-15	–	–	–
Buttler, J.C.	11	0					
Byrom, E.J.	173	2	86.50	2-64	–	–	–
Came, H.R.C.	37	0					
Campher, C.	392	4	98.00	2-84	–	–	–
Carlson, K.S.	1416	27	52.44	5-28	1	–	–
Carse, B.A.	3574	116	30.81	6-26	5	–	–
Carson, J.J.	3610	100	36.10	5-79	3	–	–
Carter, M.	2136	54	39.55	7-56	2	1	–
Chahal, Y.S.	3313	96	34.51	6-44	2	–	–
Chappell, Z.J.	3315	92	36.03	6-44	2	–	–
Charlesworth, B.G.	487	13	37.46	3-25	–	–	–
Charlesworth, L.A.	134	4	33.50	3-54	–	–	–
Clark, G.	58	2	29.00	1-10	–	–	–
Clark, J.	6381	209	30.53	6-21	5	–	–
Clark, T.G.R.	352	7	50.28	3-21	–	–	–
Clarke, J.M.	48	0					
Cliff, B.M.	116	3	38.66	2-27	–	–	–
Coad, B.O.	4983	246	20.25	6-25	11	2	1
Cobb, J.J.	1687	20	84.35	2-11	–	–	–
Cohen, M.A.R.	1777	68	26.13	5-40	3	–	–
Coles, J.M.	1147	16	71.68	3-91	–	–	–
Compton, B.G.	34	0					
Conners, S.	4197	117	35.87	5-51	4	–	1
Cook, A.N.	224	7	32.00	3-13	–	–	–
Cook, S.J.	5286	265	19.94	7-23	12	3	2
Cooke, C.B.	38	0					
Cornall, T.R.	9	0					
Coughlin, P.	4200	125	33.60	5-49	3	1	–
Cox, J.M.	3	0					
Crane, M.S.	5371	125	42.96	5-35	3	–	–
Crawley, Z.	33	0					
Critchley, M.J.J.	6126	156	39.26	6-73	3	1	–
Crocombe, H.T.	2523	58	43.50	4-47	–	–	–
Croft, S.J.	3125	72	43.40	6-41	1	–	–
Cullen, B.C.	648	14	46.28	3-30	–	–	–
Cummins, P.J.	6738	285	23.64	6-23	9	1	–
Curran, S.M.	6222	206	30.20	7-58	7	1	–

	Runs	Wkts	Avge	Best	5wI	10wM	50wS
Curran, T.K.	5709	195	29.27	7- 20	7	1	1
Currie, B.J.	630	24	26.25	6- 93	1	–	–
Currie, S.W.	364	12	30.33	4-109	–	–	–
Dal, A.K.	2299	76	30.25	6- 69	4	–	–
Dale, A.S.	1193	37	32.24	6- 41	1	–	–
Davey, J.H.	4099	182	22.52	5- 21	4	–	–
Davies, A.L.	7	0					
Davis, W.S.	3339	96	34.78	7-146	2	–	–
Dawson, L.A.	9504	296	32.10	7- 51	9	2	–
de Caires, J.M.	851	28	30.39	8-106	2	1	–
de Grandhomme, C.	6637	221	30.03	6- 24	2	–	–
de Lange, M.	10548	345	30.57	7- 23	11	2	–
de Leede, B.F.W.	494	17	29.05	4- 76	–	–	–
Denly, J.L.	3536	83	42.60	4- 36	–	–	–
Dent, C.D.J.	842	10	84.20	2- 21	–	–	–
Dickson, S.R.	54	2	27.00	1- 15	–	–	–
Dockrell, G.H.	5707	187	30.51	6- 27	8	–	–
D'Oliveira, B.L.	4185	78	53.65	7- 92	2	–	–
Douthwaite, D.A.	2360	56	42.14	4- 48	–	–	–
Drakes, D.C.	324	12	27.00	3- 17	–	–	–
Drissell, G.S.	809	9	89.88	4- 83	–	–	–
Duckett, B.M.	99	2	49.50	1- 15	–	–	–
Duke, H.G.	1	0					
Dunn, M.P.	4237	117	36.21	5- 43	4	–	–
du Plooy, J.L.	1517	27	56.18	3- 76	–	–	–
Edwards, M.W.	596	14	42.57	3- 54	–	–	–
Elgar, D.	2798	56	49.96	4- 22	–	–	–
Ellis, N.T.	1232	42	29.33	6- 43	2	–	–
Eskinazi, S.S.	4	0					
Evans, L.J.	270	2	135.00	1- 29	–	–	–
Evans, S.T.	46	0					
Evison, J.D.M.	1684	41	41.07	5- 21	1	–	–
Fernando, A.M.	4540	188	24.14	7-139	8	1	–
Fernando, M.V.T.	8290	274	30.25	5- 14	10	–	–
Ferreira, D.	201	10	20.10	3- 17	–	–	–
Finan, M.G.A.	721	21	34.33	5- 58	1	–	–
Finch, A.W.	2210	61	36.22	5- 74	2	–	–
Finch, H.Z.	118	2	59.00	1- 9	–	–	–
Finn, S.T.	16711	570	29.31	9- 37	15	1	2
Fisher, M.D.	3014	111	27.15	5- 30	4	–	–
Fletcher, L.J.	11615	447	25.98	7- 37	10	1	1
Foakes, B.T.	6	0					
Foster, M.T.	219	5	43.80	2- 38	–	–	–
Fraine, W.A.R.	25	0					
Fuller, J.K.	6723	214	31.41	6- 24	7	1	–
Garrett, G.A.	380	9	42.22	2- 53	–	–	–
Garton, G.H.S.	2049	55	37.25	5- 26	1	–	–
Gay, E.N.	95	2	47.50	1- 8	–	–	–
Geddes, B.B.A.	12	0					
Gibbon, B.J.	1574	40	39.35	4- 87	–	–	–
Gibson, O.J.	533	8	66.62	2- 25	–	–	–
Gilchrist, N.N.	1965	65	30.23	6- 61	2	–	–
Gill, S.	44	0					
Glover, B.D.	827	24	34.45	4- 83	–	–	–
Godleman, B.A.	35	0					
Goldsworthy, L.P.	103	0					
Goodman, D.C.	636	14	45.42	4- 73	–	–	–
Gorvin, A.W.	505	12	42.08	3- 88	–	–	–

	Runs	Wkts	Avge	Best	5wI	10wM	50wS
Green, B.G.F.	366	10	36.60	3- 31	–	–	–
Green, C.D.	2312	70	33.02	6- 30	3	–	–
Gregory, L.	9274	352	26.34	7- 84	16	3	1
Gubbins, N.R.T.	147	6	24.50	4- 41	–	–	–
Haider Ali	31	0					
Hain, S.R.	35	0					
Haines, T.J.	1189	25	47.56	3- 50	–	–	–
Hales, A.D.	173	3	57.66	2- 63	–	–	–
Hameed, H.	60	1	60.00	1- 0	–	–	–
Hamidullah Qadri	2249	61	36.86	6-129	3	–	–
Hammond, M.A.H.	702	6	117.00	2- 37	–	–	–
Hand, F.P.	270	4	67.50	2- 50	–	–	–
Handscomb, P.S.P.	79	0					
Hannon-Dalby, O.J.	9091	331	27.46	7- 46	13	1	2
Harmer, S.R.	23429	902	25.97	9- 80	57	14	6+2
Harris, J.A.R.	16953	571	29.69	9- 34	16	2	3
Harris, M.S.	64	0					
Harrison, C.G.	725	20	36.25	4- 28	–	–	–
Hartley, T.W.	1463	40	36.57	5- 52	1	–	–
Hassan Ali	7700	313	24.60	8-107	18	4	0+1
Hazlewood, J.R.	9559	383	24.95	6- 35	12	–	–
Head, T.M.	3897	63	61.85	4- 10	–	–	–
Helm, T.G.	4296	144	29.83	6-110	5	–	–
Henry, M.J.	10269	437	23.49	7- 23	22	3	1
Higgins, R.F.	6010	245	24.53	7- 42	7	1	2
Hill, G.C.H.	1285	47	27.34	6- 26	1	–	–
Hill, L.J.	43	0					
Hogan, M.G.	17421	695	25.06	7- 92	25	2	3
Holden, M.D.E.	460	5	92.00	2- 59	–	–	–
Holland, I.G.	2741	93	29.47	6- 60	1	–	–
Hollman, L.B.K.	1758	37	47.51	5- 65	2	1	–
Hope, S.D.	5	0					
Howell, B.A.C.	3222	96	33.56	5- 57	1	–	–
Hudson-Prentice, F.J.	2412	67	36.00	5- 68	1	–	–
Hull, J.O.	565	9	62.77	3- 68	–	–	–
Hume, G.I.	5875	317	18.53	7- 23	14	–	–
Hunt, S.F.	1707	45	37.93	3- 36	–	–	–
Hutton, B.A.	7899	310	25.48	8- 57	17	2	1
Ibrahim, D.K.	555	7	79.28	2- 9	–	–	–
Imad Wasim	4392	141	31.14	8- 81	3	1	–
Ingram, C.A.	2275	54	42.12	4- 16	–	–	–
Jacks, W.G.	1687	37	45.59	6-161	2	–	–
Jadeja, R.A.	11766	494	23.81	7- 31	31	8	0+3
James, L.W.	1894	54	35.07	6- 74	1	–	–
Jennings, K.K.	988	30	32.93	3- 37	–	–	–
Jones, M.A.	1	0					
Jones, R.P.	49	2	24.50	1- 4	–	–	–
Jordan, C.J.	10730	335	32.02	7- 43	10	–	1
Kalley, E.S.	58	0					
Karvelas, A.	2017	83	24.30	6- 71	2	–	–
Kashif Ali	93	1	93.00	1- 51	–	–	–
Kellaway, B.I.	60	0					
Kelly, D.C.	83	3	27.66	2- 55	–	–	–
Keogh, R.I.	6005	142	42.28	9- 52	2	1	–
Kerrigan, S.C.	11534	364	31.68	9- 51	16	3	2
Khawaja, U.T.	111	1	111.00	1- 21	–	–	–
Kimber, L.P.J.	219	4	54.75	1- 8	–	–	–
Klaassen, F.J.	422	9	46.88	4- 44	–	–	–

	Runs	Wkts	Avge	Best	5wI	10wM	50wS
Kohli, V.	338	3	112.66	1- 19	–	–	–
Kuhnemann, M.P.	1769	56	31.58	5- 16	5	1	–
Labuschagne, M.	3835	80	47.93	4- 81	–	–	–
Lakmal, R.A.S.	12137	370	32.80	6- 68	10	–	–
Lamb, D.J.	1525	50	30.50	4- 55	–	–	–
Lamb, M.J.	447	9	49.66	2- 38	–	–	–
Lammonby, T.A.	549	11	49.90	3- 35	–	–	–
Latham, T.W.M.	18	1	18.00	1- 7	–	–	–
Lawes, T.E.	1232	60	20.53	5- 22	3	–	–
Lawrence, D.W.	872	20	43.60	3- 98	–	–	–
Leach, J.	11937	450	26.52	6- 44	17	1	3
Leach, M.J.	12302	432	28.47	8- 85	26	4	3
Leaning, J.A.	1794	33	54.36	3- 64	–	–	–
Leech, D.J.	398	7	56.85	3- 78	–	–	–
Lees, A.Z.	96	3	32.00	2- 51	–	–	–
Lenham, A.D.	528	7	75.42	4- 84	–	–	–
Leonard, E.O.	154	2	77.00	1- 68	–	–	–
Libby, J.D.	595	9	66.11	2- 10	–	–	–
Lilley, A.M.	1428	43	33.20	5- 23	2	–	–
Linde, G.F.	6435	247	26.05	7- 29	15	3	–
Lintott, J.B.	193	3	64.33	3- 68	–	–	–
Livingstone, L.S.	1552	43	36.09	6- 52	1	–	–
Lloyd, D.L.	4344	96	45.25	4- 11	–	–	–
Loten, T.W.	152	4	38.00	2- 31	–	–	–
Lynn, C.A.	64	0					
Lyon, N.M.	24156	732	33.00	8- 50	28	5	0+1
Lyth, A.	1870	38	49.21	2- 9	–	–	–
McAlindon, S.J.C.	355	5	71.00	2- 63	–	–	–
McAndrew, N.J.	3501	117	29.92	6- 97	5	–	–
McBrine, A.R.	1789	40	44.72	6-118	1	–	–
McCollum, J.A.	88	5	17.60	5- 32	1	–	–
McDermott, B.R.	75	0					
McIlroy, J.P.	867	25	34.68	5- 34	1	–	–
McKerr, C.	1723	51	33.78	5- 54	2	1	–
McKiernan, M.H.	210	6	35.00	2- 3	–	–	–
Madsen, W.L.	1944	38	51.15	3- 45	–	–	–
Mahmood, S.	2413	83	29.07	5- 47	1	–	–
Malan, D.J.	2556	63	40.57	5- 61	1	–	–
Malan, P.J.	513	20	25.65	5- 35	1	–	–
Marsh, M.R.	5134	165	31.11	6- 84	2	–	–
Maxwell, G.J.	3236	78	41.48	5- 40	1	–	–
Mayes, T.	123	7	17.57	4- 68	–	–	–
Middleton, E.W.O.	92	1	92.00	1- 59	–	–	–
Mike, B.W.M.	3115	80	38.93	5- 37	1	–	–
Miles, C.N.	9680	344	28.13	6- 63	17	1	3
Mills, T.S.	2008	55	36.50	4- 25	–	–	–
Milnes, M.E.	4280	147	29.11	6- 53	4	–	1
Mir Hamza	8683	386	22.49	7- 59	27	6	0+1
Mitchell, D.J.	3037	98	30.98	5- 44	1	–	–
Mohammad Abbas	13586	660	20.58	8- 46	43	11	3+2
Mohammad Amir	6020	266	22.63	7- 61	13	2	0+1
Mohammed Shami	8995	332	27.09	7- 79	12	2	–
Montgomery, M.	102	2	51.00	1- 0	–	–	–
Moores, T.J.	6	0					
Moriarty, D.T.	1443	49	29.44	6- 60	6	1	–
Morley, J.P.	760	25	30.40	5- 69	1	–	–
Mousley, D.R.	124	0					
Mulder, P.W.A.	4613	166	27.78	7- 25	3	–	–

	Runs	Wkts	Avge	Best	5wI	10wM	50wS
Mullaney, S.J.	5289	144	36.72	5- 32	1	–	–
Munro, C.	1640	58	28.27	4- 36	–	–	–
Murphy, T.R.	1313	50	26.26	7-124	1	–	–
Murtagh, T.J.	23454	959	24.45	7- 82	40	5	9
Muyeye, T.S.	204	3	68.00	2- 70	–	–	–
Nair, K.K.	752	13	57.84	2- 11	–	–	–
Narine, S.P.	1398	65	21.50	8- 17	8	3	–
Naseem Shah	2766	102	27.11	6- 59	4	–	–
Naveen-ul-Haq	782	31	25.22	8- 35	1	–	–
Neser, M.G.	8212	348	23.59	7- 32	10	–	–
Nijjar, A.S.S.	1123	29	38.72	4- 67	–	–	–
Northeast, S.A.	172	1	172.00	1- 60	–	–	–
Ogborne, A.R.J.	89	3	29.66	2- 56	–	–	–
Organ, F.S.	1154	44	26.22	6- 67	2	–	–
O'Riordan, M.K.	459	11	41.72	3- 50	–	–	–
Orr, A.G.H.	12	0					
Overton, C.	10304	438	23.52	7- 57	17	1	1
Overton, J.	7136	235	30.36	6- 61	6	–	–
Parkinson, C.F.	5770	145	39.79	8-148	5	2	1
Parkinson, M.W.	4472	173	25.84	7-126	6	1	–
Parnell, W.D.	7240	242	29.91	7- 51	9	2	–
Patel, A.Y.	10882	324	33.58	10-119	24	5	–
Patel, R.S.	1173	19	61.73	6- 5	1	–	–
Patel, S.R.	13650	357	38.23	7- 68	5	1	–
Paterson, D.	12690	541	23.45	8- 52	20	2	3+2
Patterson-White, L.A.	3080	95	32.42	5- 41	4	–	–
Payne, D.A.	9705	328	29.58	6- 26	6	1	–
Pennington, D.Y.	3939	140	28.13	5- 32	1	–	–
Pettman, T.H.S.	1021	44	23.20	5- 19	2	–	–
Podmore, H.W.	4676	170	27.50	6- 36	4	–	1
Pope, O.J.D.	10	0					
Porter, J.A.	11069	466	23.75	7- 41	17	3	6
Potts, M.J.	4332	177	24.47	7- 40	7	2	2
Potts, N.J.	610	15	40.66	4- 50	–	–	–
Prest, T.J.	150	3	50.00	2- 32	–	–	–
Pretorius, M.	3811	146	26.10	6- 38	3	–	–
Price, O.J.	644	9	71.55	3- 40	–	–	–
Price, T.J.	1915	66	29.01	8- 27	3	1	–
Procter, L.A.	5291	146	36.23	7- 71	4	–	–
Pujara, C.A.	166	6	27.66	2- 4	–	–	–
Quinn, M.R.	5709	192	29.73	7- 76	2	1	–
Rahane, A.M.	75	0					
Raine, B.A.	10931	426	25.65	6- 27	13	–	4
Reece, L.M.	4282	143	29.94	7- 20	4	–	1
Revis, M.L.	1207	30	40.23	5- 50	1	–	–
Rhodes, W.M.H.	3036	89	34.11	5- 17	2	–	–
Richards, J.A.	130	5	26.00	5- 96	1	–	–
Richardson, K.W.	3505	102	34.36	5- 69	1	–	–
Rickelton, R.D.	7	0					
Roach, K.A.J.	13604	518	26.26	8- 40	22	2	–
Robinson, O.E.	8219	396	20.75	9- 78	23	6	3
Robson, S.D.	546	17	32.11	4- 46	–	–	–
Roland-Jones, T.S.	13060	522	25.01	7- 52	25	5	3
Root, J.E.	3808	81	47.01	5- 8	1	–	–
Root, W.T.	275	8	34.37	3- 29	–	–	–
Rossington, A.M.	86	0					
Roy, J.J.	495	14	35.35	3- 9	–	–	–
Rushworth, C.	14711	656	22.42	9- 52	32	6	7

	Runs	Wkts	Avge	Best	5wI	10wM	50wS
Russell, A.K.	387	6	64.50	6-175	1	–	–
Saini, N.	5057	175	28.89	6- 32	5	–	–
Sai Sudharsan, B.	17	0					
Sales, J.J.G.	460	11	41.81	4- 24	–	–	–
Salisbury, M.E.T.	4376	131	33.40	6- 37	2	–	–
Salt, P.D.	32	1	32.00	1- 32	–	–	–
Salter, A.G.	6153	134	45.91	7- 45	2	–	–
Sams, D.R.	494	13	38.00	4- 55	–	–	–
Sanderson, B.W.	7951	360	22.08	8- 73	18	3	3
Santner, M.J.	4457	101	44.12	5- 51	1	–	–
Saud Shakil	1109	23	48.21	2- 7	–	–	–
Scrimshaw, G.L.S.	539	16	33.68	5- 49	1	–	–
Scriven, T.A.R.	1178	46	25.60	4- 30	–	–	–
Seales, J.N.T.	1237	51	24.25	5- 49	2	–	–
Shadab Khan	1753	68	25.77	6- 77	2	1	–
Shaheen Shah Afridi	3592	145	24.77	8- 39	5	1	–
Shan Masood	607	8	75.87	2- 52	–	–	–
Sharma, R.G.	1154	24	48.08	4- 41	–	–	–
Shaw, J.	4648	123	37.78	5- 79	2	–	–
Shaw, P.P.	44	0					
Shipley, H.B.	2099	72	29.15	5- 37	2	–	–
Shutt, J.W.	200	5	40.00	2- 14	–	–	–
Sibley, D.P.	286	4	71.50	2-103	–	–	–
Siddle, P.M.	19653	741	26.52	8- 54	27	–	0+1
Simpson, J.A.	23	0					
Singh, J.	658	16	41.12	4- 51	–	–	–
Siraj, M.	5498	219	25.10	8- 59	7	2	–
Sisodiya, P.	443	16	27.68	4- 79	–	–	–
Slater, B.T.	214	3	71.33	1- 1	–	–	–
Smith, N.G.	2585	84	30.77	6- 54	4	–	–
Smith, R.A.J.	2413	69	34.97	5- 87	1	–	–
Smith, S.P.D.	3719	72	51.65	7- 64	1	–	–
Smith, T.M.J.	4171	82	50.86	4- 35	–	–	–
Snater, S.	2252	95	23.70	7- 98	7	–	–
Sodhi, I.S.	10015	303	33.05	7- 30	17	2	–
Sowter, N.A.	1032	20	51.60	3- 42	–	–	–
Starc, M.A.	13688	509	26.89	8- 73	21	4	–
Steel, C.T.	1297	37	35.05	4- 40	–	–	–
Steketee, M.T.	6557	254	25.81	7- 44	6	1	–
Stewart, G.	2795	81	34.50	6- 22	2	–	–
Stirling, P.R.	1118	27	41.40	2- 21	–	–	–
Stokes, B.A.	11348	376	30.18	7- 67	7	1	–
Stone, O.P.	3942	156	25.26	8- 80	6	1	–
Stoneman, M.D.	312	1	312.00	1- 34	–	–	–
Sutherland, W.J.	2471	102	24.22	6- 67	5	–	–
Swepson, M.J.	7159	199	35.97	5- 55	5	1	–
Swindells, H.J.	3	0					
Tattersall, J.A.	66	2	33.00	2- 27	–	–	–
Taylor, C.Z.	636	7	90.85	2- 16	–	–	–
Taylor, J.M.R.	3492	76	45.94	4- 16	–	–	–
Taylor, M.D.	6795	208	32.66	5- 15	7	–	1
Taylor, T.A.I.	5522	169	32.67	6- 47	5	1	–
Tector, H.T.	589	15	39.26	4- 70	–	–	–
Thain, N.R.M.	58	1	58.00	1- 44	–	–	–
Thakur, S.N.	6912	245	28.21	7- 61	13	–	0+1
Thompson, J.A.	3677	138	26.64	5- 31	3	–	–
Thomson, A.T.	3177	80	39.71	6-138	3	–	–
Tickner, B.M.	6678	190	35.14	5- 23	5	–	–

	Runs	Wkts	Avge	Best	5wI	10wM	50wS
Tongue, J.C.	4506	177	25.45	6- 97	9	–	–
Toole, R.L.	2271	84	27.03	7- 57	2	–	–
Tremain, C.P.	7158	301	23.78	7- 82	10	1	0+1
Trevaskis, L.	1655	34	48.67	5- 78	2	–	–
Turner, A.J.	537	12	44.75	6-111	1	–	–
Turner, J.A.	105	10	10.50	5- 31	1	–	–
Tye, A.J.	991	27	36.70	3- 47	–	–	–
Umar Amin	1752	50	35.04	3- 32	–	–	–
Umeed, A.R.I.	110	2	55.00	1- 19	–	–	–
Unadkat, J.D.	8893	393	22.62	8- 39	23	5	0+1
Usama Mir	1411	30	47.03	6- 91	1	–	–
van Beek, L.V.	6263	196	31.95	6- 46	8	2	–
van Buuren, G.L.	3490	104	33.55	4- 12	–	–	–
van der Gugten, T.	7137	255	27.98	7- 42	13	1	1
van der Merwe, R.E.	5069	150	33.79	5-174	1	–	–
van Meekeren, P.A.	1043	33	31.60	5- 73	1	–	–
Vasconcelos, R.S.	43	0					
Vilas, D.J.	56	0					
Vince, J.M.	1137	24	47.37	5- 41	1	–	–
Virdi, G.S.	3778	123	30.71	8- 61	5	1	–
Wagner, N.	22105	814	27.15	7- 39	36	2	0+2
Wagstaff, M.D.	88	2	44.00	2- 59	–	–	–
Waite, M.J.	1930	65	29.69	5- 16	1	–	–
Walallawita, T.N.	677	11	61.54	3- 28	–	–	–
Walker, R.I.	285	7	40.71	3- 84	–	–	–
Walter, P.I.	956	25	38.24	3- 20	–	–	–
Ward, H.D.	2	0					
Warner, D.A.	455	6	75.83	2- 45	–	–	–
Watt, M.R.J.	1137	32	35.53	5- 83	1	–	–
Weatherley, J.J.	268	5	53.60	1- 2	–	–	–
Webster, B.J.	3792	86	44.09	4- 39	–	–	–
Welch, N.R.	37	0					
Wells, L.W.P.	3897	92	42.35	5- 25	2	–	–
Westley, T.	2724	59	46.16	4- 55	–	–	–
Wharton, J.H.	114	1	114.00	1- 1	–	–	–
Wheal, B.T.J.	3668	109	33.65	6- 51	1	–	–
White, C.J.	2644	105	25.18	6- 38	5	–	1
White, G.G.	2730	65	42.00	6- 44	1	–	–
Whiteley, R.A.	2119	41	51.68	2- 6	–	–	–
Wiese, D.	9638	344	28.01	6- 58	10	1	–
Willey, D.J.	5895	198	29.77	5- 29	6	1	–
Williams, W.S.A.	4175	191	21.85	5- 26	3	–	–
Woakes, C.R.	14555	573	25.40	9- 36	22	4	3
Wood, C.P.	3174	105	30.22	5- 39	3	–	–
Wood, L.	4851	137	35.40	5- 40	3	–	–
Wood, M.A.	6386	240	26.60	6- 37	12	–	–
Worrall, D.J.	8623	321	26.86	7- 64	14	2	–
Wright, C.J.C.	18961	588	32.24	7- 53	19	–	2
Yadav, J.	7097	214	33.16	7- 58	10	1	–
Yadav, U.T.	10445	351	29.75	7- 48	15	2	–
Yates, R.M.	553	8	69.12	2- 45	–	–	–
Young, C.A.	1617	67	24.13	5- 37	2	–	–
Young, W.A.	8	0					
Zafar Gohar	8903	281	31.68	7- 79	18	4	–
Zaib, S.A.	895	25	35.80	6-115	2	–	–
Zain Ul Hassan	477	8	59.62	2- 18	–	–	–

LIMITED-OVERS CAREER RECORDS

Compiled by Philip Bailey

The following career records, to the end of the 2023 season, include all players currently registered with first-class counties or teams in The Hundred. These records are restricted to performances in limited-overs matches of 'List A' status as defined by the Association of Cricket Statisticians and Historians now incorporated by ICC into their Classification of Cricket. The following matches qualify for List A status and are included in the figures that follow: Limited-Overs Internationals; Other International matches (e.g. Commonwealth Games, 'A' team internationals); Premier domestic limited-overs tournaments in Test status countries; Official tourist matches against the main first-class teams.

The following matches do NOT qualify for inclusion: World Cup warm-up games; Tourist matches against first-class teams outside the major domestic competitions (e.g. Universities, Minor Counties etc.); Festival, pre-season friendly games and Twenty20 Cup matches.

	M	*Runs*	*Avge*	*HS*	*100*	*50*	*Wkts*	*Avge*	*Best*	*Econ*
Abbott, K.J.	112	536	16.24	56	–	1	149	29.62	5-43	5.22
Abbott, S.A.	80	832	16.97	50	–	1	123	25.45	5-43	5.19
Abell, T.B.	27	649	30.90	106	1	1	2	14.00	2-19	3.42
Ackermann, C.N.	98	2777	38.04	152*	3	19	51	41.56	4-48	4.88
Agar, W.A.	30	151	12.58	41	–	–	39	37.35	5-40	5.82
Ahmed, R.	10	97	24.25	40*	–	–	10	43.40	4-54	5.76
Aitchison, B.W.	13	60	8.57	19	–	–	15	29.00	4-39	4.80
Akhter, Z.	3	27	–	27*	–	–	5	30.80	3-56	5.92
Albert, T.E.	13	403	40.30	84*	–	2	–	–	–	–
Aldridge, K.L.	14	38	5.42	12	–	–	19	31.05	5-50	6.34
Ali, M.M.	249	5555	27.77	158	11	21	181	43.90	4-33	5.39
Ali, T.C.	1	–	–	–	–	–	1	49.00	1-49	4.90
Allison, B.M.J.	14	60	15.00	21*	–	–	10	61.10	2-33	6.09
Allison, C.W.J.	8	254	36.28	85	–	2	–	–	–	–
Alsop, T.P.	70	2271	34.93	189*	5	12	–	–	–	46/6
Anderson, J.M.	261	378	9.00	28	–	–	358	28.57	5-23	4.82
Andersson, M.K.	19	473	59.12	100	1	–	15	62.06	3-55	7.16
Archer, J.C.	35	224	17.23	45	–	–	63	24.73	6-40	4.99
Aspinwall, T.H.	8	108	27.00	47	–	–	10	29.00	4-52	5.68
Atkinson, A.A.P.	5	17	8.50	15	–	–	6	34.50	4-43	6.27
Bailey, T.E.	34	275	21.15	60	–	1	47	30.17	3-22	5.10
Bairstow, J.M.	166	5575	40.69	174	14	25	–	–	–	101/9
Baker, J.O.	17	100	14.28	25	–	–	24	31.25	3-29	5.70
Balderson, G.P.	21	463	35.61	106*	1	1	23	28.17	3-25	5.10
Ball, J.T.	95	198	8.60	28	–	–	118	33.51	5-51	5.87
Bamber, E.R.	16	85	10.62	21	–	–	27	25.59	3-27	5.05
Bancroft, C.T.	80	2644	43.34	176	4	17	–	–	–	65/2
Banton, T.	24	658	29.90	112	2	4	–	–	–	16/1
Barker, K.H.D.	72	639	18.79	56	–	1	86	31.17	4-33	5.60
Barnard, E.G.	68	1537	39.41	161	2	8	76	35.46	3-14	5.72
Bartlett, G.A.	31	732	30.50	108	1	3	–	–	–	–
Bartlett, X.C.	20	70	11.66	28	–	–	23	36.17	3-43	5.37
Bashir, S.	7	10	5.00	7	–	–	3	99.66	1-46	6.47
Bean, F.J.	9	164	18.22	61	–	1	–	–	–	–
Beard, A.P.	14	106	11.77	22*	–	–	20	35.45	4-32	6.74
Bedingham, D.G.	35	1209	39.00	152	4	7	0	–	0-25	3.84
Bell, G.J.	9	272	34.00	78*	–	2	1	20.00	1-20	6.66
Bell-Drummond, D.J.	94	3771	44.36	171*	7	25	5	24.20	2-22	4.68
Benjamin, C.G.	1	50	50.00	50	–	1	–	–	–	0/0
Benkenstein, L.M.	11	164	16.40	55	–	1	11	17.90	6-42	5.32

	M	Runs	Avge	HS	100	50	Wkts	Avge	Best	Econ
Bess, D.M.	32	317	15.09	51	–	1	27	52.40	5-37	5.87
Bethell, J.G.	16	339	24.21	66	–	3	15	28.46	4-36	5.20
Bevan, T.R.	8	218	27.25	134	1	–	–	–	–	–
Billings, S.W.	103	3125	41.66	175	7	21	–	–	–	88/9
Blake, J.W.	12	278	25.27	44	–	–	–	–	–	9/3
Blatherwick, J.M.	11	36	18.00	22*	–	–	16	28.62	4-52	6.63
Bohannon, J.J.	37	888	32.88	105	1	5	1	208.00	1-33	8.32
Boland, S.M.	63	136	6.47	19	–	–	75	40.41	5-63	5.51
Booth, M.G.	2	–	–	–	–	–	1	63.00	1-21	7.87
Borthwick, S.G.	120	1929	24.41	88	–	12	82	44.01	5-38	6.09
Bracey, J.R.	32	1374	47.37	224*	3	7	1	23.00	1-23	7.66
Briggs, D.R.	110	421	12.75	37*	–	–	114	37.61	4-32	5.09
Broad, J.	6	39	9.75	22*	–	–	0	–	0-12	7.75
Brookes, E.A.	25	356	20.94	63	–	2	9	35.55	3-15	7.32
Brookes, H.J.H.	17	25	5.00	12*	–	–	25	31.44	3-44	6.55
Brown, B.C.	99	1827	26.86	105	1	13	–	–	–	101/12
Brown, P.R.	14	5	5.00	3	–	–	21	30.90	4-51	6.32
Browne, N.L.J.	26	624	27.13	99	–	3	–	–	–	10/1
Bruce, T.C.	72	2027	32.69	100	1	17	5	50.80	3- 4	7.47
Budinger, S.G.	27	921	35.42	102	1	7	0	–	0-17	17.00
Burgess, M.G.K.	41	979	28.79	93	–	6	–	–	–	41/5
Burns, R.J.	63	1829	33.25	95	–	12	–	–	–	30/0
Bushnell, J.J.	10	203	25.37	60*	–	1	8	30.50	3-56	6.22
Buttler, J.C.	239	6988	45.08	162*	13	41	–	–	–	261/40
Byrom, E.J.	17	480	34.28	108	1	4	–	–	–	–
Came, H.R.C.	22	603	30.15	94	–	3	–	–	–	–
Carlson, K.S.	46	1181	28.80	82	–	10	18	30.55	4-41	5.79
Carse, B.A.	21	143	17.87	32	–	–	24	32.20	5-61	5.74
Carson, J.J.	6	83	20.75	20*	–	–	12	29.75	4-83	6.90
Carter, M.	16	65	7.22	21*	–	–	23	27.17	4-40	5.34
Carter, O.J.	15	267	22.25	59	–	2	–	–	–	16/3
Chappell, Z.J.	23	209	20.90	59*	–	1	30	36.10	3-35	6.35
Charlesworth, B.G.	11	458	45.80	99*	–	3	0	–	0-13	6.50
Clark, G.	53	1841	36.09	141*	4	9	4	12.50	3-18	5.55
Clark, J.	53	1028	31.15	79*	–	6	36	45.55	4-34	6.43
Clark, T.G.R.	17	436	27.25	104	1	1	0	–	0-17	5.66
Clarke, J.M.	62	1846	34.18	139	4	9	–	–	–	22/2
Cliff, B.M.	2	0	0.00	0	–	–	1	84.00	1-44	8.84
Coad, B.O.	38	142	17.75	45	–	–	41	35.90	4-63	4.87
Cobb, J.J.	99	3330	38.27	146*	7	21	35	48.91	3-34	5.84
Cohen, M.A.R.	4	16	16.00	16	–	–	3	53.33	1-17	5.00
Coles, J.M.	20	320	22.85	59	–	1	21	35.85	3-27	5.94
Compton, B.G.	26	1143	45.72	110	3	10	–	–	–	–
Conners, S.	17	69	9.85	36*	–	–	26	31.15	5-28	5.62
Cook, S.J.	15	17	5.66	6	–	–	17	35.23	3-37	4.79
Cooke, C.B.	92	2616	34.88	161	3	14	–	–	–	58/5
Coughlin, P.	37	375	15.62	77	–	1	23	49.91	3-36	5.77
Cox, J.M.	4	98	24.50	46	–	–	–	–	–	3/0
Cox, O.B.	90	1803	31.63	122*	1	10	–	–	–	98/10
Cracknell, J.B.	16	448	32.00	87	–	3	–	–	–	14/2
Crane, M.S.	47	168	21.00	31	–	–	79	29.86	4-30	5.96
Crawley, Z.	28	891	35.64	120	1	6	0	–	0-17	8.50
Critchley, M.J.J.	45	694	26.69	64*	–	2	31	55.25	4-48	6.58
Crocombe, H.T.	18	93	15.50	47	–	–	22	38.77	4-63	6.46
Croft, S.J.	175	4858	38.25	127	4	34	66	41.87	4-24	5.55
Cullen, B.C.	2	–	–	–	–	–	2	28.50	2-32	5.10

	M	Runs	Avge	HS	100	50	Wkts	Avge	Best	Econ
Curran, S.M.	75	963	22.39	95*	–	2	94	32.64	5-48	5.63
Curran, T.K.	86	739	21.11	47*	–	–	126	28.83	5-16	5.57
Currie, B.J.	12	22	11.00	18*	–	–	15	32.53	3-38	5.48
Currie, S.W.	22	181	20.11	43*	–	–	38	24.39	3-25	5.88
Dal, A.K.	25	411	22.83	110	1	1	3	98.66	1-16	5.28
Dale, A.S.	5	11	5.50	9	–	–	6	31.66	4-58	5.27
Das, R.J.	13	284	21.84	63	–	1	–	–	–	–
Davey, J.H.	93	1280	23.27	91	–	6	117	26.24	6-28	5.31
Davies, A.L.	51	1390	30.88	147	1	7	–	–	–	49/11
Davies, J.L.B.	12	261	21.75	70	–	2	–	–	–	5/0
Dawson, L.A.	165	3624	32.64	113*	3	19	172	29.85	7-15	4.74
de Caires, J.M.	10	116	12.88	43	–	–	6	49.83	3-52	5.64
de Lange, M.	98	776	15.52	58*	–	2	170	26.03	5-49	5.54
de Leede, B.F.W.	37	870	24.85	123	1	2	27	34.33	5-52	6.15
Denly, J.K.	5	78	26.00	37	–	–	4	33.75	1-20	5.29
Denly, J.L.	168	5220	36.50	150*	8	29	55	26.18	4-35	5.11
Dent, C.D.J.	90	2446	30.96	151*	5	7	12	35.00	4-43	5.67
Dickson, S.R.	65	1662	30.77	103*	1	11	0	–	0-20	10.00
D'Oliveira, B.L.	76	1389	25.25	123	1	7	65	38.90	3- 8	5.28
Donald, A.H.T.	49	1000	23.25	115	2	4	–	–	–	–
Douthwaite, D.A.	12	151	25.16	52*	–	1	13	34.53	3-43	5.81
Drissell, G.S.	17	189	18.90	37*	–	–	13	50.69	3-46	5.99
Duckett, B.M.	79	2563	38.83	220*	4	16	–	–	–	44/3
Duke, H.G.	23	737	36.85	125	2	3	–	–	–	20/3
Dunn, M.P.	21	67	13.40	34	–	–	21	40.33	2-32	6.30
du Plooy, J.L.	50	2002	54.10	155	5	11	11	38.18	3-19	6.04
Ealham, T.M.	2	9	4.50	5	–	–	0	–	0-29	4.83
Eckland, J.R.	6	91	30.33	72	–	1	–	–	–	–
Edwards, M.W.	10	29	9.66	11	–	–	11	38.81	4-31	5.82
Elgar, D.	172	5940	42.42	137	7	45	57	49.87	4-37	5.48
Ellis, N.T.	21	143	15.88	31	–	–	32	24.96	5-38	5.09
Eskinazi, S.S.	30	1434	55.15	182	6	3	–	–	–	–
Evans, L.J.	63	1735	37.71	134*	3	5	1	82.00	1-29	9.11
Evans, S.T.	6	116	38.66	60	–	1	–	–	–	–
Evison, J.D.M.	18	568	37.86	136	2	3	11	43.81	3-62	6.82
Ferreira, D.	15	308	28.00	96*	–	2	3	47.33	2-46	5.68
Finch, A.W.	14	71	14.20	24	–	–	14	43.42	3-54	6.17
Finch, H.Z.	58	1607	32.79	108	1	12	0	–	0- 2	9.00
Fisher, M.D.	35	236	26.22	36*	–	–	32	43.81	3-32	5.94
Fletcher, L.J.	79	505	20.20	53*	–	1	87	35.25	5-56	5.67
Foakes, B.T.	77	2147	38.33	106	1	19	–	–	–	88/12
Foreman, A.M.	2	63	63.00	35	–	–	2	41.00	1-40	8.20
Foster, M.T.	14	4	2.00	2*	–	–	14	31.64	3-26	5.30
Fuller, J.K.	69	884	23.26	55*	–	2	79	33.03	6-35	5.92
Garrett, G.A.	11	39	9.75	18	–	–	14	36.00	3-50	5.94
Garton, G.H.S.	24	103	11.44	38	–	–	29	34.24	4-43	6.32
Gay, E.N.	23	595	29.75	131	1	2	0	–	0-19	6.33
Geddes, B.B.A.	19	508	28.22	92	–	4	0	–	0- 8	3.00
Gibbon, B.J.	9	29	9.66	13*	–	–	13	32.53	3-58	6.22
Gibson, O.J.	10	26	5.20	6	–	–	13	35.69	3-54	6.84
Gilchrist, N.N.	20	65	8.12	33	–	–	24	34.54	5-45	7.10
Glover, B.D.	19	103	14.71	27	–	–	16	54.93	3-43	6.45
Goldsworthy, L.P.	21	882	49.00	111	1	6	11	62.63	2-30	5.55
Goodman, D.C.	2	–	–	–	–	–	0	–	0-15	5.83
Gorvin, A.W.	12	36	18.00	12*	–	–	10	46.40	2-41	5.42
Green, B.G.F.	13	356	50.85	157	1	1	12	37.58	3-64	5.74

	M	Runs	Avge	HS	100	50	Wkts	Avge	Best	Econ
Gregory, L.	79	1323	24.96	105*	1	8	110	27.66	4-23	5.95
Griffiths, L.A.	5	61	20.33	25	–	–	2	56.00	1-24	6.92
Gubbins, N.R.T.	81	3175	41.23	141	8	18	10	45.50	4-38	5.61
Guest, B.D.	24	674	32.09	88	–	5	–	–	–	20/2
Hain, S.R.	64	3004	57.76	161*	10	17	–	–	–	–
Haines, T.J.	16	619	38.68	123	1	4	0	–	0- 8	7.20
Hales, A.D.	175	6260	38.40	187*	17	32	0	–	0- 4	15.00
Hameed, H.	37	1069	34.48	114	2	6	–	–	–	–
Hamidullah Qadri	26	171	15.54	42*	–	–	34	29.82	4-36	5.68
Hammond, M.A.H.	12	315	35.00	109*	1	1	5	19.40	2-18	5.10
Handscomb, P.S.P.	137	4257	38.70	140	4	28	–	–	–	135/7
Hannon-Dalby, O.J.	60	120	13.33	21*	–	–	105	27.00	5-27	5.93
Harmer, S.R.	98	1223	21.08	68	–	1	100	38.58	4-42	4.88
Harris, J.A.R.	72	469	13.40	117	1	–	96	31.79	4-38	5.89
Harrison, C.G.	6	93	18.60	41	–	–	3	68.33	1- 0	5.51
Hartley, T.W.	5	60	30.00	23	–	–	1	215.00	1-46	5.78
Hassan Ali	91	713	16.97	59	–	3	143	28.22	5-34	5.54
Haynes, J.A.	11	469	42.63	153	1	2	–	–	–	–
Heldreich, F.J.	6	7	7.00	5	–	–	4	67.50	2-69	7.29
Helm, T.G.	40	206	12.87	30	–	–	56	31.10	5-33	5.75
Higgins, R.F.	40	967	31.19	88	–	6	35	33.60	4-33	5.43
Hill, F.J.	1	1	–	1*	–	–	–	–	–	–
Hill, G.C.H.	22	473	27.82	130	1	2	15	26.06	3-47	4.88
Hill, L.J.	67	1509	25.15	118	3	6	–	–	–	32/2
Holden, M.D.E.	24	845	42.25	166	1	5	1	104.00	1-29	4.95
Holland, I.G.	51	766	23.21	75	–	4	63	27.01	5-35	4.73
Hollman, L.B.K.	19	237	16.92	35	–	–	31	28.12	4-34	5.41
Horton, A.J.	7	81	16.20	44*	–	–	–	–	–	1/2
Hose, A.J.	30	765	31.87	101*	1	4	–	–	–	–
Howell, B.A.C.	87	2090	35.42	122	1	13	79	34.15	3-37	5.21
Hudson-Prentice, F.J.	19	564	40.28	93	–	5	18	37.55	3-37	6.16
Hughes, D.P.	39	2087	59.62	152	10	7	–	–	–	–
Hull, J.O.	9	3	–	3*	–	–	17	24.23	4-43	5.74
Hunt, S.F.	7	19	9.50	13	–	–	6	52.00	2-59	6.00
Hurst, M.F.	8	108	27.00	66	–	1	–	–	–	6/0
Hutton, B.A.	38	409	19.47	46	–	–	55	27.05	7-26	5.30
Ibrahim, D.K.	17	287	22.07	56	–	3	9	49.11	2-48	5.52
Ingram, C.A.	199	8204	48.25	155	20	52	43	34.37	4-39	5.55
Jack, E.V.	6	14	7.00	8	–	–	9	25.11	3-31	6.19
Jacks, W.G.	26	666	26.64	121	1	3	12	41.25	2-32	5.24
James, L.W.	23	484	25.47	82	–	3	13	18.23	5-48	5.64
Jennings, K.K.	90	3163	43.93	139	7	20	11	60.90	2-19	5.82
Jones, C.W.	1	0	0.00	0	–	–	1	28.00	1-28	4.00
Jones, M.A.	21	613	29.19	119	1	4	–	–	–	–
Jones, R.P.	37	1076	43.04	122	1	8	2	61.00	1- 3	6.00
Jordan, C.J.	85	648	15.42	55	–	1	122	30.18	5-28	5.75
Karvelas, A.	24	152	16.88	33	–	–	38	23.50	5-16	4.68
Kashif Ali	13	559	50.81	114	1	4	–	–	–	–
Kaushal, I.	5	7	7.00	5*	–	–	3	82.00	1-38	7.23
Kellaway, B.I.	7	195	32.50	82	–	2	13	22.92	3-41	5.41
Kelly, D.C.	7	23	11.50	17	–	–	5	53.00	2-22	6.02
Keogh, R.I.	67	1843	32.91	134	3	14	28	50.10	4-49	5.46
Khushi, F.I.N.	14	632	45.14	118	3	2	–	–	–	–
Killeen, M.J.	4	54	18.00	32	–	–	2	62.50	1-17	4.80
Kimber, L.P.J.	27	801	40.05	102	1	6	8	22.25	4-61	5.96
King, S.I.M.	3	60	20.00	37	–	–	–	–	–	–

	M	Runs	Avge	HS	100	50	Wkts	Avge	Best	Econ
Klaassen, F.J.	34	97	8.08	13	–	–	50	26.92	3-23	4.72
Kohler-Cadmore, T.	56	1808	34.11	164	3	10	–	–	–	29/0
Labuschagne, M.	74	2257	32.71	135	2	18	11	74.27	3-46	6.39
Lamb, D.J.	26	390	35.45	86*	–	2	36	33.63	5-30	5.88
Lamb, M.J.	22	619	41.26	119*	1	3	4	57.00	4-35	5.84
Lammonby, T.A.	1	6	6.00	6	–	–	–	–	–	–
Langridge, J.T.	3	6	6.00	6	–	–	2	78.00	1-17	10.40
Lavelle, G.I.D.	24	452	34.76	72	–	5	–	–	–	25/1
Lawes, T.E.	9	324	46.28	75	–	4	8	49.87	2-20	6.33
Lawrence, D.W.	28	670	26.80	115	1	4	11	54.27	3-35	6.25
Leach, J.	59	903	28.21	88	–	3	57	43.87	4-30	5.79
Leach, M.J.	17	22	7.33	18	–	–	21	33.19	3- 7	4.79
Leaning, J.A.	62	1503	32.67	137*	3	7	14	33.85	5-22	5.29
Leech, D.J.	5	42	42.00	23	–	–	5	44.80	2-34	6.22
Lees, A.Z.	72	2568	42.09	144	5	20	–	–	–	–
Lenham, A.D.	13	72	18.00	18*	–	–	12	49.08	4-59	6.33
Leonard, E.O.	11	45	15.00	32	–	–	11	49.36	3-40	6.88
Libby, J.D.	31	1085	47.17	126*	1	9	5	45.00	2-47	5.11
Lintott, J.B.	16	163	27.16	28	–	–	29	25.55	5-37	5.59
Lion-Cachet, Z.B.	1	34	34.00	34	–	–	–	–	–	–
Livingstone, L.S.	71	1988	36.81	129	1	13	33	41.69	3-16	5.24
Lloyd, D.L.	55	1240	26.95	92	–	8	22	40.81	5-53	5.94
Loten, T.W.	15	156	19.50	44	–	–	16	32.06	3-26	5.80
Luxton, W.A.	14	300	25.00	84	–	2	–	–	–	–
Lyon, N.M.	80	240	12.63	37*	–	–	90	38.84	4-10	4.90
Lyth, A.	122	3765	35.18	144	5	18	6	62.16	2-27	6.21
McAlindon, S.J.C.	7	123	30.75	50	–	1	7	42.14	4-29	6.14
McAndrew, N.J.	13	166	16.60	55	–	1	13	47.23	3-22	6.22
McDermott, B.R.	38	1610	44.72	133	5	10	–	–	–	31/0
McIlroy, J.P.	8	27	27.00	13	–	–	7	43.85	2-13	4.51
McKerr, C.	31	214	11.88	32	–	–	45	31.44	4-55	6.16
McKinney, B.S.	4	17	4.25	5	–	–	–	–	–	–
McManus, L.D.	52	1021	28.36	107	1	4	–	–	–	37/12
Madsen, W.L.	107	3398	41.43	138	6	20	16	35.81	3-27	5.14
Mahmood, S.	37	138	15.33	45	–	–	68	24.07	6-37	5.47
Majid, Y.	11	14	4.66	5*	–	–	9	49.88	3-74	5.75
Malan, D.J.	169	6157	43.97	185*	15	30	41	32.36	4-25	5.84
Martindale, B.J.R.	8	180	22.50	55	–	1	0	–	0-13	6.50
Middleton, F.S.	21	715	37.63	100	1	5	–	–	–	–
Mike, B.W.M.	15	171	14.25	41	–	–	17	36.05	4-40	7.66
Miles, C.N.	47	152	12.66	31*	–	–	56	37.16	4-29	6.21
Miller, A.H.	5	66	66.00	31	–	–	0	–	0-26	6.50
Mills, T.S.	23	7	1.75	3*	–	–	22	35.77	3-23	5.97
Milnes, M.E.	12	101	16.83	26	–	–	19	34.05	5-79	6.75
Mir Hamza	86	316	17.55	49	–	–	124	30.33	4-12	5.23
Mohammad Abbas	55	137	7.61	15*	–	–	75	29.21	4-31	4.88
Mohammad Amir	84	413	18.77	73*	–	2	123	26.65	5-30	4.63
Montgomery, M.	28	1018	48.47	104	1	7	5	83.80	2-48	6.16
Moore, H.J.	3	3	1.50	2	–	–	2	80.50	1-43	6.44
Moores, T.J.	21	566	35.37	76	–	5	–	–	–	18/5
Moriarty, D.T.	17	43	6.14	15	–	–	23	30.73	4-30	4.98
Morley, J.P.	21	13	4.33	6	–	–	21	35.38	3-40	4.95
Morris, B.J.	2	2	–	2*	–	–	0	–	0-26	7.77
Mousley, D.R.	9	338	37.55	105	1	2	7	25.42	3-32	4.23
Mulder, P.W.A.	68	1732	41.23	116*	3	11	75	29.80	4-47	5.15
Mullaney, S.J.	123	2611	35.28	124	2	19	100	34.58	4-29	5.21

	M	Runs	Avge	HS	100	50	Wkts	Avge	Best	Econ
Muyeye, T.S.	11	221	24.55	40	–	–	1	33.00	1-17	3.30
Nair, K.K.	90	2119	30.71	120	2	12	15	50.00	2-16	5.13
Naveen-ul-Haq	23	92	10.22	30	–	–	34	34.47	5-40	5.94
Neser, M.G.	63	773	22.08	122	1	2	80	32.06	5-28	5.24
Northeast, S.A.	118	3522	35.93	177*	6	19	–	–	–	–
Ogborne, A.R.J.	5	39	39.00	27*	–	–	4	61.25	3-49	6.44
Organ, F.S.	25	366	21.52	79	–	2	13	54.53	3-39	4.82
O'Riordan, M.K.	7	128	25.60	60	–	1	1	157.00	1-77	7.47
Orr, A.G.H.	14	670	47.85	206	2	3	–	–	–	–
Overton, C.	75	824	22.27	66*	–	2	95	32.16	5-18	5.32
Overton, J.	42	399	17.34	40*	–	–	57	30.54	4-42	6.28
Parkinson, C.F.	13	222	27.75	52*	–	1	4	147.25	1-34	6.40
Parkinson, M.W.	37	60	12.00	15*	–	–	64	25.50	5-51	5.29
Patel, K.K.	1	30	30.00	30	–	–	–	–	–	–
Patel, R.K.	30	790	27.24	161	2	3	–	–	–	–
Patel, R.S.	28	1060	46.08	131	4	5	5	47.60	2-65	5.92
Patel, S.R.	245	6270	35.22	136*	8	33	225	33.29	6-13	5.40
Paterson, D.	107	388	12.93	29	–	–	148	30.38	5-19	5.30
Patterson-White, L.A.	22	314	18.47	62*	–	1	32	23.21	5-19	4.88
Payne, D.A.	70	222	20.18	40	–	–	115	25.46	7-29	5.71
Pennington, D.Y.	18	109	18.16	35	–	–	31	29.51	5-67	5.97
Pepper, M.S.	7	134	26.80	63	–	1	–	–	–	0/0
Pettman, T.H.S.	4	5	–	5*	–	–	6	31.83	4-44	6.36
Phillips, J.P.	1	11	11.00	11	–	–	–	–	–	–
Podmore, H.W.	29	184	14.15	40	–	–	28	48.14	4-57	6.19
Pollock, E.J.	35	713	22.28	103*	1	2	–	–	–	–
Pope, O.J.D.	31	767	33.34	93*	–	5	–	–	–	–
Porter, J.A.	41	55	9.16	10*	–	–	40	38.70	4-29	4.88
Potts, M.J.	13	59	14.75	30	–	–	18	25.22	4-62	6.05
Potts, N.J.	7	13	13.00	6*	–	–	5	63.20	2-63	7.18
Prest, T.J.	30	1041	37.17	181	2	7	7	33.71	2-28	5.64
Price, O.J.	20	831	51.93	116*	2	3	7	36.71	2-12	5.84
Price, T.J.	16	229	20.81	45	–	–	19	36.36	4-26	5.56
Procter, L.A.	55	904	30.13	97	–	5	34	41.08	4-34	5.76
Pucovski, W.J.	14	333	27.75	137	1	2	–	–	–	–
Pujara, C.A.	124	5638	57.53	174	16	33	0	–	0- 8	8.00
Quinn, M.R.	47	166	11.85	36	–	–	59	39.28	4-71	6.25
Raine, B.A.	29	402	21.15	83	–	1	30	40.63	3-31	5.68
Ramji, U.	2	–	–	–	–	–	4	23.25	3-58	8.20
Reece, L.M.	55	1630	35.43	136	3	10	36	40.19	4-35	5.91
Revis, M.L.	23	393	23.11	58*	–	2	27	31.77	4-54	5.91
Rew, J.E.K.	21	642	30.57	114	2	1	–	–	–	18/0
Rhodes, W.M.H.	56	1470	31.27	113	1	7	33	39.03	3-22	6.04
Richards, J.A.	11	177	25.28	46	–	–	8	40.37	2-37	5.63
Roach, K.A.J.	119	400	13.33	34	–	–	156	29.69	6-27	5.01
Robinson, L.S.	2	0	0.00	0	–	–	1	56.00	1-42	7.00
Robinson, O.E.	15	122	15.25	30	–	–	16	38.93	3-31	5.97
Robinson, O.G.	26	821	39.09	206*	1	4	–	–	–	14/1
Robson, S.D.	39	1457	40.47	111	3	10	10	35.70	2-12	6.69
Roderick, G.H.	70	1678	31.07	137	3	10	–	–	–	59/6
Roland-Jones, T.S.	79	684	21.37	65	–	1	126	25.24	4-10	5.19
Root, W.T.	45	1308	45.10	113*	3	7	6	51.66	2-36	6.36
Rossington, A.M.	49	1381	37.32	97	–	11	–	–	–	34/5
Roy, J.J.	211	7252	37.96	180	19	36	0	–	0-12	12.00
Rushworth, C.	87	215	11.31	38*	–	–	140	24.40	5-31	5.17
Russell, A.K.	9	5	–	3*	–	–	6	81.50	2-69	6.43

	M	Runs	Avge	HS	100	50	Wkts	Avge	Best	Econ
Sales, J.J.G.	16	207	34.50	35*	–	–	6	69.33	2-31	6.33
Salisbury, M.E.T.	20	10	10.00	5*	–	–	24	30.62	4-55	5.28
Salt, P.D.	32	1043	35.96	137*	2	5	–	–	–	10/0
Sams, D.R.	19	392	24.50	62	–	2	24	28.83	5-46	5.26
Sanderson, B.W.	48	159	9.35	31	–	–	61	28.85	3-17	5.42
Schadendorf, D.J.	24	247	15.43	44*	–	–	–	–	–	18/5
Scrimshaw, G.L.S.	5	13	–	13*	–	–	7	30.85	3-66	7.53
Scriven, T.A.R.	20	183	22.87	42	–	–	21	28.14	5-66	5.48
Seales, J.N.T.	16	17	5.66	16*	–	–	13	47.92	3-40	5.72
Shaikh, H.	9	127	25.40	38	–	–	–	–	–	–
Shan Masood	112	5012	53.89	182*	14	31	2	8.50	2- 0	4.25
Shaw, J.	13	14	3.50	8*	–	–	13	47.76	4-36	6.22
Shaw, P.P.	57	3056	57.66	244	10	11	–	–	–	–
Sibley, D.P.	36	865	27.90	115	3	1	1	62.00	1-20	6.88
Sikandar Raza	234	7049	36.71	141	12	35	163	36.08	4-33	4.89
Simpson, J.A.	103	1782	25.82	82*	–	8	–	–	–	98/21
Singh, J.	4	24	24.00	19*	–	–	5	35.00	3-74	6.25
Sisodiya, P.	7	20	6.66	7	–	–	8	41.75	3-76	5.38
Slater, B.T.	60	2609	52.18	148*	6	17	0	–	0-17	5.66
Smale, W.T.E.	3	100	33.33	48	–	–	–	–	–	–
Smeed, W.C.F.	1	0	0.00	0	–	–	–	–	–	–
Smith, J.L.	17	434	39.45	85	–	3	–	–	–	14/2
Smith, K.	14	137	22.83	29*	–	–	–	–	–	–
Smith, N.G.	38	750	28.84	81	–	3	44	32.77	3-21	5.46
Smith, R.A.J.	21	74	8.22	14	–	–	19	39.89	4- 7	6.40
Smith, T.M.J.	106	617	19.90	65	–	2	96	38.36	4-26	5.23
Snater, S.	31	276	18.40	64	–	1	42	31.00	5-29	5.79
Sowter, N.A.	19	134	14.88	31	–	–	36	25.77	6-62	5.52
Steel, C.T.	29	515	23.40	77	–	5	24	34.25	4-33	5.46
Stewart, G.	28	334	15.18	49	–	–	26	37.34	4-42	5.66
Stone, O.P.	34	127	18.14	24*	–	–	31	40.09	4-71	5.53
Stoneman, M.D.	106	3543	37.69	144*	7	20	1	41.00	1- 8	11.18
Sutherland, W.J.	25	261	13.73	66	–	2	39	31.25	5-45	5.76
Swindells, H.J.	20	506	33.73	117*	1	4	–	–	–	16/3
Tattersall, J.A.	32	697	31.68	89	–	7	–	–	–	27/3
Taylor, J.M.R.	77	2105	42.10	121	2	18	40	32.65	4-31	5.35
Taylor, M.D.	36	106	17.66	51*	–	1	29	49.65	3-39	5.44
Taylor, T.A.I.	30	785	52.33	112	2	5	33	41.51	3-24	6.13
Tear, C.J.	2	11	5.50	11	–	–	–	–	–	2/1
Thain, N.R.M.	6	159	39.75	75*	–	2	0	–	0-25	8.66
Thomas, G.W.	10	216	21.60	75	–	1	6	34.16	2-42	5.85
Thomas, J.F.	9	59	11.80	22	–	–	6	42.66	3-40	6.56
Thompson, J.A.	1	–	–	–	–	–	0	–	0-43	8.60
Thomson, A.T.	26	441	31.50	68*	–	2	31	31.64	3-25	5.60
Tickner, B.M.	50	76	10.85	24*	–	–	63	35.60	4-37	5.71
Tongue, J.C.	15	99	19.80	34	–	–	16	45.50	2-35	6.92
Tremain, C.P.	35	316	19.75	50	–	1	56	28.76	5-25	5.64
Trevaskis, L.	32	507	23.04	76*	–	3	35	36.05	4-50	5.23
Tribe, A.M.	10	558	69.75	115*	2	3	2	91.00	1-37	5.05
Turner, J.A.	15	34	11.33	12	–	–	27	19.59	5-25	5.18
Umeed, A.R.I.	14	745	57.30	172*	3	3	3	10.33	3-31	3.87
Usama Mir	50	322	10.38	42	–	–	83	26.90	7-14	5.71
van Buuren, G.L.	86	1878	30.29	119*	2	8	68	31.80	5-35	4.78
van der Gugten, T.	67	415	15.96	49	–	–	78	34.71	5-24	5.34
van der Merwe, R.E.	188	2901	26.86	165*	1	11	251	26.62	5-26	4.87
Vasconcelos, R.S.	49	1504	32.69	112	4	7	–	–	–	33/3

	M	Runs	Avge	HS	100	50	Wkts	Avge	Best	Econ
Vince, J.M.	148	5199	39.68	190	10	25	3	54.00	1-18	5.58
Virdi, G.S.	10	31	5.16	8	–	–	7	41.42	3-38	5.80
Wagstaff, M.D.	5	74	18.50	36	–	–	–	–	–	–
Waite, M.J.	36	696	31.63	71	–	1	48	28.12	5-59	5.69
Walallawita, T.N.	9	83	11.85	29	–	–	5	87.20	2-54	5.45
Walker, R.I.	10	71	17.75	23	–	–	10	36.80	6-43	6.32
Walter, P.I.	16	253	25.30	50	–	1	14	31.00	4-37	7.07
Ward, H.D.	12	215	17.91	37	–	–	0	–	0-18	7.90
Weatherley, J.J.	30	804	32.16	105*	2	4	8	27.62	4-25	4.05
Webster, B.J.	44	988	28.22	121	1	5	26	40.76	3-38	5.68
Wells, B.J.J.	15	339	28.25	108*	1	1	–	–	–	–
Wells, L.W.P.	44	778	21.61	88	–	5	23	39.13	3-19	5.23
Westley, T.	112	3728	37.65	134	7	29	37	38.83	4-60	4.96
Wharton, J.H.	6	89	22.25	54*	–	1	–	–	–	–
Wheal, B.T.J.	32	80	7.27	18*	–	–	54	24.09	5-47	5.22
White, C.J.	20	88	14.66	29	–	–	24	31.91	4-20	5.41
White, R.G.	15	239	23.90	55	–	1	–	–	–	19/3
Whiteley, R.A.	81	1660	27.66	131	1	10	14	40.21	4-58	6.66
Willey, D.J.	150	2067	25.83	167	3	7	177	30.27	5-30	5.62
Williams, W.S.A.	54	167	9.82	19*	–	–	73	29.10	4-20	5.05
Woakes, C.R.	196	2134	22.70	95*	–	6	241	32.65	6-45	5.44
Wood, C.P.	79	400	12.90	41	–	–	106	27.96	5-22	5.38
Wood, L.	6	83	41.50	52	–	1	5	36.80	2-36	5.93
Worrall, D.J.	43	128	10.66	31*	–	–	50	38.88	5-62	5.39
Wright, C.J.C.	126	321	11.88	42	–	–	139	33.97	6-35	5.44
Yates, R.M.	25	1010	40.40	114	3	6	4	84.75	1-27	5.40
Young, W.A.	96	3548	41.74	136	10	18	–	–	–	–
Zafar Gohar	90	1071	18.15	62	–	5	125	29.72	5-56	4.78
Zaib, S.A.	25	477	25.10	136	1	1	15	42.93	4-23	5.75
Zain Ul Hassan	5	47	15.66	26*	–	–	7	26.57	4-25	6.64

TWENTY20 CAREER RECORDS

Compiled by Philip Bailey

The following career records, to the end of the 2023 season, include all players currently registered with first-class counties or teams in The Hundred. Performances in The Hundred are included.

	M	Runs	Avge	HS	100	50	Wkts	Avge	Best	Econ
Abbott, K.J.	156	324	13.50	30	–	–	157	28.56	5-14	8.27
Abbott, S.A.	146	809	12.84	110*	1	–	181	21.42	5-16	8.56
Abell, T.B.	99	2187	31.69	101*	1	10	2	50.00	1-11	10.00
Ackermann, C.N.	180	3838	26.28	85	–	21	80	29.30	7-18	7.29
Agar, W.A.	57	89	6.84	15	–	–	74	22.71	4- 6	8.79
Ahmed, R.	43	257	12.85	49	–	–	42	26.26	4-22	7.65
Aitchison, B.W.	3	2	2.00	2	–	–	4	31.50	2-30	12.60
Akhter, Z.	3	24	24.00	11*	–	–	3	31.00	2-36	8.45
Albert, T.E.	23	263	20.23	38	–	–	–	–	–	–
Aldridge, K.L.	5	43	–	32*	–	–	0	–	0-13	11.60
Ali, M.M.	297	5972	24.47	121*	2	30	197	24.86	5-34	7.62
Allen, F.H.	98	2682	28.23	101	1	18	0	–	0- 8	8.00
Allison, B.M.J.	18	17	5.66	6*	–	–	14	33.85	3-33	10.23
Alsop, T.P.	61	1285	24.71	85	–	7	–	–	–	21/3
Anderson, J.M.	44	23	5.75	16	–	–	41	32.14	3-23	8.47
Andersson, M.K.	35	265	12.04	25*	–	–	28	30.35	3-32	10.94
Archer, J.C.	135	560	16.00	36	–	–	169	23.00	4-18	7.71
Atkinson, A.A.P.	45	82	9.11	14	–	–	62	19.09	4-20	8.66
Bailey, T.E.	35	27	4.50	10	–	–	31	26.16	5-17	9.21
Bairstow, J.M.	189	4573	30.69	114	3	27	–	–	–	101/15
Baker, J.O.	8	14	3.50	5	–	–	3	68.66	2-26	9.36
Ball, J.T.	119	55	7.85	18*	–	–	158	22.33	4-11	8.98
Bamber, E.R.	7	5	–	3*	–	–	4	41.75	3-29	10.54
Bancroft, C.T.	90	2049	32.01	95*	–	15	–	–	–	42/5
Banton, T.	122	2779	23.95	107*	2	16	–	–	–	67/8
Barker, K.H.D.	65	383	13.67	46	–	–	69	23.01	4-19	7.90
Barnard, E.G.	112	832	15.12	43*	–	–	61	39.21	3-29	9.00
Bartlett, G.A.	8	148	21.14	82*	–	1	–	–	–	–
Bartlett, X.C.	29	188	37.60	42*	–	–	28	26.07	4-30	8.47
Bashir, S.	5	–	–	–	–	–	4	23.50	3-26	8.54
Beard, A.P.	21	40	13.33	13	–	–	21	25.04	4-29	9.56
Bedingham, D.G.	55	1014	20.28	73	–	6	–	–	–	15/1
Bell, G.J.	7	65	21.66	31	–	–	–	–	–	4/0
Bell-Drummond, D.J.	150	4339	31.67	112*	2	34	5	38.20	2-19	10.32
Benjamin, C.G.	53	847	24.20	68*	–	3	–	–	–	21/0
Bess, D.M.	45	119	13.22	42*	–	–	31	30.67	3-15	7.60
Bethell, J.G.	21	209	12.29	32*	–	–	1	96.00	1-21	8.72
Bevan, T.R.	4	42	14.00	21	–	–	0	–	0-24	12.00
Billings, S.W.	284	5434	23.72	95*	–	28	–	–	–	170/24
Blake, J.W.	2	–	–	–	–	–	–	–	–	4/0
Blatherwick, J.M.	5	7	7.00	7	–	–	5	29.00	2-21	9.88
Bohannon, J.J.	26	130	10.00	35	–	–	–	–	–	–
Boland, S.M.	62	71	10.14	10	–	–	75	25.36	4-30	8.33
Booth, M.G.	6	–	–	–	–	–	5	31.40	2-24	7.02
Borthwick, S.G.	116	729	17.78	62	–	1	82	25.69	4-18	8.21
Bracey, J.R.	51	809	20.22	70	–	3	–	–	–	25/12
Briggs, D.R.	233	256	11.13	35*	–	–	254	22.33	5-19	7.34
Broad, J.	15	418	38.00	62	–	3	4	33.50	2-11	8.12
Brook, H.C.	122	2982	33.50	105*	3	11	1	26.00	1-13	13.00
Brookes, H.J.H.	49	188	13.42	31*	–	–	58	25.91	5-25	9.23

	M	Runs	Avge	HS	100	50	Wkts	Avge	Best	Econ
Brooks, J.A.	76	77	12.83	33*	–	–	72	25.72	5-21	7.77
Brown, B.C.	82	840	15.00	68	–	1	–	–	–	41/7
Brown, P.R.	85	64	10.66	10*	–	–	104	24.82	4-21	9.53
Browne, N.L.J.	14	165	16.50	38	–	–	–	–	–	–
Bruce, T.C.	104	2368	27.53	93*	–	16	12	29.33	3- 9	8.98
Budinger, S.G.	14	131	10.91	24	–	–	2	10.50	2-21	5.25
Burgess, M.G.K.	66	791	17.97	64*	–	2	–	–	–	26/12
Burns, R.J.	68	826	17.20	56*	–	2	–	–	–	28/2
Bushnell, J.J.	4	73	–	40*	–	–	1	6.00	1- 6	6.00
Buttler, J.C.	387	10577	34.45	124	6	75	–	–	–	230/38
Byrom, E.J.	39	577	18.03	54*	–	1	–	–	–	–
Came, H.R.C.	23	526	23.90	56	–	2	–	–	–	–
Carlson, K.S.	60	1018	19.96	77	–	3	2	30.50	2-13	11.09
Carse, B.A.	76	738	18.45	58	–	2	40	41.95	3-23	9.04
Carter, M.	76	168	9.88	23*	–	–	71	26.54	3-14	7.75
Carter, O.J.	11	133	14.77	64	–	1	–	–	–	2/1
Chappell, Z.J.	42	110	10.00	16	–	–	58	20.58	4-33	9.36
Charlesworth, B.G.	13	299	24.91	56	–	2	1	93.00	1-32	12.40
Charlesworth, L.A.	1	1	1.00	1	–	–	1	32.00	1-32	10.66
Chohan, J.A.	13	55	18.33	37	–	–	5	49.20	1-13	7.93
Clark, G.	96	2224	25.27	102*	1	13	0	–	0- 8	15.23
Clark, J.	111	1111	22.22	60	–	1	60	30.48	4-22	8.97
Clark, T.G.R.	14	294	21.00	47	–	–	–	–	–	–
Clarke, J.M.	173	4349	27.35	136	4	27	–	–	–	73/6
Coad, B.O.	12	14	4.66	7	–	–	13	24.84	3-40	8.93
Cobb, J.J.	198	3991	23.89	103	1	24	76	31.21	5-25	7.81
Cohen, M.A.R.	12	22	22.00	7*	–	–	9	32.11	2-17	8.58
Coles, J.M.	11	122	17.42	35	–	–	1	127.00	1-15	9.07
Conners, S.	18	7	2.33	2*	–	–	13	31.30	3-25	11.20
Cook, S.J.	70	43	7.16	18	–	–	76	25.53	4-15	8.63
Cooke, C.B.	152	2593	24.23	113*	1	7	–	–	–	89/14
Coughlin, P.	62	737	21.05	53	–	1	63	24.31	5-42	9.56
Cox, J.M.	86	1798	31.54	94	–	10	–	–	–	68/6
Cox, O.B.	156	2359	25.92	61*	–	5	–	–	–	74/34
Cracknell, J.B.	46	1071	24.34	77	–	5	–	–	–	18/0
Crane, M.S.	88	86	21.50	12*	–	–	95	24.20	4-24	8.00
Crawley, Z.	62	1534	27.89	108*	1	6	–	–	–	–
Critchley, M.J.J.	123	1803	22.53	80*	–	5	104	24.72	5-28	7.98
Crocombe, H.T.	17	21	21.00	12*	–	–	14	33.14	3-31	10.79
Croft, S.J.	238	5281	31.06	101	1	29	78	28.34	3- 6	7.42
Cullen, B.C.	31	72	10.28	20*	–	–	42	21.59	4-32	9.30
Curran, S.M.	199	2624	20.18	72*	–	14	191	28.26	5-10	8.61
Curran, T.K.	192	1720	21.77	67*	–	5	202	25.46	4-22	8.84
Currie, B.J.	12	0	–	0*	–	–	17	12.29	5-13	5.97
Currie, S.W.	21	9	2.25	3	–	–	28	19.53	4-24	8.70
Dal, A.K.	25	192	13.71	35	–	–	0	–	0- 8	8.00
Dale, A.S.	3	0	0.00	0	–	–	4	29.25	2-36	10.63
Das, R.J.	19	311	19.43	72	–	2	–	–	–	–
Davey, J.H.	87	338	21.12	24	–	–	107	21.21	4-18	8.80
Davies, A.L.	126	2635	25.33	94*	–	16	–	–	–	75/19
Davies, J.L.B.	25	426	21.30	47	–	–	–	–	–	5/2
Dawson, L.A.	245	2457	18.33	82	–	6	191	25.98	5-17	7.31
de Caires, J.M.	11	105	15.00	28	–	–	8	30.87	2-34	9.14
de Lange, M.	138	398	11.37	28*	–	–	154	25.22	5-20	8.69
de Leede, B.F.W.	41	732	31.82	91*	–	5	33	20.78	3-19	8.90
Denly, J.L.	272	6559	26.88	127	5	34	47	26.91	4-19	8.03
Dent, C.D.J.	78	1543	24.10	87	–	8	5	33.60	1- 4	8.40
Dickson, S.R.	43	831	30.77	53	–	4	1	9.00	1- 9	9.00

	M	Runs	Avge	HS	100	50	Wkts	Avge	Best	Econ
D'Oliveira, B.L.	136	2150	24.43	71	–	12	77	29.23	4-11	7.69
Donald, A.H.T.	64	1009	18.68	76	–	5	–	–	–	–
Douthwaite, D.A.	49	544	18.75	53	–	2	41	27.58	4-23	9.14
Drissell, G.S.	5	0	0.00	0	–	–	1	63.00	1-20	6.87
Duckett, B.M.	184	4497	30.18	96	–	27	–	–	–	86/2
Duke, H.G.	4	–	–	–	–	–	–	–	–	3/0
Dunn, M.P.	23	4	2.00	2	–	–	27	22.88	3- 8	9.15
du Plooy, J.L.	128	2698	30.65	92	–	15	14	20.57	4-15	8.42
Edwards, M.W.	3	0	–	0*	–	–	2	42.00	1-19	9.33
Elgar, D.	82	2028	33.80	88*	–	11	29	24.93	4-23	6.91
Ellis, N.T.	118	336	9.88	24	–	–	145	23.04	4- 6	8.05
Eskinazi, S.S.	95	2839	34.20	102*	1	21	–	–	–	–
Evans, L.J.	258	5970	31.92	118*	3	38	1	35.00	1- 5	9.54
Evison, J.D.M.	10	62	31.00	46	–	–	4	55.50	3-25	9.65
Fernandes, N.S.	7	11	2.75	8	–	–	4	35.00	1- 6	10.76
Ferreira, D.	38	722	31.39	82*	–	3	10	22.30	2-18	6.96
Finch, A.W.	16	50	12.50	30*	–	–	14	38.57	3-38	9.93
Finch, H.Z.	27	310	18.23	47	–	–	–	–	–	10/0
Fisher, M.D.	45	61	8.71	19	–	–	46	27.10	5-22	9.03
Fletcher, L.J.	106	181	6.96	27	–	–	116	25.47	5-32	8.45
Foakes, B.T.	78	859	20.95	75*	–	4	–	–	–	38/10
Foster, M.T.	9	10	10.00	8	–	–	10	19.40	4-30	9.23
Fuller, J.K.	171	1616	20.20	57	–	3	148	25.91	6-28	8.73
Garrett, G.A.	2	–	–	–	–	–	1	39.00	1-19	9.75
Garton, G.H.S.	81	562	16.05	46	–	–	72	27.19	4-16	9.02
Gay, E.N.	13	290	24.16	53	–	1	0	–	0- 8	8.00
Geddes, B.B.A.	6	44	7.33	28	–	–	–	–	–	–
Gleeson, R.J.	82	51	5.66	8	–	–	91	24.31	5-33	8.25
Glover, B.D.	46	36	9.00	15	–	–	53	21.03	4-12	8.18
Goldsworthy, L.P.	25	257	19.76	48	–	–	23	21.47	3-14	7.96
Gorvin, A.W.	5	41	10.25	12	–	–	3	50.00	1-30	9.27
Green, B.G.F.	57	556	20.59	43*	–	–	64	20.26	5-29	8.99
Gregory, L.	206	2448	20.74	76*	–	7	172	25.95	5-24	8.86
Gubbins, N.R.T.	46	626	15.65	57*	–	2	10	21.20	3-27	7.85
Guest, B.D.	44	620	29.52	54	–	1	–	–	–	28/5
Hain, S.R.	122	3605	40.50	112*	1	26	–	–	–	–
Haines, T.J.	4	52	13.00	27	–	–	–	–	–	–
Hales, A.D.	418	11549	30.07	119*	6	74	0	–	0- 2	14.00
Hameed, H.	2	41	20.50	23	–	–	–	–	–	–
Hamidullah Qadri	3	–	–	–	–	–	1	66.00	1-34	8.25
Hammond, M.A.H.	94	1706	20.55	63	–	5	0	–	0-17	8.50
Handscomb, P.S.P.	120	1877	22.61	103*	1	6	–	–	–	58/14
Hannon-Dalby, O.J.	63	55	9.16	14*	–	–	75	25.58	4-20	8.82
Haris Rauf	173	218	7.26	19	–	–	230	22.43	5-27	8.21
Harmer, S.R.	167	1088	16.00	43	–	–	151	26.25	4-19	7.59
Harris, J.A.R.	60	168	10.50	18	–	–	48	34.41	4-23	9.35
Harrison, C.G.	46	151	10.06	23	–	–	45	19.11	5-11	7.64
Hartley, T.W.	82	245	12.89	39	–	–	68	26.47	4-16	7.85
Hassan Ali	173	556	11.58	45	–	–	227	21.95	5-20	7.92
Haynes, J.A.	34	761	23.06	63	–	3	–	–	–	–
Heldreich, F.J.	30	13	4.33	4	–	–	38	22.26	4-27	8.76
Helm, T.G.	89	215	11.94	28*	–	–	100	26.39	5-11	9.18
Higgins, R.F.	115	1929	26.42	77*	–	6	84	25.76	5-13	9.26
Hill, G.C.H.	14	72	12.00	19*	–	–	2	42.50	1- 9	8.09
Hill, L.J.	85	1097	18.91	59	–	4	–	–	–	34/3
Holden, M.D.E.	60	1426	26.90	121*	2	5	0	–	0-12	12.00
Holland, I.G.	23	238	26.44	65	–	1	15	22.80	2- 3	6.19
Hollman, L.B.K.	47	623	18.87	51	–	1	38	27.23	3-18	8.60

	M	Runs	Avge	HS	100	50	Wkts	Avge	Best	Econ
Horton, A.J.	4	1	1.00	1*	–	–	–	–	–	0/1
Hose, A.J.	130	3278	30.92	119	2	18	–	–	–	–
Howell, B.A.C.	208	2574	22.18	57	–	6	206	22.67	5-18	7.33
Hudson-Prentice, F.J.	41	423	16.92	49*	–	–	31	29.96	3-36	9.93
Hughes, D.P.	98	2144	27.13	96	–	13	–	–	–	–
Hull, J.O.	5	2	–	2*	–	–	6	27.33	3-35	9.64
Hutton, B.A.	9	50	16.66	18*	–	–	5	51.00	2-28	8.89
Ibrahim, D.K.	4	47	11.75	18	–	–	–	–	–	–
Ingram, C.A.	333	8188	29.45	127*	4	49	39	32.92	4-32	7.91
Jacks, W.G.	138	3655	29.95	108*	1	29	42	19.76	4-15	7.35
James, L.W.	15	154	15.40	37	–	–	2	82.50	1-23	12.22
Jennings, K.K.	84	1577	32.85	108	1	7	22	28.54	4-37	7.38
Johnson, S.H.	16	1	1.00	1*	–	–	14	29.35	3- 1	7.61
Jones, M.A.	32	760	27.14	86	–	2	–	–	–	–
Jones, R.P.	35	353	35.30	61*	–	1	0	–	0-10	10.00
Jordan, C.J.	328	1848	16.35	73	–	2	342	27.38	4- 6	8.58
Karvelas, A.	8	19	6.33	10	–	–	10	19.50	4-20	8.54
Kashif Ali	24	378	22.23	69	–	1	0	–	0-14	14.00
Kellaway, B.I.	2	4	2.00	3	–	–	0	–	0- 7	8.50
Keogh, R.I.	88	1096	26.09	59*	–	4	16	27.43	3-30	8.28
Khushi, F.I.N.	22	452	21.52	67	–	4	–	–	–	–
Kimber, L.P.J.	21	320	22.85	59*	–	3	0	–	0-16	16.00
Klaassen, F.J.	103	85	5.66	13	–	–	112	25.83	5-19	8.36
Kohler-Cadmore, T.	169	4423	29.68	127	1	33	–	–	–	93/3
Labuschagne, M.	40	978	27.16	93*	–	5	24	23.58	3-13	9.12
Lamb, D.J.	56	256	12.80	29*	–	–	43	29.95	3-23	8.84
Lamb, M.J.	10	168	24.00	39	–	–	0	–	0- 9	9.00
Lammonby, T.A.	70	860	19.54	90	–	1	15	30.53	2-32	9.19
Lavelle, G.I.D.	2	18	9.00	12	–	–	–	–	–	0/0
Lawes, T.E.	9	12	6.00	6	–	–	6	40.50	2-17	10.19
Lawrence, D.W.	107	2398	26.94	93	–	17	35	22.48	4-20	7.94
Leach, J.	54	261	10.44	24	–	–	52	26.05	5-33	9.57
Leach, M.J.	2	–	–	–	–	–	5	12.00	3-28	7.50
Leaning, J.A.	105	1854	27.67	81*	–	7	21	23.52	3-15	7.71
Leech, D.J.	4	1	1.00	1*	–	–	6	15.00	3-13	8.18
Lees, A.Z.	70	1690	28.64	90	–	10	–	–	–	–
Lenham, A.D.	21	15	15.00	7*	–	–	13	33.15	4-26	7.98
Leonard, E.O.	1	–	–	–	–	–	1	8.00	1- 8	4.00
Libby, J.D.	52	1150	30.26	78*	–	5	1	77.00	1-11	8.55
Lintott, J.B.	77	231	12.15	41	–	–	87	22.93	4-20	7.73
Livingstone, L.S.	238	5710	28.40	103	2	31	101	26.00	4-17	8.41
Lloyd, D.L.	79	1620	23.47	97*	–	10	6	31.16	2-13	8.90
Luxton, W.A.	3	11	3.66	7	–	–	–	–	–	–
Lyon, N.M.	51	60	5.45	11	–	–	57	21.87	5-23	7.34
Lyth, A.	190	4428	25.30	161	1	29	25	27.08	5-31	7.75
McAndrew, N.J.	59	250	14.70	30	–	–	54	30.90	4-31	9.07
McDermott, B.R.	152	3814	30.51	127	3	24	–	–	–	82/12
McIlroy, J.P.	15	2	1.00	2*	–	–	24	20.45	4-36	9.12
McKerr, C.	16	21	5.25	7*	–	–	13	33.46	2-19	9.88
McManus, L.D.	89	876	16.22	60*	–	2	–	–	–	45/20
Madsen, W.L.	172	4403	31.45	109*	2	30	22	34.31	2-20	8.03
Mahmood, S.	62	56	8.00	11*	–	–	78	22.16	4-14	8.72
Malan, D.J.	316	8667	32.95	117	5	56	23	31.39	2-10	7.64
Mike, B.W.M.	53	567	19.55	37	–	–	43	26.76	4-22	10.40
Miles, C.N.	55	58	7.25	11*	–	–	60	24.53	4-29	8.83
Miller, A.H.	1	5	5.00	5	–	–	–	–	–	–
Mills, T.S.	193	149	5.96	27	–	–	232	23.03	4-13	8.05
Milne, A.F.	161	402	12.18	22	–	–	182	23.48	5-11	7.71

	M	Runs	Avge	HS	100	50	Wkts	Avge	Best	Econ
Milnes, M.E.	47	64	8.00	14*	–	–	45	30.68	5-22	9.29
Mir Hamza	53	67	16.75	19*	–	–	52	30.46	4- 9	8.20
Mohammad Abbas	32	32	10.66	15*	–	–	26	37.34	3-22	8.59
Mohammad Amir	259	296	6.16	21*	–	–	303	21.83	6-17	7.11
Montgomery, M.	18	330	22.00	51	–	2	2	26.50	1- 5	7.57
Moores, T.J.	130	2113	24.56	80*	–	8	–	–	–	68/23
Moriarty, D.T.	37	29	7.25	9*	–	–	32	25.84	3-25	7.36
Mousley, D.R.	36	672	22.40	63*	–	5	28	18.85	4-28	7.38
Mulder, P.W.A.	78	1313	27.35	83*	–	8	46	28.23	2-10	8.51
Mullaney, S.J.	186	1802	17.16	79	–	3	133	28.18	4-19	7.84
Muyeye, T.S.	23	383	17.40	62	–	3	–	–	–	–
Nair, K.K.	150	2989	25.11	111	2	16	4	20.25	1- 2	6.23
Naveen-ul-Haq	145	265	9.13	25*	–	–	175	23.42	5-11	8.09
Neser, M.G.	105	582	13.53	48*	–	–	118	24.31	4-25	8.40
Northeast, S.A.	155	3791	30.08	114	1	26	–	–	–	–
Organ, F.S.	3	21	7.00	9	–	–	3	18.00	2-21	6.75
O'Riordan, M.K.	3	15	15.00	13*	–	–	3	18.33	2-24	5.50
Orr, A.G.H.	10	223	22.30	41	–	–	–	–	–	–
Overton, C.	92	407	14.53	35*	–	–	95	26.27	4-25	8.63
Overton, J.	109	991	19.82	83*	–	1	70	30.05	5-47	9.29
Parkinson, C.F.	103	298	11.03	27*	–	–	116	23.43	4-20	7.58
Parkinson, M.W.	103	74	4.62	18	–	–	139	18.96	4- 9	7.68
Patel, R.K.	42	793	20.86	104	1	1	–	–	–	–
Patel, R.S.	7	7	3.50	5*	–	–	0	–	0- 8	10.28
Patel, S.R.	392	6367	24.96	90*	–	33	332	26.06	4- 5	7.33
Paterson, D.	106	175	8.33	24*	–	–	110	25.37	4-24	8.03
Payne, D.A.	153	122	5.08	16	–	–	188	22.83	5-24	8.34
Pennington, D.Y.	57	63	9.00	10*	–	–	53	27.83	4- 9	9.03
Pepper, M.S.	59	1291	26.89	86*	–	7	–	–	–	24/0
Phillips, G.D.	217	5712	31.91	116*	5	38	17	30.05	2-11	8.13
Podmore, H.W.	24	37	5.28	9	–	–	23	28.91	3-13	9.21
Pollock, E.J.	71	1210	19.83	77	–	6	–	–	–	–
Pope, O.J.D.	47	1055	31.02	62	–	3	–	–	–	–
Porter, J.A.	25	5	5.00	1*	–	–	19	33.47	4-20	9.06
Potts, M.J.	44	136	22.66	40*	–	–	49	25.06	3- 8	8.67
Prest, T.J.	28	579	22.26	64	–	4	2	21.50	1- 8	7.16
Price, O.J.	12	193	17.54	46	–	–	10	17.80	3-21	9.28
Price, T.J.	6	44	11.00	25	–	–	1	149.00	1-29	10.64
Procter, L.A.	37	240	14.11	25*	–	–	14	31.28	3-22	8.87
Pujara, C.A.	71	1556	29.35	100*	1	9	–	–	–	–
Quinn, M.R.	74	29	14.50	8*	–	–	75	28.66	4-20	8.84
Raine, B.A.	116	1185	18.80	113	1	4	106	25.83	4-30	8.60
Rashid, A.U.	275	822	11.41	36*	–	–	307	23.17	4- 2	7.49
Rashid Khan	410	2071	13.10	79*	–	2	556	18.30	6-17	6.45
Reece, L.M.	93	1944	22.87	97*	–	16	32	31.50	3-33	8.75
Revis, M.L.	31	205	17.08	42	–	–	23	33.30	2-18	9.45
Rew, J.E.K.	1	47	47.00	47	–	–	–	–	–	0/0
Rhodes, W.M.H.	56	659	14.64	79	–	1	36	20.58	4-34	9.01
Roach, K.A.J.	46	59	7.37	12	–	–	28	43.89	3-18	8.08
Robinson, L.S.	3	–	–	–	–	–	2	37.00	2-28	10.57
Robinson, O.E.	49	92	7.07	31	–	–	45	29.02	4-15	8.86
Robinson, O.G.	46	849	25.72	69*	–	6	–	–	–	19/6
Robson, S.D.	7	128	25.60	60	–	1	–	–	–	–
Roderick, G.H.	48	262	13.10	32	–	–	–	–	–	27/1
Roland-Jones, T.S.	61	326	14.17	40	–	–	74	24.04	5-21	8.80
Root, J.E.	97	2235	31.92	92*	–	14	24	31.00	2- 7	8.58
Root, W.T.	50	634	21.13	41*	–	–	0	–	0- 6	12.33
Rossington, A.M.	151	2943	21.48	95	–	17	–	–	–	72/28

	M	Runs	Avge	HS	100	50	Wkts	Avge	Best	Econ
Roy, J.J.	333	8640	27.69	145*	6	57	1	39.00	1-23	13.00
Rushworth, C.	85	20	3.33	5	–	–	78	27.19	3-14	7.84
Russell, A.K.	3	1	–	1*	–	–	2	41.00	1-27	7.45
Sales, J.J.G.	10	42	14.00	12	–	–	1	183.00	1-16	9.63
Salisbury, M.E.T.	12	4	4.00	1*	–	–	13	29.38	2-19	9.39
Salt, P.D.	211	4805	25.28	88*	–	32	–	–	–	102/13
Sams, D.R.	147	1688	17.76	98*	–	7	179	24.21	4-14	8.78
Sanderson, B.W.	76	63	7.87	12*	–	–	87	24.64	4-21	8.67
Scrimshaw, G.L.S.	48	19	19.00	5*	–	–	64	22.93	3-16	8.86
Scriven, T.A.R.	8	40	6.66	18	–	–	9	18.44	4-21	9.22
Seales, J.N.T.	27	2	–	1*	–	–	31	20.58	4-13	8.82
Shan Masood	158	3816	27.06	103*	1	25	–	–	–	–
Shaw, J.	31	20	6.66	14	–	–	24	29.12	3-32	8.96
Shaw, P.P.	100	2507	25.32	134	1	19	–	–	–	–
Short, M.W.	81	1676	23.27	100*	1	8	24	35.45	3-14	7.42
Sibley, D.P.	35	859	29.62	74*	–	7	5	67.60	2-33	8.89
Sikandar Raza	189	3626	23.69	95	–	21	97	28.83	4- 8	7.48
Simpson, J.A.	164	2655	21.76	84*	–	9	–	–	–	88/29
Singh, J.	2	–	–	–	–	–	0	–	0-17	21.50
Sisodiya, P.	41	64	10.66	23	–	–	40	30.57	3-26	8.20
Slater, B.T.	15	305	21.78	57	–	1	–	–	–	–
Smale, W.T.E.	8	72	10.28	27	–	–	–	–	–	–
Smeed, W.C.F.	87	2232	27.21	101*	1	14	–	–	–	–
Smith, J.L.	59	871	24.88	60	–	5	–	–	–	30/8
Smith, N.G.	41	250	11.36	38*	–	–	44	23.52	5-14	8.80
Smith, R.A.J.	42	107	8.23	22*	–	–	36	31.91	4- 6	8.67
Smith, T.M.J.	175	391	17.77	36*	–	–	179	22.62	5-16	7.36
Snater, S.	45	96	8.00	16*	–	–	37	30.75	3-13	9.69
Sowter, N.A.	109	232	11.04	37*	–	–	116	23.52	5-15	7.87
Stanley, M.T.	10	10	5.00	7	–	–	9	28.33	2-24	10.33
Steel, C.T.	14	120	13.33	37	–	–	6	35.00	3-41	10.50
Stewart, G.	64	632	19.15	76	–	3	66	24.40	4-48	8.85
Stone, O.P.	66	86	7.81	22*	–	–	67	27.05	4-21	8.71
Stoneman, M.D.	77	1343	20.04	89*	–	8	–	–	–	–
Sutherland, W.J.	44	327	14.86	42*	–	–	20	44.65	3-30	9.09
Swindells, H.J.	34	495	19.80	63	–	3	–	–	–	13/3
Tattersall, J.A.	54	526	21.04	53*	–	1	–	–	–	36/6
Taylor, J.M.R.	126	1663	21.59	80	–	2	27	36.51	4-16	8.23
Taylor, M.D.	55	120	10.90	23	–	–	44	33.34	3-16	8.79
Taylor, T.A.I.	47	339	18.83	50*	–	1	48	25.72	5-28	9.27
Thompson, J.A.	97	844	15.07	74	–	4	97	25.31	5-21	9.54
Thomson, A.T.	25	111	13.87	28	–	–	20	28.60	4-35	8.28
Tickner, B.M.	78	29	4.83	10*	–	–	108	22.19	5-19	8.75
Tongue, J.C.	15	4	4.00	2*	–	–	15	26.46	3-32	9.52
Topley, R.J.W.	148	98	12.25	14*	–	–	192	21.48	4-20	8.21
Tremain, C.P.	52	80	13.33	37*	–	–	46	31.28	3- 9	8.03
Trevaskis, L.	68	379	14.57	31*	–	–	56	29.62	4-16	7.95
Tribe, A.M.	21	395	21.94	73*	–	2	–	–	–	4/2
Turner, J.A.	12	1	–	1*	–	–	22	12.22	3-15	6.66
Usama Mir	95	396	12.37	39	–	–	96	25.18	4-19	7.83
van Buuren, G.L.	81	938	23.45	64	–	4	50	26.24	5- 8	7.15
van der Gugten, T.	120	442	14.25	48	–	–	133	22.93	5-21	8.32
van der Merwe, R.E.	321	2951	21.38	89*	–	10	299	24.15	6-20	7.25
Vasconcelos, R.S.	37	903	28.21	78*	–	5	–	–	–	20/2
Vince, J.M.	350	9637	31.91	129*	5	59	3	29.00	1- 5	6.69
Waite, M.J.	27	103	10.30	35*	–	–	18	34.00	3-18	9.68
Walallawita, T.N.	15	23	4.60	10	–	–	12	28.41	3-18	8.31
Walker, R.I.	14	29	4.83	19*	–	–	19	21.89	3-15	9.07

	M	Runs	Avge	HS	100	50	Wkts	Avge	Best	Econ
Walter, P.I.	112	1551	21.54	78	–	6	62	25.51	3-20	8.89
Ward, H.D.	26	442	21.04	54	–	2	1	16.00	1- 5	7.38
Weatherley, J.J.	69	1455	27.98	71	–	6	0	–	0- 9	9.00
Webster, B.J.	67	1133	26.34	78	–	8	9	54.55	2-19	7.09
Wells, B.J.J.	9	135	16.87	43*	–	–	–	–	–	–
Wells, L.W.P.	43	557	16.38	66	–	3	23	29.65	2-19	7.93
Westley, T.	111	2569	29.19	109*	2	10	8	38.75	2-27	7.56
Wharton, J.H.	8	157	22.42	111*	1	–	–	–	–	–
Wheal, B.T.J.	56	31	6.20	16	–	–	72	21.38	5-38	8.31
White, R.G.	3	11	11.00	11*	–	–	–	–	–	1/0
Whiteley, R.A.	209	3208	23.24	91*	–	6	7	38.42	2- 2	9.60
Willey, D.J.	270	3720	23.54	118	2	14	270	22.82	4- 7	7.88
Williams, W.S.A.	37	76	25.33	29*	–	–	30	26.23	5-12	9.57
Woakes, C.R.	147	961	22.34	57*	–	2	158	25.03	4-21	8.22
Wood, C.P.	185	504	11.72	31	–	–	194	26.53	5-32	8.26
Wood, L.	122	224	8.61	33*	–	–	127	25.48	5-50	8.46
Worrall, D.J.	75	159	14.45	62*	–	1	64	30.93	4-23	8.03
Wright, C.J.C.	62	30	4.28	6*	–	–	53	34.60	4-24	9.00
Yates, R.M.	27	699	25.88	71	–	6	1	79.00	1-13	7.90
Young, W.A.	92	2131	25.98	101	1	13	–	–	–	–
Zafar Gohar	70	352	14.66	37*	–	–	74	23.86	4-14	7.68
Zaib, S.A.	60	991	24.77	92	–	5	4	60.00	1-17	8.18
Zain Ul Hassan	3	14	14.00	11	–	–	0	–	0-23	12.66
Zampa, A.	241	272	6.32	23	–	–	283	22.04	6-19	7.32

FIRST-CLASS CRICKET RECORDS

To 31 December 2023

TEAM RECORDS

HIGHEST INNINGS TOTALS

1107	Victoria v New South Wales	Melbourne	1926-27
1059	Victoria v Tasmania	Melbourne	1922-23
952-6d	Sri Lanka v India	Colombo	1997-98
951-7d	Sindh v Baluchistan	Karachi	1973-74
944-6d	Hyderabad v Andhra	Secunderabad	1993-94
918	New South Wales v South Australia	Sydney	1900-01
912-8d	Holkar v Mysore	Indore	1945-46
910-6d	Railways v Dera Ismail Khan	Lahore	1964-65
903-7d	England v Australia	The Oval	1938
900-6d	Queensland v Victoria	Brisbane	2005-06
887	Yorkshire v Warwickshire	Birmingham	1896
880	Jharkhand v Nagaland	Kolkata	2021-22
864-9d	Boost Region v Speen Ghar Region	Kandahar	2021-22
863	Lancashire v Surrey	The Oval	1990
860-6d	Tamil Nadu v Goa	Panjim	1988-89
850-7d	Somerset v Middlesex	Taunton	2007

Excluding penalty runs in India, there have been 38 innings totals of 800 runs or more in first-class cricket. Tamil Nadu's total of 860-6d was boosted to 912 by 52 penalty runs.

HIGHEST SECOND INNINGS TOTAL

770	New South Wales v South Australia	Adelaide	1920-21

HIGHEST FOURTH INNINGS TOTAL

654-5	England (set 696 to win) v South Africa	Durban	1938-39

HIGHEST MATCH AGGREGATE

2376-37	Maharashtra v Bombay	Poona	1948-49

RECORD MARGIN OF VICTORY

Innings and 851 runs: Railways v Dera Ismail Khan	Lahore	1964-65

MOST RUNS IN A DAY

721	Australians v Essex	Southend	1948

MOST HUNDREDS IN AN INNINGS

6	Holkar v Mysore	Indore	1945-46
6	Multan v Lahore Blues	Lahore	2023-24

LOWEST INNINGS TOTALS

12	†Oxford University v MCC and Ground	Oxford	1877
12	Northamptonshire v Gloucestershire	Gloucester	1907
13	Auckland v Canterbury	Auckland	1877-78
13	Nottinghamshire v Yorkshire	Nottingham	1901
14	Surrey v Essex	Chelmsford	1983
15	MCC v Surrey	Lord's	1839
15	†Victoria v MCC	Melbourne	1903-04
15	†Northamptonshire v Yorkshire	Northampton	1908
15	Hampshire v Warwickshire	Birmingham	1922

† *Batted one man short*

There have been 29 instances of a team being dismissed for under 20.

LOWEST MATCH AGGREGATE BY ONE TEAM

34 (16 and 18)	Border v Natal	East London	1959-60

LOWEST COMPLETED MATCH AGGREGATE BY BOTH TEAMS

105	MCC v Australians	Lord's	1878

FEWEST RUNS IN AN UNINTERRUPTED DAY'S PLAY

95	Australia (80) v Pakistan (15-2)	Karachi	1956-57

TIED MATCHES

Before 1949 a match was considered to be tied if the scores were level after the fourth innings, even if the side batting last had wickets in hand when play ended. Law 22 was amended in 1948 and since then a match has been tied only when the scores are level after the fourth innings has been completed. There have been 41 tied first-class matches since then. The most recent is:

Central Punjab (257-9d & 355) v Khyber Pakhtunkhwa (300 & 312)	Karachi	2021-22

BATTING RECORDS

35,000 RUNS IN A CAREER

	Career	*I*	*NO*	*HS*	***Runs***	*Avge*	*100*
J.B.Hobbs	1905-34	1315	106	316*	**61237**	50.65	197
F.E.Woolley	1906-38	1532	85	305*	**58969**	40.75	145
E.H.Hendren	1907-38	1300	166	301*	**57611**	50.80	170
C.P.Mead	1905-36	1340	185	280*	**55061**	47.67	153
W.G.Grace	1865-1908	1493	105	344	**54896**	39.55	126
W.R.Hammond	1920-51	1005	104	336*	**50551**	56.10	167
H.Sutcliffe	1919-45	1088	123	313	**50138**	51.95	149
G.Boycott	1962-86	1014	162	261*	**48426**	56.83	151
T.W.Graveney	1948-71/72	1223	159	258	**47793**	44.91	122
G.A.Gooch	1973-2000	990	75	333	**44846**	49.01	128
T.W.Hayward	1893-1914	1138	96	315*	**43551**	41.79	104
D.L.Amiss	1960-87	1139	126	262*	**43423**	42.86	102
M.C.Cowdrey	1950-76	1130	134	307	**42719**	42.89	107
A.Sandham	1911-37/38	1000	79	325	**41284**	44.82	107
G.A.Hick	1983/84-2008	871	84	405*	**41112**	52.23	136
L.Hutton	1934-60	814	91	364	**40140**	55.51	129
M.J.K.Smith	1951-75	1091	139	204	**39832**	41.84	69
W.Rhodes	1898-1930	1528	237	267*	**39802**	30.83	58
J.H.Edrich	1956-78	979	104	310*	**39790**	45.47	103
R.E.S.Wyatt	1923-57	1141	157	232	**39405**	40.04	85
D.C.S.Compton	1936-64	839	88	300	**38942**	51.85	123
G.E.Tyldesley	1909-36	961	106	256*	**38874**	45.46	102
J.T.Tyldesley	1895-1923	994	62	295*	**37897**	40.60	86
K.W.R.Fletcher	1962-88	1167	170	228*	**37665**	37.77	63
C.G.Greenidge	1970-92	889	75	273*	**37354**	45.88	92
J.W.Hearne	1909-36	1025	116	285*	**37252**	40.98	96
L.E.G.Ames	1926-51	951	95	295	**37248**	43.51	102
D.Kenyon	1946-67	1159	59	259	**37002**	33.63	74
W.J.Edrich	1934-58	964	92	267*	**36965**	42.39	86
J.M.Parks	1949-76	1227	172	205*	**36673**	34.76	51
M.W.Gatting	1975-98	861	123	258	**36549**	49.52	94
D.Denton	1894-1920	1163	70	221	**36479**	33.37	69
G.H.Hirst	1891-1929	1215	151	341	**36323**	34.13	60
I.V.A.Richards	1971/72-93	796	63	322	**36212**	49.40	114
A.Jones	1957-83	1168	72	204*	**36049**	32.89	56
W.G.Quaife	1894-1928	1203	185	255*	**36012**	35.37	72
R.E.Marshall	1945/46-72	1053	59	228*	**35725**	35.94	68
M.R.Ramprakash	1987-2012	764	93	301*	**35659**	53.14	114
G.Gunn	1902-32	1061	82	220	**35208**	35.96	62

HIGHEST INDIVIDUAL INNINGS

501*	B.C.Lara	Warwickshire v Durham	Birmingham	1994
499	Hanif Mohammed	Karachi v Bahawalpur	Karachi	1958-59
452*	D.G.Bradman	New South Wales v Queensland	Sydney	1929-30
443*	B.B.Nimbalkar	Maharashtra v Kathiawar	Poona	1948-49
437	W.H.Ponsford	Victoria v Queensland	Melbourne	1927-28
429	W.H.Ponsford	Victoria v Tasmania	Melbourne	1922-23
428	Aftab Baloch	Sindh v Baluchistan	Karachi	1973-74
424	A.C.MacLaren	Lancashire v Somerset	Taunton	1895
410*	S.A.Northeast	Glamorgan v Leicestershire	Leicester	2022
405*	G.A.Hick	Worcestershire v Somerset	Taunton	1988
400*	B.C.Lara	West Indies v England	St John's	2003-04
394	Naved Latif	Sargodha v Gujranwala	Gujranwala	2000-01
390	S.C.Cook	Lions v Warriors	East London	2009-10
385	B.Sutcliffe	Otago v Canterbury	Christchurch	1952-53
383	C.W.Gregory	New South Wales v Queensland	Brisbane	1906-07
380	M.L.Hayden	Australia v Zimbabwe	Perth	2003-04
379	P.P.Shaw	Mumbai v Assam	Guwahati	2022-23
377	S.V.Manjrekar	Bombay v Hyderabad	Bombay	1990-91
375	B.C.Lara	West Indies v England	St John's	1993-94
374	D.P.M.D.Jayawardena	Sri Lanka v South Africa	Colombo	2006
369	D.G.Bradman	South Australia v Tasmania	Adelaide	1935-36
366	N.H.Fairbrother	Lancashire v Surrey	The Oval	1990
366	M.V.Sridhar	Hyderabad v Andhra	Secunderabad	1993-94
365*	C.Hill	South Australia v NSW	Adelaide	1900-01
365*	G.St A.Sobers	West Indies v Pakistan	Kingston	1957-58
364	L.Hutton	England v Australia	The Oval	1938
359*	V.M.Merchant	Bombay v Maharashtra	Bombay	1943-44
359*	S.B.Gohel	Gujarat v Orissa	Jaipur	2016-17
359	R.B.Simpson	New South Wales v Queensland	Brisbane	1963-64
357*	R.Abel	Surrey v Somerset	The Oval	1899
357	D.G.Bradman	South Australia v Victoria	Melbourne	1935-36
356	B.A.Richards	South Australia v W Australia	Perth	1970-71
355*	G.R.Marsh	W Australia v S Australia	Perth	1989-90
355*	K.P.Pietersen	Surrey v Leicestershire	The Oval	2015
355	B.Sutcliffe	Otago v Auckland	Dunedin	1949-50
354*	L.D.Chandimal	Sri Lanka Army v Saracens	Katunayake	2020
353	V.V.S.Laxman	Hyderabad v Karnataka	Bangalore	1999-00
352	W.H.Ponsford	Victoria v New South Wales	Melbourne	1926-27
352	C.A.Pujara	Saurashtra v Karnataka	Rajkot	2012-13
351*	S.M.Gugale	Maharashtra v Delhi	Mumbai	2016-17
351	K.D.K.Vithanage	Tamil Union v SL Air	Katunayake	2014-15
350	Rashid Israr	Habib Bank v National Bank	Lahore	1976-77

There have been 240 triple hundreds in first-class cricket, W.V.Raman (313) and Arjan Kripal Singh (302*) for Tamil Nadu v Goa at Panjim in 1988-89 providing the only instance of two batsmen scoring 300 in the same innings.

MOST HUNDREDS IN SUCCESSIVE INNINGS

6	C.B.Fry	Sussex and Rest of England	1901
6	D.G.Bradman	South Australia and D.G.Bradman's XI	1938-39
6	M.J.Procter	Rhodesia	1970-71

TWO DOUBLE HUNDREDS IN A MATCH

244	202*	A.E.Fagg	Kent v Essex	Colchester	1938
201	231	A.K.Perera	Nondescripts v Sinhalese	Colombo (PSO)	2018-19

TRIPLE HUNDRED AND HUNDRED IN A MATCH

333	123	G.A.Gooch	England v India	Lord's	1990
319	105	K.C.Sangakkara	Sri Lanka v Bangladesh	Chittagong	2013-14

DOUBLE HUNDRED AND HUNDRED IN A MATCH MOST TIMES

4	Zaheer Abbas	Gloucestershire	1976-81

TWO HUNDREDS IN A MATCH MOST TIMES

8	Zaheer Abbas	Gloucestershire and PIA	1976-82
8	R.T.Ponting	Tasmania, Australia and Australians	1992-2006

MOST HUNDREDS IN A SEASON

18	D.C.S.Compton	1947	16	J.B.Hobbs	1925

100 HUNDREDS IN A CAREER

	Total		*100th Hundred*	
	Hundreds	*Inns*	*Season*	*Inns*
J.B.Hobbs	197	1315	1923	821
E.H.Hendren	170	1300	1928-29	740
W.R.Hammond	167	1005	1935	679
C.P.Mead	153	1340	1927	892
G.Boycott	151	1014	1977	645
H.Sutcliffe	149	1088	1932	700
F.E.Woolley	145	1532	1929	1031
G.A.Hick	136	871	1998	574
L.Hutton	129	814	1951	619
G.A.Gooch	128	990	1992-93	820
W.G.Grace	126	1493	1895	1113
D.C.S.Compton	123	839	1952	552
T.W.Graveney	122	1223	1964	940
D.G.Bradman	117	338	1947-48	295
I.V.A.Richards	114	796	1988-89	658
M.R.Ramprakash	114	764	2008	676
Zaheer Abbas	108	768	1982-83	658
A.Sandham	107	1000	1935	871
M.C.Cowdrey	107	1130	1973	1035
T.W.Hayward	104	1138	1913	1076
G.M.Turner	103	792	1982	779
J.H.Edrich	103	979	1977	945
L.E.G.Ames	102	951	1950	915
G.E.Tyldesley	102	961	1934	919
D.L.Amiss	102	1139	1986	1081

MOST 400s: 2 – B.C.Lara, W.H.Ponsford
MOST 300s or more: 6 – D.G.Bradman; 4 – W.R.Hammond, W.H.Ponsford
MOST 200s or more: 37 – D.G.Bradman; 36 – W.R.Hammond; 22 – E.H.Hendren

MOST RUNS IN A MONTH

1294 (avge 92.42)	L.Hutton	Yorkshire	June 1949

MOST RUNS IN A SEASON

Runs			*I*	*NO*	*HS*	*Avge*	*100*	*Season*
3816	D.C.S.Compton	Middlesex	50	8	246	90.85	18	1947
3539	W.J.Edrich	Middlesex	52	8	267*	80.43	12	1947
3518	T.W.Hayward	Surrey	61	8	219	66.37	13	1906

The feat of scoring 3000 runs in a season has been achieved 28 times, the most recent instance being by W.E.Alley (3019) in 1961. The highest aggregate in a season since 1969 is 2755 by S.J.Cook in 1991.

1000 RUNS IN A SEASON MOST TIMES

28 W.G.Grace (Gloucestershire), F.E.Woolley (Kent)

HIGHEST BATTING AVERAGE IN A SEASON

(Qualification: 12 innings)

Avge			*I*	*NO*	*HS*	*Runs*	*100*	*Season*
115.66	D.G.Bradman	Australians	26	5	278	2429	13	1938
106.50	K.C.Sangakkara	Surrey	16	2	200	1491	8	2017
104.66	D.R.Martyn	Australians	14	5	176*	942	5	2001
103.54	M.R.Ramprakash	Surrey	24	2	301*	2278	8	2006
102.53	G.Boycott	Yorkshire	20	5	175*	1538	6	1979
102.00	W.A.Johnston	Australians	17	16	28*	102	–	1953
101.70	G.A.Gooch	Essex	30	3	333	2746	12	1990
101.30	M.R.Ramprakash	Surrey	25	5	266*	2026	10	2007
100.12	G.Boycott	Yorkshire	30	5	233	2503	13	1971

FASTEST HUNDRED AGAINST AUTHENTIC BOWLING

35 min	P.G.H.Fender	Surrey v Northamptonshire	Northampton	1920

FASTEST DOUBLE HUNDRED

103 min	Shafiqullah Shinwari	Kabul Region v Boost Region	Asadabad	2017-18

FASTEST TRIPLE HUNDRED

181 min	D.C.S.Compton	MCC v NE Transvaal	Benoni	1948-49

MOST SIXES IN AN INNINGS

23	C.Munro	Central Districts v Auckland	Napier	2014-15

MOST SIXES IN A MATCH

24	Shafiqullah Shinwari	Kabul Region v Boost Region	Asadabad	2017-18

MOST SIXES IN A SEASON

80	I.T.Botham	Somerset and England		1985

MOST BOUNDARIES IN AN INNINGS

72	B.C.Lara	Warwickshire v Durham	Birmingham	1994

MOST RUNS OFF ONE OVER

36	G.St A.Sobers	Nottinghamshire v Glamorgan	Swansea	1968
36	R.J.Shastri	Bombay v Baroda	Bombay	1984-85

Both batsmen hit for six all six balls of overs bowled by M.A.Nash and Tilak Raj respectively.

MOST RUNS IN A DAY

390*	B.C.Lara	Warwickshire v Durham	Birmingham	1994

There have been 19 instances of a batsman scoring 300 or more runs in a day.

LONGEST INNINGS

1015 min	R.Nayyar (271)	Himachal Pradesh v Jammu & Kashmir	Chamba	1999-00

HIGHEST PARTNERSHIPS FOR EACH WICKET

First Wicket

561	Waheed Mirza/Mansoor Akhtar	Karachi W v Quetta	Karachi	1976-77
555	P.Holmes/H.Sutcliffe	Yorkshire v Essex	Leyton	1932
554	J.T.Brown/J.Tunnicliffe	Yorkshire v Derbys	Chesterfield	1898

Second Wicket

580	Rafatullah Mohmand/Aamer Sajjad	WAPDA v SSGC	Sheikhupura	2009-10
576	S.T.Jayasuriya/R.S.Mahanama	Sri Lanka v India	Colombo	1997-98
480	D.Elgar/R.R.Rossouw	Eagles v Titans	Centurion	2009-10
475	Zahir Alam/L.S.Rajput	Assam v Tripura	Gauhati	1991-92
465*	J.A.Jameson/R.B.Kanhai	Warwickshire v Glos	Birmingham	1974

Third Wicket

624	K.C.Sangakkara/D.P.M.D.Jayawardena	Sri Lanka v South Africa	Colombo	2006
594*	S.M.Gugale/A.R.Bawne	Maharashtra v Delhi	Mumbai	2016-17
539	S.D.Jogiyani/R.A.Jadeja	Saurashtra v Gujarat	Surat	2012-13
523	M.A.Carberry/N.D.McKenzie	Hampshire v Yorkshire	Southampton	2011

Fourth Wicket

577	V.S.Hazare/Gul Mahomed	Baroda v Holkar	Baroda	1946-47
574*	C.L.Walcott/F.M.M.Worrell	Barbados v Trinidad	Port of Spain	1945-46
538	Babul Kumar/S.Gani	Bihar v Mizoram	Kolkata	2021-22
502*	F.M.M.Worrell/J.D.C.Goddard	Barbados v Trinidad	Bridgetown	1943-44
470	A.I.Kallicharran/G.W.Humpage	Warwickshire v Lancs	Southport	1982

Fifth Wicket

520*	C.A.Pujara/R.A.Jadeja	Saurashtra v Orissa	Rajkot	2008-09
494	Marchall Ayub/Mehrab Hossain Jr	Central Zone v East Zone	Bogra	2012-13
479	Misbah-ul-Haq/Usman Arshad	Sui NGP v Lahore Shalimar	Lahore	2009-10
477*	C.N.Ackermann/P.W.A.Mulder	Leicestershire v Sussex	Hove	2022

Sixth Wicket

487*	G.A.Headley/C.C.Passailaigue	Jamaica v Tennyson's	Kingston	1931-32
461*	S.A.Northeast/C.B.Cooke	Glamorgan v Leicestershire	Leicester	2022
428	W.W.Armstrong/M.A.Noble	Australians v Sussex	Hove	1902

Seventh Wicket

460	Bhupinder Singh jr/P.Dharmani	Punjab v Delhi	Delhi	1994-95
399	A.N.Khare/A.J.Mandal	Chhattisgarh v Uttarakhand	Naya Raipur	2019-20
371	M.R.Marsh/S.M.Whiteman	Australia A v India A	Brisbane	2014
366*	J.M.Bairstow/T.T.Bresnan	Yorkshire v Durham	Chester-le-Street	2015

Eighth Wicket

433	V.T.Trumper/A.Sims	Australians v C'bury	Christchurch	1913-14
392	A.Mishra/J.Yadav	Haryana v Karnataka	Hubli	2012-13
332	I.J.L.Trott/S.C.J.Broad	England v Pakistan	Lord's	2010

Ninth Wicket

283	J.Chapman/A.Warren	Derbys v Warwicks	Blackwell	1910
268	J.B.Commins/N.Boje	SA 'A' v Mashonaland	Harare	1994-95
261	W.L.Madsen/T.Poynton	Derbys v Northants	Northampton	2012

Tenth Wicket

307	A.F.Kippax/J.E.H.Hooker	NSW v Victoria	Melbourne	1928-29
249	C.T.Sarwate/S.N.Banerjee	Indians v Surrey	The Oval	1946
239	Aqil Arshad/Ali Raza	Lahore Whites v Hyderabad	Lahore	2004-05

BOWLING RECORDS
2000 WICKETS IN A CAREER

	Career	*Runs*	*Wkts*	*Avge*	*100w*
W.Rhodes	1898-1930	69993	**4187**	16.71	23
A.P.Freeman	1914-36	69577	**3776**	18.42	17
C.W.L.Parker	1903-35	63817	**3278**	19.46	16
J.T.Hearne	1888-1923	54352	**3061**	17.75	15
T.W.J.Goddard	1922-52	59116	**2979**	19.84	16
W.G.Grace	1865-1908	51545	**2876**	17.92	10
A.S.Kennedy	1907-36	61034	**2874**	21.23	15
D.Shackleton	1948-69	53303	**2857**	18.65	20
G.A.R.Lock	1946-70/71	54709	**2844**	19.23	14
F.J.Titmus	1949-82	63313	**2830**	22.37	16
M.W.Tate	1912-37	50571	**2784**	18.16	13+1
G.H.Hirst	1891-1929	51282	**2739**	18.72	15
C.Blythe	1899-1914	42136	**2506**	16.81	14
D.L.Underwood	1963-87	49993	**2465**	20.28	10
W.E.Astill	1906-39	57783	**2431**	23.76	9
J.C.White	1909-37	43759	**2356**	18.57	14
W.E.Hollies	1932-57	48656	**2323**	20.94	14
F.S.Trueman	1949-69	42154	**2304**	18.29	12
J.B.Statham	1950-68	36999	**2260**	16.37	13
R.T.D.Perks	1930-55	53771	**2233**	24.07	16
J.Briggs	1879-1900	35431	**2221**	15.95	12

	Career	Runs	Wkts	Avge	100w
D.J.Shepherd	1950-72	47302	**2218**	21.32	12
E.G.Dennett	1903-26	42571	**2147**	19.82	12
T.Richardson	1892-1905	38794	**2104**	18.43	10
T.E.Bailey	1945-67	48170	**2082**	23.13	9
R.Illingworth	1951-83	42023	**2072**	20.28	10
F.E.Woolley	1906-38	41066	**2068**	19.85	8
N.Gifford	1960-88	48731	**2068**	23.56	4
G.Geary	1912-38	41339	**2063**	20.03	11
D.V.P.Wright	1932-57	49307	**2056**	23.98	10
J.A.Newman	1906-30	51111	**2032**	25.15	9
A.Shaw	1864-97	24580	**2026**+1	12.12	9
S.Haigh	1895-1913	32091	**2012**	15.94	11

ALL TEN WICKETS IN AN INNINGS

This feat has been achieved 82 times in first-class matches (excluding 12-a-side fixtures).
Three Times: A.P.Freeman (1929, 1930, 1931)
Twice: V.E.Walker (1859, 1865); H.Verity (1931, 1932); J.C.Laker (1956)
Instances since 1945:

W.E.Hollies	Warwickshire v Notts	Birmingham	1946
J.M.Sims	East v West	Kingston on Thames	1948
J.K.R.Graveney	Gloucestershire v Derbyshire	Chesterfield	1949
T.E.Bailey	Essex v Lancashire	Clacton	1949
R.Berry	Lancashire v Worcestershire	Blackpool	1953
S.P.Gupte	President's XI v Combined XI	Bombay	1954-55
J.C.Laker	Surrey v Australians	The Oval	1956
K.Smales	Nottinghamshire v Glos	Stroud	1956
G.A.R.Lock	Surrey v Kent	Blackheath	1956
J.C.Laker	England v Australia	Manchester	1956
P.M.Chatterjee	Bengal v Assam	Jorhat	1956-57
J.D.Bannister	Warwicks v Combined Services	Birmingham (M & B)	1959
A.J.G.Pearson	Cambridge U v Leicestershire	Loughborough	1961
N.I.Thomson	Sussex v Warwickshire	Worthing	1964
P.J.Allan	Queensland v Victoria	Melbourne	1965-66
I.J.Brayshaw	Western Australia v Victoria	Perth	1967-68
Shahid Mahmood	Karachi Whites v Khairpur	Karachi	1969-70
E.E.Hemmings	International XI v W Indians	Kingston	1982-83
P.Sunderam	Rajasthan v Vidarbha	Jodhpur	1985-86
S.T.Jefferies	Western Province v OFS	Cape Town	1987-88
Imran Adil	Bahawalpur v Faisalabad	Faisalabad	1989-90
G.P.Wickremasinghe	Sinhalese v Kalutara	Colombo	1991-92
R.L.Johnson	Middlesex v Derbyshire	Derby	1994
Naeem Akhtar	Rawalpindi B v Peshawar	Peshawar	1995-96
A.Kumble	India v Pakistan	Delhi	1998-99
D.S.Mohanty	East Zone v South Zone	Agartala	2000-01
O.D.Gibson	Durham v Hampshire	Chester-le-Street	2007
M.W.Olivier	Warriors v Eagles	Bloemfontein	2007-08
Zulfiqar Babar	Multan v Islamabad	Multan	2009-10
P.M.Pushpakumara	Colombo v Saracens	Moratuwa	2018-19
S.A.Whitehead	SW Districts v Easterns	Oudtshoorn	2021-22
A.Y.Patel	New Zealand v India	Mumbai	2021-22

MOST WICKETS IN A MATCH

19	J.C.Laker	England v Australia	Manchester	1956

MOST WICKETS IN A SEASON

Wkts		*Season*	*Matches*	*Overs*	*Mdns*	*Runs*	*Avge*
304	A.P.Freeman	1928	37	1976.1	423	5489	18.05
298	A.P.Freeman	1933	33	2039	651	4549	15.26

The feat of taking 250 wickets in a season has been achieved on 12 occasions, the last instance being by A.P.Freeman in 1933. 200 or more wickets in a season have been taken on 59 occasions, the last being by G.A.R.Lock (212 wickets, average 12.02) in 1957.

The highest aggregates of wickets taken in a season since the reduction of County Championship matches in 1969 are as follows:

Wkts		*Season*	*Matches*	*Overs*	*Mdns*	*Runs*	*Avge*
134	M.D.Marshall	1982	22	822	225	2108	15.73
131	L.R.Gibbs	1971	23	1024.1	295	2475	18.89

Since 1969 there have been 50 instances of bowlers taking 100 wickets in a season.

MOST HAT-TRICKS IN A CAREER

7	D.V.P.Wright
6	T.W.J.Goddard, C.W.L.Parker
5	S.Haigh, V.W.C.Jupp, A.E.G.Rhodes, F.A.Tarrant

ALL-ROUND RECORDS
THE 'DOUBLE'

3000 runs and 100 wickets: J.H.Parks (1937)

2000 runs and 200 wickets: G.H.Hirst (1906)

2000 runs and 100 wickets: F.E.Woolley (4), J.W.Hearne (3), W.G.Grace (2), G.H.Hirst (2), W.Rhodes (2), T.E.Bailey, D.E.Davies, G.L.Jessop, V.W.C.Jupp, J.Langridge, F.A.Tarrant, C.L.Townsend, L.F.Townsend

1000 runs and 200 wickets: M.W.Tate (3), A.E.Trott (2), A.S.Kennedy

Most Doubles: 16 – W.Rhodes; 14 – G.H.Hirst; 10 – V.W.C.Jupp

Double in Debut Season: D.B.Close (1949) – aged 18, the youngest to achieve this feat.

The feat of scoring 1000 runs and taking 100 wickets in a season has been achieved on 305 occasions, R.J.Hadlee (1984) and F.D.Stephenson (1988) being the only players to complete the 'double' since the reduction of County Championship matches in 1969.

WICKET-KEEPING RECORDS
1000 DISMISSALS IN A CAREER

	Career	*Dismissals*	*Ct*	*St*
R.W.Taylor	1960-88	**1649**	1473	176
J.T.Murray	1952-75	**1527**	1270	257
H.Strudwick	1902-27	**1497**	1242	255
A.P.E.Knott	1964-85	**1344**	1211	133
R.C.Russell	1981-2004	**1320**	1192	128
F.H.Huish	1895-1914	**1310**	933	377
B.Taylor	1949-73	**1294**	1083	211
S.J.Rhodes	1981-2004	**1263**	1139	124
D.Hunter	1889-1909	**1253**	906	347
H.R.Butt	1890-1912	**1228**	953	275
J.H.Board	1891-1914/15	**1207**	852	355
H.Elliott	1920-47	**1206**	904	302
J.M.Parks	1949-76	**1181**	1088	93
R.Booth	1951-70	**1126**	948	178
L.E.G.Ames	1926-51	**1121**	703	418
C.M.W.Read	1997-2017	**1104**	1051	53
D.L.Bairstow	1970-90	**1099**	961	138
G.Duckworth	1923-47	**1096**	753	343
H.W.Stephenson	1948-64	**1082**	748	334
J.G.Binks	1955-75	**1071**	895	176
T.G.Evans	1939-69	**1066**	816	250

	Career	Dismissals	Ct	St
A.Long	1960-80	**1046**	922	124
G.O.Dawkes	1937-61	**1043**	895	148
R.W.Tolchard	1965-83	**1037**	912	125
W.L.Cornford	1921-47	**1017**	675	342

MOST DISMISSALS IN AN INNINGS

9	(8ct, 1st)	Tahir Rashid	Habib Bank v PACO	Gujranwala	1992-93
9	(7ct, 2st)	W.R.James	Matabeleland v Mashonaland CD	Bulawayo	1995-96
8	(8ct)	A.T.W.Grout	Queensland v W Australia	Brisbane	1959-60
8	(8ct)	D.E.East	Essex v Somerset	Taunton	1985
8	(8ct)	S.A.Marsh	Kent v Middlesex	Lord's	1991
8	(6ct, 2st)	T.J.Zoehrer	Australians v Surrey	The Oval	1993
8	(7ct, 1st)	D.S.Berry	Victoria v South Australia	Melbourne	1996-97
8	(7ct, 1st)	Y.S.S.Mendis	Bloomfield v Kurunegala Youth	Colombo	2000-01
8	(7ct, 1st)	S.Nath	Assam v Tripura (*on debut*)	Gauhati	2001-02
8	(8ct)	J.N.Batty	Surrey v Kent	The Oval	2004
8	(8ct)	Golam Mabud	Sylhet v Dhaka	Dhaka	2005-06
8	(8ct)	A.Z.M.Dyili	Eastern Province v Free State	Port Elizabeth	2009-10
8	(8ct)	D.C.de Boorder	Otago v Wellington	Wellington	2009-10
8	(8ct)	R.S.Second	Free State v North West	Bloemfontein	2011-12
8	(8ct)	T.L.Tsolekile	South Africa A v Sri Lanka A	Durban	2012
8	(7ct, 1st)	M.A.R.S.Fernando	Chilaw Marians v Colts	Columbo (SSC)	2017-18

MOST DISMISSALS IN A MATCH

14	(11ct, 3st)	I.Khaleel	Hyderabad v Assam	Guwahati	2011-12
13	(11ct, 2st)	W.R.James	Matabeleland v Mashonaland CD	Bulawayo	1995-96
12	(8ct, 4st)	E.W.Pooley	Surrey v Sussex	The Oval	1868
12	(9ct, 3st)	D.Tallon	Queensland v NSW	Sydney	1938-39
12	(9ct, 3st)	H.B.Taber	NSW v South Australia	Adelaide	1968-69
12	(12ct)	P.D.McGlashan	Northern Districts v Central Districts	Whangarei	2009-10
12	(11ct, 1st)	T.L.Tsolekile	Lions v Dolphins	Johannesburg	2010-11
12	(12ct)	Kashif Mahmood	Lahore Shalimar v Abbottabad	Abbottabad	2010-11
12	(12ct)	R.S.Second	Free State v North West	Bloemfontein	2011-12
12	(12ct)	S.W.Billings	Kent v Warwickshire	Birmingham	2022

MOST DISMISSALS IN A SEASON

128 (79ct, 49st)	L.E.G.Ames	1929

FIELDING RECORDS
700 CATCHES IN A CAREER

1018	F.E.Woolley	1906-38	784	J.G.Langridge	1928-55
887	W.G.Grace	1865-1908	764	W.Rhodes	1898-1930
830	G.A.R.Lock	1946-70/71	758	C.A.Milton	1948-74
819	W.R.Hammond	1920-51	754	E.H.Hendren	1907-38
813	D.B.Close	1949-86	709	G.A.Hick	1983/84-2008

MOST CATCHES IN AN INNINGS

7	M.J.Stewart	Surrey v Northamptonshire	Northampton	1957
7	A.S.Brown	Gloucestershire v Nottinghamshire	Nottingham	1966
7	R.Clarke	Warwickshire v Lancashire	Liverpool	2011

MOST CATCHES IN A MATCH

10	W.R.Hammond	Gloucestershire v Surrey	Cheltenham	1928
9	R.Clarke	Warwickshire v Lancashire	Liverpool	2011
9	P.S.P.Handscomb	Victoria v Tasmania	Melbourne	2021-22

MOST CATCHES IN A SEASON

78	W.R.Hammond	1928	77	M.J.Stewart	1957

ICC CRICKET WORLD CUP 2023

The 13th ICC Cricket World Cup was held in England between 5 October and 19 November.

Team	*P*	*W*	*L*	*T*	*NR*	*Pts*	*Net RR*
1 India (1)	9	9	–	–	–	18	+2.57
2 South Africa (7)	9	7	2	–	–	14	+1.26
3 Australia (2)	9	7	2	–	–	14	+0.84
4 New Zealand (4)	9	5	4	–	–	10	+0.74
5 Pakistan (5)	9	4	5	–	–	8	–0.19
6 Afghanistan (10)	9	4	5	–	–	8	–0.33
7 England (3)	9	3	6	–	–	6	–0.57
8 Bangladesh (8)	9	2	7	–	–	4	–1.08
9 Sri Lanka (6)	9	2	7	–	–	4	–1.41
10 Netherlands (-)	9	2	7	–	–	4	–1.82

(*Positions from the Group Stages in 2019 in brackets*)

England's Group Stage games:

Narendra Modi Stadium, Ahmedabad, 5 October. Toss: New Zealand. **NEW ZEALAND** won by nine wickets. England 282-9 (50; J.E.Root 77, M.J.Henry 3-48). New Zealand 283-1 (36.2; D.P.Conway 152*, R.Ravindra 123*). Award: R.Ravindra.

Himachal Pradesh CA Stadium, Dharamsala, 10 October. Toss: Bangladesh. **ENGLAND** won by 137 runs. England 364-9 (50; D.J.Malan 140, J.E.Root 82, J.M.Bairstow 52, Mehedi Hasan 4-71, Shoriful Islam 3-75). Bangladesh 227 (48.2; Liton Das 76, Mushfiqur Rahim 51, R.J.W.Topley 4-43). Award: D.J.Malan.

Feroz Shah Kotla, Delhi, 15 October. Toss: England. **AFGHANISTAN** won by 69 runs. Afghanistan 284 (49.5; Rahmanullah Gurbaz 80, Ikram Alikhil 58, A.U.Rashid 3-42). England 215 (40.3; H.C.Brook 66, Rashid Khan 3-37, Mujeeb Zadran 3-51). Award: Mujeeb Zadran.

Wankhede Stadium, Mumbai, 21 October. Toss: England. **SOUTH AFRICA** won by 229 runs. South Africa 399-7 (50; H.Klaasen 109, R.R.Hendricks 85, M.Jansen 75*, H.E.van der Dussen 60, R.J.W.Topley 3-88). England 170 (22; G.W.Coetzee 3-35). Award: H.Klaasen. *England's heaviest defeat, and most runs conceded, in all LOIs.*

M.Chinnaswamy Stadium, Bengaluru, 26 October. Toss: England. **SRI LANKA** won by eight wickets. England 156 (33.2; C.B.R.L.S.Kumara 3-35). Sri Lanka 160-2 (25.4; P.N.Silva 77*, W.S.R.Samarawickrama 65*). Award: C.B.R.L.S.Kumara.

Bharat Ratna Shri Atal Bihari Vajpayee Ekana Cricket Stadium, Lucknow, 29 October. Toss: England. **INDIA** won by 100 runs. India 229-9 (50; R.G.Sharma 87, D.J.Willey 3-45). England 129 (34.5; Mohammed Shami 4-22, J.J.Bumrah 3-32). Award: R.G.Sharma.

Narendra Modi Stadium, Ahmedabad, 4 November. Toss: England. **AUSTRALIA** won by 33 runs. Australia 286 (49.3; M.Labuschagne 71, C.R.Woakes 4-54). England 253 (48.1; B.A.Stokes 64, D.J.Malan 50, A.Zampa 3-21). Award: A.Zampa.

Maharashtra CA Stadium, Pune, 8 November. Toss: England. **ENGLAND** won by 160 runs. England 339-9 (50; B.A.Stokes 108, D.J.Malan 87, C.R.Woakes 51, B.F.W.de Leede 3-74). Netherlands 179 (37.2; M.M.Ali 3-42, A.U.Rashid 3-54). Award: B.A.Stokes.

Eden Gardens, Kolkata, 11 November. Toss: England. **ENGLAND** won by 93 runs. England 337-9 (50; B.A.Stokes 84, J.E.Root 60, J.M.Bairstow 59, Haris Rauf 3-64). Pakistan 244 (43.3; Agha Salman 51, D.J.Willey 3-56). Award: D.J.Willey.

Semi-finals

Wankhede Stadium, Mumbai, 15 November. Toss: India. **INDIA** won by 70 runs. India 397-4 (50; V.Kohli 117, S.S.Iyer 105, S.Gill 80, T.G.Southee 3-100). New Zealand 327 (48.5; D.J.Mitchell 134, K.S.Williamson 69, Mohammed Shami 7-57). Award: Mohammed Shami.

Eden Gardens, Kolkata, 16 November. Toss: South Africa. **AUSTRALIA** won by three wickets. South Africa 212 (49.4; D.A.Miller 101, M.A.Starc 3-34, P.J.Cummins 3-51). Australia 215-7 (47.2; T.M.Head 62). Award: T.M.Head.

Statistical Highlights in ICC Cricket World Cup 2023

Highest total	428-5		South Africa v Sri Lanka	Delhi
Biggest victory (runs)	309		Australia beat Netherlands	Delhi
Biggest victory (wkts)	9		New Zealand beat England	Ahmedabad
Biggest victory (balls)	160		New Zealand beat Sri Lanka	Bengaluru
Most runs	765 (ave 95.62)	V.Kohli (India)		
	597 (ave 54.27)	R.G.Sharma (India)		
Highest innings	201*	G.J.Maxwell	Australia v Afghanistan	Mumbai
Most sixes (inns)	11	Fakhar Zaman	Pakistan v New Zealand	Bengaluru
Highest partnership	273*	R.Ravindra/D.P.Conway	New Zealand v England	Ahmedabad
Most wickets	24 (ave 10.70)	Mohammed Shami (India)		
	23 (ave 22.39)	A.Zampa (Australia)		
Best bowling	7-57	Mohammed Shami	India v New Zealand	Mumbai
Most economical	10-0-21-3	A.Zampa	Australia v England	Ahmedabad
Most expensive	10-0-115-2	B.F.W.de Leede	Netherlands v Australia	Delhi
Most w/k dismissals	20	Q.de Kock (South Africa)		
Most w/k dismissals (inns)	6	Q.de Kock	South Africa v Afghanistan	Ahmedabad
Most catches	11	D.J.Mitchell (New Zealand)		
Most catches (inns)	4	J.E.Root	England v Afghanistan	Delhi

Overall ICC Cricket World Cup Records

Highest total	428-5	South Africa v Sri Lanka		Delhi	2023
Lowest total	36	Canada v Sri Lanka		Paarl	2003
Biggest victory (runs)	309	Australia beat Netherlands		Delhi	2023
Biggest victory (balls)	277	England beat Canada		Manchester	1979
Most runs	2278 (ave 56.95)	S.R.Tendulkar (India)			
	1795 (ave 54.27)	V.Kohli (India)			
	1743 (ave 59.40)	R.T.Ponting (Australia)			
Highest innings	237*	M.J.Guptill	New Zealand v West Indies	Wellington	2015
Most sixes (inns)	17	E.J.G.Morgan	England v Afghanistan	Manchester	2019
Highest partnership	372	M.N.Samuels/C.H.Gayle	West Indies v Zimbabwe	Canberra	2015
Most wickets	71 (ave 18.19)	G.D.McGrath (Australia)			
	68 (ave 19.63)	M.Muralitharan (Sri Lanka)			
	65 (ave 19.29)	M.A.Starc (Australia)			
Best bowling	7-15	G.D.McGrath	Australia v Namibia	Potchefstroom	2003
Most economical	12-8-6-1	B.S.Bedi	India v East Africa	Leeds	1975
Most expensive	10-0-115-2	B.F.W.de Leede	Netherlands v Australia	Delhi	2023
Most w/k dismissals	54	K.C.Sangakkara (Sri Lanka)			
	52	A.C.Gilchrist (Australia)			
Most catches	28	R.T.Ponting (Australia)			
	25	J.E.Root (England)			

2023 ICC CRICKET WORLD CUP FINAL
INDIA v AUSTRALIA

At Narendra Modi Stadium, Ahmedabad, on 19 November.

Result: **AUSTRALIA** won by six wickets.

Toss: Australia. Award: T.M.Head. Series Award: V.Kohli.

INDIA		*Runs*	*Balls*	*4/6*	*Fall*
* R.G.Sharma	c Head b Maxwell	47	31	4/3	2- 76
S.Gill	c Zampa b Starc	4	7	–	1- 30
V.Kohli	b Cummins	54	63	4	4-148
S.S.Iyer	c Inglis b Cummins	4	3	1	3- 81
† K.L.Rahul	c Inglis b Starc	66	107	1	6-203
R.A.Jadeja	c Inglis b Hazlewood	9	22	–	5-178
S.A.Yadav	c Inglis b Hazlewood	18	28	1	9-226
Mohammed Shami	c Inglis b Starc	6	10	1	7-211
J.J.Bumrah	lbw b Zampa	1	3	–	8-214
K.Yadav	run out	10	18	–	10-240
M.Siraj	not out	9	8	1	
Extras	(LB 3, W 9)	12			
Total	**(50 overs)**	**240**			

AUSTRALIA		*Runs*	*Balls*	*4/6*	*Fall*
D.A.Warner	c Kohli b Shami	7	3	1	1- 16
T.M.Head	c Gill b Siraj	137	120	15/4	4-239
M.R.Marsh	c Rahul b Bumrah	15	15	1/1	2- 41
S.P.D.Smith	lbw b Bumrah	4	9	1	3- 47
M.Labsuchagne	not out	58	110	4	
G.J.Maxwell	not out	2	1	–	
† J.P.Inglis					
M.A.Starc					
* P.J.Cummins					
A.Zampa					
J.R.Hazlewood					
Extras	(B 5, LB 2, W 11)	18			
Total	**(4 wkts; 43 overs)**	**241**			

AUSTRALIA	O	M	R	W
Starc	10	0	55	3
Hazlewood	10	0	60	2
Maxwell	6	0	35	1
Cummins	10	0	34	2
Zampa	10	0	44	1
Marsh	2	0	5	0
Head	2	0	4	0

INDIA	O	M	R	W
Bumrah	9	2	43	2
Mohammed Shami	7	1	47	1
Jadeja	10	0	43	0
K.Yadav	10	0	56	0
Siraj	7	0	45	1

Umpires: R.K.Illingworth (*England*) and R.A.Kettleborough (*England*)

WORLD CUP WINNERS

1975	West Indies
1979	West Indies
1983	India
1987	Australia
1992	Pakistan
1996	Sri Lanka
1999	Australia
2003	Australia
2007	Australia
2011	India
2015	Australia
2019	England
2023	Australia

LIMITED-OVERS INTERNATIONALS CAREER RECORDS

These records, complete to 6 March 2024, include all players registered for county cricket for the 2024 season at the time of going to press, plus those who have appeared in LOI matches for ICC full member countries since 23 November 2022. Some players who may return to LOI action have also been listed, even if their most recent game was earlier than this date.

ENGLAND – BATTING AND FIELDING

	M	*I*	*NO*	*HS*	*Runs*	*Avge*	*100*	*50*	*Ct/St*
R.Ahmed	6	4	–	15	35	8.75	–	–	1
M.M.Ali	138	112	15	128	2355	24.27	3	6	48
J.M.Anderson	194	79	43	28	273	7.58	–	–	53
J.C.Archer	21	11	6	8*	32	6.40	–	–	6
A.A.P.Atkinson	9	6	2	35	63	15.75	–	–	1
J.M.Bairstow	107	98	8	141*	3868	42.97	11	17	55/3
J.T.Ball	18	6	2	28	38	9.50	–	–	5
T.Banton	6	5	–	58	134	26.80	–	1	2
S.W.Billings	28	23	2	118	702	33.42	1	5	19/1
S.G.Borthwick	2	2	–	15	18	9.00	–	–	–
D.R.Briggs	1	–	–	–	–	–	–	–	–
H.C.Brook	15	15	1	80	407	29.07	–	3	2
J.C.Buttler	181	154	27	162*	5022	39.54	11	26	221/37
B.A.Carse	14	9	4	32	155	31.00	–	–	3
Z.Crawley	8	8	1	58*	199	28.42	–	2	8
S.M.Curran	32	24	3	95*	468	22.28	–	1	9
T.K.Curran	28	17	9	47*	303	37.87	–	–	5
L.A.Dawson	6	5	–	20	63	12.60	–	–	2
J.L.Denly	16	13	–	87	446	34.30	–	4	7
B.M.Duckett	11	11	1	107*	395	39.50	1	3	5
B.T.Foakes	1	1	1	61*	61	–	–	1	2/1
L.Gregory	3	2	–	77	117	58.50	–	1	–
S.R.Hain	2	2	–	89	106	53.00	–	1	–
A.D.Hales	70	67	3	171	2419	37.79	6	14	27
T.W.Hartley	2	1	1	12*	12	–	–	–	–
W.G.Jacks	7	7	–	94	276	39.42	–	2	3
C.J.Jordan	35	24	9	38*	184	12.26	–	–	19
L.S.Livingstone	25	22	3	95*	558	29.36	–	3	8
S.Mahmood	8	2	–	12	20	10.00	–	–	1
D.J.Malan	30	30	4	140	1450	55.76	6	7	11
C.Overton	7	5	2	32	68	22.66	–	–	4
M.W.Parkinson	5	1	1	7*	7	–	–	–	1
S.R.Patel	36	22	7	70*	482	32.13	–	1	7
D.A.Payne	1	–	–	–	–	–	–	–	–
M.J.Potts	4	3	3	15*	21	–	–	–	–
A.U.Rashid	135	68	23	69	826	18.35	–	1	43
T.S.Roland-Jones	1	1	1	37*	37	–	–	–	–
J.E.Root	171	160	23	133*	6522	47.60	16	39	85
J.J.Roy	116	110	3	180	4271	39.91	12	21	46
P.D.Salt	19	17	–	122	619	36.41	1	3	7
G.L.S.Scrimshaw	1	–	–	–	–	–	–	–	–
J.A.Simpson	3	2	–	17	20	10.00	–	–	9
J.L.Smith	2	1	–	9	9	9.00	–	–	1
B.A.Stokes	114	99	15	182	3463	41.22	5	24	55
O.P.Stone	8	4	2	9*	14	7.00	–	–	–
R.J.W.Topley	29	14	11	15*	35	11.66	–	–	7
J.M.Vince	25	22	–	102	616	28.00	1	3	10
D.J.Willey	73	46	19	51	663	24.55	–	2	27
C.R.Woakes	122	88	24	95*	1524	23.81	–	6	50

	M	I	NO	HS	Runs	Avge	100	50	Ct/St
L.Wood	2	1	–	10	10	10.00	–	–	–
M.A.Wood	66	26	15	43*	157	14.27	–	–	14

ENGLAND – BOWLING

	O	M	R	W	Avge	Best	4wI	R/Over
R.Ahmed	47	0	233	10	23.30	4-54	1	4.95
M.M.Ali	998	13	5311	111	47.84	4-46	2	5.32
J.M.Anderson	1597.2	125	7861	269	29.22	5-23	13	4.92
J.C.Archer	189.5	14	913	42	21.73	6-40	1	4.80
A.A.P.Atkinson	63.4	0	388	11	35.27	2-28	–	6.09
J.T.Ball	157.5	5	980	21	46.66	5-51	1	6.20
S.G.Borthwick	9	0	72	0	–	–	–	8.00
D.R.Briggs	10	0	39	2	19.50	2-39	–	3.90
B.A.Carse	97.4	0	582	15	38.80	5-61	1	5.95
S.M.Curran	212.5	10	1323	33	40.09	5-48	2	6.21
T.K.Curran	218	8	1290	34	37.94	5-35	3	5.91
L.A.Dawson	44	0	284	5	56.80	2-70	–	6.45
J.L.Denly	17	0	101	1	101.00	1-24	–	5.94
L.Gregory	19	1	97	4	24.25	3-44	–	5.10
T.W.Hartley	10	0	48	0	–	–	–	4.80
W.G.Jacks	25	1	121	4	30.25	3-22	–	4.84
C.J.Jordan	276.4	5	1660	46	36.08	5-29	1	6.00
L.S.Livingstone	94.2	2	523	17	30.76	3-16	–	5.54
S.Mahmood	69.5	5	320	14	22.85	4-42	1	4.58
D.J.Malan	2.3	0	17	1	17.00	1- 5	–	6.80
C.Overton	51.2	2	291	5	58.20	2-23	–	5.66
M.W.Parkinson	34.4	0	203	5	40.60	2-28	–	5.85
S.R.Patel	197.5	4	1091	24	45.45	5-41	1	5.51
D.A.Payne	9	1	38	1	38.00	1-38	–	4.22
M.J.Potts	14	0	95	2	47.50	2-47	–	6.78
A.U.Rashid	1131.3	12	6377	199	32.04	5-27	10	5.63
T.S.Roland-Jones	7	2	34	1	34.00	1-34	–	4.85
J.E.Root	273	2	1587	27	58.77	3-52	–	5.81
G.L.S.Scrimshaw	8.4	0	66	3	22.00	3-66	–	7.61
B.A.Stokes	518.2	8	3137	74	42.39	5-61	2	6.05
O.P.Stone	53	2	317	8	39.62	4-85	1	5.98
R.J.W.Topley	223	17	1202	46	26.13	6-24	3	5.39
J.M.Vince	7	0	38	1	38.00	1-18	–	5.42
D.J.Willey	538.2	34	2975	100	29.75	5-30	5	5.52
C.R.Woakes	956.1	52	5193	173	30.01	6-45	14	5.43
L.Wood	10	0	59	0	–	–	–	5.90
M.A.Wood	549.5	18	3039	77	39.46	4-33	2	5.52

AUSTRALIA – BATTING AND FIELDING

	M	I	NO	HS	Runs	Avge	100	50	Ct/St
S.A.Abbott	21	15	1	69	297	21.21	–	2	11
A.C.Agar	22	18	5	48*	322	24.76	–	–	10
W.A.Agar	2	2	–	41	50	25.00	–	–	–
X.C.Bartlett	2	–	–	–	–	–	–	–	–
S.M.Boland	14	4	1	4	9	3.00	–	–	3
A.T.Carey	72	66	11	106	1814	32.98	1	8	82/8
P.J.Cummins	88	57	21	37	492	13.66	–	–	24
T.H.David	4	4	–	35	45	11.25	–	–	–
N.T.Ellis	8	7	4	18	63	21.00	–	–	2

AUSTRALIA – BATTING AND FIELDING (continued)

	M	I	NO	HS	Runs	Avge	100	50	Ct/St
J.M.Fraser-McGurk	2	2	–	41	51	25.50	–	–	1
C.D.Green	26	22	8	89*	552	39.42	–	2	11
P.S.P.Handscomb	22	20	1	117	632	33.26	1	4	14
A.M.Hardie	4	3	–	26	31	10.33	–	–	2
J.R.Hazlewood	86	32	25	23*	125	17.85	–	–	27
T.M.Head	65	62	5	152	2397	42.05	5	16	17
J.P.Inglis	21	19	1	65	411	22.83	–	3	20/2
S.H.Johnson	1	1	1	0*	0	–	–	–	–
M.Labuschagne	52	47	3	124	1656	37.63	2	11	27
N.M.Lyon	29	14	10	30	77	19.25	–	–	7
B.R.McDermott	5	5	–	104	223	44.60	1	1	–
M.R.Marsh	89	85	11	177*	2672	36.10	3	18	35
G.J.Maxwell	138	127	17	201*	3895	35.40	4	23	85
L.R.T.Morris	2	–	–	–	–	–	–	–	–
M.G.Neser	4	4	–	6	11	2.75	–	–	1
T.S.Sangha	2	1	–	0	0	0.00	–	–	–
M.W.Short	4	3	–	41	52	17.33	–	–	2
S.P.D.Smith	158	142	18	164	5446	43.91	12	33	84
M.A.Starc	121	71	25	52*	571	12.41	–	1	44
M.P.Stoinis	70	63	8	146*	1487	27.03	1	6	18
W.J.Sutherland	2	1	–	18	18	18.00	–	–	1
C.P.Tremain	4	3	2	23*	23	23.00	–	–	1
D.A.Warner	161	159	6	179	6932	45.30	22	33	71
D.J.Worrall	3	1	1	6*	6	–	–	–	1
A.Zampa	99	48	18	36	293	9.76	–	–	18

AUSTRALIA – BOWLING

	O	M	R	W	Avge	Best	4wI	R/Over
S.A.Abbott	165.1	9	894	28	31.92	3-23	–	5.41
A.C.Agar	183	4	958	21	45.61	2-31	–	5.23
W.A.Agar	11	1	39	0	–	–	–	3.54
X.C.Bartlett	16.1	1	38	8	4.75	4-17	2	2.35
S.M.Boland	119.2	3	725	16	45.31	3-67	–	6.07
P.J.Cummins	763.5	44	4042	141	28.66	5-70	7	5.29
T.H.David	2	0	20	1	20.00	1-20	–	10.00
N.T.Ellis	64	1	382	10	38.20	2-13	–	5.96
C.D.Green	125.4	0	714	18	39.66	5-33	1	5.68
A.M.Hardie	18	2	89	3	29.66	2-62	–	4.94
J.R.Hazlewood	752.3	58	3556	135	26.34	6-52	4	4.72
T.M.Head	175.3	0	999	18	55.50	2-21	–	5.69
S.H.Johnson	8	0	61	0	–	–	–	7.62
M.Labuschagne	33.5	1	230	2	115.00	2-19	–	6.79
N.M.Lyon	271	11	1334	29	46.00	4-44	1	4.92
M.R.Marsh	364.5	9	2009	56	35.87	5-33	2	5.50
G.J.Maxwell	619.5	12	3384	70	48.34	4-40	4	5.45
L.R.T.Morris	14.3	3	72	2	36.00	2-13	–	4.96
M.G.Neser	36.4	2	239	3	79.66	2-46	–	6.51
T.S.Sangha	18	0	125	2	62.50	1-61	–	6.94
M.W.Short	12	0	66	0	–	–	–	5.50
S.P.D.Smith	179.2	1	971	28	34.67	3-16	–	5.41
M.A.Starc	1040	50	5420	236	22.96	6-28	21	5.21
M.P.Stoinis	342.1	4	2059	48	42.89	3-16	–	6.01
W.J.Sutherland	8.3	0	33	2	16.50	2-28	–	3.88
C.P.Tremain	40	0	255	7	36.42	3-64	–	6.37
D.A.Warner	1	0	8	0	–	–	–	8.00

AUSTRALIA – BOWLING (continued)

	O	M	R	W	Avge	Best	4wI	R/Over
D.J.Worrall	26.2	0	171	1	171.00	1-43	–	6.49
A.Zampa	866.3	14	4742	169	28.05	5-35	12	5.47

SOUTH AFRICA – BATTING AND FIELDING

	M	I	NO	HS	Runs	Avge	100	50	Ct/St
K.J.Abbott	28	13	4	23	76	8.44	–	–	7
T.Bavuma	38	37	4	144	1512	45.81	5	4	26
N.Burger	3	2	1	7	8	8.00	–	–	–
G.W.Coetzee	14	7	–	22	57	8.14	–	–	4
Q.de Kock	155	155	7	178	6770	45.74	21	30	209/17
M.de Lange	4	–	–	–	–	–	–	–	–
T.de Zorzi	5	5	1	119*	276	69.00	1	1	–
D.Elgar	8	7	1	42	104	17.33	–	–	4
B.C.Fortuin	5	3	1	1	2	1.00	–	–	–
B.E.Hendricks	10	4	1	18	24	8.00	–	–	4
R.R.Hendricks	34	34	2	102	929	29.03	1	7	20
C.A.Ingram	31	29	3	124	843	32.42	3	3	12
M.Jansen	23	19	5	75*	422	30.14	–	1	6
H.Klaasen	54	50	7	174	1723	40.06	4	6	46/6
S.S.B.Magala	8	5	2	6*	18	6.00	–	–	2
K.A.Maharaj	44	23	5	40	238	13.22	–	–	9
A.K.Markram	68	65	7	175	2121	36.56	3	10	28
D.A.Miller	173	149	43	139	4458	42.05	6	24	83
P.W.A.Mulder	15	12	4	19*	82	10.25	–	–	7
L.T.Ngidi	56	22	14	19*	91	11.37	–	–	14
A.A.Nortje	22	7	1	10	40	6.66	–	–	3
W.D.Parnell	73	43	15	56	574	20.50	–	1	13
D.Paterson	4	–	–	–	–	–	–	–	2
A.L.Phehlukwayo	78	51	18	69*	853	25.84	–	2	17
K.Rabada	101	42	18	31*	360	15.00	–	–	37
R.D.Rickelton	2	2	–	14	17	8.50	–	–	2/2
T.Shamsi	51	14	10	11*	38	9.50	–	–	8
T.Stubbs	1	1	–	6	6	6.00	–	–	–
H.E.van der Dussen	62	56	11	134	2360	52.44	6	14	25
L.B.Williams	4	1	–	2	2	2.00	–	–	–

SOUTH AFRICA – BOWLING

	O	M	R	W	Avge	Best	4wI	R/Over
K.J.Abbott	217.1	13	1051	34	30.91	4-21	2	4.83
T.Bavuma	6.1	0	22	0	–	–	–	3.56
N.Burger	24.4	1	129	5	25.80	3-30	–	5.22
G.W.Coetzee	111	1	720	31	23.22	4-44	2	6.48
M.de Lange	34.5	1	198	10	19.80	4-46	1	5.68
D.Elgar	16	1	67	2	33.50	1-11	–	4.18
B.C.Fortuin	31	2	175	6	29.16	2-46	–	5.64
B.E.Hendricks	64.2	2	346	10	34.60	3-59	–	5.37
R.R.Hendricks	7	0	47	1	47.00	1-13	–	6.71
C.A.Ingram	1	0	17	0	–	–	–	17.00
M.Jansen	179.2	8	1138	35	32.51	5-39	1	6.34
H.Klaasen	5	0	33	0	–	–	–	6.60
G.F.Linde	15	1	72	3	24.00	2-32	–	4.80
S.S.B.Magala	57	4	381	15	25.40	5-43	1	6.68
K.A.Maharaj	369.2	13	1686	55	30.65	4-33	2	4.56
A.K.Markram	146.5	1	833	18	46.27	2-18	–	5.67
P.W.A.Mulder	74	0	422	12	35.16	2-59	–	5.70
L.T.Ngidi	436.3	26	2508	88	28.50	6-58	5	5.74

SOUTH AFRICA – BOWLING (continued)

	O	M	R	W	Avge	Best	4wI	R/Over
A.A.Nortje	167.4	4	982	36	27.27	4-51	3	5.85
W.D.Parnell	537.2	23	3010	99	30.40	5-48	5	5.60
D.Paterson	34.5	1	217	4	54.25	3-44	–	6.22
A.L.Phehlukwayo	499.1	17	2889	91	31.74	4-22	3	5.78
K.Rabada	861.5	60	4361	157	27.77	6-16	8	5.06
T.Shamsi	413.3	8	2284	72	31.72	5-49	4	5.52
H.E.van der Dussen	1	0	3	1	3.00	1- 3	–	3.00
L.B.Williams	35.4	2	238	5	47.60	2-56	–	6.67

WEST INDIES – BATTING AND FIELDING

	M	I	NO	HS	Runs	Avge	100	50	Ct/St
A.S.Athanaze	10	10	–	66	288	28.80	–	2	6
T.J.Bishop	1	1	–	0	0	0.00	–	–	–
S.S.J.Brooks	29	29	1	101*	842	30.07	1	4	14
Y.Cariah	14	7	1	52	93	15.50	–	1	3
K.U.Carty	22	20	3	88	578	34.00	–	3	3
J.Charles	58	58	–	130	1537	26.50	2	7	25/2
R.L.Chase	45	34	4	94	783	26.10	–	4	19
D.C.Drakes	3	2	–	8	11	5.50	–	–	1
M.W.Forde	4	4	1	19	39	13.00	–	–	2
J.P.Greaves	5	5	–	12	38	7.60	–	–	2
S.O.Hetmyer	53	50	3	139	1515	32.23	5	4	21
K.A.R.Hodge	4	3	–	26	37	12.33	–	–	–
J.O.Holder	138	114	24	99*	2237	24.85	–	12	65
S.D.Hope	124	119	16	170	5177	50.26	16	25	128/13
A.J.Hosein	38	28	9	60	266	14.00	–	1	16
A.Jordan	2	1	1	3*	3	–	–	–	2
A.S.Joseph	68	41	16	49	425	17.00	–	–	22
B.A.King	37	37	2	112	1054	30.11	2	6	11
K.R.Mayers	28	26	–	120	660	25.38	2	2	10
G.Motie	13	9	3	39*	70	11.66	–	–	5
K.Y.Ottley	4	4	–	24	41	10.25	–	–	1
K.M.A.Paul	30	22	7	46*	320	21.33	–	–	15
N.Pooran	61	58	8	118	1983	39.66	3	11	23/2
R.Powell	51	48	3	101	979	21.75	1	2	16
R.A.Reifer	6	5	–	27	51	10.20	–	–	–
K.A.J.Roach	95	60	36	34	308	12.83	–	–	22
S.E.Rutherford	3	3	–	63	72	24.00	–	1	1
J.N.T.Seales	10	5	2	16*	17	5.66	–	–	1
R.Shepherd	31	25	3	50	398	18.09	–	1	5
K.Sinclair	7	3	1	25	38	19.00	–	–	6
O.F.Smith	9	8	1	46	199	28.42	–	–	1
O.R.Thomas	25	14	8	7	22	3.66	–	–	1
H.R.Walsh †	22	12	3	46*	148	16.44	–	–	4

WEST INDIES – BOWLING

	O	M	R	W	Avge	Best	4wI	R/Over
A.S.Athanaze	1	0	7	0	–	–	–	7.00
Y.Cariah	99.3	1	622	13	47.84	2-26	–	6.25
K.U.Carty	4.1	0	28	0	–	–	–	6.72
J.Charles	0.5	0	12	0	–	–	–	14.40
R.L.Chase	258.5	6	1255	27	46.48	3-30	–	4.84
D.C.Drakes	19	2	73	2	36.50	2-29	–	3.84
M.W.Forde	23	1	138	5	27.60	3-29	–	6.00
K.A.R.Hodge	18	0	113	2	56.50	2-46	–	6.27
J.O.Holder	1067	64	5878	159	36.96	5-27	7	5.50

WEST INDIES – BOWLING (continued)

	O	*M*	*R*	*W*	*Avge*	*Best*	*4wI*	*R/Over*
A.J.Hosein	348.2	12	1687	57	29.59	4-39	1	4.84
A.Jordan	11	2	56	1	56.00	1-36	–	5.09
A.S.Joseph	577.2	23	3158	111	28.45	5-56	5	5.46
K.R.Mayers	114.2	3	632	14	45.14	2-30	–	5.52
G.Motie	110.1	5	436	22	19.81	4-23	1	3.95
K.M.A.Paul	208.5	4	1238	34	36.41	3-34	–	5.92
N.Pooran	28.1	0	174	6	29.00	4-48	1	6.17
R.Powell	46.4	0	275	3	91.66	1- 7	–	5.89
R.A.Reifer	26.5	0	149	6	24.83	2-23	–	5.55
K.A.J.Roach	763.1	53	3885	125	31.08	6-27	6	5.09
S.E.Rutherford	4	0	24	1	24.00	1-24	–	6.00
J.N.T.Seales	73.1	3	445	6	74.16	1-21	–	6.08
R.Shepherd	195	6	1083	27	40.11	3-37	–	5.55
K.Sinclair	63.3	1	282	11	25.63	4-24	2	4.44
O.F.Smith	47.1	0	261	10	26.10	2-26	–	5.53
O.R.Thomas	153.2	1	1034	31	33.35	5-21	2	6.74
H.R.Walsh	171.1	1	923	28	32.96	5-39	2	5.39

† *H.R.Walsh has also made 1 appearance for the USA v PNG, scoring 27 and taking 0-9.*

NEW ZEALAND – BATTING AND FIELDING

	M	*I*	*NO*	*HS*	*Runs*	*Avge*	*100*	*50*	*Ct/St*
F.H.Allen	22	21	–	96	582	27.71	–	5	9
A.Ashok	2	1	–	10	10	10.00	–	–	1
T.A.Blundell	12	12	3	68	266	29.55	–	2	13/2
T.A.Boult	114	52	28	21*	216	9.00	–	–	43
C.J.Bowes	6	6	–	51	99	16.50	–	1	4
M.G.Bracewell	19	16	5	140	510	42.50	2	–	9
M.S.Chapman	23	20	3	124*	486	28.58	2	–	4
J.A.Clarkson	3	2	–	16	17	8.50	–	–	1
D.P.Conway	32	31	3	152*	1246	44.50	5	3	17
J.A.Duffy	6	2	1	1*	1	1.00	–	–	–
L.H.Ferguson	65	30	13	19	122	7.17	–	–	14
D.Foxcroft	1	1	–	0	0	0.00	–	–	–
M.J.Henry	82	35	12	48*	255	11.08	–	–	28
K.A.Jamieson	13	6	2	25*	83	20.75	–	–	2
T.W.M.Latham	147	134	17	145*	4099	35.03	7	24	125/15
B.G.Lister	3	3	2	5*	10	10.00	–	–	–
C.E.McConchie	6	5	2	64*	126	42.00	–	1	3
A.F.Milne	49	22	8	36	180	12.85	–	–	23
D.J.Mitchell	39	35	5	134	1577	52.56	6	5	25
J.D.S.Neesham	76	65	12	97*	1495	28.20	–	7	27
H.M.Nicholls	75	73	15	124*	2056	35.44	1	15	28
W.P.O'Rourke	3	1	–	1	1	1.00	–	–	–
G.D.Phillips	30	24	3	72	735	35.00	–	4	16
R.Ravindra	25	21	1	123*	820	41.00	3	3	6
M.J.Santner	104	78	29	67	1355	27.65	–	3	43
H.B.Shipley	8	6	1	7	18	3.60	–	–	2
I.S.Sodhi	51	24	4	35	201	10.05	–	–	11
T.G.Southee	161	96	35	55	740	12.13	–	1	44
B.M.Tickner	13	7	5	6*	16	8.00	–	–	5
K.S.Williamson	165	157	17	148	6810	48.64	13	45	66
W.A.Young	31	31	3	120	1244	44.42	3	8	8

NEW ZEALAND – BOWLING

	O	M	R	W	Avge	Best	4wI	R/Over
A.Ashok	10.1	1	65	1	65.00	1-63	–	6.39
T.A.Boult	1030	76	5146	211	24.38	7-34	16	4.99
M.G.Bracewell	123	4	634	15	42.26	3-21	–	5.15
J.A.Clarkson	12	0	73	3	24.33	2-24	–	6.08
J.A.Duffy	47.4	1	321	11	29.18	3-51	–	6.73
L.H.Ferguson	550	13	3124	99	31.55	5-45	3	5.68
M.J.Henry	712.5	54	3722	141	26.39	5-30	12	5.22
K.A.Jamieson	100.4	9	511	14	36.50	3-45	–	5.07
B.G.Lister	26	0	158	4	39.50	3-69	–	6.07
C.E.McConchie	28	1	135	4	33.75	2-18	–	4.82
A.F.Milne	373.4	8	2027	57	35.56	4-34	1	5.42
D.J.Mitchell	48.3	1	275	13	21.15	3-25	–	5.67
J.D.S.Neesham	408	6	2556	71	36.00	5-27	4	6.26
W.P.O'Rourke	18.5	0	115	5	23.00	3-47	–	6.10
G.D.Phillips	77	1	471	12	39.25	3-37	–	6.11
R.Ravindra	139.1	1	839	18	46.61	4-60	1	6.02
M.J.Santner	812.3	18	3960	107	37.00	5-50	2	4.87
H.B.Shipley	64.3	4	359	15	23.93	5-31	1	5.56
I.S.Sodhi	407.1	12	2251	63	35.73	6-39	2	5.52
T.G.Southee	1345.5	80	7448	221	33.70	7-33	8	5.53
B.M.Tickner	103.5	4	679	16	42.43	4-50	1	6.53
K.S.Williamson	244.3	2	1310	37	35.40	4-22	1	5.35

INDIA – BATTING AND FIELDING

	M	I	NO	HS	Runs	Avge	100	50	Ct/St
Aavesh Khan	8	4	1	10	23	7.66	–	–	3
Arshdeep Singh	6	3	1	18	34	17.00	–	–	–
R.Ashwin	116	63	20	65	707	16.44	–	1	31
J.J.Bumrah	89	26	14	16	91	7.58	–	–	18
Y.S.Chahal	72	14	5	18*	77	8.55	–	–	16
D.L.Chahar	13	9	3	69*	203	33.83	–	2	1
R.D.Gaikwad	6	6	–	71	115	19.16	–	1	1
S.Gill	44	44	7	208	2271	61.37	6	13	301
D.J.Hooda	10	7	1	33	153	25.50	–	–	3
S.S.Iyer	59	54	6	128*	2383	49.64	5	18	24
R.A.Jadeja	197	132	47	87	2756	32.42	–	13	74
I.P.Kishan	27	24	2	210	933	42.40	1	7	13/2
V.Kohli	292	280	44	183	13848	58.67	50	72	151
P.M.Krishna	17	7	5	2*	2	1.00	–	–	3
Kuldeep Yadav	103	37	18	19	190	10.00	–	–	15
Mohammed Shami	101	48	20	25	220	7.85	–	–	31
Mukesh Kumar	6	2	1	6	10	10.00	–	–	1
K.K.Nair	2	2	–	39	46	23.00	–	–	–
H.H.Pandya	86	61	9	92*	1769	34.01	–	11	32
R.R.Pant	30	26	1	125*	865	34.60	1	5	26/1
A.R.Patel	57	36	10	64*	489	18.80	–	2	23
R.M.Patidar	1	1	–	22	22	22.00	–	–	–
C.A.Pujara	5	5	–	27	51	10.20	–	–	–
K.L.Rahul	75	70	14	112	2820	50.35	7	18	62/5
B.Sai Sudharsan	3	3	1	62	127	63.50	–	2	1
S.V.Samson	16	14	5	108	510	56.66	1	3	9/2
K.R.Sen	1	1	1	2*	2	–	–	–	–
Shahbaz Ahmed	3	1	–	0	0	0.00	–	–	1
R.G.Sharma	262	254	36	264	10709	49.12	31	55	93
P.P.Shaw	6	6	–	49	189	31.50	–	–	2
R.K.Singh	2	2	–	38	55	27.50	–	–	1
M.Siraj	41	14	8	9*	46	7.66	–	–	6

	M	I	NO	HS	Runs	Avge	100	50	Ct/St
S.N.Thakur	47	25	6	50*	329	17.31	–	1	9
N.T.Tilak Varma	4	4	1	52	68	22.66	–	1	1
Umran Malik	10	4	3	2*	2	2.00	–	–	2
J.D.Unadkat	8	–	–	–	–	–	–	–	1
M.S.Washington Sundar	19	11	1	51	265	26.50	–	1	4
S.A.Yadav	37	35	5	72*	773	25.76	–	4	17

INDIA – BOWLING

	O	M	R	W	Avge	Best	4wI	R/Over
Aavesh Khan	59.2	5	329	9	36.55	4-27	1	5.54
Arshdeep Singh	40.1	2	184	10	18.40	5-37	2	4.58
R.Ashwin	1050.3	37	5180	156	33.20	4-25	1	4.93
J.J.Bumrah	763.2	57	3509	149	23.55	6-19	8	4.59
Y.S.Chahal	623.1	14	3283	121	27.13	6-42	7	5.26
D.L.Chahar	85	5	489	16	30.56	3-27	–	5.75
S.Gill	2	0	11	0	–	–	–	5.50
D.J.Hooda	25	1	119	3	39.66	1- 6	–	4.76
S.S.Iyer	6.1	0	39	0	–	–	–	6.32
R.A.Jadeja	1625	56	7936	220	36.07	5-33	9	4.88
V.Kohli	110.2	1	680	5	136.00	1-13	–	6.16
P.M.Krishna	132.2	7	742	29	25.58	4-12	2	5.60
Kuldeep Yadav	864.5	29	4370	168	26.01	6-25	9	5.05
Mohammed Shami	830.5	51	4618	195	23.68	7-57	15	5.55
Mukesh Kumar	39	4	217	5	43.40	3-30	–	5.56
H.H.Pandya	533.1	15	2960	84	35.23	4-24	1	5.55
A.R.Patel	434.3	19	1972	60	32.86	3-24	–	4.53
B.Sai Sudharsan	0.3	0	8	0	–	–	–	16.00
K.R.Sen	5	0	37	2	18.50	2-37	–	7.40
Shahbaz Ahmed	26	0	125	3	41.66	2-32	–	4.80
R.G.Sharma	99.4	2	522	9	58.00	2-27	–	5.23
R.K.Singh	1	0	2	1	2.00	1- 2	–	2.00
M.Siraj	304.1	29	1550	68	22.79	6-21	3	5.09
S.N.Thakur	323.2	10	2014	65	30.98	4-37	3	6.22
N.T.Tilak Varma	7	0	39	0	–	–	–	5.57
Umran Malik	61	2	399	13	30.69	3-57	–	6.54
J.D.Unadkat	57	5	225	9	25.00	4-41	1	3.94
M.S.Washington Sundar	106	2	521	18	28.94	3-30	–	4.91
S.A.Yadav	2	0	17	0	–	–	–	8.50

PAKISTAN – BATTING AND FIELDING

	M	I	NO	HS	Runs	Avge	100	50	Ct/St
Abdullah Shafiq	12	12	–	113	416	34.66	1	4	5
Agha Salman	21	17	5	58	487	40.58	–	4	13
Babar Azam	117	114	13	158	5729	56.72	19	32	50
Faheem Ashraf	34	24	3	28	224	10.66	–	–	10
Fakhar Zaman	82	81	6	210*	3492	46.56	11	16	42
Haris Rauf	37	15	7	35	68	8.50	–	–	10
Haris Sohail	45	44	5	130	1749	44.84	2	14	17
Hassan Ali	66	38	11	59	383	14.18	–	2	13
Iftikhar Ahmed	28	24	8	109*	614	38.37	1	1	17
Ihsanullah	1	–	–	–	–	–	–	–	–
Imam-ul-Haq	72	71	6	151	3138	48.27	9	20	15
Kamran Ghulam	1	–	–	–	–	–	–	–	–
Mohammad Abbas	3	–	–	–	–	–	–	–	–
Mohammad Amir	61	30	10	73*	363	18.15	–	2	8

	M	I	NO	HS	Runs	Avge	100	50	Ct/St
Mohammad Haris	6	5	1	17*	30	7.50	–	–	5/2
Mohammad Hasnain	9	5	3	28	47	23.50	–	–	2
Mohammad Nawaz	37	28	6	53	406	18.45	–	1	14
Mohammad Rizwan	74	67	15	131*	2088	40.15	3	13	76/3
Mohammad Wasim	20	9	2	17*	80	11.42	–	–	4
Naseem Shah	14	4	3	18*	31	31.00	–	–	2
Saud Shakil	15	12	1	68	317	28.81	–	3	5
Shadab Khan	70	44	11	86	855	25.90	–	4	19
Shaheen Shah Afridi	53	29	17	25	196	16.33	–	–	11
Shan Masood	9	9	–	50	163	18.11	–	1	2
Usama Mir	12	6	–	20	40	6.66	–	–	7
Zafar Gohar	1	1	–	15	15	15.00	–	–	–
Zaman Khan	1	–	–	–	–	–	–	–	–

PAKISTAN – BOWLING

	O	M	R	W	Avge	Best	4wI	R/Over
Agha Salman	69	0	399	4	99.75	2-42	–	5.78
Faheem Ashraf	232.2	9	1204	26	46.30	5-22	1	5.18
Fakhar Zaman	22.3	0	111	1	111.00	1-19	–	4.93
Haris Rauf	305.5	11	1822	69	26.40	5-18	5	5.95
Haris Sohail	107	0	613	11	55.72	3-45	–	5.72
Hassan Ali	531.2	16	3084	100	30.84	5-34	6	5.80
Iftikhar Ahmed	132.4	4	742	16	46.37	5-40	1	5.59
Ihsanullah	8	0	60	0	–	–	–	7.50
Mohammad Abbas	27	0	153	1	153.00	1-44	–	5.66
Mohammad Amir	502.1	34	2400	81	29.62	5-30	2	4.77
Mohammad Hasnain	77.1	5	497	12	41.41	5-26	1	6.44
Mohammad Nawaz	295.3	4	1507	42	35.88	4-19	3	5.09
Mohammad Wasim	160.2	7	856	34	25.17	4-36	1	5.33
Naseem Shah	115.5	3	543	32	16.96	5-33	2	4.68
Saud Shakil	7.5	0	37	1	37.00	1-14	–	4.72
Shadab Khan	564.4	13	2960	85	34.82	4-27	5	5.24
Shaheen Shah Afridi	449.1	24	2490	104	23.94	6-35	9	5.54
Usama Mir	106	0	634	15	42.26	4-43	1	5.98
Zafar Gohar	10	0	54	2	27.00	2-54	–	5.40
Zaman Khan	6	1	39	0	–	–	–	6.50

SRI LANKA – BATTING AND FIELDING

	M	I	NO	HS	Runs	Avge	100	50	Ct/St
S.S.D.Arachchige	5	3	–	57	89	29.66	–	1	2
K.I.C.Asalanka	56	49	8	110	1772	43.21	3	11	14
K.N.A.Bandara	6	5	1	55*	141	35.25	–	2	3
P.V.D.Chameera	52	35	12	29	266	11.56	–	–	8
L.D.Chandimal	157	142	21	111	3854	31.85	4	24	62/8
S.D.L.Daniel	1	1	–	12	12	12.00	–	–	–
D.M.de Silva	90	82	10	93	1865	25.90	–	10	41
P.W.H.de Silva	51	43	7	80*	846	23.50	–	4	15
A.M.Fernando	7	2	1	1*	1	1.00	–	–	–
M.N.K.Fernando	4	4	–	50	75	18.75	–	1	–
W.I.A.Fernando	35	35	–	127	1178	33.65	3	7	14
M.A.D.I.Hemantha	5	4	2	22	39	19.50	–	–	1
C.Karunaratne	26	24	6	75	451	25.05	–	1	6
F.D.M.Karunaratne	50	46	4	103	1316	31.33	1	11	17
C.B.R.L.S.Kumara	28	16	6	10	55	5.50	–	–	6
P.A.D.Lakshan	3	2	–	2	4	2.00	–	–	1
P.M.Liyanagamage	6	3	–	15	17	5.66	–	–	2

	M	I	NO	HS	Runs	Avge	100	50	Ct/St
L.D.Madushanka	21	10	8	19	36	18.00	–	–	4
A.D.Mathews	226	195	48	139*	5916	40.24	3	40	53
B.K.G.Mendis	127	124	10	122	3755	32.93	3	28	86/6
M.Pathirana	12	7	2	5	11	2.20	–	–	2
M.D.K.J.Perera	116	111	5	135	3237	30.53	6	17	50/3
M.K.P.A.D.Perera	40	30	6	50*	291	12.12	–	1	14
C.A.K.Rajitha	34	19	7	33	117	9.75	–	–	5
W.S.R.Samarawickrama	38	35	5	108	1152	38.40	1	8	9
M.D.Shanaka	71	63	5	108*	1299	22.39	2	4	18
P.N.Silva	52	52	5	210*	2074	44.12	5	13	19
M.M.Theekshana	40	22	8	38*	248	17.71	–	–	7
J.D.F.Vandersay	22	14	4	25	111	11.10	–	–	4
K.L.J.Vimukthi	6	3	–	95	169	56.33	–	2	1
D.N.Wellalage	19	15	3	42*	207	17.25	–	–	6

SRI LANKA – BOWLING

	O	M	R	W	Avge	Best	4wI	R/Over
S.S.D.Arachchige	7	0	28	1	28.00	1-18	–	4.00
K.I.C.Asalanka	29.4	1	149	5	29.80	4-18	1	5.02
K.N.A.Bandara	1	0	8	0	–	–	–	8.00
P.V.D.Chameera	360	16	1970	56	35.17	5-16	4	5.47
D.M.de Silva	375	1	1907	44	43.34	3-32	–	5.08
P.W.H.de Silva	402.3	19	2031	78	26.03	7-19	6	5.04
A.M.Fernando	45	1	269	5	53.80	2-23	–	5.97
M.N.K.Fernando	2	0	22	0	–	–	–	11.00
M.A.D.I.Hemantha	35	0	193	2	96.50	2-49	–	5.51
C.Karunaratne	132.5	4	765	24	31.87	4-43	1	5.75
F.D.M.Karunaratne	2.4	0	18	0	–	–	–	6.75
C.B.R.L.S.Kumara	188.3	4	1223	37	33.05	3-22	–	6.48
P.A.D.Lakshan	11	0	76	1	76.00	1-43	–	6.90
P.M.Liyanagamage	36.2	1	249	11	22.63	4-75	1	6.85
L.D.Madushanka	158.2	9	946	37	25.56	5-80	2	5.97
A.D.Mathews	887.2	56	4110	126	32.61	6-20	3	4.63
B.K.G.Mendis	3.2	0	28	0	–	–	–	8.40
M.Pathirana	84.4	2	616	17	36.23	4-32	1	7.27
M.K.P.A.D.Perera	332.3	5	1715	58	29.56	6-29	4	5.15
C.A.K.Rajitha	254.3	5	1553	43	36.11	4-50	2	6.10
M.D.Shanaka	176	3	999	27	37.00	5-43	1	5.67
M.M.Theekshana	331.1	12	1541	55	28.01	4-25	5	4.65
J.D.F.Vandersay	153	6	849	27	31.44	4-10	1	5.54
K.L.J.Vimukthi	12	1	77	1	77.00	1-17	–	6.41
D.N.Wellalage	132.2	2	716	23	31.13	5-40	1	5.41

P.W.H.de Silva is also known as W.Hasaranga; P.M.Liyanagamage is also known as P.Madushan; M.K.P.A.D.Perera is also known as A.Dananjaya; P.N.Silva is also known as P.Nissanka; K.L.J.Vimukthi is also known as J.Liyanage.

ZIMBABWE – BATTING AND FIELDING

	M	I	NO	HS	Runs	Avge	100	50	Ct/St
G.S.Ballance †	5	5	1	64*	157	39.25	–	2	5
R.P.Burl	52	44	6	83	938	24.68	–	6	23
T.L.Chatara	87	57	25	23	206	6.43	–	–	8
C.J.Chibhabha	109	109	2	99	2474	23.12	–	16	34
T.L.Chivanga	8	6	3	8*	25	8.33	–	–	1
C.R.Ervine	119	115	13	130*	3376	33.09	4	20	56
B.N.Evans	15	13	3	33*	121	12.10	–	–	7

	M	I	NO	HS	Runs	Avge	100	50	Ct/St
Faraz Akram	2	1	–	1	1	1.00	–	–	2
J.Gumbie	12	12	–	78	354	29.50	–	2	10
L.M.Jongwe	43	36	5	46	430	13.87	–	–	12
I.Kaia	19	19	1	110	450	25.00	1	2	4
T.Kaitano	11	11	1	42	157	15.70	–	–	2
T.S.Kamunhukamwe	12	12	–	51	131	10.91	–	1	1
C.Madande	15	11	1	74	231	23.10	–	2	7/1
W.N.Madhevere	36	34	–	72	705	20.73	–	5	9
T.Marumani	12	11	1	45	157	15.70	–	–	1
W.P.Masakadza	38	24	4	40	208	10.40	–	–	11
B.A.Mavuta	12	8	2	28*	88	14.66	–	–	2
T.Mufudza	2	1	–	1	1	1.00	–	–	–
T.T.Munyonga	7	6	1	30*	92	18.40	–	–	1
B.Muzarabani	48	36	13	17*	122	5.30	–	–	13
R.Ngarava	44	27	12	35	168	11.20	–	–	7
V.M.Nyauchi	10	6	–	26	43	7.16	–	–	2
M.Shumba	10	9	2	26	57	8.14	–	–	3
Sikandar Raza	142	134	20	141	4154	36.43	7	21	57
S.C.Williams	156	151	20	174	4986	38.06	8	35	58

ZIMBABWE – BOWLING

	O	M	R	W	Avge	Best	4wI	R/Over
R.P.Burl	121.4	2	766	19	40.31	5-10	2	6.29
T.L.Chatara	709	55	3752	115	32.62	4-33	1	5.29
C.J.Chibhabha	279.5	12	1631	35	46.60	4-25	1	5.82
T.L.Chivanga	50.1	0	295	4	73.75	1-38	–	5.88
B.N.Evans	87.2	5	521	13	40.07	5-54	1	5.96
Faraz Akram	20	0	101	2	50.50	2-58	–	5.05
L.M.Jongwe	235.5	12	1339	40	33.47	5- 6	1	5.67
I.Kaia	4.4	0	22	0	–	–	–	4.71
W.N.Madhevere	134.2	1	683	13	52.53	3-36	–	5.08
W.P.Masakadza	258	8	1266	32	39.56	4-21	1	4.90
B.A.Mavuta	66	0	349	10	34.90	2-30	–	5.28
T.Mufudza	17	0	75	0	–	–	–	4.41
T.T.Munyonga	1	0	10	0	–	–	–	10.00
B.Muzarabani	385.2	22	1962	60	32.70	5-49	4	5.09
R.Ngarava	326.1	22	1739	56	31.05	5-32	2	5.33
V.M.Nyauchi	67	5	353	7	50.42	2-65	–	5.26
M.Shumba	6.5	0	42	0	–	–	–	6.14
Sikandar Raza	768.2	24	3738	88	42.47	4-55	1	4.86
S.C.Williams	798.4	34	3946	83	47.54	4-43	1	4.94

† *G.S.Ballance also made 16 appearances for England, scoring 297 runs at an average of 21.21, HS 79, 8ct.*

BANGLADESH – BATTING AND FIELDING

	M	I	NO	HS	Runs	Avge	100	50	Ct/St
Afif Hossain	31	27	6	93*	600	28.57	–	3	12
Anamul Haque	48	45	–	120	1340	29.77	3	5	14
Ebadat Hossain	12	6	4	1*	3	1.50	–	–	1
Hasan Mahmud	22	14	4	15	49	4.90	–	–	2
Khaled Ahmed	2	2	1	1	1	1.00	–	–	–
Liton Das	89	88	8	176	2563	32.03	5	12	55/4
Mahmudullah	229	199	51	128*	5348	36.13	4	28	81
Mehedi Hasan	94	66	11	112*	1294	23.52	2	3	38
Mohammad Naim	8	7	–	28	95	13.57	–	–	4
Mrittunjoy Chowdhury	1	1	–	8	8	8.00	–	–	2

	M	I	NO	HS	Runs	Avge	100	50	Ct/St
Mushfiqur Rahim	268	250	40	144	7657	36.46	9	49	229/56
Mustafizur Rahman	103	51	30	20	160	7.61	–	–	16
Nasum Ahmed	15	9	2	44	156	22.28	–	–	3
Nazmul Hossain	42	41	2	117	1202	30.82	2	8	12
Nurul Hasan	7	5	3	45*	165	82.50	–	–	6/4
Rishad Hossain	2	1	–	6	6	6.00	–	–	2
Rony Talukdar	1	1	–	4	4	4.00	–	–	1
Shakib Al Hasan	247	234	31	134*	7570	37.29	9	56	60
Shamim Hossain	4	4	–	16	33	8.25	–	–	1
Sheikh Mehedi Hasan	11	10	2	29*	122	15.25	–	–	2
Shoriful Islam	33	20	9	16	83	7.54	–	–	3
Soumya Sarkar	66	62	4	169	1941	33.46	3	11	35
Taijul Islam	18	12	1	39*	110	10.00	–	–	3
Tamim Iqbal	243	240	12	158	8357	36.65	14	56	68
Tanzid Hasan	14	13	–	51	179	13.76	–	1	4
Tanzim Hasan Sakib	5	3	2	14*	32	32.00	–	–	–
Taskin Ahmed	70	38	11	21	199	7.37	–	–	11
Towhid Hridoy	27	23	2	92	727	34.61	–	6	6
Yasir Ali	9	7	–	50	102	14.57	–	1	3
Zakir Hasan	1	1	–	1	1	1.00	–	–	–

BANGLADESH – BOWLING

	O	M	R	W	Avge	Best	4wI	R/Over
Afif Hossain	15.4	1	91	3	30.33	1- 0	–	5.80
Ebadat Hossain	90	4	504	22	22.90	4-42	2	5.60
Hasan Mahmud	159.3	7	963	30	32.10	5-32	1	6.03
Khaled Ahmed	13.2	1	72	3	24.00	3-60	–	5.40
Mahmudullah	725	14	3791	82	46.23	3- 4	–	5.22
Mehedi Hasan	735.3	32	3566	102	34.96	4-25	5	4.84
Mrittunjoy Chowdhury	8	0	64	0	–	–	–	8.00
Mustafizur Rahman	824.5	34	4268	162	26.34	6-43	10	5.17
Nasum Ahmed	121.1	12	550	12	45.83	3-19	–	4.53
Nazmul Hossain	13.2	0	75	1	75.00	1-10	–	5.62
Rishad Hossain	12.2	0	66	0	–	–	–	5.35
Shakib Al Hasan	2095.5	101	9360	317	29.52	5-29	14	4.46
Shamim Hossain	2	0	18	0	–	–	–	9.00
Sheikh Mehedi Hasan	88	2	436	14	31.14	4-71	1	4.95
Shoriful Islam	245.2	12	1360	51	26.66	4-21	3	5.54
Soumya Sarkar	80.4	1	483	14	34.50	3-18	–	5.98
Taijul Islam	162	9	708	30	23.60	5-28	2	4.37
Tamim Iqbal	1	0	13	0	–	–	–	13.00
Tanzim Hasan Sakib	36.3	3	202	8	25.25	3-14	–	5.53
Taskin Ahmed	541.2	24	2937	95	30.91	5-28	6	5.42
Yasir Ali	1	0	2	0	–	–	–	2.00

IRELAND – BATTING AND FIELDING

	M	I	NO	HS	Runs	Avge	100	50	Ct/St
M.R.Adair	46	32	12	32	396	19.80	–	–	21
A.Balbirnie	106	100	8	145*	3003	32.64	8	16	35
C.Campher	35	27	2	120	872	34.88	1	6	10
M.Commins	2	1	–	6	6	6.00	–	–	1
G.J.Delany	21	18	5	22	234	18.00	–	–	9
G.H.Dockrell	122	84	28	91*	1335	23.83	–	6	47
S.T.Doheny	9	7	–	84	162	23.14	–	1	3
G.I.Hume	13	4	3	15*	27	27.00	–	–	2
M.J.Humphreys	2	1	1	4*	4	–	–	–	–

IRELAND – BATTING AND FIELDING (continued)

	M	I	NO	HS	Runs	Avge	100	50	Ct/St
J.B.Little	36	14	5	29	80	8.88	–	–	5
A.R.McBrine	86	57	13	79	826	18.77	–	2	33
B.J.McCarthy	44	29	7	41	212	9.63	–	–	14
P.R.Stirling	159	152	3	177	5645	37.88	14	28	60
H.T.Tector	43	39	6	140	1606	48.66	4	11	20
L.J.Tucker	49	40	5	83	753	21.51	–	3	63/3
T.F.van Woerkom	2	–	–	–	–	–	–	–	1
B.C.White	2	–	–	–	–	–	–	–	–
C.A.Young	44	24	11	40*	125	10.41	–	–	12

IRELAND – BOWLING

	O	M	R	W	Avge	Best	4wI	R/Over
M.R.Adair	340.3	21	1955	56	34.91	4-19	4	5.74
A.Balbirnie	10	0	68	2	34.00	1-26	–	6.80
C.Campher	164.4	4	967	28	34.53	4-37	1	5.87
G.J.Delany	65	0	410	7	58.57	2-52	–	6.30
G.H.Dockrell	795.2	31	3854	106	36.35	4-24	4	4.84
G.I.Hume	90.3	4	500	20	25.00	4-34	2	5.52
M.J.Humphreys	11	0	95	0	–	–	–	8.63
J.B.Little	288.5	11	1757	56	31.37	6-36	4	6.08
A.R.McBrine	669.5	37	3031	85	35.65	5-29	3	4.52
B.J.McCarthy	364.4	14	2124	70	30.34	5-46	3	5.82
P.R.Stirling	406.5	8	1942	43	45.16	6-55	2	4.77
H.T.Tector	32	0	200	3	66.66	1- 5	–	6.25
T.F.van Woerkom	8	0	75	1	75.00	1-47	–	9.37
B.C.White	18	0	118	1	118.00	1-59	–	6.55
C.A.Young	345.2	15	1871	73	25.63	5-46	2	5.41

AFGHANISTAN – BATTING AND FIELDING

	M	I	NO	HS	Runs	Avge	100	50	Ct/St
Abdul Rahman	3	3	1	4*	10	5.00	–	–	–
Azmatullah Omarzai	25	19	6	149*	696	53.53	1	5	4
Fareed Ahmad	17	7	4	17	42	14.00	–	–	3
Fazalhaq Farooqi	30	16	11	6*	16	3.20	–	–	2
Gulbadin Naib	81	70	8	82*	1223	19.72	–	5	24
Hashmatullah Shahidi	76	76	12	97*	2106	32.90	–	19	15
Ibrahim Zadran	31	31	3	162	1358	48.50	5	6	11
Ikram Alikhil	24	19	5	86	373	26.64	–	3	9/4
Karim Janat	3	3	–	22	32	10.66	–	–	–
Mohammad Nabi	159	140	15	136	3359	26.87	2	16	71
Mohammad Saleem	2	–	–	–	–	–	–	–	1
Mujeeb Zadran	75	40	14	64	236	9.07	–	1	11
Najibullah Zadran	92	84	13	104*	2060	29.01	1	15	40
Naveen-Ul-Haq	15	10	5	10*	37	7.40	–	–	4
Noor Ahmad	9	4	1	26	31	10.33	–	–	1
Qais Ahmad	3	2	–	11	12	6.00	–	–	–
Rahmanullah Gurbaz	38	38	1	151	1295	35.00	5	4	22/2
Rahmat Shah	109	105	4	114	3724	36.87	5	28	27
Rashid Khan	103	81	14	60*	1316	19.64	–	5	33
Riaz Hassan	5	4	–	50	120	30.00	–	1	3
Shahidullah	3	3	–	37	39	13.00	–	–	2
Sharafuddin Ashraf	20	12	4	21	70	8.75	–	–	6
Yamin Ahmadzai	9	5	2	5	9	3.00	–	–	4
Zia-ur-Rehman	1	1	–	5	5	5.00	–	–	–

AFGHANISTAN – BOWLING

	O	*M*	*R*	*W*	*Avge*	*Best*	*4wI*	*R/Over*
Abdul Rahman	17.2	0	133	1	133.00	1-83	–	7.67
Azmatullah Omarzai	129.4	2	764	16	47.75	3-56	–	5.89
Fareed Ahmad	115	5	649	23	28.21	3-56	–	5.64
Fazalhaq Farooqi	222	13	1294	39	33.17	4-34	3	5.82
Gulbadin Naib	462.3	12	2561	72	35.56	6-43	4	5.53
Hashmatullah Shahidi	3	0	25	0	–	–	–	8.33
Karim Janat	13	0	90	0	–	–	–	6.92
Mohammad Nabi	1248.2	47	5357	164	32.66	4-30	4	4.29
Mohammad Saleem	10.2	0	70	0	–	–	–	6.77
Mujeeb Zadran	661.2	39	2863	101	28.34	5-50	4	4.32
Najibullah Zadran	5	0	30	0	–	–	–	6.00
Naveen-Ul-Haq	115.1	2	708	22	32.18	4-42	1	6.14
Noor Ahmad	75	1	454	8	56.75	3-49	–	6.05
Qais Ahmad	21.4	0	133	6	22.16	3-32	–	6.13
Rahmat Shah	90.3	2	532	15	35.46	5-32	1	5.87
Rashid Khan	883.2	32	3748	183	20.48	7-18	10	4.24
Shahidullah	3	0	16	0	–	–	–	5.33
Sharafuddin Ashraf	147.2	4	652	13	50.15	3-29	–	4.42
Yamin Ahmadzai	56.4	4	304	7	43.42	2-34	–	5.36
Zia-ur-Rehman	3.3	0	22	0	–	–	–	6.28

ASSOCIATES – BATTING AND FIELDING

	M	*I*	*NO*	*HS*	*Runs*	*Avge*	*100*	*50*	*Ct/St*
C.N.Ackermann (Neth)	16	15	–	81	427	28.46	–	3	8
S.W.Currie (Scot)	2	1	–	5	5	5.00	–	–	–
J.H.Davey (Scot)	31	28	6	64	497	22.59	–	2	10
B.F.W.de Leede (Neth)	43	41	2	123	976	25.02	1	3	22
B.D.Glover (Neth)	9	6	4	18	29	14.50	–	–	3
I.G.Holland (USA)	15	14	–	75	368	26.28	–	2	6
M.A.Jones (Scot)	12	12	–	87	354	29.50	–	3	4
F.J.Klaassen (Neth)	19	15	7	13	68	8.50	–	–	5
S.Snater (Neth)	4	4	1	17*	33	11.00	–	–	5
C.J.Tear (Scot)	1	1	1	54*	54	–	–	1	1
A.R.I.Umeed (Scot)	1	1	–	8	8	8.00	–	–	–
T.van der Gugten (Neth)	8	4	–	49	54	13.50	–	–	–
R.E.van der Merwe (Neth) †	14	10	–	57	128	12.80	–	1	6
B.T.J.Wheal (Scot)	13	7	3	14	16	4.00	–	–	3

ASSOCIATES – BOWLING

	O	*M*	*R*	*W*	*Avge*	*Best*	*4wI*	*R/Over*
C.N.Ackermann	91.2	3	451	9	50.11	2-39	–	4.93
S.W.Currie	15	3	62	3	20.66	2-16	–	4.13
J.H.Davey	216.5	18	1082	49	22.08	6-28	3	4.99
B.F.W.de Leede	219	2	1362	43	31.67	5-52	2	6.21
B.D.Glover	73	2	444	9	49.33	3-43	–	6.08
I.G.Holland	104.4	6	466	19	24.52	3-11	–	4.45
F.J.Klaassen	174.3	12	753	32	23.53	3-23	–	4.31
S.Snater	25	1	188	2	94.00	1-41	–	7.52
T.van der Gugten	54	7	195	12	16.25	5-24	1	3.61
R.E.van der Merwe	105	1	527	12	43.91	2-33	–	5.01
B.T.J.Wheal	114.3	9	508	23	22.08	3-34	–	4.43

† *R.E.van der Merwe has also made 13 appearances for South Africa (see above).*

LIMITED-OVERS INTERNATIONALS RESULTS

1970-71 to 27 February 2024

This chart excludes all matches involving multinational teams.

	Opponents	*Matches*	*Won*													*Tied*	*NR*
			E	*A*	*SA*	*WI*	*NZ*	*I*	*P*	*SL*	*Z*	*B*	*Ire*	*Afg*	*Ass*		
England	Australia	156	63	88	–	–	–	–	–	–	–	–	–	–	–	2	3
	South Africa	70	30	–	34	–	–	–	–	–	–	–	–	–	–	1	5
	West Indies	105	53	–	–	46	–	–	–	–	–	–	–	–	–	–	6
	New Zealand	96	44	–	–	–	45	–	–	–	–	–	–	–	–	3	4
	India	107	44	–	–	–	–	58	–	–	–	–	–	–	–	2	3
	Pakistan	92	57	–	–	–	–	–	32	–	–	–	–	–	–	–	3
	Sri Lanka	79	38	–	–	–	–	–	–	37	–	–	–	–	–	1	3
	Zimbabwe	30	21	–	–	–	–	–	–	–	8	–	–	–	–	–	1
	Bangladesh	25	20	–	–	–	–	–	–	–	–	5	–	–	–	–	–
	Ireland	15	11	–	–	–	–	–	–	–	–	–	2	–	–	–	2
	Afghanistan	3	2	–	–	–	–	–	–	–	–	–	–	1	–	–	–
	Associates	19	17	–	–	–	–	–	–	–	–	–	–	–	1	–	1
Australia	South Africa	110	–	51	55	–	–	–	–	–	–	–	–	–	–	3	1
	West Indies	146	–	79	–	61	–	–	–	–	–	–	–	–	–	3	3
	New Zealand	142	–	96	–	–	39	–	–	–	–	–	–	–	–	–	7
	India	151	–	84	–	–	–	57	–	–	–	–	–	–	–	–	10
	Pakistan	108	–	70	–	–	–	–	34	–	–	–	–	–	–	1	3
	Sri Lanka	103	–	64	–	–	–	–	–	35	–	–	–	–	–	–	4
	Zimbabwe	33	–	29	–	–	–	–	–	–	3	–	–	–	–	–	1
	Bangladesh	22	–	20	–	–	–	–	–	–	–	1	–	–	–	–	1
	Ireland	5	–	4	–	–	–	–	–	–	–	–	0	–	–	–	1
	Afghanistan	4	–	4	–	–	–	–	–	–	–	–	–	0	–	–	–
	Associates	17	–	17	–	–	–	–	–	–	–	–	–	–	0	–	–
S Africa	West Indies	64	–	–	45	16	–	–	–	–	–	–	–	–	–	1	2
	New Zealand	72	–	–	42	–	25	–	–	–	–	–	–	–	–	–	5
	India	94	–	–	51	–	–	40	–	–	–	–	–	–	–	–	3
	Pakistan	83	–	–	52	–	–	–	30	–	–	–	–	–	–	–	1
	Sri Lanka	81	–	–	46	–	–	–	–	33	–	–	–	–	–	1	1
	Zimbabwe	41	–	–	38	–	–	–	–	–	2	–	–	–	–	–	1
	Bangladesh	25	–	–	19	–	–	–	–	–	–	6	–	–	–	–	–
	Ireland	8	–	–	6	–	–	–	–	–	–	–	1	–	–	–	1
	Afghanistan	2	–	–	2	–	–	–	–	–	–	–	–	0	–	–	–
	Associates	22	–	–	20	–	–	–	–	–	–	–	–	–	1	–	1
W Indies	New Zealand	68	–	–	–	31	30	–	–	–	–	–	–	–	–	–	7
	India	142	–	–	–	64	–	72	–	–	–	–	–	–	–	2	4
	Pakistan	137	–	–	–	71	–	–	63	–	–	–	–	–	–	3	–
	Sri Lanka	64	–	–	–	31	–	–	–	30	–	–	–	–	–	–	3
	Zimbabwe	49	–	–	–	36	–	–	–	–	11	–	–	–	–	1	1
	Bangladesh	44	–	–	–	21	–	–	–	–	–	21	–	–	–	–	2
	Ireland	15	–	–	–	11	–	–	–	–	–	–	3	–	–	–	1
	Afghanistan	9	–	–	–	5	–	–	–	–	–	–	–	3	–	–	1
	Associates	30	–	–	–	27	–	–	–	–	–	–	–	–	2	1	–
N Zealand	India	118	–	–	–	–	50	60	–	–	–	–	–	–	–	1	7
	Pakistan	116	–	–	–	–	51	–	61	–	–	–	–	–	–	1	3
	Sri Lanka	102	–	–	–	–	52	–	–	41	–	–	–	–	–	1	8
	Zimbabwe	38	–	–	–	–	27	–	–	–	9	–	–	–	–	1	1
	Bangladesh	45	–	–	–	–	33	–	–	–	–	11	–	–	–	–	1
	Ireland	7	–	–	–	–	7	–	–	–	–	–	0	–	–	–	–
	Afghanistan	3	–	–	–	–	3	–	–	–	–	–	–	0	–	–	–
	Associates	17	–	–	–	–	17	–	–	–	–	–	–	–	0	–	–
India	Pakistan	135	–	–	–	–	–	57	73	–	–	–	–	–	–	–	5
	Sri Lanka	168	–	–	–	–	–	99	–	57	–	–	–	–	–	1	11
	Zimbabwe	66	–	–	–	–	–	54	–	–	10	–	–	–	–	2	–
	Bangladesh	41	–	–	–	–	–	32	–	–	–	8	–	–	–	–	1

	Opponents	Matches	Won													Tied	NR
			E	A	SA	WI	NZ	I	P	SL	Z	B	Ire	Afg	Ass		
	Ireland	3	–	–	–	–	–	3	–	–	–	–	0	–	–	–	–
	Afghanistan	4	–	–	–	–	–	3	–	–	–	–	–	0	–	1	–
	Associates	26	–	–	–	–	–	24	–	–	–	–	–	–	2	–	–
Pakistan	Sri Lanka	157	–	–	–	–	–	–	93	59	–	–	–	–	–	1	4
	Zimbabwe	62	–	–	–	–	–	–	54	–	4	–	–	–	–	2	2
	Bangladesh	39	–	–	–	–	–	–	34	–	–	5	–	–	–	–	–
	Ireland	7	–	–	–	–	–	–	5	–	–	–	1	–	–	1	–
	Afghanistan	8	–	–	–	–	–	–	7	–	–	–	–	1	–	–	–
	Associates	26	–	–	–	–	–	–	26	–	–	–	–	–	0	–	–
Sri Lanka	Zimbabwe	64	–	–	–	–	–	–	–	49	12	–	–	–	–	–	3
	Bangladesh	54	–	–	–	–	–	–	–	42	–	10	–	–	–	–	2
	Ireland	5	–	–	–	–	–	–	–	5	–	–	0	–	–	–	2
	Afghanistan	15	–	–	–	–	–	–	–	10	–	–	–	4	–	–	1
	Associates	23	–	–	–	–	–	–	–	22	–	–	–	–	1	–	–
Zimbabwe	Bangladesh	81	–	–	–	–	–	–	–	–	30	51	–	–	–	–	–
	Ireland	22	–	–	–	–	–	–	–	–	8	–	10	–	–	1	3
	Afghanistan	28	–	–	–	–	–	–	–	–	10	–	–	18	–	–	–
	Associates	58	–	–	–	–	–	–	–	–	44	–	–	–	11	1	2
Bangladesh	Ireland	16	–	–	–	–	–	–	–	–	–	11	2	–	–	–	3
	Afghanistan	16	–	–	–	–	–	–	–	–	–	10	–	6	–	–	–
	Associates	27	–	–	–	–	–	–	–	–	–	18	–	–	9	–	–
Ireland	Afghanistan	30	–	–	–	–	–	–	–	–	–	–	13	16	–	–	1
	Associates	66	–	–	–	–	–	–	–	–	–	–	48	–	14	1	3
Afghanistan	Associates	42	–	–	–	–	–	–	–	–	–	–	–	28	13	–	1
Associates	Associates	304	–	–	–	–	–	–	–	–	–	–	–	–	294	3	7
		4727	400	606	410	420	379	559	512	420	151	157	80	77	348	43	165

MERIT TABLE OF ALL L-O INTERNATIONALS

	Matches	Won	Lost	Tied	No Result	% Won (exc NR)
South Africa	672	410	235	6	21	62.98
Australia	997	606	348	9	34	62.92
India	1055	559	443	9	44	55.29
Pakistan	970	512	428	9	21	53.95
England	797	400	357	9	31	52.21
West Indies	873	420	412	11	30	49.82
New Zealand	824	379	395	7	43	48.52
Afghanistan	164	77	82	1	4	48.12
Sri Lanka	915	420	450	5	40	48.00
Ireland	199	80	101	3	15	43.47
Bangladesh	435	157	268	–	10	36.94
Zimbabwe	572	151	398	8	15	27.10
Associate Members (v Full*)	372	54	308	3	7	14.79

* Results of games between two Associate Members and those involving multi-national sides are excluded from this list; Associate Members have participated in 676 LOIs, 304 LOIs being between Associate Members.

TEAM RECORDS

HIGHEST TOTALS

† Batting Second

498-4	(50 overs)	England v Netherlands	Amstelveen	2022
481-6	(50 overs)	England v Australia	Nottingham	2018
444-3	(50 overs)	England v Pakistan	Nottingham	2016

443-9	(50 overs)	Sri Lanka v Netherlands	Amstelveen	2006
439-2	(50 overs)	South Africa v West Indies	Johannesburg	2014-15
438-9†	(49.5 overs)	South Africa v Australia	Johannesburg	2005-06
438-4	(50 overs)	South Africa v India	Mumbai	2015-16
434-4	(50 overs)	Australia v South Africa	Johannesburg	2005-06
428-5	(50 overs)	South Africa v Sri Lanka	Delhi	2023-24
418-5	(50 overs)	South Africa v Zimbabwe	Potchefstroom	2006-07
418-5	(50 overs)	India v West Indies	Indore	2011-12
418-6	(50 overs)	England v West Indies	St George's	2018-19
417-6	(50 overs)	Australia v Afghanistan	Perth	2014-15
416-5	(50 overs)	South Africa v Australia	Centurion	2023-24
414-7	(50 overs)	India v Sri Lanka	Rajkot	2009-10
413-5	(50 overs)	India v Bermuda	Port of Spain	2006-07
411-8†	(50 overs)	Sri Lanka v India	Rajkot	2009-10
411-4	(50 overs)	South Africa v Ireland	Canberra	2014-15
410-4	(50 overs)	India v Netherlands	Bengaluru	2023-24
409-8	(50 overs)	India v Bangladesh	Chittagong	2022-23
408-5	(50 overs)	South Africa v West Indies	Sydney	2014-15
408-9	(50 overs)	England v New Zealand	Birmingham	2015
408-6	(50 overs)	Zimbabwe v USA	Harare	2023
404-5	(50 overs)	India v Sri Lanka	Kolkata	2014-15
402-2	(50 overs)	New Zealand v Ireland	Aberdeen	2008
401-3	(50 overs)	India v South Africa	Gwalior	2009-10
401-6	(50 overs)	New Zealand v Pakistan	Bengaluru	2023-24
399-6	(50 overs)	South Africa v Zimbabwe	Benoni	2010-11
399-9	(50 overs)	England v South Africa	Bloemfontein	2015-16
399-1	(50 overs)	Pakistan v Zimbabwe	Bulawayo	2018
399-5	(50 overs)	India v Australia	Indore	2023-24
399-7	(50 overs)	South Africa v England	Mumbai	2023-24
399-8	(50 overs)	Australia v Netherlands	Delhi	2023-24
398-5	(50 overs)	Sri Lanka v Kenya	Kandy	1995-96
398-5	(50 overs)	New Zealand v England	The Oval	2015
397-5	(44 overs)	New Zealand v Zimbabwe	Bulawayo	2005
397-6	(50 overs)	England v Afghanistan	Manchester	2019
397-4	(50 overs)	India v New Zealand	Mumbai	2023-24
393-6	(50 overs)	New Zealand v West Indies	Wellington	2014-15
392-6	(50 overs)	South Africa v Pakistan	Centurion	2006-07
392-4	(50 overs)	India v New Zealand	Christchurch	2008-09
392-4	(50 overs)	India v Sri Lanka	Mohali	2017-18
392-8	(50 overs)	Australia v South Africa	Bloemfontein	2023-24
391-4	(50 overs)	England v Bangladesh	Nottingham	2005
390-5	(50 overs)	India v Sri Lanka	Karyavattom	2022-23
389	(48 overs)	West Indies v England	St George's	2018-19
389-4	(50 overs)	Australia v India	Sydney	2020-21
388	(49.2 overs)	Australia v New Zealand	Dharamsala	2023-24
387-5	(50 overs)	India v England	Rajkot	2008-09
387-5	(50 overs)	India v West Indies	Visakhapatnam	2019-20

The highest score for Ireland is 359-9 (v NZ, Dublin, 2022), for Bangladesh is 349-6 (v Ire, Sylhet, 2022-23) and for Afghanistan is 339-6 (v SL, Pallekele, 2023-24).

HIGHEST MATCH AGGREGATES

872-13	(99.5 overs)	South Africa v Australia	Johannesburg	2005-06
825-15	(100 overs)	India v Sri Lanka	Rajkot	2009-10
807-16	(98 overs)	West Indies v England	St George's	2018-19

LARGEST RUNS MARGINS OF VICTORY

317 runs	India beat Sri Lanka	Karyavattom	2022-23
309 runs	Australia beat Netherlands	Delhi	2023-24

304 runs	Zimbabwe beat USA	Harare	2023
302 runs	India beat Sri Lanka	Mumbai	2023-24
290 runs	New Zealand beat Ireland	Aberdeen	2008
275 runs	Australia beat Afghanistan	Perth	2014-15
272 runs	South Africa beat Zimbabwe	Benoni	2010-11
258 runs	South Africa beat Sri Lanka	Paarl	2011-12
257 runs	India beat Bermuda	Port of Spain	2006-07
257 runs	South Africa beat West Indies	Sydney	2014-15
256 runs	Australia beat Namibia	Potchefstroom	2002-03
256 runs	India beat Hong Kong	Karachi	2008
255 runs	Pakistan beat Ireland	Dublin	2016
245 runs	Sri Lanka beat India	Sharjah	2000-01
244 runs	Pakistan beat Zimbabwe	Bulawayo	2018
243 runs	Sri Lanka beat Bermuda	Port of Spain	2006-07
243 runs	India beat South Africa	Kolkata	2023-24
242 runs	England beat Australia	Nottingham	2018
238 runs	Pakistan beat Nepal	Multan	2023
234 runs	Sri Lanka beat Pakistan	Lahore	2008-09

LOWEST TOTALS (Excluding reduced innings)

35	(18.0 overs)	Zimbabwe v Sri Lanka	Harare	2003-04
35	(12.0 overs)	USA v Nepal	Kirtipur	2019-20
36	(18.4 overs)	Canada v Sri Lanka	Paarl	2002-03
38	(15.4 overs)	Zimbabwe v Sri Lanka	Colombo (SSC)	2001-02
43	(19.5 overs)	Pakistan v West Indies	Cape Town	1992-93
43	(20.1 overs)	Sri Lanka v South Africa	Paarl	2011-12
44	(24.5 overs)	Zimbabwe v Bangladesh	Chittagong	2009-10
45	(40.3 overs)	Canada v England	Manchester	1979
45	(14.0 overs)	Namibia v Australia	Potchefstroom	2002-03
50	(15.2 overs)	Sri Lanka v India	Colombo (RPS)	2023-24
54	(26.3 overs)	India v Sri Lanka	Sharjah	2000-01
54	(23.2 overs)	West Indies v South Africa	Cape Town	2003-04
54	(13.5 overs)	Zimbabwe v Afghanistan	Harare	2016-17
55	(28.3 overs)	Sri Lanka v West Indies	Sharjah	1986-87
55	(19.4 overs)	Sri Lanka v India	Mumbai	2023-24
58	(18.5 overs)	Bangladesh v West Indies	Mirpur	2010-11
58	(17.4 overs)	Bangladesh v India	Mirpur	2014
58	(16.1 overs)	Afghanistan v Zimbabwe	Sharjah	2015-16
59-9	(19.2 overs)	Afghanistan v Pakistan	Hambantota	2023
61	(22.0 overs)	West Indies v Bangladesh	Chittagong	2011-12
63	(25.5 overs)	India v Australia	Sydney	1980-81
63	(18.3 overs)	Afghanistan v Scotland	Abu Dhabi	2014-15
64	(35.5 overs)	New Zealand v Pakistan	Sharjah	1985-86
65	(24.0 overs)	USA v Australia	Southampton	2004
65	(24.3 overs)	Zimbabwe v India	Harare	2005
67	(31.0 overs)	Zimbabwe v Sri Lanka	Harare	2008-09
67	(24.4 overs)	Canada v Netherlands	King City	2013
67	(24.0 overs)	Sri Lanka v England	Manchester	2014
67	(25.1 overs)	Zimbabwe v Pakistan	Bulawayo	2018
68	(31.3 overs)	Scotland v West Indies	Leicester	1999
69	(28.0 overs)	South Africa v Australia	Sydney	1993-94
69	(22.5 overs)	Zimbabwe v Kenya	Harare	2005-06
69	(23.5 overs)	Kenya v New Zealand	Chennai	2010-11
70	(25.2 overs)	Australia v England	Birmingham	1977
70	(26.3 overs)	Australia v New Zealand	Adelaide	1985-86
70	(23.5 overs)	West Indies v Australia	Perth	2012-13

70	(24.4 overs)	Bangladesh v West Indies	St George's	2014
70	(24.4 overs)	Zimbabwe v Sri Lanka	Pallekele	2021-22

The lowest for England is 86 (v A, Manchester, 2001) and for Ireland is 77 (v SL, St George's, 2007).

LOWEST MATCH AGGREGATES

71-12	(17.2 overs)	USA (35) v Nepal (36-2)	Kirtipur	2019-20
73-11	(23.2 overs)	Canada (36) v Sri Lanka (37-1)	Paarl	2002-03
75-11	(27.2 overs)	Zimbabwe (35) v Sri Lanka (40-1)	Harare	2003-04
78-11	(20.0 overs)	Zimbabwe (38) v Sri Lanka (40-1)	Colombo (SSC)	2001-02

BATTING RECORDS
6500 RUNS IN A CAREER

		LOI	*I*	*NO*	*HS*	***Runs***	*Avge*	*100*	*50*
S.R.Tendulkar	I	463	452	41	200*	**18426**	44.83	49	96
K.C.Sangakkara	SL/Asia/ICC	404	380	41	169	**14234**	41.98	25	93
V.Kohli	I	292	280	44	183	**13848**	58.67	50	72
R.T.Ponting	A/ICC	375	365	39	164	**13704**	42.03	30	82
S.T.Jayasuriya	SL/Asia	445	433	18	189	**13430**	32.36	28	68
D.P.M.D.Jayawardena	SL/Asia	448	418	39	144	**12650**	33.37	19	77
Inzamam-ul-Haq	P/Asia	378	350	53	137*	**11739**	39.52	10	83
J.H.Kallis	SA/Afr/ICC	328	314	53	139	**11579**	44.36	17	86
S.C.Ganguly	I/Asia	311	300	23	183	**11363**	41.02	22	72
R.S.Dravid	I/Asia/ICC	344	318	40	153	**10889**	39.16	12	83
M.S.Dhoni	I/Asia	350	297	84	183*	**10773**	50.57	10	73
R.G.Sharma	I	262	254	36	264	**10709**	49.12	31	55
C.H.Gayle	WI/ICC	301	294	17	215	**10480**	37.83	25	54
B.C.Lara	WI/ICC	299	289	32	169	**10405**	40.48	19	63
T.M.Dilshan	SL	330	303	41	161*	**10290**	39.27	22	47
Mohammad Yousuf	P/Asia	288	272	40	141*	**9720**	41.71	15	64
A.C.Gilchrist	A/ICC	287	279	11	172	**9619**	35.89	16	55
A.B.de Villiers	SA/Afr	228	218	39	176	**9577**	53.50	25	53
M.Azharuddin	I	334	308	54	153*	**9378**	36.92	7	58
P.A.de Silva	SL	308	296	30	145	**9284**	34.90	11	64
Saeed Anwar	P	247	244	19	194	**8824**	39.21	20	43
S.Chanderpaul	WI	268	251	40	150	**8778**	41.60	11	59
Yuvraj Singh	I/Asia	304	278	40	150	**8701**	36.55	14	52
D.L.Haynes	WI	238	237	28	152*	**8648**	41.37	17	57
L.R.P.L.Taylor	NZ	236	220	39	181*	**8607**	47.55	21	51
M.S.Atapattu	SL	268	259	32	132*	**8529**	37.57	11	59
M.E.Waugh	A	244	236	20	173	**8500**	39.35	18	50
Tamim Iqbal	B	243	240	12	158	**8357**	36.65	14	56
V.Sehwag	I/Asia/ICC	251	245	9	219	**8273**	35.05	15	38
H.M.Amla	SA	181	178	14	159	**8113**	49.46	27	39
H.H.Gibbs	SA	248	240	16	175	**8094**	36.13	21	37
Shahid Afridi	P/Asia/ICC	398	369	27	124	**8064**	23.57	6	39
S.P.Fleming	NZ/ICC	280	269	21	134*	**8037**	32.40	8	49
M.J.Clarke	A	245	223	44	130	**7981**	44.58	8	58
E.J.G.Morgan	E/Ire	248	230	34	148	**7701**	39.29	14	47
Mushfiqur Rahim	B	268	250	40	144	**7657**	36.46	9	48
Shakib Al Hasan	B	247	234	31	134*	**7570**	37.29	9	56
S.R.Waugh	A	325	288	58	120*	**7569**	32.90	3	45
Shoaib Malik	P	287	258	40	143	**7534**	34.55	9	44
A.Ranatunga	SL	269	255	47	131*	**7456**	35.84	4	49
Javed Miandad	P	233	218	41	119*	**7381**	41.70	8	50
M.J.Guptill	NZ	198	195	19	237*	**7346**	41.73	18	39

		LOI	I	NO	HS	Runs	Avge	100	50
Younus Khan	P	265	255	23	144	**7249**	31.24	7	48
Salim Malik	P	283	256	38	102	**7170**	32.88	5	47
N.J.Astle	NZ	223	217	14	145*	**7090**	34.92	16	41
G.C.Smith	SA/Afr	197	194	10	141	**6989**	37.98	10	47
W.U.Tharanga	SL/Asia	235	223	17	174*	**6951**	33.74	15	37
D.A.Warner	A	161	159	6	179	**6932**	45.30	22	33
M.G.Bevan	A	232	196	67	108*	**6912**	53.58	6	46
K.S.Williamson	NZ	165	157	17	148	**6810**	48.64	13	45
G.Kirsten	SA	185	185	19	188*	**6798**	40.95	13	45
S.Dhawan	I	167	164	10	143	**6793**	44.11	17	39
A.Flower	Z	213	208	16	145	**6786**	35.34	4	55
Q.de Kock	SA	155	155	7	178	**6770**	45.74	21	30
I.V.A.Richards	WI	187	167	24	189*	**6721**	47.00	11	45
B.R.M.Taylor	Z	205	203	15	145*	**6684**	35.55	11	39
Mohammad Hafeez	P	218	216	15	140*	**6614**	32.90	11	38
G.W.Flower	Z	221	214	18	142*	**6571**	33.52	6	40
Ijaz Ahmed	P	250	232	29	139*	**6564**	32.33	10	37
A.R.Border	A	273	252	39	127*	**6524**	30.62	3	39
J.E.Root	E	171	160	23	133*	**6522**	47.60	16	39

The most runs for Ireland is 5645 by P.R.Stirling (152 innings) and for Afghanistan 3724 by Rahmat Shah (105 innings).

HIGHEST INDIVIDUAL INNINGS

264	R.G.Sharma	India v Sri Lanka	Kolkata	2014-15
237*	M.J.Guptill	New Zealand v West Indies	Wellington	2014-15
219	V.Sehwag	India v West Indies	Indore	2011-12
215	C.H.Gayle	West Indies v Zimbabwe	Canberra	2014-15
210*	Fakhar Zaman	Pakistan v Zimbabwe	Bulawayo	2018
210*	P.N.Silva	Sri Lanka v Afghanistan	Pallekele	2023-24
210	Ishan Kishan	India v Bangladesh	Chittagong	2022-23
209	R.G.Sharma	India v Australia	Bengaluru	2013-14
208*	R.G.Sharma	India v Sri Lanka	Mohali	2017-18
208	S.Gill	India v New Zealand	Hyderabad	2022-23
201*	G.J.Maxwell	Australia v Afghanistan	Mumbai	2023-24
200*	S.R.Tendulkar	India v South Africa	Gwalior	2009-10
194*	C.K.Coventry	Zimbabwe v Bangladesh	Bulawayo	2009
194	Saeed Anwar	Pakistan v India	Chennai	1996-97
193	Fakhar Zaman	Pakistan v South Africa	Johannesburg	2020-21
189*	I.V.A.Richards	West Indies v England	Manchester	1984
189*	M.J.Guptill	New Zealand v England	Southampton	2013
189	S.T.Jayasuriya	Sri Lanka v India	Sharjah	2000-01
188*	G.Kirsten	South Africa v UAE	Rawalpindi	1995-96
186*	S.R.Tendulkar	India v New Zealand	Hyderabad	1999-00
185*	S.R.Watson	Australia v Bangladesh	Mirpur	2010-11
185	F.du Plessis	South Africa v Sri Lanka	Cape Town	2016-17
183*	M.S.Dhoni	India v Sri Lanka	Jaipur	2005-06
183	S.C.Ganguly	India v Sri Lanka	Taunton	1999
183	V.Kohli	India v Pakistan	Mirpur	2011-12
182	B.A.Stokes	England v New Zealand	The Oval	2023
181*	M.L.Hayden	Australia v New Zealand	Hamilton	2006-07
181*	L.R.P.L.Taylor	New Zealand v England	Dunedin	2017-18
181	I.V.A.Richards	West Indies v Sri Lanka	Karachi	1987-88
180*	M.J.Guptill	New Zealand v South Africa	Hamilton	2016-17
180*	Fakhar Zaman	Pakistan v New Zealand	Rawalpindi	2023
180	J.J.Roy	England v Australia	Melbourne	2017-18

179	D.A.Warner	Australia v Pakistan	Adelaide	2016-17
179	J.D.Campbell	West Indies v Ireland	Dublin	2019
178*	H.Masakadza	Zimbabwe v Kenya	Harare	2009-10
178	D.A.Warner	Australia v Afghanistan	Perth	2014-15
178	Q.de Kock	South Africa v Australia	Centurion	2016-17
177*	J.N.Malan	South Africa v Ireland	Dublin	2021
177*	M.R.Marsh	Australia v Bangladesh	Pune	2023-24
177	P.R.Stirling	Ireland v Canada	Toronto	2010
176*	E.Lewis	West Indies v England	The Oval	2017
176	A.B.de Villiers	South Africa v Bangladesh	Paarl	2017-18
176	Liton Das	Bangladesh v Zimbabwe	Sylhet	2019-20
175*	Kapil Dev	India v Zimbabwe	Tunbridge Wells	1983
175	H.H.Gibbs	South Africa v Australia	Johannesburg	2005-06
175	S.R.Tendulkar	India v Australia	Hyderabad	2009-10
175	V.Sehwag	India v Bangladesh	Mirpur	2010-11
175	C.S.MacLeod	Scotland v Canada	Christchurch	2013-14
175	A.K.Markram	South Africa v Netherlands	Johannesburg	2022-23

The highest for Afghanistan is 162 by Ibrahim Zadran (v SL, Pallekele, 2022-23).

HUNDRED ON DEBUT

D.L.Amiss	103	England v Australia	Manchester	1972
D.L.Haynes	148	West Indies v Australia	St John's	1977-78
A.Flower	115*	Zimbabwe v Sri Lanka	New Plymouth	1991-92
Salim Elahi	102*	Pakistan v Sri Lanka	Gujranwala	1995-96
M.J.Guptill	122*	New Zealand v West Indies	Auckland	2008-09
C.A.Ingram	124	South Africa v Zimbabwe	Bloemfontein	2010-11
R.J.Nicol	108*	New Zealand v Zimbabwe	Harare	2011-12
P.J.Hughes	112	Australia v Sri Lanka	Melbourne	2012-13
M.J.Lumb	106	England v West Indies	North Sound	2013-14
M.S.Chapman	124*	Hong Kong v UAE	Dubai (ICA)	2015-16
K.L.Rahul	100*	India v Zimbabwe	Harare	2016
T.Bavuma	113	South Africa v Ireland	Benoni	2016-17
Imam-ul-Haq	100	Pakistan v Sri Lanka	Abu Dhabi	2017-18
R.R.Hendricks	102	South Africa v Sri Lanka	Pallekele	2018
Abid Ali	112	Pakistan v Australia	Dubai (DSC)	2018-19
Rahmanullah Gurbaz	127	Afghanistan v Ireland	Abu Dhabi	2020-21

Shahid Afridi scored 102 for P v SL, Nairobi, 1996-97, in his second match having not batted in his first.

Fastest 100	31 balls	A.B.de Villiers (149)	SA v WI	Johannesburg	2014-15
Fastest 50	16 balls	A.B.de Villiers (149)	SA v WI	Johannesburg	2014-15

16 HUNDREDS

		Inns	***100***	*E*	*A*	*SA*	*WI*	*NZ*	*I*	*P*	*SL*	*Z*	*B*	*Ire*	*Afg*	*Ass*
V.Kohli	I	280	**50**	3	8	5	9	6	–	3	10	1	5	–	–	–
S.R.Tendulkar	I	452	**49**	2	9	5	4	5	–	5	8	5	1	–	–	5
R.G.Sharma	I	254	**31**	2	8	3	3	2	–	2	6	1	3	–	1	–
R.T.Ponting	A	365	**30***	5	–	2	2	6	6	1	4	1	1	–	–	1
S.T.Jayasuriya	SL	433	**28**	4	2	–	1	5	7	3	–	1	4	–	–	1
H.M.Amla	SA	178	**27**	2	1	–	5	2	2	3	5	3	2	1	–	1
A.B.de Villiers	SA	218	**25**	2	1	–	5	1	6	3	2	3	1	–	–	1
C.H.Gayle	WI	294	**25**	4	–	3	–	2	4	3	1	3	1	–	–	4
K.C.Sangakkara	SL	380	**25**	4	2	2	–	2	6	2	–	–	5	–	–	2
D.A.Warner	A	159	**22**	2	–	5	–	2	3	4	3	–	1	–	1	1
S.C.Ganguly	I	300	**22**	1	1	3	–	3	–	2	4	3	1	–	–	4
T.M.Dilshan	SL	303	**22**	2	1	2	–	3	4	2	–	2	4	–	–	2

		Inns	100	E	A	SA	WI	NZ	I	P	SL	Z	B	Ire	Afg	Ass
Q.de Kock	SA	155	**21**	3	3	–	–	1	6	1	4	–	2	1	–	–
L.R.P.L.Taylor	NZ	220	**21**	5	2	1	1	–	3	3	2	2	2	–	–	–
H.H.Gibbs	SA	240	**21**	2	3	–	5	2	2	2	1	2	1	–	–	1
Saeed Anwar	P	244	**20**	–	1	–	2	4	4	–	7	2	–	–	–	–
Babar Azam	P	114	**19**	2	3	1	5	2	–	–	3	2	–	–	–	1
B.C.Lara	WI	289	**19**	1	3	3	–	2	–	5	2	1	1	–	–	1
D.P.M.D.Jayawardena	SL	418	**19***	5	–	–	1	3	4	2	–	–	1	–	1	1
M.J.Guptill	NZ	195	**18**	2	1	2	2	–	1	1	2	2	3	1	–	1
M.E.Waugh	A	236	**18**	1	–	2	3	3	3	1	1	3	–	–	–	1
A.J.Finch	A	142	**17**	7	–	2	–	–	4	2	1	–	–	–	–	1
S.Dhawan	I	164	**17**	–	4	3	2	–	–	1	4	1	–	1	–	1
D.L.Haynes	WI	237	**17**	2	6	–	–	2	2	4	1	–	–	–	–	–
J.H.Kallis	SA	314	**17**	1	1	–	4	3	2	1	3	1	–	–	–	1
S.D.Hope	WI	119	**16**	1	–	1	–	–	3	1	2	1	3	1	1	2
J.E.Root	E	160	**16**	–	–	2	4	3	3	1	2	–	1	–	–	–
N.J.Astle	NZ	217	**16**	2	1	1	1	–	5	2	–	3	–	–	–	1
A.C.Gilchrist	A	279	**16***	2	–	2	–	2	1	1	6	1	–	–	–	–

* = Includes hundred scored against multi-national side.

The most for Zimbabwe is 11 by B.R.M.Taylor (203 innings), for Bangladesh 14 by Tamim Iqbal (240), for Ireland 14 by P.R.Stirling (152), and for Afghanistan 6 by Mohammad Shahzad (84).

HIGHEST PARTNERSHIP FOR EACH WICKET

1st	365	J.D.Campbell/S.D.Hope	West Indies v Ireland	Dublin	2019
2nd	372	C.H.Gayle/M.N.Samuels	West Indies v Zimbabwe	Canberra	2014-15
3rd	258	D.M.Bravo/D.Ramdin	West Indies v Bangladesh	Basseterre	2014
4th	275*	M.Azharuddin/A.D.Jadeja	India v Zimbabwe	Cuttack	1997-98
5th	256*	D.A.Miller/J.P.Duminy	South Africa v Zimbabwe	Hamilton	2014-15
6th	267*	G.D.Elliott/L.Ronchi	New Zealand v Sri Lanka	Dunedin	2014-15
7th	177	J.C.Buttler/A.U.Rashid	England v New Zealand	Birmingham	2015
8th	202*	G.J.Maxwell/P.J.Cummins	Australia v Afghanistan	Mumbai	2023-24
9th	132	A.D.Mathews/S.L.Malinga	Sri Lanka v Australia	Melbourne	2010-11
10th	106*	I.V.A.Richards/M.A.Holding	West Indies v England	Manchester	1984

BOWLING RECORDS
200 WICKETS IN A CAREER

		LOI	Balls	R	W	Avge	Best	5w	R/Over
M.Muralitharan	SL/Asia/ICC	350	18811	12326	**534**	23.08	7-30	10	3.93
Wasim Akram	P	356	18186	11812	**502**	23.52	5-15	6	3.89
Waqar Younis	P	262	12698	9919	**416**	23.84	7-36	13	4.68
W.P.J.U.C.Vaas	SL/Asia	322	15775	11014	**400**	27.53	8-19	4	4.18
Shahid Afridi	P/Asia/ICC	398	17620	13632	**395**	34.51	7-12	9	4.62
S.M.Pollock	SA/Afr/ICC	303	15712	9631	**393**	24.50	6-35	5	3.67
G.D.McGrath	A/ICC	250	12970	8391	**381**	22.02	7-15	7	3.88
B.Lee	A	221	11185	8877	**380**	23.36	5-22	9	4.76
S.L.Malinga	SL	226	10936	9760	**338**	28.87	6-38	8	5.35
A.Kumble	I/Asia	271	14496	10412	**337**	30.89	6-12	2	4.30
S.T.Jayasuriya	SL	445	14874	11871	**323**	36.75	6-29	4	4.78
Shakib Al Hasan	B	247	12575	9360	**317**	29.52	5-29	4	4.46
J.Srinath	I	229	11935	8847	**315**	28.08	5-23	3	4.44
D.L.Vettori	NZ/ICC	295	14060	9674	**305**	31.71	5- 7	2	4.12
S.K.Warne	A/ICC	194	10642	7541	**293**	25.73	5-33	1	4.25
Saqlain Mushtaq	P	169	8770	6275	**288**	21.78	5-20	6	4.29
A.B.Agarkar	I	191	9484	8021	**288**	27.85	6-42	2	5.07
Z.Khan	I/Asia	200	10097	8301	**282**	29.43	5-42	1	4.93

		LOI	Balls	R	W	Avge	Best	5w	R/Over
J.H.Kallis	SA/Afr/ICC	328	10750	8680	**273**	31.79	5-30	2	4.84
A.A.Donald	SA	164	8561	5926	**272**	21.78	6-23	2	4.15
Mashrafe Mortaza	B/Asia	220	10922	8893	**270**	32.93	6-26	1	4.88
J.M.Anderson	E	194	9584	7861	**269**	29.22	5-23	2	4.92
Abdul Razzaq	P/Asia	265	10941	8564	**269**	31.83	6-35	3	4.69
Harbhajan Singh	I/Asia	236	12479	8973	**269**	33.35	5-31	3	4.31
M.Ntini	SA/ICC	173	8687	6559	**266**	24.65	6-22	4	4.53
Kapil Dev	I	225	11202	6945	**253**	27.45	5-43	1	3.72
Shoaib Akhtar	P/Asia/ICC	163	7764	6169	**247**	24.97	6-16	4	4.76
K.D.Mills	NZ	170	8230	6485	**240**	27.02	5-25	1	4.72
M.G.Johnson	A	153	7489	6038	**239**	25.26	6-31	3	4.83
H.H.Streak	Z/Afr	189	9468	7129	**239**	29.82	5-32	1	4.51
M.A.Starc	A	121	6240	5420	**236**	22.96	6-28	9	5.21
D.Gough	E/ICC	159	8470	6209	**235**	26.42	5-44	2	4.39
C.A.Walsh	WI	205	10822	6918	**227**	30.47	5- 1	1	3.83
C.E.L.Ambrose	WI	176	9353	5429	**225**	24.12	5-17	4	3.48
T.G.Southee	NZ	161	8075	7448	**221**	33.70	7-33	3	5.53
R.A.Jadeja	I	197	9750	7936	**220**	36.07	5-33	2	4.88
T.A.Boult	NZ	114	6180	5146	**211**	24.38	7-34	6	4.99
Abdur Razzak	B	153	7965	6065	**207**	29.29	5-29	4	4.56
C.J.McDermott	A	138	7460	5018	**203**	24.71	5-44	1	4.03
C.Z.Harris	NZ	250	10667	7613	**203**	37.50	5-42	1	4.28
C.L.Cairns	NZ/ICC	215	8168	6594	**201**	32.80	5-42	1	4.84

The most wickets for Ireland is 114 by K.J.O'Brien (153 matches) and for Afghanistan 183 by Rashid Khan (103).

BEST FIGURES IN AN INNINGS

8-19	W.P.J.U.C.Vaas	Sri Lanka v Zimbabwe	Colombo (SSC)	2001-02
7-12	Shahid Afridi	Pakistan v West Indies	Providence	2013
7-15	G.D.McGrath	Australia v Namibia	Potchefstroom	2002-03
7-18	Rashid Khan	Afghanistan v West Indies	Gros Islet	2017
7-19	P.W.H.de Silva	Sri Lanka v Zimbabwe	Colombo (RPS)	2023-24
7-20	A.J.Bichel	Australia v England	Port Elizabeth	2002-03
7-30	M.Muralitharan	Sri Lanka v India	Sharjah	2000-01
7-32	Ali Khan	USA v Jersey	Windhoek	2022-23
7-33	T.G.Southee	New Zealand v England	Wellington	2014-15
7-34	T.A.Boult	New Zealand v West Indies	Christchurch	2017-18
7-36	Waqar Younis	Pakistan v England	Leeds	2001
7-37	Aqib Javed	Pakistan v India	Sharjah	1991-92
7-45	Imran Tahir	South Africa v West Indies	Basseterre	2016
7-51	W.W.Davis	West Indies v Australia	Leeds	1983
7-57	Mohammed Shami	India v New Zealand	Mumbai	2023-24
6- 4	S.T.R.Binny	India v Bangladesh	Mirpur	2014
6-11	S.Lamichhane	Nepal v PNG	Al Amerat	2021
6-12	A.Kumble	India v West Indies	Calcutta	1993-94
6-13	B.A.W.Mendis	Sri Lanka v India	Karachi	2008
6-14	G.J.Gilmour	Australia v England	Leeds	1975
6-14	Imran Khan	Pakistan v India	Sharjah	1984-85
6-14	M.F.Maharoof	Sri Lanka v West Indies	Mumbai (BS)	2006-07
6-15	C.E.H.Croft	West Indies v England	Kingstown	1980-81
6-16	Shoaib Akhtar	Pakistan v New Zealand	Karachi	2001-02
6-16	K.Rabada	South Africa v Bangladesh	Mirpur	2015
6-16	S.Lamichhane	Nepal v USA	Kirtipur	2019-20
6-18	Azhar Mahmood	Pakistan v West Indies	Sharjah	1999-00
6-19	H.K.Olonga	Zimbabwe v England	Cape Town	1999-00

6-19	S.E.Bond	New Zealand v Zimbabwe	Bulawayo	2005
6-19	J.J.Bumrah	India v England	The Oval	2022
6-20	B.C.Strang	Zimbabwe v Bangladesh	Nairobi	1997-98
6-20	A.D.Mathews	Sri Lanka v India	Colombo (RPS)	2009-10
6-21	M.Siraj	India v Sri Lanka	Colombo (RPS)	2023-24
6-22	F.H.Edwards	West Indies v Zimbabwe	Harare	2003-04
6-22	M.Ntini	South Africa v Australia	Cape Town	2005-06
6-23	A.A.Donald	South Africa v Kenya	Nairobi	1996-97
6-23	A.Nehra	India v England	Durban	2002-03
6-23	S.E.Bond	New Zealand v Australia	Gqeberha	2002-03
6-24	Imran Tahir	South Africa v Zimbabwe	Bloemfontein	2018-19
6-24	R.J.W.Topley	England v India	Lord's	2022
6-24	P.W.H.de Silva	Sri Lanka v UAE	Bulawayo	2023
6-25	S.B.Styris	New Zealand v West Indies	Port of Spain	2002
6-25	W.P.J.U.C.Vaas	Sri Lanka v Bangladesh	Pietermaritzburg	2002-03
6-25	Kuldeep Yadav	India v England	Nottingham	2018
6-26	Waqar Younis	Pakistan v Sri Lanka	Sharjah	1989-90
6-26	Mashrafe Mortaza	Bangladesh v Kenya	Nairobi	2006
6-26	Rubel Hossain	Bangladesh v New Zealand	Mirpur	2013-14
6-26	Yasir Shah	Pakistan v Zimbabwe	Harare	2015-16

The best figures for Ireland are 6-36 by J.B.Little (v Z, Harare, 2023-24).

HAT-TRICKS

Jalaluddin	Pakistan v Australia	Hyderabad	1982-83
B.A.Reid	Australia v New Zealand	Sydney	1985-86
C.Sharma	India v New Zealand	Nagpur	1987-88
Wasim Akram	Pakistan v West Indies	Sharjah	1989-90
Wasim Akram	Pakistan v Australia	Sharjah	1989-90
Kapil Dev	India v Sri Lanka	Calcutta	1990-91
Aqib Javed	Pakistan v India	Sharjah	1991-92
D.K.Morrison	New Zealand v India	Napier	1993-94
Waqar Younis	Pakistan v New Zealand	East London	1994-95
Saqlain Mushtaq	Pakistan v Zimbabwe	Peshawar	1996-97
E.A.Brandes	Zimbabwe v England	Harare	1996-97
A.M.Stuart	Australia v Pakistan	Melbourne	1996-97
Saqlain Mushtaq	Pakistan v Zimbabwe	The Oval	1999
W.P.J.U.C.Vaas	Sri Lanka v Zimbabwe	Colombo (SSC)	2001-02
Mohammad Sami	Pakistan v West Indies	Sharjah	2001-02
W.P.J.U.C.Vaas[1]	Sri Lanka v Bangladesh	Pietermaritzburg	2002-03
B.Lee	Australia v Kenya	Durban	2002-03
J.M.Anderson	England v Pakistan	The Oval	2003
S.J.Harmison	England v India	Nottingham	2004
C.K.Langeveldt	South Africa v West Indies	Bridgetown	2004-05
Shahadat Hossain	Bangladesh v Zimbabwe	Harare	2006
J.E.Taylor	West Indies v Australia	Mumbai (BS)	2006-07
S.E.Bond	New Zealand v Australia	Hobart	2006-07
S.L.Malinga[2]	Sri Lanka v South Africa	Providence	2006-07
A.Flintoff	England v West Indies	St Lucia	2008-09
M.F.Maharoof	Sri Lanka v India	Dambulla	2010
Abdur Razzak	Bangladesh v Zimbabwe	Mirpur	2010-11
K.A.J.Roach	West Indies v Netherlands	Delhi	2010-11
S.L.Malinga	Sri Lanka v Kenya	Colombo (RPS)	2010-11
S.L.Malinga	Sri Lanka v Australia	Colombo (RPS)	2011
D.T.Christian	Australia v Sri Lanka	Melbourne	2011-12
N.L.T.C.Perera	Sri Lanka v Pakistan	Colombo (RPS)	2012
C.J.McKay	Australia v England	Cardiff	2013

Rubel Hossain	Bangladesh v New Zealand	Mirpur	2013-14
P.Utseya	Zimbabwe v South Africa	Harare	2014
Taijul Islam	Bangladesh v Zimbabwe	Mirpur	2014-15
S.T.Finn	England v Australia	Melbourne	2014-15
J.P.Duminy	South Africa v Sri Lanka	Sydney	2014-15
K.Rabada	South Africa v Bangladesh	Mirpur	2015
J.P.Faulkner	Australia v Sri Lanka	Colombo (RPS)	2016
Taskin Ahmed	Bangladesh v Sri Lanka	Dambulla	2016-17
P.W.H.de Silva	Sri Lanka v Zimbabwe	Galle	2017
Kuldeep Yadav	India v Australia	Kolkata	2017-18
D.S.M.Kumara	Sri Lanka v Bangladesh	Mirpur	2017-18
Imran Tahir	South Africa v Zimbabwe	Bloemfontein	2018-19
T.A.Boult	New Zealand v Pakistan	Abu Dhabi	2018-19
Mohammed Shami	India v Afghanistan	Southampton	2019
T.A.Boult	New Zealand v Australia	Lord's	2019
Kuldeep Yadav	India v West Indies	Visakhapatnam	2019-20
W.N.Madhevere	Zimbabwe v Netherlands	Harare	2022-23

[1] The first three balls of the match. Took four wickets in opening over (W W W 4 wide W 0).
[2] Four wickets in four balls.

WICKET-KEEPING RECORDS
150 DISMISSALS IN A CAREER

Total			*LOI*	*Ct*	*St*
482†‡	K.C.Sangakkara	Sri Lanka/Asia/ICC	360	384	98
472‡	A.C.Gilchrist	Australia/ICC	287	417	55
444	M.S.Dhoni	India/Asia	350	321	123
424	M.V.Boucher	South Africa/Africa	295	402	22
287‡	Moin Khan	Pakistan	219	214	73
283	Mushfiqur Rahim	Bangladesh	253	227	56
258	J.C.Buttler	England	180	221	37
242†‡	B.B.McCullum	New Zealand	185	227	15
233	I.A.Healy	Australia	168	194	39
226	Q.de Kock	South Africa	154	209	17
220‡	Rashid Latif	Pakistan	166	182	38
206‡	R.S.Kaluwitharana	Sri Lanka	187	131	75
204‡	P.J.L.Dujon	West Indies	169	183	21
189	R.D.Jacobs	West Indies	147	160	29
188	D.Ramdin	West Indies	139	181	7
187	Kamran Akmal	Pakistan	154	156	31
181	B.J.Haddin	Australia	126	170	11
165	D.J.Richardson	South Africa	122	148	17
165†‡	A.Flower	Zimbabwe	213	133	32
163†‡	A.J.Stewart	England	170	148	15
154‡	N.R.Mongia	India	140	110	44

† *Excluding catches taken in the field.* ‡ *Excluding matches when not wicket-keeper.*

The most for Ireland is 96 by N.J.O'Brien (103 matches) and for Afghanistan 88 by Mohammad Shahzad (84).

SIX DISMISSALS IN AN INNINGS

6	(6ct)	A.C.Gilchrist	Australia v South Africa	Cape Town	1999-00
6	(6ct)	A.J.Stewart	England v Zimbabwe	Manchester	2000
6	(5ct/1st)	R.D.Jacobs	West Indies v Sri Lanka	Colombo (RPS)	2001-02
6	(5ct/1st)	A.C.Gilchrist	Australia v England	Sydney	2002-03
6	(6ct)	A.C.Gilchrist	Australia v Namibia	Potchefstroom	2002-03
6	(6ct)	A.C.Gilchrist	Australia v Sri Lanka	Colombo (RPS)	2003-04
6	(6ct)	M.V.Boucher	South Africa v Pakistan	Cape Town	2006-07

6	(5ct/1st)	M.S.Dhoni	India v England	Leeds	2007
6	(6ct)	A.C.Gilchrist	Australia v India	Vadodara	2007-08
6	(5ct/1st)	A.C.Gilchrist	Australia v India	Sydney	2007-08
6	(6ct)	M.J.Prior	England v South Africa	Nottingham	2008
6	(6ct)	J.C.Buttler	England v South Africa	The Oval	2013
6	(6ct)	M.H.Cross	Scotland v Canada	Christchurch	2013-14
6	(5ct/1st)	Q.de Kock	South Africa v New Zealand	Mt Maunganui	2014-15
6	(6ct)	Sarfraz Ahmed	Pakistan v South Africa	Auckland	2014-15
6	(6ct)	Q.de Kock	South Africa v Afghanistan	Ahmedabad	2023-24

FIELDING RECORDS
100 CATCHES IN A CAREER

Total			*Inns*
218	D.P.M.D.Jayawardena	Sri Lanka/Asia	448
160	R.T.Ponting	Australia/ICC	375
156	M.Azharuddin	India	334
151	V.Kohli	India	292
142	L.R.P.L.Taylor	New Zealand	236
140	S.R.Tendulkar	India	463
133	S.P.Fleming	New Zealand/ICC	280
131	J.H.Kallis	South Africa/Africa/ICC	328
130	Younus Khan	Pakistan	262
130	M.Muralitharan	Sri Lanka/Asia/ICC	350
127	A.R.Border	Australia	273
127	Shahid Afridi	Pakistan/Asia/ICC	398
124	R.S.Dravid	India/Asia/ICC	271
124	C.H.Gayle	West Indies/ICC	301
123	S.T.Jayasuriya	Sri Lanka/Asia	445
120	C.L.Hooper	West Indies	227
120	B.C.Lara	West Indies/ICC	299
118	T.M.Dilshan	Sri Lanka	327
113	Inzamam-ul-Haq	Pakistan/Asia	378
111	S.R.Waugh	Australia	325
109	R.S.Mahanama	Sri Lanka	213
108	P.D.Collingwood	England	197
108	M.E.Waugh	Australia	244
108	H.H.Gibbs	South Africa	248
108	S.M.Pollock	South Africa/Africa/ICC	303
106	M.J.Clarke	Australia	245
105	M.E.K.Hussey	Australia	185
105	G.C.Smith	South Africa/Africa	197
105	J.N.Rhodes	South Africa	245
104	M.J.Guptill	New Zealand	198
102	S.K.Raina	India	226
100	I.V.A.Richards	West Indies	187
100	S.C.Ganguly	India/Asia	311

The most for Zimbabwe is 86 by G.W.Flower (220), for Bangladesh 81 by Mahmudullah (228), for Ireland 68 by W.T.S.Porterfield (141), and for Afghanistan 71 by Mohammad Nabi (159).

FIVE CATCHES IN AN INNINGS

5	J.N.Rhodes	South Africa v West Indies	Bombay (BS)	1993-94

APPEARANCE RECORDS
250 MATCHES

463	S.R.Tendulkar	India
448	D.P.M.D.Jayawardena	Sri Lanka/Asia
445	S.T.Jayasuriya	Sri Lanka/Asia
404	K.C.Sangakkara	Sri Lanka/Asia/ICC
398	Shahid Afridi	Pakistan/Asia/ICC
378	Inzamam-ul-Haq	Pakistan/Asia
375	R.T.Ponting	Australia/ICC
356	Wasim Akram	Pakistan
350	M.S.Dhoni	India/Asia
350	M.Muralitharan	Sri Lanka/Asia/ICC
344	R.S.Dravid	India/Asia/ICC
334	M.Azharuddin	India
330	T.M.Dilshan	Sri Lanka
328	J.H.Kallis	South Africa/Africa/ICC
325	S.R.Waugh	Australia
322	W.P.J.U.C.Vaas	Sri Lanka/Asia
311	S.C.Ganguly	India/Asia
308	P.A.de Silva	Sri Lanka
304	Yuvraj Singh	India/Asia
303	S.M.Pollock	South Africa/Africa/ICC
301	C.H.Gayle	West Indies/ICC
299	B.C.Lara	West Indies/ICC
295	M.V.Boucher	South Africa/Africa
295	D.L.Vettori	New Zealand/ICC
292	V.Kohli	India
288	Mohammad Yousuf	Pakistan/Asia
287	A.C.Gilchrist	Australia/ICC
287	Shoaib Malik	Pakistan
283	Salim Malik	Pakistan
280	S.P.Fleming	New Zealand/ICC
273	A.R.Border	Australia
271	A.Kumble	India/Asia
269	A.Ranatunga	Sri Lanka
268	M.S.Atapattu	Sri Lanka
268	S.Chanderpaul	West Indies
268	Mushfiqur Rahim	Bangladesh

265	Abdul Razzaq	Pakistan/Asia	251	V.Sehwag	India/Asia/ICC
265	Younus Khan	Pakistan	250	C.Z.Harris	New Zealand
262	R.G.Sharma	India	250	Ijaz Ahmed	Pakistan
262	Waqar Younis	Pakistan	250	G.D.McGrath	Australia/ICC
260	B.B.McCullum	New Zealand			

The most for England is 225 by E.J.G.Morgan, for Zimbabwe 221 by G.W.Flower, for Ireland 159 by P.R.Stirling, and for Afghanistan 159 by Mohammad Nabi.
The most consecutive appearances is 185 by S.R.Tendulkar for India (Apr 1990-Apr 1998).

100 MATCHES AS CAPTAIN

			W	*L*	*T*	*NR*	*% Won (exc NR)*
230	R.T.Ponting	Australia/ICC	165	51	2	12	75.68
218	S.P.Fleming	New Zealand	98	106	1	13	47.80
200	M.S.Dhoni	India	110	74	5	11	58.20
193	A.Ranatunga	Sri Lanka	89	95	1	8	48.10
178	A.R.Border	Australia	107	67	1	3	61.14
174	M.Azharuddin	India	90	76	2	6	53.57
150	G.C.Smith	South Africa/Africa	92	51	1	6	63.88
147	S.C.Ganguly	India/Asia	76	66	–	5	53.52
139	Imran Khan	Pakistan	75	59	1	4	55.55
138	W.J.Cronje	South Africa	99	35	1	3	73.33
129	D.P.M.D.Jayawardena	Sri Lanka	71	49	1	8	58.67
126	E.J.G.Morgan	England	76	40	2	8	64.40
125	B.C.Lara	West Indies	59	59	–	7	50.42
118	S.T.Jayasuriya	Sri Lanka	66	47	2	3	57.39
113	W.T.S.Porterfield	Ireland	50	55	2	6	46.72
109	Wasim Akram	Pakistan	66	41	2	–	60.55
106	A.D.Mathews	Sri Lanka	49	51	1	5	48.51
106	S.R.Waugh	Australia	67	35	3	1	63.80
105	I.V.A.Richards	West Indies	67	36	–	2	65.04
103	A.B.de Villers	South Africa	59	39	1	4	59.59

The most for Zimbabwe is 86 by A.D.R.Campbell, for Bangladesh 88 by Mashrafe Mortaza, and for Afghanistan 59 by Asghar Afghan.

150 LOI UMPIRING APPEARANCES

231	Alim Dar	Pakistan	16.02.2000	to	05.07.2023
209	R.E.Koertzen	South Africa	09.12.1992	to	09.06.2010
200	B.F.Bowden	New Zealand	23.03.1995	to	06.02.2016
181	S.A.Bucknor	West Indies	18.03.1989	to	29.03.2009
174	D.J.Harper	Australia	14.01.1994	to	19.03.2011
174	S.J.A.Taufel	Australia	13.01.1999	to	02.09.2012
172	D.R.Shepherd	England	09.06.1983	to	12.07.2005
154	R.B.Tiffin	Zimbabwe	25.10.1992	to	22.07.2018

ENGLAND TWENTY20 INTERNATIONALS CAREER RECORDS

These records, complete to 4 April 2024, include all players registered for county cricket for the 2024 season at the time of going to press.

BATTING AND FIELDING

	M	*I*	*NO*	*HS*	*Runs*	*Avge*	*100*	*50*	*Ct/St*
R.Ahmed	7	5	1	11	33	8.25	–	–	2
M.M.Ali	82	69	17	72*	1154	22.19	–	7	19
J.M.Anderson	19	4	3	1*	1	1.00	–	–	3
J.C.Archer	13	3	1	18*	19	9.50	–	–	4
A.A.P.Atkinson	3	1	1	8*	8	–	–	–	–
J.M.Bairstow	70	64	13	90	1512	29.64	–	10	45/1
J.T.Ball	2	–	–	–	–	–	–	–	1
T.Banton	14	14	–	73	327	23.35	–	2	9
S.W.Billings†	36	32	5	87	474	17.55	–	2	17/2
S.G.Borthwick	1	1	–	14	14	14.00	–	–	1
D.R.Briggs	7	1	1	0*	0	–	–	–	1
H.C.Brook	29	26	6	81*	544	27.20	–	2	18
P.R.Brown	4	1	1	4*	4	–	–	–	2
J.C.Buttler	114	105	21	101*	2927	34.84	1	22	65/11
B.A.Carse	3	1	1	0*	0	–	–	–	–
M.S.Crane	2	–	–	–	–	–	–	–	–
S.M.Curran	46	28	8	50	260	13.00	–	1	19
T.K.Curran	30	13	7	14*	64	10.66	–	–	8
L.A.Dawson	11	5	1	34	57	14.25	–	–	2
J.L.Denly	13	12	2	30	125	12.50	–	–	4
B.M.Duckett	12	12	2	70*	315	31.50	–	1	6
B.T.Foakes	1	–	–	–	–	–	–	–	1
G.H.S.Garton	1	1	–	2	2	2.00	–	–	–
R.J.Gleeson	6	2	–	2	2	1.00	–	–	4
L.Gregory	9	7	1	15	45	7.50	–	–	–
A.D.Hales	75	75	8	116*	2074	30.95	1	12	39
W.G.Jacks	11	11	–	40	181	16.45	–	–	2
C.J.Jordan	88	54	24	36	434	14.46	–	–	43
L.S.Livingstone	38	32	7	103	617	24.68	1	1	19
S.Mahmood	12	7	4	7*	22	7.33	–	–	2
D.J.Malan	62	60	8	103*	1892	36.38	1	16	22
T.S.Mills†	15	5	2	7	8	2.66	–	–	2
M.W.Parkinson	6	4	–	5	5	1.25	–	–	1
S.R.Patel	18	14	2	67	189	15.75	–	1	3
A.U.Rashid	104	33	16	22	101	5.94	–	–	29
J.E.Root	32	30	5	90*	893	35.72	–	5	18
J.J.Roy	64	64	1	78	1522	24.15	–	8	19
P.D.Salt	21	20	2	119	639	35.50	2	2	13/1
B.A.Stokes	43	36	9	52*	585	21.66	–	1	22
O.P.Stone	1	1	–	0	0	0.00	–	–	–
R.J.W.Topley	25	8	6	9	13	6.50	–	–	6
J.M.Vince	17	17	–	59	463	27.23	–	2	7
D.J.Willey	43	26	11	33*	226	15.06	–	–	17
C.R.Woakes	33	17	8	37	147	16.33	–	–	12
L.Wood	5	1	–	3	3	3.00	–	–	1
M.A.Wood	28	3	3	5*	11	–	–	–	3

BOWLING

	O	M	R	W	Avge	Best	4wI	R/Over
R.Ahmed	24	0	228	9	25.33	3-39	–	9.50
M.M.Ali	151.3	1	12162	45	28.04	3-24	–	8.33
J.M.Anderson	70.2	1	552	18	30.66	3-23	–	7.84
J.C.Archer	58	1	444	18	24.66	4-33	1	7.65
A.A.P.Atkinson	8.5	0	84	6	14.00	4-20	1	9.50
J.T.Ball	7	0	83	2	41.50	1-39	–	11.85
S.G.Borthwick	4	0	15	1	15.00	1-15	–	3.75
D.R.Briggs	18	0	199	5	39.80	2-25	–	11.05
P.R.Brown	13	0	128	3	42.66	1-29	–	9.84
B.A.Carse	8	0	66	4	16.50	3-23	–	8.25
M.S.Crane	8	0	62	1	62.00	1-38	–	7.75
S.M.Curran	144.5	1	1159	49	23.65	5-10	1	8.00
T.K.Curran	98	1	907	29	31.27	4-36	1	9.25
L.A.Dawson	34	0	242	6	40.33	3-27	–	7.11
J.L.Denly	12	0	93	7	13.28	4-19	1	7.75
G.H.S.Garton	4	0	57	1	57.00	1-57	–	14.25
R.J.Gleeson	21	1	187	9	20.77	3-15	–	8.90
L.Gregory	13	0	117	2	58.50	1-10	–	9.00
W.G.Jacks	2	0	19	1	19.00	1- 5	–	9.50
C.J.Jordan	304.4	2	2658	96	27.68	4- 6	3	8.72
L.S.Livingstone	63	0	549	18	30.50	3-17	–	8.71
S.Mahmood	38	0	398	7	56.85	3-33	–	10.47
D.J.Malan	2	0	27	1	27.00	1-27	–	13.50
T.S.Mills	53.4	1	474	14	33.85	3-27	–	8.83
M.W.Parkinson	20	0	198	7	28.28	4-47	1	9.90
S.R.Patel	42	0	321	7	45.85	2- 6	–	7.64
A.U.Rashid	365.2	4	2698	107	25.21	4- 2	2	7.38
J.E.Root	14	0	139	6	23.16	2- 9	–	9.92
B.A.Stokes	102	1	856	26	32.92	3-26	–	8.39
O.P.Stone	4	0	36	0	–	–	–	9.00
R.J.W.Topley	89.4	0	735	28	26.25	3-22	–	8.19
D.J.Willey	144.1	1	1180	51	23.13	4- 7	1	8.18
C.R.Woakes	101.5	1	822	31	26.51	3- 4	–	8.07
L.Wood	18	0	174	8	21.75	3-24	–	9.66
M.A.Wood	99.3	1	831	45	18.46	3- 9	–	8.35

† *S.W.Billings and T.S.Mills also played one game for an ICC World XI v West Indies at Lord's in 2018.*

INTERNATIONAL TWENTY20 RECORDS

From 1 January 2019, the ICC granted official IT20 status to all 20-over matches between its 105 members. As a result, there has been a vast increase in the number of games played, many featuring very minor nations. In the records that follow, except for the first-ranked record, only those IT20s featuring a nation that has also played a full LOI are listed.

MATCH RESULTS

2004-05 to 26 February 2024

	Opponents	*Matches*	*Won*													*Tied*	*NR*
			E	*A*	*SA*	*WI*	*NZ*	*I*	*P*	*SL*	*Z*	*B*	*Ire*	*Afg*	*Ass*		
England	Australia	23	11	10	–	–	–	–	–	–	–	–	–	–	–	–	2
	South Africa	25	12	–	12	–	–	–	–	–	–	–	–	–	–	–	1
	West Indies	29	12	–	–	17	–	–	–	–	–	–	–	–	–	–	–
	New Zealand	27	15	–	–	–	10	–	–	–	–	–	–	–	–	1	1
	India	23	11	–	–	–	–	12	–	–	–	–	–	–	–	–	–
	Pakistan	29	18	–	–	–	–	–	9	–	–	–	–	–	–	1	1
	Sri Lanka	14	10	–	–	–	–	–	–	4	–	–	–	–	–	–	–
	Zimbabwe	1	1	–	–	–	–	–	–	–	0	–	–	–	–	–	–
	Bangladesh	4	1	–	–	–	–	–	–	–	–	3	–	–	–	–	–
	Ireland	2	0	–	–	–	–	–	–	–	–	–	1	–	–	–	1
	Afghanistan	3	3	–	–	–	–	–	–	–	–	–	–	0	–	–	–
	Associates	2	0	–	–	–	–	–	–	–	–	–	–	–	2	–	–
Australia	South Africa	25	–	17	8	–	–	–	–	–	–	–	–	–	–	–	–
	West Indies	22	–	11	–	11	–	–	–	–	–	–	–	–	–	–	–
	New Zealand	19	–	13	–	–	5	–	–	–	–	–	–	–	–	1	–
	India	31	–	11	–	–	–	19	–	–	–	–	–	–	–	–	1
	Pakistan	25	–	11	–	–	–	–	12	–	–	–	–	–	–	1	1
	Sri Lanka	26	–	15	–	–	–	–	–	10	–	–	–	–	–	1	–
	Zimbabwe	3	–	2	–	–	–	–	–	–	1	–	–	–	–	–	–
	Bangladesh	10	–	6	–	–	–	–	–	–	–	4	–	–	–	–	–
	Ireland	2	–	2	–	–	–	–	–	–	–	–	0	–	–	–	–
	Afghanistan	1	–	1	–	–	–	–	–	–	–	–	–	0	–	–	–
	Associates	1	–	1	–	–	–	–	–	–	–	–	–	–	0	–	–
S Africa	West Indies	19	–	–	11	8	–	–	–	–	–	–	–	–	–	–	–
	New Zealand	15	–	–	11	–	4	–	–	–	–	–	–	–	–	–	–
	India	26	–	–	11	–	–	14	–	–	–	–	–	–	–	–	1
	Pakistan	22	–	–	10	–	–	–	12	–	–	–	–	–	–	–	–
	Sri Lanka	17	–	–	11	–	–	–	–	5	–	–	–	–	–	1	–
	Zimbabwe	6	–	–	5	–	–	–	–	–	0	–	–	–	–	–	1
	Bangladesh	8	–	–	8	–	–	–	–	–	–	0	–	–	–	–	–
	Ireland	5	–	–	5	–	–	–	–	–	–	–	0	–	–	–	–
	Afghanistan	2	–	–	2	–	–	–	–	–	–	–	–	0	–	–	–
	Associates	3	–	–	2	–	–	–	–	–	–	–	–	–	1	–	–
W Indies	New Zealand	19	–	–	–	4	10	–	–	–	–	–	–	–	–	3	2
	India	30	–	–	–	10	–	19	–	–	–	–	–	–	–	–	1
	Pakistan	21	–	–	–	3	–	–	15	–	–	–	–	–	–	–	3
	Sri Lanka	15	–	–	–	7	–	–	–	8	–	–	–	–	–	–	–
	Zimbabwe	4	–	–	–	3	–	–	–	–	1	–	–	–	–	–	–
	Bangladesh	16	–	–	–	9	–	–	–	–	–	5	–	–	–	–	2
	Ireland	8	–	–	–	3	–	–	–	–	–	–	3	–	–	–	2
	Afghanistan	7	–	–	–	4	–	–	–	–	–	–	–	3	–	–	–
	Associates	1	–	–	–	0	–	–	–	–	–	–	–	–	1	–	–
N Zealand	India	25	–	–	–	–	10	12	–	–	–	–	–	–	–	3	–
	Pakistan	39	–	–	–	–	17	–	21	–	–	–	–	–	–	–	1
	Sri Lanka	23	–	–	–	–	13	–	–	7	–	–	–	–	–	2	1
	Zimbabwe	6	–	–	–	–	6	–	–	–	0	–	–	–	–	–	–
	Bangladesh	20	–	–	–	–	15	–	–	–	–	4	–	–	–	–	1
	Ireland	5	–	–	–	–	5	–	–	–	–	–	0	–	–	–	–
	Afghanistan	1	–	–	–	–	1	–	–	–	–	–	–	0	–	–	–
	Associates	12	–	–	–	–	11	–	–	–	–	–	–	–	1	–	–

	Opponents	Matches	Won													Tied	NR
			E	A	SA	WI	NZ	I	P	SL	Z	B	Ire	Afg	Ass		
India	Pakistan	12	–	–	–	–	–	8	3	–	–	–	–	–	–	1	–
	Sri Lanka	29	–	–	–	–	–	19	–	9	–	–	–	–	–	–	1
	Zimbabwe	8	–	–	–	–	–	6	–	–	2	–	–	–	–	–	–
	Bangladesh	13	–	–	–	–	–	12	–	–	–	1	–	–	–	–	–
	Ireland	7	–	–	–	–	–	7	–	–	–	–	0	–	–	–	–
	Afghanistan	8	–	–	–	–	–	6	–	–	–	–	–	0	–	1	1
	Associates	7	–	–	–	–	–	6	–	–	–	–	–	–	0	–	1
Pakistan	Sri Lanka	23	–	–	–	–	–	–	13	10	–	–	–	–	–	–	–
	Zimbabwe	18	–	–	–	–	–	–	16	–	2	–	–	–	–	–	–
	Bangladesh	19	–	–	–	–	–	–	16	–	–	3	–	–	–	–	
	Ireland	1	–	–	–	–	–	–	1	–	–	–	0	–	–	–	–
	Afghanistan	7	–	–	–	–	–	–	4	–	–	–	–	3	–	–	–
	Associates	12	–	–	–	–	–	–	12	–	–	–	–	–	0	–	–
Sri Lanka	Zimbabwe	6	–	–	–	–	–	–	–	5	1	–	–	–	–	–	–
	Bangladesh	13	–	–	–	–	–	–	–	9	–	4	–	–	–	–	–
	Ireland	3	–	–	–	–	–	–	–	3	–	–	0	–	–	–	–
	Afghanistan	8	–	–	–	–	–	–	–	5	–	–	–	3	–	–	–
	Associates	9	–	–	–	–	–	–	–	8	–	–	–	–	1	–	–
Zimbabwe	Bangladesh	20	–	–	–	–	–	–	–	–	7	13	–	–	–	–	–
	Ireland	15	–	–	–	–	–	–	–	–	7	–	8	–	–	–	–
	Afghanistan	15	–	–	–	–	–	–	–	–	1	–	–	14	–	–	–
	Associates	38	–	–	–	–	–	–	–	–	24	–	–	–	12	2	–
Bangladesh	Ireland	8	–	–	–	–	–	–	–	–	–	5	2	–	–	–	1
	Afghanistan	11	–	–	–	–	–	–	–	–	–	5	–	6	–	–	–
	Associates	16	–	–	–	–	–	–	–	–	–	12	–	–	4	–	–
Ireland	Afghanistan	23	–	–	–	–	–	–	–	–	–	–	6	16	–	1	–
	Associates	78	–	–	–	–	–	–	–	–	–	–	46	–	28	1	3
Afghanistan	Associates	41	–	–	–	–	–	–	–	–	–	–	–	32	9	–	–
Associates	Associates	1291	–	–	–	–	–	–	–	–	–	–	–	–	1249	12	30
		2481	94	100	96	79	107	140	134	83	46	59	66	77	1308	32	60

MATCH RESULTS SUMMARY

	Matches	Won	Lost	Tied	NR	% Won (ex NR)
India	219	140	68	5	6	65.72
Afghanistan	127	77	47	2	1	61.11
Pakistan	228	134	85	3	6	60.36
South Africa	173	96	73	1	3	56.47
Australia	188	100	81	3	4	54.34
England	182	94	80	2	6	53.40
New Zealand	211	107	88	10	6	52.19
Sri Lanka	186	83	97	4	2	45.10
Ireland	157	66	82	2	7	44.00
West Indies	191	79	99	3	10	43.64
Bangladesh	158	59	95	0	4	38.31
Zimbabwe	140	46	91	2	1	33.09
Associates (v Full)	220	59	154	3	4	27.31

Results of games between two Associate Members and Pakistan's three IT20s v a World XI in 2017 (W2, L1) and West Indies' IT20 v an ICC World XI in 2018 (W1) are excluded from these figures.

INTERNATIONAL TWENTY20 RECORDS

(To 1 March 2023)

TEAM RECORDS

HIGHEST INNINGS TOTALS

† Batting Second

314-3	Nepal v Mongolia	Hangzhou	2023-24
278-3	Afghanistan v Ireland	Dehradun	2018-19
267-3	England v West Indies	Tarouba	2023-24
263-3	Australia v Sri Lanka	Pallekele	2016
260-6	Sri Lanka v Kenya	Johannesburg	2007-08
260-5	India v Sri Lanka	Indore	2017-18
259-4†	South Africa v West Indies	Centurion	2022-23
258-5	West Indies v South Africa	Centurion	2022-23
254-5	New Zealand v Scotland	Edinburgh	2022
252-3	Scotland v Netherlands	Dublin	2019
248-6	Australia v England	Southampton	2013
245-6	West Indies v India	Lauderhill	2016
245-5†	Australia v New Zealand	Auckland	2017-18
245-1	Canada v Panama	Coolidge	2021-22
245-2	Scotland v Italy	Edinburgh	2023
244-4†	India v West Indies	Lauderhill	2016
243-5	New Zealand v West Indies	Mt Maunganui	2017-18
243-6	New Zealand v Australia	Auckland	2017-18
241-6	South Africa v England	Centurion	2009-10
241-3	England v New Zealand	Napier	2019-20
241-4	Australia v West Indies	Adelaide	2023-24
240-3	Namibia v Botswana	Windhoek	2019
240-3	India v West Indies	Mumbai	2019-20
239-6	Bermuda v Bahamas	Coolidge	2021-22
238-3	New Zealand v West Indies	Mt Maunganui	2020-21
238-3	Nepal v Netherlands	Kirtipur	2021
237-3	India v South Africa	Guwahati	2022-23
237-5	Kenya v Lesotho	Kigali	2022-23
236-6†	West Indies v South Africa	Johannesburg	2014-15
236-3	Nepal v Bhutan	Kirtipur	2019-20
236-5	Zimbabwe v Singapore	Bulawayo	2022
235-4	India v Australia	Karyavattom	2023-24

The highest total for Pakistan is 232-6 (v E, Nottingham, 2021), for Bangladesh 215-5 (v SL, Colombo (RPS), 2017-18), and for Ireland 226-4 (v Austria, Edinburgh, 2023).

LOWEST COMPLETED INNINGS TOTALS

† Batting Second

10	(8.4)	Isle of Man v Spain	Cartagena	2022-23
30	(10.4)	Mali v Kenya	Kigali	2022-23
30†	(11.3)	Cayman Is v Canada	Hamilton	2023-24
36	(15.2)	Philippines v Oman	Al Amerat	2021-22
37†	(17.2)	Panama v Canada	Coolidge	2021-22
38†	(10.4)	Hong Kong v Pakistan	Sharjah	2022
39	(10.3)	Netherlands v Sri Lanka	Chittagong	2013-14
39	(18.2)	Mali v Kenya	Benoni	2023-24
41†	(13.1)	Mongolia v Nepal	Hangzhou	2023-24
41	(12.4)	China v Hong Kong	Mong Kok	2023-24
44	(10.0)	Netherlands v Sri Lanka	Sharjah	2021-22
45†	(11.5)	West Indies v England	Basseterre	2018-19
45†	(17.0)	Philippines v PNG	Port Moresby	2023
46	(12.1)	Botswana v Namibia	Kampala	2019
48	(14.2)	Cameroon v Kenya	Benoni	2022
48	(16.2)	Cameroon v Kenya	Benoni	2023-24
48-8†	(20.0)	China v Hong Kong	Mong Kok	2023-24

53	(14.3)	Nepal v Ireland	Belfast	2015
55	(14.2)	West Indies v England	Dubai (DSC)	2021-22
56†	(18.4)	Kenya v Afghanistan	Sharjah	2013-14
60†	(15.3)	New Zealand v Sri Lanka	Chittagong	2013-14
60-9†	(13.4)	West Indies v Pakistan	Karachi	2017-18
60	(16.5)	New Zealand v Bangladesh	Mirpur	2021
60†	(10.2)	Scotland v Afghanistan	Sharjah	2021-22

The lowest total for England is 80 (v I, Colombo (RPS), 2012-13.

LARGEST RUNS MARGIN OF VICTORY

273 runs	Nepal beat Mongolia	Hangzhou	2023-24
208 runs	Canada beat Panama	Coolidge	2021-22
172 runs	Sri Lanka beat Kenya	Johannesburg	2007
168 runs	India beat New Zealand	Ahmedabad	2022-23
167 runs	Kenya beat Lesotho	Kigali	2022-23
166 runs	Scotland beat Austria	Edinburgh	2023
166 runs	Canada beat Cayman Is	Hamilton	2023-24
163 runs	Canada beat Panama	Hamilton	2023-24
155 runs	Pakistan beat Hong Kong	Sharjah	2022
155 runs	Scotland beat Italy	Edinburgh	2023

There have been 52 victories by ten wickets, with Spain beating Isle of Man by a record margin of 118 balls remaining (Cartagena, 2022-23). England's biggest win by 137 runs (v WI, Basseterre, 2018-19).

BATTING RECORDS
2000 RUNS IN A CAREER

Runs			*M*	*I*	*NO*	*HS*	*Avge*	*50*	*R/100B*
4037	V.Kohli	I	117	109	31	122*	51.75	38	138.1
3974	R.G.Sharma	I	151	143	18	121*	31.79	34	139.9
3698	Babar Azam	P	109	103	14	122	41.55	36	129.1
3531	M.J.Guptill	NZ	122	118	7	105	31.81	22	135.7
3438	P.R.Stirling	Ire	134	133	11	115*	28.18	24	135.7
3120	A.J.Finch	A	103	103	12	172	34.28	21	142.5
3099	D.A.Warner	A	103	103	11	100*	33.68	27	142.6
2981	Mohammad Rizwan	P	90	78	17	104*	48.86	27	127.5
2927	J.C.Buttler	E	114	105	21	101*	34.84	23	144.6
2547	K.S.Williamson	NZ	89	87	12	95	33.96	18	123.6
2514	Mohammad Hafeez	P	119	108	13	99*	26.46	14	122.0
2468	G.J.Maxwell	A	106	98	16	145*	30.09	15	155.5
2458	E.J.G.Morgan	E	115	107	21	91	28.58	14	136.1
2435	Shoaib Malik	P/ICC	124	111	33	75	31.21	9	125.6
2382	Shakib Al Hasan	B	117	116	16	84	23.82	12	122.4
2277	Q.de Kock	SA	80	79	9	100	32.52	15	137.3
2268	D.A.Miller	SA/Wd	116	101	34	106*	33.85	8	144.5
2265	K.L.Rahul	I	72	68	8	110*	37.75	24	139.1
2141	S.A.Yadav	I	60	57	10	117	45.55	21	171.5
2140	B.B.McCullum	NZ	71	70	10	123	35.66	15	136.2
2122	Mahmudullah	B	121	113	23	64*	23.57	6	117.3
2094	A.Balbirnie	Ire	98	94	4	83	23.26	10	124.7
2074	A.D.Hales	E	75	75	8	116*	30.95	13	138.3
2048	Mohammad Shahzad	Afg	73	73	3	118*	29.25	13	132.1
2032	R.D.Berrington	Scot	85	77	15	100	32.77	11	132.4
2019	Mohammad Nabi	Afg	118	110	21	89	22.68	5	138.9
2018	Virandeep Singh	Malay	67	66	12	116*	37.37	14	127.4

HIGHEST INDIVIDUAL INNINGS

Score	*Balls*				
172	76	A.J.Finch	A v Z	Harare	2018
162*	62	Hazratullah Zazai	Afg v Ire	Dehradun	2018-19
156	63	A.J.Finch	A v E	Southampton	2013
145*	65	G.J.Maxwell	A v SL	Pallekele	2016

137*	50	K.Malla	Nepal v Mong	Hangzhou	2023-24
137	62	F.H.Allen	NZ v P	Dunedin	2023-24
133*	73	M.P.O'Dowd	Neth v Malay	Kirtipur	2021
132	61	H.G.Munsey	Scot v Austria	Edinburgh	2023
127*	56	H.G.Munsey	Scot v Neth	Dublin	2019
127*	53	O.J.Hairs	Scot v Italy	Edinburgh	2023
126*	63	S.Gill	I v NZ	Ahmedabad	2022-23
125*	62	E.Lewis	WI v I	Kingston	2017
124*	71	S.R.Watson	A v I	Sydney	2015-16
124	62	K.J.O'Brien	Ire v HK	Al Amerat	2019-20
123*	57	R.D.Gaikwad	I v A	Guwahati	2023-24
123	58	B.B.McCullum	NZ v B	Pallekele	2012-13
122*	61	V.Kohli	I v Afg	Dubai (DSC)	2022
122	60	Babar Hayat	HK v Oman	Fatullah	2015-16
122	59	Babar Azam	P v SA	Centurion	2021
121*	59	A.Johnson	Can v Panama	Hamilton	2023-24
121*	69	R.G.Sharma	I v Afg	Bengaluru	2023-24
120*	55	G.J.Maxwell	A v WI	Adelaide	2023-24
119	56	F.du Plessis	SA v WI	Johannesburg	2014-15
119	57	P.D.Salt	E v WI	Tarouba	2023-24
118*	67	Mohammad Shahzad	Afg v Z	Sharjah	2015-16
118	43	R.G.Sharma	I v SL	Indore	2017-18
118	46	J. Charles	WI v SA	Centurion	2022-23
117*	51	R.E.Levi	SA v NZ	Hamilton	2011-12
117*	68	Shaiman Anwar	UAE v PNG	Abu Dhabi	2017
117	57	C.H.Gayle	WI v SA	Johannesburg	2007-08
117	51	S.A.Yadav	I v E	Nottingham	2022
116*	56	B.B.McCullum	NZ v A	Christchurch	2009-10
116*	64	A.D.Hales	E v SL	Chittagong	2013-14
115*	75	P.R.Stirling	Ire v Z	Bready	2021

The highest score for Sri Lanka is 104* by T.M.Dilshan (v A, Pallekele, 2011), for Zimbabwe 94 by S.F.Mire (v P, Harare, 2018) and for Bangladesh 103* by Tamim Iqbal (v Oman, Dharamsala, 2015-16).

MOST SIXES IN AN INNINGS

16	Hazratullah Zazai (162*)	Afg v Ire	Dehradun	2018-19
16	F.H.Allen (137)	NZ v P	Dunedin	2023-24
14	A.J.Finch (156)	A v E	Southampton	2013
14	H.G.Munsey (127*)	Scot v Neth	Dublin	2019
13	R.E.Levi (117*)	SA v NZ	Hamilton	2011-12
12	E.Lewis (125*)	WI v I	Kingston	2017
12	K.Malla (137*)	Nepal v Mong	Hangzhou	2023-24

HIGHEST PARTNERSHIP FOR EACH WICKET

1st	258*	L.Yamamoto-Lake/K.S.Fleming	Japan v China	Hong Kong	2023-24
2nd	183	O.J.Hairs/B.McMullen	Scot v Italy	Edinburgh	2023
3rd	193	K.Malla/R.K.Paudel	Nepal v Mong	Hangzhou	2023-24
4th	174*	Q.de Kock/D.A.Miller	SA v I	Guwahati	2022-23
5th	190*	R.G.Sharma/R.K.Singh	I v Afg	Bengaluru	2023-24
6th	139	S.E.Rutherford/A.D.Russell	WI v A	Perth	2023-24
7th	92	M.P.Stoinis/D.R.Sams	A v NZ	Dunedin	2020-21
8th	80	P.L.Mommsen/S.M.Sharif	Scot v Neth	Edinburgh	2015
9th	132*	Saber Zakhil/Saqlain Ali	Belg v Austria	Waterloo	2021
10th	62*	K.B.Ahir/N.Ahir	Panama v Arg	North Sound	2021-22

BOWLING RECORDS
75 WICKETS IN A CAREER

Wkts			*Matches*	*Overs*	*Mdns*	*Runs*	*Avge*	*Best*	*R/Over*
157	T.G.Southee	NZ	123	446.5	6	3635	23.15	5-18	8.13
140	Shakib Al Hasan	B	117	422.3	3	2869	20.49	5-20	6.79
132	I.S.Sodhi	NZ	111	379.5	–	3048	23.09	4-28	8.02

Wkts			Matches	Overs	Mdns	Runs	Avge	Best	R/Over
130	Rashid Khan	Afg/IC	82	312.2	1	1925	14.80	5- 3	6.16
111	M.J.Santner	NZ	100	345.2	2	2457	22.13	4-11	7.11
107	S.L.Malinga	SL	84	299.5	1	2225	20.79	5- 6	7.42
107	A.U.Rashid	E	104	365.2	4	2698	25.21	4- 2	7.38
105	Mustafizur Rahman	B	88	311.4	6	2338	22.26	5-22	7.50
104	Shadab Khan	P	92	325.1	3	2301	22.12	4- 8	7.07
102	P.W.H.de Silva	SL	64	232.4	1	1587	15.55	4- 9	6.82
102	M.R.Adair	Ire	74	261.5	2	2011	19.71	4-13	7.68
98	S.Lamichhane	Nep/Wd	52	195.5	5	1233	12.58	5- 9	6.29
98	Shahid Afridi	P/Wd	99	361.2	4	2396	24.44	4-11	6.63
96	S.O.Ngoche	Ken	96	273.4	12	1641	17.09	4-14	5.99
96	Y.S.Chahal	I	80	294.0	2	2409	25.09	6-25	8.19
96	C.J.Jordan	E	88	304.4	2	2658	27.68	4- 6	8.72
92	Bilal Khan	Oman	64	230.1	7	1489	16.18	4-19	6.46
92	A.Zampa	A	80	285.5	1	2082	22.63	5-19	7.28
92	Mohammad Nabi	Afg	118	349.4	5	2577	28.01	4-10	7.36
90	H.Senyondo	Ugan	73	243.4	8	1298	14.42	4- 4	5.32
90	Haris Rauf	P	66	239.1	1	1963	21.81	4-18	8.20
90	B.Kumar	I	87	298.3	10	2079	23.10	5- 4	6.96
85	Umar Gul	P	60	200.3	2	1443	16.97	5- 6	7.19
85	Saeed Ajmal	P	64	238.2	2	1516	17.83	4-19	6.36
83	G.H.Dockrell	Ire	128	261.2	1	1878	22.62	4-20	7.18
79	K.C.Karan	Nep	55	184.3	5	1412	17.87	5-21	7.65
78	T.Shamsi	SA	65	234.4	1	1732	22.20	5-24	7.38
78	D.J.Bravo	WI	91	250.5	–	2036	26.10	4-19	8.11
76	Ehsan Khan	HK	56	209.0	4	1264	16.63	4-24	6.04

The most wickets for Zimbabwe is 62 by T.L.Chatara (56 matches).

BEST FIGURES IN AN INNINGS

7- 8	Syazrul Idrus	Malay v China	Kuala Lumpur	2023
6- 7	D.L.Chahar	I v B	Nagpur	2019-20
6- 8	B.A.W.Mendis	SL v Z	Hambantota	2012-13
6-10	J.J.Smit	Nam v Uganda	Windhoek	2022
6-11	A.Bohara	Nep v Mald	Hangzhou	2023-24
6-12	N.Rana	HK v PNG	Kuala Lumpur	2023-24
6-16	B.A.W.Mendis	SL v A	Pallekele	2011
6-17	O.C.McCoy	WI v I	Basseterre	2022
6-17	P.K.Langat	Ken v Mali	Kigali	2022-23
6-24	J.N.Frylinck	Nam v UAE	Dubai (ICA)	2021-22
6-25	Y.S.Chahal	I v E	Bengaluru	2016-17
6-30	A.C.Agar	A v NZ	Wellington	2020-21
5- 3	H.M.R.K.B.Herath	SL v NZ	Chittagong	2013-14
5- 3	Rashid Khan	Afg v Ire	Greater Noida	2016-17
5- 4	Khizar Hayat	Malay v HK	Kuala Lumpur	2019-20
5- 4	B.Kumar	I v Afg	Dubai (DSC)	2022
5- 6	Umar Gul	P v NZ	The Oval	2009
5- 6	Umar Gul	P v SA	Centurion	2012-13
5- 6	S.L.Malinga	SL v NZ	Pallekele	2019
5- 9	C.Viljoen	Nam v Bots	Kampala	2019
5- 9	S.Lamichhane	Nep v Ken	Nairobi	2022
5- 9	K.V.Morea	PNG v Phil	Port Moresby	2023
5-10	S.M.Curran	E v Afg	Perth	2022-23
5-11	Karim Janat	Afg v WI	Lucknow	2019-20
5-12	V.Patel	Ken v Nig	Kigali	2021-22
5-12	S.N.Netravalkar	USA v Sing	Bulawayo	2022
5-13	Elias Sunny	B v Ire	Belfast	2012
5-13	Samiullah Shenwari	Afg v Ken	Sharjah	2013-14
5-13	B.J.Currie	Scot v Ire	Edinburgh	2023
5-14	Imad Wasim	P v WI	Dubai	2016-17

5-15	K.M.A.Paul	WI v B	Mirpur	2018-19
5-15	D.A.Ravu	PNG v Vanu	Apia	2019
5-15	Aamir Kaleem	Oman v Nep	Al Amerat	2019-20

The best figures for South Africa are 5-17 by D.Pretorius (v P, Lahore, 2020-21), for New Zealand 5-18 by T.G.Southee (v P, Auckland, 2010-11), for Zimbabwe 4-8 by Sikandar Raza (v Neth, Bulawayo, 2022), and for Ireland 4-11 by A.R.Cusack (v WI, Kingston, 2013-14).

HAT-TRICKS

B.Lee	Australia v Bangladesh	Melbourne	2007-08
J.D.P.Oram	New Zealand v Sri Lanka	Colombo (RPS)	2009
T.G.Southee	New Zealand v Pakistan	Auckland	2010-11
N.L.T.C.Perera	Sri Lanka v India	Ranchi	2015-16
S.L.Malinga	Sri Lanka v Bangladesh	Colombo (RPS)	2016-17
Faheem Ashraf	Pakistan v Sri Lanka	Abu Dhabi	2017-18
Rashid Khan†	Afghanistan v Ireland	Dehradun	2018-19
S.L.Malinga†	Sri Lanka v New Zealand	Pallekele	2019
Mohammad Hasnain	Pakistan v Sri Lanka	Lahore	2019-20
Khawar Ali	Oman v Netherlands	Al Amerat	2019-20
N.Vanua	PNG v Bermuda	Dubai (ICA)	2019-20
D.L.Chahar	India v Bangladesh	Nagpur	2019-20
A.C.Agar	Australia v South Africa	Johannesburg	2019-20
M.K.P.A.D.Perera	Sri Lanka v West Indies	Coolidge	2020-21
N.T.Ellis	Australia v Bangladesh	Mirpur	2021
E.Otieno	Kenya v Uganda	Entebbe	2021
C.Campher†	Ireland v Netherlands	Abu Dhabi	2021-22
P.W.H.de Silva	Sri Lanka v South Africa	Sharjah	2021-22
K.Rabada	South Africa v England	Sharjah	2021-22
J.O.Holder†	West Indies v England	Bridgetown	2021-22
K.C.Karan	Nepal v PNG	Kirtipur	2021-22
J.J.Smit	Namibia v Uganda	Windhoek	2022
L.V.van Beek	Netherlands v Hong Kong	Bulawayo	2022
M.G.Bracewell	New Zealand v Ireland	Belfast	2022
K.P.Meiyappan	UAE v Sri Lanka	Geelong	2022-33
J.B.Little	Ireland v New Zealand	Adelaide	2022-23
T.G.Southee	New Zealand v India	Mt Maunganui	2022-23
M.J.Henry	New Zealand v Pakistan	Lahore	2023
Karim Janat	Afghanistan v Bangladesh	Sylhet	2023
K.V.Morea	PNG v Philippines	Port Moresby	2023
Sikandar Raza	Zimbabwe v Rwanda	Windhoek	2023-24

† Four wickets in four balls.

WICKET-KEEPING RECORDS – 60 DISMISSALS IN A CAREER

Dis			*Inns*	*Ct*	*St*
92	Q.de Kock	South Africa	78	76	16
91	M.S.Dhoni	India	98	57	34
83	I.A.Karim	Kenya	53	59	24
72	J.C.Buttler	England	96	61	11
63	D.Ramdin	West Indies	71	43	20
62	Mushfiqur Rahim	Bangladesh	84	32	30
61	Mohammad Shahzad	Afghanistan	72	33	28
60	Kamran Akmal	Pakistan	53	28	32

MOST DISMISSALS IN AN INNINGS

5 (3ct, 2st)	Mohammad Shahzad	Afghanistan v Oman	Abu Dhabi	2015-16
5 (5ct)	M.S.Dhoni	India v England	Bristol	2018
5 (2ct, 3st)	I.A.Karim	Kenya v Ghana	Kampala	2019
5 (5ct)	K.Doriga	PNG v Vanuatu	Apia	2019
5 (5ct)	I.A.Karim	Kenya v Uganda	Kigali	2021-22
5 (4ct, 1st)	I.A.Karim	Kenya v Mali	Kigali	2022-23

FIELDING RECORDS – 50 CATCHES IN A CAREER

Total			Matches	Total			Matches
77	D.A.Miller	South Africa/Wd	115	60	R.G.Sharma	India	151
68	M.J.Guptill	New Zealand	122	58	D.A.Warner	Australia	103
65	T.G.Southee	New Zealand	123	52	V.Kohli	India	117
62	Mohammad Nabi	Afghanistan	118	50	A.J.Finch	Australia	103
62	G.H.Dockrell	Ireland	128	50	Shoaib Malik	Pakistan/ICC	124

MOST CATCHES IN AN INNINGS

5	W.J.Malinda	Maldives v Qatar	Doha	2023-24
4	D.J.G.Sammy	West Indies v Ireland	Providence	2009-10
4	P.W.Borren	Netherlands v Bangladesh	The Hague	2012
4	C.J.Anderson	New Zealand v South Africa	Gqeberha	2012-13
4	L.D.Chandimal	Sri Lanka v Bangladesh	Chittagong	2013-14
4	A.M.Rahane	India v England	Birmingham	2014
4	Babar Hayat	Hong Kong v Afghanistan	Mirpur	2015-16
4	D.A.Miller	South Africa v Pakistan	Cape Town	2018-19
4	L.Siaka	PNG v Vanuatu	Apia	2019
4	C.S.MacLeod	Scotland v Ireland	Dublin	2019
4	T.H.David	Singapore v Scotland	Dubai	2019-20
4	C.de Grandhomme	New Zealand v England	Wellington	2019-20
4	P.Sarraf	Nepal v Malaysia	Bangkok	2019-20
4	M.G.Erasmus	Namibia v UAE	Dubai (ICA)	2021-22
4	K.Bhurtel	Nepal v Malaysia	Kirtipur	2022
4	Saim Ayub	Pakistan v New Zealand	Auckland	2023-24
4	W.P.Masakadza	Zimbabwe v Sri Lanka	Colombo (RPS)	2023-24
4	S.A.Abbott	Australia v West Indies	Hobart	2023-24

APPEARANCE RECORDS – 105 APPEARANCES

151	R.G.Sharma	India	117	V.Kohli	India
134	P.R.Stirling	Ireland	117	Shakib Al Hasan	Bangladesh
128	G.H.Dockrell	Ireland	116	D.A.Miller	South Africa/World
124	Shoaib Malik	Pakistan/ICC	115	E.J.G.Morgan	England
123	T.G.Southee	New Zealand	114	J.C.Buttler	England
122	M.J.Guptill	New Zealand	111	I.S.Sodhi	New Zealand
121	Mahmudullah	Bangladesh	110	K.J.O'Brien	Ireland
119	Mohammad Hafeez	Pakistan	109	Babar Azam	Pakistan
118	Mohammad Nabi	Afghanistan	106	G.J.Maxwell	Australia

The most appearances for West Indies is 101 by K.A.Pollard, for Sri Lanka 94 by M.D.Shanaka, and for Zimbabwe 81 by Sikandar Raza.

50 MATCHES AS CAPTAIN

			W	*L*	*T*	*NR*	*%age wins*
76	A.J.Finch	Australia	40	32	1	3	54.79
72	M.S.Dhoni	India	41	28	1	2	58.57
72	E.J.G.Morgan	England	42	27	2	1	59.15
71	Babar Azam	Pakistan	42	23	–	6	64.61
71	K.S.Williamson	New Zealand	37	32	1	1	52.85
56	W.T.S.Porterfield	Ireland	26	26	–	4	50.00
54	R.G.Sharma	India	41	12	1	–	75.92
52	Asghar Stanikzai	Afghanistan	42	9	1	–	80.76
52	A.Balbirnie	Ireland	19	31	1	1	37.25
50	V.Kohli	India	30	16	2	2	62.50

INDIAN PREMIER LEAGUE 2023

The 16th IPL tournament was held in India between 31 March and 29 May.

Team	*P*	*W*	*L*	*T*	*NR*	*Pts*	*Net RR*
1 Gujarat Titans	14	10	4	–	–	20	+0.80
2 Chennai Super Kings	14	8	5	–	1	17	+0.65
3 Lucknow Super Giants	14	8	5	–	1	17	+0.28
4 Mumbai Indians	14	8	6	–	–	16	–0.50
5 Rajasthan Royals	14	7	7	–	–	14	+0.14
6 Royal Challengers Bangalore	14	7	7	–	–	14	+0.13
7 Kolkata Knight Riders	14	6	8	–	–	12	–0.23
8 Punjab Kings	14	6	8	–	–	12	–0.30
9 Delhi Capitals	14	5	9	–	–	10	–0.80
10 Sunrisers Hyderabad	14	4	10	–	–	8	–0.59

1st Qualifying Match: At M.A.Chidambaram Stadium, Chennai, 23 May (floodlit). Toss: Gujarat Titans. **CHENNAI SUPER KINGS** won by 15 runs. Chennai Super Kings 172-7 (20; R.D.Gaikwad 60, D.P.Conway 40). Gujarat Titans 157 (20; S.Gill 42). Award: R.D.Gaikwad.

Eliminator: At M.A.Chidambaram Stadium, Chennai, 24 May (floodlit). Toss: Mumbai Indians. **MUMBAI INDIANS** won by 81 runs. Mumbai Indians 182-8 (20; C.D.Green 41, Naveen-ul-Haq 4-38, Y.R.Thakur 3-34). Lucknow Super Giants 101 (16.3; M.P.Stoinis 40, A.Madhwal 5-5). Award: A.Madhwal.

2nd Qualifying Match: At Narendra Modi Stadium, Ahmedabad, 26 May (floodlit). Toss: Mumbai Indians. **GUJARAT TITANS** won by 62 runs. Gujarat Titans 233-3 (20; S.Gill 129, S.Sudharsan 43). Mumbai Indians 171 (18.2; S.A.Yadav 61, N.T.T.Varma 43, M.M.Sharma 5-10). Award: S.Gill.

FINAL: At Narendra Modi Stadium, Ahmedabad, 28, 29 May (floodlit). Toss: Chennai Super Kings. **CHENNAI SUPER KINGS** won by five wickets (DLS method). Gujarat Titans 214-4 (20; S.Sudharsan 96, W.P.Saha 54). Chennai Super Kings 171-5 (15/15; D.P.Conway 47, M.M.Sharma 3-36). Award: D.P.Conway. Series award: S.Gill (GT).

IPL winners:				
	2008	Rajasthan Royals	2009	Deccan Chargers
	2010	Chennai Super Kings	2011	Chennai Super Kings
	2012	Kolkata Knight Riders	2013	Mumbai Indians
	2014	Kolkata Knight Riders	2015	Mumbai Indians
	2016	Sunrisers Hyderabad	2017	Mumbai Indians
	2018	Chennai Super Kings	2019	Mumbai Indians
	2020	Mumbai Indians	2021	Chennai Super Kings
	2022	Gujarat Titans		

TEAM RECORDS – HIGHEST TOTALS

263-5 (20)	Bangalore v Pune	Bangalore	2013
257-5 (20)	Lucknow v Punjab	Mohali	2023

LOWEST TOTALS

49 (9.4)	Bangalore v Kolkata	Kolkata	2017
58 (15.1)	Rajasthan v Bangalore	Cape Town	2009

LARGEST MARGINS OF VICTORY

146 runs	Mumbai (212-3) beat Delhi (66)	Delhi	2017
87 balls	Mumbai (68-2) beat Kolkata (67)	Mumbai	2008

There have been 14 victories in IPL history by ten wickets.

BATTING RECORDS – MOST RUNS IN IPL

7263	V.Kohli	Bangalore	2008-23
6617	S.Dhawan	Deccan, Delhi, Mumbai, Punjab, Hyderabad	2008-23

850 RUNS IN A SEASON

Runs			*Year*	*M*	*I*	*NO*	*HS*	*Ave*	*100*	*50*	*6s*	*4s*	R/100B
973	V.Kohli	Bangalore	2016	16	16	4	113	81.08	4	7	38	83	152.0
890	S.Gill	Gujarat	2023	17	17	2	129	59.33	3	4	33	85	157.8
863	J.C.Buttler	Rajasthan	2022	17	17	2	116	57.53	4	4	45	83	149.0

HIGHEST SCORES

Runs	*Balls*				
175*	66	C.H.Gayle	Bangalore v Pune	Bangalore	2013
158*	73	B.B.McCullum	Kolkata v Bangalore	Bangalore	2008
140*	70	Q.de Kock	Lucknow v Kolkata	Mumbai	2022

K.P.Pietersen 103* (Delhi v Deccan at Delhi, 2012), B.A.Stokes 103* (Pune v Gujarat at Pune, 2017) and 107* (Rajasthan v Mumbai at Abu Dhabi, 2020), J.M.Bairstow 114 (Hyderabad v Bangalore at Hyderabad, 2019), H.C.Brook 100 (Hyderabad v Kolkata at Kolkata, 2023) and J.C.Buttler (five times, best of 124 Rajasthan v Hyderabad in 2021 and four more times in 2022) are the only England-qualified centurions in the IPL.

FASTEST HUNDRED

30 balls	C.H.Gayle (175*)	Bangalore v Pune	Bangalore	2013

MOST SIXES IN AN INNINGS

17	C.H.Gayle	Bangalore v Pune	Bangalore	2013

HIGHEST STRIKE RATE IN A SEASON (Qualification: 100 runs or more)

R/100B	*Runs*	*Balls*		
216.66	130	60	Rashid Khan Gujarat	2023

HIGHEST STRIKE RATE IN AN INNINGS (Qualification: 30 runs, 370+ strike rate)

R/100B	*Runs*	*Balls*				
422.2	38*	9	C.H.Morris	Delhi v Pune	Pune	2017
387.5	31	8	A.B.de Villiers	Bangalore v Pune	Bangalore	2013
375.0	30*	8	K.D.Karthik	Bangalore v Hyderabad	Mumbai	2022
373.3	56*	15	P.J.Cummins	Kolkata v Mumbai	Pune	2022
372.7	41	11	A.B.de Villiers	Bangalore v Mumbai	Bangalore	2015

BOWLING RECORDS – MOST WICKETS IN IPL

187	Y.S.Chahal	Bangalore, Mumbai, Rajasthan	2013-23
183	D.J.Bravo	Chennai, Gujarat, Mumbai	2008-22

30 WICKETS IN A SEASON

Wkts			*Year*	*P*	*O*	*M*	*Runs*	*Avge*	*Best*	*4w*	*R/Over*
32	H.V.Patel	Bangalore	2021	15	56.2	–	459	14.34	5-27	2	8.14
32	D.J.Bravo	Chennai	2013	18	62.3	–	497	15.53	4-42	1	7.95
30	K.Rabada	Delhi	2020	17	65.4	1	548	18.26	4-24	2	8.34

BEST BOWLING FIGURES IN AN INNINGS

6-12	A.S.Joseph	Mumbai v Hyderabad	Hyderabad	2019
6-14	Sohail Tanvir	Rajasthan v Chennai	Jaipur	2008
6-19	A.Zampa	Pune v Hyderabad	Visakhapatnam	2016
5-5	A.Kumble	Bangalore v Rajasthan	Cape Town	2009
5-5	A.Madhwal	Mumbai v Lucknow	Chennai	2023

A.D.Mascarenhas 5-25 (Punjab v Pune at Mohali, 2012) and M.A.Wood 5-14 (Lucknow v Delhi at Lucknow, 2023) are the only England-qualified bowlers to take five wickets in an innings in the IPL.

MOST ECONOMICAL BOWLING ANALYSIS

O	*M*	*R*	*W*				
4	1	6	0	F.H.Edwards	Deccan v Kolkata	Cape Town	2009
4	1	6	1	A.Nehra	Delhi v Punjab	Bloemfontein	2009
4	1	6	1	Y.S.Chahal	Bangalore v Chennai	Chennai	2019

MOST EXPENSIVE BOWLING ANALYSIS

O	*M*	*R*	*W*				
4	0	70	0	B.Thampi	Hyderabad v Bangalore	Bangalore	2018
4	0	69	0	Y.Dayal	Gujarat v Kolkata	Ahmedabad	2023

THE MEN'S HUNDRED 2023

The third edition of The Hundred, featuring eight franchise sides in matches of 100 balls per side, took place between 1 and 27 August. The second-and third-placed sides played off for a place in the final, held at Lord's. (2022's positions in brackets.)

	P	W	L	T	NR	Pts	Net RR
1. Oval Invincibles (5)	8	6	1	1	–	13	+0.56
2. Manchester Originals (2)	8	4	3	–	1	9	+0.52
3. Southern Brave (7)	8	4	3	–	1	9	+0.06
4. Welsh Fire (8)	8	4	3	1	–	9	–0.05
5. Trent Rockets (1)	8	3	4	–	1	7	+0.18
6. Birmingham Phoenix (4)	8	2	4	–	2	6	–0.08
7. London Spirit (3)	8	2	4	–	2	6	–0.65
8. Northern Superchargers (6)	8	2	5	–	1	5	–0.70

LEADING AGGREGATES AND RECORDS 2023

BATTING (235 runs)	M	I	NO	HS	Runs	Avge	100	50	R/100b	Sixes
J.C.Buttler (Originals)	10	10	1	82	391	43.44	–	3	145.3	17
F.H.Allen (Brave)	9	9	–	69	240	26.66	–	1	144.5	11
H.C.Brook (Superchargers)	8	7	2	105*	238	47.60	1	1	196.6	14

BOWLING (12 wkts)	Balls	R	W	Avge	BB	4w	R/100b
T.S.Mills (Brave)	160	209	16	13.06	4-13	1	130.6
R.J.W.Topley (Superchargers)	145	208	13	16.00	3-29	–	143.4
D.R.Sams (Rockets)	134	215	12	17.91	3-17	–	160.4

Highest total	201-3	Originals v Brave		The Oval
	201-3	Superchargers v Brave		Southampton
Biggest win (runs)	94	Invincibles (186-5) beat Originals (92)		The Oval
Biggest win (balls)	41	Brave (91-1) beat Fire (87)		Cardiff
Highest innings	105*	H.C.Brook	Superchargers v Fire	Leeds
Most sixes	17	H.Klaasen (Invincibles), J.C.Buttler (Originals)		
Highest partnership	127*	J.D.S.Neesham/T.K.Curran	Invincibles v Originals	Lord's
Best bowling	5-11	C.G.Harrison	Originals v Superchargers	Manchester
Most economical	20b-1-3	S.H.Johnson	Invincibles v Originals	The Oval
Most expensive	20b-53-1	D.A.Payne	Fire v Superchargers	Leeds
Most w/k dismissals	11	J.C.Buttler (Originals)		
Most catches	7	J.L.du Plooy (Brave), N.A.Sowter (Invincibles), D.Wiese (Superchargers)		

OVERALL RECORDS

Highest total	208-5	Originals v Superchargers		Leeds	2022
Biggest win (runs)	94	Invincibles (186-5) beat Originals (92)		The Oval	2023
Biggest win (balls)	41	Brave (91-1) beat Fire (87)		The Oval	2023
Most runs	707	P.D.Salt (Originals)			2021-23
Highest innings	108*	W.G.Jacks	Invincibles v Brave	The Oval	2022
Most sixes	46	L.S.Livingstone (Phoenix)			2021-23
Highest partnership	127*	J.D.S.Neesham/T.K.Curran	Invincibles v Originals	Lord's	2023
Most wickets	31	A.U.Rashid (Superchargers)			2021-23
Best bowling	5-11	C.G.Harrison	Originals v Superchargers	Manchester	2023
Most economical	20b-1-3	S.H.Johnson	Invincibles v Originals	The Oval	2023
Most expensive	20b-53-1	D.Wiese	Superchargers v Originals	Leeds	2022
	20b-53-1	D.A.Payne	Fire v Superchargers	Leeds	2023
Most w/k dismissals	20	A.M.Rossington (Spirit)			2021-23
Most catches	13	H.C.Brook (Superchargers), T.W.Hartley (Originals), J.M.Vince (Brave)			2021-23

2023 THE HUNDRED FINAL MANCHESTER ORIGINALS v OVAL INVINCIBLES

At Lord's, London, on 27 August (floodlit).

Result: **OVAL INVINCIBLES** won by 14 runs.

Toss: Manchester Originals. Award: T.K.Curran.

OVAL INVINCIBLES		*Runs*	*Balls*	*4/6*	*Fall*
J.J.Roy	c Buttler b Gleeson	0	3	–	1- 0
W.G.Jacks	c Walter b Hartley	14	14	2	5-34
P.R.Stirling	c Walter b Gleeson	5	5	1	2-15
S.M.Curran	c Buttler b Little	0	1	–	3-15
†*S.W.Billings	c Buttler b Walter	10	11	2	4-28
J.D.S.Neesham	not out	57	33	7/1	
T.K.Curran	not out	67	34	4/5	
R.A.Whiteley					
A.A.P.Atkinson					
N.A.Sowter					
D.R.Briggs					
Extras	(B 2, LB 1, NB 2, W 3)	8			
Total	**(5 wkts; 100 balls)**	**161**			

MANCHESTER ORIGINALS		*Runs*	*Balls*	*4/6*	*Fall*
P.D.Salt	c S.M.Curran b T.K.Curran	25	16	4/1	1- 34
†*J.C.Buttler	b Briggs	11	15	1	2- 44
M.D.E.Holden	lbw b S.M.Curran	37	25	4/1	6-114
W.L.Madsen	b Sowter	4	3	1	3- 48
L.J.Evans	c Sowter b Jacks	1	3	–	4- 51
P.I.Walter	b Jacks	7	11	1	5- 72
J.Overton	not out	28	19	–/1	
T.W.Hartley	not out	16	8	1/1	
J.B.Little					
Zaman Khan					
R.J.Gleeson					
Extras	(LB 7, W 11)	18			
Total	**(6 wkts; 100 balls)**	**147**			

ORIGINALS	*B*	*0*	*R*	*W*	**INVINCIBLES**	*B*	*0*	*R*	*W*
Gleeson	20	7	37	2	S.M.Curran	20	4	31	1
Little	20	11	21	1	Atkinson	20	6	47	0
Walter	15	5	20	1	T.K.Curran	20	7	25	1
Overton	10	3	14	0	Sowter	20	9	24	1
Hartley	20	1	35	1	Briggs	5	3	2	1
Zaman Khan	15	4	31	0	Jacks	15	7	11	2

Umpires: M.Burns and A.G.Wharf

THE HUNDRED WINNERS

2021 Southern Brave
2022 Trent Rockets
2023 Oval Invincibles

Eliminator: At The Oval, London, 26 August. Toss: Manchester Originals. **MANCHESTER ORIGINALS** won by seven wickets. Southern Brave 196-1 (100 balls; F.H.Allen 69, J.M.Vince 56*, D.P.Conway 51*). Manchester Originals 201-3 (96 balls; J.C.Buttler 82, P.D.Salt 47). Award: J.C.Buttler.

IRELAND INTERNATIONALS

The following players have played for Ireland in any format of international cricket since 1 December 2022. Details correct to 6 March 2024.

ADAIR, George **Ross**, b Belfast 21 Apr 1994. Elder brother of M.R.Adair (*see below*). RHB, LB. Northern Knights debut 2021 (not f-c). **IT20**: 7 (2022-23 to 2023); HS 65 v Z (Harare) 2022-23. LO HS 76 Northern v NW (Bready) 2023. LO BB 2-32 Northern v NW (Belfast) 2023. T20 HS 111. T20 BB 2-24.

ADAIR, Mark Richard (Sullivan Upper S, Holywood), b Belfast 27 Mar 1996. Younger brother of G.R.Adair (*see above*). 6'2". RHB, RMF. Warwickshire 2015-16. Northern Knights debut 2018. Ireland Wolves 2018-19 to 2020-21. Essex 2023. **Tests**: 5 (2019 to 2023-24); HS 88 v E (Lord's) 2023; BB 5-39 v Afg (Abu Dhabi) 2023-24. **LOI**: 46 (2019 to 2023-24); HS 32 v E (Dublin) 2019; BB 4-19 v Afg (Belfast) 2019. **IT20**: 74 (2019 to 2023-24); HS 72 v Scot (Edinburgh) 2023; BB 4-13 v Austria (Edinburgh) 2023. HS 91 Northern v Leinster (Dublin, Sandymount) 2018. BB 5-39 (*see Tests*). LO HS 108 Northern v Munster (Cork) 2022. LO BB 4-19 (*see LOI*). T20 HS 72. T20 BB 4-13.

BALBIRNIE, Andrew (St Andrew's C, Dublin; UWIC), b Dublin 28 Dec 1990. 6'2". RHB, OB. Cardiff MCCU 2012-13. Ireland debut 2012. Middlesex 2012-15. Leinster Lightning debut 2017. Ireland Wolves 2017-18. Glamorgan 2021. **Tests**: 8 (2018 to 2023-24, 5 as captain); HS 95 v SL (Galle) 2023; BB –. **LOI**: 106 (2010 to 2023-24, 37 as captain); HS 145* v Afg (Dehradun) 2018-19; BB 1-26 v Afg (Dubai, DSC) 2014-15. **IT20**: 98 (2015 to 2023-24, 52 as captain); HS 83 v Neth (Al Amerat) 2018-19. HS 205* Ire v Neth (Dublin) 2017. BB 4-23 Leinster v NW (Bready) 2017. LO HS 160* IW v Bangladesh A (Dublin, CA) 2018. LO BB 1-26 (*see LOI*). T20 HS 99*.

CAMPHER, Curtis (St Stithians C), b Johannesburg, South Africa 20 Apr 1999. RHB, RMF. Ireland Wolves 2020-21. Somerset 2023. Leinster Lightning 2020 (not f-c). Munster Reds debut 2021 (not f-c). **Tests**: 5 (2022-23 to 2023-24); HS 111 v SL (Galle) 2023; BB 2-13 v Afg (Abu Dhabi) 2023-24. **LOI**: 35 (2020 to 2023-24); HS 120 v Scot (Bulawayo) 2023; BB 4-37 v Z (Harare) 2023-24. **IT20**: 44 (2021 to 2023-24); HS 72* v Scot (Hobart) 2022-23; BB 4-25 v USA (Lauderhill) 2021-22. HS 111 (*see Tests*). BB 2-13 (*see Tests*). LO HS 120 (*see LOI*). LO BB 4-37 (*see LOI*). T20 HS 72*. T20 BB 4-20.

COMMINS, Murray, b Cape Town, South Africa 2 Jan 1997. Son of J.B.Commins (W Province, Boland & South Africa 1985-86 to 1994-95); grandson of K.T.Commins (W Province & Boland 1951-52 to 1960-61). RHB, RMF. SW Districts 2016-17. Boland 2017-18 to 2018-19. Northern Knights 2019. Munster Reds debut 2021 (not f-c). **Tests**: 2 (2022-23 to 2023); HS 5 v B (Mirpur) 2022-23. **LOI**: 2 (2022-23); HS 6 v Z (Harare) 2022-23. HS 93 Ire Emerging v WI Acad (Coolidge) 2023-24. LO HS 125 Munster v Northern (Belfast) 2021. T20 HS 102.

DELANY, Gareth James, b Dublin 28 Apr 1997. Cousin of D.C.A.Delany (Leinster, Northern, Munster & Ireland 2017 to date). RHB, LBG. Leinster Lightning 2017-19. Ireland Wolves 2018-19 to 2020-21. Leicestershire 2020 (T20 only). Munster Reds debut 2021 (not f-c). **LOI**: 21 (2019-20 to 2023); HS 22 v E (Southampton) 2020 and 22 v NZ (Dublin) 2022; BB 2-52 v SL (Bulawayo) 2023. **IT20**: 64 (2019 to 2023-24); HS 89* v Oman (Abu Dhabi) 2019-20; BB 3-16 v WI (Hobart) 2022-23. HS 22 IW v Sri Lanka A (Colombo, SSC) 2018-19. BB 3-48 Leinster v Northern (Belfast) 2017. LO HS 104 and LO BB 5-39 IW v Namibia A (Windhoek) 2021-22. T20 HS 89*. T20 BB 3-8.

DOCKRELL, George Henry (Gonzaga C, Dublin), b Dublin 22 Jul 1992. 6'3". RHB, SLA. Ireland debut 2010. Somerset 2011-14. Sussex 2015. Leinster Lightning debut 2017. Ireland Wolves 2017-18. Essex 2023. **Tests**: 2 (2018-19 to 2023); HS 39 and BB 2-63 v Afg (Dehradun) 2018-19. **LOI**: 122 (2009-10 to 2023-24); HS 91* v Oman (Bulawayo) 2023; BB 4-24 v Scot (Belfast) 2013. **IT20**: 128 (2009-10 to 2023-24); HS 58* v Afg (Belfast) 2022; BB 4-20 v Neth (Dubai) 2009-10. HS 92 Leinster v NW (Bready) 2018. BB 6-27 Sm v Middx (Taunton) 2012. LO HS 100* Leinster v Northern (Dublin, SP) 2021. LO BB 5-21 Leinster v Northern (Dublin, V) 2018. T20 HS 69*. T20 BB 4-20.

DOHENY, Stephen Thomas (Catholic Uni S, Dublin), b Dublin 29 Aug 1998. RHB, WK, occ OB. Leinster Lightning 2018-19. Ireland Wolves 2018-19 to 2020-21. North West Warriors debut 2021 (not f-c). **LOI**: 3 (2022-23 to 2023); HS 84 v Z (Harare) 2022-23. **IT20**: 3 (2022-23); HS 15 v Z (Harare) 2022-23. HS 58 IW v Sri Lanka A (Hambantota) 2018-19. BB 1-4 Leinster v Northern (Dublin) 2019. LO HS 97 NW v Northern (Belfast) 2022. T20 HS 74*.

HAND, Fionn Philip (Ardgillan Community C; Queen's C, Taunton), b Dublin 1 Jul 1998. RHB, RMF. Leinster Lightning debut 2019. Munster Reds 2021-22 (not f-c). **Tests**: 1 (2023); HS 7 and BB 1-113 v E (Lord's) 2023. **IT20**: 10 (2022 to 2022-23); HS 36 v Afg (Belfast) 2022; BB 1-11 v Afg (Belfast) 2022 – separate matches. HS 48 and BB 2-50 Ire v Essex (Chelmsford) 2023. LO HS 49* Munster v NW (Cork) 2021. LO BB 3-51 Leinster v NW (Bready) 2023. T20 HS 44*. T20 BB 3-32.

HUME, Graham Ian, b Johannesburg, South Africa 23 Nov 1990. LHB, RMF. Gauteng 2009-10 to 2012-13. KZN Inland 2013-14 to 2018-19. Dolphins 2014-15. North West Warriors debut 2019. Ireland Wolves 2020-21. **Tests**: 3 (2022-23 to 2023); HS 14 v B (Mirpur) 2022-23 and 14 v E (Lord's) 2023; BB 1-85 v E (Lord's) 2023. **LOI**: 13 (2022 to 2023-24); HS 15* v Oman (Bulawayo) 2023; BB 4-34 v Z (Harare) 2023-24. **IT20**: 4 (2022 to 2022-23); HS 20* v B (Chittagong) 2022-23; BB 3-17 v Z (Harare) 2022-23. HS 105 Gauteng v SW Districts (Johannesburg) 2011-12. BB 7-23 KZN Inland v Northerns (Centurion) 2017-18. LO HS 44* NW v Leinster (Dublin, SP) 2021. LO BB 4-18 NW v Northern (Bready) 2022. T20 HS 52. T20 BB 4-7.

HUMPHREYS, Matthew James, b 28 Sep 2002. RHB, SLA. Northern Knights debut 2022 (not f-c). **Tests**: 1 (2023); HS 7 v SL (Galle) 2023; BB –. **LOI**: 2 (2022-23); HS 4* v B (Sylhet) 2022-23; BB –. **IT20**: 1 (2022-23); HS – ; BB 2-10 v B (Chittagong) 2022-23. HS 7 (*see Tests*). BB –. LO HS 20 Northern v NW (Belfast) 2022. LO BB 3-43 Northern v Leinster (Dublin, SP) 2022. T20 HS 7. T20 BB 5-13.

KANE, Tyrone Edward (Catholic Uni S, Dublin; University C, Dublin), b Dublin 8 Jul 1994. RHB, RMF. Leinster 2017-19. Munster Reds debut 2021 (not f-c). **Tests**: 1 (2018); HS 14 v P (Dublin) 2018; BB –. **IT20**: 9 (2015 to 2022-23); HS 26* v Scot (Bready) 2015; BB 3-19 v PNG (Belfast) 2015. HS 75 and BB 3-45 Leinster v Northern (Dublin, CA) 2017. LO HS 83 Munster v Leinster (Dublin, SP) 2023. LO BB 6-42 Leinster v Northern (Belfast) 2019. T20 HS 66*. T20 BB 5-22.

LITTLE, Joshua Brian (St Andrew's C), b Dublin 1 Nov 1999. RHB, LFM. Leinster Lightning debut 2018. Ireland Wolves 2018-19. IPL: GT 2023. Manchester Originals 2022 to date. **LOI**: 36 (2019 to 2023-24); HS 29 v E (Nottingham) 2023; BB 6-36 v Z (Harare) 2023-24 – Ire record. **IT20**: 63 (2016 to 2023-24); HS 15* v SA (Dublin) 2021; BB 4-23 v SL (Abu Dhabi) 2021-22. HS 27 Leinster v NW (Bready) 2018. BB 3-95 Leinster v Northern (Dublin) 2018. LO HS 29 (*see LOI*). LO BB 6-36 (*see LOI*). T20 HS 27*. T20 BB 5-13.

McBRINE, Andrew Robert, b Londonderry 30 Apr 1993. Son of A.McBrine (Ireland 1985-92), nephew of J.McBrine (Ireland 1986). LHB, OB. Ireland debut 2013. North West Warriors debut 2017. Ireland Wolves 2017-18. **Tests**: 7 (2018-19 to 2023-24); HS 86* v E (Lord's) 2023; BB 6-118 v B (Mirpur) 2022-23. **LOI**: 86 (2014 to 2023-24); HS 79 v SL (Dublin) 2016; BB 5-29 v Afg (Abu Dhabi) 2020-21. **IT20**: 32 (2013-14 to 2022); HS 36 v Oman (Al Amerat) 2021-22; BB 2-7 v PNG (Townsville) 2015-16. HS 86* (*see Tests*). BB 6-118 (*see Tests*). LO HS 117 NW v Northern (Belfast) 2022. LO BB 5-29 (*see LOI*). T20 HS 52*. T20 BB 3-19.

McCARTHY, Barry John (St Michael's C, Dublin; University C, Dublin), b Dublin 13 Sep 1992. 5'11". RHB, RMF. Durham 2015-18. Leinster Lightning debut 2019. **Tests**: 1 (2023-24); HS 5 and BB 3-48 v Afg (Abu Dhabi) 2023-24. **LOI**: 44 (2016 to 2023); HS 41 v E (Nottingham) 2023; BB 5-46 v Afg (Sharjah) 2017-18. **IT20**: 46 (2016-17 to 2023-24); HS 51* v I (Dublin) 2023; BB 4-30 v USA (Lauderhill) 2021-22. HS 51* Du v Hants (Chester-le-St) 2016. BB 6-63 Du v Kent (Canterbury) 2017. LO HS 110 Leinster v Northern (Dublin, SP) 2022. LO BB 6-39 Leinster v Munster (Dublin, SP) 2021. T20 HS 51*. T20 BB 4-12.

McCOLLUM, James Alexander (Methodist C, Belfast; Durham U), b Craigavon 1 Aug 1995. RHB, RM. Durham MCCU 2017. Northern debut 2017. Ireland Wolves 2018-19 to 2020-21. **Tests**: 6 (2018-19 to 2023); HS 39 v Afg (Dehradun) 2018-19. **LOI**: 10 (2018-19 to 2020-21); HS 73 v Z (Belfast) 2019. HS 119* Northern v Leinster (Belfast) 2017. BB 5-32 Northern v NW (Bready) 2018. LO HS 102 Ire W v Sri Lanka A (Colombo, RPS) 2018-19. LO BB 1-14 Northern v NW (Eglinton) 2018. T20 HS 79*.

MOOR, Peter Joseph (St John's C, Johannesburg; Tuks U, Pretoria), b Harare, Zimbabwe 2 Feb 1991. RHB, WK, occ OB. Mashonaland Eagles 2010-11 to 2012-13. Mid West Rhinos 2012-13 to 2015-16. Midlands Rhinos 2016-17 to 2017-18. Rhinos 2018-19 to 2019-20. Tuskers 2020-21. Mountaineers 2021-22 to date. Munster Reds debut 2021 (not f-c). **Tests** (Z/Ire): 13 (8 for Z 2016 to 2018; 5 for Ire 2022-23 to 2023-24); HS 83 Z v B (Mirpur) 2018-19. **LOI** (Z): 49 (2014-15 to 2019); HS 58* v UAE (Harare) 2019. **IT20** (Z): 21 (2015-16 to 2019-20); HS 92* v Singapore (Singapore) 2019-20. HS 157 Z A v Pakistan A (Bulawayo) 2016-17. LO HS 152 Munster v Leinster (Dublin, SP) 2022. T20 HS 95*.

ROCK, Neil Alan, b Dublin 24 Sep 2000. LHB, WK. Northern Knights debut 2018. Ireland Wolves 2018-19. Munster Reds 2020 (T20 only). **LOI**: 3 (2021-22); HS 5 v WI (Kingston) 2021-22. **IT20**: 19 (2021 to 2023); HS 36 v Austria (Edinburgh) 2023. HS 85 IW v Sri Lanka A (Hambantota) 2018-19. LO HS 102 Northern v Munster (Cork) 2023. T20 HS 79*.

STIRLING, Paul Robert (Belfast HS), b Belfast, N Ireland 3 Sep 1990. Father Brian Stirling was an international rugby referee. 5'10". RHB, OB. Ireland 2007-08 to date. Middlesex 2013-19; cap 2016. Northamptonshire 2020 (T20 only). Northern Knights debut 2020 (not f-c). Warwickshire 2022 to date (T20 only). Southern Brave 2021-22. Oval Invincibles 2023. **Tests**: 6 (2018 to 2023-24); HS 103 v SL (Galle) 2023; BB –. **LOI**: 159 (2008 to 2023-24, 9 as captain); HS 177 v Canada (Toronto) 2010 – Ire record; BB 6-55 v Afg (Greater Noida) 2016-17 – Ire record. **IT20**: 134 (2009 to 2023-24, 19 as captain); HS 115* v Z (Bready) 2021; BB 3-21 v B (Belfast) 2012. HS 146 Ire v UAE (Dublin) 2015. CC HS 138 and BB 2-21 M v Glamorgan (Radlett) 2019. LO HS 177 (*see LOI*). LO BB 6-55 (*see LOI*). T20 HS 119. T20 BB 4-10.

TECTOR, Harry Tom, b Dublin 6 Nov 1999. Younger brother of J.B.Tector (Leinster 2017 to date). RHB, OB. Northern Knights 2018-21. Ireland Wolves 2018-19 to 2020-21. Gloucestershire 2023. Leinster Lightning debut 2022 (not f-c). **Tests**: 5 (2022-23 to 2023-24); HS 85 v SL (Galle) 2023; BB –. **LOI**: 43 (2020 to 2023-24); HS 140 v B (Chelmsford) 2023; BB 1-5 v Z (Harare) 2023-24. **IT20**: 67 (2019 to 2023-24); HS 64* v I (Dublin) 2022; BB 2-17 v Z (Harare) 2022-23. HS 146 Northern v Leinster (Dublin) 2019. BB 4-70 Northern v NW (Bready) 2018. LO HS 140 (*see LOI*). LO BB 5-36 Northern v NW (La Manga) 2019. T20 HS 91. T20 BB 4-21.

TUCKER, Lorcan John, b Dublin 10 Sep 1996. RHB, WK. Leinster Lightning debut 2017. Ireland Wolves 2018-19 to 2020-21. **Tests**: 5 (2022-23 to 2023-24); HS 108 v B (Mirpur) 2022-23 – on debut. **LOI**: 49 (2019 to 2023-24); HS 83 v Afg (Abu Dhabi) 2020-21. **IT20**: 62 (2016 to 2023-24); HS 94* v Austria (Edinburgh) 2023. HS 108 (*see Tests*). LO HS 133 Leinster v NW (Dublin, V) 2023. T20 HS 94*.

VAN WOERKOM, Theo Francis (Christchurch BHS; Canterbury U), b Christchurch, New Zealand 26 Jul 1993. RHB, SLA. Canterbury 2015-16 to 2022-23. Northern Knights debut 2023 (not f-c). **Tests**: 1 (2023-24); HS 1 and BB 1-43 v Afg (Abu Dhabi) 2023-24. **LOI**: 2 (2023 to 2023-24); HS – ; BB 1-47 v E (Bristol) 2023. **IT20**: 1 (2023-24); HS and BB –. HS 63* Cant v Wellington (Christchurch) 2018-19. BB 5-42 Cant v Auckland (Lincoln) 2021-22. LO HS 41 Cant v Otago (Dunedin) 2021-22. LO BB 4-63 Northern v Munster (Cork) 2023. T20 HS 13*. T20 BB 3-27.

WHITE, Benjamin Charlie, b Dublin 29 Aug 1998. RHB, LB. Northern Knights 2021-22 (not f-c). Munster Reds debut 2023 (not f-c). **Tests**: 3 (2022-23 to 2023); HS 1 v SL (Galle) 2023; BB 2-71 v B (Mirpur) 2022-23. **LOI**: 2 (2023); HS – ; BB 1-59 v Scot (Bulawayo) 2023. **IT20**: 20 (2021 to 2023); HS 7* v Scot (Edinburgh) 2023; BB 2-10 v Jersey (Edinburgh) 2023. HS 1 and BB 2-71 (*see Tests*). LO HS 17* Munster v Northern (Cork) 2023. LO BB 4-49 IW v Namibia A (Windhoek) 2021-22. T20 HS 12*. T20 BB 5-13.

YOUNG, Craig Alexander (Strabane HS; North West IHE, Belfast), b Londonderry 4 Apr 1990. RHB, RM. Ireland debut 2013. North West Warriors debut 2017. Ireland Wolves 2018-19. **Tests**: 1 (2023-24); HS 1* and BB 3-24 v Afg (Abu Dhabi) 2023-24. **LOI**: 44 (2014 to 2023-24); HS 40* v E (Nottingham) 2023; BB 5-46 v Scot (Dublin) 2014. **IT20**: 59 (2015 to 2023-24); HS 22 v SA (Belfast) 2021; BB 4-13 v Nigeria (Abu Dhabi) 2019-20. HS 23 and BB 5-37 NW v Northern (Eglinton) 2017. LO HS 40* (*see LOI*). LO BB 5-46 (*see LOI*). T20 HS 22. T20 BB 5-15.

ENGLAND WOMEN INTERNATIONALS

The following players have played for England since 1 December 2022 and are still available for selection or have a central contract. Details correct to 18 March 2024.

BEAUMONT, Tamsin ('**Tammy**') Tilley, b Dover, Kent 11 Mar 1991. RHB, WK. MBE 2018. Kent 2007-19. Diamonds 2007-12. Sapphires 2008. Emeralds 2011-13. Surrey Stars 2016-17. Adelaide Strikers 2016-17 to 2017-18. Southern Vipers 2018-19. Melbourne Renegades 2019-20 to date. Lightning 2020 to date. Sydney Thunder 2020-21 to 2022-23. London Spirit 2021. Welsh Fire 2022 to date. The Blaze 2023. *Wisden* 2018. **Tests**: 9 (2013 to 2023-24); HS 208 v A (Nottingham) 2023 – E record. **LOI**: 109 (2009-10 to 2023); HS 168* v P (Taunton) 2016. **IT20**: 99 (2009-10 to 2021-22); HS 116 v SA (Taunton) 2018.

BELL, Lauren Katie, b Swindon, Wilts 2 Jan 2001. Younger sister of C.J.Bell (Berkshire & Buckinghamshire 2016-19). RHB, RM. Berkshire 2015-19. Southern Vipers 2020 to date. Southern Brave 2021 to date. Sydney Thunder 2023-24. **Tests**: 3 (2022 to 2023-24); HS 8 and BB 3-67 v I (Mumbai) 2023-24. **LOI**: 8 (2022 to 2023); HS 11* v I (Canterbury) 2022; BB 4-33 v WI (North Sound) 2022-23. **IT20**: 14 (2022 to 2023-24); HS –; BB 4-12 v WI (Bridgetown) 2022-23.

BOUCHIER, Maia Emily (Dragon S; Rugby S; Oxford Brookes U), b Kensington, London 5 Dec 1998. RHB, RM. Middlesex 2014-18. Auckland 2017-18. Southern Vipers 2018 to date. Hampshire 2019. Southern Brave 2021 to date. W Australia 2021-22. Melbourne Stars 2021-22 to date. **LOI**: 3 (2023); HS 95 v SL (Leicester) 2023. **IT20**: 23 (2021 to 2023-24); HS 34 v I (Derby) 2022.

CAPSEY, Alice Rose (Bede's S), b Redhill, Surrey 11 Aug 2004. RHB, OB. Surrey 2019 to date. South East Stars 2020 to date. Oval Invincibles 2021 to date. Melbourne Stars 2022-23 to date. Delhi Capitals 2022-23 to date. **LOI**: 10 (2022 to 2023); HS 40 v A (Bristol) 2023; BB 1-12 v SL (Chester-le-St) 2023. **IT20**: 24 (2022 to 2023-24); HS 51 v Ire (Paarl) 2022-23 and 51 v SL (Hove) 2023; BB 1-10 v SA (Worcester) 2022.

CROSS, Kathryn ('**Kate**') Laura, b Manchester, Lancs 3 Oct 1991. RHB, RMF. Lancashire 2005-19. Sapphires 2007-08. Emeralds 2012. W Australia 2017-18 to 2018-19. Brisbane Heat 2015-16. Lancashire Thunder 2016-19. Perth Scorchers 2018-19. Thunder 2020 to date. Manchester Originals 2021-22. Northern Superchargers 2023. **Tests**: 8 (2013-14 to 2023-24); HS 16 v I (Mumbai) 2023-24; BB 4-63 v SA (Taunton) 2022. **LOI**: 59 (2013-14 to 2023); HS 29 v NZ (Leicester) 2021; BB 5-24 v NZ (Lincoln) 2014-15. **IT20**: 16 (2013-14 to 2023); HS 2 v SL (Derby) 2023; BB 2-18 v I (Guwahati) 2018-19.

DAVIDSON-RICHARDS, Alice Natica, b Tunbridge Wells, Kent 29 May 1994. RHB, RFM. Kent 2010-19. Sapphires 2011-12. Emeralds 2013. Otago 2018-19. South East Stars 2020 to date. Yorkshire Diamonds 2016-19. Northern Superchargers 2021 to date. **Tests**: 1 (2022); HS 107 and BB 1-39 v SA (Taunton) 2022. **LOI**: 6 (2017-18 to 2023); HS 50* v I (Hove) 2022; BB 3-35 v SA (Leicester) 2022. **IT20**: 8 (2017-18 to 2022-23); HS 24 v A (Mumbai) 2017-18; BB 3-5 v WI (Bridgetown) 2022-23.

DAVIES, Freya Ruth, b Chichester, Sussex 27 Oct 1995. RHB, RMF. Sussex 2012-19. Western Storm 2016-19. South East Stars 2020 to date. London Spirit 2021-22. Welsh Fire 2023. **LOI**: 9 (2019-20 to 2022-23); HS 10* v I (Lord's) 2022; BB 2-36 v B (Wellington) 2021-22. **IT20**: 26 (2018-19 to 2023); HS 1* v NZ (Wellington) 2020-21; BB 4-23 v NZ (Wellington) 2020-21 – separate matches.

DEAN, Charlotte ('**Charlie**') Ellen (Portsmouth GS), b Burton-upon-Trent, Staffs 22 Dec 2000. Daughter of S.J.Dean (Staffordshire and Warwickshire 1986-2002 – List-A only). RHB, OB. Hampshire 2016-19. Southern Vipers 2017 to date. London Spirit 2021 to date. **Tests**: 2 (2021-22 to 2023-24); HS 20* and BB 4-68 v I (Mumbai) 2023-24. **LOI**: 25 (2021 to 2023); HS 47 v I (Lord's) 2022; BB 5-31 v SL (Leicester) 2023. **IT20**: 17 (2021-22 to 2023-24); HS 34 v SL (Chelmsford) 2023; BB 4-19 v WI (Bridgetown) 2022-23.

DUNKLEY, Sophia Ivy Rose, b Lambeth, Surrey 16 Jul 1998. RHB, LB. Middlesex 2013-19. Surrey Stars 2016-18. Lancashire Thunder 2019. South East Stars 2020 to date. Southern Brave 2021-22. Welsh Fire 2023. Melbourne Stars 2023-24. **Tests**: 5 (2021 to 2023-24); HS 74* v I (Bristol) 2021; BB –. **LOI**: 31 (2021 to 2023); HS 107 v SA (Bristol) 2022; BB 1-1 v WI (North Sound) 2022-23. **IT20**: 50 (2018-19 to 2022-23); HS 61* v I (Chester-le-St) 2022; BB 1-6 v SL (Colombo, PSS) 2018-19.

ECCLESTONE, Sophie (Helsby HS), b Chester 6 May 1999. 5'11". RHB, SLA. Cheshire 2013-14. Lancashire 2015-19. Lancashire Thunder 2016-19. Thunder 2020 to date. Manchester Originals 2021 to date. Sydney Sixers 2022-23. **Tests**: 7 (2017-18 to 2023-24); HS 35 v SA (Taunton) 2022; BB 5-63 (10-192 match) v A (Nottingham) 2023. **LOI**: 58 (2016-17 to 2023); HS 33* v WI (Dunedin) 2021-22; BB 6-36 v SA (Christchurch) 2021-22. **IT20**: 76 (2016 to 2023-24); HS 33* v SA (Derby) 2022; BB 4-18 v NZ (Taunton) 2018.

FARRANT, Natasha (**'Tash'**) Eleni (Sevenoaks S), b Athens, Greece 29 May 1996. LHB, LMF. Kent 2012-19. Sapphires 2013. W Australia 2016-17. Southern Vipers 2016-19. South East Stars 2020 to date. Oval Invincibles 2021. **LOI**: 6 (2013-14 to 2021-22); HS 22 v NZ (Worcester) 2021; BB 2-31 v NZ (Christchurch) 2020-21. **IT20**: 18 (2013 to 2021); HS 3* v A (Mumbai, BS) 2017-18; BB 2-15 v P (Loughborough) 2013.

FILER, Lauren Louise, b Bristol 22 Dec 2000. RHB, RFM. Somerset 2018-19. Western Storm 2020 to date. Welsh Fire 2022. London Spirit 2023. **Tests**: 2 (2023 to 2023-24); HS 11 and BB 2-49 v A (Nottingham) 2023. **LOI**: 3 (2023); HS –; BB 3-27 v SL (Chester-le-St) 2023.

GAUR, Mahika (Sedbergh S), b Reading, Berks 6 Mar 2006. RHB, LFM. Lancashire Thunder 2023. Manchester Originals 2023. **LOI**: 2 (2023); HS –; BB 3-26 v SL (Chester-le-St) 2023. **IT20** (UAE/E): 23 (19 for UAE 2018-19 to 2022-23; 4 for E 2023); HS 6* UAE v Hong Kong (Dubai, ICA) 2021-22; BB 3-21 UAE v SL (Sylhet) 2022-23. She made her international debut aged 12y 316d.

GIBSON, Danielle Rose, b Cheltenham, Glos 30 Apr 2001. RHB, RMF. Gloucestershire 2015-17. Wales 2018-19. Western Storm 2020 to date. London Spirit 2021 to date. Adelaide Strikers 2023-24. **IT20**: 7 (2023 to 2023-24); HS 21 v SL (Derby) 2023; BB 1-9 v SL (Chelmsford) 2023.

GLENN, Sarah, b Derby 27 Feb 1999. RHB, LB. Derbyshire 2013-18. Worcestershire 2019. Loughborough Lightning 2017-19. Central Sparks 2020-22. Perth Scorchers 2020-21. Trent Rockets 2021-22. The Blaze 2023. Brisbane Heat 2023-24. **LOI**: 14 (2019-20 to 2023); HS 22* v A (Southampton) 2023; BB 4-18 v P (Kuala Lumpur) 2019-20. **IT20**: 46 (2019-20 to 2023-24); HS 26 v WI (Derby) 2020; BB 4-23 v I (Chester-le-St) 2022.

HEATH, Bess Alice May, b Chesterfield, Derbys 20 Aug 2001. RHB, WK. Derbyshire 2015-19. Northern Diamonds 2020 to date. Northern Superchargers 2021 to date. Melbourne Stars 2022-23. Brisbane Heat 2023-24. **LOI**: 1 (2023); HS 21 v SL (Leicester) 2023. **IT20**: 1 (2023-24); HS 1 v I (Mumbai) 2023-24.

JONES, Amy Ellen, b Solihull, Warwicks 13 Jun 1993. RHB, WK. Warwickshire 2008-19. Diamonds 2011. Emeralds 2012. Rubies 2013. Loughborough Lightning 2016-19. Sydney Sixers 2016-17 to 2017-18. W Australia 2017-18. Perth Scorchers 2018-19 to date. Central Sparks 2020 to date. Birmingham Phoenix 2021 to date. Sydney Thunder 2022-23. **Tests**: 6 (2019 to 2023-24); HS 64 v A (Taunton) 2019. **LOI**: 82 (2012-13 to 2023); HS 94 v I (Nagpur) 2017-18. **IT20**: 94 (2013 to 2023-24); HS 89 v P (Kuala Lumpur) 2019-20.

KEMP, Freya Grace (Cunmor House S; Bede's S), b Westminster, London 21 Apr 2005. LHB, LMF. Sussex 2019 to date. Southern Vipers 2022 to date. Southern Brave 2022 to date. **LOI**: 2 (2022); HS 12 v I (Canterbury) 2022; BB 2-24 v I (Lord's) 2022. **IT20**: 15 (2022 to 2023-24); HS 51* v I (Derby) 2022; BB 2-14 v SL (Birmingham) 2022.

KNIGHT, Heather Clare, b Rochdale, Lancs 26 Dec 1990. RHB, OB. OBE 2018. Devon 2008-09. Emeralds 2008-13. Berkshire 2010-19. Sapphires 2011-12. Tasmania 2014-15 to 2015-16. Hobart Hurricanes 2015-16 to 2019-20. Western Storm 2016 to date. Sydney Thunder 2020-21 to date. London Spirit 2021 to date. Royal Challengers Bangalore 2022-23. *Wisden* 2017. **Tests**: 12 (2010-11 to 2023-24, 7 as captain); HS 168* v A (Canberra) 2021-22; BB 2-7 v I (Bristol) 2021. **LOI**: 134 (2009-10 to 2023, 79 as captain); HS 106 v P (Leicester) 2017; BB 5-26 v P (Leicester) 2016. **IT20**: 107 (2010-11 to 2023-24, 74 as captain); HS 108* v Thai (Canberra) 2019-20; BB 3-9 v I (North Sound) 2018-19.

LAMB, Emma Louise, b Preston, Lancs 16 Dec 1997. Sister of D.J.Lamb (*see SUSSEX*). RHB, RM. Lancashire 2012 to date. Thunder 2020 to date. Manchester Originals 2021 to date. **Tests**: 2 (2022 to 2023); HS 38 v SA (Taunton) 2022; BB –. **LOI**: 11 (2021-22 to 2023); HS 102 v SA (Northampton) 2022; BB 3-42 v SA (Leicester) 2022. **IT20**: 1 (2021); HS 0*.

SCIVER-BRUNT, Natalie Ruth (Epsom C), b Tokyo, Japan 20 Aug 1992. Wife of K.H.Sciver-Brunt (England 2004 to 2022-23). RHB, RM. Surrey 2010-19. Rubies 2011. Emeralds 2012-13. Melbourne Stars 2015-16 to 2020-21. Surrey Stars 2016-19. Perth Scorchers 2017-18 to date. Northern Diamonds 2020-22. Trent Rockets 2021 to date. Mumbai Indians 2022-23 to date. The Blaze 2023. *Wisden* 2017. **Tests**: 10 (2013-14 to 2023-24); HS 169* v SA (Taunton) 2022; BB 3-41 v A (Canberra) 2021-22. **LOI**: 100 (2013 to 2023, 1 as captain); HS 148* v A (Christchurch) 2021-22; BB 4-59 v SA (Northampton) 2022. **IT20**: 113 (2013 to 2023-24, 10 as captain); HS 82 v WI (Derby) 2020. BB 4-15 v A (Cardiff) 2015.

WINFIELD-HILL, Lauren, b York 16 Aug 1990. RHB, WK. Yorkshire 2007-19. Diamonds 2011. Sapphires 2012. Rubies 2013. Brisbane Heat 2015-16 to 2016-17. Yorkshire Diamonds 2016-19. Hobart Hurricanes 2017-18. Adelaide Strikers 2019-20. Northern Diamonds 2020 to date. Northern Superchargers 2021. Oval Invincibles 2022 to date. Melbourne Stars 2022-23. Queensland 2023-24. Perth Scorchers 2023-24. **Tests**: 5 (2014 to 2021-22); HS 35 v I (Wormsley) 2014 and 35 v I (Bristol) 2021. **LOI**: 55 (2013 to 2021-22); HS 123 v P (Worcester) 2016. **IT20**: 44 (2013 to 2022-23); HS 74 v SA (Birmingham) 2014 and 74 v P (Bristol) 2016.

WONG, Isabelle Eleanor Chih Ming ('**Issy**') (Shrewsbury S), b Chelsea, London 15 May 2002. RHB, RMF. Worcestershire 2018. Warwickshire 2019-22. Southern Vipers 2019. Central Sparks 2020 to date. Birmingham Phoenix 2021 to date. Sydney Thunder 2021-22. Mumbai Indians 2022-23. **Tests**: 1 (2022); HS –; BB 2-46 v SA (Taunton) 2022. **LOI**: 3 (2022); HS –; BB 3-36 v SA (Bristol) 2022. **IT20**: 10 (2022 to 2023); HS 13 v SL (Chelmsford) 2023; BB 2-10 v SL (Birmingham) 2022 and 2-10 v NZ (Birmingham) 2022.

WYATT, Danielle ('**Danni**') Nicole, b Stoke-on-Trent, Staffs 22 Apr 1991. RHB, OB/RM. Staffordshire 2005-12. Emeralds 2006-08. Sapphires 2011-13. Victoria 2011-12 to 2015-16. Nottinghamshire 2013-15. Melbourne Renegades 2015-16 to 2019-20. Sussex 2016-19. Lancashire Thunder 2016. Southern Vipers 2017 to date. Southern Brave 2021 to date. Brisbane Heat 2022-23. Tests: 2 (2023 to 2023-24); HS 54 v A (Nottingham) 2023. **LOI**: 105 (2009-10 to 2023); HS 129 v SA (Christchurch) 2021-22; BB 3-7 v SA (Cuttack) 2012-13. **IT20**: 151 (2009-10 to 2023-24); HS 124 v I (Mumbai, BS) 2017-18; BB 4-11 v SA (Basseterre) 2010.

WOMEN'S TEST CRICKET RECORDS

1934-35 to 4 April 2024
RESULTS SUMMARY

	Opponents	*Tests*					*Won by*						*Drawn*
			E	*A*	*NZ*	*SA*	*WI*	*I*	*P*	*SL*	*Ire*	*H*	
England	Australia	52	9	13	–	–	–	–	–	–	–	–	30
	New Zealand	23	6	–	0	–	–	–	–	–	–	–	17
	South Africa	7	2	–	–	0	–	–	–	–	–	–	5
	West Indies	3	2	–	–	–	0	–	–	–	–	–	1
	India	15	1	–	–	–	–	3	–	–	–	–	11
Australia	New Zealand	13	–	4	1	–	–	–	–	–	–	–	8
	South Africa	1	–	1	–	0	–	–	–	–	–	–	–
	West Indies	2	–	0	–	–	0	–	–	–	–	–	2
	India	11	–	4	–	–	–	1	–	–	–	–	6
New Zealand	South Africa	3	–	–	1	0	–	–	–	–	–	–	2
	India	6	–	–	0	–	–	0	–	–	–	–	6
South Africa	India	2	–	–	–	0	–	2	–	–	–	–	–
	Netherlands	1	–	–	–	1	–	–	–	–	–	0	–
West Indies	India	6	–	–	–	–	1	1	–	–	–	–	4
	Pakistan	1	–	–	–	–	0	–	0	–	–	–	1
Pakistan	Sri Lanka	1	–	–	–	–	–	–	0	1	–	–	–
	Ireland	1	–	–	–	–	–	–	0	–	1	–	–
		148	20	22	2	1	1	7	0	1	1	0	93

	Tests	*Won*	*Lost*	*Drawn*	*Toss Won*
England	100	20	16	64	58
Australia	79	22	11	46	30
New Zealand	45	2	10	33	21
South Africa	14	1	6	7	6
West Indies	12	1	3	8	6†
India	40	7	6	27	19†
Pakistan	3	–	2	1	1
Sri Lanka	1	1	–	–	1
Ireland	1	1	–	–	–
Netherlands	1	–	1	–	1

† *Results of tosses in five of the six India v West Indies Tests in 1976-77 are not known*

TEAM RECORDS – HIGHEST INNINGS TOTALS

575-9d	Australia v South Africa	Perth	2023-24
569-6d	Australia v England	Guildford	1998
525	Australia v India	Ahmedabad	1983-84
517-8	New Zealand v England	Scarborough	1996
503-5d	England v New Zealand	Christchurch	1934-35
497	England v South Africa	Shenley	2003
473	Australia v England	Nottingham	2023
467	India v England	Taunton	2002
463	England v Australia	Nottingham	2023
455	England v South Africa	Taunton	2003
448-9d	Australia v England	Sydney	2017-18
440	West Indies v Pakistan	Karachi	2003-04
428	India v England	Mumbai	2023-24
427-4d	Australia v England	Worcester	1998
426-7d	Pakistan v West Indies	Karachi	2003-04
426-9d	India v England	Blackpool	1986

420-8d	Australia v England	Taunton	2019
417-8d	England v South Africa	Taunton	2022
414	England v New Zealand	Scarborough	1996
414	England v Australia	Guildford	1998
406	India v Australia	Mumbai	2023-24
404-9d	India v South Africa	Paarl	2001-02
403-8d	New Zealand v India	Nelson	1994-95
400-6d	India v South Africa	Mysore	2014-15

The highest totals for countries not included above are:

316	South Africa v England	Shenley	2003
193-3d	Ireland v Pakistan	Dublin	2000
108	Netherlands v South Africa	Rotterdam	2007

LOWEST INNINGS TOTALS

35	England v Australia	Melbourne	1957-58
38	Australia v England	Melbourne	1957-58
44	New Zealand v England	Christchurch	1934-35
47	Australia v England	Brisbane	1934-35
50	Netherlands v South Africa	Rotterdam	2007
53	Pakistan v Ireland	Dublin	2000

The lowest innings totals for countries not included above are:

65	India v West Indies	Jammu	1976-77
67	West Indies v England	Canterbury	1979
76	South Africa v Australia	Perth	2023-24

BATTING RECORDS – 1000 RUNS IN TESTS

		Career	*M*	*I*	*NO*	*HS*	*Avge*	*100*	*50*
1935	J.A.Brittin (E)	1979-98	27	44	5	167	49.61	5	11
1676	C.M.Edwards (E)	1996-2015	23	43	5	117	44.10	4	9
1594	R.Heyhoe-Flint (E)	1960-79	22	38	3	179	45.54	3	10
1301	D.A.Hockley (NZ)	1979-96	19	29	4	126*	52.04	4	7
1164	C.A.Hodges (E)	1984-92	18	31	2	158*	40.13	2	6
1110	S.Agarwal (I)	1984-95	13	23	1	190	50.45	4	4
1078	E.Bakewell (E)	1968-79	12	22	4	124	59.88	4	7
1030	S.C.Taylor (E)	1999-2009	15	27	2	177	41.20	4	2
1007	M.E.Maclagan (E)	1934-51	14	25	1	119	41.95	2	6
1002	K.L.Rolton (A)	1995-2009	14	22	4	209*	55.66	2	5

HIGHEST INDIVIDUAL INNINGS

242	Kiran Baluch	P v WI	Karachi	2003-04
214	M.D.Raj	I v E	Taunton	2002
213*	E.A.Perry	A v E	Sydney	2017-18
210	A.J.Sutherland	A v SA	Perth	2023-24
209*	K.L.Rolton	A v E	Leeds	2001
208	T.T.Beaumont	E v A	Nottingham	2023
204	K.E.Flavell	NZ v E	Scarborough	1996
204‡	M.A.J.Goszko	A v E	Shenley	2001
200	J.Broadbent	A v E	Guildford	1998
193	D.A.Annetts	A v E	Collingham	1987
192	M.D.T.Kamini	I v SA	Mysore	2014-15
190	S.Agarwal	I v E	Worcester	1986
189	E.A.Snowball	E v NZ	Christchurch	1934-35
179	R.Heyhoe-Flint	E v A	The Oval	1976
177	S.C.Taylor	E v SA	Shenley	2003
176*	K.L.Rolton	A v E	Worcester	1998
169*	N.R.Sciver	E v SA	Taunton	2022

168*	H.C.Knight	E v A	Canberra	2021-22
167	J.A.Brittin	E v A	Harrogate	1998
161*	E.C.Drumm	E v A	Christchurch	1994-95
160	B.A.Daniels	E v NZ	Scarborough	1996
158*	C.A.Hodges	E v NZ	Canterbury	1984
157	H.C.Knight	E v A	Wormsley	2013
150	M.Kapp	SA v E	Taunton	2022

‡ *On debut*

FIVE HUNDREDS

				Opponents								
		M	*I*	*E*	*A*	*NZ*	*SA*	*WI*	*Ind*	*P*	*SL*	*Ire*
5	J.A.Brittin (E)	27	44	–	3	1	–	–	1	–	–	–

HIGHEST PARTNERSHIP FOR EACH WICKET

1st	241	Kiran Baluch/Sajjida Shah	P v WI	Karachi	2003-04
2nd	275	M.D.T.Kamini/P.G.Raut	I v SA	Mysore	2014-15
3rd	309	L.A.Reeler/D.A.Annetts	A v E	Collingham	1987
4th	253	K.L.Rolton/L.C.Broadfoot	A v E	Leeds	2001
5th	138	J.Logtenberg/C.van der Westhuizen	SA v E	Shenley	2003
6th	229	J.M.Fields/R.L.Haynes	A v E	Worcester	2009
7th	157	M.D.Raj/J.N.Goswami	I v E	Taunton	2002
8th	181	S.J.Griffiths/D.L.Wilson	A v NZ	Auckland	1989-90
9th	107	B.A.Botha/M.Payne	SA v NZ	Cape Town	1971-72
10th	119	S.Nitschke/C.R.Smith	A v E	Hove	2005

BOWLING RECORDS – 50 WICKETS IN TESTS

Wkts		*Career*	*M*	*Balls*	*Runs*	*Avge*	*Best*	*5wI*	*10wM*
77	M.B.Duggan (E)	1949-63	17	3734	1039	13.49	7- 6	5	–
68	E.R.Wilson (A)	1948-58	11	2885	803	11.80	7- 7	4	2
63	D.F.Edulji (I)	1976-91	20	5098†	1624	25.77	6- 64	1	–
60	M.E.Maclagan (E)	1934-51	14	3432	935	15.58	7- 10	3	–
60	C.L.Fitzpatrick (A)	1991-2006	13	3603	1147	19.11	5- 29	2	–
60	S.Kulkarni (I)	1976-91	19	3320†	1647	27.45	6- 99	5	–
57	R.H.Thompson (A)	1972-85	16	4304	1040	18.24	5- 33	1	–
55	J.Lord (NZ)	1966-79	15	3108	1049	19.07	6-119	4	1
51	K.H.Brunt (E)	2004-22	14	2611	1098	21.52	6- 69	3	–
50	E.Bakewell (E)	1968-79	12	2697	831	16.62	7- 61	3	1

TEN WICKETS IN A TEST

13-226	Shaiza Khan	P v WI	Karachi	2003-04
12-165	A.K.Gardner	A v E	Nottingham	2023
11- 16	E.R.Wilson	A v E	Melbourne	1957-58
11- 63	J.M.Greenwood	E v WI	Canterbury	1979
11-107	L.C.Pearson	E v A	Sydney	2002-03
10- 65	E.R.Wilson	A v NZ	Wellington	1947-48
10- 75	E.Bakewell	E v WI	Birmingham	1979
10- 78	J.N.Goswami	I v E	Taunton	2006
10-107	K.Price	A v I	Lucknow	1983-84
10-118	D.A.Gordon	A v E	Melbourne	1968-69
10-137	J.Lord	NZ v A	Melbourne	1978-79
10-192	S.Ecclestone	E v A	Nottingham	2023

SEVEN WICKETS IN AN INNINGS

8-53	N.L.David	I v E	Jamshedpur	1995-96
8-66	A.K.Gardner	A v E	Nottingham	2023
7- 6	M.B.Duggan	E v A	Melbourne	1957-58
7- 7	E.R.Wilson	A v E	Melbourne	1957-58

7-10	M.E.Maclagan	E v A	Brisbane	1934-35
7-18	A.Palmer	A v E	Brisbane	1934-35
7-24	L.J.Johnston	A v NZ	Melbourne	1971-72
7-34	G.E.McConway	E v I	Worcester	1986
7-41	J.A.Burley	NZ v E	The Oval	1966
7-51	L.C.Pearson	E v A	Sydney	2002-03
7-59	Shaiza Khan	P v WI	Karachi	2003-04
7-61	E.Bakewell	E v WI	Birmingham	1979

HAT-TRICKS

E.R.Wilson	Australia v England	Melbourne	1957-58
Shaiza Khan	Pakistan v West Indies	Karachi	2003-04
R.M.Farrell	Australia v England	Sydney	2010-11

WICKET-KEEPING AND FIELDING RECORDS – 25 DISMISSALS IN TESTS

Total			*Tests*	*Ct*	*St*	
58	C.Matthews	Australia	20	46	12	1984-95
43	J.Smit	England	21	39	4	1992-2006
36	S.A.Hodges	England	11	19	17	1969-79
28	B.A.Brentnall	New Zealand	10	16	12	1966-72

EIGHT DISMISSALS IN A TEST

9 (8ct, 1st)	C.Matthews	A v I	Adelaide	1990-91
8 (6ct, 2st)	L.Nye	E v NZ	New Plymouth	1991-92

SIX DISMISSALS IN AN INNINGS

8 (6ct, 2st)	L.Nye	E v NZ	New Plymouth	1991-92
6 (2ct, 4st)	B.A.Brentnall	NZ v SA	Johannesburg	1971-72
6 (6ct)	A.E.Jones	E v A	Canberra	2021-22

20 CATCHES IN THE FIELD IN TESTS

Total			*Tests*	
25	C.A.Hodges	England	18	1984-92
21	S.Shah	India	20	1976-91
20	L.A.Fullston	Australia	12	1984-87

APPEARANCE RECORDS – 25 TEST MATCH APPEARANCES

27	J.A.Brittin	England	1979-98

12 MATCHES AS CAPTAIN

			Won	*Lost*	*Drawn*	
14	P.F.McKelvey	New Zealand	2	3	9	1966-79
12	R.Heyhoe-Flint	England	2	–	10	1966-76
12	S.Rangaswamy	India	1	2	9	1976-84

England Results Since April 2023

At Trent Bridge, Nottingham, 22-26 June. Toss: Australia. **AUSTRALIA** won by 89 runs. Australia 473 (A.J.Sutherland 137*, E.A.Perry 99, T.M.McGrath 61, S.Ecclestone 5-129) and 257 (B.L.Mooney 85, A.J.Healy 50, S.Ecclestone 5-63). England 463 (T.T.Beaumont 208, N.R.Sciver-Brunt 78, H.C.Knight 57, A.K.Gardner 4-99) and 178 (D.N.Wyatt 54, A.K.Gardner 8-66). England debuts: L.L.Filer, D.N.Wyatt. Award: A.K.Gardner.

At Dr D.Y.Patil Sports Academy, Mumbai, 14-16 December. INDIA won by 347 runs. India 428 (S.Shubha 69, J.I.Rodrigues 68, D.B.Sharma 67, Y.H.Bhatia 66) and 186-6d (C.E.Dean 4-68). England 136 (N.R.Sciver-Brunt 59, D.B.Sharma 5-7) and 131 (D.B.Sharma 4-32). Award: D.B.Sharma.

WOMEN'S LIMITED-OVERS RECORDS

1973 to 1 March 2024

RESULTS SUMMARY

	Matches	*Won*	*Lost*	*Tied*	*No Result*	*% Won (exc NR)*
Thailand	9	8	1	–	–	88.88
Australia	364	288	67	2	7	80.67
England	383	227	142	2	12	61.18
South Africa	239	125	99	5	10	54.58
India	307	165	136	2	4	54.45
New Zealand	379	186	182	3	8	50.13
West Indies	215	93	110	3	9	45.14
Sri Lanka	181	60	114	–	7	34.48
Trinidad & Tobago	6	2	4	–	–	33.33
Ireland	173	49	116	1	7	29.51
Pakistan	203	59	138	3	3	29.50
Bangladesh	63	17	39	2	5	29.31
Jamaica	5	1	4	–	–	20.00
Netherlands	110	20	89	–	1	18.34
Denmark	33	6	27	–	–	18.18
Scotland	11	2	9	–	–	18.18
International XI	18	3	14	–	1	17.64
Young England	6	1	5	–	–	16.66
Zimbabwe	14	1	12	1	–	7.14
Japan	5	–	5	–	–	0.00

TEAM RECORDS – HIGHEST INNINGS TOTALS

491-4	(50 overs)	New Zealand v Ireland	Dublin	2018
455-5	(50 overs)	New Zealand v Pakistan	Christchurch	1996-97
440-3	(50 overs)	New Zealand v Ireland	Dublin	2018
418	(49.5 overs)	New Zealand v Ireland	Dublin	2018
412-3	(50 overs)	Australia v Denmark	Mumbai	1997-98
397-4	(50 overs)	Australia v Pakistan	Melbourne	1996-97
378-5	(50 overs)	England v Pakistan	Worcester	2016

LARGEST RUNS MARGIN OF VICTORY

408 runs	New Zealand beat Pakistan	Christchurch	1996-97
374 runs	Australia beat Pakistan	Melbourne	1996-97

LOWEST INNINGS TOTALS

22	(23.4 overs)	Netherlands v West Indies	Deventer	2008
23	(24.1 overs)	Pakistan v Australia	Melbourne	1996-97
24	(21.3 overs)	Scotland v England	Reading	2001

BATTING RECORDS – 3500 RUNS IN A CAREER

Runs		*Career*	*M*	*I*	*NO*	*HS*	*Avge*	*100*	*50*
7805	M.D.Raj (I)	1999-2022	232	211	57	125*	50.68	7	64
5992	C.M.Edwards (E)	1997-2016	191	180	23	173*	38.16	9	46
5589	S.W.Bates (NZ)	2006-2023	157	151	16	168	41.40	13	33
5521	S.R.Taylor (WI)	2008-2023	154	148	22	171	43.81	7	40
4844	B.J.Clark (A)	1991-2005	118	114	12	229*	47.49	5	30
4814	K.L.Rolton (A)	1995-2009	141	132	32	154*	48.14	8	33
4639	A.E.Satterthwaite (NZ)	2007-2022	145	138	17	137*	38.33	7	27
4602	M.M.Lanning (A)	2011-2023	103	102	16	152*	53.51	15	21
4101	S.C.Taylor (E)	1998-2011	126	120	18	156*	40.20	8	23
4066	D.A.Hockley (NZ)	1982-2000	118	115	18	117	41.91	4	34
4056	S.J.Taylor (E)	2006-2019	126	119	13	147	38.26	7	20
3894	E.A.Perry (A)	2007-2024	144	117	40	112*	50.57	2	34
3765	H.C.Knight (E)	2010-2023	134	128	26	106	36.91	2	26
3760	M.du Preez (SA)	2007-2022	154	141	27	116*	32.98	2	18
3726	D.J.S.Dottin (WI)	2008-2022	143	135	13	150*	30.54	3	22
3676	S.F.M.Devine (NZ)	2006-2023	143	130	12	145	31.15	7	15
3650	T.T.Beaumont (E)	2009-2023	109	100	9	168*	40.10	9	18
3613	L.Wolvaardt (SA)	2016-2024	92	91	10	149	44.60	5	31

HIGHEST INDIVIDUAL INNINGS

232*	A.C.Kerr	New Zealand v Ireland	Dublin	2018
229*	B.J.Clark	Australia v Denmark	Mumbai	1997-98
188	D.B.Sharma	India v Ireland	Potchefstroom	2017
178*	A.M.C.Jayangani	Sri Lanka v Australia	Bristol	2017
176*	Sidra Ameen	Pakistan v Ireland	Lahore	2022-23
173*	C.M.Edwards	England v Ireland	Pune	1997-98
171*	H.Kaur	India v Australia	Derby	2017
171	S.R.Taylor	West Indies v Sri Lanka	Mumbai	2012-13
170	A.J.Healy	Australia v England	Christchurch	2021-22
168*	T.T.Beaumont	England v Pakistan	Taunton	2016
168	S.W.Bates	New Zealand v Pakistan	Sydney	2008-09
157	R.H.Priest	New Zealand v Sri Lanka	Lincoln	2015-16
156*	L.M.Keightley	Australia v Pakistan	Melbourne	1996-97
156*	S.C.Taylor	England v India	Lord's	2006
154*	K.L.Rolton	Australia v Sri Lanka	Christchurch	2000-01
153*	J.Logtenberg	South Africa v Netherlands	Deventer	2007
152*	M.M.Lanning	Australia v Sri Lanka	Bristol	2017
151	K.L.Rolton	Australia v Ireland	Dublin	2005
151	S.W.Bates	New Zealand v Ireland	Dublin	2018
150*	D.J.S.Dottin	West Indies v South Africa	Johannesburg	2021-22

HIGHEST PARTNERSHIP FOR EACH WICKET

1st	320	D.B.Sharma/P.G.Raut	India v Ireland	Potchefstroom	2017
2nd	295	A.C.Kerr/L.M.Kasperek	New Zealand v Ireland	Dublin	2018
3rd	244	K.L.Rolton/L.C.Sthalekar	Australia v Ireland	Dublin	2005
4th	224*	J.Logtenberg/M.du Preez	South Africa v Netherlands	Deventer	2007
5th	188*	S.C.Taylor/J.Smit	England v Sri Lanka	Lincoln	2000-01
6th	142	S.E.Luus/C.L.Tryon	South Africa v Ireland	Dublin	2016
7th	122	S.Rana/P.Vastrakar	India v Pakistan	Mt Maunganui	2021-22
8th	88	N.N.D.de Silva/O.U.Ranasinghe	Sri Lanka v England	Hambantota	2018-19
9th	77	A.K.Gardner/K.J.Garth	Australia v South Africa	Sydney (NS)	2023-24
10th	76	A.J.Blackwell/K.M.Beams	Australia v India	Derby	2017

BOWLING RECORDS – 120 WICKETS IN A CAREER

		LOI	*Balls*	*Runs*	*W*	*Avge*	*Best*	*4w*	*R/Over*
J.N.Goswami (I)	2002-2022	204	10005	5622	**255**	22.04	6-31	9	3.37
S.Ismail (SA)	2007-2022	127	6170	3812	**191**	19.95	6-10	8	3.70
C.L.Fitzpatrick (A)	1993-2007	109	6017	3023	**180**	16.79	5-14	11	3.01
A.Mohammed (WI)	2003-2022	141	6252	3735	**180**	20.75	7-14	13	3.58
K.H.Sciver-Brunt (E)	2005-2022	141	6841	4074	**170**	23.96	5-18	8	3.57
E.A.Perry (A)	2007-2024	144	5638	4114	**163**	25.23	7-22	4	4.37
M.Kapp (SA)	2009-2024	140	6156	3907	**157**	24.88	5-45	5	3.80
S.R.Taylor (WI)	2008-2023	154	5700	3375	**153**	22.05	4-17	5	3.55
Sana Mir (P)	2005-2019	120	5942	3665	**151**	24.27	5-32	8	3.70
L.C.Sthalekar (A)	2001-2013	125	5965	3646	**146**	24.97	5-35	2	3.66
N.L.David (I)	1995-2008	97	4892	2305	**141**	16.34	5-20	6	2.82
J.L.Jonassen (A)	2012-2023	93	4161	2764	**141**	19.60	5-27	8	3.98
D.van Niekerk (SA)	2009-2021	107	4576	2642	**138**	19.14	5-17	8	3.46
J.L.Gunn (E)	2004-2019	144	5906	3822	**136**	28.10	5-22	6	3.88
L.A.Marsh (E)	2006-2019	103	5328	3463	**129**	26.84	5-15	4	3.89
H.A.S.D.Siriwardene (SL)	2003-2019	118	5449	3578	**124**	28.85	4-11	6	3.93
A.Khaka (SA)	2012-2024	97	4580	3151	**122**	25.82	5-26	3	4.12
M.Schutt (A)	2012-2024	89	4127	2897	**121**	23.94	4-18	5	4.21

SIX OR MORE WICKETS IN AN INNINGS

7- 4	Sajjida Shah	Pakistan v Japan	Amsterdam	2003
7- 8	J.M.Chamberlain	England v Denmark	Haarlem	1991
7-14	A.Mohammed	West Indies v Pakistan	Mirpur	2011-12
7-22	E.A.Perry	Australia v England	Canterbury	2019
7-24	S.Nitschke	Australia v England	Kidderminster	2005
6- 6	T.Putthawong	Thailand v Zimbabwe	Bangkok	2022-23
6-10	J.Lord	New Zealand v India	Auckland	1981-82

6-10	M.Maben	India v Sri Lanka	Kandy	2003-04
6-10	S.Ismail	South Africa v Netherlands	Savar	2011-12
6-20	G.L.Page	New Zealand v Trinidad & T	St Albans	1973
6-20	D.B.Sharma	India v Sri Lanka	Ranchi	2015-16
6-20	Khadija Tul Kobra	Bangladesh v Pakistan	Cox's Bazar	2018-19
6-31	J.N.Goswami	India v New Zealand	Southgate	2011
6-31	C.Murray	Ireland v Zimbabwe	Harare	2023-24
6-32	B.H.McNeill	New Zealand v England	Lincoln, NZ	2007-08
6-36	S.E.Luus	South Africa v Ireland	Dublin	2016
6-36	S.Ecclestone	England v South Africa	Christchurch	2021-22
6-45	S.E.Luus	South Africa v New Zealand	Hamilton	2019-20
6-46	A.Shrubsole	England v India	Lord's	2017
6-46	L.M.Kasperek	New Zealand v Australia	Mt Maunganui	2020-21

WICKET-KEEPING AND FIELDING RECORDS – 100 DISMISSALS IN A CAREER

Total			*LOI*	*Ct*	*St*
182	T.Chetty	South Africa	134	131	51
136	S.J.Taylor	England	126	85	51
133	R.J.Rolls	New Zealand	104	90	43
114	J.Smit	England	109	69	45
103	M.R.Aguillera	West Indies	112	76	27
100	A.J.Healy	Australia	107	68	32

SIX DISMISSALS IN AN INNINGS

6	(4ct, 2st)	S.L.Illingworth	New Zealand v Australia	Beckenham	1993
6	(1ct, 5st)	V.Kalpana	India v Denmark	Slough	1993
6	(2ct, 4st)	Batool Fatima	Pakistan v West Indies	Karachi	2003-04
6	(4ct, 2st)	Batool Fatima	Pakistan v Sri Lanka	Colombo (PSS)	2011

50 CATCHES IN THE FIELD IN A CAREER

Total			*LOI*	*Career*
80	S.W.Bates	New Zealand	157	2006-2023
69	J.N.Goswami	India	204	2002-2022
68	S.R.Taylor	West Indies	154	2008-2023
64	M.D.Raj	India	232	1999-2022
56	A.E.Satterthwaite	New Zealand	145	2007-2022
56	D.van Niekerk	South Africa	107	2009-2021
55	A.J.Blackwell	Australia	144	2003-2017
52	L.S.Greenway	England	126	2003-2016
52	C.M.Edwards	England	191	1997-2016
51	H.Kaur	India	130	2009-2024
50	M.M.Lanning	Australia	101	2011-2023

FOUR CATCHES IN THE FIELD IN AN INNINGS

4	Z.J.Goss	Australia v New Zealand	Adelaide	1995-96
4	J.L.Gunn	England v New Zealand	Lincoln, NZ	2014-15
4	Nahida Khan	Pakistan v Sri Lanka	Dambulla	2017-18
4	A.C.Kerr	New Zealand v India	Queenstown	2021-22

APPEARANCE RECORDS – 150 APPEARANCES

232	M.D.Raj	India	1999-2022
204	J.N.Goswami	India	2002-2022
191	C.M.Edwards	England	1997-2016
157	S.W.Bates	New Zealand	2006-2023
154	M.du Preez	South Africa	2007-2022
154	S.R.Taylor	West Indies	2008-2023

100 CONSECUTIVE APPEARANCES

109	M.D.Raj	India	17.04.2004 to 07.02.2013
101	M.du Preez	South Africa	08.03.2009 to 05.02.2018

100 MATCHES AS CAPTAIN

			Won	*Lost*	*No Result*	
155	M.D.Raj	India	89	63	3	2004-2022
117	C.M.Edwards	England	72	38	7	2005-2016
101	B.J.Clark	Australia	83	17	1	1994-2005

WOMEN'S INTERNATIONAL TWENTY20 RECORDS

2004 to 24 February 2024

As for the men's IT20 records, in the section that follows, except for the first-ranked record and the highest partnerships, only those games featuring a nation that has also played a full LOI are listed.

MATCH RESULTS SUMMARY

	Matches	*Won*	*Lost*	*Tied*	*NR*	*Win %*
Zimbabwe	52	40	12	–	–	76.92
England	187	133	49	3	2	71.89
Australia	183	123	51	4	5	69.10
New Zealand	163	93	64	3	3	58.12
India	179	94	79	1	5	54.02
West Indies	165	81	75	6	3	50.00
South Africa	152	66	80	–	6	45.20
Pakistan	159	65	87	3	4	41.93
Ireland	115	45	69	–	1	39.47
Bangladesh	110	43	66	–	1	39.44
Sri Lanka	137	43	90	–	4	32.33

WOMEN'S INTERNATIONAL TWENTY20 RECORDS

TEAM RECORDS – HIGHEST INNINGS TOTALS † Batting Second

427-1	Argentina v Chile	Buenos Aires	2023-24
255-2	Bangladesh v Maldives	Pokhara	2019-20
250-3	England v South Africa	Taunton	2018
226-3	Australia v England	Chelmsford	2019
226-2	Australia v Sri Lanka	Sydney (NS)	2019-20
217-4	Australia v Sri Lanka	Sydney (NS)	2019-20
216-1	New Zealand v South Africa	Taunton	2018
213-4	Ireland v Netherlands	Deventer	2019
213-5	England v Pakistan	Cape Town	2022-23
213-3†	West Indies v Australia	Sydney (NS)	2023-24
212-6	Australia v West Indies	Sydney (NS)	2023-24

LOWEST COMPLETED INNINGS TOTALS † Batting Second

6	(9.0)	Mali v Rwanda	Rwanda	2019
6†	(12.1)	Maldives v Bangladesh	Pokhara	2019-20
17	(9.2)	Eswatini v Zimbabwe	Gaborone	2021
21-9	(20.0)	Myanmar v Thailand	Kuala Lumpur	2023
24	(17.4)	France v Scotland	Cartagena	2021
24	(16.1)	France v Ireland	Cartagena	2021
27†	(13.4)	Malaysia v India	Kuala Lumpur	2018
27†	(16.0)	Malaysia v Thailand	Bangkok	2018-19
28†	(15.5)	Japan v Tanzania	Wong Nai	2023-24
29†	(11.0)	Namibia v Netherlands	Schiedam	2022

The lowest score for England is 87 (v Australia, Hove, 2015).

BATTING RECORDS – 2500 RUNS IN A CAREER

Runs			*M*	*I*	*NO*	*HS*	*Avge*	*50*	*R/100B*
4118	S.W.Bates	NZ	152	149	12	124*	30.05	28	108.9
3405	M.M.Lanning	A	132	121	28	133*	36.61	17	116.3
3236	S.R.Taylor	WI	117	114	23	90	35.56	22	100.8†
3204	H.Kaur	I	161	145	29	103	27.62	12	106.3†
3107	S.F.M.Devine	NZ	127	124	16	105	28.76	19	121.7
3104	S.S.Mandhana	I	128	124	11	87	27.46	23	121.5
2870	Bismah Maroof	P	140	133	29	70*	27.59	12	91.3

Runs			M	I	NO	HS	Avge	50	R/100B
2795	A.J.Healy	A	153	135	21	148*	24.51	17	129.1
2764	B.L.Mooney	A	95	89	22	117*	41.25	24	123.5
2697	D.J.S.Dottin	WI	127	125	20	112*	25.68	14	122.8†
2651	A.M.C.Jayangani	SL	121	120	3	113	22.65	9	106.2
2605	C.M.Edwards	E	95	93	14	92*	32.97	12	106.9
2602	D.N.Wyatt	E	151	130	12	124	22.05	15	127.2

† *No information on balls faced for games at Roseau on 22 and 23 February 2012.*

HIGHEST INDIVIDUAL INNINGS

Score	Balls				
169	84	L.Taylor	Arg v Chile	Buenos Aires	2023-24
148*	61	A.J.Healy	A v SL	Sydney (NS)	2019-20
133*	63	M.M.Lanning	A v E	Chelmsford	2019
132	64	H.K.Matthews	WI v A	Sydney (NS)	2023-24
126*	76	S.L.Kalis	Neth v Ger	Cartagena	2019
126	65	M.M.Lanning	A v Ire	Sylhet	2013-14
124*	66	S.W.Bates	NZ v SA	Taunton	2018
124	64	D.N.Wyatt	E v I	Mumbai (BS)	2017-18
117*	70	B.L.Mooney	A v E	Canberra	2017-18
116*	71	S.A.Fritz	SA v Neth	Potchefstroom	2010-11
116	52	T.T.Beaumont	E v SA	Taunton	2018

HIGHEST PARTNERSHIP FOR EACH WICKET

1st	182	S.W.Bates/S.F.M.Devine	NZ v SA	Taunton	2018
2nd	174	H.K.Matthews/S.R.Taylor	WI v A	Sydney (NS)	2023-24
3rd	236*	Nigar Sultana/Fargana Haque	B v Mald	Pokhara	2019-20
4th	147*	K.L.Rolton/K.A.Blackwell	A v E	Taunton	2005
5th	129*	A.K.Gardner/G.M.Harris	A v I	Mumbai (BS)	2022-23
6th	84	M.A.A.Sanjeewani/N.N.D.de Silva	SL v P	Colombo (SSC)	2017-18
7th	75*	Salma Khatun/Ritu Moni	B v Ken	Kuala Lumpur	2021-22
8th	47*	A.K.Gardner/A.M.King	A v I	Birmingham	2022
9th	50	H.C.Knight/C.E.Dean	E v I	Mumbai	2023-24
10th	37*	P.Vastrakar/R.S.Gayakwad	I v A	Carrara	2021-22

BOWLING RECORDS – 100 WICKETS IN A CAREER

Wkts			Matches	Overs	Mdns	Runs	Avge	Best	R/Over
133	M.Schutt	A	108	366.3	8	2337	17.57	5-15	6.37
130	Nida Dar	P	141	455.2	13	2512	19.32	5-21	5.51
125	A.Mohammed	WI	117	395.3	6	2206	17.64	5-10	5.57
125	E.A.Perry	A	151	401.5	8	2349	18.79	4-12	5.84
123	S.Ismail	SA	113	396.5	21	2291	18.62	5-12	5.77
116	N.Boochatham	Thai	82	277.1	21	1099	9.47	5- 5	3.96
114	K.H.Sciver-Brunt	E	112	392.1	17	2188	19.19	4-15	5.57
113	S.F.M.Devine	NZ	127	317.3	6	2035	18.00	4-22	6.40
113	D.B.Sharma	I	104	360.0	12	2186	19.34	4-10	6.07
109	S.Ecclestone	E	76	279.3	10	1636	15.00	4-18	5.85
102	A.Shrubsole	E	79	266.2	10	1587	15.55	5-11	5.95

BEST FIGURES IN AN INNINGS

7- 3	F.C.J.Overdijk	Neth v Fra	Cartagena	2021
7- 3	A.Stocks	Arg v Peru	Seropedica	2022-23
6-11	E.Mbofana	Z v Eswatini	Gaborone	2021
6-17	A.E.Satterthwaite	NZ v E	Taunton	2007
5- 3	M.J.McColl	Scot v France	Cartagena	2021
5- 4	C.Sutthiruang	Thai v Indon	Bangkok	2018-19
5- 5	D.J.S.Dottin	WI v B	Providence	2018-19
5- 5	N.Boochatham	Thai v Myan	Kuala Lumpur	2023
5- 6	L.N.M.Phiri	Z v Bot	Gaborone	2021

5-7	P.Marange	Z v Uganda	Entebbe	2023-24
5-8	S.E.Luus	SA v Ire	Chennai	2015-16
5-8	T.Putthawong	Thai v Neth	Utrecht	2023
5-8	Nahida Akter	B v P	Chittagong	2023-24

The best figures for England are 5-11 by A.Shrubsole, v NZ, Wellington, 2011-12.

HAT-TRICKS IN ENGLAND MATCHES

Asmavia Iqbal	Pakistan v England	Loughborough	2012
N.R.Sciver	England v New Zealand	Bridgetown	2013-14
A.Shrubsole	England v South Africa	Gros Islet	2018-19

WICKET-KEEPING RECORDS – 70 DISMISSALS IN A CAREER

Dis			*Inns*	*Ct*	*St*
118	A.J.Healy	Australia	137	59	59
74	S.J.Taylor	England	88	23	51
73	R.H.Priest	New Zealand	74	41	32
70	T.Chetty	South Africa	82	42	28
70	M.R.Aguilleira	West Indies	85	36	34

FIVE DISMISSALS IN AN INNINGS

5 (1ct, 4st)	K.A.Knight	West Indies v Sri Lanka	Colombo (RPS)	2012-13
5 (1ct, 4st)	Batool Fatima	Pakistan v Ireland	Dublin	2013
5 (1ct, 4st)	Batool Fatima	Pakistan v Ireland	Dublin	2013
5 (3ct, 2st)	B.M.Bezuidenhout	New Zealand v Ireland	Dublin	2018
5 (1ct, 4st)	S.J.Bryce	Scotland v Netherlands	Arbroath	2019
5 (2ct, 3st)	M.Rathnayake	Italy v Scotland	Almeria	2023
5 (2ct, 3st)	S.J.Bryce	Scotland v Netherlands	Almeria	2023

FIELDING RECORDS – 45 CATCHES IN A CAREER

Total			*Matches*	*Total*			*Matches*
81	S.W.Bates	New Zealand	152	57	N.R.Sciver-Brunt	England	113
61	H.Kaur	India	161	54	L.S.Greenway	England	85
58	J.L.Gunn	England	104	45	M.M.Lanning	Australia	132

FOUR CATCHES IN AN INNINGS

4	L.S.Greenway	England v New Zealand	Chelmsford	2010
4	V.Krishnamurthy	India v Australia	Providence	2018-19
4	S.W.Bates	New Zealand v West Indies	North Sound	2022-23
4	T.Brits	South Africa v England	Cape Town	2022-23
4	H.Kaur	India v Australia	Mumbai (DYP)	2023-24

APPEARANCE RECORDS – 130 APPEARANCES

161	H.Kaur	India	151	D.N.Wyatt	England
153	A.J.Healy	Australia	141	Nida Dar	Pakistan
152	S.W.Bates	New Zealand	140	Bismah Mahroof	Pakistan
151	E.A.Perry	Australia	132	M.M.Lanning	Australia

65 MATCHES AS CAPTAIN

			W	*L*	*T*	*NR*	*%age wins*
106	H.Kaur	India	59	42	1	4	57.84
100	M.M.Lanning	Australia	76	18	1	5	80.00
93	C.M.Edwards	England	68	23	1	1	73.91
76	A.M.C.Jayangani	Sri Lanka	28	47	–	1	37.33
74	H.C.Knight	England	54	18	1	1	73.97
73	M.R.Aguilleira	West Indies	39	29	3	2	54.92

THE WOMEN'S HUNDRED 2023

The Women's Hundred was launched in 2021, featuring eight franchise sides in matches of 100 balls per side, with all games played alongside the men's version. The second- and third-placed sides played off for a place in the final, held at Lord's.

	P	*W*	*L*	*T*	*NR*	*Pts*	*Net RR*
1. Southern Brave (2)	8	7	1	–	–	14	+0.68
2. Northern Superchargers (5)	8	6	2	–	–	12	+0.35
3. Welsh Fire (8)	8	5	2	–	1	11	+0.60
4. Trent Rockets (3)	8	3	4	–	1	7	–0.00
5. Oval Invincibles (1)	8	3	4	–	1	7	–0.36
6. London Spirit (7)	8	2	4	–	2	6	+0:34
7. Manchester Originals (6)	8	2	4	–	2	6	–0.77
8. Birmingham Phoenix (4)	8	–	7	–	1	1	–0.92

Eliminator: At The Oval, London, 26 August. Toss: Welsh Fire. **NO RESULT**. Welsh Fire 104-2 (75 balls; S.I.R.Dunkley 38, T.T.Beaumont 37*).

FINAL: At Lord's, 27 August. Toss: Northern Superchargers. **SOUTHERN BRAVE** won by 34 runs. Southern Brave 139-6 (100 balls; D.N.Wyatt 59, F.G.Kemp 31, K.L.Cross 3-21). Northern Superchargers 105 (94 balls; K.Moore 3-15, L.K.Bell 3-21). Award: D.N.Wyatt. Series award: M.Kapp (Oval Invincibles).

LEADING AGGREGATES AND RECORDS 2023

BATTING (275 runs)	*M*	*I*	*NO*	*HS*	*Runs*	*Avge*	*100*	*50*	*R/100b*	*Sixes*
D.N.Wyatt (Brave)	9	9	–	67	295	32.77	–	3	141.1	4
T.T.Beaumont (Fire)	8	8	1	118	290	41.42	1	1	153.4	5
P.Litchfield (Superchargers)	10	9	1	68	279	34.87	–	1	132.8	3

BOWLING (12 wkts)	*Balls*	*R*	*W*	*Avge*	*BB*	*4w*	*R/100b*
G.L.Adams (Brave)	180	205	16	12.81	4-11	1	113.8

Highest total	181-3	Fire v Rockets		Cardiff
Biggest win (runs)	73	Spirit (172-5) beat Phoenix (99)		Birmingham
Biggest win (balls)	36	Rockets (110-1) beat Originals (107-5)		Nottingham
Highest innings	118	T.T.Beaumont	Fire v Rockets	Cardiff
Most sixes	8	B.F.Smith (Rockets)		
Highest partnership	100	T.T.Beaumont/S.J.Bryce	Fire v Rockets	Cardiff
Best bowling	5-7	F.M.K.Morris	Originals v Phoenix	Manchester
Most economical	20b-7-3	G.Wareham	Superchargers v Originals	Manchester
Most expensive	20b-52-0	B.F.Smith	Rockets v Fire	Cardiff
Most w/k dismissals	11	R.Southby (Brave)		
Most w/k dismissals (inns)	4	R.Southby	Brave v Superchargers	Southampton
Most catches	7	P.J.Scholfield (Invincibles), G.Wareham (Superchargers)		
Most catches (inns)	3	L.C.N.Smith	Superchargers v Brave	Southampton

PRINCIPAL WOMEN'S FIXTURES 2024

F	Floodlit match
100	The Hundred
LOI	Limited-Overs International
RHF	Rachael Heyhoe Flint Trophy (50 overs)
CEC	Charlotte Edwards Cup (Twenty20)
IT20	Vitality International Twenty20

Sat 20 April

RHF	Birmingham	Sparks v Blaze
RHF	Chester-le-St	Diamonds v Thunder
RHF	Beckenham	SE Stars v Vipers
RHF	Cardiff	Storm v Sunrisers

Wed 24 April

RHF	Leicester	Blaze v SE Stars
RHF	Leeds	Diamonds v Storm
RHF	Wormsley	Vipers v Sparks
RHF	Sale	Thunder v Sunrisers

Sat 27 April

RHF	Beckenham	SE Stars v Sparks
RHF	Southampton	Vipers v Diamonds
RHF	Chelmsford	Sunrisers v Blaze
RHF	Manchester	Thunder v Storm

Wed 1 May

RHF	Worcester	Sparks v Sunrisers
RHF	Scarborough	Diamonds v Blaze
RHF	Wormsley	Vipers v Thunder
RHF	Taunton	Storm v SE Stars

Sat 4 May

RHF	Birmingham	Sparks v Diamonds
RHF	Northampton	Sunrisers v SE Stars
RHF	Bristol	Storm v Vipers

Mon 6 May

RHF	Nottingham	Blaze v Thunder

Wed 8 May

RHF	Nottingham	Blaze v Storm
RHF	Beckenham	SE Stars v Diamonds
RHF	Radlett	Sunrisers v Vipers
RHF	Manchester	Thunder v Sparks

Thu 9 May

T20	Leicester	ECB Dev v Pakistan

Sat 11 May

IT20	**Birmingham**	**England v Pakistan**

Fri 17 May

IT20[F]	**Northampton**	**England v Pakistan**

Sat 18 May

CEC	Southampton	Vipers v Blaze

Sun 19 May

IT20	**Leeds**	**England v Pakistan**
CEC	Worcester	Sparks v Sunrisers
CEC	Manchester	Thunder v Diamonds
CEC	Bristol	Storm v SE Stars

Tue 21 May

50ov	Northampton	ECB Dev v Pakistan

Wed 22 May

CEC[F]	Taunton	Storm v Sparks

Thu 23 May

LOI[F]	**Derby**	**England v Pakistan**
CEC[F]	Nottingham	Blaze v Diamonds

Fri 24 May

CEC	Beckenham	SE Stars v Thunder
CEC[F]	Chelmsford	Sunrisers v Vipers

Sun 26 May

LOI	**Taunton**	**England v Pakistan**
CEC	Loughborough	Blaze v Thunder

Mon 27 May

CEC	Leeds	Diamonds v Sparks
CEC	Beckenham	SE Stars v Storm
CEC	Arundel	Vipers v Sunrisers

Wed 29 May

LOI[F]	**Chelmsford**	**England v Pakistan**

Thu 30 May

CEC	Southampton	Vipers v Storm
CEC	Manchester	Thunder v Sparks

Fri 31 May

CEC	Nottingham	Blaze v Sparks
CEC	Chester-le-St	Diamonds v SE Stars
CEC	Taunton	Storm v Sunrisers

Sun 2 June

CEC	The Oval	SE Stars v Vipers
CEC	Northampton	Sunrisers v Diamonds
CEC	Manchester	Thunder v Blaze

Thu 6 June
CEC Lord's Sunrisers v SE Stars

Fri 7 June
CEC Leicester Blaze v Storm
CEC Manchester Thunder v Vipers

Sat 8 June
CEC Birmingham Sparks v Diamonds

Sun 9 June
CEC Leeds Diamonds v Blaze
CEC Canterbury SE Stars v Sparks
CEC Blackpool Thunder v Sunrisers
CEC Bristol Storm v Vipers

Thu 13 June
CEC Lord's Sunrisers v Blaze
CEC Cardiff Storm v Thunder

Fri 14 June
CEC Birmingham Sparks v Thunder
CEC Southampton Vipers v Diamonds

Sun 16 June
CEC Derby Blaze v SE Stars
CEC Worcester Sparks v Vipers
CEC Leeds Diamonds v Storm

Wed 19 June
CEC Birmingham Sparks v Blaze
CEC Chester-le-St Diamonds v Thunder
CEC Hove Vipers v SE Stars
CEC Chelmsford Sunrisers v Storm

Fri 21 June
50ov Leicester ECB Dev v New Zealand

Sat 22 June
CEC Derby Semi-finals and FINAL

Wed 26 June
LOI^F Chester-le-St England v New Zealand

Sat 29 June
LOI Worcester England v New Zealand

Sun 30 June
RHF Scarborough Diamonds v Sparks
RHF Beckenham SE Stars v Blaze
RHF Hove Vipers v Storm
RHF Chelmsford Sunrisers v Thunder

Wed 3 July
LOI^F Bristol England v New Zealand

Fri 5 July
RHF Chesterfield Blaze v Vipers

Sat 6 July
IT20 Southampton England v New Zealand

Sun 7 July
RHF Radlett Sunrisers v Sparks
RHF Blackpool Thunder v SE Stars
RHF Cheltenham Storm v Diamonds

Tue 9 July
IT20^F Hove England v New Zealand

Wed 10 July
RHF Worcester Sparks v Thunder
RHF York Diamonds v Sunrisers
RHF Newbury Vipers v SE Stars
RHF Cheltenham Storm v Blaze

Thu 11 July
IT20^F Canterbury England v New Zealand

Fri 12 July
RHF Worcester Sparks v Storm

Sat 13 July
IT20 The Oval England v New Zealand

Sun 14 July
RHF Lincoln Blaze v Diamonds
RHF Beckenham SE Stars v Sunrisers
RHF Sedbergh Thunder v Vipers

Wed 17 July
IT20^F Lord's England v New Zealand

Tue 23 July
100 The Oval Invincibles v Phoenix

Wed 24 July
100 Southampton Brave v Spirit

Thu 25 July
100 Manchester Originals v Fire

Fri 26 July
100 Leeds Superchargers v Rockets

Sat 27 July
100 Lord's Spirit v Phoenix

Sun 28 July
100 Cardiff Fire v Invincibles

Mon 29 July
100 Manchester Originals v Rockets

Tue 30 July
100 Leeds Superchargers v Brave

Wed 31 July
100 Nottingham Rockets v Phoenix

Thu 1 August
100 Lord's Spirit v Fire
100 Southampton Brave v Originals

Fri 2 August
100 The Oval Invincibles v Superchargers

Sat 3 August
100 Birmingham Phoenix v Brave
100 Nottingham Rockets v Fire

Sun 4 August
100 Lord's Spirit v Invincibles
100 Leeds Superchargers v Originals

Mon 5 August
100 Cardiff Fire v Brave

Tue 6 August
100 Manchester Originals v Invincibles
100 Birmingham Phoenix v Superchargers

Wed 7 August
100 Nottingham Rockets v Spirit

Thu 8 August
100 Cardiff Fire v Superchargers
100 The Oval Invincibles v Brave

Fri 9 August
100 Lord's Spirit v Originals

Sat 10 August
100 Southampton Brave v Rockets
100 Cardiff Fire v Phoenix

Sun 11 August
100 The Oval Invincibles v Spirit
100 Manchester Originals v Superchargers

Mon 12 August
100 Birmingham Phoenix v Rockets

Tue 13 August
100 Leeds Superchargers v Spirit

Wed 14 August
100 Southampton Brave v Fire
100 Nottingham Rockets v Invincibles

Thu 15 August
100 Birmingham Phoenix v Originals

Sat 17 August
100 The Oval Eliminator

Sun 18 August
100 Lord's FINAL

Mon 26 August
RHF Beckenham SE Stars v Thunder
RHF Arundel Vipers v Blaze
RHF Chelmsford Sunrisers v Diamonds
RHF Taunton Storm v Sparks

Fri 30 August
RHF Worcester Sparks v Vipers

Sat 31 August
RHF Derby Blaze v Sunrisers
RHF Beckenham SE Stars v Storm

Sun 1 September
RHF Southport Thunder v Diamonds

Wed 4 September
RHF tbc Sparks v Stars
RHF Leeds Diamonds v Vipers
RHF Radlett Sunrisers v Storm
RHF Sale Thunder v Blaze

Sat 7 September
RHF tbc Blaze v Sparks
RHF Chester-le-St Diamonds v SE Stars
RHF Southampton Vipers v Sunrisers
RHF Taunton Storm v Thunder

Sat 14 September
RHF tbc Semi-finals 1 & 2

Sat 21 September
RHF Leicester FINAL

NATIONAL COUNTIES FIXTURES 2024

Sun 28 April	**TWENTY20 COMPETITION**
Gosforth	Northumberland v Cumbria (1)
Knypersley	Staffordshire v Cheshire (1)
Exning	Cambridgeshire v Suffolk (2)
Gt Witchingham	Norfolk v Lincolnshire (2)
Wargrave	Berkshire v Hertfordshire (3)
High Wycombe	Buckinghamshire v Bedfordshire (3)
Wormsley	Oxfordshire v Shropshire (4)
Llandysul	Wales NC v Herefordshire (4)
Werrington	Cornwall v Devon (5)
Wimborne	Dorset v Wiltshire (5)
Sun 5 May	**TWENTY20 COMPETITION**
Toft	Cheshire v Cumbria (1)
Burslem	Staffordshire v Northumberland (1)
Bracebridge Heath	Lincolnshire v Cambridgeshire (2)
Sprowston	Norfolk v Suffolk (2)
Newbury	Berkshire v Buckinghamshire (3)
West Herts	Hertfordshire v Bedfordshire (3)
Wormsley	Oxfordshire v Wales NC (4)
Oswestry	Shropshire v Herefordshire (4)
Wadebridge	Cornwall v Dorset (5)
Exeter	Devon v Wiltshire (5)
Mon 6 May	**TWENTY20 COMPETITION**
Alderley Edge	Cheshire v Northumberland (1)
Carlisle	Cumbria v Staffordshire (1)
Exning	Cambridgeshire v Norfolk (2)
Ipswich School	Suffolk v Lincolnshire (2)
Ampthill Town	Bedfordshire v Berkshire (3)
Beaconsfield	Buckinghamshire v Hertfordshire (3)
Brockhampton	Herefordshire v Oxfordshire (4)
Brymbo	Wales NC v Shropshire (4)
Wimborne	Dorset v Devon (5)
South Wilts	Wiltshire v Cornwall (5)
Sun 12 May	**NCCA TROPHY**
Keswick	Cumbria v Bedfordshire (1)
Jesmond	Northumberland v Lincolnshire (1)
Sprowston	Norfolk v Herefordshire (2)
Mildenhall	Suffolk v Staffordshire (2)
Henley	Berkshire v Devon (3)
Wormsley	Oxfordshire v Buckinghamshire (3)
Dorchester	Dorset v Cheshire (4)
Marlborough Coll	Wiltshire v Hertfordshire (4)
Sun 19 May	**TWENTY20 COMPETITION**
tbc	Super 12s
Sun 26 May	**TWENTY20 COMPETITION**
Chester Boughton	Finals Day (Reserve day 27 May)
Sun 2 June	**NCCA TROPHY**
Luton Town & Ind	Bedfordshire v Northumberland (1)
Fenners	Cambridgeshire v Cumbria (1)
Shifnal	Shropshire v Suffolk (2)
Smethwick	Staffordshire v Norfolk (2)
St Austell	Cornwall v Berkshire (3)
Sidmouth	Devon v Oxfordshire (3)
Welwyn Garden	Hertfordshire v Dorset (4)
Pontarddulais	Wales NC v Wiltshire (4)
Sun 9 June	**NCCA TROPHY**
Woodhall Spa	Lincolnshire v Bedfordshire (1)

Gosforth	Northumberland v Cambridgeshire (1)
Eastnor	Herefordshire v Staffordshire (2)
Gt Witchingham	Norfolk v Shropshire (2)
High Wycombe	Buckinghamshire v Devon (3)
Banbury	Oxfordshire v Cornwall (3)
Alderley Edge	Cheshire v Hertfordshire (4)
Wimborne	Dorset v Wales NC (4)
Sun 16 June	**NCCA TROPHY**
Sawston & Babraham	Cambridgeshire v Lincolnshire (1)
Kendal	Cumbria v Northumberland (1)
Whitchurch	Shropshire v Herefordshire (2)
Sudbury	Suffolk v Norfolk (2)
Newbury	Berkshire v Oxfordshire (3)
Redruth	Cornwall v Buckinghamshire (3)
Panteg	Wales NC v Cheshire (4)
Warminster	Wiltshire v Dorset (4)
Sun 23 June	**NCCA TROPHY**
Southill Park	Bedfordshire v Cambridgeshire (1)
Bourne	Lincolnshire v Cumbria (1)
Colwall	Herefordshire v Suffolk (2)
Moddershall & Oulton	Staffordshire v Shropshire (2)
Chesham	Buckinghamshire v Berkshire (3)
Cornwood	Devon v Cornwall (3)
Didsbury	Cheshire v Wiltshire (4)
Hitchin	Hertfordshire v Wales NC (4)
Sun 30 June	**NCCA TROPHY**
Quarter-final A	Winner Gp 1 v Runner-up Gp 2
Quarter-final B	Winner Gp 2 v Runner-up Gp 1
Quarter-final C	Winner Gp 3 v Runner-up Gp 4
Quarter-final D	Winner Gp 4 v Runner-up Gp 3
Sun 7 – Tue 9 July	**CHAMPIONSHIP**
Sleaford	Lincolnshire v Buckinghamshire (E1)
Checkley	Staffordshire v Bedfordshire (E1)
Peterborough T	Cambridgeshire v Hertfordshire (E2)
Jesmond	Northumberland v Cumbria (E2)
Helston	Cornwall v Oxfordshire (W1)
North Devon	Devon v Berkshire (W1)
St Georges	Shropshire v Dorset (W2)
Corsham	Wiltshire v Herefordshire (W2)
Sun 14 – Tue 16 July	**CHAMPIONSHIP**
Dunstable Town	Bedfordshire v Lincolnshire (E1)
Tring Park	Buckinghamshire v Suffolk (E1)
Kendal	Cumbria v Cambridgeshire (E1)
Bishop's Stortford	Hertfordshire v Norfolk (E2)
Wargrave	Berkshire v Cornwall (W1)
Thame Town	Oxfordshire v Cheshire (W1)
Wimborne	Dorset v Wiltshire (W2)
Eastnor	Herefordshire v Wales NC (W2)
Sun 21 July	**SHOWCASE GAMES**
Fenners	Cambridgeshire v Surrey
Nantwich	Cheshire v Derbyshire
Truro	Cornwall v Somerset
Sedbergh	Cumbria v Lancashire
Wimbourne	Dorset v Hampshire
Lindum	Lincolnshire v Nottinghamshire
Horsford	Norfolk v Northamptonshire
Jesmond	Northumberland v Durham
tbc	Oxfordshire v Middlesex
Wellington	Shropshire v Yorkshire
Knypersley	Staffordshire v Warwickshire

Woolpit	Suffolk v Essex
Arundel	Sussex v Hertfordshire
Sudbrook	Wales NC v Worcestershire
Swindon	Wiltshire v Glamorgan
Tue 23 July	**SHOWCASE GAMES**
Dunstable Town	Bedfordshire v Kent
Slough	Berkshire v Sussex
Exmouth	Devon v Somerset
Sun 28 – Tue 30 July	**CHAMPIONSHIP**
Cleethorpes	Lincolnshire v Staffordshire (E1)
Bury St Edmunds	Suffolk v Bedfordshire (E1)
Netherfield	Cumbria v Hertfordshire (E2)
Jesmond	Northumberland v Norfolk (E2)
Nantwich	Cheshire v Berkshire (W1)
Truro	Cornwall v Devon (W1)
Ebbw Vale	Wales NC v Dorset (W2)
South Wilts	Wiltshire v Shropshire (W2)
Sun 4 August	**NCCA TROPHY**
Semi-final	Winner Match B v Winner Match A
Semi-final	Winner Match D v Winner Match C
	(Reserve day 5 August)
Sun 11 – Tue 13 August	**CHAMPIONSHIP**
Flitwick	Bedfordshire v Buckinghamshire (E1)
Stafford	Staffordshire v Suffolk (E1)
Fenners	Cambridgeshire v Northumberland (E2)
Horsford	Norfolk v Cumbria (E2)
Newbury	Berkshire v Oxfordshire (W1)
Sidmouth	Devon v Cheshire (W1)
Wimborne	Dorset v Herefordshire (W2)
Bridgnorth	Shropshire v Wales NC (W2)
Sun 18 – Tue 20 August	**CHAMPIONSHIP**
High Wycombe	Buckinghamshire v Staffordshire (E1)
Copdock & OI	Suffolk v Lincolnshire (E1)
Hertford	Hertfordshire v Northumberland (E2)
Horsford	Norfolk v Cambridgeshire (E2)
Chester Boughton	Cheshire v Cornwall (W1)
Banbury	Oxfordshire v Devon (W1)
Eastnor	Herefordshire v Shropshire (W2)
Abergavenny	Wales NC v Wiltshire (W2)
Sun 25 August	**NCCA TROPHY**
Wormsley	FINAL (Reserve day 26 August)
Sun 1 – Wed 4 September	**CHAMPIONSHIP**
West Brom Dartmouth	FINAL

SECOND XI CHAMPIONSHIP FIXTURES 2024

(NB: All fixtures are subject to change.)

FOUR-DAY MATCHES

(three-day matches are shown with a †)

APRIL		
Mon 8	Beckenham	Kent v Essex
	Taunton Vale	Somerset v Glamorgan
	Kidderminster	Worcs v Glos
	Bradford PA	Yorkshire v Lancashire
Tue 9	Birm EFSG	Warwicks v Derbyshire†
Mon 15	Manchester	Lancashire v Durham
	Kibworth	Leics v Worcs
	Overstone	Northants v Glamorgan
	Horsham	Sussex v Middlesex
	Birm EFSG	Warwicks v Essex
	Leeds	Yorkshire v Somerset
Tue 16	Beckenham	Kent v Notts†
Mon 22	Radlett	Middlesex v Hampshire
	Guildford	Surrey v Sussex
	Scarborough	Yorkshire v Leics
Tue 23	tbc	Lancashire v Warwicks
	Notts SC	Notts v Derbyshire
Mon 29	Newport	Glamorgan v Glos
	Southampton	Hampshire v Essex
	Polo Farm, Cant	Kent v Middlesex
	Kibworth	Leics v Northants
	Notts SC	Notts v Yorkshire
	Birm EFSG	Warwicks v Sussex
	Barnt Green	Worcs v Somerset
MAY		
Mon 6	Repton	Derbyshire v Durham†
	Billericay	Essex v Somerset
	Birm EFSG	Warwicks v Glamorgan
	Kidderminster	Worcs v Lancashire
Tue 7	Southampton	Hampshire v Glos†
	Guildford	Surrey v Kent
Mon 13	Belper Mead	Derbyshire v Leics
	New Malden	Surrey v Middlesex
Tue 14	Abergavenny	Glamorgan v Lancashire
	Beckenham	Kent v Sussex
	Notts SC	Notts v Warwicks
JUNE		
Mon 17	Burnopfield	Durham v Yorkshire†
	Billericay	Essex v Lancashire
	Rockhampton	Glos v Derbyshire
	Southampton	Hampshire v Sussex
	Notts SC	Notts v Leics
	Taunton Vale	Somerset v Middlesex
	New Malden	Surrey v Glamorgan†
Mon 24	tbc	Lancashire v Middlesex
	Notts SC	Notts v Durham
	Taunton Vale	Somerset v Northants
	New Malden	Surrey v Hampshire
	Birm EFSG	Warwicks v Worcs
Tue 25	Rockhampton	Glos v Glamorgan†
AUGUST		
Mon 12	Rockhampton	Glos v Sussex
Mon 19	Newport	Glamorgan v Leics
	Rockhampton	Glos v Essex
Tue 20	Chesterfield	Derbyshire v Yorkshire
	tbc	Durham v Northants†
Mon 26	Denby	Derbyshire v Lancashire
	Burnopfield	Durham v Warwicks†
	Billericay	Essex v Sussex
	Rockhampton	Glos v Somerset†
	Loughborough	Leics v Notts
	Radlett	Middlesex v Worcs
Tue 27	Southampton	Hampshire v Kent
	York	Yorkshire v Surrey
SEPTEMBER		
Mon 2	Billericay	Essex & Kent v Surrey
	Newport	Glamorgan v Hampshire
	Scarborough	Yorkshire v Durham†
Tue 3	Blackstone	Sussex v Derbyshire
Mon 9	Gosforth	Durham v Notts†
	Billericay	Essex v Middlesex
	Southport	Lancashire v Yorkshire
	Peterborough	Northants v Leics
	Taunton Vale	Somerset v Warwicks
	Barnt Green	Worcs v Derbyshire
Mon 16	Northwood	Middlesex v Yorkshire
	Dunstable	Northants v Worcs
	Taunton Vale	Somerset v Hampshire
	Blackstone	Sussex v Glamorgan
	Birm EFSG	Warwicks v Surrey

SECOND XI TWENTY20 CUP FIXTURES 2024

MAY		
Mon 20	Kibworth	Leics v Derbyshire
	Droitwich	Worcs v Somerset
Tue 21	Horsham	Sussex v Surrey
	Birm EFSG	Warwicks v Somerset
Wed 22	Kibworth	Leics v Notts
	Horsham	Sussex v Essex
	Birm EFSG	Warwicks v Worcs
Thu 23	Chester-le-St	Durham v Lancashire
	Southend	Essex v Middlesex
	Polo Farm, Cant	Kent v Surrey
	Arundel	Sussex v Hampshire
Fri 24	Chester-le-St	Durham v Lancashire
	Taunton Vale	Somerset v Worcs
Mon 27	Derby	Derbyshire v Lancashire
	Gosforth	Durham v Notts
	Southend	Essex v Sussex
	Tunbridge W	Kent v Middlesex
	Taunton Vale	Somerset v Glos
Tue 28	Gosforth	Durham v Notts
	Rockhampton	Glos v Somerset
Wed 29	Derby	Derbyshire v Leics
	Cheltenham	Glos v Northants (x 2)
	Polo Farm, Cant	Kent v Essex
	tbc	Lancashire v Yorkshire
	Birm EFSG	Warwicks v Glamorgan
Thu 30	Newport	Glamorgan v Somerset
	Enfield	Middlesex v Hampshire
JUNE		
Mon 3	Leicester	Leics v Durham
	Uxbridge	Middlesex v Kent
	Taunton Vale	Somerset v Warwicks
	Worcester	Worcs v Glos
Tue 4	Southampton	Hampshire v Middlesex
	Leicester	Leics v Durham
	Worksop	Notts v Derbyshire (x 2)
	New Malden	Surrey v Sussex
	Worcester	Worcs v Glamorgan
Wed 5	Newport	Glamorgan v Glos
	Tunbridge W	Kent v Sussex
	Taunton Vale	Somerset v Northants (x 2)
Thu 6	Southampton	Hampshire v Essex
	Worksop	Notts v Lancashire (x 2)
	Leeds	Yorkshire v Durham (x 2)
Mon 10	Tunbridge W	Kent v Hampshire (x 2)
	Leicester	Leics v Yorkshire
	New Malden	Surrey v Middlesex
Tue 11	Newport	Glamorgan v Northants (x 2)
	Blackpool	Lancashire v Derbyshire
	New Malden	Surrey v Essex
	Horsham	Sussex v Kent
	Birm EFSG	Warwicks v Glos
Wed 12	Caldicot	Glamorgan v Worcs
	Radlett	Middlesex v Sussex
Thu 13	Sheffield Col	Yorkshire v Leics
	Southampton	Hampshire v Surrey
Tue 18	Bromsgrove	Worcs v Warwicks
Fri 28	Duffield	Derbyshire v Yorkshire
JULY		
Mon 1	Southend	Essex v Hampshire
	Cardiff	Glamorgan v Warwicks
	Richmond	Middlesex v Surrey
Tue 2	Chester-le-St	Durham v Derbyshire
	Mansfield	Notts v Leics
	Barnsley	Yorkshire v Lancashire
Wed 3	Chester-le-St	Durham v Derbyshire
	Rockhampton	Glos v Worcs
	Teddington	Middlesex v Essex
	Milton Keynes	Northants v Warwicks (x 2)
	Taunton Vale	Somerset v Glamorgan
	New Malden	Surrey v Kent
Thu 4	Leeds, Weet	Yorkshire v Notts (x 2)
Fri 5	New Malden	Surrey v Hampshire
Mon 8	Chelmsford	Essex v Kent
	Rockhampton	Glos v Warwicks
	Horsham	Sussex v Middlesex
Tue 9	Southend	Essex v Surrey
	Rockhampton	Glos v Glamorgan
	Southampton	Hampshire v Sussex
	Leicester	Leics v Lancashire (x 2)
	Sheffield Col	Yorkshire v Derbyshire
Wed 10	Northampton	Northants v Worcs (x 2)
Tue 16	Wormsley	Semi-finals and FINAL

THE HUNDRED FIXTURES 2024

Tue 23 July
100F The Oval Invincibles v Phoenix

Wed 24 July
100F Southampton Brave v Spirit

Thu 25 July
100F Manchester Originals v Fire

Fri 26 July
100F Leeds Superchargers v Rockets

Sat 27 July
100F Lord's Spirit v Phoenix

Sun 28 July
100F Cardiff Fire v Invincibles

Mon 29 July
100F Manchester Originals v Rockets

Tue 30 July
100F Leeds Superchargers v Brave

Wed 31 July
100F Nottingham Rockets v Phoenix

Thu 1 August
100 Lord's Spirit v Fire
100F Southampton Brave v Originals

Fri 2 August
100F The Oval Invincibles v Superchargers

Sat 3 August
100 Birmingham Phoenix v Brave
100F Nottingham Rockets v Fire

Sun 4 August
100 Lord's Spirit v Invincibles
100F Leeds Superchargers v Originals

Mon 5 August
100F Cardiff Fire v Brave

Tue 6 August
100 Manchester Originals v Invincibles
100F Birmingham Phoenix v Superchargers

Wed 7 August
100F Nottingham Rockets v Spirit

Thu 8 August
100 Cardiff Fire v Superchargers
100F The Oval Invincibles v Brave

Fri 9 August
100F Lord's Spirit v Originals

Sat 10 August
100 Southampton Brave v Rockets
100F Cardiff Fire v Phoenix

Sun 11 August
100 The Oval Invincibles v Spirit
100F Manchester Originals v Superchargers

Mon 12 August
100F Birmingham Phoenix v Rockets

Tue 13 August
100F Leeds Superchargers v Spirit

Wed 14 August
100 Southampton Brave v Fire
100F Nottingham Rockets v Invincibles

Thu 15 August
100F Birmingham Phoenix v Originals

Sat 17 August
100F The Oval Eliminator

Sun 18 August
100F Lord's FINAL

PRINCIPAL FIXTURES 2024

CC1	County Championship Division 1
CC2	County Championship Division 2
F	Floodlit
FCF	First-Class Friendly
LOI	Limited-Overs International
MBC	Metro Bank One-Day Cup
T20	Vitality Blast
IT20	Vitality Twenty20 International
TM	Test Match

Fri 5 – Mon 8 April

CC1	Chester-le-St	Durham v Hampshire
CC1	Canterbury	Kent v Somerset
CC1	Manchester	Lancashire v Surrey
CC1	Nottingham	Notts v Essex
CC1	Birmingham	Warwicks v Worcs
CC2	Derby	Derbyshire v Glos
CC2	Lord's	Middlesex v Glamorgan
CC2	Hove	Sussex v Northants
CC2	Leeds	Yorkshire v Leics

Fri 12 – Mon 15 April

CC1	Chelmsford	Essex v Kent
CC1	Southampton	Hampshire v Lancashire
CC1	Nottingham	Notts v Worcs
CC1	The Oval	Surrey v Somerset
CC1	Birmingham	Warwicks v Durham
CC2	Cardiff	Glamorgan v Derbyshire
CC2	Bristol	Glos v Yorkshire
CC2	Leicester	Leics v Sussex
CC2	Northampton	Northants v Middlesex

Fri 19 – Mon 22 April

CC1	Chelmsford	Essex v Lancashire
CC1	Southampton	Hampshire v Warwicks
CC1	Canterbury	Kent v Surrey
CC1	Taunton	Somerset v Notts
CC1	Kidderminster	Worcs v Durham
CC2	Derby	Derbyshire v Leics
CC2	Lord's	Middlesex v Yorkshire
CC2	Northampton	Northants v Glamorgan
CC2	Hove	Sussex v Glos

Fri 26 – Mon 29 April

CC1	Chester-le-St	Durham v Essex
CC1	The Oval	Surrey v Hampshire
CC1	Birmingham	Warwicks v Notts
CC1	Kidderminster	Worcs v Somerset
CC2	Bristol	Glos v Middlesex
CC2	Leicester	Leics v Northants
CC2	Leeds	Yorkshire v Derbyshire

Fri 3 – Mon 6 May

CC1	Manchester	Lancashire v Kent
CC1	Taunton	Somerset v Essex
CC2	Derby	Derbyshire v Sussex
CC2	Lord's	Middlesex v Leics
CC2	Leeds	Yorkshire v Glamorgan

Fri 10 – Mon 13 May

CC1	Southampton	Hampshire v Durham
CC1	Canterbury	Kent v Worcs
CC1	Nottingham	Notts v Lancashire
CC1	The Oval	Surrey v Warwicks
CC2	Cardiff	Glamorgan v Sussex
CC2	Northampton	Northants v Glos

Fri 17 – Mon 20 May

CC1	Chelmsford	Essex v Warwicks
CC1	Blackpool	Lancashire v Durham
CC1	Nottingham	Notts v Hampshire
CC1	Taunton	Somerset v Kent
CC1	The Oval	Surrey v Worcs
CC2	Derby	Derbyshire v Northants
CC2	Cardiff	Glamorgan v Middlesex
CC2	Leicester	Leics v Glos
CC2	Hove	Sussex v Yorkshire

Wed 22 May

IT20F	**Leeds**	**England v Pakistan**

Fri 24 – Mon 27 May

CC1	Chester-le-St	Durham v Somerset
CC1	Southampton	Hampshire v Surrey
CC1	Canterbury	Kent v Essex
CC1	Manchester	Lancashire v Warwicks
CC1	Worcester	Worcs v Notts
CC2	Bristol	Glos v Derbyshire
CC2	Leicester	Leics v Glamorgan
CC2	Lord's	Middlesex v Sussex
CC2	Northampton	Northants v Yorkshire

Sat 25 May

IT20	**Birmingham**	**England v Pakistan**

Tue 28 May

IT20F	**Cardiff**	**England v Pakistan**

Thu 30 May

IT20F	**The Oval**	**England v Pakistan**
T20F	Bristol	Glos v Essex
T20F	Southampton	Hampshire v Surrey
T20F	Manchester	Lancashire v Durham
T20F	Northampton	Northants v Derbyshire
T20F	Leeds	Yorkshire v Worcs

Fri 31 May

T20F	Chester-le-St	Durham v Warwicks
T20F	Cardiff	Glamorgan v Surrey
T20F	Leicester	Leics v Yorkshire
T20F	Chelmsford	Middlesex v Kent
T20F	Nottingham	Notts v Northants
T20F	Taunton	Somerset v Essex
T20F	Hove	Sussex v Glos
T20	Worcester	Worcs v Lancashire

Sat 1 June

T20	Birmingham	Derbyshire v Leics
T20F	Birmingham	Warwicks v Notts

Sun 2 June

T20	Chelmsford	Essex v Middlesex
T20	Cardiff	Glamorgan v Sussex
T20	Southampton	Hampshire v Kent
T20	Manchester	Lancashire v Derbyshire
T20	Northampton	Northants v Yorkshire
T20	The Oval	Surrey v Somerset

Thu 6 June

T20F	Lord's	Middlesex v Glamorgan
T20F	Nottingham	Notts v Worcs

Fri 7 June

T20F	Derby	Derbyshire v Notts
T20F	Chelmsford	Essex v Glamorgan
T20F	Bristol	Glos v Hampshire
T20F	Canterbury	Kent v Somerset
T20F	Manchester	Lancashire v Warwicks
T20F	Leicester	Leics v Durham
T20F	Northampton	Northants v Worcs
T20F	The Oval	Surrey v Sussex

Sat 8 June

T20	Birmingham	Warwicks v Durham

Sun 9 June

T20	Bristol	Glos v Sussex
T20	Canterbury	Kent v Middlesex
T20	Leicester	Leics v Worcs
T20	Nottingham	Notts v Lancashire
T20	Taunton	Somerset v Hampshire
T20	Leeds	Yorkshire v Derbyshire

Tue 11 June

T20F	Lord's	Middlesex v Somerset

Wed 12 June

T20F	Chester-le-St	Durham v Leics

Thu 13 June

T20F	Cardiff	Glamorgan v Hampshire
T20F	Lord's	Middlesex v Essex

Fri 14 June

T20F	Derby	Derbyshire v Northants
T20F	Chelmsford	Essex v Sussex
T20F	Southampton	Hampshire v Middlesex
T20F	Leicester	Leics v Lancashire
T20F	Taunton	Somerset v Kent
T20F	The Oval	Surrey v Glos
T20F	Birmingham	Warwicks v Yorkshire
T20	Worcester	Worcs v Notts

Sat 15 June

T20	Nottingham	Notts v Durham
T20	Hove	Sussex v Surrey

Sun 16 June

T20	Derby	Derbyshire v Warwicks
T20	Chester-le-St	Durham v Lancashire
T20	Canterbury	Kent v Glos
T20	Taunton	Somerset v Glamorgan
T20	Worcester	Worcs v Northants
T20	Leeds	Yorkshire v Leics

Thu 20 June

T20F	Chelmsford	Essex v Hampshire
T20F	Cardiff	Glamorgan v Glos
T20F	Lord's	Middlesex v Surrey
T20F	Hove	Sussex v Kent
T20F	Birmingham	Warwicks v Northants
T20F	Leeds	Yorkshire v Lancashire

Fri 21 June

T20F	Chester-le-St	Durham v Yorkshire
T20F	Bristol	Glos v Somerset
T20F	Southampton	Hampshire v Sussex
T20F	Canterbury	Kent v Essex
T20F	Northampton	Northants v Leics
T20F	Nottingham	Notts v Derbyshire
T20F	The Oval	Surrey v Glamorgan
T20	Worcester	Worcs v Warwicks

Sun 23 – Wed 26 June

CC1	Chelmsford	Essex v Durham
CC1	Canterbury	Kent v Lancashire
CC1	Nottingham	Notts v Somerset
CC1	Birmingham	Warwicks v Hampshire
CC1	Worcester	Worcs v Surrey
CC2	Cardiff	Glamorgan v Northants
CC2	Lord's	Middlesex v Derbyshire
CC2	Hove	Sussex v Leics
CC2	Scarborough	Yorkshire v Glos

Sun 30 June – Wed 3 July

CC1	Chester-le-St	Durham v Worcs
CC1	Southampton	Hampshire v Kent
CC1	Southport	Lancashire v Notts
CC1	Taunton	Somerset v Warwicks
CC1	The Oval	Surrey v Essex
CC2	Chesterfield	Derbyshire v Yorkshire
CC2	Cheltenham	Glos v Glamorgan

CC2	tbc	Leics v Middlesex
CC2	Northampton	Northants v Sussex

Wed 3 – Sat 6 July

FCF	Beckenham	FCC Select v West Indians

Fri 5 July

T20F	Chester-le-St	Durham v Worcs
T20F	Chelmsford	Essex v Somerset
T20	Cheltenham	Glos v Kent
T20F	Northampton	Northants v Lancashire
T20F	Nottingham	Notts v Leics
T20F	The Oval	Surrey v Middlesex
T20F	Hove	Sussex v Glamorgan
T20F	Leeds	Yorkshire v Warwicks

Sat 6 July

T20F	Leicester	Leics v Derbyshire
T20	Radlett	Middlesex v Hampshire

Sun 7 July

T20	Chesterfield	Derbyshire v Yorkshire
T20	Cardiff	Glamorgan v Essex
T20	Manchester	Lancashire v Worcs
T20	Northampton	Northants v Durham
T20	Nottingham	Notts v Warwicks
T20	Taunton	Somerset v Glos
T20	The Oval	Surrey v Kent

Wed 10 – Sun 14 July

TM1	**Lord's**	**ENGLAND v WEST INDIES**

Wed 10 July

T20F	Hove	Sussex v Hampshire

Thu 11 July

T20F	Derby	Derbyshire v Lancashire
T20F	Chelmsford	Essex v Kent
T20	Cheltenham	Glos v Middlesex
T20	Worcester	Worcs v Leics
T20F	Leeds	Yorkshire v Durham

Fri 12 July

T20F	Chester-le-St	Durham v Notts
T20F	Cardiff	Glamorgan v Middlesex
T20F	Southampton	Hampshire v Glos
T20F	Canterbury	Kent v Sussex
T20F	Manchester	Lancashire v Yorkshire
T20F	Leicester	Leics v Northants
T20F	Taunton	Somerset v Surrey
T20F	Birmingham	Warwicks v Worcs

Sat 13 July

T20	Hove	Sussex v Essex

Sun 14 July

T20	Chester-le-St	Durham v Northants
T20	Chelmsford	Essex v Surrey
T20	Cheltenham	Glos v Glamorgan
T20	Southampton	Hampshire v Somerset
T20	Leicester	Leics v Notts
T20	Birmingham	Warwicks v Derbyshire
T20	Worcester	Worcs v Yorkshire

Tue 16 July

T20F	Canterbury	Kent v Glamorgan

Wed 17 July

T20F	Manchester	Lancashire v Notts

Thu 18 – Mon 22 July

TM2	**Nottingham**	**ENGLAND v WEST INDIES**

Thu 18 July

T20F	Chelmsford	Middlesex v Glos
T20F	Northampton	Northants v Warwicks
T20F	Taunton	Somerset v Sussex
T20F	The Oval	Surrey v Hampshire
T20	Worcester	Worcs v Derbyshire

Fri 19 July

T20F	Derby	Derbyshire v Durham
T20F	Cardiff	Glamorgan v Somerset
T20F	Southampton	Hampshire v Essex
T20F	Canterbury	Kent v Surrey
T20F	Manchester	Lancashire v Northants
T20F	Hove	Sussex v Middlesex
T20F	Birmingham	Warwicks v Leics
T20F	Leeds	Yorkshire v Notts

Wed 24 July

MBC	Chelmsford	Essex v Warwicks
MBC	Sedbergh	Lancashire v Durham
MBC	Leicester	Leics v Notts
MBC	Northampton	Northants v Derbys
MBC	Worcester	Worcs v Middlesex

Thu 25 July

MBC	Cardiff	Glamorgan v Glos
MBC	The Oval	Surrey v Yorkshire

Fri 26 – Tue 30 July

TM3	**Birmingham**	**ENGLAND v WEST INDIES**

Fri 26 July

MBC	Southampton	Hampshire v Northants
MBCF	Leicester	Leics v Warwicks
MBC	Mansfield	Notts v Sussex
MBCF	Taunton	Somerset v Kent

Sat 27 July

MBC	Derby	Derbyshire v Middlesex

Sun 28 July

MBC	Bristol	Glos v Essex
MBC	Southampton	Hampshire v Somerset
MBC	Blackpool	Lancashire v Kent
MBC	Mansfield	Notts v Yorkshire

MBC	The Oval	Surrey v Glamorgan
MBC	Hove	Sussex v Warwicks
MBC	Worcester	Worcs v Durham

Mon 29 July

MBC	Radlett	Middlesex v Northants

Tue 30 July

MBC	The Oval	Surrey v Glos

Wed 31 July

MBC	Derby	Derbyshire v Lancashire
MBC	Chester-le-St	Durham v Somerset
MBC	Chelmsford	Essex v Leics
MBC	Neath	Glamorgan v Notts
MBC	Beckenham	Kent v Hampshire
MBC	York	Yorkshire v Sussex

Fri 2 August

MBC	Derby	Derbyshire v Worcs
MBC	Chester-le-St	Durham v Northants
MBC	Neath	Glamorgan v Sussex
MBC[F]	Taunton	Somerset v Lancashire
MBC	Rugby	Warwicks v Surrey
MBC	York	Yorkshire v Glos

Sun 4 August

MBC	Chelmsford	Essex v Glamorgan
MBC	Bristol	Glos v Warwicks
MBC	Southampton	Hampshire v Lancashire
MBC	Beckenham	Kent v Middlesex
MBC	Northampton	Northants v Worcs
MBC	Taunton	Somerset v Derbyshire
MBC	Guildford	Surrey v Notts
MBC	Hove	Sussex v Leics

Tue 6 August

MBC	tbc	Leics v Surrey
MBC	Radlett	Middlesex v Durham
MBC	Scarborough	Yorkshire v Essex

Wed 7 August

MBC	Bristol	Glos v Sussex
MBC	Southampton	Hampshire v Derbyshire
MBC	Northampton	Northants v Somerset
MBC	Worcester	Worcs v Kent

Thu 8 August

MBC	Manchester	Lancashire v Middlesex
MBC	Birmingham	Warwicks v Glamorgan
MBC	Scarborough	Yorkshire v Leics

Fri 9 August

MBC	Derby	Derbyshire v Kent
MBC	Gosforth	Durham v Hampshire
MBC[F]	Chelmsford	Essex v Surrey
MBC	Nottingham	Notts v Glos
MBC	Taunton	Somerset v Worcs

Sunday 11 August

MBC	Canterbury	Kent v Durham
MBC	Leicester	Leics v Glamorgan
MBC	Lord's	Middlesex v Somerset
MBC	Northampton	Northants v Lancashire
MBC	Nottingham	Notts v Essex
MBC	Hove	Sussex v Surrey
MBC	Rugby	Warwicks v Yorkshire
MBC	Worcester	Worcs v Hampshire

Wed 14 – Sat 17 August

FCF	Worcester	England Lions v Sri Lankans

Wed 14 August

MBC	Chester-le-St	Durham v Derbyshire
MBC	Cardiff	Glamorgan v Yorkshire
MBC	Bristol	Glos v Leics
MBC	Canterbury	Kent v Northants
MBC	Manchester	Lancashire v Worcs
MBC	Northwood	Middlesex v Hampshire
MBC	Hove	Sussex v Essex
MBC	Rugby	Warwicks v Notts

Fri 16 August

MBC	tbc	Quarter-finals 1 & 2

Sun 18 August

MBC	tbc	Semi-finals 1 & 2

Wed 21 – Sun 25 August

TM1	**Manchester**	**ENGLAND v SRI LANKA**

Thu 22 – Sun 25 August

CC1	Chester-le-St	Durham v Notts
CC1	Southampton	Hampshire v Essex
CC1	The Oval	Surrey v Lancashire
CC1	Birmingham	Warwicks v Somerset
CC1	Worcester	Worcs v Kent
CC2	Derby	Derbyshire v Glamorgan
CC2	Bristol	Glos v Leics
CC2	Northwood	Middlesex v Northants
CC2	Scarborough	Yorkshire v Sussex

Thu 29 August – Mon 2 September

TM2	**Lord's**	**ENGLAND v SRI LANKA**

Thu 29 August – Sun 1 September

CC1	Chelmsford	Essex v Worcs
CC1	Manchester	Lancashire v Hampshire
CC1	Nottingham	Notts v Surrey
CC1	Taunton	Somerset v Durham
CC1	Birmingham	Warwicks v Kent
CC2	Cardiff	Glamorgan v Leics
CC2	Bristol	Glos v Northants
CC2	Hove	Sussex v Derbyshire
CC2	Leeds	Yorkshire v Middlesex

Tue 3 September

T20^{F}	tbc	Quarter-final 1

Wed 4 September

T20^{F}	tbc	Quarter-final 2

Thu 5 September

T20^{F}	tbc	Quarter-final 3

Fri 6 – Tue 10 September

TM3	**The Oval**	**ENGLAND v SRI LANKA**

Fri 6 September

T20^{F}	tbc	Quarter-final 4

Mon 9 – Thu 12 September

CC1	Chester-le-St	Durham v Lancashire
CC1	Chelmsford	Essex v Notts
CC1	Canterbury	Kent v Hampshire
CC1	Taunton	Somerset v Surrey
CC1	Worcester	Worcs v Warwicks
CC2	Leicester	Leics v Yorkshire
CC2	Lord's	Middlesex v Glos
CC2	Northampton	Northants v Derbyshire
CC2	Hove	Sussex v Glamorgan

Wed 11 September

IT20^{F}	Southampton	**England v Australia**

Fri 13 September

IT20^{F}	Cardiff	**England v Australia**

Sat 14 September

T20	Birmingham	Semi-finals and FINAL

Sun 15 September

IT20	Manchester	**England v Australia**

Tue 17 – Fri 20 September

CC1	Southampton	Hampshire v Worcs
CC1	Canterbury	Kent v Notts
CC1	Manchester	Lancashire v Somerset
CC1	The Oval	Surrey v Durham
CC1	Birmingham	Warwicks v Essex
CC2	Derby	Derbyshire v Middlesex
CC2	Cardiff	Glamorgan v Yorkshire
CC2	Bristol	Glos v Sussex
CC2	Northampton	Northants v Leics

Thu 19 September

LOI^{F}	**Nottingham**	**England v Australia**

Sat 21 September

LOI	**Leeds**	**England v Australia**
MBC	Nottingham	FINAL

Tue 24 September

LOI^{F}	**Chester-le-St**	**England v Australia**

Thu 26 – Sun 29 September

CC1	Chester-le-St	Durham v Kent
CC1	Chelmsford	Essex v Surrey
CC1	Nottingham	Notts v Warwicks
CC1	Taunton	Somerset v Hampshire
CC1	Worcester	Worcs v Lancashire
CC2	Cardiff	Glamorgan v Glos
CC2	Leicester	Leics v Derbyshire
CC2	Hove	Sussex v Middlesex
CC2	Leeds	Yorkshire v Northants

Fri 27 September

LOI^{F}	**Lord's**	**England v Australia**

Sun 29 September

LOI	**Bristol**	**England v Australia**

First published in 2024

by HEADLINE PUBLISHING GROUP

1

Cataloguing in Publication Data is available from the British Library

ISBN 978 1 0354 1177 1

Typeset in Times by
Letterpart Limited, Caterham on the Hill, Surrey

Printed and bound in Great Britain by
Clays Ltd St Ives plc

Headline's policy is to use papers that are natural, renewable and recyclable products and made from wood grown in sustainable forests. The logging and manufacturing processes are expected to conform to the environmental regulations of the country of origin.

HEADLINE PUBLISHING GROUP

An Hachette UK Company
Carmelite House
50 Victoria Embankment
London EC4Y ODZ

www.headline.co.uk
www.hachette.co.uk